The Contemporary
American Family

❁ THE ❁ CONTEMPORARY AMERICAN FAMILY

BY

ERNEST R. GROVES

AND

GLADYS HOAGLAND GROVES

J. B. LIPPINCOTT COMPANY
CHICAGO   PHILADELPHIA   NEW YORK

PREFACE

IN THE writing of this edition of *The Contemporary American Family* we have kept steadily in mind the purpose of the book. This is to give the reader an understanding of American family life that will help him handle his own problems whether they are associated with premarriage, marriage, or parenthood experiences. He who studies the family rightly expects to gain insight and preparedness that will function in his own personal career. Our desire to fulfill this expectation has directed us throughout the book, determining what has gone in and what has been left out of the discussions. We have sought a presentation that will, when tested in life, prove useful, and at no point have we been led away from this object in order to create a book impressive by its bulk or quantity of detail. Instead, references are given that will enable the reader to pursue any special interest and become familiar at first hand with the many sources of information that have contributed to our knowledge of the American family. The influences that affect domestic experience are so many that it can rightly be said that nothing humanly important is foreign to the family. The college student who elects a course in the family, however, seeks a discriminating, applicatory interpretation that will later aid him in gathering the satisfactions that successful adjustments bring, when he establishes his own family.

In order to accomplish the purpose of the book, we have divided it into four parts. Part I, "The Development of the Family," deals with the development of the American family and provides background. It includes also a discussion of the study of the family and the significance of the family as a social institution. Part II, "Psychological Aspects of American Family Experience," emphasizes the emotional and psychological aspects of our present domestic manner of life. Part III, "Social Problems of the American Family," discusses important social problems associated with American family life. The final Part IV, "Specialized Programs for the Conservation of the American Family," considers the resources available for the improving and strengthening of family life. Here the interests of the family as a social organization and the potential values of marriage and parenthood for the individual are both emphasized.

The widespread and serious interest in problems of the American family in recent years is reflected in the instruction offered in colleges and universities by departments of sociology and home economics. The family as a social institution has been lifted out of emotional controversy and has become for serious men and women a subject deserving scientific interpretation and objective study in college courses. The development of instruction in the family and its allied problems has been extraordinarily rapid. So much has happened since the senior author's *Social Problems of the Family,* the first college text, was published in 1927, that it is difficult to realize that the former book, when it first appeared, was a pioneer in presenting the family and its problems as a major subject for college instruction in sociology. Now, a similar development appears to be taking place in courses dealing with marriage problems, as distinct from those of the family, and what has been perhaps the most emotional of all the topics of discussion within the field of social experience is passing over to the scientist for investigation and to the college instructor for systematic and practical exposition.

As the contents of this book make clear, the authors are indebted to the great quantity of literature which expresses the investigation and the thinking of a host of persons interested in the family and its problems. In addition to this acknowledgment, we wish especially to recognize the following: the Institute for Research in Social Science for the assistance and opportunity which made this book possible; Professor Benjamin R. Andrews for his critical reading of the manuscript and valuable suggestions; Edgar Schmiedeler, Catholic University, Washington, D. C.; L. Foster Wood, Federal Council of Churches; Rabbi Sidney Goldstein; our colleagues, Donald S. Klaiss and

Rupert B. Vance; Robert L. Dickinson, M.D., of New York City; Joseph K. Folsom, Vassar College; Lester W. Dearborn, Counseling Service, Boston, for many stimulating discussions of marriage and family problems; Anna Greene Smith for her revision of the fiction, plays, and biographical material suggested as sources for a literary study of American family life; John S. Bradway, Director, Legal Aid Clinic, Duke University, for help in regard to legal problems; Georgia H. Faison for help in checking references; Ruth Ferris and Grace Welch Behrman for the preparation of the manuscript; and Catherine Groves for assistance and penetrating criticisms.

E. R. G.
G. H. G.

Contents

xi

PART III

Social Problems of the American Family

PART IV

Specialized Programs for the Conservation of the American Family

Part I

The Development of the Family

Chapter 1

SOCIAL SIGNIFICANCE
OF THE FAMILY

FOREWORD. Malinowski, one of the most widely read of modern anthropologists, calls attention to the impossibility of understanding any form of social organization without the insight given us by the family structure.[1] This recent statement of the social significance of the family finds its counterpart in various assertions made by those whom we know as the earliest recorded thinkers who were interested in and who reflected upon social experience. Thus, for example, we find Plato and Aristotle recognizing the basic importance of the family and wrestling with its problems as they attempted to build a rational program for social life.

Because of the family's contribution to the establishing and maintaining of society and its causal influence on the individual as appears in the building of both his personality and his conduct, this text starts with a discussion of the social significance of the family. In order to realize how secure the family is and how tied up with the development of man and his culture, it is needful that we both investigate the biological basis of the family and retrace its sociological unfolding. This consideration in turn reveals the survival function of the family and the consequences of this as expressed in the institutionalizing of the mother-father-child relationships. Thus kinship association brought forth an organization, which not only throughout the historic period has contributed to the structure and the security of society, but which has itself also reacted to the prevailing social milieu.

This reaction of the present-day American family to its

---

[1] Malinowski, Bronislaw, "Kinship," *Encyclopedia Britannica*, 14th edition, Vol. 13, p. 403.

social situation, especially as it appears in the behavior of the individual family members, has a personal meaning for the student who seeks from his study not only a better understanding of the influences of the home as they have operated on his own personality, but also a greater preparedness for the responsibilities and opportunities anticipated in his own marriage and parenthood. If his study of the family is to have practical value, it must stress the concreteness and individuality of family experience. As a sociological institution the home may remain an abstraction, but when we seek to understand the meaning of family experience, its relationships and interactions, its values and its problems, it becomes necessary to envisage the family as it operates in the lives of individual men, women, and children.

The biological basis of the family. As one would expect of so ancient a human organization as the family, science cannot trace its evolution with exactness. Although the gradual emergence of human marriage and the family is a matter of conjecture, any attempt to search out the beginning uncovers their biological foundations. The effort to reconstruct the history of this human institution, even though the stages of its coming cannot be made a continuous record, leads us backward into the simpler life of the lower animals. We find in all biological organisms two fundamental sets of activities, the one providing self-maintenance and the other the perpetuation of the species. It is in this second line of behavior that we find developing the activities and interests most closely related to what in its present human maturity we designate as family experience. Accompanying the increasing complexity of the animal organism, we find the general trend toward a widening of the meaning of the reproductive activities and a greater stress of the co-operation of male and female which has reached its fullest and most intricate expression in the family life of the human. Once reproduction requires the union of the male and female organisms, we have the basis of this association that appears in highest form in the human family.

The more important progress, however, toward the human experience found in the animal world is within the field of mother-offspring relationship. With the appearance of the male-female method of reproduction biological changes appear in both types of organisms, that each may be the better equipped to

carry on its specialized activity in reproduction. This same readjustment of a physical organism to meet new circumstances is
even more significant along the lines of development ushered in
by the mother-offspring relationship. It is here chiefly that the
general evolutionary trend occurs which in a much more complex form appears in the family experience of primitive peoples.

Biological intimation of the family. Although we find
pairing among the lower animals, it is, as a rule, a temporary
relationship and as such affords no provision for the simplest
kind of family experience. We see the beginnings in the mother-
offspring relationship of what, when highly developed, constitutes the family. Once this comes under the dominancy of an
instinct, making the association relatively permanent as we find
it, for example, in our household pets or domestic animals, we
have the start of a passionate care on the one side and a dependency on the other which lead the mother and infant to maintain a special and close relationship, an intimation of what on
the human level becomes the family.

The instinct, however, which creates this protective-de-
pendency alliance also in due time destroys it, and then the
mother drives her offspring away and all sense of belonging is
lost by both animals. While the mother-spirit persists the animal
accepts her role with patience, courage, diligence, and a willingness to sacrifice self even unto death.[2] In the handling of so
highly developed a domestic animal as the dog, it has to be
recognized how greatly parenthood may, especially in its beginning, modify the disposition of the mother and drive her to a
ferocious attack if she is made to feel that her pups are being
hurt. The aggressiveness of the female under such circumstances
has become an axiom among hunters of wild animals.

In spite of the strength of the instinct which shows itself
in the mother attitude, it is precarious and may under adverse
conditions disappear. A very common illustration of this disappearance of elemental mother-love is found in the effect that the
attempt to domesticate the wild animal frequently has. So long
as favorable conditions prevail parent birds generally show themselves devoted to their young, but if something amiss happens
these parents may quickly lose concern. Thus the disturbing of

---

[2] Needham, James G., *About Ourselves*, pp. 116–117.

the nest may lead to the birds abandoning their young.[3] Hudson, the naturalist, reports the case of a female robin who paid no attention to her offspring which had been pushed out of the nest by an alien cuckoo which she had hatched. Although the young robin was near and in full sight for hours, the mother robin gave it no attention whatsoever and continued to warm and feed the parasite stealthily forced upon her.[4]

An experienced French aviculturist, M. Delacour, reports that in his attempts to breed turacos, large brightly colored African birds related to the cuckoo, he found that he could not succeed with the first brood because the male invariably killed the young as soon as they were hatched. Three years in succession the male invariably did this after the first hatching but allowed the young of the second brood to live. The breeder had a similar experience with several other species of birds.[5]

The mother-offspring relationship, once it arrives, offers opportunity for a new line of behavior which in the higher animals begins to assume a significance that finally comes forth in fullness in the infancy period of the human career. This new mode of animal behavior is a product of biological need, and, although we think of it as the expression of maternal instinct, the relationship shows marked variations in strength, in duration, and in forms of expression. Undoubtedly it is awakened, supported, and brought to an end by physiological changes of the animal's body. This therefore cannot be faithfully interpreted, however strong it appears, as having in full vigor the sentimental and conceptual characteristics normally found in the mother-child relationship on the human level. It is an intimation rather than a distinct copy of the human experience, but, as we should suppose, among the higher animals this relationship closely approximates the weakest and most primitive forms of the human mother-child attachment.

The mother-offspring status brings a new set of activities which in turn give new meaning to the function of reproduction. Not only is the career of the female modified by the prominent place in her activities given to the care of offspring, but changes

[3] Friedmann, Herbert, "The Instinctive Emotional Life of Birds," *Psychoanalytic Review*, Vol. 21, p. 381.

[4] Hudson, W. H., *Hampshire Days*, p. 24.

[5] Friedmann, *ibid.*, p. 271.

in her functioning are reflected in the male who is gradually brought through his interest in his mate to co-operate in the care of the helpless offspring. This incorporating of the male in the new and more complex method of reproduction does not go on in a continuous line of development which would permit us to retrace the modern form of family life backward through the experience of simpler people into that of the higher animals to the first beginning of the alliance of male and female in the rearing of young. What we do find is different illustrations of helping by the male in, as Jennings says, various, isolated, and unexpected ways.[6] For example, among some fish we find the male helping to build and protect the nest and even defending the young when first they start swimming. This bringing of the male into the mother-offspring relationship for the purpose of maintenance and defense proves a new and important step in the evolution that finally reaches human expression.

We have instances among the lower animals of the mating of a male and female continuing for a duration which leads some to designate their living together an animal marriage.[7] Some species change their mates with each brood, others continue together until the end of the season, and still others mate for life. In the first two cases, when one of the two dies the other quickly finds a new mate; but in the case of birds mating for life, there is a longer time before the survivor seeks another life-partner, and because of this a breeding season may be missed.[8] The majority of birds are monogamous even though their breeding may be for so short a period as a month or two. This is not true of all of them and we find some practicing pologyny, promiscuity, and perhaps polyandry. As an illustration of this variation from a monogamous relationship, we have the reports of the behavior of the South American cowbird. The female of this species when she has exhausted the opportunity for safe nests in the territory presided over by her mate moves on until she finds another place where she can build a nest in security, and then she mates with the male of that district. Her conduct is perhaps best described as a short monogamy, while the various mates are clearly polygamous.[9] The majority of birds may be credited with a temporary

[6] Jennings, H. S., The Biological Basis of Human Nature, p. 257.
[7] Reuter, Edward Byron, and Runner, Jessie Ridgway, The Family, p. 61.
[8] Friedmann, op. cit., Psychoanalytic Review, p. 261.
[9] Friedmann, Herbert, The Cowbirds, pp. 271–272.

but genuine family relationship during which the parent birds not only feed the offspring but minister to their comfort and protection. There are exceptions, however, and some species are parasitic. They place their eggs in the nests of other birds, leaving to the foster parents of their choice the task of hatching and then caring for the unrelated strangers forced upon them.

In the family of primitive peoples we shall see pressure coming from economic and social circumstances to force the male to assume greater responsibility for the care of mother and child. Influences coming forth from the lengthening of the human infancy period are the greater helplessness of the child and the increasing need of support and protection for the mother as she gives herself to the care of her offspring. Thus we find biological needs, which on lower levels of animal life are temporary, fixed in form, and instinctive in character, spreading under the pressure of social necessities into varied, permanent, and self-conscious expression.

The family as a social institution.   The evolution of organisms, with the ever increasing complexity of the allied functions of self-maintenance and reproduction, proceeds along two distinct lines. One develops into the family type of behavior that we find in birds, the higher anthropoids, and man, while the other finds its goal in the highly specialized society of insects, such as the bees and the ants. The second destroys the basis of family life by making reproduction the mere laying of eggs by a single fertilized female or queen, while the hatching of the eggs and the caring for the young are given over to the group of workers. Along the line of development in which man thus far has had his career, the family, on the other hand, has had such prominence that it is no exaggeration to call it the "nursery of all modern institutions." [10]

Although birds are used as examples among the higher animals of the establishment of a simple but genuine family relationship, they also reveal in high degree the ability to develop socialization and to learn as flocks to act together for their common interest. Thus the instinct which leads them to individualize their concern for their offspring in ways that suggest the reactions of the human parent does not prevent their working together for group welfare. Kropotkin tells us that some par-

---

[10] Dealey, J. Q., *The Family in Its Sociological Aspects*, p. 4.

rots reach so high a level in their practices as to suggest normal human intelligence and sympathy.[11] The source of such co-operative practices is found by some authors in a mother-love that spreads, is imparted to the offspring, continued, and enlarged until it becomes a capacity for socialization.[12]

The human family has had a double role to play. It has served as a medium by which the infancy period has been able to perform its biological and social purposes. Thus the family has given the child the means of survival by providing for him in his years of weakness a favorable environment. Activities carried on for the protecting and training of the child have reacted upon the parents themselves so that the home has been for them also a specialized social environment out of which have come consequences that have gone beyond the mere care of the child itself. This does not mean that the man or woman has sought parenthood with the deliberate intent either to perpetuate the race or to gain through the experience its social results, but rather that the coming of the child has brought for the parent a new social situation rarely foreseen. Indeed in the unsophisticated experience of simple peoples these consequences of parenthood have not even been clearly conscious.

It is interesting to find in the contrast of these two different lines of development of organic life testimony to the importance of the family as the source of individualization. On the human level it has been recognized from Plato on by social reformers tending toward some sort of communistic state that the family must necessarily be their chief obstacle because of its inherent tendency to develop, strengthen, and express the significance of each member as an individual in the household.

John Fiske, by his contribution of the meaning of the infancy period, added an important clue to the evolution which distinguishes man from other animal life. The length of the nurture period permits the development of a nervous system which can support the complexity and flexibility which human conduct requires. It is reasonable to assume that this was not merely a growth of greater nervous capacity but that as it proceeded there was a corresponding enlargement of social activities and that the family by its basic, instinctive regard for others

---

[11] Kropotkin, Peter, *Mutual Aid*, p. 31.
[12] Reuter and Runner, *op. cit.*, p. 60.

and the opportunity it provided for the expansion of this other-than-self concern became the breeding place of that recognition of others which was prerequisite to the establishment of any kind of social institution. Mother-love inherently possessed incentives not only for its own enlargement and strengthening but also as a consequence of this extension for the development of a social tendency which carried mother-love and later parental affection beyond itself. Thus evolution reflected the advantages of a lengthening infancy which increased the significance of the family, enabling it to assume the task of extending that awareness of, and concern for, others which the emerging primitive man required for his socialization.[13]

The family and social evolution. Evolution assumes that the increase of the infancy period which permitted a longer, thereby more complex, preparedness for life was a gradual process ranging over a long period of time and finally reaching its climax in the human species. It is unreasonable to suppose that this was a mere enlargement of brain capacity since we know that such structural development must have been accompanied by an increasing function of the higher nervous system. At least that is what now takes place as the human individual moves toward maturity. The growth of brain and its refinement are associated with an increase of activity which becomes more complex and in its earliest stages replaces instinct and the simple reflex by the conditioned reflex, by habit and self-consciousness.

Since the socializing processes that became characteristic of man could not have awaited the coming of a certain period in this prolonging of infancy before becoming themselves a part of the evolution, the family, because of the character of its activities and the possibility these offered for increasing socialization, must have played the basic role as this greater dominance of brain functioned socially. Looking backward from the present with our understanding of the basic motivations for life that come out of family experience, we find in the feeling of identity first enforced by instinct, as is still true of the animals nearest man, an incentive leading toward socialization. The organism no longer adapted itself merely to the pressure of its

[13] Groves, E. R., *The Family and Its Social Functions,* Chs. 4–6.

environment. In addition there was an inward pressure that came from the feeling of identity between mother and offspring. Out of this came the parental impulses in response to dependency that, although not the only incitement of sympathy, were surely stronger and more secure than any other.

This holding together of mother and offspring, which itself was an increasing experience as the infancy period lengthened, by its awakening and maintaining this relationship of belonging encouraged the coming of other incentives, and as the greater brain capacity began to show itself there followed an increase in that richness of memory and imagination which is distinctive of man. The sense of identity could be carried forward into the future so that the mother-offspring relationship, although it might change, would not dissolve as is true of the animals under the control of instinct. Thus began another line of development providing a new quality in association. This would be rooted in the incentive of perpetuity, motivations coming not from the strength but from the persistence of parental attitudes.

The third contribution to man's socialization arising from the family represents a maturity which assumes not only the full development of brain capacity but also a high quality in the parent-child relationship. It was possible only when the sense of identity had taken on great emotional meaning and the impulse to continue this had become so strong that to the parent the belonging of the infant was both realized in the present and projected into the future. The family by the development it had already made and the demands that it had made conscious was carried beyond itself. Then appeared and grew the incentives of transcendence, and the socialization which had been nurtured and matured within the family was carried beyond the family experience.

No one who appreciates the gradations that the hypothesis of human evolution assumes, the immense period of time involved, and the influence that each advancement has in encouraging another will suppose that these family motivations stood out distinctly or that they represented disconnected lines of development. Such an analysis results from our interpretation as we now seek to retrace and describe the slow emergence of man and the strengthening of his social interests, as this went hand in hand with an increasing capacity of brain resources associated with the lengthening of the infancy period.[14]

Biologically the mother and father transmit their hereditary traits to the child; socially they build into his growing personality his social heritage as they maintain for him the protective environment necessary for his survival.

What is family experience?   The family is essentially conduct. It is not an establishment as is the house, but a group of activities that have a core of common significance. It is not just people, but people who live together that make a home. The study of the social problems of the family is the investigation of human behavior in the relationships characteristic of family grouping. Family life is one type of social conduct, and everything we know about the behavior of men, women, and children in their other relationships helps us to understand the problems of the family; every fact that we gather concerning family situations has a value in understanding human conduct in its wider aspects. The family is a social institution, but it is such because it is an organization which provides a peculiar opportunity for the interaction of individual human beings. It is essentially not a status but a distinct complex of behavior. It is life expressed at close quarters with the intense personal reactions characteristic of people living together in intimate emotional relationship.

Family life, because of its intimacy and privacy, provides a unique opportunity for the free expression of personality. It is in this closeness of relationship that the family meets its severest strain. It is also in this very intimacy of home associations that we find the power of the family to influence character and satisfy human cravings. Thus the family permits in the largest possible manner "the intimate face-to-face associations and co-operation," which Cooley has told us are characteristic of the primary groups.[15]

The family is the meeting place of adult and child. One, a social product already largely shaped, becomes the chief influence in fashioning the other and helping him to adapt himself to his social environment. The family is something more than the prototype of society; it is itself a society, the first into which

---

[14] Groves, E. R., *The Family and Its Social Functions*, Chs. 4, 5, and 6.
[15] Cooley, C. H., *Social Organization*, Ch. 3.

we all enter, and the most powerful in changing raw human nature into a socialized personality.

Because the family presents a social microcosm, it offers the best opportunity for the study of social behavior. It provides the psychologist and the sociologist, as well as the psychiatrist, a laboratory where in relative simplicity compared with the complexities of modern life the motivations and reactions of individuals socially tied to one another can best be unraveled and traced with a measure of definiteness. The human individual even in the family setting is too complex and too subtle for a complete causal understanding. Nevertheless, his social behavior as a family member is more open to investigation and explanation than when outside the home he reacts to the more extensive and diverse environment of the social group. It is therefore not merely the priority of family experience which gives it its lasting significance in the life of each individual but, in addition, its distinguishing characteristic, an intensifying of social experience because it occurs within a grouping limited in number but unrestricted in the opportunity it offers for emotional expression and response.

The family and changing culture. The family, although providing for its members a social microcosm, does not, of course, exist by itself uninfluenced by outside social conditions. Much of the family behavior is actually derivative, having its origin in the out-of-the-home experiences of the various members who compose it. In this way the family is kept in close contact with the social environment and is forced to adapt itself to the conditions of a group life larger than that of the home.

We are prone in thinking of the family to regard it as static, having reached by social evolution a final form which is fully adjusted to an unchanging situation. As we look backward we easily see the variations in family conditions and the necessity for them, but in our own time and place it is natural to feel that at last the family has arrived and must be protected against further change. It is our faulty human wish for permanence of conditions that have become comfortable by being made habitual that creates the idea of the family as an unalterable social institution.

The quickest way to become dislodged from a restricted

view of the family, conceived from one's own personal experience and contact with other households essentially similar to one's own, is to visit vicariously through literature families that are in structure and in much of their functioning considerably different from those with whom the reader is familiar. This explains the attention given other types of family life in the conventional texts which seek to interpret the family of the United States. Through his consideration of other forms of familial experience, the student translates the abstract realization of the great variability of the family as an institution into a concrete appreciation of this diversity, and through the contrast he recognizes he is all the more prepared to understand the family type to which he himself belongs.

Knowledge of family life in different parts of the world and at different periods of time helps also to impress the fact that as an institution the family is always in process of adaptation to its own environment. This contact, however, cannot be regarded as having to do merely with the physical and material conditions which Le Play, the pioneering student of the economic aspect of the family, described [16] but also with adjustment to the deposit of cultural experience which is transmitted by custom and tradition. Frequently, in interpreting family traits that differ greatly from our own conventional form, the clue to the peculiarity is found in the reaction not to the physical environment but to cultural characteristics which have been socially transmitted.

Much of the pessimism regarding the family is born of the conviction, held with the tenacity characteristic of strong emotional bias, that any change in family life is an evil; or it comes from a failure to recognize that the family in its attempt at adaptation must suffer disturbances and losses. It is only by internal readjustments that the family in common with other institutions can adapt itself to human need and accomplish its social task.

The history of the family reveals the fact that we cannot estimate its importance on a purely quantitative basis. By that measurement recent changes in the family may give the impression that the family is fading away since it does not maintain

---

[16] Zimmerman, Carle C., and Frampton, Merle E., *Family and Society*, p. 74.

as many kinds of activities as formerly. For example, when the Industrial Revolution led to mills that took away the livelihood of persons who had carried on cottage production, all the members of the family of sufficient age taking their part in the weaving or spinning which gave the household its means of support, one might easily have prophesied that the family was disappearing. What was happening was a change in family life. If household co-operation was lost, it was equally true that the machine was to bring greater leisure, thus providing fellowship for family members far superior to that permitted by their mere being together as workers. The changes in the family that are inevitable in a nonstatic society have their gains and their losses, but in any attempt to estimate the strength or the security of the family as an institution attention must be given to the qualitative aspect of familial experience as well as the quantitative.

It is interesting at present, for example, to find the vitality of the American family questioned because of the family's loss of functions while at the same time it is also criticized because of too great parental devotion to children on account of its smaller size and an increased attention to the individual child. Sometimes we find the critic both deploring the lessening significance of the family while indicting it for meaning too much to the family members. It is evident that in so far as this situation is adequately described as an American trend it illustrates a parenthood change in quantity in one direction and a change in quality in another direction so that there is both more and less parenthood experience.

The family must remain sensitive to the varying circumstances of group life; it cannot settle into a self-satisfied stiffness. Traditions passed from one generation to another within the family group frequently leave no place for family adaptability, but change takes place in spite of this, only with more emotional stress for the representatives of the two periods of time, who, with differing viewpoints, contend for power to shape the family.

The family reflects.   The family is, of course, an abstraction. This does not mean that the family is a fiction but rather that it is a necessary term for human experience that is composite. It is only when the word "family" is used to cover up its concreteness and the multiplicity and diversity of its content that the term becomes misleading. The concept is necessary if we are to think intelligently of the vast mass of particular happenings and behavior, interests and values which center about that special relationship which constitutes the home. What the student needs to keep steadily in mind is that whenever we come close to familial reality we find not the family but always only families.

What exists as actual human experience is families, each with distinguishable peculiarities similar to those that we find among individual persons. The amount of variation between families, however, is influenced by the state of social culture, the difference becoming greater the more complex the social environment. As a consequence, in any discussion of the family, attention must always be given to the cultural conditions of the time and the place. In the background of the modern family, the influences of economic status, education, race, nationality, and religious faith are especially prominent. Thus the family reflects the mores that surround it. In our present complex society, especially in the United States, we detect the working of a selective process so that individual families respond to standards that exist at different levels and in different sections. But this fact must not be interpreted to mean that American family life has escaped mores control. Even though a family offers to its members a restricted area for social interaction, it cannot because of this maintain isolation, for its members also enter the larger social environment expressive of the prevailing culture. Not only does the family have contact in this way with the out-of-home conditions, but its life also responds to these outside influences just as the individual member has to make his personal adjustment to his total environment.

Under unusual circumstances the family life may be chiefly influenced by conditions distant in place or time or by an environment that is being built deliberately and artificially. An American family in Haiti on a coffee plantation twenty miles from the nearest white neighbor illustrates the first; religious groups attempting to resurrect the family of the Hebrew period of Genesis, the second; while the Oneida Community is a striking example of the third. Even in these unusual types there is not complete removal from the impact of the ordinary surrounding culture, as appears in the final breaking up of the Oneida colony not chiefly because of internal dissatisfaction or dissension but on account of the hostility of outside public opinion.

The family originates.   The individual family never lives independent of the surrounding culture with which it has contact. It is, however, not a mere facsimile of the prevailing environment. Besides transmitting what the sociologist calls *social inheritance,* it also provides through the intimacies of personal experience and the interaction of one member with another something unique which makes it unlike any other familial cluster. In this way the family furnishes the child with an original setting from which come influences that enter his growing personality, peculiar to the home life in which fate has placed him.

These influences have, of course, greater significance for the developing child than for the parents, who react in greater degree to the conditions of their own childhood situation. It is because of this peculiarity of home conditions that each family gives to the child original stimuli that are not a mere reproduction of the general culture. This provides opportunity for variation so that in different degrees individual families originate as well as transmit culture. In the family life of primitive peoples we find this originating activity reduced to its minimum, and this in turn helps to perpetuate the relative unchangeableness of preliterate society.

Since the family's original contribution enters culture through the medium of the personalities that develop within the domestic circle, the career of the nonconformist, of the reformer, and of the social leader who plays a prominent part in some cultural change, all show the results of family circumstances. The psychoanalysts, especially through their effort to interpret the character effects of the family environment, have added a new line of approach to historical criticism, and already we have an attempt to unravel the formative influences that operated upon Napoleon, Lincoln, Darwin, and others who have played a large role in modern civilization. With greater clearness the psychoanalysts discover in the early childhood of neurotic and maladjusted adults influences that appear largely responsible for their difficulties.

Through its power to originate, the family may become a source of social antagonism and maladjustment. The most widely accepted theory of the origin of functional mental disease finds in the early family situation the chief cause of trouble. During the first years of the child when the emotional habits were taking form the environment provided by the family proved harmful, and as a consequence the emotional life of the adult at a later time drove the individual into some kind of social maladjustment. One of the common causes of difficulty is retardation of growth as the family obstructs the self-expression and independent development of the boy or girl. This takes many forms and frequently is the product of circumstances that injured the maturing of the father or mother during childhood. Among the immigrant families in the United States there often appears an attempt to retard growth, as a result of the parents' policy of attempting to preserve as much as possible the cultural patterns of the country from which they have migrated, while the child in his out-of-the-family environment is exposed to the prevailing cultural traits of the United States.

We also have families that attempt to maintain for their children the domestic situations characteristic of past periods, so that the impact of modern life at every point meets with resistance and the child from his infancy forward becomes a victim of two persistent, antagonizing lines of influence. Under such circumstances he may develop an emotional dualism which renders him an alien member of his own social culture while at the same time preventing his wholehearted acceptance of the traditions of his early home. Since the family is a slow-changing institution, the home, when traditional and unresponsive to new conditions, becomes for many children the source of social confusion, conflict, and emotional instability.

The modern American family situation.   The flow of material and social culture has become so rapid in our time that it is universally recognized as one of the most distinctive features of contemporary civilization. Not only do people generally realize what is happening, but they also see its cause. The enormous progress made during the last two centuries through discoveries, inventions, and the application of science has changed and is changing constantly the activities, the beliefs, the desires, and the relationships of men, women, and children. Nothing that feels the force of the cultural current remains stationary. Just as government, business, religion, education, and vocations change, so does the family. That this is especially true in the United States is also generally recognized. It is, however, a grave mistake to regard the changing family as something peculiar to the American environment. It is the modern character of our culture rather than its distinctive American features that chiefly accounts for the disorganization so clearly recognized in our prevailing family life. Nowhere in the world has the momentum of material progress been greater than here, and as a consequence our culture reflects the disturbances that come from so rapid a change in the ways of living.

This great influence, which the United States shares with most other countries, has been the effect of a rapidly developing machine culture based upon even greater advances in applied science. Even though many believe the family has been more conservative perhaps than any other institution in reacting to these environmental changes, it has responded, and as we look backward over our social trends, in recent years we see in greater or less degree confusion and conflict as individual families feel the impact of the new striking the conditions and habits drawn from the past. In a great measure this collision has been the cause of tension between the older and the younger members of families. It cannot, however, be limited merely to this expression of stress, since it to some extent is always found where there is close and free expression between youth and their elders. Instead we find in young people and in children considerable strain because they present in their own inner life a battleground for the struggle of the old with the new.

The anchorage of the type of patriarchal family life that became established in the United States during the eighteenth and nineteenth centuries has been or is being swept away, and in consequence there is great confusion, unrest, and instability in American marriage and family relationships. Although family life everywhere in the world where modern conditions prevail reveals greater or less change, our situation has been heightened by the disturbance brought about by the influx of immigrants during the nineteenth century with their great variation in family traditions, standards, and ideals. The attempt to assimilate such a diversity of culture added greatly to the strain brought forth by the modern development of science. The tension appeared more in family experience than elsewhere, since it was

in the home that the immigrant could take refuge in his fight
to maintain his former habits of living. In a later chapter we
shall need to consider in greater detail the social changes that
have influenced and are influencing American family life.

Increasing difficulty of family tasks.   No social institution
adjusts itself easily, for its organization always tends toward
conservatism and the advocacy of letting things be as they have
been. The family suffers especially in its attempts at social adaptation, for it has more of sentiment connected with it than have
other institutions.

The meaning of individual family difficulties expressed in
quarrels, separations, and divorces is the failure of the persons
concerned to adapt themselves to the needs of the family situation. Such failures bear testimony to the fact that for many
people the shifting demands of business, morals, and beliefs are
more easily met than those of the home.

The difficulty is increased by the common notion that the
family is a stable institution. Ideas of what constitutes a satisfactory family condition may clash, each individual assuming
that the proper thing is what he or she has seen or personally
experienced in other homes. Again, the conflict may result from
an individual's attempting for selfish reasons to block changes
that another member of the family believes imperative.

The family in common with the other fundamental social
institutions finds its task of adaptation becoming ever more difficult as a result of the growing complexity of civilization and the
higher standards of living. In comparison with the family life
of savages, or even of people a half-century ago, the modern
home has to make much more delicate adjustments or fail to
bring to its members the satisfactions they want.

Social pressure in the form of fashion, conventional behavior, and such standards as are popularly regarded as ideals for
home life, keeps the family ever in a process of attempting to do
what is expected of it.

Of course it is true that this pressure is felt by the family
members individually to a large degree rather than by the family
as a whole, but the home group reacts to the situation as a result
of the individuals' responses. If, for example, fashion demands
of the marriageable daughter of the house, who contributes to
the family income, the expenditure of a relatively larger part of
her earnings that she may have the fur coat she needs to meet the

matrimonial competition of her girl friends and rivals, then the family as a whole feels the drain made on her wages by a luxury she could not really afford.

The relationships of the various members of the family are more difficult to maintain satisfactorily to each person when there is an increase of leisure, with its heightening of desires and usually of sensitiveness, because there is time to develop the competitions that normally arise in the modern home. It often seems to children (and usually they are quite right about it) that what one of them has or does explains the necessity of the others' going without this or some other much-sought pleasure.

It is also true that as the child comes more under the dominance of outside social organizations such as school and church— and such institutions are continually encroaching farther upon what was once entirely family territory—it is harder to adjust the various codes of conduct and the differing standards and purposes. The family has to assume the role of arbitrator; it must help the child adjust not only to the conflicting demands of outside institutions but also to the opposing interests expressed in the home program and that of other social organizations. The husband and wife in their response to out-of-the-home conditions have to meet difficulties similar to those encountered by the children. The family may have less function than in former times, but what it does becomes more complex and difficult.

The study of the family. Its importance in modern life and in the past of human experience, so far as this is known to science, justifies the attention the family is now receiving from psychologists, psychiatrists, social scientists, and all serious students of human behavior. Introductory courses dealing with the family, and advanced courses stressing some special phase of familial experience, are now widely offered by colleges and universities. Such courses provided by the departments of home economics and of sociology have developed rapidly during the last twenty years in institutions of higher learning in the United States and have already attained a prominent place in the curricula of modern educational institutions. To scarcely a less degree this interest in the family is appearing in the curricula of the more progressive high schools.[17]

---

[17] Folsom, Joseph K., *Youth, Family and Education*, Ch. 6; Goodykoontz, Bess, and Coon, Beulah I., *Family Living and Our Schools*, Ch. 5; and American Association of School Administrators, *Education for Family Life*.

Anyone interested in personality problems or looking forward to a vocation that requires understanding of people has need of becoming familiar with the history of the family, its influence upon character, and its present problems brought forth by modern conditions. For students interested in contemporary civilization, especially for those majoring in some field of social science, the study of the family becomes in turn imperative. In none of our social institutions is it easier to detect influences of our present material and social conditions and in no portion of the individual's experience can we discover the origin of the social inadequacy and maladjustment which produce our major social problems more clearly than in that which reveals the failure of the home.

A study of the family in accord with the tendency of the sciences concerned with human behavior encourages the analytic interpretation of personality. We are no longer content to describe or classify people; we seek to understand them as products of the various and complex influences that have worked upon them from conception through infancy into childhood and finally adulthood. Nearly always throughout this period during which the characteristics of the personality are developed and expressed, the family makes the chief contribution. From the study of the functioning of the family we develop ability to reconstruct and understand the formative background, a knowledge which proves indispensable whenever we attempt a scientific interpretation of personality.

Sources of knowledge. Our knowledge of the contemporary American family has to be gathered from many sources. For an understanding of the simpler forms of the family we turn to anthropology. History furnishes us with the evolution of the family during the period that we have had written records. In our effort to get at the significance of familial relationship, the interaction of person with person in the frankest and most intimate of contacts, we explore psychology, psychiatry, and sociology. Sociology furnishes us with a description of the problems of the family. Many features of the family are measurable, and for knowledge of these we turn to the statistician. Certain phases of family life carry us into law, politics, economics, education, ethics, and religion.

Even literature has an important contribution to make to

the understanding of contemporary American family life. This is particularly true of the domestic novel in which we find the artist attempting through character study to portray family situations and to disclose their causes and results.

Danger of bias and prejudice.   The student of the modern family meets all the difficulties that attend the study of any social institution and some that are peculiar to the family itself.

In no other experience is there so much of feeling and self-deception as is characteristic of family relationships. It is next to impossible to view without bias one's own home situation. The visitor in a brief period generally can see the significant conditions of a family in a clearer light than can the members themselves. Emotional attitudes are almost inevitable in the everyday contacts of a home. One's ideas of family matters are bound to be colored by feelings that forbid calm, objective judgments since everything which happens within the family is so likely to have a personal interest for each member.

Sentiment also hampers a just appraisal of any definite family. We look backward through the colored lights of emotion; our forward vision is distorted by our hopes, fears, or wishes. The exact facts are hard to get. This does not mean necessarily that the interested person is trying to hide or change facts, but rather that our family relationships, past, present, and even future in so far as imagined, are too shot through with personal meaning to be treated with unprejudiced judgment.

Because the home is so vivid a part of childhood and childhood so pleasant a portion of memory, it is easy for the emotions to color interpretations of the family. Problems of family life are favorite topics in the novel and the drama. Poetry portrays home experiences. In fiction and poetry the appeal to sentiment in the treatment of family topics is in harmony with the purpose of the author and is expected, even demanded, by the reader.

A scientific interpretation of the family requires, on the other hand, a purely objective attitude on the part of both author and reader. This does not mean that the human sympathies that relate to family experience are obstacles to the scientific understanding of the family. It is quite otherwise; but it is necessary that the emotional attitudes that would color the study of the family be held in check, for in no other social investigation is there such risk that personal experience or desire obstruct the effort to discover the facts. The chief value of a scientific study of the family as a social institution consists in the demand such an investigation makes that we consider the family with its problems apart from our own personal and emotional attitudes toward it. By disentangling our own experiences from the subject of our study, we gain a richer and more accurate understanding of the social significance of the family in modern life.

The family also hides itself behind a privacy not shared by any other institution. If law regards a man's home as his castle, convention and tradition make the happenings of the home more private than the inner counsels of the most secret fraternal organizations. It is bad taste to talk without great care of one's own or even another's home conditions. Curiosity may wish to pry into the secrecy of family situations, but unless protected by the guise of serious purpose it is considered socially disreputable.

When we enter our homes we become by common consent socially isolated and our privacy is protected by a conventional code of conduct which the well bred are expected to follow and which shuts in the family more effectively than high walls. Even those who turn to the court for legal separation or divorce are expected by public opinion to hide as far as possible the truth regarding their unhappiness. This regard for family privacy has become so ingrained in our social attitudes that we observe it without thought as a matter of course.

The idea of family rights is firmly fixed in law, and only an experienced social worker knows how heavy is the burden of proof assumed by one who asks of the court legal authority to interfere in a family situation which seems socially intolerable.

It is clear, therefore, that these emotional reactions, sentiments, and concealments hamper the scientist who attempts an objective study of the family. Certain facts of great importance present no difficulty. We can, for example, tabulate the number of divorces, the marriage rate, the birth rate, and a quantity of valuable information. It is when we attempt the explanation of some of these facts in concrete human behavior that we find ourselves on uncertain ground. It is one thing to know that divorces are increasing; it is quite another to discover what motives are operating to produce this increase. We can easily discover the low birth-rate record of any particular group of men or women, but it is more difficult to see what social or psychic causes are at work to bring about this situation.

In spite of the perplexities in the way of a scientific interpretation of family problems, the effort is bound to be made by students interested in the family, and not without result. Scientists can at least bring together some suggestive material that will help those who must deal practically with family problems. All investigations of human behavior when they try to disclose psychic and social causes encounter baffling problems. Such studies are attempted, nevertheless, and our fund of knowledge is slowly increased.

Traits of the contemporary American family. If the students of any sizable class will write out briefly what to them seems characteristic of the contemporary families with which they are familiar, although there will be minor differences influenced by section, class, and social background, a rather general agreement will appear in the statements of the individual members. This results from the fact that most of us living in this country are familiar with our foremost domestic traits and therefore can start the study of the family with an understanding of the object of our analysis.

It will be found when a summary of such individual descriptions is made that the following are generally regarded as distinctive of American family life. The family as compared with that of earlier periods reveals a loss of functions; many of its former activities are now carried on by other agencies, especially the school, and this tendency is continuing. The change in the economic function of the family has been greatest. It has moved from a largely household-producing unit to a consuming economy. The housewife is increasingly a manager who buys, plans, and distributes foods and goods furnished by commerical enterprises, and, even though she continues to carry on the duties of a housekeeper, her managerial function in comparison with the past has an importance that distinguishes our modern contemporary family life. The birth rate has decreased and there is, in a large proportion of American families, a trend toward spacing children by voluntary control of reproduction. In the professional classes marriages occur relatively late.

Within the family there is expression of the American social

trend toward the equality of men and women. In a large proportion of homes, indeed, the woman appears to be dominant,
especially in the training of children. Although there are wide
variations between families, the characteristic ideal is toward a
democratic household. There is less discipline of children than
formerly but a better understanding of the responsibilities of
child nurture. The parents' control of children has lessened as
the school has taken over greater responsibility, and this seems
to be in accord with the wishes of the majority of mothers and
fathers. Family life shows considerable instability, and the increasing divorce rate, one expression of this, suggests that this is
greater at present than when the family performed a greater
quantity of services. Love has become the conventional motivation for marriage and affection is generally regarded as the basic
tie of the family. During the last decade there has been a marked
drift from the former American ideal of self-responsibility and
a greater dependence upon the state, especially in the attitude
of children toward their aged parents. The disposition to look
toward the state for security has also lessened emphasis on thrift,
formerly in America a necessary and much emphasized domestic
virtue.

In this text the American development of family life is
studied for the purpose of explaining its origin; describing its
present characteristics, difficulties, and opportunities; and discussing the movements that are strengthening and improving
American domestic experience. Thus the contents of the book
aim at answering the questions: how our family life has come to
be; what it is; what are its present adjustments, interactions, and
relationships; what are some of its most significant problems;
and what important contributions are now being made to its
more successful functioning.

Definition of family.   The term "family" needs definition,
since in different periods and cultures it has been used to denote
various types of groupings. In Roman law it referred to household members, including slaves and servants, united as a unit
of production and consumption rather than as persons connected by blood or marriage relationship. In the days of American slavery in the old South on the better plantations, the slave,
especially the household servant in contrast with the field
worker, considered himself a member of the family to which he

belonged and a relationship which included responsibilities was recognized by the owner. Within this larger and looser grouping, however, there was another, smaller, closer, and different in quality, determined by common descent or marriage, and from which the slave considered himself excluded.

The family has been defined as a unit of interaction, and this stresses one of its important functions; but this is a relationship shared by other groupings, for example, a class of students and a teacher. Le Play, a French student of the family, regarded the normal family or desirable family as one made up of a parent household (the stem), the foundation of society, and a number of individual members (the branches), who go out from the home in order to take advantage of the greater economic opportunity found in industrial and urban environments.[18]

The term "family," as it is used in the tabulation of the results of the 1930 Census, "is limited in the main to what might be called private families, excluding the institutions and hotel or boarding-house groups which have been counted as families in previous censuses. A family may therefore be defined in general as a group of persons related either by blood or by marriage or by adoption, who live together as one household usually sharing the same table. Single persons living alone are counted as families, however, as are a few small groups of unrelated persons sharing the same living accommodations as 'partners.' Households reporting more than ten lodgers are classified as boarding or lodging houses rather than as families. Two or more related persons occupying permanent quarters in a hotel are counted as a private family rather than as a part of the hotel group." [19]

In the 1940 Census there is a slight difference in order to place greater emphasis on the household as a place of dwelling. The last two sentences of the previous statement disappear, being replaced by the following: "A dwelling unit is defined as the living quarters occupied by one family or household. In an apartment house there are, therefore, as many dwelling units as there are separate apartments." [20]

In this book, the word "family" is used to mean the group-

---

[18] Zimmerman, Carle C., and Frampton, Merle E., *Family and Society*, p. 47.
[19] *Abstract of the Fifteenth Census of the United States*, 1930, p. 401.
[20] *Statistical Abstract of the Sixteenth Census of the United States*, 1941, p. 49.

ing of persons maintaining the relationship recognized as that of parents and children. As the context indicates the term at times also refers to the period in this relationship when the parents and children live together. The grouping is usually based on an acknowledged sex commitment of the parents and the blood kinship of the children, but adoption also brings a child into the parent-child relationship.

Chapter 2

THE STUDY OF THE FAMILY

FOREWORD. It saves time and confusion for the student of the family to be introduced at the beginning of his interest to important contributions made by various specialists in the field of marriage and the family. Such a presentation is the purpose of this chapter. It reveals what a wide territory of human experience is covered by the family and the need of interpreting family life along many differing lines of investigation. Familial experience is not exclusively possessed by any particular division of science. Unless this is recognized, the student is led toward a partial and distorting portrayal of family life. Even within a special field of science we frequently find great diversity in the direction that the analysis of the family takes. It is important also that the student at the beginning of his work become familiar with representative studies of marriage and the family, and in this chapter each type described is also illustrated by reference to some book accessible to the student. It would be a mistake for anyone studying the family to ignore current, popular literature, especially material appearing in our newspapers and magazines and in fiction, plays, and biography.

Difficulty. The first impression when one considers research of the family is that it should prove relatively easy to undertake, since the family provides for nearly all men and women the first and most vivid experiences. Only those children who from the first have been brought up in some sort of an institution have failed to enter life through the family gateway, and most of these have had, in the better type of orphan asylum, the best possible substitute provided by the cottage system.

29

Family experience also constitutes so large a portion of social life that it would seem that the investigator would be favored by the great abundance of material awaiting study.

It is the universality of family experience and our familiarity with it that present the chief difficulties of research. The fact that one's personal reaction to a family means so much explains the danger of prejudice, which was discussed in the first chapter. The quantity of family data also creates a problem for the investigator on account of the great complexity of this material. It is easy to trace causal relationship arbitrarily in the analysis of the happenings of family life, but it is rare for these deductions to have objective validity.

There is also an added problem which comes from the natural reluctance of family members to uncover in perfect frankness the more intimate meanings of their association together, particularly when any disclosure antagonizes their self-respect. It is true that Le Play, a pioneer in the scientific study of social experience, chose the family as the unit of his investigation in France, but it must be noticed that this was because the family provided the means by which he could classify the economic conditions of individuals. This was his interest and he made little attempt to explore the inner workings of the individual family. Since his day there have been many valuable sociological studies that have utilized the family as a social unit, but it is recognized by all modern investigators that the study of family life, particularly successful family life, challenges the ingenuity as well as the objectivity of any investigator.

The need for, and the difficulty of getting, objective criteria concerning the family has to be recognized, as has frequently been pointed out. This is especially true when we seek to get at influences that make for successful family life.[1] People in trouble are as a rule made self-conscious of their own convictions as to the causes of their trouble. Whether the individual examining his domestic career considers it a success or a failure, he is apt to allow his emotional attitudes to obscure the actual conditions, and he is liable also to read into his experience explanations that merely repeat ideas that he has gathered during his formative period from his religious or moral teachings. Thus,

---

[1] Frank, Lawrence K., "The Need for Objective Criteria of Successful Family Life," *Social Forces*, Vol. 8, No. 4, pp. 538–539.

although his explanations are convincing to himself, they have a subjective basis and may not at all agree with what are the facts in the case. This is most likely to occur when the individual is asked to state his findings in self-appraisal at the request of someone who is making a research of family experience. It is this which leads to the discounting of any collection gathered by the questionnaire method of conditions that make for successful family living. They are indeed, as Frank points out, usually mere verbalizations. In any case they are certainly not verifiable data; therefore, upon them cannot be built an objective satisfactory program for success in marriage or parenthood. They are not without value in so far as they encourage seriousness in the student and a thoughtful searching of motives and qualifications for matrimony or family life. Even when so used they must be stated with caution lest the student be given the idea that he should strive for certain virtues that can be abstractly stated rather than for the complex, concrete adaptation successful living together requires.

It is also of the greatest importance for the student of the family to recognize that the experience which he seeks to understand cannot be delegated to any one science. Especially is this true of marriage. The causes that are the chief explanation of a problem which seems to be within the field of psychology or sociology may, for example, find their origin in a physical condition the interpretation of which belongs to medicine or in a mental pathology which is the task of the psychiatrist to interpret. This is merely a simple illustration of the great complexity of the causations which operate upon marriage and the home. It follows, therefore, that any complete program of research on any aspect of family life is likely to require the co-operative effort of a great variety of scientists. This concerted attack on domestic problems is rarely possible at present; instead we have limited undertakings in research. It becomes the business of the instructor, however, as is suggested elsewhere, to recognize this wide territory of family experience and to draw constantly from the resources of sciences with which he has intellectual contact even though they are not in his particular specialty. The significance of this is bound to increase the more teachers in the family become specialists and the more they attempt to relate their instruction to the actual problems of domestic life. Fortunately, the trend toward this more thorough grasping of the character of familial experience is accentuated by the pressure that comes from students in courses in marriage and the family who demand a factual instruction that yields personal preparedness for their own family career.

The student.   As was suggested in the first chapter, the student necessarily has a social background that gives him a characteristic family slant. His first task, therefore, upon undertaking any sort of investigation of family life, is to analyze his personal experience as impartially as possible and to recognize its consequences, especially in his emotional attitudes. Just as a counselor of human behavior requires self-knowledge, which he usually gets through some kind of psychoanalysis with the assistance of another specialist, so the investigator of the family profits from a searching of his own attitude and the influences that explain it. Thus he needs as a first step in any investigation to discover his own familial latitude and longitude. Only so can he avoid entering upon his study with some axe to grind.

It must be noticed also that there are influences that operate besides those coming from the events of childhood and parenthood relationship. The imagination works early and often prolifically in building concepts that have much to do with the shaping of matrimonial and family ideals. There are also effects that come from influences of section, class, and religious belief that during childhood become embedded in the concepts of the family.

Even if the student is not committed to research of the family, it will profit him as an observer of life, always in contact with family experience, to sound his prejudices and convictions that he may more readily discover the objective facts of any domestic group with which he associates.

This attempt to explore personal family experience may well be designated as socioanalysis in distinction to psychoanalysis, and one of the purposes of this text is to make such a scientific attitude toward the family possible. It will help the student to understand himself as a family product if he attempts observation of some particular family experience and records it objectively and systematically. In the effort to do this he will become aware of the necessity of putting aside personal feeling and also of the temptation to distort by an exaggeration of the dramatic or because of the desire to see things simply.

The successful family.   There is much greater knowledge of family failure than of success. Family disaster is more interesting in the sense that it is more apt to attract attention. The scientist, however, knowing how difficult it is to gather knowledge of successful family experience and how valuable it proves, is more concerned with such data. It is always easier to gather information regarding the maladjustments of marriage and the family, and possibly such material is also easier to analyze than the more subtle interactions that lead to happiness and success. In any case those who are dissatisfied in their family experience are more vocal and, once their pride has been passed, more willing to uncover the intimacies of their experience. On the other hand, those who are well adjusted are apt to take for granted their situation and any attempt to get their co-operation in analyzing their circumstances for the purpose of gaining information is usually difficult even when it is not resented.

There is also a question that confronts any investigation of the successful family, which comes from the relativity of social experience. When does a family become a success? To determine this there has to be a precise and objective understanding of extremely subjective and emotional reactions. Just as noise gets its degree of unpleasantness for the person suffering from a headache in proportion to the seriousness of the individual's discomfort, so characteristics of personality may magnify or minimize the happenings of family experience so that discordant interactions in the one case are reacted to as maladjustment while in another they are minor differences embodied in the greater unity. Difficult as the appraisal of these subjective variations is, there can be no escape from the undertaking the moment one attempts to interpret accurately any concrete relationship in family experience.

Research.   The family in some form has contact with nearly every expression of human culture. It so spreads itself through human behavior that there is no investigator in any field of psychological or sociological science who does not find himself concerned at some point in his research with the outcoming of family experience. As a consequence the research of the family invites the attention of a great variety of specialists. This manifold character of the family appears as soon as one attempts to catalog the various studies that have been made. They have to do with every aspect of human conduct and may be classified according to the major interests of psychological and social science. The following examples illustrate this: in anthropology, E. Westermarck's *The History of Human Marriage;* in history, A. W. Calhoun's *Social History of the American Family;* in biology, H. S. Jennings' *The Biological Basis of Human Nature,* Ch. 11; in psychology, J. E. Wallin's *Minor Mental Adjustments in Normal People,* Ch. 13; in psychiatry, Leo Kanner's *Child Psychiatry;* in psychoanalysis, J. C. Flügel's *The Psychoanalytical Study of the Family;* in economics, Margaret G. Reid's *Economics of Household Production;* in sociology, Joseph K. Folsom's *The Family;* in home economics, Ivol Spafford's *The Functioning Program of Home Economics;* in ethics, Walter Lippmann's *A Preface to Morals,* Ch. 14; in religion, E. R. Groves' *Christianity and the Family;* in race, E. Franklin Frazier's *Negro Family in Chicago;* in law, Chester G. Vernier's *American Family Laws;* in philosophy, Arthur Schopenhauer's *World as Will and Idea,* Vol. 3, pp. 338–361; in statistics, E. R. Groves and William F. Ogburn's *American Marriage and Family Relationships,* Part II; in regionalism, Margaret J. Hagood's *Mothers of the South;* in social pathology, Harriet R. Mowrer's *Personality Adjustment and Domestic Discord;* in medicine, Robert L. Dickinson and Lura Beam's *A Thousand Marriages;* in population, Alva Myrdal's *Nation and Family,* a Swedish experiment in democratic family and population policy; in eugenics, Frederick Osborn's *Preface to Eugenics;* in sex, Carney Landis and Others' *Sex in Development;* in child care, Marion E. Faegre and John E. Anderson's *Child Care and Training.*

Family research not only takes many forms; it is also carried on by all the methods available to the social scientists. The significance of each of these needs consideration.

The statistical method. The statistical method yields the most accurate and precise data when the nature of the study permits its use. It is best adapted to the measurement of changes and trends in certain aspects of family experience. Statistical studies have been made of changes of family size, age at marriage, the increasing or decreasing tendency toward divorce, illegitimacy, marriage, and similar problems. It can be used wherever quantitative material has been or can be gathered. One of the most complete statistical studies of a definite aspect of family life thus far made is W. F. Ogburn's "A Statistical Study of American Marriage," Part II of *American Marriage and Family Relationships*. It is a study of statistical correlation and is chiefly based upon data gathered by the United States Census Department.

Valuable as is the statistical method of family research, it has its limitations, as is generally recognized to be true of this methodology along certain lines of investigation in both the physical and the social sciences.[2]

As Lundberg states, we cannot at present statistically study certain phases of social behavior because of lack of instruments of objective observation, including the lack of standardized units and terminology.[3] The emotional character of family experience in addition to the uniqueness of each individual group especially hampers the statistical method of investigation.

The case method. The case method is an attempt in as objective a manner as possible to record and interpret all the pertinent facts of a family situation or problem. The case study presents a comprehensive picture of an individual family or member of a family as a means of insight in getting at the peculiarity of each specific relationship. As Bogardus has said, it penetrates the interesting personal experiences of all the individuals involved and out of these experiences it arrives at an understanding of the various stimuli and responses that have functioned.[4] It has especially proved useful to the social worker engaged in family rehabilitation and suggests the technique of the physician who gathers all the pertinent information obtainable from his patient as an aid to diagnosis. There is, however, seldom an exact parallelism, since the doctor usually can test the reliability and value of some of the statements made by the patient by utilizing the resources of the laboratory and experimentation.

[2] See H. W. Odum and K. Jocher, *An Introduction to Social Research*, pp. 296–297; C. E. Gehlke, "The Use and Limitation of Statistics in Sociological Research," *Publications of the American Sociological Society*, Vol. 21, pp. 141–148; and L. L. Bernard, "Development of Methods in Sociology," *The Monist*, April, 1928, pp. 306–314.

[3] Lundberg, George A., *Social Research*, p. 169.

[4] Bogardus, E. S., *Making Social Science Studies*, p. 50.

The value of the life history or case history as a means of interpreting social experience has been increased in recent years by the development of better techniques in recording and analyzing the data given.[5] It is important to notice that this material seeks not only to discover facts but also the meaning these have for the individual. Although the interviewer attempts to separate the actual occurrences from the feelings and ideas that the individual being interviewed has toward them, the inaccuracy of the statements made does not take away their significance in the understanding of the personality involved. On the contrary, their very lack of substance may be most revealing to the inquirer who is seeking not an impersonal, itemized chronicle of happenings but rather a personalized life-revelation which gives the insight needed for diagnosis and therapeutic effort. Again the interviewer has a problem similar to that which occasionally confronts the physician and very often the psychiatrist. To the latter the recitals of daydreaming which the subject recognizes as fictitious may be much more valuable as a means of disclosing the essential personality than the most careful and reliable statement of objective facts. Thus it is with family counseling, but here, as it is true of the physician, every effort has to be made by the specialist to separate the two types of information.

The Problem Child at Home, by Mary B. Sayles, a study in parent-child relationships, illustrates the importance of information gathered concerning aspects of family experience by means of the case method. This technique has been particularly fruitful as a means of tracing the life of an individual in its sequence so as to uncover the influences that have shaped personality. The material gathered is not obtained by the methods of the psychoanalyst but the data has a similar purpose in attempting a causal understanding of the individual. The personality is so decidedly a family product that the greater portion of such case studies falls within the province of family research.

It is obvious that the case method, like the others, has its limitations. It is difficult to eliminate subjectivity entirely, in spite of the attempt of the investigator to be impartial. There is also the difficulty of correctly reporting the facts without distortion or exaggeration, and since any conclusion is an attempt at

---

[5] Lundberg, George A., *Social Research*, 2nd edition, p. 379.

generalization it offers opportunity for prejudice and inaccuracy.

The questionnaire. The questionnaire method is an attempt to direct self-analysis by a series of questions which are expected to bring the information desired. It suggests the questions asked by the physician of his patients. It has the advantage of concentrating upon the information desired, thus avoiding the great quantity of irrelevant data that usually appears in extended case history. Much use has been made of the questionnaire method in the effort to penetrate the privacy of the home in the exploring of the individual family career.

The questionnaire is generally confidential and may be anonymous. It permits unemotional answers at one's leisure. It is relatively inexpensive. So many questionnaires, however, have been issued in recent years that it is becoming difficult to get busy, intelligent people to co-operate in making returns unless the contemplated study has an especial appeal to the person questioned. In addition to this difficulty there are inherent limitations in the questionnaire method which lessen its value for the student of the family. There is always the risk of rationalization on the part of the person who fills it out, and this need not be a deliberate attempt to put one's best foot forward. The individual memory always proves a faulty instrument for the reconstruction of one's own past history because it is motivated by attitudes and purposes that are often without conscious recognition. The truth may be told but not the full truth, or it may be so stated as to lead to a mistaken interpretation. Since the person who fills out the questionnaire ordinarily has only the printed questions, there is frequently a misunderstanding of their significance and as a consequence an erroneous answer. The nearer the questionnaire keeps to activities and happenings rather than motives and goals, the more useful it is.

One of the best studies of this sort is Ernest W. Burgess and Leonard S. Cottrell's *Predicting Success or Failure in Marriage.* Not only does the content of this book especially interest the student of marriage and the family, but also in its methodology it is an example of the most careful type of investigation carried through by the questionnaire. The authors state clearly the basis of the questionnaire which they used, its construction, and distribution, and also discuss the background of those from whom they sought information.[6] It is apparent that the authors gathered their data with all the safeguards their means of research provided. It is also clear that the basis of their findings had to be in great measure the subjective self-appraisal of those who were willing to co-operate with them.

Youth, Marriage and Parenthood is a study that was directed by Lemo D. Rockwood and Mary E. Ford at Cornell University. It was built upon the answers of juniors and seniors at the university to an exhaustive list of questions which attempted to gather the attitudes of the students toward marriage and its problems. Three hundred and sixty-four of these students elected the course given in preparation for marriage, first offered in 1938, and one hundred and thirty-two who did not enroll in the course also answered the questions. The study sought the opinion of these students on the following:

1. Matters that they were presumed to have observed, such as, "Which of the following do you consider the most frequent sources of disagreement between husbands and wives? (Check the three which seem to you most frequent.)"

Jealousy	Having children
Drinking	Rearing children
Money	In-laws and relatives
Sex	"Little things"
Others, such as_____	

2. Matters of judgment, such as, "What monthly income would you consider necessary before marriage?"[7]

3. The ideas of the students at the time in anticipation of marriage, such as, "Would you marry a person who you knew could not have children?"[8]

Many of these questions were such as students hesitate to answer frankly even when they merely have to check a questionnaire; others had to do with future hypothetical reactions. It is the most comprehensive of such studies of special interest to American youth who wish to know what a group of college stu-

---

[6] *Op. cit.,* pp. 17–29.

[7] Rockwood, Lemo D., and Ford, Mary E., *Youth, Marriage and Parenthood,* p. 233.

[8] *Ibid.,* p. 231.

dents stated as their opinions regarding various experiences and problems of courtship, engagement, and marriage.

The method of the schedule. The schedule is a provision for the gathering of answers to definite questions by a personal interview, using questions that can be answered by "Yes" or "No" or by a check mark or number. The question has to be simple, clear, and precise. No data should be gathered that is not pertinent for the study that is being made, and it should all appear in a form that forbids ambiguity of meaning. The schedule used for the periodic making of the federal census is the best known example of this type of methodology, and an important feature of the census is the questions that concern family life. A. C. Kinsey's impressive study of human sex behavior is based on material gathered by the schedule method.[9] The chief purpose of the schedule is to provide quantitative data that can be statistically interpreted.

The survey and the interview. The survey is a scrutiny of some social situation or organization. Often it is an examination of an entire community. The investigation of *The Life and Labor of the People of London,* begun in 1886 by Charles Booth, was one of the first and most comprehensive, reliable, and impressive of all social surveys. A later study of equal quality is that of an Indiana city made by the Lynds and published under the title *Middletown, A Study in Contemporary American Culture.* This first investigation, published in 1929, was followed in 1937 by the second, *Middletown in Transition.*

The community survey always contains material of interest to students of the family, and there is usually data of value in interpreting some phase of family life in the more restricted surveys such as the survey of a specific school system, the survey of crime, of delinquency, of vice, or of recreation.

Most of the material gathered in the making of a social survey is obtained by means of the interview. This is a personal visitation for the purpose of gathering information. The technique of the interview is so large and important in securing frank, accurate, and definite information that it has been studied as a sociological process, particularly by those who are engaged in social work that requires frequent use of this method. Like the questionnaire, the interview provides opportunity for rationali-

---

[9] Research project at Indiana University, under Medical Divisions of Rockefeller Foundation and of the National Research Council.

zation, and care has to be taken by the investigator to detect the attitude of the person interviewed and to estimate the amount of subjectivity. The investigator may misinterpret due to his own prejudices.

The survey and the interview permit a comprehensive portrayal of conditions beyond the possibility of the questionnaire or the life history. Anyone familiar with the second part of the book by the Lynds would enter the midwestern city they studied with a better understanding of the family situation than that of any of the citizens living there who had never read *Middletown*.

Other methods of study. Description based upon a wide and varied gathering of data has been frequently used to interpret family conditions. The summarizing of statistical investigation has often taken this form, for only so can a comprehensive picture be given. An example of this is W. F. Ogburn's chapter on "The Family" in *Recent Social Trends in the United States*. Another illustration of this method is T. J. Woofter's *Black Yeomanry*, Ch. 10.

Regarding this method of approach Katharine Jocher writes: "It fills an important need, for it is a valuable means of education. Moreover, it is entirely sound when based on accurate observation and substantiated facts. It calls attention to existing conditions, stimulates thought, and frequently points the way to a possible solution. When supported and strengthened by authentic and authoritative figures, it becomes doubly valuable." [10]

Experiment. The student of the family is hampered, as is true of all social scientists, by the fact that he can only to a limited extent make use of the experimental method of investigation which has proved so fruitful in the natural sciences. It is obvious that experiments in family functioning would require much time, great expense, and often would violate morality, even would be unlawful. For example, the Kaspar Hauser experience as it has come to us by tradition could be repeated under strict scientific control. However, any attempt to gain insight as to the significance of the family by bringing a child to maturity without conscious contact with any other human being seems too barbarous even to contemplate.

---

[10] *The Family*, Vol. 9, No. 3, pp. 80–85. Quoted by permission.

For the most part in the use of this methodology we are restricted to a study of social experiments that have special significance for the family. An example is the federal legislation giving aid to the state for the promotion of the welfare and hygiene of maternity and infancy which was passed by the Sixty-seventh Congress in 1921. Laws relating to child labor, the employment of women, minimum wage, old-age pensions, and a multitude of others are social experiments through legislation that are of direct concern to the family. These may be studied chiefly by the methodology already discussed. The specific, controlled, and limited experiment so common in natural science is rarely possible in the investigation of family life.

Representative research in the family.   It is interesting to analyze the methodology used in special studies of the family.

1. *Factors in the Sex Life of Twenty-Two Hundred Women,* by Katharine B. Davis. This investigation was carried on by an eight-page questionnaire which was sent to ten thousand women in all parts of the United States. Five thousand were selected by a large national organization which has representatives in practically every town and city in this country. It was requested that the names be those of normal married women of sufficient background to appreciate the questionnaire. One thousand, five hundred names were taken from membership of the general federation of women's clubs; two thousand, five hundred additional women were chosen from the alumni registers of women's colleges. Ten thousand additional names of unmarried women were taken from alumni registers of women's colleges and coeducational institutions, and to them a twelve-page questionnaire was sent. One thousand answers from the first group and twelve hundred from the second were made the basis of this study.

2. *A Research in Marriage,* by G. V. Hamilton. This investigation was undertaken to penetrate the reticence of domestic relationship in the attempt to discover the important happenings during the childhood of a hundred men and a hundred women and to discover the sex and marriage experience of these individuals as adults. It was carried on by a modified form of the interview which was designed to reduce suggestion and ra-

tionalization to the smallest proportion possible and to encourage frankness and freedom of expression.

3. *A Thousand Marriages,* by Robert Dickinson and Lura Beam. The data upon which this book is based were obtained from medical case records. These are given statistical interpretation and description by a specialist who brought to his task an extraordinary background of a long professional career. Since this material came from the interviews of Dr. Dickinson and his patients and was from the point of view of the latter incidental and minor to securing medical assistance, it has the added value of naturalness and spontaneity, making possible one of the most useful books dealing with its topic ever written.

4. *The Family in the Present Social Order,* by Ruth Lindquist. This study is based upon the questionnaire method chiefly, but has the peculiarity of being addressed to a group of persons especially interested in the problems presented and unusually well qualified to give information. A questionnaire was sent out in three sections to the alumni and honorary membership of Omicron Nu and Phi Upsilon Omicron, two honor home economics sororities.

5. *The Polish Peasant,* by W. I. Thomas and F. Znaniecki. In this study the family organization is interpreted in its significance as an institution of social control by the case analysis method.

6. *Sex and Culture,* by J. D. Unwin. This book is an attempt by a comparative study of cultures to discover the patterns of behavior relating to marriage among peoples who are primitive, meaning uncivilized rather than primeval, so as to construct a frame of reference permitting the grouping of various societies according to their rank in distance or nearness to the monogamic ideal. In contrast with earlier studies of anthropological data that concern students of the family of which Herbert Spencer's discussion of marriage is an example, Unwin in this book seeks to place together peoples of similar culture before he attempts to interpret his findings.

7. *Chicago Families,* by Day Monroe. The material of this study comes mostly from schedules of the 1920 census. Unpublished data were used relating to 23,373 families scattered throughout the city, only Negroes being excluded.

8. *The Family: A Study of Member Roles,* by K. D. Lumpkin. This is an example of the descriptive type of study based upon case material gathered from the observation of forty-six families who were clients of a family society in New York City, selected because a quantity of information had been recorded concerning them in a form available for scientific analysis.

9. *The Step-Father in the Family,* by Adele Stuart Meriam. This is an interesting illustration of a highly specialized study which combines case material with legal decisions. We are given a brief statement of the essential facts of significant controversies, the decisions rendered, and the logical arguments upon which they were based.

10. *Adventuring in Adoption,* by L. M. and E. C. Brooks. In this book another treatment is given of a special problem concerning the family. It has first a consideration of the personal problems faced by the person who wishes to adopt a child and then in its second part a discussion of the social and legal background of adoption, including a summary of the laws of the various states as they existed at the time the book was published.

11. *The Family Encounters the Depression,* by Robert C. Angell. This study is another example of this type of specialized contribution. It was a product of the case method of investigation.

12. *Married Life in an African Tribe,* by I. S. Schapera. This is one of the best examples of a searching, scientific observation of the life patterns of behavior relating to marriage and the family in a definite tribe of uncivilized people. It discusses the family of the Kgattas in a culture changing because of contact with a more complex civilization, choice of mate, getting married, the adjustments of married life, the economic system as it affects the family, household routine, relationship of parents and children, the consequences of death in a family, and other aspects of democratic life, giving us a detailed picture of a family in great contrast with our own.

13. *Endocrinology of Women,* by E. C. Hamblen. This is an example of a highly technical book which for that reason is not likely to attract the attention of the student of the family but which contains information of great value in understanding certain domestic problems, in this particular book those of adoles-

cence, fertility, and the climacteric. Fortunately, in this instance a portion of this information has been popularized by the same author under the title *Facts for Childless Couples*.

Our knowledge of the family, and this is true of the other social institutions, has been greatly advanced by a quantity of investigations each dealing with some particular feature of familial experience which could be delimited and investigated.

The instructor in courses in marriage and the family finds his task of knowing and interpreting such highly specialized literature, especially as it appears in the field of natural science, an exacting one, but it is this contact with contributions of specialists majoring in other fields of science which provides the insight that helps to make courses in marriage and the family practical, factual, and helpful to the students.

The value of fiction, drama, and biography. The student of the family may through the reading of fiction and biography stimulate his interest, increase his discrimination, and broaden his imagination. Family experience and marriage as problems of human interaction receive extensive treatment in the novel and the play, and the significance of childhood and family contact is beginning to get in biography and autobiography more adequate consideration than has been true in the past. This literary material is dramatic and concrete, permitting the reader's penetration into the intricacies of family association, but it necessarily lacks the exactness and impartiality that characterize the more objective products of science.

The trend in recent fiction has been toward character analysis and a portrayal of situation rather than an emphasis upon plot. This makes the characteristic novel of the period more useful to the student of the family. Nothing tends so to widen the sympathy of the student and to impress upon him the complexities and difficulties of matrimonial and family adjustments as the reading of the literature being produced by the psychologically and psychoanalytically inclined artist.

When fiction and biography are used for insight in family problems, care must be taken to keep the story in the background and to concentrate upon the material that reveals the author's analysis of the marriage or family situation.

In Appendix A on pages 755 to 759 are listed novels, plays,

and biographies suggested for the study of domestic experience. An effort has been made to provide discussions of a great variety of family problems from which selection can be made by the instructor and student according to their interests and emphasis.

Since love, marriage, and parent-child relationships are the most universal and dramatic in character of the personality revealing occurrences in the human period, they provide an inexhaustible source of themes for literary creation.

The development of the study of the family.   Intellectual interest in marriage and the family is not recent, but its factual study is, especially as this has developed in courses of instruction. This development appeared first in the colleges in the United States leading in time to a similar attention to the family in the high schools and differently and more recently in the grades. This spread did not occur, however, until on the college level the movement accepted as its purpose the task of preparing for marriage and family life, since a mere academic consideration provided no incentive for this type of instruction in the secondary schools.

The philosophic period.   The philosophers early gave testimony to the fact that there could not be serious thinking about the major problems of society without consideration being given to marriage and the family. Thus we find Plato and Aristotle attempting to fit the family into their theories of society. The former made his scheme for marriage the basis of his ideal society in the *Republic* and he also discussed the significance of love in *Phaedras* and especially in the *Symposium*. Aristotle writes in opposition to his famous teacher, stating his conception of the social function of the family in his *Politics*. Jean Jacques Rousseau was another philosopher of great influence who found it necessary to give a major place in his social thinking to domestic matters. In his *Emile* and his *La Nouvelle Heloise* he especially concerned himself with the mating problem. Arthur Schopenhauer in the nineteenth century gave prominence in his philosophic system to mating and especially to the significance of love between man and woman.

During the Middle Ages the church leaders dominated the thinking concerning marriage and the family as was true in other fields of intellectual interest. They also assumed in considerable measure the responsibility of regulations and decisions concerning matrimonial problems,[11] thus accepting the control which at present is chiefly in the hands of the civil court, as the regulation of marriage has become primarily a function of statutory law and court decisions. The student must beware of the impression that during this period when serious thinking was so largely taking a theological form there was little interest in practical problems having a domestic origin. Indeed we find in a much earlier period in India the beginning of a valuable erotic literature concerned with the physical adjustments of marriage. Some writers on this aspect of marriage have made liberal use of the insight that has developed among the Hindus, and not always have they given credit to the contributions that have been made by Indian students of the art of love over a long period of time. Vatsya Yana's *Kama Sutra*, written it is thought between the first and sixth centuries of the Christian era, is not only valuable in itself, but because it is a compilation of earlier writings it reveals the length of time there has been in India a serious interest in the physical compatibility of marriage.

Evolutionary hypothesis and the family.   Among the controversies following the publicizing of Charles Darwin's theory of evolution and the teaching and writing of his disciples was a debate as to the origin of the family and its prehistoric development. Some of the contributions to this newly awakened interest in the family came directly from Darwin's influence, while others reflected interest in the question of origins, a topic of thought of even wider appeal than the Darwinian hypothesis. Among the important writers dealing with this phase of the family was Sir Henry Maine (1822–1888) who in his *Ancient Law,* published in 1861, argued for a primitive family similar to that of the earlier patriarchal Roman family. This point of view met with opposition from Herbert Spencer, who included the domestic institution in his attempt at a complete philosophic system. John F. McLennan (1827–1881) in his *The Patriarchal Theory* insisted that an original promiscuity was replaced by a marriage system based on kinship traced through the female line. Because of the scarcity of women on account of female infanticide among primitive people, it became necessary for many to go outside the tribe to obtain wives by capture. Lewis H. Morgan (1818–1881), an

---

[11] Smith, Charles Edward, *Papal Enforcement of Some Medieval Marriage Laws.*

American lawyer interested in the Seneca-Iroquois Indians, in his *Systems of Consanguinity and Affinity of the Human Family* and his later work *Ancient Society* traced the evolution of marriage from a universal promiscuity to a communal marriage system of a group of kinsfolk leading through stages of development to a final monogamy. During the first stage, marriage was a group affair similar to the scheme that Plato advocated; then there came the stressing of the mother and kinship with succession proceeding along the female line and finally the patriarchal period with the father replacing the mother with his dominance supreme.

Edward A. Westermarck brought to the controversy the advantages of a more factual anthropological background, and he discusses in three volumes with great detail the growth of the family as a social institution (5th edition, 1923). Marriage originated as a natural consequence of the social maturing of primitive people. Monogamy was always the standard type of marriage, being affected, however, by changes in the ratio of the sexes. He denied that there was ever a state of general promiscuity. Robert Briffault continued this searching for an explanation of the origin of marriage and the family and found his explanation in the mother-offspring relationship and the strength of the maternal impulses (1927).

George F. Howard's three volumes entitled *History of Matrimonial Institutions,* 1904, summarized and criticized the earlier anthropological theories of the origin of marriage and the family, carrying his discussion through the historic period with emphasis upon the legal aspects of the growth of the institutions. This scholarly product is the definitive contribution within its range. The author's interest was also expressed in instruction he developed in the field of the family at the University of Nebraska. On a similar base of interest but from an ethnological background, Elsie Clews Parsons gave lectures on the family at Barnard College, Columbia University, 1899–1905, and in 1906 published a text on the family for the use of college lecturers and directors of home reading clubs. According to the words of the author, this was an anthropological and historical outline with descriptive notes. In the last lecture of the book her attention is turned to the modern, which she calls also the simple, family. Here we find evidence of the beginning of an interest that was soon not only to bring courses of the family into the conventional American college program but also to change the nature of the instruction.

Aside from this main academic development there were many writers dealing with various phases of marriage and the family. Otis T. Mason directed his attention to the primitive status of woman and her contributions to culture. Mrs. Helen Bosanquet and Charlotte Perkins Gilman were especially concerned with economic problems of the family, Havelock Ellis was mainly concerned with sex, Ellen Key with the divorce problem, and Willystine Goodsell summarized the history of marriage and the family up to the modern period.

The sociologist and the family.   The sociologist from the days of Comte onward gave considerable attention to the family. Auguste Comte considered it a unit of society. Familial experience in his theory was the original source of society. Lester F. Ward also gave a prominent place to the family in his system of sociology, especially emphasizing the social significance of parental and romantic love. He also accepted the hypothesis of the dominance of the mother in the primitive period of evolution. William Graham Sumner, whose interpretation of society was at the opposite pole from Ward's, nevertheless agreed in his writings with this emphasis upon the evolutionary significance of the family. His thinking takes mature form in Sumner and Keller's *Science of Society*.[12] Franklin Giddings saw in the family the simplest form of genetic aggregation, and he bases his scheme of social organization on kinship.[13] Charles H. Cooley brought to the interpretation of family experience a new point of view showing how within the home originate the incentives to self-development and also the great importance of primary contacts during this period of the child's growth. George H. Mead interpreted the family as the association through which developed both the individual consciousness of self and the awareness of others, the double source of social relationship.

Instruction in marriage and the family as preparation for life.   The attention the family received following Darwin's *Origin of Species* shows how much his hypothesis of evolution stimulated thought concerning the earliest developments of

---

[12] See Vol. 3, pp. 1485–2056.
[13] Giddings, Franklin, *The Principles of Sociology*, pp. 154–170, 245.

the institution of marriage and the family. It is evident that the interest in questions of origin was then much greater than at present and that there was also greater confidence that the veil of time could be put aside permitting the recapture of knowledge of those earliest stages during which the family was established as a human institution. In the writings that appeared in the later part of this period of debate over origins began a transition to the more practical effort of analyzing the contemporary family and of dealing with its present problems. This swinging away from a concentration on the question of origins is evident in the writings of Ward, Sumner, Cooley, Mead, John Dewey, and a host of others. It was inevitable that this new attitude should mature into an instruction which attempted to prepare students for their own personal career as husbands, wives, and parents. Its development proceeded over a wide territory. Two American women pioneered in this transition. Charlotte Perkins Gilman drove home to popular audiences the necessity of facing the domestic problems originating from changing social conditions. Anna Garlin Spencer in an even more pointed way carried the same message to college students. She started lecturing at Teachers College, Columbia University, in the summer session of 1919 and continued this for twelve years, finally bringing out, at the suggestion of Benjamin R. Andrews, Professor of Household Economics at the same institution, *The Family and Its Members* (1923).

The senior author of *The Contemporary American Family* inaugurated in 1922 at Boston University the first college credit course in preparation for family life. The following announcements gave the purpose and the content of the instruction:

Present Status of the Family. This course treats the influences in modern life that are most seriously changing family life and creating the problems of the modern home. It is a rapid, comprehensive survey of the present situation of the family, and is designed for those who wish an understanding of the forces operating upon family life. It will also prove a useful introductory course for those who plan to elect other specialized courses relating to family problems. There will be six sessions of one and one-quarter hours each, on *Monday evenings, beginning February 4,* at 8.00, in University Building, 688 Boylston Street, corner of Exeter. Professor Groves will give the lectures. Time will be allowed at each session for discussion and questions. One-half point of credit toward the degree of Bachelor of Science in Education or Master of Education will be given those who attend all lectures and complete the assignments. The course may be attended by any one interested in the subject-matter whether academic credit is sought or not.

Social Adjustment in Family Life. An analysis of the difficulties of family associations as they appear in the modern home, with emphasis upon their psychological and sociological origins. The course is intended for those who desire knowledge of the conditions that hamper the construction of wholesome family life as well as for those who deal with special problems of family adjustment. It is not a course in family rehabilitation from the viewpoint of the social worker, but an investigation of problems of personal relationships within the family itself. Illustrations will be drawn from actual family situations.

Six sessions of one and one-quarter hours each, on Monday evenings, at 8:00, *beginning March 24,* at the University Building, Boylston and Exeter Streets. Credit (if desired) one-half point. Professor Groves, lecturer.

Two years later through the influence of Dr. Andrews he offered two courses of similar character at Teachers College, one, an introductory course; the other for graduates:

TEACHERS COLLEGE, COLUMBIA UNIVERSITY. In 1925 Summer Session. Social Science S 196. *Social and Economic Problems of the Family.* Professor Ernest R. Groves. Two points.

The psychological and economic organization of the family group and present readjustments to increase its personal and social values. Early family types and their relation to present problems. Biological and eugenic considerations. The modern family—its significance as mutual aid, as personal development, as permanent friendship. The psychological basis—individual and social; the adjusting personalities—husband, wife, child, parent; family types, rural and urban, stable and unstable, etc. Relation of family to economic production, distribution, consumption; adjustments with industry, household income, expenditure and standards of living.

SOCIAL SCIENCE S 296. *Introduction to Research in Modern Family Problems.* Professor Ernest R. Groves. Three points.

Open to students prepared to begin research on problems of the type indicated in Social Science S 196.

This instruction went on for several summers. Since it was elected by many working in the field of home economics who came from all sections of the country, it led to a rapid spread of interest in instruction in the family and its addition to the curricula of departments of home economics, always with an emphasis upon its relation to life problems, as was characteristic of the other courses in this rapidly growing academic specialty of applied science. To encourage this new development, at the suggestion of Dr. Andrews, the author's *Social Problems of the Family* was published in 1927. This was the predecessor of the present text and has been designated the first college text which dealt with problems of the modern family.[14] The first college text on the family had been written by Dr. Willystine Goodsell, also at Teachers College. This book which appeared in 1915 dealt with the history of the family as a social and legal institution and was entitled *A History of the Family as a Social and Educational Institution.*

Interest in the contemporary problems of the family and the effort to meet them by training was not limited to courses in the family in the colleges. There were many varied expressions of what was to become a conventional part of the educational program in the United States. In 1923 at Vassar College a program in euthenics stressing training for homemaking and for parenthood was started. It was inaugurated by Miss Annie Louise McLeod, now director of the Department of Home Economics at Syracuse University. This in 1926 expanded into the Vassar Summer Institute of Euthenics, including instruction for children from 2–4 years in the Nursery School, and from 4–9 years in the Progressive School. Parents, chiefly mothers, attended lectures and discussions dealing with pedagogical principles that concern parenthood and with problems of the American home life. These ranged over a wide territory of interests. Largely through the influence of Mrs. William Dummer of Chicago, who was following the development of the instruction for preparation for marriage and the family with a keen and discerning interest, a section on the family appeared in 1924 on the annual program of the American Sociological Society.

Home economics and family courses. Not only did the leaders in home economics welcome this emerging instruction

---

[14] Rockwood, Lemo D., "History and Status of the Movement for Education in Family Life at the High School and College Levels," *Parent Education*, Vol. 2, No. 2, pp. 10–16, 47.

as a preparation for family life; they also encouraged modern attitudes toward domestic problems independently along other lines. A committee of the American Home Economics Association in drawing up a syllabus of home economics in 1913 recognized the problems of child care. These were chiefly limited to physical aspects of the growing child, topics which came generally under the heading of home nursing. Between 1915 and 1919 courses in child welfare began to appear among the curricula offered by home economics teachers. These chiefly gave attention to the physical needs of infants and young children. Apparently the first effort to enlarge this interest in children and to provide preparation for child management was a bulletin on child care and child welfare brought out by the Federal Board for Vocational Education in 1921. It had a section discussing child mentality and child management. Pioneering in this field had taken place earlier, the following having been the chief contributors: G. Stanley Hall in *The Investigation of Childhood;* Bird Baldwin, who at the University of Iowa organized a statewide service for parents and children, bringing to them along many lines the advantages of applied science while at the same time carrying on various studies in the effort to understand both the child and the parent better; and L. E. Holt, who, working in the medical field largely through his extremely popular book *Care and Feeding of Children,* greatly improved the physical care of infants and children in the United States and also the physician's technique in both diagnosing and caring for sick children. Dr. Holt's influence dominated the development of American pediatrics, a branch of medicine which accepts the health problems of children as its specialty.[15] Among other pioneers in the new concern of the problems of the modern home were Dorothy Canfield Fisher, one of the greatest of American novelists, who popularized the modern attitude toward the family in *Mothers and Children,* and Edna N. White, a specialist in home economics, who in 1920 organized the Merrill Palmer School of Motherhood Home Training at Detroit, Michigan.

At the University of North Carolina upon petition of the students following a lecture given by Chloe Owens, then representing the American Social Hygiene Society, a course in prepa-

---

[15] Duffus, R. L., and Holt, L. E., Jr., *Pioneer of a Children's Century,* p. VIII.

ration for marriage was offered in 1925 for the election of senior men. At that time there were few women in the University. This course was taken over by the author in 1927 and developed independently from the instruction also offered in the family, using factual material gathered from the various specialties dealing with different aspects of marriage. The course from the beginning was taught in the spirit of the natural sciences. Its expansion was rapid and by 1940 it was given in seven sections during the year: four for men, two for women, and one for men and women together.[16] This instruction after several years began to appear in other institutions and also to influence courses in the family which came to include more attention to mating and the husband-and-wife relationship.

<hr />

[16] Groves, E. R., *Marriage,* 1st edition, 1933, 2nd edition, 1941, New York: Henry Holt and Co.; and Klaiss, Donald, *The Program of Marriage Instruction at the University of North Carolina,* Social Forces, Vol. 18, No. 4, May, 1940, pp. 536–539.

Chapter 3

THE PRIMITIVE FAMILY

FOREWORD. It is desirable that the student have a clear idea not only as to the meaning of the primitive family which is discussed in this chapter but also the purpose of its study. The question might well be raised as to why attention should be given to a family experience which is either distant from the American family in its characteristics or so far away in time that no certainty exists as to what its traits were. Consideration of the primitive family appears in this text for two reasons: to provide a background which as a means of contrast helps illuminate features of the modern American family that are distinctive and to answer questions that would surely arise in the mind of any person seeking to understand any type of modern family life. As the chapter states in greater detail we are not motivated in our interest in a primitive family by the belief that we must find in primitive experience the basis and the security of what has become conventional with us. Also it is impressive to recognize the very great diversity in the customs and practices in the domestic institution of people whom we call primitive because their culture is simpler than ours. This group of people, unlike the prehistoric, we do know through the studies of trained observers. No longer, however, do these investigators seek to force such differing types of family life into some prearranged classification which supports a favored hypothesis, but instead there is an acceptance of the fact that so great a diversity of domestic culture exists. Perhaps the realization of this is the most important contribution that the discussion of this chapter can bring the student. Since the American Indians were the primitive people with whom the European settlers of North America had contact and later the men and women who also developed our western territory, this chapter uses our own natives as an example of primitive family life. Since there was considerable variation between various Indian tribes, it seems best to use for this illustration of primitive domestic experience a group that has been carefully studied and whose family therefore has been accurately described.

The meaning and significance of the primitive family. That portion of man's life on the earth which falls within the historic period, and of which we have record, is a small part of his total existence. The researches of anthropologists in recent years have pushed back the boundaries of man's prehistoric life. It represents a vast quantity of cultural experience which we cannot reconstruct, although science can trace it in part along the lines of physical and material evolution and can build hypotheses regarding much more. The domestic experience within this period of elemental human culture is often referred to by those using the term *primitive family*. They are groping after the beginning of the family and marriage and are seeking to describe their origin and earliest form. These writers are attempting to interpret happenings outside history and therefore have to be content with conjectures and hypotheses.

The term *primitive family* is employed also in another sense. It then denotes the relatively simpler experiences of savage or preliterate people. About these forms of the family and marriage we now know a great deal, much of which has been gathered recently by skilled investigators who have gone to live with and study particular groups of those whom we commonly designate as natives. These scientists have gone on a fact-finding quest, free from prejudice and *a priori* theories. They have found that the family and married life of primitive peoples are much less simple than was once thought and often more diverse even than the racial and national differences we find in modern life. The variety of experience they have reported is so great that their findings confuse the student who is seeking a typical, stereotyped form of the family or marriage among primitive people. These preliterate groups, although contemporary with us, are assumed to represent the earlier stages of human culture. We attempt through them to get some clue to the evolution of the family and marriage.

It is natural for the student interested in the family to attempt to retrace as far as possible its evolution. This is in part because it has become a habit to start every kind of study with the historic development of the subject of inquiry. To suppose that by studying the family life of the past one can get a great deal of help in understanding its present problems is a mistake. It is a fallacy to consider evolution as a continuous advancement. There is no such thing in social experience as consistent progress, and particularly is this true of the family.

The value of studying the primitive family is merely that one gains a background for appreciating its present-day characteristics. Nobody can safely go to the family of the past to get standards for the family of today. Much of the controversy of earlier students of savage society has been futile, for the authors of these discussions have tried to determine by their investigations what is the normal home life for all time. Some writers have tried to show that our present conventional monogamy has always been the usual thing, fearing if they did not prove that, the family in its existing form would not be so secure. Others have tried to show that in the beginning mating was promiscuous, believing that would prove our present morals scientifically unsound. It matters little what the first form of marriage was, so far as the stability of married life today is concerned. We have no motive for reaching into the past and trying to force our findings into the preconceived form that seems to us necessary to establish the kind of family life we now think good.

It is impossible to get at the very beginning of the family. Concerning the housing customs of primitive man we have a definite body of knowledge; we have discovered some of the caverns in which people lived a great many thousands of years ago, and we have seen a few of the utensils they used; we can tell something about their daily life from the pictures they left on the cavern walls. But in our attempt to ascertain the facts regarding their family life we cannot go beyond history because tradition does not help us.

This explains why we study with such assiduity the domestic experience of the simpler preliterate people who still survive. We no longer expect to gather from them information that will permit us to reconstruct in orderly fashion the evolution of the human family and marriage through its cultural stages.

We recognize that contemporary savage peoples, even in those instances in which we have reason to believe that they have been long retarded or have degenerated from a previous higher level of culture, in their ways of living are far removed from the simpler beginnings of prehistoric and primitive man.

Nor do we any longer jump over this great duration of cultural darkness seeking to find in the animal the starting point of the development of the human family and marriage. As was said in the preceding chapter, we do find a linking between the domestic life that man has achieved and the behavior of animals, since in both we discover the basic biological function of sex and reproduction. We find among some animals intimations of the human institution of the family, and these are highly suggestive in showing the original instinctive foundation of what has now become a culture-supported, human pattern of behavior.

Among animals we find the parental instinct widely showing itself in some form of expression, and the biologists insist that family life in one form or another is not uncommon.[1] Child tells us that the true family can be found at least in temporary or periodic form even in certain fishes and in many species among the higher vertebræ. It is, however, as Briffault shows,[2] chiefly the mother-offspring attachment which provides the stable and significant relationship which antecedes the human institution of the family. The male remains outside; his function is sexual rather than familial. According to Briffault, even the anthropoid apes, nearest to man in their evolution, maintain a family life with which the male is not more closely associated than in other species.[3] Thus Briffault challenges the statement made by Westermarck[4] that the gorilla was monogamous, an assertion upon which, according to Briffault, Westermarck had based his theory of the evolution of marriage.[5]

The evolution of marriage. Any attempt to understand the primitive family leads to the investigation of its derived social institution, marriage. Marriage in some form appears to be universal among human groups, but at times it brings so

---

[1] Jennings, H. S., *The Biological Basis of Human Nature*, pp. 258–263; and Child, C. M., *Physiological Foundations of Behavior*, p. 274.

[2] Briffault, R., *The Mothers*, Vol. 1, pp. 188–194.

[3] *Ibid.*, p. 189.

[4] Westermarck, E., *The History of Human Marriage*, pp. 33–38.

[5] Briffault, *op cit.*, Vol. 1, pp. 168–180.

little change in the relationship of those concerned or is so lacking in permanence as to be scarcely distinguishable as a definite status.[6] The origin of marriage is, and long has been, a matter of speculation. How early and persistent this effort has been to draw aside the curtain of time and see marriage first appearing is attested by the countless myths that have appeared to explain its origin all over the world. Science also has wrestled with the problem and has offered many hypotheses.

The early attempt to retrace man's social evolution, stimulated by the Darwinian hypothesis, brought forth the theory of an original period of promiscuity which preceded the institution of marriage and led to its coming. It is, of course, reasonable to assume in the words of Darwin that "The habit of marriage in any strict sense of the word has been gradually developed." It is true that no group of people, however low in culture at present, reproduces the conditions of man's earliest society.

If there ever existed a time when among humans there was no regulation of sex and therefore a society without marriage, it was so far distant in the past as to be for us lost experience. No state of promiscuity has been found among simple people.

Lowie's statement of the situation is representative of the modern viewpoint regarding the theory of promiscuity in human history:

Sexual communism as a condition taking the place of the individual family exists nowhere at the present time; and the arguments for its former existence must be rejected as unsatisfactory. This conclusion will find confirmation in the phenomena of primitive family life.[7]

Reports in some instances have been made of a state of near promiscuity. As a rule these statements have grown out of a misinterpretation of customs unfamiliar to the observer. The theory of L. H. Morgan, one of the writers of the evolutionary school, may be used as an example. He said that among peoples with a rudimentary family life each generation married within itself promiscuously, so that all the younger men and women were mates, and the members of the elder generation, their parents; a child could not distinguish his own father and mother

---

[6] Briffault, *op. cit.*, Vol. 2, pp. 78–79.
[7] Lowie, R. H., *Primitive Society*, p. 2. Quoted by permission.

from the group of his potential fathers and mothers. This idea Morgan got from the fact that in the Hawaiian Islands, as in some other groups, the children call all the men father. The confusion apparently resulted from a misunderstanding of the meaning of the word "father"; to Morgan the word meant what we mean by father, to the Hawaiians it meant men of the older generation. The savage was simply classifying the two generations. Likewise, when the young people used a certain term in speaking of each other it did not follow that they were mingling freely in their sex life, but that they were recognizing the fact that they belonged to the generation within which they would later marry.[8]

There are, as one would expect, great differences among groups of savages both in premarital license and also in the amount of regulation prescribed by marriage. But even when these codes of conduct vary greatly from those of modern civilization, they cannot be justly described as survivals of an earlier promiscuity.

Although marriage is a social institution regulating sex relationship, it is clearly not a creation of sex impulse. Sex desire provided one of the needs for marriage; it did not in itself furnish the motive. Marriage is, and supposedly was from the first, a social invention, a regulation useful to the group as a whole. It was the development of the family that made marriage possible and led to its necessity. The economic association of husband and wife with its advantage of a division of labor, and the social need for regulating sex conduct, both products of a growth in the family status, were among preliterate peoples the chief influences that established the institution of marriage. Malinowski describes the social situation in which we see the father assuming the economic responsibility for a mother and her child even when the physical facts of fatherhood are unknown.[9] Public opinion will not tolerate the fatherless child, but not because there is recognition of the meaning of paternity. It is possible, however, that even so astute an investigator as Malinowski may have been led astray by reticence in answering the white man's questions or an eagerness to respond in accord with what were supposed to be the white man's ideas or a

[8] Tozzer, A. M., *Social Origins and Social Continuities,* pp. 141–144.
[9] Malinowski, B., *The Father in Primitive Psychology,* pp. 82–85.

combination of these reactions. It is not uncommon for pre-literate people to fall into the role that they assume they are expected to take. In any case it is difficult to explain how men who understood breeding of animals had no conception of the process of fertilization among humans. We have plenty of evidence that reproduction is an experience concerning which there is sometimes reluctance to discuss on the part of the natives or a taboo which makes the primitive less frank in his statements than when he talks about other happenings in his social life.

The consanguineous family and mother right. The predominant relationship among peoples of simple culture is, as with us, that of identity of blood. Such evidence as we have suggests that the family grouping in its elemental stage was consanguineous in character. The bond of mother and offspring constituted its foundation even when the entire tribe was conceived of as a community of one common blood. The special identification of mother and child was early recognized, built upon the idea of blood unity. This notion did not require knowledge of the meaning of physiological maternity, for the period of pregnancy, the appearance of blood at birth, the experience of lactation, and the infant's helplessness, led to the belief in a common identity of mother and child which was interpreted as a tie of blood. This concept of blood unity was extended to include the consanguineous relationship of the woman's children to each other and to her kinfolks since they were all possessors of the same blood. This basic relationship provided the means of tracing descent and fixing one's identity as need of these arose with the evolution of culture.

The mother-child relationship provided the original basis for tracing descent and defining succession, once the idea of an hereditary office developed. The mother-child connection received attention from the first because it was so clear and precise, while the physiological significance of the male remained for later discovery.

Kaberry reports that although the Australian Aborigines emphasize the physical relationship of the mother and the child this does not lessen the affection between the father and his offspring. Like the modern father he may see less of his child than does the mother on account of the fact that the division of labor keeps him away from the household and the camp much of the time, but when he is in the presence of the child he makes much of the latter and shows his pride as a parent. If he has any reasons for so doing, he upbraids his wife for not taking better care of the child. The inheritance that determines horde country and dream totems is transmitted through the father. This does not mean that the mother's blood tie is ignored or becomes socially insignificant.[10]

This priority of mother-child relationship led to the theory that in the earliest stages of human culture the authority of the female was dominant. This doctrine was maintained by Bachofen in his *Das Mutterrecht,* published in 1861. Lester Ward later brought forward his thesis of the gynæcocracy or the female rule. As recently as 1906 Ward maintained that during the time when descent was traced through the mother the woman was socially dominant.[11] He regarded this as the long stage in the evolution of society. The theories of Bachofen and Ward are no longer held, for the anthropologists find no facts to support them. On the contrary, even when descent was traced only through the mother, and the mother-child relationship represented the basic tie, woman depended for protection upon either the male members of her own family or upon the man who maintained with her the special status out of which came marriage. In either case authority accompanied this responsibility for protection.

Father family and the patriarchy. Even though, as we have seen, the reckoning of descent through the mother did not of necessity bring social dominance to the female, it did from the first establish the family with an inherent weakness, since authority was shifted to the male relatives of the mother. These brothers and uncles constituted a divided responsibility. They were themselves supposed to go outside their blood family for their own mating and were frequently absent during hunting or war expeditions. Moreover, with economic advancement, especially when the agriculture stage was reached, the role of the husband as the provider for his wife and children grew, and with it his authority increased. The transition to a father type of family was in accord with the demands of the social situation, and once knowledge of the male's part in pro-

---

[10] Kaberry, Phyllis M., *Aboriginal Woman,* pp. 59–60.
[11] Dealey, J. Q., and Ward, L. F., *The Text Book of Sociology,* p. 110.

creation arose, his position as head of the household was strengthened. Out of the father type of family developed the patriarchy which gave to the male head of the household priority in politics, religion, economics, and social standing.

Once a sense of private property developed, the significance of the father was increased by tracing descent through him as the means of establishing and regulating inheritance. We have instances of property being handed down through a family line of inheritance and then either the mother or the father may be the basis of the transmission.[12] This may include also a conveyance of rights such as a reservation for fishing as well as tools, weapons, or other movable property. If the idea of property does not happen to be represented by any word in the vocabulary of the group, this does not necessarily mean that the natives have no experience of possession and transmission. The fact may be recognized even though the concept is absent from the speech of the people.[13]

One of the influences in primitive life that tended to make the male prominent was exerted by the religious doctrines, for from the first the male had the advantage at this point since he had control of the ceremonial part of life and often left out the woman, not permitting her to have any part in religion.

Secret societies also added to the inequality of women. These societies were organized by men for men, against women. One that flourished among the natives of Africa had an occasional celebration, usually at night, when the members, wearing masks so they would not be known, would frighten the women and whip any who had been troublesome to men during the preceding season.[14] This was a sort of taming society that kept women in their place.

One needs to be cautious in interpreting mother and father types of primitive family experience, for there is nothing like the consistent, clear-cut stages of familial relationship, in the practices of existing primitive groups, required for the reconstruction of these early family forms with definiteness and certainty.

[12] Firth, Raymond, *Primitive Economics of the New Zealand Maori,* p. 113.
[13] *Ibid.,* p. 335.
[14] Thomas, William I., *The Source Book of Primitive Origins,* pp. 802–803.

We find survivals and transitional types of familial organizations. The situation is confused by the prevalence of customs and traditions that appear to come down from an earlier time and that are out of accord with the dominant features of the existing family form.

Matrilocal and patrilocal marriage. The place of residence of the family is one of the influences that enhance the mother's or father's status. When the husband comes to live with his wife's relatives we have the matrilocal marriage and a tendency to trace the descent through the mother. When the opposite is true, in the patrilocal marriage, descent is patrilineal. In some instances we find the family dividing its time between the wife's and the husband's residential group. Although the place of abode naturally encourages one or the other of the two systems of descent, it must not be assumed, as it sometimes has been by writers, that this is the exclusive influence. Often we find an intermediate type of family organization with only a slight stress on either the father or mother status.

The result of the attempt to correlate the culture of primitive peoples with their means of livelihood, made by Hobhouse, Wheeler, and Ginsberg, brings out the impossibility of accounting for the matrilineal or patrilineal family as the product of any one influence. These authors classify preliterate groups, according to their economic activity, in seven divisions: two stages of culture among the hunters, two among the pastoral, and three among the agricultural peoples. What they found in this study

	I	II	III	IV	V
Lower Hunters	22½	8	7	0	0
Higher Hunters	14	10	3	4	0
Agricultural I	9½	7	0	0	0
Pastoral I	1	4	2	0	0
Agricultural II	19½	23	2	6½	0
Pastoral II	0	6	1	0	0
Agricultural III	14	18	8	1	1½
	80½	76	23	11½	1½ *

* Doubtful classifications are counted ½.

of the family type appears in the table on page 63.[15] The first column represents the stages of matrilineal or matrilocal family or both types in conjunction; the second, patrilineal or patrilocal or both; the third, matrilineal and patrilineal in conjunction; the fourth, matrilineal descent with patrilocal marriage; and the fifth, patrilineal descent with matrilocal marriage.

Polygyny. Polygyny is the form of marriage in which several women are legally bound to one man. In most primitive tribes it is permitted even when it is not a common form of marriage. We are apt to get the idea that it is common because it is permissible, but it cannot be common unless there are many more women than men. This does not often happen among savages. If one man has many wives, others will have none unless there is a great inequality of the sexes. Where permissible, it is often checked by the fact that it is too costly. On the other hand, it may be just the opposite because each woman is an additional worker and it is an economic advantage to have more than one wife. Polygyny is frequently limited by the fact that the man has to live with his wife and she has to live with her kinspeople. Since she represents their property, the clan will not let her go outside their territory. A man who has several wives would have to live first with one, then with another, much as some of the Mormons used to do. This traveling household naturally restricted the polygynous type of family.

Polygyny is not necessarily unpopular with women. In the kind of life the savage lives, economic conditions may be so hard that the lone wife is overworked and urges her husband to take another wife so that she may have help with her household labors. As the first wife is usually the dominant one, every time the man adds another wife she gets an additional helper, while the new wives also benefit by the arrangement since the more women there are in the family, the lighter the duties of each and the more prosperous the group as a whole. Instances are reported of wives in China encouraging their husbands to add concubines to their households because the latter would help with the work of the former.

When polygyny thrives among people whose life is not so

[15] Hobhouse, L. T., Wheeler, G. C., and Ginsberg, M., *The Material Culture and Social Institutions of the Simpler Peoples,* p. 152. Quoted by permission.

hard that many women are needed to do the work, it will usually be found to emphasize sex, as it has done in the very wealthy Turkish family of the past, where the women were little more than legalized sex companions of the man, keeping to their own part of the house and sharing few interests or activities with the head of the house. This is the sort of polygynous family life we have in mind when we think of polygyny as degrading women and debasing the function of the home.

When the family lifts itself above the physical level to a possibility of comradeship and affection, the polygynous form of family life shows its handicap. Although Turkey has entirely done away with polygyny, making it a criminal offense for a man to have more than one wife, this is but the legal crystallization of a trend that was noticeable early in the century. In 1914 Stanwood Cobb, a keen observer of Turkish life, wrote:

Polygamy is now a waning custom in Islam. The influence of European culture has been steadily creating a sentiment against it among progressives, and the Young Turk almost universally restricts himself to one wife. It is only in the passing generation that the harem exists. The Young Turk aspires to the happiness of a real union—a home built up by the love and devotion of two people, one for the other—a partnership between man and wife. And he knows this is impossible if he has more than one wife. He also desires his wife to be educated, so that she can be his intellectual and spiritual companion.[16]

In the reconstruction of Turkey in both its political and civil life following World War I, marriage was placed firmly on a monogamic basis. But this reform was the natural outcome of the trend away from the polygynous family which was proving so out of accord with conditions of modern life.

Besides the economic advantage of polygyny in the lower stages of culture, it may be a means by which the man of wealth or position adds to his political authority and social prestige.

Polyandry. Polyandry is the opposite of polygyny, one woman having several husbands. It is very uncommon, only rarely being found among savages. When it does exist it may be due to an unusual disproportion between the sexes, caused perhaps by female infanticide or by the carrying away of women

---

[16] *The Real Turk*, p. 74. Quoted by permission.

by an alien tribe, or to such hard economic conditions that it takes the combined efforts of several men to support one family.

There are two kinds of polyandry, the fraternal and the nonfraternal. Fraternal polyandry is the marriage of brothers to one woman; nonfraternal polyandry is the marriage of several men not brothers to one woman. In the case of the brothers, the family usually lives in one place and the fatherhood of the children is likely to be decided by seniority, the first born being conceded to be the child of the eldest brother, the second child going to the second brother, and so on; though the fatherhood of the children may be decided in the fraternal as in the nonfraternal family by the performance of some such ceremony as the shooting of an arrow in a certain way. Each father has special control over his own child. The nonfraternal family is a migratory affair, the wife moving about and spending a few months with one husband after another, then coming back where she started.

Although polyandry is generally considered a result of oppressive poverty or of an unnatural shortage of women, this is not always true. In Toda, a part of India, the people have been very poor and have maintained polyandry; when they became more prosperous, observers expected to see the polyandrous family disappear, but instead of that the Toda family became in many instances at the same time polyandrous and polygynous, the brothers continuing to live together but having several wives instead of one as in earlier times, so that the whole group was married, each woman having several husbands and each man several wives.

Individual cases of polyandry are sometimes found as exceptional and abnormal variations. As a system it is chiefly found in Tibet, in parts of India, and in ancient Arabia. In Tibet polyandry takes the fraternal type. The brothers live together and possess the wife in common, and the children born are sometimes regarded as belonging to the oldest male. In other instances the mother apparently establishes the paternity by stating at the child's birth which of the men was its father. Among the Mayers of southwest India the woman when she becomes pregnant announces which of her husbands, who are unrelated, shall act as father and assume responsibility for the child's maintenance and education.

Testimony comes from students of Australian Aborigines as to the influence social conditions have upon the form of marriage. It is reported that in the Wikmunken tribe [17] plural marriage because of the burden of pregnancy, childbearing, and food-gathering is an economic necessity. No woman by herself is equal to the bearing, rearing, and caretaking of babes and children while at the same time carrying through the household needs, the procuring of food and firewood, and the preparing of the daily meals. Another observer states that in the Murngin tribe polygamy becomes the cause of constant strife because of the scarcity of women and the intense desire of the younger men to attain mates.[18] The situation is complicated by the killing of young men below twenty-five years of age in warfare. There had been over a hundred deaths of this sort among the Murngin men during the last twenty years. From Queensland comes the assertion that the majority of marriages among the natives of that section are monogamous, that a man only takes additional wives when this is in accord with the wishes of his first wife.[19] In 1913, from the information then available, Malinowski concluded that polygyny among the Australian Aborigines appeared to be limited to the older and more influential men and to be exceptional rather than the usual type of marriage, although it was found in all the tribes.[20] In the Lunga territory Kaberry among 174 marriages found 150 monogamous and 22 polygynous, or 12.6 per cent of the total. Of the latter nineteen men had two wives and one had four and two had five.[21] The same investigator found in the Djaru tribe 130 monogamous marriages and only 9 that were polygynous, or 7.4 of the total. These were all older men. In the Lunga tribe plural marriage was possible, not on account of the fact that males were killed in warfare, but because girls married at puberty and the boys later at the age of twenty or twenty-five.[22]

Monogamy. Monogamy, the marriage of one man to one woman, is not only the most common among the existing forms of marriage, but is also the norm of marital relationship. As

[17] Kaberry, Phyllis M., *Aboriginal Woman*, pp. 113.
[18] *Op. cit.*, p. 114.
[19] *Ibid.*
[20] *Ibid.*
[21] *Ibid.*
[22] *Ibid.*, p. 115.

Malinowski states, both polyandry and polygyny are compound marriages built upon the pattern of monogamy.[23] Monogamy is nearly always found even among peoples where one or the other type of plural marriage predominates. It is the kind of family that is most stable, because it leads to concentration of authority among simple people and a convergence of affection in the love union characteristic of modern culture. It is held by some authorities that a temporary monogamic relationship constituted the earliest form of marriage.

Monogamy offers opportunity for co-operation between man and woman that is difficult in any form of plural marriage. Private property and the rights of inheritance encourage it. It has proved expedient for the child and an advantage to the group in its struggle for political survival. Monogamy has favored the advancement of woman even though usually it has imposed upon her a far greater concentration of sex within the family than has been exacted by the social code for man. It is interesting to note that the sex jealousy which in our culture so strongly enforces monogamy and strengthens the monogamic code of conduct is less often found among primitive peoples whether their system of marriage is plural or singular.

Marriage contract. The most common marriage contracts were exchange and purchase. Exchange was the giving of one woman for another, one family pledging its daughter to marry into another family, which in turn promised a daughter to be given in marriage to a man in the first family. Still oftener brides were bought from their parents by the payment of animals or other goods. This enabled a wealthy man to buy several wives if that were permitted in his tribe, while a poor man might not be able to afford any.

The Old Testament story of Jacob working seven years for his wife and then getting the wrong sister is an illustration of marriage by purchase. Marriage by purchase implies that the woman was considered property and was treated as such, but this does not necessarily follow; rather this type of marriage meant that a woman was recognized as having social value, and therefore was not carelessly allowed to drift about from one family attachment to another. In England in feudal times the lord of a manor demanded a considerable payment if the daugh-

---

[23] *Encyclopedia Britannica*, 14th edition, Vol. 14, p. 950.

ter of one of his villeins married a man living elsewhere, until finally it was seen that for every girl who married outside her home group a girl from another estate was brought in as bride to one of the tenants.

At times the gifts made to the relatives of a primitive bride were replied to by presents from her kin to those of the bridegroom, much in the manner of our Christmas giving. This represented a ceremony, somewhat like our own giving of wedding presents, rather than actual marriage by purchase. Such an exchange of gifts takes place in the opera *Madame Butterfly*.

Not long ago a case of marriage by purchase in this country attracted wide attention. A gypsy sold his daughter to the man who wanted to marry her, and the characteristic gypsy wedding ceremony was enacted; but the girl soon afterward left her husband and ran away with the man of her choice, whereupon the man who had bought her as his bride wanted his money back from the father. In the ensuing publicity, it came out that the custom of buying their wives was widespread among the gypsies in America, but that the girls were growing less and less willing to abide by the conventions of their people, frequently running away from their allotted husbands, as this girl had done.

There was among primitive people what is known as marriage by capture. It was rather the stealing of property than the securing of a mate who came to have the legal status of wedlock. The woman was a part of the booty that had been gathered by an attack upon some neighboring group and the man who came into possession of her added her to his household because thus she could be made most useful. Several ceremonies connected with savage weddings hint at an earlier period of marriage by capture, and this is also suggested by some of our own marriage customs, but the present anthropological thought is that capture was a minor form of marriage contract which came about occasionally when men found it impossible to get enough wives and had to go out and steal them from some other tribe. If this had been common there would have been perpetual warfare among savages, and that was not true; besides, the weaker tribes would soon have lost all their women, which did not often happen. Moreover, a captured woman usually became not a wife but a concubine as in the Old Testament, the men not being allowed to marry the women they captured, though permitted to keep them as concubines. This also provided at times incentive for wife-stealing since the woman thus obtained was denied the right of the status of wife and literally was the man's slave. On the other hand, fear of reprisal tended to discourage this foraging for women.

The anthropologists explain the suggestions of earlier marriage by capture which persist in savage and civilized wedding customs today by saying that those rites represent the male's desire to show his strength and skill.

In the midst of the wedding feast the Bushman bridegroom suddenly snatches his bride away from her people, when he is immediately assailed by her relatives, who beat him unmercifully; if he is able to endure this pommeling without letting go of his prize, the young woman is declared his wife, but if his powers of endurance fail and his bride eludes his grasp the whole performance must be gone through successfully at a later date before the couple can become man and wife.[24]

To argue that the carrying out of a mimic seizure of the bride by forcible means in the face of the frenzied opposition of her kin as part of a primitive wedding ceremony is valid evidence of the earlier prevalence of marriage by capture in that tribe is no more sensible, says Westermarck, than to suppose that the custom in some tribes of treating the bride and bridegroom as a king and queen is proof that marriage used to be confined to royalty.[25]

Such modern customs as the wearing of the wedding veil, the honeymoon avoidance of friends and relatives, and the lifting of the bride over the threshold when she first enters her new home have been supposed by some writers to be relics of prehistoric marriage by capture. No such far-fetched explanation is needed, since these conventions can be shown to have sprung directly from much more simple and common impulses, such as modesty.[26]

The marriage ceremony. The marriage ceremony is as universal as the institution itself. In addition to the wedding customs, frequently the betrothal is also celebrated. Since

---

[24] Westermarck, E., *History of Human Marriage*, Vol. 2, p. 255.
[25] *Ibid.*, p. 261.
[26] *Ibid.*, p. 277.

primitive peoples carry on a great quantity of ceremonial behavior, especially in connection with eventful happenings such
as birth, death, and war, marriage ceremonies are in accord with
their general practice. In none of the customs of primitive
people do we find greater diversity than in the rites connected
with marriage. However trivial the form of marriage ceremony
may seem to us, it fulfills the same purpose as our own wedding
by giving the union public recognition. At a time when there
were no records and the mating regulations were strict and
frequently complex, there was great need of making the marriage
known and of establishing before witnesses the new status of
the man and woman.

Since ideas of magic have a large place in the beliefs and
practices of savage groups, it is not strange that the wedding
ceremony so often took some form that was assumed to have
significance in making the union fruitful, or in protecting the
new household against the dangers of evil spirits, or in cleansing
the woman when she was regarded as the possessor of magic
power that rendered her dangerous to the man. Often the ceremony used symbolism to emphasize the change in the relationship of the man and the woman and the significance of their
union. One of the common ceremonies was for the man and
woman to eat from the same dish. Always we find some recognition of the fact that the two people are attempting a new undertaking and mutually bind themselves to accept their new
obligations.

Endogamy.   Preliterate society never permits any man to
marry any woman without regard to tribal law. Instead we find
many regulations that limit freedom of choice, although usually
there is opportunity for individual preference. The individual
may be prohibited from marrying one who is not a member of
a definite group, or he may be denied the right to marry anyone who does not belong outside a certain group. These opposite
types of regulation may exist together, but in such a case they
do not refer to the same grouping. For example, as is commonly
true, the man has to marry a woman who is a member of his own
tribe but one who does not belong to the same clan as himself.
Thus we have endogamic regulations so far as the tribe is concerned and exogamic on the basis of clan grouping. Endogamy
renders the woman taboo to men outside her group, but it must

be remembered that wife-capture provides the means by which the man may escape restriction and obtain an out-of-the-group woman who may be his wife in all but legal status. The taboos that enforce endogamy may not only prevent marriage but also sexual relations between persons who are not within the same grouping. Endogamy is found at present among those in India who are forbidden to marry outside their caste. But an endogamic attitude exists wherever public opinion frowns upon marriage outside one's race, class, or religious faith.

Exogamy. Exogamy is the more common form of marriage restriction among preliterate people. This prohibition is against a member of a particular group marrying some other member of the same group. Usually the prohibition is based on the idea of relationship of persons who consider themselves of the same blood or the same line of descent. A common name even without blood relationship may be the basis of the prohibition.

There has been much speculation as to the origin of the idea of exogamy and its allied problem, the horror of incest. It is held by some that exogamy was a conscious attempt to prevent inbreeding. The trouble with this theory is that it is hard to see how the savage could find out that inbreeding was bad, if it was, for present-day biologists have no conclusive evidence that inbreeding of humans is necessarily harmful. Many biologists go so far as to maintain that the intermarriage of close relatives is dangerous only if the strain is markedly poor in important characteristics. On the other hand, the breeder of animals considers it important not to allow his stock to become inbred; if that happens he thinks he gets inferior results. Yet here again are conflicting stands; Darwin reported that the English racehorse was an example of as close inbreeding as one could hope to find. Some of the smaller animals, such as rats, which produce offspring at the age of three months, have been very closely inbred for many generations in laboratory experimentation without loss of vitality. Since it is so difficult to determine the status of human inbreeding today, one can scarcely imagine the savage holding such definite ideas on the subject as to impel him to set up the strong taboos of exogamy.

It has been insisted by some that there is an instinct against incest which led to the practice of exogamy. There appears to be no such instinct. For example, we have numerous cases of brothers and sisters, ignorant of their relationship, having been adopted perhaps by two different families, marrying, or planning to marry, and at the last moment learning of their true identity. We also know from our study of the delinquent girl that frequently her first introduction of sex experience is at the hands of a father, brother, uncle, or close relative. It appears generally to be true that constant familiar association in childhood lessens sex attraction, so that one naturally seeks marriage with someone he has not seen so frequently. This, however, is not always true and we have cases of unrelated persons brought up in the same household marrying.

It is held by some students that the purpose of exogamy is to bring the tribes into unity by scattering the marriages, much as the royal marriages of Europe are arranged with a view to bringing the nations into harmony. It is obvious that the exogamous regulations, by scattering marriage ties, would tend to strengthen tribal security.

The problem is a difficult one and at present there is no convincing solution. Even horror of incest has not been so universal as it is often thought. Although brother and sister marriages have not been common except among the Incas of Peru and at the time of the later Pharaohs and Ptolemies in Egypt, such unions occasionally occurred among various nationalities in antiquity and incited no social taboo. Among primitive peoples such marriage was not only permitted by some groups, but under certain circumstances it was even regarded as preferable and at times as a moral obligation. Whatever its origin, incest has become one of our strongest and most universal taboos.

The levirate, sororate, and couvade. A common practice in primitive life is for a brother to marry his widowed sister-in-law. This is known as the levirate. When a younger brother takes over a wife, or wives, of the deceased, we have what is known as junior levirate. Sometimes the widow is permitted to choose the new husband from her former husband's kin. The levirate was a moral obligation among the Jews, as Deuteronomy clearly expresses. "If brethren dwell together, and one of them die, and have no child, the wife of the dead shall not marry without unto a stranger; her husband's brother shall go in unto her, and take her to him to wife, and perform the duty of an husband's brother unto her. And it shall be that the first-born which she beareth shall succeed in the name of his brother which is dead, that his name be not put out of Israel." [27]

The various theories that have been advanced to explain the levirate afford a good example of the difficulty of finding the origin and purpose of many of the customs associated with the primitive family. Tozzer believes that the levirate expresses the desire for offspring and stresses the fact that marriage was between families rather than individuals. Rivers considers it nothing more than a method of keeping the property and children of the husband within his family or clan. Westermarck interprets it as a form of inheritance of property, the wife being looked upon as one of the man's possessions. Briffault regards it as related to fraternal polyandry, a survival of an earlier group marriage system. Frazer also finds in it a survival of an earlier group marriage. Lippert interprets it as having had its beginning in the desire to provide a son for the husband who has died in order that the latter's cult may be continued. It may be that the custom as it appeared in different parts of the world had more than one explanation. Indeed, more than a single influence may account for its appearance in any particular group.

The sororate describes the situation where it is customary for the man who marries the elder sister of a family to become the husband of the other sisters. If the husband cannot afford to marry his wife's sisters as they approach the marriageable period, or if in any particular case he does not desire to do so, he may transfer his right to some other man. For such a union his consent is necessary, and sometimes the purchase price of the bride must be paid to him rather than to the woman's relatives.

The couvade is another curious custom among primitive people which has disappeared from our social practices,[28] although rarely one comes across instances in modern life in which men reproduce the experience as they react pathologically to their wife's pregnancy. It was not an uncommon custom among primitive people for the husband to act as if he were ill during the pregnancy of his wife and at childbirth, thus assuming the role of the female while the wife carried on her ordinary activities as far as possible without attention to her condition.

---

[27] *Deuteronomy*, 25: 5–6.
[28] Crawley, Ernest, and Besterman, Theodore, *Mystic Rose*, Vol. II, pp. 177–188.

Sometimes the husband was expected to counterfeit the pains of childbirth and upon him also were often placed taboos associated with pregnancy and birth.

The couvade must not be interpreted as a purposeless custom. It had a meaning in that it gave the father a domestic and social status, not through his usual responsibilities as a male member of the group, but because he assumed a part in the feminine role by imitating the mother's childbirth experience. Thus the distinction between the father and the mother which would have left him out of the childbirth process was removed. He shared the ordeal of bringing the child into the world even though it was through the fiction of a ritual.[29] To the primitive mind this behavior of the father that seems so curious at first to us attested the infant's belonging to the father as well as to the mother.

Domestic experience of primitive people. The student of primitive family life is bewildered by the great amount of variation in the customs of the peoples he reads about, and most especially in their forms of marriage. As he looks at the practices of individual tribes and their changes in new circumstances, he finds much that is different from modern life, but it seems as if there is nothing to make a clear-cut picture, for there is no one definite form of family. What the student does find is all sorts of family life, so that he must generalize with a great deal of caution. The primitive family varies from place to place far more than the modern family as we know it, though that differs from nation to nation.

Another thing that stands out clearly is the fact that there is no progression from simple to complex family life so as to make an increasing evolution. The typical characteristics of the family at a certain level of experience differ from those at another level, but it is impossible to say that one type is higher or lower; the family life of a people is usually adapted to the life they have to live, or at least to their ideas with reference to that life. Thus the family has many different forms, each one fulfilling its function fairly well.

Little is gained by merely recording what a certain primitive people believe concerning the status of women or the institution of marriage, because that is largely theoretical. Only

---

[29] Allen, Frederick H., *Psychotherapy with Children*, p. 32.

by following the practices of the people throughout the whole of their social life can the real characteristics of their family life be determined. For instance, if it is the custom for the males to live by themselves, this changes the entire complexion of the family. There can then be only a limited family life with smaller function than where there is no club life; and many of the functions that we think of as peculiar to the family are carried on by the men in their clubhouse, even the housekeeping duties of the women shrinking to a very small place.

The difference between theory and practice in the savage home is shown by the fact that the beliefs of a people may be such as to make one infer that the woman is abused, while actually she may receive fair treatment. Even though theoretically ill-used, she may be hedged about with protection.

A marked economic division of labor is to be found in the family of primitives which throws light on the question whether the woman is exploited. When, for instance, the warrior coming home sees the camp fire and drops his game, which the wife goes out and gets, dragging it up to the fire and dressing it, because by custom no warrior brings home game when within sight of the camp fire, it sounds as if she were unfairly treated. Or if the wife and children may not eat until the men are satisfied, but must sit around on the hillside watching their menfolk feast and wondering if there will be anything but the scraps left for them, it seems to us like rank exploitation; but we do not take into account all the practical considerations. When there is not food enough for all, the men must be fed as well as may be, so they will be strong enough to go forth to seek more food for the group and able to repel the sudden attack of an enemy who may be waiting for a favorable time to make raids.

Both men and women often go hungry and overwork; neither of them is likely to be long-lived. The more we study the situation, the less sure we are that the woman is exploited compared with the man. Both are in hard circumstances and try to adjust themselves to the necessities of their existence.

The strength of the primitive family is based on its economic rather than its social or moral value. The family does, however, have social significance. The children are considered a wealth that belongs to the tribe, and a large part of the early history of the family revolves about the question: Who shall have control of the children? This is particularly true of the male children; it is often not true of the females because they are reckoned a less valuable tribal asset.

Besides its significance as the producer of children, the family has another function that is socially valuable: it transmits culture just as the modern family does. The primitive family transmits very satisfactorily and much more efficiently than our modern family, because the culture to be handed on is simple, with few perplexing problems or discords.

The child is taught just those things that seem important, consisting primarily of traditions, information leading to the skill which his way of living requires, and the ideas of magic and misinterpretation of causes which we label superstition and which occupy so large a place in primitive culture.

Kaberry bears testimony to the value of the preparation that the native girl of Australia receives. She becomes familiar with the routine of the household, the getting and the preparing of food, and learns the facts of sexual intercourse in her play with boys when she is eight or ten, so that when she is given to her future husband at the age of from nine to twelve she has some understanding of the domestic responsibilities belonging to her and has some knowledge of sex.[30]

The happiness of the primitive family. Ordinarily the primitive family is happy. This surprises those who cannot get away from the notion that the woman is exploited, but she seems to be at least as happy as the modern woman. She does not have the sensitiveness or unrest of the latter, but regards her life as the natural one and accepts it as it comes because she is accustomed to it; she does not complain because she has no motive for complaining.

In asking some of the women of Australian tribes the question whether they were happy, Kaberry tells us that they were puzzled as to what answer they should give. Evidently they had accepted their career as a matter of course. The impression gathered by the investigator was that although there was considerable grumbling concerning domestic matters from time to time none of the women could conceive of an existence that did not include marriage. Although there was no doubt of the importance of sex in the thinking of these natives and they

[30] Kaberry, *op. cit.*, pp. 92–93.

frankly admitted it as a motive in their marriages, there was also emphasis upon the economic co-operative aspects and on the importance of legitimatizing the children. It was clear also that in addition to the general advantages that were associated with marriage, there was at times the same mutual affection leading to the union that is the conventional motive in our own society.

Older men and women are also treated well, from a modern viewpoint too well, for they are often permitted to have too much power. One of the reasons why young boys and girls treat the elders so well is that among some tribes all the elders are relatives in the eyes of the child, there being in their thinking nothing like our idea of uncles and aunts but everybody being "related" if of the same clan. Even though the elders are sometimes put to death by their sons at the proper age for that proceeding, as has been true of the Eskimo, they are well treated up to that time.

The mother-in-law is controlled by very rigorous taboos, sometimes not being allowed even to speak to her son-in-law. Just why this should be is one of the puzzling questions. It is assuming a good deal to suppose that the savage plans this purposely to avoid trouble, for he is not so wise in other ways, but at any rate the taboo works out most advantageously. Freud thinks there is a feeling that the mother-in-law might be jealous of her daughter and have an affection for the son-in-law, but that seems absurd in view of the absence of jealousy among savages. The two families often live together without any difficulty. Tozzer lived for a year next to a savage family, both houses having roofs but no walls to afford privacy, so that if there had been any quarrels he would have known it. The primitive family consisted of a mother, three sons, and three daughters-in-law, all living together with never a quarrel of any sort in all that time.[31] This is a characteristic picture of primitive family life.

Sex control.   A superficial acquaintance with savage society leaves many people with the idea that sex control is a very modern thing and that savage people are lacking in sex discipline. There are so many variations from our way of living that

---

[31] Tozzer, *op. cit.*, pp. 130–131.

it seems as if that must be the fact, and missionaries, travelers, and traders, because they go so rapidly through the country or because they are so biased, often get this impression. But the theory that the evolution of man has been from a very loose to a very rigorous sex life is contrary to fact. What is true is that there are enormous differences among savages, some having a very strict sex life and others having considerable license, so that it is almost impossible to generalize. Often the facts have been misinterpreted by persons not scientific in their point of view, who do not linger long enough among a savage people to understand them. Sometimes the trouble has been an incorrect translation of words used by the savages. At other times the observers have not grasped the complexity of marriage relationships and have assumed that no standard marriage existed because they did not comprehend what it was.

Primitive people have also been ignorantly charged with a lack of modesty. This has been the result of a misinterpretation of strange customs. There is, of course, great variation between preliterate groups in their sense of shame and in their clothing of the body. It must be remembered, however, as the anthropologists insist, that vanity, with its influence upon ornamentation, had more to do with the development of clothing than either the idea of shame or the need of comfort. It is clear that among simple people there is no correlation between modesty and morality and the amount of clothing used. The presence or absence of modesty can only be discovered through familiar and sympathetic contacts of the trained observer; it cannot be inferred by measuring similarity or deviation from our prevailing fashion of dress, assumed as the standard of propriety.

Schapera in his *Married Life in an African Tribe* tells us that among the Kgatla there was a frankness concerning the sexual aspect of marriage, an absence of prudery which impressed him. Although there were standards determining propriety in dress and speech, there was no hesitation in talking freely about sexual matters. From an early age children were well acquainted with the nature of intercourse and many of their plays were distinctly sexual in character. As they grew older they were given definite instruction concerning sex. This was especially true of the girls, who were taught by their mothers. As soon as they had passed through puberty both boys and girls were given great freedom, and it was assumed that by the time they married each had had personal experience in intercourse.[32]

In her report on the Australian Aborigines, Kaberry states that mutual fidelity was expected by both the husband and wife, and the laxities of the former were not condoned. Instead, both guarded their rights jealously, and when the husband was away his relatives and her own were expected to see that she remained faithful. The author reports several instances of quarrels and final separations because one of the spouses had discovered the unfaithfulness of the other and took strong measures in protest. It is apparent that the elders did their best as a rule to suppress these domestic disturbances. If a lover ran away with a man's wife, when reconciliation could not take place some sort of compensation would be arranged. Discussions of intertribal meetings frequently concerned themselves with such illicit affairs, though most of these domestic upheavals were thrashed out beforehand in the camp between husband, wife, and lover.[33]

Divorce. Although marriage among primitive peoples, as with us, is usually expected to last for life, there are numerous exceptions and the right to divorce is common. In the practice of divorce we find, as usual, great diversity. Among some of the lower hunters it is claimed to be unknown or extremely rare. On the other hand, we sometimes find divorce frequent while in other tribes of a similar cultural level it is an occasional happening. In general, we detect the influence of economic conditions. The family remain together so long as it is for their material advantage but have recourse to divorce when it appears otherwise. Contrary to the modern situation, it is more often the man who obtains the divorce than the woman. It is rarely the result of the jealousy that plays so important a part in modern life, but instead it is sought for economic reasons or for personal comfort. Examples of this are divorces for inefficiency in housekeeping, such as bad cooking, accusation of witchcraft, troublesome talkativeness, or merely that the wife is no longer desired. Divorce is not considered a disgrace and does not hinder a second marriage. Sometimes there is a ceremony

---

[32] *Op. cit.,* pp. 180–181.
[33] *Op. cit.,* pp. 143–145.

connected with it, but ordinarily the needful publicity is furnished by rites connected with a second marriage. Barrenness is one of the frequent reasons for divorce.

In interpreting divorce among primitive people we must take care not to assume its frequency merely because it is something easily obtained. We may discover that in some tribe the savage can divorce his wife by simply throwing a kitchen utensil after her as she goes out of the door. This does not mean necessarily that there is nothing to restrain the man from getting rid of a wife. The fact that the purchase price has to be returned leads to a public opinion which may have much influence in limiting divorces. There is also the necessity of the man's having property with which to purchase another wife. The fact that there are children may also tend to prevent divorce just as it does in modern society.

Tribal custom may restrict divorce even when the grounds for securing it seem to the European extremely lax. Although divorce is more open to the man, it must not be inferred that it is always difficult for the wife or that she never seeks it. Rules governing the division of property and the menace of family feuds also restrain husbands from attempting to break their marriage ties. Generally it may be said that the economic motive has a greater influence in leading to divorce or in preventing it than does the happiness of the individual in the domestic association. The prevalence of divorce does not permit us to classify the stage of matrimonial culture, since it is a matter influenced by many economic and social conditions. The position of woman also in any definite primitive group cannot be inferred on the mere basis of the ease of divorce. The question always is not what may be, but what, as the result of public opinion, actually happens. Usually divorce, as is true of marriage, is a private affair which at most does not extend beyond the concern of the relatives of the man and woman. Sometimes it is in the hands of the chief, the council, or the governing group of old men, the last being more frequent among the Australians. When there is an intervention of some public authority outside the kinsfolk concerned, it is for the purpose of avoiding violations of regulations or to prevent dissension and feud.

Schapera [34] tells us that of the three hundred and four

---

[34] *Op. cit.,* p. 294.

marriages concerning which he had collected information in making up his genealogical records only nine had been divorced and of the eighty-eight cases tried in the chief's court from July, 1935, to June, 1939, only two had been concerned with divorce. The husband among these African peoples studied hesitates to seek divorce, since this will at least deprive him of a useful service. He is therefore not likely to seek to be rid of his wife unless she is barren, repeatedly unfaithful, or utterly neglectful of her household responsibilities. Because the wife by being divorced loses the prestige and the material advantage of being married and generally the possession of her children, she also is not likely to ask for a divorce unless she is constantly ill treated or is denied the maintenance that she has a right to expect.

It is interesting to notice that among the Kimberley natives there appeared to be no distinction made between the barren and the fruitful marriage, although the former in some cases appeared to be the cause of a polygynous union.[35]

Children. Children are usually treated generously. Indeed, they are sometimes indulged too much, contrary to our general thought; but as a rule they are so severely disciplined concerning the bigger things that they are obedient, while in the smaller they are allowed to do very much as they please and their life might seem enviable to the modern child whose life is so much regulated.

In spite of the fact that, aside from observation of the taboos and other regulations that are supposed to have great social importance, little effort is made to interfere with the behavior of the child, the education that the boy and girl receive from their close contact with nature, which teaches the wisdom of co-operating with the older people and following their precepts, leads irresistibly to self-discipline. Public praise and blame also contribute to this end. The children are in a position to realize the need of following the demands of the elders as, for example, when on a hunting expedition, because they see immediately the consequences of disobedience. The son's failure to remain motionless in accord with the gesture of the parent may mean the escape of the animal. Although the savage when possessed by anger or some other strong emotion may be so cruel

---

[35] Kaberry, *op. cit.*, p. 156.

to the child as to appear to us destitute of feeling or sanity, as a rule he treats his children with kindness, for they are highly valued not only by their immediate family but by all the adults of the tribe.

Testimony has been given to the weakening of family discipline and the lessening authority of the parents in the training of children as a consequence of the contact of natives with civilization. The school, the church, and industry have replaced to some extent the home as an educational agency among the natives, and, as a result, the complaint that children are lacking in manners and respect for their elders is common. Youth seem less willing to work, the girls show less interest in domestic matters, and children are less conscientious in supporting their parents. The youth of this native tribe are also indicted for looseness in morals and promiscuity and characterized as having concern for nothing except their own pleasure. These criticisms were more than merely fondness for "the good old days"; they also laid bare the difficulties of cultural transition.[36]

It is important to notice the value of the home in the development of the primitive child because during the earlier years of childhood he is permitted to enter so freely into the activities of adults and is not placed under the supervision characteristic of the modern home and later is not subjected to the regimentation of a rigid educational system. His preparation for life therefore in large measure comes from contact with his parents. The boy hunts with his father and other men whom he has known from infancy; likewise, the girl associates with her mother and other women as food is gathered and prepared. The child accumulates gradually through observation and imitation skills based upon habit and develops ability to adjust himself not only to the conditions of his physical environment but also to cultural demands that are put upon him through traditions, customs, and taboos.[37] The break from childhood is recognized by the initiating ceremony, which usually has greater significance for the boy than for the girl.

The American Indian. The Europeans who made colonial settlements in North America found themselves in contact with primitive groups which came to be known as the American

---

[36] Schapera, *op. cit.*, pp. 265–266.
[37] Kaberry, *op. cit.*, pp. 71–83.

Indians. Although there were considerable differences among these native people in their cultural development, they were all backward and primitive as compared with the men and women from the old world, and as a consequence of this a survival conflict resulted. As the new settlements expanded, they encroached more and more upon the hunting grounds which were the Indians' means of sustenance. The interactions that took place, sometimes co-operations but usually conflicts, play so large a part in our colonial history as to give this particular primitive group special significance to the student of the American family.

It is necessary, therefore, as we trace the beginnings of our type of family, to keep in mind that the early settler not only had to conquer the wilderness but also the native tribes and that many of these were in their methods of fighting not only well adapted to their environmental conditions but also unsurpassed in carrying on a kind of warfare most difficult for the Europeans to encounter. In the annals of such contests between peoples of simpler culture with those further advanced and therefore possessing greater resources, there is none that excels in fierceness that which took place in North America during the period of settlement and the later winning of the west. Man for man the Indian was a more dangerous antagonist than would have been true under similar circumstances of soldiers from any of the various national armies of Europe. The headway that the colonists made was the result of their superiority in offensive weapons, a more mature social organization, and a greater population increase both through births and immigration. From the beginning they had to deal with the Indian as a neighbor, although compared with European experience an elusive one, as a trader, and always as a potential enemy. A peaceful settlement of difficulties would have been under any circumstances doubtful because the settlers and the Indians for the most part had such unlike purposes in their use of the land. No treaty could change this fundamental clashing. Then also the rights of the territory were ill defined and in constant dispute even among the natives themselves. As a result the treaties made with certain tribes were not recognized by others while the white people on their side frequently had no intention of making a just treaty, and even when such settlement did occur there was no way by which individual frontiersmen could be restrained from encroaching constantly on the hunting grounds of the Indians as the American civilization moved westward.

The situation led to the keenest type of survival warfare because of the cruelties practiced by both parties in the conflict. The Indian judged by European codes did his fighting in ways that led to unmerciful retaliation. When a comparison is made between the conditions that faced the American colonies and those existing in Australia when its early settlers came in conflict with the aborigines, then it becomes clear that in our country the traits of the Indians were such as to make them throughout the history of the American frontier an important influence in the development of the nation as it took place beyond the Alleghenies. The long continuing conflict between the whites and the Indians was one of the sources of the independence, self-reliance, initiative, and intense localism that characterized the frontier men and women who contributed so greatly to the distinctive traits of the American people and thus became one of the most important social influences that shaped the American family.

The family life of the American Indian. *The Social Organization of the Tewa of New Mexico,* by Elsie Clews Parsons, presents a detailed picture of the family life of a group of the Pueblo Indians. When a child is born the lying-in period of the mother is three days. She gets up on the fourth, when the infant is named. The day of birth is counted as the first of the three during which she is permitted to recuperate from the ordeal of delivery. There is an elaborate ceremony associated with the birth of the child, who on the fourth day is carried out of the house early in the morning. Within a week or two he is taken to church, where he receives his Mexican name. In this group of Indians there is considerable restriction of marriage-choice, a limitation based on recognized blood ties between collateral relations on both the maternal and paternal side. Descendants of the same grandparents are not permitted to marry although concerning this there seem to exist irregularity and inconsistency. Betrothal and marriage proceed according to a stereotyped pattern of ceremony which in the case of the former stresses responsibilities of the boy as a provider. As a rule, the married sons and daughters seek their own home, although occasionally as many as three generations are found living together. The older widows and widowers either live with a married child or carry on with adopted grandchildren. Two or even three houses may be owned by a family group, the husband and the wife each possessing a house, and they may live in each alternately or use one for storage purposes.[38] There is at least in theory equality of male and female offspring in the inheritance of property including land, cattle, horses and houses.[39]

Adultery and changing of spouses appear in the folk tales, but it is difficult to discover how common these are as social practices. The influence of the church is against separation and remarriage. There is considerable promiscuity among the unmarried and there are many births out of wedlock.[40]

The basic principle of social classification among the Tewa is that of summer and winter. Moiety grouping is patrilineal, while the clanship is frequently matrilineal. Illegitimate children are given the same moiety as their mother as well as the same clan. Occasionally the moiety may be changed or the clan, in either case requiring similar change in the other classification.[41] There appears to be no opposition to members of the same moiety marrying, although the occasional changing of both boys and girls from one moiety to the other suggests that formerly the moiety was strictly endogamous.[42]

Cochiti marriage customs. *The Social and Ceremonial Organization of Cochiti,* by Esther Schiff Goldfrank, presents an interesting example of family customs. Cochiti, a Keres Pueblo village, is situated on the banks of the Rio Grande, some thirty miles northwest of Santa Fe. Its customs express a culture which seems to be about halfway between that of the southern Pueblos with their strong clanship and the northern Pueblos who stress the ceremonial moieties. In this village there is evidence that the culture of the natives has been influenced by the nearness of their Mexican neighbors and intermarriage that has occurred. Apparently this has led to a degeneration of the meaning of clan and a considerable diffusion of Mexican traits.[43] Although the investigator discovered marriages within the clan,

---

[38] *Op. cit.,* p. 37.
[39] *Ibid.,* p. 38.
[40] *Ibid.,* p. 36.
[41] *Ibid.,* p. 93.
[42] *Ibid.,* p. 96.
[43] *Op. cit.,* p. 11.

the villagers on the whole seem to be conscious of the exogamic custom and eager to observe it. This is illustrated by the belief that the death of three children in one family where members of the same clan had married was a consequence of their violation of the law.[44] In this group of the Pueblo Indians, in contrast with the Tewa, the moiety is merely a ceremonial organization with an unstable membership. The children join that of their fathers, the daughters in marriage adopt their husbands', and, at times, on account of some quarrel, an entire family may change its affiliations. In addition to the exogamy of the clan, marriage is still more limited by the influence of the Church, which does not permit or sanction the union of blood cousins or their children.[45] Monogamy is the rule. A boy announces to his father that he intends to marry, the relatives are informed, the father then visits the girl's father, who in turn notifies his relatives. A few nights later the relatives of the boy meet at his house, and at the same time the girl's relatives meet at her home. After each group has been asked to give consent to the marriage, the girl's father goes to the boy's home and tells him that he can have the girl. Both groups of relatives prepare for the wedding. They feast first at the girl's and then later at the boy's home. The boy gives to his future wife all her wedding clothes. Formerly the couple after the wedding lived at the girl's house; now it is becoming more common for them to go immediately to their own home, the boy having already built a house. After the two have been married for some time, the wife carries food to the boy's family in return for what they brought to the wedding feast.[46] When the wife becomes pregnant she procures a perfect ear of blue corn and keeps it in her house. Once the child is born she places a stirring stick beside this ear of corn with a light beside the baby to ward off evil spirits. Sometimes these remain until the child is baptized. The father may be present at the birth of the child and some female, either the woman's mother or aunt, will also be near.

The Giant Shaman is usually called in when it appears the child is about to be born. He is prepared to assist the woman in her delivery of the child. The lying-in period is four days. The child cannot receive any name of any living person, but there is

[44] *Ibid.*, p. 12.
[45] *Ibid.*, p. 15.
[46] *Ibid.*, p. 84.

a tendency to revive names of relatives who have died. This does not mean however that the spirit of the dead person enters the newborn child. After confinement the heavy work is done for the woman by her female relatives. During this time intercourse is not permitted. Occasionally a newborn child is taken by a woman who is sterile to her own home in the hope that this will make her fertile. She keeps the child four days and treats it as her own, having it nursed by some friend, but not by the mother. During this time none of the child's immediate family is allowed to see it. The woman who has borrowed a child in this manner is regarded as a foster mother and is always called mother by the child. She chooses the godfather and godmother whom usually the parents select after the child has received his Indian name.[47]

Through the influence of the church, sex relations before marriage are disapproved by the Indians themselves. There is no ceremony connected with the coming of adolescence in the case of the girl, but she is informed as to the meaning of menstruation when it occurs and the boys also during adolescence are informed concerning this function in women. After menstruation has started, the girl does not have as great freedom in her play with boys as was previously true.

Customs and beliefs concerning pregnancy have a decided influence on conduct. The following are examples: If a young girl drinks water behind a grinding stone before menstruation commences, it will be painful. A pregnant woman may not chew gum, or her baby will cry. If a pregnant woman peeps out of a door or window, labor will be prolonged as the baby will only peep through. If a pregnant woman stretches her arms, the child will do likewise, and labor will be difficult. If a pregnant woman puts her shoes on the mattress, the afterbirth will not follow quickly. A pregnant woman should not sew, because the baby's cord would wind itself around the neck of the child, just as the stitches run over the cloth. If a pregnant woman leaves her lunch before she has entirely finished it, she may not touch it again. If she did, her labor pains would be prolonged. If a woman opens her eyes and "looks scared," she will have a boy. If a woman does not go out and look at the moon when it is red and half-full, her child will be born without an upper lip.

---

[47] *Ibid.*, pp. 76–78.

Chapter 4

THE PATRIARCHAL FAMILY

FOREWORD. It is desirable that the student who is beginning his study of the family should become familiar with the family types of the ancient world that indirectly have contributed most to the background of the American family and especially with that aspect in their development which was most influential. This explains the title of this chapter—"The Patriarchal Family."

The following are featured as examples of this type of family: the Hebrew family because of its Old Testament setting and the significant part these writings have played in American civilization; the Greek family because of the contribution of the Greek literature to the Renaissance and the reconstruction of Europe; and the Roman on account of the role its culture played in the building of Europe during the Middle Ages and especially the legal aspect of this family system as it has affected family law in this country. The purpose of this choice has decided the content of the chapter. No effort is made to deal with any one of the three exhaustively but rather to use each as an example of the patriarchal family that has meaning for the student of the American family.

THE HEBREW FAMILY

The Hebrew family. The development of the family in the ancient world took various forms and all of them have interest for the student. We, however, are concerned in this text only with the types of family life that have had direct influence upon the American. From this viewpoint the Hebrew, the Greek, and the Roman are most significant, not only because of what each has contributed directly to its modern evolution, but also in a greater degree on account of the influence each had upon the development of the Christian Church, from which chiefly came the background of the occidental modern family. Even though for our present purpose it is necessary to treat the Hebrew family as a development by itself, it must be remembered that it is a portion of a larger evolution which comprises the family life of all the Semitic people. The Greek and Roman types likewise are specialized forms of the family that have relations to preceding developments in Asia and Europe. This is clearly seen in the case of the Roman family, since its history reveals both Greek and Germanic influences. The Hebrew family has not only greatly affected the direction taken by the Christian family, but it also has been perpetuated and has been handed on to us with less change than any of the others in the contemporary orthodox Jewish family.

The stages of the Hebrew family.   Our chief sources for the history of the Hebrew family are the Old Testament and the Talmud. Both record an evolution which continued over centuries of time and disclose marriage and family situations at various stages. In the interpreting of the Old Testament, this fact must be recognized in arriving at a true understanding of the Hebrew family. For example, in the story of creation, as recorded in Genesis, we find two distinct statements. The first presents the man and woman as equals, while in the second the woman's existence is derived from that of the man. There emerged from the critical study of the Bible, which began in the nineteenth century, a realization that the first six books of the Old Testament, upon which we rely for the reconstruction of the early Jewish family, are built upon four distinguishable sources which are known to scholars as the J, E, D, and P documents. Their antiquity varies, the J material going back probably to about 850 B.C., while the P may in part come down to 400 B.C. Obviously we should expect the family to reveal different stages of development in these basic documents, and that is what happened.[1] In tracing the history of the Hebrew family, it is necessary also to realize that the religious thinking and practices reveal a long-continued struggle between the

---

[1] Cross, E. B., *The Hebrew Family,* p. 6; and *The History of Christianity in the Light of Modern Knowledge,* A Collective Work, p. 712.

priestly and the prophetic leaders. As a consequence of these various stages and different emphases, we are forbidden a static description of the Hebrew family. History presents us with a changing picture of family life among a people held together at first by nationalistic ties and later unified by their common faith.

Religious significance of the Hebrew family.   Throughout the evolution of the Jewish family we find a marked predominance of religion. The patriarch was not merely the head of the household; he was also priest of the domestic circle, upon whom fell the responsibility for the proper observation of rites and ceremonies. These were precise and elaborate and woven into the activities of everyday life. In the earlier period every home was the center of religious sacrifice and the patriarch was the celebrant. Although his functions lessened with the development of the local synagogue and the temple of Jerusalem, his role as the religious leader continued. Upon him fell the responsibility for the carrying out of the fasts and feasts that had so large a place in the Hebrew religion. Every day brought to the Hebrew home solemn duties of ritual in addition to these celebrations of great events in the history of the nation. The observance of these, in which the father of the household assumed leadership, whether daily or seasonable, grew rigid with time and had to be carried out in minute detail and with exactness. It was this mechanical observance built into the domestic life that the prophets persistently challenged.

Vestiges of the metronymic family.   The vestiges of a former metronymic culture that appear in the Old Testament records are in accord with the family evolution that one would expect. Cross tells us that out of twenty-nine instances of the naming of children given in the J document of the Hexateuch, which, it should be remembered, is the oldest document, twenty-one and possibly twenty-two describe the naming of the child by the mother.[2] In later writings the trend has changed. In the five cases of the naming of children according to the E document, only one is metronymic.

Another evidence of a former metronymic culture comes from instances in which the half-brother marries the half-sister. Since under the metronymic system the man and woman, in spite

---

[2] Cross, *op. cit.*, p. 7.

of a common father, belong each to the family of the mother,
they are therefore unrelated. An example of this is the marriage
of Abram and Sarah, according to the E document. In the code of
Deuteronomy which appeared in the seventh century B.C. we
find such marriages prohibited, it being unlawful for the brother
to take his sister as a wife whether she be the daughter of his
father or of his mother.[3] Three times in Leviticus in what is
known as the "Holiness Code," which was later than the Deu-
teronomic, we find protest against the brother and sister marrying. Apparently the former metronymic practice lingered up to
the time of the exile. The Old Testament narrative also reveals
cases of matrilocal residence. The man goes to live with his wife's
people and his children come under the charge of her male relatives. In Exodus we read: "And Moses was content to dwell with
the man: and he gave Moses Zipporah his daughter." [4] Cross believes the evidence is even clearer in the case of Samson's marriage to the woman of Timnah, and Gideon's union with a
woman in Shechem, and Ithra's connection with Abigail. After
the exile we find in the book of Ezra the children of Barzillai,
who took a wife of the daughters of Barzillai the Gileadite, expelled from the priesthood on account of their inability to prove
their patronymic genealogy, the former metronymic folkways
being by this time forgotten.[5]

The patriarchal family.   The patriarchal type of family
which developed among the Hebrews and smothered out that
which had gone before grew to such strength that it has come
to seem the prototype of this form of domestic organization. The
most common picture brought out by the word patriarch is that
of the male head of the Jewish family. The theology of the Old
Testament presents to us a patriarchal God for whom the father,
head of the family, acts as representative and interpreter. In all
ways the male predominates. The woman belongs to a lower
order and her inequality is enforced by religious practices. Since
she is denied the right to take part in the sacrifices and rituals,
the household altar and the holy of holies of the temple are to
her taboo. She lives her life under the control of some male except, perhaps, when upon the death of her husband she goes to

---

[3] *Deuteronomy,* 27:22.
[4] *Exodus,* 2:21.
[5] Cross, *op. cit.,* p. 27.

live at the home of a son. In spite of this general picture of patri-archal authority which makes the official head of the house an overlord in control of the younger men and women, the servants, and even the stranger within the gates, and reduces, at least at first, the woman to the status of mere property, we find in the Old Testament narrative glimpses of a domestic life inconsistent with this prevailing social pattern. We are introduced to affec-tionate relationships, husband-wife co-operation, and the re-hearsal of family joys and sorrows which appear inconsistent with the rigid and powerful patriarchal system. Unquestionably the religious and cultural trend led to a softening of patriarchal authority, even though the system itself remained intact as a form of family organization and survives in contemporary Jew-ish orthodoxy.

The ethical code so far as it was concerned with sex conduct reflects in Jewish culture the patriarchal viewpoint. Emphasis was placed upon ceremony, including the rites of purification, and upon taboo. Adultery was dealt with severely. Not to marry was considered a religious sin. Celibacy was not permitted even to the priest. Marriage was required of men who had passed twenty.

The Essenes, one of the three Judaistic parties flourishing at the time of Jesus, to some extent practiced celibacy, appar-ently believing, as later was taught by some of the Christian Fathers, that by so doing they achieved a higher level of spiritual purity.

Marriage among the Hebrews. As every reader of the Old Testament narrative knows, the ancient Hebrews were polygy-nous. Cross tells us that nowhere in the Old Testament litera-ture can we find any clear presentation of monogamy as the ideal relationship for men and women. Hebrew polygyny met the same difficulty due to the approximate equality in number of males and females that the system always encounters, so that it was largely confined to the wealthy, who had the means of pur-chasing several wives.

The usual way of procuring a wife was by purchase, pay-ment being made to the girl's father. The bride went to the husband's house and this completed the marriage. There ap-pears at first to have been no ceremony or wedding ritual. As a matter of fact, in her social status the wife was so subordinated to her husband as to be only in degree of subjection distinguishable from the slave. We find in the Hebrew narrative cases of departure from the standard form of marriage. One of these variations was a temporary union, of which Samson's marriage to Delilah is an example.[6] These and the occasional matrilocal unions were possibly substitutes for the polygynous marriages denied men of small means. We also have illustrations of wife capture. The most spectacular of these is the story of the vengeance the Hebrew tribes inflicted upon Jabesh-gilead, capturing four hundred young virgins and turning them over to the males of the tribe of Benjamin, who had survived earlier massacre.[7]

Inheritance. The inheritance of property among the Hebrews followed patriarchal traditions, emphasizing the unity of the family and leading to the desire for male heirs. In the passing down of property from father to son in the earlier nomadic stage the right of inheritance went to the eldest son and with it nearly all the property of the father. The son took over the patriarchal leadership from the father. It was this that Jacob stole from his twin brother Esau when by trickery he obtained from his dying father the blessing which commissioned his primogeniture.[8] In the later agricultural stage the property was divided among the sons, the eldest receiving a double portion. If there were no children, the slave might inherit the property of his master. There is evidence that after the exile the daughters were permitted to inherit in cases where there were no male heirs. A record appears in the E document of female inheritance which is ascribed to the time of Moses, but the historical character of this incident is disputed. In the division of property in this later period the sons of the subordinate wife, unless through intrigue they were denied their rights, received their share of their father's estate. The levirate was an established custom among the Hebrews. Although the brother was expected to marry the wife of the man who had died childless, provision was made, in case he objected, for his release from his obligation, but his refusal had to be publicly made and in the presence of

---

[6] *Judges*, Ch. 16.
[7] *Ibid.*, Ch. 21.
[8] *Genesis*, Ch. 27.

the widow, who was permitted a ceremonial expression of protest.

Divorce among the Hebrews.   Divorce in the earlier patriarchal period appears as a masculine prerogative, in agreement with the general practices of this cultural level in the evolution of the family of other nations and races. We find Abraham, at the insistence of his wife Sarah, sending Hagar into the wilderness provided only with a small quantity of water and bread. This incident may not reveal what was customary in divorce proceedings, because Hagar enjoyed only a slave's status and was therefore as much the property of her master to do with as he wished as were his cattle. At a later time Michal was divorced from David on the grounds of desertion. David had fled from the presence of Saul, who had grown suspicious of David's ambition. Since this divorce involves the power of a king, it also may not be representative. The same complication enters when later David, who had become king, required Abner, who held the throne of Israel, to return Michal, as the condition of an alliance, thus forcing her to leave her husband. "And her husband went with her, weeping as he went, and followed her to Bahurim. Then said Abner unto him, 'Go, return.' And he returned." [9] David married Michal, but again we do not know whether this was a special privilege possible because of his position or an ordinary practice. In the seventh century B.C. the Code of Deuteronomy legalizes divorce but attempts to protect the woman from hasty decision on the part of her husband by requiring a legal document. The woman is allowed to remarry, but union between her and her first husband is prohibited. "When a man taketh a wife and marrieth her, then it shall be if she find no favor in his eyes, because he hath found some unseemly thing in her, that he shall write her a bill of divorcement and give it in her hand and send her out of his house." [10] The protest against the practice of divorce appeared first in the denunciation of Malachi, the prophet, in the period after the exile. The P document, which reflects the period after the exile, makes no reference to divorce. Possibly this reveals a growing hostility to the practice.

---

[9] *II Samuel,* 3:16.
[10] *Deuteronomy,* 24:1.

The enactment of Deuteronomy has a special significance. The Old Testament expression "uncleanness," as the grounds for divorce was differently interpreted by two rival rabbinical schools at the time of Jesus. The followers of Hillel insisted that it meant for any cause satisfactory to the husband, while the disciples of Shammai held that it was restricted to adultery or its moral equivalent. This difference explains why the question of which was correct was put before Jesus. His decision as it has been generally understood—for from the early period of the Church until now there has been controversy as to its meaning —has been the determining influence in the Church's attitude toward divorce.[11]

Home life of the Hebrews.   The characteristic strength of the modern Jewish family life suggests that it has deep historic roots, and this is the impression gathered from the study of Hebrew literature. A mere rehearsal of the most important features of the Hebrew family system does not present a just picture of home life. It is true that the family was strongly masculine and that inequality was placed upon the woman. This did not sap the unity of family life or create in the woman restlessness and dissatisfaction. The glimpses we gather of the Hebrew family in action portray a closely knit, co-operative, pious home life which moves toward monogamic standards and the modern relationship of affection. Discipline of the home was strict, but it was accepted as a matter of course and was tempered by religious responsibility and concern for the moral success of the children. The women seem to have been better treated and more nearly equal to men than in other Eastern family systems. The life was hard, recreation meager, and education limited, but this was characteristic of the period. Slavery was milder than in other Eastern countries, considerably more so than that which developed in the Western world. A mere summary of patriarchal authority does not bring out the quality of the Hebrew home. Lew Wallace's description in _Ben Hur_ is more to be trusted than the regulations of the Code of Deuteronomy.

Evolution of the Hebrew family.   Although in the family life of modern Italy and Greece we find the historic representatives of their ancient Roman and Greek predecessors, they do not maintain the distinctive characteristics of their origin in the

---

[11] Norcross, F. H., _Christianity and Divorce._

way that is true of the modern Hebrew or Jewish family. The latter because of its religious basis constitutes a development that continues its distinguishing traits from the earliest Biblical records up to the present time. This does not of course mean that there have been no changes but rather that at all periods in its history the Hebrew family has been sharply marked off from other types and in every social and national environment has perpetuated its individuality. Its long evolution, exceeding a thousand years, has been classified [12] as the Biblical, Talmudic, Medieval, and Modern types. These cannot accurately be separated into periods since the second overlaps in time all three, extending from the last of the first through, in some parts of the world, the fourth. The Hebrew family as portrayed during the Old Testament history has been discussed in the preceding pages, since its traditions and ideals have influenced the evolution of the American family.

The Talmudic type. The Biblical rules and commandments as they concern marriage and the family were interpreted and enlarged by the writers of the Talmud, which contained the official teachings of the Jewish church. An authoritative literature, it interpreted and applied the principles of the Old Testament in a somewhat similar way to that in which the decisions of the American courts are based upon the common law. The orthodox Jewish family was expected to follow the precepts of the Talmud, as still is true. Although dispersed over the continents of Asia, Europe, and Africa, the Jewish people, especially during the Medieval period when orthodoxy flourished, endeavored to follow the family program described in the Talmud.[13] During the first centuries of the Christian era, marriage, previously regarded as the normal way of life, was construed as a divine ordinance. Celibacy was frowned upon and was rarely found. Early marriages were encouraged, but according to the authoritative teaching no man was entitled to a wife who did not have the means of supporting her. Although the Jews frequently married while still minors, child marriages were contrary to Talmudic ruling.[14] This prohibition was at times set aside because of the persecutions. In the twelfth century one

---

[12] Brav, Stanley, *Jewish Family Solidarity*, p. 3.
[13] *Ibid.*, p. 7.
[14] Jung, Leo, *The Jewish Library*, p. 130.

authority explains that the custom of betrothing daughters before they were twelve years of age was the result of the fear of
their fathers that if they waited longer they might be unable to
provide a suitable dowry. Living as the Jews were, in constant
danger of being plundered and massacred, it was wise to arrange
for their daughters while they were able to furnish the dowry,
without which marriage was likely never to occur. A later ruling
given in the fourteenth century affirmed that the prohibition of
child marriages applied only where Jewish families were settled
in the same town and that when they were scattered and their
numbers reduced by persecutions it was expedient that the child
be married whenever an eligible husband appeared.[15] According
to Talmudic teaching, the purpose of marriage was the begetting
of children. It was expected that the unions would be arranged
by the parents. Betrothal was a formal act making the woman the
legal wife of the man. Twelve months was considered the normal
period between the agreement and the consummation of the
marriage in the case of a maid. The time for a widow was less.
Polygyny was considered legitimate, but it was not common. It
was discouraged by the Rabbinical marriage contract and settlement. The single code of morals that found expression in the
Bible was enforced and extended in Talmudic literature. Monogamy, which for as many as fifteen hundred years had been
customary, became the legal requirement for the Jews of the
Western world about the year 1000 of the Christian era.[16] In
alien environments, without any national existence of their own,
the Jews frequently met with difficulties as they tried to maintain a family life consistent with Talmudic teaching. At times
they had to modify their practices because of the prevailing
customs of the Gentiles. These deviations from orthodoxy appeared in the Medieval period but in much greater degree in
the modern world and in the West as compared with the East.

The Medieval Jewish family. In this period the Jewish
family reveals its vitality in maintaining its peculiar traits. It
also discloses its inability to escape altogether the social conditions of its time and place. For example, although in accord
with the spirit of the period the Jewish woman was given an
inferior status as compared with the man, this inequality was

---

15 *Ibid.*, p. 7.
16 Brav, Stanley, *op. cit.*, p. 11.

tempered by the relatively higher position given woman in Jewish theology in contrast to that in the teaching of the early Church Fathers. Since the Jewish home was the scene of many of the religious rites and its sanctity was enforced by tradition, it was inevitable that both the wife and the child would profit by this emphasis upon the domestic aspects of religious faith. The home was a place of refuge from the inferiorities and persecutions that the Jew faced in Gentile contacts. This enhancement of family life naturally encouraged monogamy so that, in spite of the fact that polygyny was permissible, custom and Talmudic teaching reflected the incentives of the high quality of domestic fellowship and discouraged plural marriages. In comparison with the general atmosphere concerning sex, Jewish literature of post-Biblical times was distinguished by its refined treatment of the subject of intercourse between husband and wife.[17] From the tenth century onward there was growing protest against permitting the man to divorce his wife against her will.[18] Some men were brutal enough to force their wives to consent to a divorce, but this was less a problem than wife desertion. The proneness of men to travel led to problems of separation, and in the twelfth century an effort was made to protect the wife by limiting the husband's absence to eighteen months. For this, formal permission had to be obtained from the communal authorities. The husband was required upon his return to remain at home for at least six months, and he was not permitted during the first year of marriage to go away on any considerable journey.[19] It came about, in order to prevent the wife's being left by the long absence of a husband neither a maid, wife, nor widow, that the husband planning a long trip away from home was required to give his wife a conditional divorce which would take effect only if he did not return within a stated period.[20] Another remarkable provision was the imperfect divorce which was made use of to protect the wife from the persecution of tax-hungry government officials during the absence of her husband. Even when the wife was divorced by the husband he was not free from all responsibilities but was expected to show consideration in case she

[17] Abrahams, Israel, *Jewish Family Life in The Middle Ages,* p. 86.
[18] *Ibid.,* p. 89.
[19] *Ibid.,* p. 90.
[20] *Ibid.*

had need of assistance. The Talmud had made this an obligation, insisting that the husband "should remember that she had been his flesh and must stretch out his hand to succor her." This command was generally enforced during the Middle Ages.

The Rabbi, unlike the priest, was not only permitted to marry but was required to do so, and the great respect given religious leadership by orthodox Jews tended to elevate and enhance marriage. Prostitution was said to have been nonexistent among Jews during the Middle Ages. In accord with the Old Testament and the spirit of the patriarchal organization of family life, children honored their parents, especially the father. The Jewish son stood if he came into the presence of his father and never occupied the parent's seat or left or entered the room before him.[21] The life of the child during the Medieval period was at best hard. In contrast with the Gentile situation the Jewish child, especially the boy, was relatively more fortunate. Discipline, however, was severe and corporal punishment customary. It was the duty of the Jewish boy to marry at least upon reaching his eighteenth year and an earlier marriage was considered praiseworthy.[22] Arrangements for marriage were nearly always made through the parents and were usually brought about through the services of the professional matchmaker or shadchan. More emphasis was placed, especially among Eastern Jews, upon the learning of the son-in-law than upon his wealth. The highest prestige was given to the young man preparing to be a Rabbi. Friday was the favored day for the wedding in spite of the fact that the Talmud approved the marriage of the single girl on Wednesday and of the widow on Thursday. The wedding ceremonies were elaborate in accord with both custom and religious precepts. The one-time chuppa, the actual physical consummation of marriage privately in the bridal chamber during the ceremony, disappeared in Europe by the fourteenth century, being replaced by the symbolic canopy that became known as the tallith. This symbol of the earlier room where the couple cohabited was typified by a veil or garment which was thrown over the heads of the bridal pair.[23]

It was expected that every Jew should have at least one son

---

[21] *Ibid.*, p. 123.
[22] Brav, Stanley, *op. cit.*, p. 11.
[23] Abrahams, Israel, *op. cit.*, p. 200.

and one daughter. During the period when polygyny prevailed, if the wife proved barren the husband had a right to take a second wife. After the ban of Gershom the argument was advanced that bigamy was less cruel to the wife than divorce. It was generally held that after ten years of marriage the Jew who found himself childless should divorce his wife and take another, the assumption being that the woman was the one that was barren.[24]

The modern Jewish family. Aside from its influence as a significant part of the historic background of the American family, the Jewish family is of great interest because of the part it has had in the survival, in spite of hardship and persecution, of the Jewish people. The regenerative forces of those preserving the Jewish faith were strengthened greatly by the large role religion played in the Jewish institution of marriage. Through the Talmudic writings the entire domestic life of the Jew, including his sexual interest, came under the rigid control of religion. This proved a tremendous advantage in the struggle of the Jewish people for survival. The home shared with the synagogue the religious rites which did so much to give cohesion to the Jewish believers. The Rabbinical writers took the middle ground between elevating marriage into a sacrament and considering it a mere contract in civil law. They avoided the asceticism that entered Christianity through the influence of the words of Paul. Instead they regarded marriage as a necessary social institution. To them the marriage relationship was unique, the establishment of a communion between husband and wife which was termed sanctification.[25] A Rabbi who remained unmarried brought forth from his colleagues the following condemnations: A Jew who has no wife lives without joy, without blessing and without good; a Jew who has no wife is not a man.[26] The minute regulation of family life tended to accentuate the religious peculiarities of the people but at the same time to strengthen the unity of the home.

With this historic background the Jewish family entered the Modern period exposed to the many forces antagonizing the security of family life. The practices of the Jews in Eastern coun-

[24] Baron, Salo W., *A Social and Religious History of the Jews*, Vol. 2, p. 113.
[25] *Op. cit.*, Vol. 1, p. 263.
[26] *Ibid.*

tries have been more resistant to the changing social environment of the modern world than in the West and in America where there has been a great measure of adaptation. Even in the United States there are variations in the customs, ceremonies, laws, and conditions of marriage according to whether the Jewish household clings to Eastern tradition or modifies its practices as it adjusts to American life. Even in the individual family, tension comes when some members face one way and the others in the opposite direction. In this country the Jews recognize that they live under the jurisdiction not of Jewish law but that of the state of which they are legal residents.[27] In one state only, Rhode Island, does the civil law make an exception allowing a Jewish man to marry his niece providing the marriage ceremony is performed by a Rabbi, although such a relationship is prohibited to the non-Jew.[28] Although the Jewish marriage in this country must conform to the legal authority of the state, former customs, once the requirements of the Jewish law, may be continued as ceremony emphasizing Jewish tradition and the religious significance of marriage. The betrothal has become in the West simply the ordinary engagement even though it receives a religious sanction in the synagogue when the bridegroom on the Sabbath following is called up to the reading of the law.[29]

If the engagement later is broken, the girl turns to the law of the state or nation if she seeks redress. The religious solemnization of marriage is essentially the same in its significant features in all lands. The festive celebrations vary greatly.[30] The birth of the child, especially the male, is celebrated by a variety of customs, partly religious and partly an expression of ancient folkways. The most important of these is circumcision in the case of the male. This occurs on the eighth day following his birth. In comparison with the various celebrations that according to orthodox custom will occur during the boy's career, the reception given the girl is exceedingly simple and is expressed by announcing her birth and Hebrew name in the synagogue on the following Sabbath morning, but even this in the West is disappearing, and the mere registration of her birth in the office

---

[27] Goldstein, Sidney E., *The Meaning of Marriage and the Foundations of the Family*, p. 40.

[28] *Ibid.*, p. 49.

[29] Cohen, Israel, *Jewish Life in Modern Times*, p. 39.

[30] *Ibid.*

of the civil authorities is regarded as sufficient.[31] The orthodox household in the United States, as elsewhere, observes special dietary laws associated with the Jewish faith and seeks to follow the regulations both in the cooking and the eating of the food.

It is clear that while Western Jews have to a remarkable degree maintained the separateness of their domestic traits emphasized by their religious regulations, they have not escaped the disorganizing influences of modern life. This is indicated by the first chapter of Rabbi Goldstein's valuable, Jewish interpretation of the meaning of marriage and the foundation of the family. There he presents his statement of the crisis in marriage and the family as a point of departure in his portrayal of Jewish domestic experience.[32] As Cohen points out, the Jews are chiefly town people and are therefore subjected to the social conditions of modern city life. This appears in the lessening of their birth rate, their tendency to have small families, their delay of marriage, and the increasing number who do not marry at all. They contribute their share to the increasing divorce rate of the United States and even family relationships are lessened, especially as housing conditions forbid making the home the center of family interest. The Jew as much as the Gentile finds that it is not possible to rear the right kind of family in the wrong kind of home.

THE GREEK FAMILY

The Greek family. At the outset it is necessary to notice that Greece presents not a single line of family development but several, of which two, the Athenian and the Spartan, stand in sharp contrast. The Greek evolution also presents class distinctions with differences so great as to constitute four separate groups, each contributing to the background from which Greek domestic life developed. Thus the Greek adult population was divided in four parts—the male citizen, the conventional wife, the prostitute, and the slave.

There is also a general trend in woman's status so unmistakable that it forces attention. Unlike the evolution of the Hebrew family, we find, so far as woman's role is concerned, a reversed line of change. The woman of Homer's time approxi-

[31] *Ibid.*, p. 42.
[32] Goldstein, Sidney E., *op. cit.*, p. 8.

mated the man in social status and shared his fellowship but receded from this until at the time of Pericles she had fallen to such an inequality and discrimination that she was denied her husband's respect, much less his comradeship. Although this takes different form in the three outstanding cities—Athens, Sparta, and Corinth—in each of them we find a decided loss in the standing of women. As a consequence, Greek civilization as it advanced intellectually pushed the family backward, away from the possibility of the sharing of affection toward which the Hebrew family moved.

According to Kipling, "East is East, and West is West, and never the twain shall meet." It was the destiny of Greece to develop its civilization in the corridor that separated Eastern and Western culture. In this debasement of woman we detect a portion of the influence that spread from the Orient and which in turn was later to be transmitted as Greek thinking and customs traveled westward and permeated Roman life. This trend must not be thought of as something of significance only to woman. Her loss of prestige and opportunity, her narrowed outlook and activities, brought her life down to a lower level, but with her descent there went a diminishing of the function of the family and a lessening of the significance of domestic relationship from which man, in turn, in spite of his political and intellectual attainment, could not escape the consequences. Denied fellowship in the home where the wife was chiefly a bearer of children, and at best the household manager and at worst a drudge, he sought it in association in the prostitute class who furnished sex appeal and, in the case of the most favored, also intellectual stimulus.

The importance of Greek family life. The direct importance of the Greek evolution of the family upon contemporary American domestic experience is so slight that were it not for the indirect significance of the Greek evolution as it became a part of the European background there would be no reason for including it in this discussion. It is, of course, interesting to the student of the family, as is each definite type of family development, but there is a greater reason than this for considering it in this interpretation of the American family background. It has been chiefly through the impression its intellectual achievement made upon the leadership of the Church during the first twelve centuries that Greek culture has influenced the Christian doctrine regarding marriage and the family.

Influence of Greek philosophy. In the beginning there was a great gulf between the Greek and Roman philosophers and the followers of Jesus, who were humble-minded folk, in great proportion drawn from the ranks of those socially exploited and ostracized by the officials, the wealthy, and the intelligentsia. With the onward sweep of time the chasm was bridged and there steadily moved into Christian thinking influences that issued from Greek thought. Thus it was that Greek philosophy furnished the thought-environment of the leadership that became dominant in the theology of the growing Church.

Plato and Aristotle, who were chiefly influential, reflect, in spite of their genius, the domestic situation of their time and place. It was not so much their direct teachings regarding the nature of woman that carried over, for these were minor and incidental. It was rather the fact that woman had been excluded from the creative thinking of Greece, and this conveyed the sense of her inferiority more potently than any declaration. Aristotle, who in time came to have the greater influence, assumed that the Greek domestic situation was in accord with nature's decree, as the following abstract from his *Politics* reveals.

Again, the male is by nature superior, and the female inferior; and the one rules, and the other is ruled; this principle, of necessity, extends to all mankind. . . . The rule of a household is a monarchy, for every house is under one head: whereas constitutional rule is a government of freemen and equals. . . . For the slave has no deliberative faculty at all; the woman has, but it is without authority, and the child has, but it is immature. So it must necessarily be with the moral virtues also; all may be supposed to partake of them, but only in such manner and degree as is required by each for the fulfillment of his duty. Hence the ruler ought to have moral virtue in perfection, for his duty is entirely that of a master artificer, and the master artificer is reason; the subjects, on the other hand, require only that measure of virtue which is proper to each of them. Clearly, then, moral virtue belongs to all of them; but the temperance of a man and of a woman, or the courage and justice of a man and of a woman, are not, as Socrates maintained, the same; the courage of a man is shown in commanding, of a woman in obeying.

Plato, in his fanciful picture of the *Republic,* argues that woman should have the same educational preparation for life as man, but this is contrary to his acceptance elsewhere of the notion of woman's inferiority.

Man versus woman. The subordinated, restricted life forced upon the conventional woman suggests the influence of the Eastern harem. Mahaffy suggests that the contempt and isolation of woman that grew up in Imperial Athens reflects Asiatic jealousy and was the result of the influence of Asia Minor on the aristocratic youth of Athens who, traveling abroad, returned with the desire to imitate the fashions and luxuries of the Asiatic cities.[33] In any case, man assumed not only the headship of the household but monopolized the world of affairs. The woman was relegated to the home, a home that was narrowly conceived. Even Xenophon's sympathetic discussion of woman's education assumes that her responsibilities begin and end in household efficiency. The women were assigned to their special apartment, usually in the second story of the house. They were denied attendance at banquets; indeed, it was customary for the men to eat by themselves and not to present their wives even when they had guests. The state suppressed the independence of the male citizen, who, in turn, as household lord destroyed the individuality of the wife. As Xenophon says, the man's duties were out of doors and the task of the woman within doors.

The unconventional woman. In Athens and throughout Attica there was a considerable number of women living outside the established custom, who comprised a class by itself. Possibly the word *courtesan* best interprets their career, but it does not convey the idea of the difference that existed between the three distinct groups that had in common only their freedom from the conventional life followed by other women and their sex promiscuity. The three types were the *Dicteriades,* the *Auletrides,* and the *Hetairai.*[34] The first resembles the modern prostitute; the second, the geisha girls of Japan; and the third were the flute players who went about giving private entertainment at the homes of male citizens or appeared at public festivals. The last were most like the courtesan of French history. It was this third group, the hetairai, the best educated of the three, that

---

[33] Mahaffy, J. P., *Social Life in Greece,* p. 147.
[34] LaCroix, P., *History of Prostitution,* p. 97.

associated with the leading men of Greece. Undoubtedly the social prestige of the hetairai as a class has been exaggerated because individual women belonging to it appear in Greek literature as social equals of poets, philosophers, and men of authority. From this has come a misinterpretation of the social status usually held by the three types of unconventional women. The two lower grades were largely foreigners, but the other was made up of citizens. All three were regulated by the state. Even the courtesans were not free to leave the Republic without special permission. They were taxed by the state and were a source of considerable revenue. In return they were given tolerance and protection.

The Spartan family. The family that developed in Sparta was unlike that of the rest of Greece. The life of women was regulated as strictly as elsewhere but with a eugenic motive. As the career of the Spartan male was consummated in becoming a good soldier, so the mission of the woman was to be the mother of soldiers. This explains the rigid physical training imposed upon boys and girls alike. As compared with the Athenian woman, the Spartan woman was more nearly the equal of man, but this is true because both man and woman were reduced to a regimen imposed by the state which had as its ideal for both sexes essentially the development of a healthy animal. In spite of this eugenic emphasis the Spartans degenerated. Their experiment in breeding for military efficiency contributed nothing to the European background of the American family.

Marriage customs. Marriages were arranged by the families of the two persons concerned. In Homer's time gifts, and this usually meant cattle, were presented to the father of the bride. Sometimes they had to be paid in installments. Following the financial transaction the woman was handed over to her husband with a simple ceremony and a wedding feast. At a later time the general custom was to separate these two preliminaries of marriage, the betrothal consisting of the payment of dowry and a legal agreement, followed by the nuptials, which were celebrated with an elaborate ceremony. One feature was the eating by the guest of a portion of a cake made of honey and sesame seeds. Another was the sacrifice offered to the god of marriage by the father and the utterance of a formula which released the bride from his control and from the worship of his family gods.

Then came the wedding banquet at which the women were permitted to be present, seated by themselves. Then followed a torchlight procession to the groom's home at which there was further ritual and ceremony.

THE ROMAN FAMILY

Evolution of the Roman family.   The evolution of the Roman family presents two distinct but inconsistent lines of development. Along one we see the softening of patriarchal authority, which at the beginning, in the heroic age, was never more absolute or better established, and an increase in the social status and freedom of the woman. Accompanying this was a weakening of the family, which perhaps reached its greatest instability in the late period of the Republic. These two trends were both the result of cultural changes. Although there can be no doubt that in its earlier period the Roman family was a well-ordered household, extremely patriarchal, it must not be forgotten that we see it chiefly through the eyes of writers who look back upon it in retrospective sentiment. On the other hand, the evils that appeared in the civilization of the later period of the Republic and during the Empire tend to be exaggerated by critics who assumed a golden age in the past. Allowing for these distortions we recognize in the first scenes of Rome's historic drama a simple, hard-working, man-dominated, rural family life, while, throughout the entire third act, marriage and the home are struggling to maintain their integrity in the restless, cosmopolitan civilization of a world empire.

First period.   In the first period the family, as a rule, was that of the farmer and his housekeeping wife. Slaves and servants were few and a life of manual labor was the common lot of all. The children were brought up carefully and simply. Manual labor was universally respected. To the American this period of Roman family life suggests that of our own frontier.

The authority of the male head of the household, the patriarch, was never greater, and in accord with the Roman temper, it was legally defined as early as 450 B.C., in the Laws of the Twelve Tables. His *patria potestas* brought under his control all members of his household, including the wife. It was for him to say whether the child at birth should be permitted to live or be put to death. He arranged the marriages of his children and took charge of their earnings, and had the right to scourge them, to banish them, to sell them into slavery, or even to punish them by death. Before deciding to punish the child for some offense with slavery or death, however, he had to call in session the male members of his gens and obtain their judgment. This having been done, he remained free to follow his own inclinations. The fact that there appears to be no record of a father selling his child into slavery emphasizes the need of distinguishing between the authority given the father and his customary practices.[35]

At marriage the wife transferred from the *potestas* of her father to that of her husband. Control of the wife by the husband was known as *manus*. The day she committed any serious offense her husband became judge, but before deciding upon her death he had to call together his and her male relatives, except in case he discovered her in the act of adultery. Under that circumstance he could put her to death immediately. The wife's status can be summarized by the statement that legally through marriage she became her husband's daughter, subject to the same control he exercised over his other children.

The Roman family of this period maintained an independent existence and we detect neither Greek nor Asiatic influence. Although girls married early, as it seems to us, that was in accord with their rapid maturing, for Oriental child marriages were unknown. Plural marriages also were never legal. The betrothal of children through agreement of their fathers was, however, a conventional practice.

The second period. The type of Roman family life characteristic of the first period was incompatible with the civilization that later developed. The culture of which we hear most in Roman literature had become distinctly urban in character. An aristocracy, controlling vast estates, maintaining themselves in luxury and display, and possessing city and country residences, had developed, and as a class these rulers, men of affairs, and idle rich, were extravagant, ostentatious, and unsocial.

Yet caution is necessary in painting a picture of the later stages of Roman civilization. It is the upper classes of which we know most, and of their family life we have only fragmentary evidence. Even the history of the period is aristocratic; the litera-

---

[35] Goodsell, W., *A History of the Family as a Social and Educational Institution*, p. 114.

ture almost ignores the middle and lower classes.[36] The glimpses we get of family life among the upper classes is in sharpest contrast with that prevailing during the earlier period. The home had lost its discipline. Although the Roman law still defined the husband as the ruler of his wife, a new kind of marriage, without *manus,* had appeared after the expansion brought about by the Roman wars of conquest, and in the later period of the Republic this had become an established custom. Although the husband still enjoyed the income of the formal dowry, he no longer possessed it as a part of his estate, for its ownership remained in the hands of the wife's father. Since it was common for the wealthy father to endow his daughter at marriage with a money gift, she often had an independent income over which the husband had no authority.

The women of wealth were addicted to the same vices as the men. They squandered their money in following the costly fashions; attended the theater, the circus, the baths, and other places of dissipation; took up the religious cults of the East, and in smaller numbers stimulated a dilettante interest in literature and philosophy. The earlier monogamy was displaced by concubinage, prostitution, and frequent divorce. Celibacy and childless marriages had reached a popularity that led to legislation being passed against them.

Marriage customs. Marriages were arranged by the families concerned, and on both sides there was consideration of rank, lineage, and finances. With the selection of husband and wife so often determined by social or political ambition or avarice rather than by mutual attraction, there was little basis for domestic congeniality. The wife was usually between thirteen and sixteen when she married. A woman who had not become a mother by twenty was liable to the penalties legislated by Augustus to discourage celibacy and childlessness. The males were punished if they remained childless at the age of twenty-five. Apparently in the middle and lower classes men did not usually marry until they were eighteen or twenty. The absence of courtship is attested by the fact that in Latin we have no words meaning to woo, or to court. The girls were frequently betrothed in childhood, the arrangements being made by the families concerned through intermediaries who acted as marriage brokers.

---

[36] Friedländer, L., *Roman Life and Manners,* Vol. I, p. 264.

The wedding, at least among the upper classes, was elaborate. The bride was expected to have an expensive trousseau, including ornaments and jewelry, which were given by the bridegroom. On the wedding day the homes of both families, elaborately decorated, were opened wide to guests. The wedding took place at the house of the bride's father. After the omens had been announced as favorable, the bride and groom came together into the largest room of the house and the wedding proceeded. First came the ceremony, the essential part of which was the statement of consent to marry in the presence of witnesses. Then followed the festivities, the most spectacular features being a torch-lighted procession from the bride's former home to her new residence, and the banquet that followed her arrival there, unless, as was more usual, it had been held at her father's home. Lavish expenditures were expected. Augustus attempted to restrict the cost of weddings, but apparently without success.

The marriage could be with or without *manus*. In the former case the wife became legally subjected to her husband. In the other she continued her former legal status in her father's household, at least in theory. Actually she maintained a large independence. There were three kinds of marriage ceremonies. The first, *confarreatio*, was the more aristocratic form of ceremony and was usual among the members of the patrician class in Rome. It consisted of an elaborate religious ceremony suggestive of our most formal church wedding. The *coemptio* consisted of a fictitious sale of the bride in the presence of at least five witnesses. A single coin of small value but symbolic of the wife's status was placed in the scales held by an official. This was followed by prayer, sacrifice, and festivities. The third method of marrying was the *usus*. It appears to have been something like our common-law marriage, validating the union of a man and woman who had cohabited together for a year during which the woman had not been absent from the home three days.

In addition to these three modes of performing marriage between social equals, or *matrimonium justum*, as it was called, there was a legal status known as *matrimonium non justum*, or the marriage of a citizen to a woman of inferior social rank. It was a sort of legalized concubinage, and if children were born they were not permitted to inherit the property of their father and were not considered members of his family.

Divorce. In the earlier period the patriarch had the right to divorce, as we know, because it is provided for in the Laws of the Twelve Tables, but there is every reason to suppose that it was extremely rare. Not so in the later Roman civilization. In the last years of the Republic divorce became common. By the time of Augustus the frequency of divorce and remarriage had become a public scandal. For example, Statilea Messalina, one of Nero's wives, had already been married four times. Juvenal speaks of women having eight husbands in five years.

Divorce was a private matter between the two people concerned, and its procedure was merely the delivering of a written statement in the presence of seven witnesses, stating that the writer intended to abolish the relationship, and authorizing the other to take his property. No reason need be given. The divorce might be by mutual consent or against the wishes of one of the pair. Only when there were disputes about the future of the children or the division of property was there any judicial procedure. The extent to which the divorce habit grew appears in the legislation enacted for the purpose of curbing it.

Contribution of Roman family life. Aside from the influence upon our domestic law that accompanied the basic contribution of Roman law to the building of our jurisprudence, the Roman family entered for the most part indirectly in the building of the European background out of which came the beginning of the American evolution of family life. The significance of the Roman family consists for us primarily in the effect it had upon Christian ideals and practices. Early Christian teaching stands out from its Roman background and is in contrast with it. That this has led to an exaggeration of the immorality of Rome, including the breaking down of the family, there can be no doubt. It is probable that the early Christian writers as well as the pessimistic Roman critics overstate the depravity of the period. The luxuries of the Empire of which we hear much were certainly nothing like those characteristic of our own time. Unquestionably licentiousness was more prevalent during the last days of the Republic than during the Empire. Admitting the exaggeration of Christians, writing in the midst of the greatest collision between opposite moral forces in human history, in their denunciation of the social evil of Rome, it remains true that family instability had reached a point from which the new religious movement was bound to recoil. The unrest which had become characteristic of Roman civilization, the loss of standards, the terrific burden imposed by slavery, the agrarian ruin, cruel corruption, and cynicism necessarily registered in Christian consciousness until Rome personified the Anti-Christ. Undoubtedly Roman family life at least maintained as great stability as the other social institutions. Nevertheless, those who directed the growing Christian Church saw in its salient features unmixed evil. Among these the relative independence of women and freedom of divorce were outstanding.

The attitude of the Church Fathers during the first centuries of the growth of Christianity cannot be understood apart from the impression made upon them by the breaking down of Roman civilization. In their general reaction we find preachment and legislation concerning the family, and these in turn greatly influenced the thinking and practices that were built into the European evolution of the family.

The patriarchal system.   Although the family life of the Hebrews, the Greeks, and the Romans gives us with a different coloring a domestic institution firmly patriarchal, it is evident also that this does not necessarily mean in individual households despotic control by the man or even on his part dominance in family matters. In interpreting the law and even the customs that supported the traditions and standards associated with home life, it is necessary always to recognize that these may be greatly softened in practice and in individual cases largely ignored. We find, as a matter of fact, in both the primitive and classical patriarchal family life that the disposition of the individual man and woman finds expression and that this sometimes leads to a practical dominance on the part of the woman even though in outward form the superiority of the man is recognized.

Moreover there are many things permissible in the code of patriarchal authority that are nevertheless discouraged by social attitudes. We see this frequently in modern life, and it is not safe to forget that this same inconsistency also appears among people of very simple culture. Thus, even though the outline formed by folkways, the mores, and the laws is clearly drawn, when we seek to interpret domestic experience, we find that much of this does not follow the pattern formally prescribed by the group. We classify types of family life as patriarchal, but we have to be cautious not to use this description as a means of defining in any detail the family life that actually is practiced. The student in interpreting every type of family life must recognize how frequently there are exceptions to what logically should be expected from the particular domestic system studied. It is therefore for the student of the family to distinguish between the patriarchal type and the expressions of this in the everyday behavior of men and women.

 Indirect contributions to the American family. The influence of the Greek and Roman families on the American family has been almost entirely indirect through their contribution to the family life of western Europe, especially England, in which our own domestic institution was chiefly rooted. Both of them furnished material which became a part of the amalgam out of which the European medieval family emerged. Plato's proposals in *The Republic* encouraged speculation and criticism in regard to the conventional family and Roman law made its contribution. Nevertheless, the greater significance is the legacy of these two dominant ancient civilizations to the rebuilding of the institution of the family in the setting of western Europe. The Hebrew family made its impression through its early history as recorded in the Old Testament and the relation between Jewish domestic tradition and practices of early Christianity. Although the Christian family discarded the regulations and customs that the Jewish faith built into the orthodox home practices, the basic concept of monogamic marriage was taken over as the new religion broke from the old.

Chapter 5

THE EUROPEAN BACKGROUND
OF THE AMERICAN FAMILY

FOREWORD. The development of the American family cannot be understood if it is conceived as a sort of social upstart whose history is a record of spontaneous and consistent adaptation to the new environment of the western world. The domestic traditions and practices of European origin that were brought both by the early settlers and the later immigrants have to be recognized as causal influences that helped to produce the conditions, customs, and ideals that characterized the family in the United States. The importance of the European background appears when we consider how differently our domestic life would have shaped itself if this country had been established by peoples from the oriental rather than the occidental world. The European civilization from which we drew so heavily was, of course, itself a development and in turn can only be understood as a cultural evolution, complex rather than simple, ever-changing rather than static.

Among the various influences contributing to the building of the European foundation for our family life none was greater than Christianity. Its influence, however, must not be regarded as consistent or unchanged during the centuries from its introduction to the migration of the various national and religious groups to the new land. On the contrary, unless the student apprehends the great meaning of this diversity of domestic background and the mobility of its underlying ideals during the European evolution, he loses the clue that explains the differences and contrasts expressed in our own domestic behavior and standards. The schism in Christianity made manifest by the Reformation multiplied theological differences and brought forth influences that played a large part in the shaping of the family during our colonial period. It is not possible to interpret these results as they came out of Protestantism as consistent because they took various forms. Especially is it important to consider the consequences of its ascetic trend and the various motivations that led to this development. From the beginning of the American settlements there was considerable variation in the religious background of family life between the various sections and groups along the Atlantic coast. This religious regionalism affected both domestic thinking and practices and to find their roots one must go back to their European religious origin. Chivalry and the romantic development in which the troubadours took the prominent part also must be recognized as important sources of the influences that affected domestic trends in Europe. Finally in the following chapter the attention of the student is directed toward the great contrasts that existed between the most important domestic traditions that were maintained by the leading European groups that established themselves in the new world.

Rome and Christianity. Students of the history of Christianity have frequently pointed out that conditions in Rome at the time that Christianity was introduced by Paul and other missionaries were favorable for the spread of the new religion. Rome had brought the greater part of the western world under its authority and developed effective means of communication throughout the great area of the empire while at the same time there had developed inwardly corruption, vice, and a slave economy which had sapped the moral vitality of the Roman people, leaving them spiritually empty and discontented. The poor and enslaved classes especially felt the void that had come from the decay of former religious beliefs, and this explains their responding so favorably to the new aggressive gospel.

It is difficult now to retrace this introductory period of Christianity and bring into proper perspective its contact with Roman culture. The new religion certainly attracted little attention from the government at first, and when finally recognized it was greeted generally with toleration. Soon, however, the uncompromising crusading spirit of Christianity made the Roman officials realize that the new teaching, spiritually motivated and secured, was forcing a life-and-death struggle with the authoritative conventional civilization of the empire. We who know the outcome of this conflict find it difficult not to over-estimate the social force of Christianity in its days of frail begin-ning and also not to exaggerate the Roman evils and social in-stability of the period. The fact that we have gathered much of our conception of this breaking down of the Roman Empire from the polemic writings of the early Christian leaders who were in the thick of an uncompromising fight and not inclined to picture Roman political and social life judiciously adds to our difficulty of getting a just interpretation of one of the most revolutionary cultural conflicts of human history.

Looking backward we detect that there was not a complete replacement of the old by the new but rather an amalgamation in which neither of the contending forces remained unchanged, a blending in which Christianity was the impregnating influ-ence. In this fusing of a new and an old philosophy of life and of two unlike social systems, the family was especially resistant. Its privacy, highly emotional experience, and incidental but ef-fective functioning as a means of social transmission necessarily made it obstinate to Christianity's attempt to transform tradition and practices and bring them into accord with the new way of life. Paul in his letters bears testimony to the difficulties that the Christian churches encountered in their effort to bring and to keep the family on the level of Christian principles. His admoni-tions are directed more toward domestic problems and less to-ward political, industrial, and social behavior than we in these days could expect. He is sensitive to the dangers to the churches that might come from mere unconventional behavior which from the pagan point of view might seem scandalous. This ex-plains his attention to the proprieties of husbands and wives, men and women, and accounts for his statements concerning marriage, which lifted out of their time and place seem antago-nistic to the American trend toward domestic equality.

Influence of Christianity. Judged merely by its social consequences, the spread of Christianity throughout the Roman Empire was one of the most influential events in human history. It supremely affected the evolution of family life in Europe in which was rooted our own development. It must not be thought, however, that the significance of Christianity is to be found solely in specific church legislation concerning marriage and the family, for the changes it brought in the general patterns of life were of more fundamental consequence. Nor does it square with the facts to assume that at any period the contribution of Christianity was simple and consistent. On the contrary, it was from the beginning complex and dualistic, as the result of the historic circumstances in which the spreading faith found itself.

In the teaching of Jesus we find only incidental references to family life. Monogamy was taken for granted, and there is no effort to bring about any change in the prevailing patriarchal domestic type. Some of the sayings of Jesus have been interpreted as a discounting of the importance of the home, but this is contrary to the spirit of his gospel and the effect his message had on his immediate followers. These assertions have to be read in their historic setting. "For I have come to set a man at variance against his father, the daughter against her mother" is a realistic statement of what actually did occur in many Jewish homes, as a result of a divided religious allegiance. "He that loveth father and mother more than me is not worthy of me" could be affirmed without challenge by every great leader whose cause permitted no rivalry because of loyalty to unbelieving parents. "Call no man your father on the earth, for one is your Father even He Who is in heaven" is an attempt to show the supreme significance of spiritual relationship with God. Nowhere do we find the direct attack on the family which would have resulted from any feeling that the home was a rival rather than an ally in the spread of the kingdom of God.

Paul in his letters to the churches had to deal more specifically with matters that concerned family life. Not only did he assume the patriarchal family with which he was familiar, but he supported it while cautioning his followers to set a good example to the unbelievers. As a missionary entrusted with the difficult task of securely establishing the new faith he preached, it is difficult to see how he could have done otherwise. He had no reason to reconstruct the family customs unless they antagonized the spirit of his teachings. It is true that the principles of Christianity were to speed the movement toward the democratic household, but in his time and place the domestic folkways, patriarchal in character, did not appear at variance with the gospel. Then, even as now, it was the spirit of domestic fellowship rather than the form that was supremely important. Paul illustrated this realistic attitude when confronted with the much more questionable problem of human slavery. He was content to send the slave convert back to his master asking that he be received no longer as a servant but more than a servant, a brother beloved. It does not, however, seem just in these days of greater social maturity to misuse Paul's words to uphold patriarchal despotism any more than it would be to quote his letter to Philemon as a defense of human slavery.

As the spread of Christianity widened and groups of converts with non-Jewish background arose in various parts of the Roman Empire, Christianity began to reflect influences born of its new constituency. Its ecclesiastical organization and canonical legislation were directed along the course suggested by the political efficiency of the Empire and its well-matured legal system. Its thought environment was, however, not single but double. In addition to that of distinctly Christian origin, there was the Greek philosophy with its offshoot in Latin form. Medieval theology was the fruit of both, and in its development there came from the second source of influence the depreciation of woman with which Greek and Roman philosophy was saturated. Antagonistic as this fundamentally was to the teaching of Jesus, it permeated the thinking of the Church and its canons.

The ascetic trend.   One of the consequences of this fading of the attitude toward woman found in the Gospels was the encouragement of the ascetic trend already appearing among Christians. This movement also is composite in origin. Nothing is clearer now than that with the coming of Christianity appeared a new moral force which demonstrated itself through the lives of men and women. The maintaining of the high level of early Christian ethics in an environment such as the Roman Empire presented was from the beginning a difficult problem. Even in the first century Paul had to face it, and some of his admonitions addressed to his converts now make strange reading.

As Christianity spread and its followers multiplied, its earlier homogeneity became impossible. By the beginning of the third century we discover a tendency to separate the requirements of Christianity into higher and lower obligations. The latter represented the average Christian experience and was less exacting than that practiced by the first believers. The other program was for those who were willing to sacrifice for a life holier than that required for salvation. There were many reasons why this should drift toward an antisex and antimarriage program. Already this had been foreshadowed by a group among the Essenes, motivated no doubt by impulses which only of late, with the help of psychoanalysis, we are beginning to understand.

In addition to this morbid tendency of human nature, the influence of Greek philosophy as it entered Christian theology carried with it an attitude toward woman that led the idealist, especially if he reacted against earlier laxity, to find in sex his chief temptation. As early as the beginning of the second century we find Saturninus saying, "Marriage and procreation are of Satan." [1] The fact that the first Christians led a life apart, committing themselves to the Kingdom of God without compromise, inclined them toward asceticism, and faith in the second coming of Jesus encouraged the decision not to marry, for under such circumstances not to start a family was good judgment. Paul exhorts the Corinthians, "Brethren the time is shortened, that henceforth both those that have wives may be as though they had none; and those that weep, as though they wept not; and those that rejoice, as though they rejoiced not; and they that buy, as though they possessed not; and those that use the world, as not using it to the full: for the fashion of this world passeth away." [2] As this confidence in the second advent of Jesus faded away, nothing was more natural than that the teaching of Paul should fuse with influences coming from Greek thought in the building of ascetic doctrine. There were other words of Paul to give impetus to this trend. His patriarchal outlook upon the family appears in such statements as, "For a man ought not to cover his head forasmuch as he is the image and glory of God but the woman is the glory of the man," and his "Let your women keep silence in the churches, for it is not permitted for them to speak. They are commanded to be under obedience as also says the law." His doctrine of the warfare of flesh and spirit was easily translated into the idea that the struggle for higher living was a fight to get rid of the sex dominance of women. Tertullian was representative of this sentiment when he declared, "And do you not know that you are [each] an Eve? . . . You are the devil's

---

[1] Briffault, R., *The Mothers,* Vol. 3, p. 371.
[2] *I Corinthians,* 7:29–31.

gateway; . . . You are the first deserter of that divine law: . . . you are she who persuaded him whom the devil was not valiant enough to attack. You destroyed so easily God's image, man." [3]

The whole force of such teaching can be realized only when one remembers that there was a widespread belief in the existence of demons and that human lust was considered the means by which these evil spirits gained possession of a man. Since it was unquestionably Paul's opinion that celibacy was to be ranked higher than married life, it was inevitable that the ascetic trend should establish as the primary test of the holier life for both men and women the suppression of sex and the renunciation of marriage. Virginity became the ideal and marriage a mere sop to the weakness of human nature provided for those who could be Christians only on the lower level of behavior.

Family life before the Renaissance. There was a barbarian infusion into Christianity that added its influence to the medieval evolution of the family. No culture could have been more distant from the Eastern civilization with its ascetic trend. The northern Teutonic and Celtic peoples of Europe revealed evidence of matriarchal tradition.[4] The little information we have concerning them is gathered from their sagas in which we get glimpses of strong-minded women, often acting as leaders and commonly possessing powers associated with priestesses. They choose their husbands and get rid of them at their pleasure. In culture these northern people were little, if at all, above the level of the most developed of North American Indians.[5] These were the people potentially strong, but rough and backward, who became the physical conquerors of the Roman Empire and whom the Church had to convert, absorb, and Christianize until, after being nearly a thousand years in process, a new Europe appeared at the Renaissance, a consolidation of eastern and western influences contributed by the Greeks, the Romans, the Christians, the Celts, and the Germans.

At no point in the spiritual assimilation of these northern conquerors of Rome did the Church find greater difficulty than along the lines of its sex teachings and marriage program. The

[3] *Ante-Nicene Fathers,* Vol. 11, p. 305; and Goodsell, W., *A History of the Family as a Social and Educational Institution,* p. 163.

[4] Briffault, R., *op. cit.,* Vol. 1, p. 418.

[5] Adams, G. B., *Civilization During the Middle Ages,* p. 7.

hordes at the behest of rulers could be converted in the mass, but this afforded no magical qualities that would rub away their barbarian habits and equip them with the Christian sentiments taught by the Church. Throughout the Middle Ages we see charge and countercharge of these unlike social forces, Christian and pagan, ecclesiastical and secular, each changing and being changed as some fundamental incompatibility revealed itself in one contest after another.

The important social organization that developed in this tumultuous period was the feudal system, and with it came a characteristic family life to which both barbarian and Christian influences contributed.

Domestic life appears again in patriarchal form but with a new centralizing of authority. It was the military chieftain who acquired a position corresponding to the patriarchal head of the household in the early Roman and Greek family development. Since the ownership of land was based upon the ability to perform military service at the command of the overlord, it followed that the widow inheriting from her husband, or the daughter from her father, had to surrender her property, being unable to fulfill her obligations, and as a consequence woman lost the economic rights that had been given to the Roman matron in the later part of Roman civilization. Deprived of her power to inherit, woman tended toward a civil status similar to that imposed upon her by the theology and regulations of the Church. In the development of feudalism the woman seems to have lost her guardianship of her children, which had been given by Anglo-Saxon law, and her former right was assumed by the overlord. This power carried with it authority to decide the marriage of the ward, and the decision, especially when the girl belonged to a wealthy family, was made with a view to strengthening the overlord's position rather than to providing for the girl's welfare. The widow also had to look to the overlord for permission to remarry, for if she took a second husband without his approval she lost her dowry.

The inferiority put upon women by the feudal system should not conceal the advantages that came to women in the end through the organization of these fragmentary political groups around the neighborhood castle which made possible in the well-nigh social anarchy the preservation of a remnant of

Roman civilization. As culture again advanced and the scattered political authority grew toward unity, there went along with it a general progress which brought an easier existence to woman and gradually gave her an increasing independence. It is the lady of the castle who first profited by assuming, during the frequent absences of her husband on military expeditions, the responsibility for keeping up and directing the various activities of the castle and community, a leadership which she was often successful in continuing upon his death.

The authority of the Church in the sphere of domestic relations was limited by the feudal organization, and in the general confusion of the period it contented itself chiefly with the effort to protect the integrity of marriage along three lines of ecclesiastical regulations. One was the insistence on an age of consent which, for the girl, was twelve years. Although this seems low, the position of the Church met with popular resistance. The second, the theory of free consent, was held pugnaciously even though under the prevailing conditions this freedom was for the woman more formal than actual. Nevertheless, the Church continued the idea, which logically antagonized the dependency the feudal system enforced. Third, the Church insisted upon an unconsanguineous marriage. In the days of the Empire even the marriage of first cousins met with no protest. The opposition of the Church to the marriage of related persons grew until it reached its climax in the prohibiting of the marriage of persons related in the seventh degree from a common ancestor.

Divorce during the Middle Ages. The Church uncompromisingly denied the right to divorce. It insisted that marriage was an indissoluble and lifelong union. At first some of the Church Fathers had interpreted the words of Jesus to mean that in case of adultery divorce was proper, some adding desertion as a rightful cause. Through the influence of St. Augustine, the Church officially decreed in 140 that marriage was a sacrament and indissoluble. In spite of this stand of the Church, the state continued for several centuries the Roman attitude toward divorce. From the sixth century onward the Church struggled to practice its theories regarding marriage as it encountered opposition from those it was trying to Christianize.

The Church by the canon law did its utmost to preserve the sanctity of marriage. It sought to secure the mutual free consent of those entering marriage, since this was regarded as an absolute necessity for a valid marital union. It attempted, therefore, to prevent marriages between those who were lacking in physical, mental, or spiritual qualities required for a valid marriage. These were termed impediments, and unless a dispensation was secured they prohibited marriage or enforced the separation of those who ostensibly married. There were two sorts of impediments: the *impedientia* type, preventing marriage; and the *dirimentia*, ending a union that had already been established. Since mutual consent was required, a valid union could not be contracted if one or both of the parties lacked the mental faculty for a binding contract because of insanity or any other condition demanded in making a responsible choice of mate. The Church was also called upon to define the relationships between spouses that precluded valid marriage. *Divortium a vinculo matrimonii* was the setting aside of a marriage as null and void because of impediments. There was a second method of ending an invalid union, *divortium a mensa et thoro*. This permitted the separation of husband and wife for adultery, heresy or apostasy, and cruelty. In case a marriage, however, was pronounced null and void, the man and woman were free to remarry. This separation was not a divorce but rather recognition that an invalid union had been attempted. If the marriage had been invalid from the start, it was, of course, not a sacrament.

The Church held religious sway over a great territory, including peoples representing various degrees of spiritual and social culture and with variant attitudes toward the institution of marriage. As was to be expected under such circumstances, ecclesiastical courts were organized to pass judgment upon many specific unions the validity of which had to be determined. There appeared to be no authentic papal decretals dealing with consanguinity as an impediment to marriage prior to the pontificate of Gregory I (590–604), who issued a decision prohibiting anyone taking as wife one of his kindred in the seventh degree of relationship.[6] This prohibition was made less severe by the Fourth Lateran Council (1215) when it was decided that all marriages among those who were related beyond the fourth degree were valid. The ecclesiastical legislation also prohibited the

---

[6] Smith, Charles Edward, *Papal Enforcement of Some Medieval Marriage Laws,* p. 18.

union of persons related through marriage or carnal intercourse. There was considerable confusion because of the difficulty of determining the degree of kinship, but from the time of Pope Alexander III the method of counting one generation as a degree was generally adopted.[7] Although the validity of marriage bonds was usually determined by ecclesiastical courts organized for that purpose, papal intervention was sometimes made in response to the appeal of the parties concerned or local ecclesiastical authorities who were in doubt about some particular case. The Pope's decisions were as a rule attempts to enforce justice and to uphold the law of the Church.

Luther (1483–1546), who started the Protestant Reformation, had toward divorce an attitude similar to that of the Church to which he had originally belonged. In the earlier period of his career he appears to have preferred bigamy to divorce. He was also strongly hostile to the idea that the Pope had rightfully the authority to annul marriage. He expressed himself at one time in the following words:

As to divorce, it is still a moot question whether it is allowable. For my part, I so greatly detest divorce that I should prefer bigamy to it, but whether it is allowable I do not venture to decide. . . . Christ permits divorce, but for the cause of fornication only. The Pope, therefore, must be in error when he grants a divorce for any other cause, and no one should feel safe who has obtained a dispensation by this temerity of the Pope.[8]

Luther's later consenting to the bigamy of Philip, Landgrave of Hesse, was given according to his own statement out of pressure as a result of Philip's insistence that if necessary he would seek annulment of his marriage from the Pope,[9] and Luther's approval was given only on condition that it remain a secret. His attitude when the facts became known brought a great storm of protest from Protestant leaders. When Luther declared that if the second marriage was made public he would not accept any responsibility, Philip became angry at what he regarded as Luther's deception. This brought the following reply from Luther:

---

[7] *Ibid.*, p. 198.
[8] Lenski, G. E., *Marriage in the Lutheran Church*, p. 178.
[9] *Ibid.*, p. 197.

If your Grace should publish this marriage you could not get the world to recognize its legality if a hundred Luthers and Melanchthons defend it. . . .

As to what you say about not wishing your second wife to pass as a whore, I do not see why your Grace should mind that, for she has had to pass for one hitherto, at least, before the world, though we three persons and God know that she is a wedded concubine. . . .

Your Grace should think what an offense it would be were it published, and also whether you could answer for it to the Emperor. . . .

Wherefore I advise you to give an ambiguous answer by which you could remain. I commend you to God and assure you that I advise you to do exactly what I should advise my own soul.[10]

The monastery. In the Middle Ages the ascetic trend which had appeared so early in Christianity led to the establishment of monasteries. The monastery not only permitted those who sought the holier life to band together and to remove from the ordinary secular life, but afforded an opportunity for service beyond that of the regular priesthood and provided a social environment superior to that presented by the outside world. It became the headquarters of a spiritual aristocracy and was one of the most potent influences making for a more refined and moral civilization. It antagonized marriage. But if it led many away from family experience, it must be credited with one advantage. It provided an avenue of escape for any woman who rebelled against entering upon the inferiority imposed by marriage with its masculine dominance of state and church. There was seldom any other choice for her. She must marry or become a nun. Unquestionably, by providing an escape from the conventional life of the woman of the time, the convent contributed to the influences that lessened the hardships and limitations put upon women by marriage.

The important role that the monastery played in the preservation of culture is likely to be minimized. It is easy to point out instances in which the intellectual life of the inmates fell to low levels, but such criticisms are most misleading if they conceal the important function the monastery had in keeping alive under untoward circumstances knowledge of the writings of

---

[10] *Ibid.*, pp. 200–201.

intellectual and theological leaders. It is no exaggeration to regard them as constituting oases in a social environment relatively a desert in its intellectual life and interests. It is difficult now to see how Christianity could have preserved its intellectual vitality so effectively as by this concentration of men and women who had taken vows of special responsibility in small communities such as the monasteries and convents became.

Since they carried on in the social disorganization resulting from the effort to transfuse paganism with medieval Christianity, it is not surprising that occasionally individuals who had assumed the high calling were indicted for behavior at variance with their vows. The chief criticism that was directed against them was, however, their disregard of social responsibility, their selfish withdrawal from the world which so greatly needed spiritual incentive and moral encouragement. Open to this censure for being self-contained and indifferent to the common weal as they frequently were, it is only fair to remember that their spiritual purpose depended upon their maintaining a life apart. The flaw that appeared in their system has always sooner or later come to the surface in every social and religious movement that has committed itself to separatism.

Chivalry.   Chivalry was an institutional development that flourished in the later part of the Middle Ages, originating in France, where it reached its perfection. Starting in the eleventh century, it reached its height in the twelfth and thirteenth, and during the next two centuries declined and disappeared. It was a strange mixture expressed in sentiment and practices, laws and customs, that brought together the discordant motivations of war, religion, and sexual love. Supported by the ruling classes, it was an attempt to idealize and direct knighthood, the anachronistic survival of feudalism, which with its armor-clad horseman and fortified castle had earlier developed as a means of local protection which the feeble central government could not give. The knight, the hero of chivalry, vowed a life of service to his feudal lord, his sovereign, and his lady love. The attitude of the Church, which in the days of the early Fathers was absolutely committed to peace and against all fighting, had changed. One of the reasons that Christians had been persecuted by the Roman authorities was the refusal of members of the Church to accept military service and their preaching of pacifism; chivalry, on the contrary, tied war and religion together through the Crusades.

Although the Church deserves high praise for the success of its efforts to curb the ferocious feudal knight who, a one-time needful contributor to social order, had continued out of season, chivalry never achieved such a success that the lofty ideals accepted as the knight's commission were actually put in practice by the bulk of those who took the vows. Even so, this restraining of a social group tending to cruelty and lawlessness was no small accomplishment, especially since the priestly conception of the ideal knight who devoted his life to generous service was attained by individuals of the chivalric orders.[11] Both the ideals of chivalry and the practices of the knights had domestic significance. With the passing of the struggle between feudalized Christendom and the pagan or infidel invaders, the castle became the center of social intercourse, and the knight who was now free to remain at home instituted a court which offered to women an opportunity for the expression of feminine graces and interests. This has been described as a domestic renaissance.[12] The knight fully committed to war and indifferent to feminine charms was replaced by the new type of warrior who went to combat to win the favor of his lady love. Then eventually came the idea that a man could not be a perfect knight unless he was the perfect lover.

This change of attitude which lifted the woman of noble birth from her former state when, even though possessing beauty, she was less esteemed than a "good lance thrust or a fine charger" [13] occurred in the middle of the twelfth century. This transformation was associated with the troubadours, and their importance requires a separate discussion. The romantic offshoot of chivalry which centered about woman evolved a code of morals so unlike our own of Puritan origin that we are apt not to see the contribution the troubadours made to the emergence of woman from a status of inferiority and to condemn their system of gallantry with a judgment as severe as at the time was the opposition of the Church.

---

[11] Prestlege, Edgar, editor, *Chivalry, A Series of Studies to Illustrate Its Historical Significance and Civilizing Influence*, by Members of Kings College, London, pp. 20–21.

[12] *Ibid.*, p. 16.

[13] *Ibid.*, p. 60.

Chivalry was thoroughly aristocratic. It assumed an innate connection of birth and character, and the gulf it interposed between the higher and the lower classes was one of the causes of its final passing. This separation of classes was bridged more successfully in England than in France, and this explains why we have in the former country a remnant surviving even in our own time. The common people when chivalry flourished were mere social pawns and being left outside chivalry concerned them little except as they suffered from the cruelties and disturbances of the knight on horseback whose eminence was soon to be challenged by the European introduction of gunpowder in warfare.

Romanticism.   It is not possible with balanced judgment to appraise this romantic movement unless through imagination we place ourselves back in a historic setting very unlike that with which we are now familiar. The popular idea of chivalry, which has found substantial support in such literature as the novels of Sir Walter Scott, Tennyson's *Idylls of the King,* and their earlier sources such as Mallory's *Morte D'Arthur* must be recognized as highly colored literary creations rather than realistic descriptions even of the medieval aristocracy. Christianity was making headway in its lifting of the barbaric standard of sexual morals that confronted it when it began its conversion of pagan Europe, but its task was difficult and therefore its progress slow. Much licentiousness and immodesty appears to have been common in every class of society.[14]

Just as the idealization of chivalry as it appeared in literature of the eighteenth century [15] gives a false picture of the characteristic life of Europe in the Middle Ages, so also the content and treatment of the poetry of the troubadours may lead to an exaggeration in the opposite direction. These wandering poets did not create their theme of illicit love, but their exploiting of the intrigues and license of the times in accord with their interest denies them the role of trustworthy interpreters. Christianity was making headway, and its triumph finally appeared in the transforming of even this literature of passion which attempted to idealize the moral looseness with which the troubadours were so well acquainted. They finally disappeared because

14 Briffault, Robert, *The Mothers,* Vol. 3, p. 12.
15 For example, see James Lane Allen's *The Reign of Law.*

they had allied themselves with paganism in its struggle with Christianity, and their romances were then given either a transmutation which brought them into accord with higher standards of morality or they were proscribed by church authority and passed out of circulation, replaced by religious romances.

There were two types of troubadours. One was composed of wealthy amateurs, the other of the professionals who earned their livelihood as poets and songsters traveling about from court to court. Troubadours did not create but found among the secular knights a conception of marriage which made it a mere commercial enterprise, an assignment forced upon the two interested parties by their overlords and guardians and destitute of love. Through their songs the troubadours gave the erotic passion aesthetic coloring which so frequently was expressed outside the matrimonial commitment. It was an achievement thus to give passion this emotional idealization and to permit it to recover meaning as a medium for the expression of affection. The next step which the modern development of the concept of marriage has made possible came through the refining of a love relationship developed within marriage and matured beyond mere physical passion, thus forming the basic support of an abiding affection between husband and wife. This has become an essential feature of the concept of monogamic marriage in occidental culture.

This does not mean, however, that never before had love been experienced in the fellowship of individual men and women. We have abundant evidence to the contrary. Even among people of simple culture testimony is given to the strength of affection that develops in the marriage relationship. Among primitive people, rarely demonstrative in revealing their feelings, an old man many years married, for example, may openly express his love for his wife as he helps her with her burdens.[16]

The bulk of the provincial poetry of the troubadours was undoubtedly in part a reaction against the teaching of Christianity, especially its doctrine of marriage. Many medieval Europeans, in spite of their outward allegiance to Christianity, were still at heart pagan.[17] Their inner rebellion against the restraints

---

[16] Kaberry, Phyllis, *Aboriginal Woman*, p. 154.
[17] De Rougemont, Denis D., *Love in the Western World*, p. 71.

of the Christian code and the teaching of the Church found a way of escape in the new type of literature they created. They sought relief from the bans of official Christianity, and thus while simulating conversion to the Christian principles they sought emancipation through mystic and allegoric poetry from what seemed to them an oppressive way of life.

Romanticism in England.   It is the medieval development of romanticism in England that is most closely related as a contributing influence to the development of the American family. At the time of the troubadours it was common among the higher classes of England to pledge small children as bride and bridegroom, or even for the parents to sell or barter them into matrimony as children or later when they had become adults. We have record of the occasional case of a daughter, for example, being cruelly punished by her mother because of her refusal to consent to the marriage arranged by her parents. Elizabeth Paston, because she was unwilling to marry an unattractive widower of fifty years, was brutally whipped once or twice a week and sometimes twice the same day until eventually her will was broken.[18] Among the child marriages we have one instance where a boy of three was coached by the clergyman into repeating the marriage vows that tied him for life to a girl of five.[19]

A medieval household.   Fortunately, we have a record in some detail of a household in Paris in the fourteenth century. Even though we cannot regard it as a typical French home it is certainly representative and affords an illuminating and interesting glimpse of medieval domestic experience. It is found in a book written between 1392 and 1394 by a man of wealth who desired to instruct his young wife in her household responsibilities and routine.[20] It is not strange that he expected her to be inexperienced, for we find that she was only fifteen years of age when she was married. The author states that discrepancies in age between husband and wife were frequent in the Middle Ages. The theme of the book is the wife's function to make her husband's declining years comfortable. He exhibits a paternal feeling toward his young spouse as he seeks to make it easier for her to prove a good wife. The book was in answer to the desire

---

[18] Trevelyan, G. M., *English Social History*, p. 65.
[19] *Ibid.*, p. 69.
[20] Power, Aline, "The Ménagier's Wife," *Medieval People*, pp. 85–110.

expressed by the young girl that her husband not be too critical but help her to correct her faults and to carry on her household tasks according to his wishes. From time to time he urges her to become efficient, lest after his death, and when she marries again, her habits might discredit him to her second husband.

The book is divided into three parts. The first takes up her religious and moral duties. She has two commanding ethical obligations, one the salvation of her own soul and the second the providing of comfort for her husband. Both of these are discussed in considerable detail and impressed by numerous illustrations gathered from his reading and his experience. The second section of the book concerns itself with household management. Here the author's knowledge is impressive, for he ranges over a mass of household interests, for example, giving instruction in how to get out grease spots from dresses and furs, how to catch fleas, how to keep flies out of the bedroom, how to care for the wine, how to superintend the farming, how to care for the horses, and how to choose and prepare food. In this section considerable attention is given to the art of cooking, including numerous recipes. The third part of the book, left unfinished, is devoted to indoor amusements and out-of-door recreation, especially hawking, which appears to have been in favor with women of leisure.

The chief purpose of the book is clearly to help the wife understand how to minister to her husband's comfort. This subject appears again and again throughout the discussion. It is interesting to notice that the author includes advice as to how a wife can get back the love of an unfaithful husband. In accord with the spirit of the time, the wife is expected to respond wholeheartedly to the desires of her husband without regard to her own feeling. The cookbook section suggests long feasts with many courses and dishes of highly spiced food. Considerable counsel is given regarding marketing, and here is included a list of all the meat markets in Paris. The modern wife will find nothing to envy in this housekeeper's program with its multitude of responsibilities always centering about the husband and ranging from seeing that he would always be greeted in winter by a good fire to being sure that in summer all fleas were driven from his bed.

The Renaissance. The Renaissance was a cultural rejuvenescence which, although associated with a reawakened interest in the classics, was the breaking forth of the new ideas and ways of living made possible at last by the slow social progress that had been going on in the Middle Ages. It announced the closing of the medieval epoch and the beginning of the modern. Marriage and family experience, like all other social experiences, were responsive to its influence. It enlarged the opportunities, along intellectual lines chiefly, of the women of rank. The effect of the changing conditions did not register in the sphere of the average woman until the second reconstruction of society brought about by the Reformation. The financial and legal inequality of woman was little changed. In spite of these persisting handicaps, woman had started a new adventure, unlike that with which she had grown familiar during the preceding centuries of human existence, which after much travel was to bring her to the near-equality which she has now achieved in contemporary American life.

The conventions of behavior as well as those of thought were broken into by the force of the rapidly moving cultural changes, and domestic relationship did not escape the general instability. Lax morals, illegitimacy, and seduction reveal the social strain. To prevent the evils of clandestine and irregular marriages, Pope Innocent the Third, as early as 1215, required that the banns of marriage be three times announced in the Church before the wedding could take place. Later the Council of Trent made this prerequisite to a valid marriage. The Church continued its position regarding the indissoluble character of marriage, and since annulment of the marriage was the only way out of an unhappy union, it was sought by people of wealth and position.

The Reformation. The Reformation was the result of a disturbing gap between a growing individualism brought forward by the general advance in social conditions and the static ecclesiastical dogma of the period. It brought to an issue the increasing demand among forward-looking intellectuals that Christianity return to the practices and teachings of its earlier days and that each person be free to find for himself through the study of the Bible his own religious faith. In Luther it found a leader of extravertive mind who, turning the protest away from mysticism and mere intellectual discussion, led it into action. It was chiefly directed against the Church because this was the institution that had been most resistant to the changing conditions resulting from the Renaissance. Luther and his followers insisted that marriage was not a sacrament but a civil contract, established for social perpetuation and human welfare. He advised the clergy to break their vows and marry, and himself set the example. Spiritual kinship impediments to marriage were removed and unions were permitted between those whose blood relationship was not closer than the third degree of consanguinity.

The emphasis placed upon the rights of the individual, plus the influence that came from the development of commerce and the rise of the middle class, gave the coloring to the European background out of which came the American marriage and family.

The Puritan tradition. The Puritan ancestry carried straight back to the primitive asceticism of the Christian followers. In its Protestant form, however, it represented restraint rather than renunciation of the world and retreat from its practical affairs. The Puritan and the Calvinist cultivated restraint in their use of worldly things. Committed to a program of self-denial as the essential test of true religion, it was not strange that they became people of thrift and prospered in the new commercial era. They were ideally prepared to meet the testing of the American wilderness. Whatever their peculiar emphasis—Pilgrim, English Puritan, Calvinist, Dutch Reformer, or the Huguenot—all shared a seriousness and a confidence in their co-working with God that gave them a stern but important role in the development of the new nation.

The Dutch tradition. Protestantism as it had developed in the Netherlands had done well by women. They were accustomed to an independence not yet attained by women elsewhere. They had greater educational advantages, more legal protection, and larger opportunities for self-expression than in other countries in Europe. Boys and girls were educated in the same elementary schools. The property rights of the wife were in accord with her high social status. She could bequeath her dowry according to her will and if childless could, after the death of her husband, will to her relatives half of what he had acquired after his marriage. Children inherited equally, and one third of the father's property had to be left to them. Only for serious reasons, approved by law, was a man permitted to disinherit any of his children. Although Bradford tells us that one of the reasons why the Pilgrims left their refuge in Holland and came to America was the danger of their children's being led astray from their faith because of the influences of the alien environment, there can be no doubt that the twelve years' residence of the Pilgrims in Holland had much to do with the liberal policy of the colony on Cape Cod.[21] Recording the first marriage in the new country, Bradford writes:

May 12 was ye first marriage in this place which according to ye laudable custome of ye Low Cuntries in which they had lived was thought most requisite to be performed by the magistrate as being a civill thing, upon which many questions aboute inheritances doe depende with other things most proper to their cognizans and most consonante to ye scriptures.[22]

The Quaker tradition. In an unprecedented manner the Quakers combined mystic thinking with practical efficiency. Of all the religious sects that came into existence after the Reformation, none was more democratic than this group of Separatists who were so afraid of worldly distinction that they refused to bare their heads even in the presence of royalty itself. From the beginning Fox had taught that the inner life from which the Quaker obtained his spiritual guidance was as open to the woman as to the man. This doctrine provided for the woman in the Quaker meetinghouse the same opportunity to reveal her experience and express her conviction that was given to the man. Such a position, so far in advance of the conventional thinking of the period, led to the insistence on education for the girl as well as for the boy. Fox started as early as 1667 a special school for girls at Shacklewell, England, and urged his followers to attend to the need of providing training for the girl as well as for the boy.

Although the woman was given the same opportunities as the man for expression at the religious gatherings, she was expected to become efficient in the duties of the housewife. If her business was chiefly in the home, she enjoyed an equality there

[21] Calhoun, A. W., *Social History of the American Family*, Vol. 1, pp. 49–50.
[22] Bradford, W., *History of Plymouth Plantation*, p. 122.

with her husband. No religious group has ever come closer to the conditions of primitive Christianity, and the practical character of their faith was reflected within the household. Of course, believing in no sacrament, they emphasized Luther's idea that marriage was a civil contract, but they went further than other Protestants in refusing to allow priest or minister to officiate at the marriage ceremony. Instead the bride and groom married each other in the presence of the meeting. So easy an entrance into matrimony appeared scandalous to outsiders, but the Quakers were by no means lax in their regulating of marriage. Fox stood against child marriages, unions of persons near of blood, and hasty remarriages. It is interesting to find him advocating a register of marriages and the refusal of marriage to any unable to present a certificate from parents or relatives permitting the union.

The English traditional family. The conventional family of England remained throughout the seventeenth and eighteenth centuries distinctly patriarchal in type. Although minor changes were made in the law of advantage to woman, her legal status continued one of subordination to man. The masculine dominance was not only authorized by law but was also supported by the mores, as is vividly portrayed in Richardson's *Clarissa Harlowe.*

Up to the reign of Henry VIII, the Established Church of England, in accord with Roman Catholic teaching, held to the indissolubility of marriage and its sacramental character. After the English Church separated from the Church of Rome, the canon law was permitted to remain in force in the ecclesiastical courts. Henry VIII appointed a commission to revise the regulations, and had he lived to carry out these recommendations, divorce would have been granted on the grounds of adultery, desertion, long absence, cruelty, and an attempt on the life of one of the spouses by the other, or deadly hatred between the spouses. It was recommended that separation of bed and board be abolished. With his death the Church continued the former policy concerning divorce.[23] The ecclesiastical courts, although refusing legal divorce, did grant a judicial separation known as divorce *a mensa et thoro.* This could be had on clear proof of grave misconduct on the part of husband or wife, such as adultery or

[23] Drummond, I., *Getting a Divorce,* p. 20.

cruelty. It did not dissolve the marriage bond but merely permitted separation and did not take the dowry away from the wife or remove from the husband his legal claims on her property. In addition to this separation the ecclesiastical courts also pronounced decrees of nullity known as divorce *a vinculo,* when lack of capacity made the union impossible. Eventually there developed in England the rare practice of securing divorces *a vinculo matrimonii* by act of parliament.[24]

In interpreting the domestic life of England during the seventeenth and eighteenth centuries, there must be recognition of the significance of class differences and of the meaning of the extraordinary careers of women like Queen Elizabeth, who, surmounting the handicap of sex, achieved distinction and power. These were exceptional cases that may easily lead to the misinterpreting of the conventional situation of English women.

The Cavalier tradition. One of the important influences in the early making of the United States, distinctly carrying its own type of domesticity, was a class tradition which can be best described as that of the Cavalier. It represented a new-world imitation of the country squire of England. From the earliest days of its settlement Virginia was strongly Anglican and Royalist in sympathy,[25] and, because of this, during the English Civil War and the ascendance of Cromwell, many of the Royalists who fled from their native country settled in Virginia. Those who remained after the return to the throne of Charles II strengthened the aristocratic culture of the tidewater inhabitants. Although this Cavalier background was especially prominent in eastern Virginia, it was not limited to that colony but instead dominated the tidewater communities of all the southern colonies. Agriculture in this section took the plantation form and was chiefly given over to the raising of tobacco. Once slavery was introduced, the plantation system established itself on the basis of Negro labor. The planter constituted the head of a small community maintaining artisans [26] as well as field workers and depending chiefly on the English market for the sale of its products. He frequently spent vacations in London

[24] Madden, J. W., *Cases on Domestic Relations,* p. 630.
[25] Andrews, Charles M., *The Colonial Period of American History,* Vol. 1, p. 234.
[26] Wertenbaker, Thomas J., *The First Americans,* pp. 44–45.

or Glasgow and sent his children, at least the boys, to English schools. Thus strong cultural ties were maintained with the motherland. The farmers of the uplands were not sympathetic with this tidewater aristocracy. After the Seven Years War they took over political control with leaders such as Richard Henry Lee, Patrick Henry, and Thomas Jefferson.

Largely on account of the influence of literature the Cavalier tradition has been overemphasized in the uncritical thinking about the South. In spite of this exaggeration it must be recognized as having contributed significantly to the culture of the southern states. Because of the portrayal it has received through fiction, southern life is popularly thought of as social gaiety, luxurious living expressed in leisure, hunting, the consuming of the rich and abounding food and drink of the gourmet, and romance, rapid courtship, early marriage, and for the most part undemocratic attitudes in sharpest contrast with the practices and thinking of the western people. With the development of the western Southeast, the plantation system with its aristocratic tendencies passed beyond its tidewater origin, especially with the later expansion of cotton culture.[27]

The French and Spanish settlements. The English colonies were enclosed by French and Spanish settlements, maintaining the domestic traditions of their European motherland. This wall of alien cultures was, except in the Canadian North and the Louisiana of the South, fragmentary and thin. As the migrants of the colonists spread westward, these barriers were broken through and the domestic habits of the earlier settlers supplanted by those of American origin. Thus it was that the original development at St. Louis disappeared and left nothing to suggest in our time its earlier history. Not so, however, in New Orleans. Here from the first we find a vigorous growth of non-English culture which still, especially through the influences that come down to us from the period of French occupation, reveals itself in New Orleans and its environs. New Orleans is unlike any other city of the United States, and so it was from the beginning. During the period of the dominance of French-Spanish culture—for the two easily amalgamated—it was the most cosmopolitan and distinctive city on the North

---

[27] Odum, Howard W., *An American Epoch*, Ch. 3.

American continent. By the time it had come under American rule it had developed into the new-world Paris.

The picture we get of domestic life is a pleasant one. The Louisiana planters were kind and affectionate to their children, lenient to their slaves. The Spaniards in the new world appear to have been the mildest slaveholders, cheerful in disposition, and fond of good living. Contrary to English habit, the settlers were not unwilling to marry native women.[28] The Church did not approve of these mixed marriages but recorded them as *mariages naturels*. In New Orleans numerous freed girls of Negro blood had much to do with the lax sex morals which gave the city notoriety. The marriage ceremony took place in the churches, the priest consecrating the nuptial vows. Banns were published, but due to the infrequency of the visits of priests at times in some localities, one public notice was deemed sufficient.

The legal system of Louisiana perhaps best reveals today the strength of the earlier French influence, but this is not the exclusive remnant that comes down to us. In spite of American political administration, as late as 1848 we find New Orleans the most European of American cities, and it is still strikingly unlike our other cities.[29] To what now remains of the original Latin influences we have added those that come through the commercial contact of New Orleans and Spanish America. In a similar way the survivals of the former Spanish occupation throughout the Southwest are being reinforced by the recent influx of Mexicans.

The American tradition. Thus from various cultural backgrounds came types of family life that under the determining influence of a new environment were to be amalgamated into a form of domestic experience distinctly different from anything European. On this side of the ocean developed domestic standards and ideals as original as were the political thought and systems which came forth in North America. In the next chapter we shall be concerned with this evolution of the American family.

---

[28] Wallace, J., *History of Illinois and Louisiana Under the French Rule*, p. 412.

[29] Jones, H. M., *America and French Culture*, p. 123.

Chapter 6

THE COLONIAL AND FRONTIER AMERICAN FAMILY

FOREWORD. The American family is not a European institution transplanted to a new environment and slightly changed by this transferring. Instead it represents an original development which so reconstructed the contributions of European culture as to bring forth a family type in its characteristics clearly distinctive from the original European institutions. Western Europe contributed the people and the traditions, and if this be thought of as the raw material, the processes that brought about the change must be found in the environmental conditions of the New World. The purpose of this and the following chapter is to uncover these influences as they work together to shape our domestic traits. Briefly, because of necessary limitations of space, the most important of the social consequences of life in the new world are discussed as they are related to the evolution of marriage and the family. The frontier was the most significant of these, that is, the most causal in creating what distinguishes our family type. It is because this reconstruction of European family traits started as soon as settlements were firmly made in the new land that we turn to the colonial period. This discussion should not be thought of as a mere rehearsal of social history, an epoch in our national life, but as the first disclosure of the frontier's influence in the making of the American family. Although these settlements were not generally regarded either in the old or the new world as leading to the breaking away from the dominance of the European culture, this severance began at once to be a necessity for survival in the American wilderness, and from then until its final passing as a major influence on American life the frontier was the chief causal source of the distinctive characteristics of the American people.

The effect of geographical distance.   Each group of European colonies brought with them to the new land a definite cultural background. Rarely did they show any disposition to get rid of the old culture in order to develop something new. Even those who felt themselves most estranged from the ruling class of the old land assumed as a matter of course that the traditions, conventions, and ways of living to which they were accustomed would be continued in their new environment. Indeed, the desire to maintain without interference the kind of culture they had developed, especially along religious lines, was second only to the economic motive as a cause of their migration.

The European social pattern which they brought over and attempted to follow included traditions, customs, and laws relating to marriage and domestic life of concern to us. On neither side of the ocean was there any general realization that the colonists must inevitably be changed by their new environment. A simple illustration of the attempt of the migrants to follow the practices with which they were familiar was the building of thatched roofs at the Plymouth settlement, a custom that appears to have lingered in New England for more than forty years, in spite of the fact that there was an abundance of wood suitable for a better type of roofing, while the thatch had to be artificially cultivated.

It is difficult for us now to imagine the significance of the mere distance of the new settlement from the old country. The Atlantic Ocean, which in our time can be so quickly crossed in a nonstop airplane, over which in a second the spoken voice can be passed, was in the seventeenth century a wedge between the old country and the new, which was destined in time to sever even the political ties which on both sides seemed at first secure against change. The only means of travel over the three thousand miles of ocean was the slow sailing vessel which at best could not make the crossing in less than a month. This also was the only means of communication between the settlements and the motherland. As a consequence, the colonies gradually drifted away not only from their political loyalties but from the cultural background of their European origin. Their survival depended upon an adjustment to new conditions, and this they could not accomplish unless they were willing to reconstruct their manner of living and achieve considerable cultural independence. The process of change was gradual but persistent. The seriousness of the differences between the old and the new was slowly recognized on both sides, although the efforts of the old country to prevent change by long-distance legal control made the colonists the more conscious of what was happening.

Sectional differences. The fact that the new environment began from the first days of the settlement to operate upon the colonists and to force them to an adaptation to the new conditions does not mean that the former cultural experiences had no significance. Especially was this not true in domestic relationships. The family tradition is slow-changing and there was greater resistance at this point to the influences of the new environment than in other aspects of the social life. This resulted in considerable variation between the groups of colonists. Being different from the start, they continued their distinctions. Moreover, the environment itself, especially in its effect upon economic activity, was diverse and tended to build up sectional differences. For example, the fishing folk of the New England seacoast were vocationally more distant than they were in space from the tobacco growers of Virginia.

Here we see two different major influences coming out of the physical environment of the new country. One tended to wipe out European practices and led to the building of common interests between the northern, the middle, and the southern colonies. Along with this went also the effects of the differences of the environment, and these, of course, at that time were far more significant than is true now when modern science has lessened the peculiarities of different sections and increased the fund of common possessions and common interests. Even now the traveler who crosses the United States from east to west or from north to south notices a degree of sectionalism in the thinking and habits of life, and even in political philosophy, that is the result of environmental conditions. Our prevailing ideas of marriage, domestic habits, and even divorce practices reveal still these sectional differences. In the building of the American family there entered three distinct influences. One was the original domestic background brought by the settlers from their European homeland. Another was the result of distance from the old countries and of exposure to the new conditions of frontier life. The third resulted from the environmental peculiarities which led the various colonies to develop each its own distinct type of adaptation to land, climate, and geographical situation.

It is natural to think of the colonial settlers as English folk because the majority of them were and their language prevailed throughout the territory that finally became the original United States of America. Nevertheless, the European stock in the New World from Massachusetts down the coast to Georgia was not exclusively English. The Swedes made a short-lived settlement on the Delaware, but although their colony disappeared the people who had founded it remained and were amalgamated with the English. The Dutch maintained their colony a longer period and their influence was more pronounced. Culturally it was more significant than was indicated by the size of the Dutch population, which was finally incorporated into the English-speaking population. There were settlers also who came from Germany; they chiefly established themselves in Pennsylvania. From France came the Huguenots, who established themselves in small groups in Massachusetts, Rhode Island, New York, Virginia, and South Carolina, who also in time blended with the prevailing English. Immigrants from Wales, especially Quakers, and from Scotland, although we think of them as English, represented a somewhat different background than those coming from England itself. Thus it is apparent that from the very beginning the stock that developed into the people of the United States of America was not exclusively English. Almost from their earliest days the colonies provided a cross-fertilization of culture which encouraged an original social evolution.

It is an advantage in discussing marriage and the family to divide the colonies roughly into three types: New England, the Middle States from New York to Maryland, and the South from Maryland to Georgia. It must not be forgotten, however, that in each division there was considerable variation. For example, not only may we find life in Virginia considerably different from that in Georgia, but even within a colony we may find great differences because of diversity of settlement. For example, in North Carolina the early seaboard settlements were made chiefly by people straight from England, while in the western part, Quakers, Moravians, Irish Presbyterians, and other groups entered the province through the Shenandoah Valley of Virginia. Time led to a large measure of consolidation of these diverse elements within each colony, but in the process each made its contribution.

Courtship.   Courtship was adjusted to the environmental conditions. It was, as one would expect, frank and generally brief. Although the conscientious parent kept a watchful eye upon his daughter, the frontier environment forbade seclusion. It was natural, also, in settlements made up of persons of kindred spirit, often largely relatives and friends, that the girl should be permitted greater freedom than would have been granted by the same parents in Europe. Courtship had to conform to the limited space of the houses, and, until the singing school came in New England to help provide an opportunity for the youth to come together, much of the courting had to take place in the living-room, sometimes in the presence of their elders. Restricted quarters, without question, explain the revival of the old folkway, bundling, in colonial New England. Although from the beginning frowned upon by some, it was current from New York northward, but most common in Massachusetts and Connecticut. It is interesting to notice that it was attacked vigorously after the return of the colonial youth from the French and Indian wars, when their loose morals turned it to vice and it became a public scandal.[1]

The new conditions on this side of the ocean made it difficult from the first to maintain the patriarchal control of daughters. In Massachusetts, as early as 1647, a situation arose which led to the passing of the statute fining any person who should endeavor "directly or indirectly, to draw away the affection of any maid in this jurisdiction under pretense of marriage, before he hath obtained liberty and allowance from her parents or governors (or in absence of such) of the nearest magistrate. . . ."[2] This same unconventionality appears in the New Haven colony. In 1660 a young man was haled into court for violating a similar law. When the young maiden concerned insisted that the fault was hers, she was fined by the court and declared to be a "bould virgin." Timothy Edwards, father of

---

[1] Calhoun, A. W., *Social History of the American Family*, Vol. 1, p. 129.
[2] Lawrence, H. W., *The Not-Quite Puritans*, pp. 28–29.

Jonathan, refused to baptize the child of a father who had married without getting the consent of the bride's parents. He also refused to allow the bridegroom, Joseph Diggens, to transfer to another parish.[3]

The colonial habit of keeping a diary has preserved for us some detailed records of courtship. One of the most interesting of these was that of Judge Samuel Sewall, of Boston. During his matrimonial career of forty years he had at least six courtships, three of which led to marriage, his third wife surviving him. In the diary of the Reverend Doctor Cotton Mather, of Boston, we have record of a different sort of courtship, a story of a woman's aggression that, although not typical, gives evidence that the new environment was stimulating in some women greater self-assertion. His wife having died in December, 1702, Mather found himself the following February faced with a proposal of marriage from a twenty-year-old maiden of his congregation who was, he states, "a young gentlewoman of incomparable accomplishments, no woman in English America having had a more polite education." He writes that having been tempted by nature to wed this remarkable girl, but having refused because the mere notion that he was courting her having gone abroad had raised a mighty noise, he finally made his rejection clear.

July 17, 1703

The Rage of that young Gentlewoman, whom out of obedience to God, I have rejected, (and never more pleased God than in rejecting of her Addresses to me,) is transporting her; to threaten that she will be a Thorn in my Side, and contrive all possible Wayes to vex me, affront me, disgrace me, in my Attempting a Return to the married State with another Gentlewoman. . . .[4]

It is, of course, impossible with any degree of certainty to compare the morals of different periods. It is clear, however, that the colonies were not free from serious courtship problems. In spite of the greater stress of religion in the New England colonies, we have no reason to suppose that they were for this reason less troubled than the other settlements. In the southern colonies, for example, one of the most common crimes that

[3] Winslow, Elizabeth, *Jonathan Edwards,* p. 226.
[4] Hanscom, E. D., *The Heart of the Puritan,* p. 71.

brought women before the courts was that of bastardy.[5] Every effort was made by law to enforce morality in Virginia from the days of Jamestown, where we find adultery punished by death and fornication dealt with very severely. During the nineteenth century down to 1860, in North Carolina, fornication, adultery, and bastardy were offenses often appearing in criminal indictments.[6] At least there seems to have been little protest against fornication, if it was eventually followed by marriage, no matter how long this was delayed. In 1722 a group of Harvard students seriously debated the question whether sex intimacy before marriage was truly fornication if matrimony was intended. Jonathan Edwards seems to have lost his pulpit at Northampton in part because of his opposition to such practices. In New York in 1695, according to the report of a traveler, such an antenuptial relationship was not considered a sin and apparently, Adams tells us, was not an uncommon practice. He states that in one Massachusetts church, of which we seem to have a complete record, this practice was followed in practically every marriage, while a church in Connecticut made a rule that seven-month children should be considered legitimate.[7] In the South we find toward the end of the seventeenth century an increasing problem of miscegenation as a consequence of the sex temptation brought by slavery. In any description of the laxities common among the colonists, it must be remembered that conditions in the seventeenth and eighteenth centuries in Europe from whence the settlers had come were even more coarse and vicious. Nowhere in America were conditions so bad as those found in the slums of London.[8]

Marriage. Colonial conditions led to early marriage. Of Connecticut youth, for example, it was said by one writing in 1704, "They generally marry very young, the males oftener, as I am told, under twenty years than above." The girls often married at sixteen or younger, and an unmarried woman at twenty-five entered the ranks of the old maids. Calhoun tells us that "New England family policy pressed as heavily upon the unattached man as on the isolated woman. Bachelors were rare

---

[5] Spruill, Julia Cherry, *Women's Life and Work in the Southern Colonies*, p. 314.

[6] Johnson, Guion Griffis, *Ante-Bellum North Carolina*, p. 657.

[7] Adams, J. T., *Provincial Society 1690–1763*, p. 159.

[8] George, M. Dorothy, *London Life in the XVIIIth Century*, Ch. 2.

and were viewed with disapproval. They were almost in the class of suspected criminals. . . . In Hartford solitary men were taxed twenty shillings a week." [9]

After the Revolutionary War we find the same tendency toward early marriage in the new frontier over the Alleghenies. In Kentucky early marriages were common, men of eighteen or twenty wedding girls of fourteen or sixteen.[10]

The social conditions that led to early marriage also encouraged the remarriage of widows and widowers and cut short their period of formal mourning. Although the first marriage in Plymouth Colony was an exceptional case, it was indicative of a situation that demanded that family ties broken by death be replaced by others as quickly as possible. In this marriage Edward Winslow, who had been a widower only seven weeks, was married to Susannah White, who had lost her husband twelve weeks earlier.[11]

It is stated that a governor of colonial New Hampshire married a lady whose previous husband had been dead just ten days. It is possible, however, for us to exaggerate the influence of frontier conditions in inducing early marriage and quick remarriage. The fact that we find these trends in the seventeenth century English mores is evidence that we are not dealing here merely with the difficulty of meeting pioneering conditions unmated. The American frontier, nevertheless, favored the continuation of such customs and also provided opportunity that made it easy for the young people, accustomed to hard work, to leave the home of their parents, knowing that courage and industry would soon enable them to win from the unclaimed wilderness conditions as pleasant as those they had left.

In all the American colonies it was required by law that there be public announcement of intention to marry. The general custom was to have the banns read three times publicly. In Virginia, for example, this was done on three successive Sundays or holidays at the divine service. In Pennsylvania a notice had to be posted on the court or meetinghouse door one month before the wedding. In New Jersey such a public statement had to be made two weeks prior to the solemnizing of the

[9] Calhoun, A. W., *op. cit.*, pp. 67–68.
[10] *Ibid.*, Vol. 2, p. 14.
[11] *Ibid.*, Vol. I, p. 69.

marriage or the banns proclaimed three weeks in succession in a church. In the southern states the solemnizing of the marriage was performed by the clergyman, and at first he had to be of the Church of England. As early as 1728 the Carolinas provided for a marriage in the absence of a clergyman of the Church of England, or with his consent. Under such circumstances a lawful magistrate could perform the service.

In Maryland, while the Catholics were in control, either a religious or a civil marriage was considered legal. Later a clergyman of the Church of England, or of the Catholic Church, or of one of the dissenting churches, had to officiate. In Pennsylvania, as a result of Quaker influence, a marriage performed according to the form of any religious organization was held as legal. In New England marriage was at first a civil contract and had to be performed by a public magistrate. In 1646 the Massachusetts Bay Colony forbade their clergy to officiate. Later this ban was removed and finally ministers of all denominations were permitted to take charge of the wedding ceremony.

Throughout the colony it was the general practice to require registration of marriage. In New England the town clerk was responsible for keeping a record of marriages, births, and deaths. In Virginia the minister of every parish was required to keep a record of all his weddings. In North Carolina the governor appointed one of three freeholders nominated by the people to act as register of deeds. Nowhere was what we now know as common-law marriage authorized by law, but there can be no doubt that many such marriages occurred even though they were punishable as illegal and held to be invalid.

Status of the colonial wife. The popular religion of the colonists, particularly in New England, though it can scarcely be said to be the product of the hard life of the frontier, was certainly in harmony with the setting in which the people found themselves. It was largely taken from the Old Testament and emphasized, so far as the family was concerned, the patriarchal character of the Jewish home. Family conditions were linked with the Scriptures until they appeared divinely sanctioned. The husband, of course, sat in the seat of power as the patriarch. It was the business of his spouse to demonstrate by obedience and subordination her piety and religious fervor.

In law woman's status was always that of inferiority. The

colonists, whether Cavaliers or Puritans, had been trained among legal traditions that defined woman as legally inferior to man. The English law became our Common Law, and it placed woman in so great an economic dependence upon man that even the clothing and ornaments of a married woman were the property of the husband and could be disposed of by him according to his wish, while on the contrary his property was his absolute possession, to which she could lay no claim. The following excerpt taken from Blackstone's Commentaries, published in 1765, reveals the temper of the English law as it attempted to define the legal status of woman:

By marriage the husband and wife are one person in law: that is, the very being or legal existence of the woman is suspended during the marriage, or at least is incorporated and consolidated into that of the husband: under whose wing, protection, and *cover*, she performs everything; . . . Upon this principle, of an union of person in husband and wife, depend most of the legal rights, duties, and disabilities, that either of them acquire by the marriage. . . . For this reason a man cannot grant anything to his wife, or enter into covenant with her, for the grant would be to suppose her separate existence: and to covenant with her would be only to covenant with himself: and therefore it is also generally true that all compacts made between husband and wife, when single, are voided by the intermarriage. . . .

The husband also (by the old law) might give his wife moderate correction. For, as he is to answer for her behavior, the law thought it reasonable to instruct him with this power of restraining her, by domestic chastisement, in the same moderation that a man is allowed to correct his apprentices or children, for whom the master or parent is also liable in some cases to answer. But this power of correction was confined within reasonable bounds. . . . The civil law gave the husband the same, or a larger, authority over his wife: . . . But with us in the politer reign of Charles the Second, this power of coercion began to be doubted: and a wife may now have security of the peace against her husband; or, in return, a husband against his wife. Yet the lower rank of people, who were always fond of the old common law, still claim and exert their ancient privilege; and the courts of law still permit a husband to restrain a wife of her liberty, in case of any gross misbehavior.

These are the chief legal effects of marriage during the coverture; upon which we may observe, that even the disabilities which the wife lies under are for the most part intended for her protection and benefit. So great a favorite is the female sex of the laws of England.[12]

If the husband of the period was chiefly interested in defining his wife's subordination because of its significance for his control of the property of the family, his wife doubtless suffered most in her loss of legal rights from the greater power the husband had in the control of their children. How deeply this was embedded in the common law that colored American jurisprudence comes out when we learn of such facts as the following:

In 1911 there were, for instance, still seven states in which the father could by will prevent the mother from being the guardian of her own children after his death. There were twenty-four states in which the mother during the lifetime of the father had no legal right whatever in the control of the children, that is, states in which the father was the sole guardian.[13]

Harsh as was the definition of woman's status in the colonial period, it was nevertheless true that the husband was forced to accept some responsibilities in his marriage; he had to support her in the manner justified by his circumstances, and he was liable not only for the debts she contracted after marriage, but for those she had at the time of the ceremony. Colonial law also assured to the wife her dowry rights. In most of the colonies she was protected from the beating of the husband, although this was a right he had long enjoyed under English law.

In spite of the fact that woman's subordination was legally maintained and socially upheld, there is clear evidence that the new environment was from the first an influence leading to her greater independence and equality. This was true in all the colonies, but most marked in New England because of the greater democracy there and the prevailing emphasis upon personal industry. It was chiefly through the new vocational opportunities that the colonial women began to advance their social and legal status. There were, as is true in every society, outstanding women such as Abigail Adams, wife of John Adams, who through unusual ability and personality achieved distinction, but even in these cases opportunity reinforced native

---

[12] *Commentaries on the Laws of England*, 15th Edition, Vol. 1, pp. 441–445.
[13] Wolfe, A. B., *Readings in Social Problems*, p. 447.

intelligence. Because of the many long absences of the husband, it became necessary for someone to take over his responsibilities when he was away, and these were assumed by the wife.

For the most part woman's advance was along the line of industry and business. As a rule, this came about through the death of the husband or his desertion. Women took charge of taverns, became merchants, managed small businesses such as dyeing, candlemaking, coachmaking, ropemaking, and even horseshoeing. A few undertook to give medical advice, and midwifery for over a century remained entirely a woman's vocation. Women, both married and single, taught school, managed farms in the North and plantations in the South, and even ran newspapers.[14] Opportunities for women were more numerous in the North than in the South, in part because of its more diversified economic life.

From the seventeenth on into the eighteenth century those who entered professions had very little special training. They had to gain their fitness through experience; therefore, there was nothing but social attitudes to curb a woman's desire to enter a profession. Women could not enter the ministry, although they occasionally became preachers among the sects that did not require ordination or pay salaries. Women also did not enter the practice of law, nor did they seek a military or political career. Some of them did take over the function of the doctor, especially that part which is now the practice of obstetrics. Indeed, midwifery may be said to have been the first profession generally regarded as a proper career for women. Soon, however, it became the custom to call in male physicians whenever a childbirth was difficult. This attitude is illustrated by the following words written by Thomas Jefferson to his daughter who was facing the ordeal of delivery: "Some female friend of your mamma's (I forgot whom) used to say it was no more than a job of the elbow. The material thing is to have scientific aid in readiness, that if anything uncommon takes place it may be redressed on the spot, and not be made serious by delay. It is a case which least of all will wait for doctors to be sent for: therefore with single precaution nothing is ever to be feared."[15] Em-

[14] Dexter, E. A., *Colonial Women of Affairs.*
[15] Spruill, *op. cit.*, p. 51.

ployment of men as midwives, however, met with fierce opposition from some who regarded it as an attack on female modesty.[16] In the South the wife of the plantation owner or of the overseer carried the responsibility of seeing that the slave mother was properly cared for during delivery and the lying-in period. Nursing throughout the colonies also was largely in the hands of women, some of them making it a means of livelihood. As a rule, care of the sick was carried on by women as a part of their household or neighborhood service. Although during the first century of American colonial life most teachers were men, we have records of women entering the profession in which later they were to predominate. In the South, for example, as early as 1657 there is record of a Mrs. Peacock who apparently became mistress of a small school in Rappahannock County in Virginia.[17]

Birth rate and death rate.   Early marriage and other social conditions stimulated the American birth rate. As a consequence, the colonial fecundity was one of the highest on record. Francis A. Walker, an authoritative American statistician, has said:

There is not the shadow of a statistical reason for attributing to the native American population prior to the War of Secession a deficiency in reproductive vigor compared with any people that ever lived.

Public opinion was favorable to the high birth rate. After the formation of the Union there was a national sentiment which encouraged large families. With the industrial development of the nation, a rapid increase in population was also for the advantage of the large land-owner and of those engaged in trade and manufacturing. Along with the high birth rate went a correspondingly high death rate. In many a large family the majority of the children did not travel beyond childhood. Preventive medicine had not originated; even curative medicine could do little to curb most infectious diseases. An inscription on a Plymouth gravestone is said to read, "Here lies ———— ———— with twenty small children." Fortunately such a family history was not characteristic even of the colonial period. In spite of

[16] *Ibid.*, p. 275.
[17] *Ibid.*, p. 255.

the high mortality of children, the excess of births over deaths was such as to send the population steadily upward.

The scant medical knowledge of the time contributed to the high death rate of children. Medical superstition was widespread and even practicing doctors knew almost nothing about the causes or cures of disease. Not until the discovery of bacteria had been made could there be much understanding of infectious diseases and their treatment, and as a consequence the death rate of children was high everywhere up to the time of Pasteur. When one reads the recipes for the compounding of medicines to be given children, it seems remarkable that any survived, but alongside the prevailing ignorance must be placed the advantages that came from the colonists' way of living. Those who did not succumb to epidemics were likely to reach old age. We have interesting evidences of this in the town records of Hingham, Massachusetts. From 1635, the time of its first settlement, 837 persons are mentioned in the first period of the town's history. The length of life of these persons is recorded: One hundred and five reached the age of eighty; nineteen lived to be ninety or more; and three reached a hundred years.[18]

In the diary of Judge Sewall we find record of a William Lee, born in 1637, who lived ninety-four years and "Had issue from his Loyns in his Life-time two hundred lacking two." This was the record: children, seventeen; grandchildren, seventy-eight; great-grandchildren, one hundred and three. A certain Maria Hazard who lived for a hundred years in Rhode Island had, it is said, five hundred children, grandchildren, great-grandchildren, and great-great-grandchildren. Upon her death, two hundred and five were alive, and a granddaughter of hers had been a grandmother nearly fifteen years.[19]

The American setting as a result of its social and economic influences stimulated desire for large families. Both husbands and wives usually wanted as many children as they could have and defended their policy on both scriptural and patriotic grounds. The motives, however, which led to the high birth rate were pride and the feeling that children were a good investment, an insurance against old age. Schooling as a rule was scanty, a great part of the time of the child being used in labor

[18] Wertenbaker, T. J., *The First Americans*, p. 181.
[19] Lawrence, H. W., *The Not-Quite Puritans*, pp. 82–83.

on the farm or in the house, the sons helping the father and the daughters the mother. It was taken for granted that the chief purposes of women in addition to their religious obligations were to bear children and carry on housekeeping. The burden placed upon women was frequently too great and they died early from excessive childbearing. This domestic tragedy of women dying before they reached middle age after having borne many children was regarded as one of the inscrutable decrees of Providence. Thomas Jefferson's letter to his daughter naturally had behind it an anxiety that proved well founded. The daughter succumbed in her first ordeal of childbirth, as her mother had died shortly after delivering her sixth child during her ten years of marriage.

Divorce.   The American colonies, as is the case at present in our states, differed greatly in their laws concerning divorce. In New England we find the idea of civil marriage in the place of an ecclesiastical marriage, and also divorce by the power of the colony. The Puritans were more influenced by what they considered the spirit of the New Testament than by the English law to which they had been accustomed. They practically did away with the canonical decree of separation "from bed and board" and replaced it with divorce, which was granted for various causes.

In Massachusetts, after 1692, the control of matrimony and divorce was placed in the hands of the governor and his council. Governor Hutchinson, who for many years presided over the divorce court, states in his history of Massachusetts that what would have been considered a just cause for separation in a spiritual court was usually considered sufficient ground for an absolute divorce. Divorce was always granted automatically in the case of female adultery, and after considerable debate on the subject it was decided that in the case of male adultery divorce was not justified.

Connecticut was particularly liberal and modern in its attitude toward divorce; in 1670 this colony permitted remarriage to a woman who had not heard from her husband for eight years or more. Although the wives of New England received greater consideration than those of the other colonies, they were nevertheless discriminated against as compared with men. The trend in this section was to grant divorces most often on the grounds of cruelty, desertion, and failure of the husband to support.

In the middle colonies we find a more conservative policy concerning divorce. New Netherlands had granted few divorces for adultery or separation, but after the colony came under English rule it followed the English tradition, that placed the power to decree separation from bed and board in the ecclesiastical court, which, however, was denied the power of granting absolute divorce. As New York did not provide an ecclesiastical court for the trying of such cases, few separations were ever granted. The same situation existed in Pennsylvania, except that while New York had granted a few special separations by act of the governor, who apparently acted without legal power, in the case of the neighboring colony the legislature acted in two cases to grant absolute divorce.

The southern colonies followed the teaching of the Church of England, but their failure to establish ecclesiastical courts to handle cases asking for separation resulted in there not being any power by which a legalized separation could be brought about. Separations, however, occurred and it was necessary for the courts to handle the question of maintenance. Record is made of such a case in Maryland; and in Virginia the county courts appear to have taken over the power of granting alimony, although they seem to have acted without statutory authority. It is interesting to notice that the English home government did not challenge the New England colonies in their policy of granting divorces, even though this was contrary to the English law.

Family discipline.   The discipline of children was generally severe and the atmosphere of the home, at least in New England, repressive. Reverence for authority and respect for elders were taught children from their first years. There was great confidence in the value of the rod as a means of child training. Fathers exercised their authority with the knowledge that the neighbor's eyes were on them and that any laxity would be frowned upon.

Under the shadow of New England theology childhood appears to us darkened with morbid suggestion. Trivial expressions of immaturity were given serious interpretation. The fear of death was used to force upon the boy or girl obedience and what was interpreted as righteous living. Whether typical or not of the time, the diary of Cotton Mather discloses the harsh outlook upon life to which children of the northern colonies were often introduced.

> I took my little Daughter, Katy into my Study; and there I told my Child, that I am to *dy* shortly, and shee must, when I am *Dead,* Remember every Thing, that I said unto her.
>
> I sett before her, the sinful and woful Condition of her *Nature,* without ceasing, that God for the Sake of Jesus Christ would give her a *New Heart,* and *pardon* Her Sins, and make her a *Servant* of His. . . .[20]

These words were addressed to a child who was between eight and nine years of age. Again, we find the father writing regarding his son, Sammy, who was then between ten and eleven years old.

> I must think of some exquisite and obliging Wayes, to abate *Sammy's* inordinate Love of Play. His play wounds his Faculties. I must engage him in some nobler Entertainments.
>
> What shall be done, for the raising of *Sammy's* Mind, above the debasing Meannesses of Play!
>
> Entertain *Sammy* betimes, with the first Rudiments of Geography and Astronomy, as well as History; and so raise his Mind above the sillier Diversions of Childhood.[21]

As late as the childhood of Henry Ward Beecher we find his father, one of the best-known clergymen of the period, inflicting upon his children a moral discipline nearly as harsh and morbid as that of the earlier period. It is possible, however, to exaggerate the burdens of the colonial child. There were undoubtedly parents who were sympathetic and affectionate, nor must it be forgotten that rigorous times tend to make stern parents.

Home life in the colonial period.   With the settlement of America, European culture was introduced into a new environment. This culture of the Old World was no sooner injected into the new surroundings than it began to be changed by the effort of the colonists to adapt themselves better to their actual condi-

---

[20] Hanscom, E. D., *The Heart of the Puritan,* pp. 86–87.
[21] *Ibid.,* p. 90.

tions of living. It was, of course, the European family that was transported to the western shores, particularly the traditional family of England. In the development of the thirteen colonies, in spite of a considerable proportion of non-English people in the population, made up of Dutch, Swedes, and Germans, the culture of the Old World which influenced the inhabitants of the territory that was to become the United States was, in both its legal and social expressions, more and more predominantly English.[22]

The colonial family, therefore, attempted to set itself in the English form. The experiences of the Virginia plantation had early taught those interested in the settlement of the New World that the colonists could not become prosperous or stable unless some provision was made for the furnishing of wives to the single men who had migrated across the water. With the establishment of permanent homes, there began at once an evolution of American family life which disclosed the influences of the new physical, economic, religious, and political conditions.

England in the seventeenth century was not without its class distinctions and religious parties. These differences were brought to the new continent by the original settlers and at once showed themselves in social customs and family life. The environmental differences of the thirteen colonies, especially as shown in their various kinds of economic activity, also made uniformity of family life from New Hampshire to Georgia impossible. In sketching the general characteristics of family life in the New World, one must not forget that the complete picture will contain religious, class, and sectional variations.

The frontier character of the early settlements led, as one would suppose, to a closeness of family ties. The family of the pioneer had to be self-reliant, depending largely upon itself for existence. Food, clothing, education, religion, recreation, and even medical care had to be provided by the family working as a unit, that its existence under hard circumstances might be maintained. The severity of life in the wilderness and scattered communities reinforced the natural sympathy of the family and encouraged its harmonious working. It is not surprising that under such circumstances family interests were intensified to such an extent as to produce the clannish spirit which still shows

---

[22] Harlow, R. V., *Growth of the United States,* p. 70.

itself in rural New England and the pride of family which became characteristic of southern aristocracy.

There was hard work for all the members of the family, including the children old enough to contribute their labor, but the woman was given the heaviest load, since she had not only to be housewife but mother as well. Even though she took her hard lot as a matter of course, she aged prematurely, just as does the woman of the pioneering family among the mountain whites of our own times.

In any description of home life in the colonial period, the difference between conditions in the North and in the South must be recognized. Throughout the entire thirteen colonies the influence of the frontier appears, and the difference between physical conditions of the North and the South influenced the development of the family. It is easier to describe the family life of the northern section because it tends toward greater uniformity. There we find the rural family farming an estate relatively small compared to the plantations of the South. The village center furnishes artisans of specialized skills, even though on every farm the need of developing mechanical ability was taken as a matter of course. In the South the cultivation of tobacco, the main commercial crop, tended toward the plantation system of farming. The estates were large and there was greater need of developing in connection with the main industry the various skills that would permit the plantation to be largely self-sustaining. Since George Washington at Mount Vernon managed one of the largest of southern plantations, the units that he developed may be taken as an example. Under his control we find a smithy, charcoal burners, brickmakers, carpenters, masons, shoemakers, a flour mill, and even a sailing vessel to carry his products to market. A visit to Mount Vernon or Monticello convinces one that Washington and Jefferson were proprietors of community enterprises rather than farmers in the New England sense.

Even in the North, family life was not absolutely uniform, for the merchants and professional people in the towns could not follow the routine commonly found among the farming class. It is from the latter that we draw our picture of New England home life. The household arose early. The farmer, who was likely first to be up, started in a great fireplace by a flint and

steel the fire necessary for the cooking of breakfast. While his
wife and daughter prepared breakfast, he and his sons were feeding the stock. When these chores were done, the family gathered
around the fireplace for morning prayer. Then came a simple
breakfast, probably of mush or of bread and milk. The simple
meal finished, the men folks, including hired men on the large
farms, went their way to out-of-door labor, to plant, hoe, mow
the grass or hay, cut wood for fuel or lumber, build stone walls,
or carry on some other toil, according to the season.

While the men were at their work the women were equally
busy at various household activities. This usually followed a
weekly schedule and included more than cooking and caring for
the house, since upon the women fell the responsibility for the
carding, the weaving, the dyeing, the soapmaking, the salting of
fish, pickling and jellymaking, and a host of other occupations
that are not now normally performed by the American housewife. Dinner was a heavier meal than breakfast and supper. It
was followed by a program of work similar to that of the morning. Before supper the men drove the stock to the barn where
the cows were milked. Then the animals were fed, and man's
work for the day was done. Supper followed, and again there
were prayers, followed by a brief sitting around the fireplace,
and possibly reading by the light of a pine knot or tallow candle.
At eight o'clock it was time to go to bed that the household
might be ready to start early the work of the next day.

The picture of home life that has come to seem typical of
the South is that characteristic of the large plantation. Time has
given this a romance that leads us to forget that the description
does not at all fit the life of a large proportion of the families
living in the southern colonies. In 1701 in Virginia, we are told,
the average family unit on the plantation consisted of eleven
members. This was not much larger than the average family unit
elsewhere.[23] The ties between the southern aristocrat and the
mother country were stronger than those between men of wealth
and prominence in the North and the old country. The southern
planter sold his crop in England and bought there much of his
supplies. To England his sons went for their higher education,
particularly in the earlier half of colonial history. One of the
consequences of this close relationship with the motherland was

---

[23] Wertenbaker, T. J., *op. cit.*, p. 31.

the perpetuation of the ideal of the English country squire by the planters who attempted to imitate in America the rural aristocracy of England. Their copy, because of frontier conditions, could not be complete.

The institution of slavery also added a new element, as did the need of making the plantation mechanically and vocationally as self-supporting as possible. By comparison with usual American conditions, the owners of the larger plantations approached a life of luxury, but it was not one of leisure or freedom. Upon the planter and his wife fell a large burden of managerial responsibility. To raise and sell the tobacco, oversee the slaves and indentured servants, and maintain the hospitality that went with his position, day by day, was a task that required close application as well as judgment. Jefferson and others gave testimony that any prolonged absence, even when the planter had expert subordinates, meant risk of financial losses and of running into debt. Often under economic stress the planter had to sell part of his estate in order to meet his obligations. On the well-managed plantation the planter's wife also had managerial responsibility that made her burden, although different, no lighter than that of the farmer's wife in the North. Life on the larger plantations tended from the beginning toward the "big house" which we now associate with southern life in ante-bellum days. Nothing impresses on us the amount of business associated with the large plantation more than the cataloging of food required during a year for the maintenance of one of these big houses. This is the estimate: "twenty beeves, twenty-seven thousand pounds of pork, five hundred bushels of wheat and unmeasured corn, along with four hogsheads of rum and three barrels of whiskey, not to reckon the Madeira. For the twenty-eight fireplaces a cart with six oxen hauling four loads a day no more than sufficed for winter needs." [24]

The western frontier. The basic influences that have shaped family life in the United States have come from the physical environment of America, the political evolution of the nation, the development of industry and modern science, immigration and, most recently, the rapid growth of cities. Among these, the frontier conditions have from the first been largely

---

[24] Odum, H. W., *An American Epoch,* p. 35. Quoted by permission of the author.

responsible for what is distinctive in the American family situation.

The modern American family represents no synthesis compounded of various European traditions. It is a product that chiefly came from the experiences of the men and women who pushed into the frontier, settling and ruralizing it while they struggled to triumph over a wilderness as formidable as ever challenged any civilization and to dislodge the Indians, the most cruel and resourceful natives ever encountered by peoples of European origin. As the American population from the original settlements pressed over the Appalachian Mountains and scattered through the great stretches of wilderness, the frontier life of the early colonial period was continued, but with definite social modifications. Just as the English people who planted themselves along the Atlantic seaboard were gradually forced by their distance from the homeland and the changes in their environment to construct a new culture which, although English in its basic elements, was largely different, so also the American migrants from the South, New York, and New England in like manner were led by the necessity of adapting themselves to new conditions into the building of a social life distinctly their own.[25]

By 1730 the Presbyterian Irish were coming to America in large numbers. They landed chiefly at Charleston and Philadelphia but did not tarry in the seaboard cities. They went into the unsettled foothills and valleys along the mountains, coming for the most part from western Pennsylvania into Virginia and the Carolinas. They broke at once their European ties and developed scant relationship with the tidewater peoples. They amalgamated with like-minded migrants who had moved out from the seaboard settlements into the western wilderness. In a generation these, with others straight from Europe, principally Germans and French Huguenots, became, in spite of their differing European and racial origins, one people in sentiment, interests, and traits, with little in their character to suggest their motherlands, for which they had neither sympathy nor concern. They were the first of those frontiersmen who, in building a distinctive American culture, gave form to our characteristic family life.

---

[25] Turner, F. J., *The Frontier in American History*, Ch. 13.

The frontier was a continuing influence until its disappearance, when finally the entire territory between the Atlantic and the Pacific became settled and easy access to the land came to an end. This western expansion has been divided into three periods, which may be roughly described as the occupation of the territory up to the Appalachian Mountains, then in the Middle West as far as the west bank of the Missouri River, and lastly to the Pacific Coast. Although in each of these periods of settlement frontier conditions prevailed that affected the social life of the nation, they were not duplications. There were differences in the physical environment, including climate, soil, rainfall, topography, and the like. The differences in time and the changing political and cultural conditions in the well-settled part of the nation were also reflected in frontier experience, thus conditioning the meaning this had at different periods of our national growth. For example, improved transportation greatly affected the second, and especially the third, frontier when they were opened up to settlement by the coming of the transcontinental railways.

In spite of these differences there were general trends common to all three frontiers: an aggressive individualism, desire for independence, emphasis upon physical and moral qualities, disregard of family background, and educational and even financial status. No term has better revealed the quality of frontier civilization in the United States than that of "rugged individualism." There was also throughout the west a trend toward equalitarianism, and this was especially emphasized in the attitude taken toward women. Not only was there among western people an aloofness from European culture, expressed in either indifference or hostility, but frequently a similar feeling toward the ideas and attitudes of the older, well-settled portion of the country.

The first settlers of the Western frontier were mostly from the South. Shortly an ever increasing number from New England, New York, and the Middle States poured into the new territory. Later, Germans, Irish Catholics, and Scandinavians appeared, and each of these groups of settlers added something to the social life of the towns and cities of the rapidly developing West.

The family life and the frontier.   The family life that formed under frontier circumstances was of necessity a product of this mingling of people trained previously in such widely differing cultures and of the influences that came out of the environment itself. While the New England habits and traditions largely prevailed, the family life was less stern, in part as a result of the contacts of Yankee parents with the more indulgent southern and European fathers and mothers. The patriarchal home of the early New England theology was also out of season, for, with the passing of the years, this paternal authority had softened even in its place of origin in this country. The western people, freer of ancient traditions and readier in adaptation, moved more rapidly toward establishing a happier childhood and a greater equality of the sexes.

It was the more prolific families of the East that went into the frontier. It has been estimated that the population of Kentucky doubled every fifteen years from natural increase, but this is probably an exaggeration.[26] The conditions of the West also encouraged parents to have many children, for, as always when new and cheap lands are being brought under cultivation, a large family was an economic advantage.

Whatever the motives that led the individual family to trek to the wilderness, confidence in the future and a willingness to break from the past were always prominent. The pioneers held firmly to the idea of equality, because in practice they recognized no distinctions other than those that came from industry and personal character. In such an atmosphere the doctrine of woman's subordination was difficult to maintain, particularly in communities where there were more men than women. Never was there a clearer illustration of the social working of the law of supply and demand than in the results of the relative scarcity of women on the American frontier. The isolation which led to a concentration of family interests and strengthened domestic ties also tended to elevate the status of women, while distance from the older region weakened the traditions of European origin that had been established in the first settlements along the seaboard.

Although manners were rough and conversation among the males often coarse, the prevailing domestic ethics were on a high level. During the first two periods of this frontier movement

---

[26] Roosevelt, T., *Winning of the West*, Vol. 1, p. 308.

divorce was rare and vice uncommon. In the third period, especially where there were few women, there were communities where life was wild, and gambling, drinking, and prostitution flourished. In the less settled parts everyone was well known to his neighbors, and, as a consequence, there was a keen sense of the force of public opinion. Girls were given a large measure of social freedom in the belief, which was largely justified, that they were fully capable of taking care of themselves. The self-reliance of the modern American girl, which is everywhere recognized as a characteristic product of our culture, developed especially from the freedom of the girl on the western frontier.

It was to be expected that the coeducational college should start and thrive in the West. Its origin was not merely the economical desire to escape duplication of equipment. It was the natural issue of the free contacts of boys and girls from early childhood on through their schooling. When higher education was provided, it was the logical step and in accord with the attitude of public opinion that both men and women were given entrance into the new institutions, and thus continued their study in the advanced subjects in an association to which they had long been accustomed. Indiana, in its constitution of 1816, expressed the democratic trend of the West when it accepted as a matter of course the idea of equal educational opportunities for both sexes in its provision for a "general system of education ascending in regular gradations from township schools to a State University, wherein tuition shall be gratis and equally open to all." [27]

---

[27] Turner, F. J., *op. cit.*, p. 282.

Chapter 7

THE MODERN AMERICAN FAMILY

FOREWORD. This chapter continues the discussion of the influences that shaped the American family. It does not attempt to summarize the history from the colonial settlements to the present but rather to select from this period those features which appeared during this development which were of special concern to the family. It must be remembered that during most of this time the frontier influences previously discussed continued to affect American life and to bring out its distinguishing traits. It would, however, be an exaggeration to charge to this source all that is characteristic of American culture, especially as expressed in domestic experience. The other basic contributions are the slave system; the Civil War; World Wars I and II; the development of modern industry; urbanization; immigration; progress of science; and the advancement of the status of women, including woman suffrage and the changes that increased woman's vocational and professional opportunities, bringing her closer to equality with men.

Manners and social standards. Manners and social standards were a continuing influence on domestic relations. Nevertheless, any generalization is difficult, even more so than is generally true in a long settled, homogenous population. Social life was fluid, and into it were constantly introduced by immigrants from many European countries folkways and mores developed in their former backgrounds. There were also great variations among the natives according to class, section, religious training, and vocational or educational opportunities. In spite of this great diversity in manners and standards, constantly changing, there was on the part of European travelers who wrote books based on their visits to America no hesitation in describing and criticizing the characteristics of the people of the United States. These visitors, who usually made their coming profitable, differed in the details of their indictment of American manners and standards but agreed in affirming that they were low. First of these major critics was William Cobbett, who later became one of the greatest of England's agitators. He made two visits to the United States and both of them for a longer period than was true of most of the writers. At the end of his first sojourn in 1800, he departed cursing the corruption of most Americans and the tyranny of their institutions. Seventeen years later, after a trying period in England, his reaction to American conditions was more favorable. Perhaps none of the critics except Charles Dickens wrote up America more impressively than Harriet Martineau, who made her visit in 1836. She was particularly severe in condemning the conventional boardinghouses which were so common throughout the country and much of the life she saw in the southern states which of course she looked at through the eyes of an ardent abolitionist.[1] Captain Marryat, who came shortly after Harriet Martineau, also found much to condemn in American social life.[2] Frances M. Trollope, who lived temporarily in America between 1827 and 1831, wrote her impressions during this period in two volumes entitled *Domestic Manners of the Americans* and revealed an underlying hostility to our democratic traits which led her to a biased and exaggerated impeachment of American habits and standards. She can perhaps be dismissed because, as has been said, she came seeking a fortune and failed in getting it.[3]

Of all these foreign critics the one that created the most feeling among Americans was Charles Dickens. He was genuinely sympathetic toward much that he saw in the United States. He was, for example, especially enthusiastic about the conditions that he found in the Lowell mills[4] and the attempts that were made by the factory owners to safeguard women workers. Nevertheless, his popularity as a novelist among the Americans appeared to increase their resentment when he criticized those aspects of American life which he did disapprove, especially his

---

[1] Martineau, Harriet, *Society in America*.

[2] Marryat, Frederick, *A Diary in America*.

[3] Courtney, Janet E., *The Adventurous Thirties*, p. 128.

[4] Dickens, Charles, *American Notes*.

treatment of Americans in his novel *Martin Chuzzlewit*. This, of course, was a caricature of American manners and customs. The same assertion could be made of his novels dealing with English life, but for some reason his readers on this side were not prepared to accept a similar interpretation of their ways of life, thus reacting oppositely to the English who took in good part his ridicule of their faulty customs and even his attack on their social evils. Among the American travelers one of the most discerning was Frederick Olmsted, who just before the breakout of the Civil War went through the South attempting to portray its social conditions.[5] Although he made a sincere effort to paint southern life realistically, there was much of it that escaped him.[6] James S. Buckingham, an English visitor, had previously tried to describe this southern section and achieved considerable objective insight. He wrote:

> Here, too, as elsewhere, there is a great difference between the condition of the field slaves on the plantations and the domestic slaves about the houses of respectable families. These last are as well fed and as well clad as the free domestic servants of many countries of Europe, though far inferior to those of England; . . . In the domestic service of most private establishments here, there are often more slaves than are necessary for the labour required of them, many being kept for state, or ostentation; and as the coachman, footman, lady's maid, butler, cook, and other household servants are continually passing before the eyes of the master and mistress, as well as their visitors and guests, they are almost sure of being well clad and kindly treated, because the sight of dirty and miserable-looking attendants would be painful to those by whom they are surrounded, as well as to themselves.[7]

The following were common indictments of American customs and standards: the almost universal chewing of tobacco and spitting of the men; bad eating habits, especially the overuse of the knife; poor cooking and faulty diet; the common complaint of indigestion, apparently due in part to the rapid way people ate; the overdressing of the upper middle and wealthy class in the cities, particularly women; the sensationalism of the

---

[5] Olmsted, Frederick L., *A Journey in the Back Country* and *Journey and Exploration in the Cotton Kingdom*.

[6] Odum, Howard W., *An American Epoch*, p. 36.

[7] Buckingham, J. S., *The Slave States in America*, Vol. 1, pp. 199–200.

American newspapers; the slums of the great cities; and the low standards of taste in music and literature.

After the Civil War, criticism of American social evils came chiefly from native writers and speakers. The war brought inflation, encouraged speculation, and became a source of much graft and corruption. During the next two decades the deterioration of both public and private morals was so apparent that it forced the attention of thoughtful people. In the large cities political bosses developed, typified by Boss Tweed in New York, who brought political life to a new level of disrepute. Men in public office frequently grew wealthy rapidly, and money was freely used to decide elections. Corporations were able to get charters by buying off legislators, public funds were squandered, and even the Federal government became tainted. The most scandalous occurrence in Congress was the Credit Mobilier, the sale of railroad stock to members of both Houses of Congress for far less than their actual value. The standards of public service were so low that some of these congressmen, who had practically been given bribes in return for their influence, were unable to recognize that they had done anything blameworthy.[8]

The police systems in the large cities were corrupted. Gambling and prostitution were permitted to flourish provided they paid a part of their income to the police. This graft money was apportioned according to rank so that the high administrators soon became wealthy. Although prostitution prevailed in all the larger cities, New York, Chicago, and San Francisco were especially notorious for the grafting by the police and the open way that prostitution advertised its presence. During the first World's Fair at Chicago, thousands of prostitutes gathered, and they rivaled the fair itself as a sensational attraction for men.[9] The situation in Chicago became so bad that finally leading reformers, including Dean Sumner, an Episcopalian clergyman, and Jane Addams, of Hull House, brought about the organization of a commission that studied the vice situation. Their report, made in 1911, which was a factual statement based on carefully gathered data, made a tremendous impression. The details of this report were such that the United States post office department refused to allow it to go through the mail. From that time, al-

---

[8] Nevins, Allan, *The Emergence of Modern America*, p. 190.
[9] Washburn, Charles, *Come into My Parlor*.

though there was ebb and flow in the strength of the political reform movement, conditions in most of the cities improved. They reached a low level again with the coming of prohibition.

Slavery and family life. In the colonial period we find slaves both North and South. The plantation system, and in particular the development of cotton growing as the major agricultural interest in the South, led to the prolongation and extension of the slave system of production in the section below the Mason and Dixon line. Once firmly established upon a slave basis, the southern people found it difficult to discover the archaic and uneconomic character of slavery, especially after emotions were stirred by the bitter attacks of northern reformers.

As slavery colored all the social life of the South, so it stamped its influence upon the family. The Negroes on the whole had a meager and uncertain home life. Their domestic situation was largely dependent on the attitude of the owner. At best it was precarious; at its worst it revealed the most serious moral hazards of slavery.

White children on the plantations were not and could not be segregated from the Negroes. Negro servants often cared for their master's children practically from birth. The black and white children came in contact constantly; not infrequently they played together. When cruelty was practised against the blacks, white children were coarsened and hurt. Because of their superstitious and vicious topics, Negro conversations were frequently harmful in the young life of listening children. Slavery of necessity perpetuated among the Negroes the social standards of an illiterate and irresponsible people. White children could not be entirely protected from the influences of a social environment made up in part of elements contributed by the Negro slaves.

Without exaggeration of the worst results of slavery as they appeared in miscegenation and remembering the sympathy and affection which so often existed between the owner's family and the slaves, the strength of which was given vivid demonstration by the loyalty of slaves to their masters during the testing of the Civil War, it is nevertheless clear that slavery as a system struck at the roots of wholesome family life for the whites as well as the blacks. Family life tended to keep to a social level in accord with the attempt to continue a system which was becoming more and more an anachronism. The passing of slavery relieved the southern family of burden in the same way that the wage system of industry has stimulated the prosperity of the southern states.

The ending of the slave system, in spite of the violence with which this was brought about, proved a relief to the white women of the South, upon whom fell so heavily the responsibilities of the plantation. Some have testified that the burden was getting too great to be carried. It represented something very far from a life of leisure and luxury. How exacting was the routine of these women appears in the description of the daily tasks of the wife of General Leonidas Polk.[10]

It is a pity, however, that American statesmanship was unequal to the task of transmuting the slave system into that of free labor without the social costs of the Civil War. The war between the states struck the southern home immediately a crushing blow, and the suffering that followed delayed the commercial and cultural contributions that the South is now giving in fuller measure to our national life.

The Civil War and family life.   The Civil War affected the northern family also. The conflict was of course temporarily a great impetus to business, especially manufacturing. The number of producers being restricted, those who remained at home had plenty of employment, and the mills multiplied, even though often working day and night. As men went out of industry, women were drawn in. In the West, women, as in the World Wars, engaged in various forms of agriculture; in the East they were drained from rural sections into the towns and cities to carry on in mills work formerly given to men.

Many women had their horizons widened by the new occupations and opportunities that came to them through the war. Some acted as nurses and, through their service, exchanged their former environment for the more exciting contacts at Washington or some base hospital. Some entered government work as clerks at Washington. Others carried on activities that previously had been considered exclusively man's.

Women were taught by their humanitarian and patriotic enterprises to co-operate in various kinds of public activity. It was inevitable that these experiences should strengthen the demands of women for a greater share of self-expression and more

---

[10] Polk, W. M., *Life of Leonidas Polk*, Vol. 1, pp. 200–202.

social independence. Their growing sense of power was reflected in a less docile acceptance of the inferiority which men had come to consider one of the unchanging fundamentals of society. Agitation for social equality was stimulated.

The war with its great loss of life, North and South, accelerated the immigration of Europeans, who replaced the wastage of native stock and flooded industry with the cheap labor necessary for the rapid development of manufacturing. Cities became more magnetic and drew an ever increasing multitude from rural sections. Congestion of population arose in the Northern cities, creating slums as menacing to social welfare as those of the Old World.

The moral strain of the war showed itself in various experiences of corruption in the government that were revealed in the years following the war.[11] During the period of slavery there was little venereal disease among American Negroes. Their exposure to syphilis and gonorrhea during the war led to a wide distribution of both diseases. It is estimated that there is ten times as much syphilis among Negroes in this country as among whites.[12] The rapid growth of cities, with the segregation of different nationalities in colonies that kept a considerable amount of their Old World customs, made possible the political machine and boss, and the low level of political life percolated back into the homes.

Many of the soldiers who had enlisted from rural communities when very young came into contact with vices of which they had previously known nothing. In the decades following the war, as just suggested, commercial prostitution appeared in the cities in the proportions of a serious social evil, corrupting the police and becoming a most profitable source of graft. Although bound to grow with the rapid development of cities, particularly where immigration crowded into the Atlantic seaboard cities, prostitution without question got a firmer foothold because of the influence of war conditions.

Modern industry and the American family. The Industrial Revolution, which changed manufacturing from a household factory system, developed more slowly in the United States than in England, in part because England attempted to keep

---

[11] Harlow, R. V., *Growth of the United States*, p. 556.
[12] U. S. Public Health Service Selective Surveys.

secret its inventions and to prevent its machinery from being exported to the New World, and in part because the old country with its more thickly settled territory was riper for the change.

Factories did, however, develop in the northern states, although delayed by English policy and by the rural character of the population. With the coming of the factories a new field of employment was offered women, since men continued in agriculture and trade, both of which seemed more profitable. The mills depended largely upon women from rural communities, and about 1830 we find the beginning of the movement of workers toward the mill towns.[13] These women who came to Lawrence, Lowell, New Bedford, and other manufacturing places were mostly from the country; they entered the mills without loss of caste since millwork at that time had the same dignity for women that farming had for their fathers and brothers. The situation changed later when the mills were filled with foreigners as a result of the influx of immigrants from Europe.

The women were young and were rarely married. Sometimes married women worked for a time to help their husbands pay for a home. Widows also found in the manufacturing towns opportunities to earn a living by keeping boarders. Dickens, a keen observer who visited Lowell, gives this testimony in his American Notes in 1842 regarding the condition of the young women workers:

These girls were all well dressed; and that phrase necessarily includes extreme cleanliness. They had serviceable bonnets, good warm cloaks and shawls; and were not above clogs and pattens. Moreover, there were places in the mill in which they could deposit these things without injury; and there were conveniences for washing. They were healthy in appearance, many of them remarkably so, and had the manners and deportment of young women: not of degraded brutes of burden. . . .

The rooms in which they worked were as well ordered as themselves. In the windows of some, there were green plants, which were trained to shade the glass; in all there was as much fresh air, cleanliness, and comfort as the nature of the occupation would possibly admit of. . . .

They reside in various boarding-houses near at hand. The owners of the mills are particularly careful to allow no persons to enter

---

[13] "Population Growth in Southern New England," *American Statistical Association Publications*, Vol. 15, p. 813.

upon the possession of these houses, whose characters have not undergone the most searching and thorough inquiry. Any complaint that is made against them, by the boarders, or by any one else, is fully investigated; and if good ground of complaint be shown to exist against them, they are removed, and their occupation is handed over to some more deserving person. . . . There is a joint-stock piano in a great many of the boarding-houses. Nearly all these young ladies subscribe to circulating libraries. They have got up among themselves a periodical called *The Lowell Offering,* "A repository of original articles, written exclusively by females actively employed in the mills,"—which is duly printed, published, and sold; and whereof I brought away from Lowell four hundred good solid pages, which I have read from beginning to end. . . . Of the merits of *The Lowell Offering* as a literary production, I will only observe, putting entirely out of sight the fact of the articles having been written by these girls after the arduous labours of the day, that it will compare advantageously with a great many English Annuals.

The new immigration. After the Civil War the flow of immigration from Europe increased greatly. There were many reasons for this. Trouble in Ireland between the people there and the English government increased the number of Irish coming to America. The Austro-Prussian conflict affected Germans and Austrians in the same manner. The effort of steamship companies to entice Europeans to leave for the United States because of the great profit made in transporting them was no small influence. This and the need of cheap labor through the rapid expansion of industry led to many immigrants entering the country from Italy, the Balkan states, Poland, and Russia. Not only were many of these people from eastern and southeastern Europe less familiar with the democratic tendencies of American life than those who had been coming from Scandinavia, Ireland, and England, but like the Irish they settled chiefly in the large cities and tended to cluster together. Soon there were great alien groups in our chief cities attempting to maintain as far as possible old country habits and ways of life while at the same time seeking the economic advantages of American commerce and industry which had been their motive for coming to this country. Frequently they were disillusioned. They constituted an important part of the voting support of the city bosses.[14]

---

[14] Wendt, Lloyd, and Kogan, Herman, *Lords of the Levee.*

The rapid urbanization of the country was in itself a great social problem and of great significance in its effects on the domestic life of the American people, and its evils also were increased by the establishment of European groups in our chief cities who unlike the earlier immigrants did not lose themselves by mixing with the natives but to a great extent maintained an alien cultural existence. Public education was expected to Americanize their children and in large measure succeeded. The influx, however, was too great for the assimilation processes to achieve the success attained before the Civil War. Increasing efforts to restrict European immigration by legislation did not accomplish much until a bill limiting entrance to this country on a quota basis became a law in 1921. The restrictions were still further strengthened in 1924, and in 1927 immigration was limited to 150,000 a year; the quota was based upon national origins, favoring immigration from Great Britain. However, preceeding this there were several enactments by Congress that attempted to improve the quality of the immigration coming to the United States.

Child labor. Children were employed in the mills from their first establishment. This was not strange, for child labor was in accord with the Puritan's notion of childhood and his attitude toward play. The child was safe if at work. Idleness—and play was not uncommonly interpreted as idleness—was the Devil's opportunity.

It was, of course, nothing new for children to work. They had long been accustomed to working with their parents either on the farm or in the household industries. The factory merely provided a different kind of work. There was no realization on the part of many that machine industry necessarily meant overstrain for the child and that an industry that was run for profits had no interest in the child's welfare. Factory labor was nothing like the tasks of the home as a training experience for life; the factory owner was, even when humane in his purposes, unable to give his child workers the safeguards furnished by parents of normal affection.

Samuel Slater, who started the first cotton mill in Rhode Island, followed the English custom of employing entire families, though it is stated that during 1790 and 1791 his operatives were almost exclusively children of seven to twelve years of age.[15] The Committee on Manufactures in 1816 estimated that there were 24,000 boys under seventeen and 66,000 women and girls in the total number of 100,000 workers in cotton mills.

The first attack on child factory labor came from the governor of Rhode Island in 1818. Massachusetts in 1825 ordered an investigation of child labor in "incorporated manufacturing companies." It was stated after an investigation that the boys and girls in the mills worked twelve or thirteen hours a day. Beginning with Connecticut and Massachusetts in 1842, several states passed laws attempting to regulate the hours of child labor in the factories. None of these laws provided adequate means of enforcement, and as a result they did little more than record a growing sentiment against the exploitation of child life by modern industry. Laws regarding school attendance were more effectual, and in this movement Massachusetts led with a law passed in 1836, which provided that children under fifteen years of age must attend school three months out of twelve. The report of the Massachusetts Labor Commission in 1866 proves that this law was not well enforced. From a Woonsocket manufacturer comes this statement regarding the working hours of children:

From eight years old and upwards, they work full time—rise at four and a half A.M., having thirty minutes for breakfast, forty-five minutes for dinner, and leave work at seven P.M., fourteen and a half hours. . . . Manufacturers in Massachusetts and in Rhode Island pay little regard to the law respecting the employment of children.[16]

The following testimony was given by one who knew conditions in Fall River:

Question.—Was there any one who ever tried to cause the children to be sent to school?
Answer.—Not since old man Robeson died.
Q.—Why do not the parents send them to school?
A.—Small help is scarce; a great deal of the machinery has been stopped for want of small help, so the overseers have been going

---

[15] Cheney, W. L., *Industry and Human Welfare*, p. 51.
[16] *Ibid.*, p. 54.

around to draw the small children from the schools into the mills;
the same as a draft in the army.[17]

A laborer from the same city testified that children as young
as seven were employed in the mills. He had his own children
work because their earnings were necessary for the maintenance
of the family. His attitude toward child labor was expressed with
pathetic simplicity:

I don't know that I have any more to say, except that I have
two little boys, one eleven and the other about eight and a half. I
am no scholar myself because I have always been working in the
mill, and I am sorry for it. I don't want my children to be brought
up the same way. I wish to get them to work a little less hours so
that I can send them to night school. I want, if it is possible, to get
a law so that they can go to school and know how to read and write
their own names.[18]

Growth of cities.   A marked feature of great significance
to the family was the shift in this country during the nineteenth
and the present century from the once distinctly rural culture
to one predominantly urban. This trend toward urbanization
which still continues was the result of the decrease of farming as
a means of livelihood and its replacement by industry. Factories
developed in or about cities. The commercial organizations that
naturally concentrated in urban centers grew in power. The
personal relations of the open country and villages disappeared
since the conditions of city life destroyed the basis for the intimacies and interests characteristic of neighborhood contacts.
In 1790 in the United States 5.1 per cent of the people lived in
cities of 2500 and over; in 1940 city dwellers constituted 56.5 per
cent of the population.[19] The increase in the size of cities is even
more impressive. New York in 1790 was the largest city, with
nearly 50,000 people; in 1940 it had grown to 7,454,995. In that
year there were 199 cities that had 50,000 or more population.
This shift was more than the mere moving of people from
the country and village to the cities. It was equally a change in

---

[17] *Ibid.*, p. 55.
[18] *Ibid.*
[19] Sixteenth Census of the United States; *Population: Characteristics of the Population,* Vol. 2, Pt. 1, p. 18.

manner of life, interests, and outlook. These social and psychic differences between rural and urban people were increased because there were also corporations, labor unions, and various types of political and social organizations that acted as centers of education, propaganda, political pressure, and reform. These were dominated by urban leadership. City life tended to intensify economic struggle, class, and race differences and to take away from a large portion of the population, commonly designated as the masses, the feeling of security. As a consequence, the individualism which has been so characteristic of American rural life lessened, and in its place there grew the disposition to seek through government activities—city, state, and nation—protection from competition and a means of security. This trend appeared less in the family than in industry, but the family as well as the individual revealed the change. In the cities developed also centers of culture, education, and recreation that could not be maintained in small communities. These became a magnet, drawing from the country and village those who had talent and ambition that could not find expression except where these advantages of urban culture flourished. However, much as these people preferred nonurban ways of life, they were forced to live in or near cities and to use their abilities to increase urban prestige. In chapter eleven the effect of this urban dominance on family life will be discussed in greater detail.

Unorthodox family life. Of the various peculiar types of family life that developed in the United States, that of the Mormons is by far the most important. The doctrine of plural marriages based upon a literal interpretation of Old Testament practices was not at first a part of the theology of the new church but appeared early. It was without question due to their teaching of polygyny that the Mormons were treated with such hostility when as a rule all sorts of religious sects and doctrines were received with characteristic tolerance by the orthodox Americans. To the Mormons, in spite of early opposition on the part of some of the leaders, polygyny came to be the normal family form built upon a divine sanction. Marriage was for eternity, if accompanied by the ecclesiastical ceremony of "sealing," and was a necessary preparation for heavenly bliss. A man could be sealed to any number of women but a woman to only one man. Polygyny made possible the giving of earthly bodies to a multitude of spirits which had long waited opportunity for incarnation.

It has been pointed out that the system of celestial marriage offered the basis for security for women who from a monogamous background attempted to adjust to the system of plural marriage.[20] The wife by becoming a member of a large family was assured in her future life a larger measure of post-mortem glory because of the large number of her husband's descendents. This religious support of polygamous marriage undoubtedly helped many of these women, proselytes from a monogamous social and religious code, to adjust to the new situation. There were other influences both from within and without the family that also helped to give these women a feeling of assurance as they carried on as members of a different kind of home. It would be a mistake, however, to assume that this transition from one to another type of family was always difficult because of the previous bringing up and experience in the monogamous environment. The experience of women in the Oneida Community as well as that of the Mormons reveals, as does the matrimonial career of some modern women, that there are among females as well as males those who if left to their own inclinations would prefer plural marriage experience rather than the code that western culture has made conventional.

Eastern agitation against Mormon polygyny was carried on with a zeal only less than that which had marked the attack on southern slavery. The orthodox churches were determined to destroy the western monster that disgraced the land, and when missionary enterprise proved futile they demanded laws forbidding polygyny. Laws were easy to pass in Washington but difficult to enforce in Utah. The eastern reformers forgot that the Mormon family life, although built upon a polygynous basis, had the same tenacious sentiments that always gather about the home and make regulation of the family difficult to legislate with success.

The Mormon experiment in family organization was made possible by abnormal conditions of temporary character. The members of the Church of the Latter Day Saints, held together by strong religious faith and constant persecutions in Ohio,

---

[20] Hulett, J. E., Jr., "Social Role and Personal Security in Mormon Polygamy," *The American Journal of Sociology*, Vol. 45, p. 543.

Illinois, and Missouri, took refuge in the Utah wilderness. The leaders felt that their safety depended upon increasing their numbers as rapidly as possible. Since they believed that man had no holier mission than to multiply and replenish the earth, the notion of plural marriages was in accord with both their theology and their purposes. There was also another problem, rarely found in a frontier settlement. They had made more converts among women than among men and as a consequence in Utah the females outnumbered the males.

The agitation against plural marriages came from the east and chiefly from the women. Among the Mormon women themselves we find little evidence of discontent. Some even wanted their husbands to add other wives to the household, while some acquiesced in what they did not really desire. Whatever the feeling of the woman, she accepted what had come to be an accepted teaching of the Church. As a matter of fact, the importance of plural marriages among the Mormons has been greatly exaggerated. Apparently at no time were more than 4 per cent of all the families of Utah practicing polygynists.[21] Moreover, it was not a matter that could be decided by the husband himself. The Church leaders authorized in each instance the taking of an additional wife. There were men who repeatedly asked for permission and who were denied the right to have more than one wife. On the other hand, there were men who did not desire to change from monogamy but were forced to do so by command of the Church officials. Undoubtedly eugenic considerations as well as economic influenced the Church leaders in their decision. In addition to the principle of polygyny, other teachings of the Old Testament having to do with sex taboo were practiced by the Mormons, and a consequence of this was the strengthening of motives that led to plural marriages.

When the repressive legislation passed by Congress in the effort to destroy polygyny in Utah was upheld by the United States Supreme Court, it became evident to the Church leaders that it was best to abandon what had always been a minority practice. Once the Church announced its change of policy, an

---

[21] President Joseph F. Smith, in the *Desert News* of March 5, 1904, quotes figures to show that the polygynous marriage never exceeded 3 per cent. Mr. Lofter Bjarnason, of Salt Lake City, assures me that 4 per cent is a conservative estimation.

era of good feeling followed, and soon the territory was admitted to the Union as a state. Without question social conditions were already making ground against polygyny in a way law failed to do. Modern life with its economic competition and popularizing of high standards of life, coupled with the passing of cheap land, would in any case have put an end to Mormon polygyny except as the sporadic luxury of a few wealthy leaders. Already the existence of the early polygynous family has become to the younger Mormons of today a fact as much out of harmony with their personal preferences as it would be for any other group of American youth.[22] Of one thing there can be no doubt: among the Mormons at present is to be found family life of a very high order not excelled elsewhere in its strength of ties, co-operative spirit, and affection.

Another interesting departure from the conventional form of marriage and family was developed by the Bible Communists of Oneida Community. The founder of this organization, as in the case of the Mormons, was a Vermonter, who found it necessary to remove from local prejudices. Going from Putney, Vermont, the members of the new fellowship established themselves at Oneida, New York, where after a short period of hardship they began to prosper.

Their communism extended to the family and resulted in a definite kind of group marriage. In spite of their radical teaching and practices with reference to sex relations, the community was not disturbed; indeed, as a result of their high business ethics, the members enjoyed the respect and friendliness of those who came to know them locally.

The founder of this community, John H. Noyes, had from the first stated that social opposition might force them to abandon their peculiar family organization, and in 1879, as a result of agitation led by church organizations of central New York, they gave up their complex marriage and reorganized their business by incorporation as a stock company.

Noyes had no sympathy with what he termed free love; his statement is this:

Our Communities are *families* as distinctly bounded and separated from promiscuous society as ordinary households. The tie that

_____
[22] Werner, M. R., *Brigham Young*, p. 372.

binds us together is as permanent and sacred, to say the least, as that of common marriage, for it is our religion. We receive no new members (except by deception and mistake) who do not give heart and hand to the family interest for life and for ever. Community of property extends just as far as freedom of love. Every man's care and every dollar of the common property are pledged for the maintenance and protection of the women and the education of the children of the Community.[23]

Although in sociological time this community based on a system of group marriage had a very brief existence, its experiences have value as a peculiar experiment in domestic relationships. The program of controlled mating to which was given the term *stirpiculture* was an attempt to practice eugenics, and in spite of the meager scientific knowledge upon which it was based its results as measured later in the longevity and physical and mental health of those born from this scheme of planned parenthood were extraordinary, instituting perhaps the most successful eugenic procreation of which we have record. It is apparent that the inhibition of romantic ties between the sexes, the denial of any special relationship between a man and a woman, ran contrary to the natural inclination of some of the members of the community and in the second generation especially became a cause of tension and dissatisfaction. The child, although well cared for physically and given a training for life superior to what was customary for most children at the time, felt an insecurity which is impressively revealed by the confessions of Pierrepont Noyes in his book *My Father's House*.

The sexual aspect of the experiment has special interest for the sexologist, but unfortunately this has been disclosed only partially. The community was founded on religious zeal, but it repudiated the conventional morality. Noyes insisted that the seventh commandment was "good penitentiary morality," a lockstep code that was rooted in laziness. Constant and great pressure was placed upon every member to hold to the group type of sexual fellowship, but there is evidence that the temptation to develop a monogamic concentration constantly appeared and required discipline. This is shown by the importance of this disposition in the confessions of individuals and the criti-

---

[23] *Encyclopedia Britannica*, 11th edition, Vol. 20, p. 107.

cisms of their fellows, the method of catharsis given the term, *krinopathy*, which was accepted by the community not only for therapeutic purposes, including the treatment of illness, but also for moral growth. It became a periodic obligation for every adult and was used even at times to rid children of ailments such as croup.

Noyes insisted that the amative and propagative functions of sex should be recognized as distinct, and in the effort to make this separation practical he advocated a peculiar method of birth control. Not until sometime in the future when the records of the community are released in fullness will be known what this social-laboratory experiment has to teach concerning sexual experiences in a plural marriage system.

The Shaker experiment is interesting as an extraordinary basis for a religious organization, but, built as it was on the idea of celibacy as one of the cardinal commands of the spiritual life, it could not have social significance. It has gradually dwindled and has now all but passed.

Robert Owen in his unsuccessful socialistic experiment at New Harmony, Indiana, appears not to have advocated the marriage ideas he expressed at a later time, but he did develop a dormitory care for the children as soon as they could leave their parents safely and a nursery school. His enterprise has no greater interest for the student of the family than have Brook Farm and the other communistic communities that during this period sprung up and died in various parts of the United States.

Science and home life. The rapid development of science and industry during the nineteenth century influenced the family both directly and indirectly. Directly family life profited by higher standards of living and an enormous increase in comfort and in leisure. The indirect influences came from the changes of social and economic conditions such as are discussed in a later chapter. Transportation and communication made greater progress during the nineteenth and the early period of the twentieth century than in all previous times. The isolated family, once commonplace, ceased to exist. Provincialism decreased through the ease and cheapness of travel. Improvement in the means of production made the factory a successful competitor of the home. As a consequence, the housewife was relieved of much of her former drudgery.

The improved methods of heating, lighting, and furnishing houses are representative of a great multitude of improvements that have added to the comfort, safety, and satisfactions of domestic life. The inconvenient kitchen with its limited equipment became transformed when it took over the better equipment science brought, and this metamorphosis is still in process. One of the first changes that came was the use of tin utensils in place of the heavy iron and copper ware of the colonial period. This innovation brought the tin peddler, who became, to rural and village families, virtually a missionary for more efficient housekeeping. Although the most radical transformation took place in the kitchen, every part of the house responded to the new discoveries of science and the greater efficiency of production. The coming of improved plumbing, which in turn made possible the modern bathroom, was one of the most important of the many changes that took place.

Household remedies in the field of medicine were largely replaced by patent medicines. These in turn, as a result of greater intelligence, have been somewhat driven out of use as the need of individual diagnosis has become generally realized. Patent-medicine sales are still a large factor in the current expenditures for sickness, as the recent report of the Committee on the Costs of Medical Care shows, and constitute a major problem of medical ignorance.[24]

Perhaps the most striking change has been in the more varied and more wholesome diet which has become typical of American homes and is in such sharp contrast with the heavy food that once tried the digestion of the American people. Unquestionably there has also been in the average home an improvement in the selection, combining, and preparation of food. The development of the art of commercial canning has proved a great advantage, putting an end to the meager winter diet which was followed in the spring by sulphur and molasses and other supposed purifiers of the blood. Now the winter monopoly of canned goods is being shaken by the new process of rapid-freezing fresh vegetables and fruits.

Inventions and discoveries.   The history of American civilization from the colonial period to the present is a record of a

---

[24] See *Abstract of Report* by Rufus Rorem and Robert P. Fischelis on the Costs of Medicines, p. 3.

constantly rising material standard of living as a consequence of the increasing advantages provided by a machine culture. Inventions and discoveries have affected domestic life both directly and in the rebound that has come from changing conditions outside the home. A great quantity of activities formerly a necessary part of housekeeping have been industrialized, not only lessening household labor but also frequently improving the quality and increasing the quantity of materials once produced within the home. Dependence on the baker for bread is an apt illustration of a host of services once performed by the housewife and her children that have been handed over to industry. Laundering is another example, although it has not in equal measure been transferred, in part because the electrically driven washing machine and the electric iron have so lessened the time and strength once required in the cleaning of clothes as to encourage many families to continue their own laundering.

Electricity has become the great drudgery remover as it has provided power in the home for refrigeration, cooking, sewing, and almost every sort of labor. Even air conditioning has made a start, and there is promise that this soon will become a rather common means of comfort within the home. Electricity allied with fuel oil has greatly reduced the problem of heating, and whatever the future there is no doubt that heating of houses in America will never again demand either the time or the strength formerly required. Electricity has become the almost universal means of lighting, and its recent progress in rural areas indicates that, except in rare cases of great isolation, electric lights and power will be universally used and the telephone will become almost an American necessity. The dominance of canned food is now being challenged by quick-frozen fruits and vegetables and the improved processes of dehydrating food materials. These new methods will change household practices as greatly as canning did. The discovery of vitamins and their dietary values also are revolutionizing American food habits.

The radio has accomplished what not so many years ago appeared to be the fantastic dream of a social reformer.[25] It has made effective a new method of contact which rivals in significance both the primary and secondary contacts of the sociologists

---

[25] Bellamy, Edward, *Looking Backward*.

and deserves the distinction of tertiary contact.[26] Already this peculiar relationship established electrically between persons at a distance, even continents apart, promises to be greatly enlarged as a result of the television already in use and bound to improve and become more available. The motion picture, an electric product, has become the most potent source of social influence for a multitude of persons, especially adolescents. Although for the most part it flourishes outside the home as a commercial enterprise, its effects constantly appear within the family, influencing standards and practices and providing a means of spreading modern culture which promises to put an end to sectionalism and isolation.

Discoveries, especially in medicine, dietetics, chemistry, and in psychology and psychiatry, have had profound consequences for the family. The resources for health have been multiplied, including the means of detecting, curing, or retarding diseases. These advances have not only lengthened the life span and lowered the death rate, but they have also added to the security and efficiency of the home. Our increasing knowledge of bacteriology, resulting in preventive inoculations, has also lessened illness and conserved life.

As is recognized by everyone, the automobile has influenced social life in myriad ways, and its popularity and importance as related to the home is revealed by the term "family car." Its availability through mass production has already made it, at least as instrumental in bringing about social changes in and out of the home, the most effective invention aside from the use of electrical power. It is already beginning to have as a means of rapid transportation a rival in the airplane. Undoubtedly both will become commonplace soon as means of travel, and many families now depending on the automobile will turn to the airplane for long-distance journeys. Already in a comparatively short period of time great progress has been made in increasing safety in flying, and, as a result of the incentive of World War II, mass production of the airplane has been achieved. This prophesies the same lessening of cost in producing the airplane that has been accomplished with the automobile. Lower costs, interest in flying, and the present air-mindedness of Americans, especially youth, will stimulate airplane use by private owners as

---

[26] Groves, E. R., and Moore, H. E., *Introduction to Sociology*, pp. 218–220.

well as mass commercial plane travel. It is certain that this will become another source of social change affecting family life just as happened through the popularizing of the automobile.

The family and the depression. Business cycles have been a continuous economic phenomena in this country throughout its history. Depressions have occurred approximately every five years and have lasted about eighteen months.[27] The last depression varied greatly from all previous experiences in its duration, continuing in various degrees throughout the 1930 decade, and also in the number of persons who received relief and the source from which it came. The first two months of 1934, 28 million persons representing 8 million households were receiving aid, chiefly from the federal government.[28] It has been estimated that at the peak of the depression in 1932 and 1933, 14 to 16 million persons were unemployed as compared with 3 or 4 million during the prosperous year of 1929. Depressions obviously bring dire consequences that adversely affect a multitude of families, creating problems such as lowering of standards of living, loss of security, complacent acceptance of dependency on private or public charity, or both, and also more subtle results that appear in personal and family tension and conflict. The significance of familial individuality immediately shows itself in a wide range of reactions. A relief status may be accepted by one family or by certain individuals within the family, while in other instances it brings great emotional protest, feelings of disgrace, and bitterness. An economic ordeal may be met by a greater clinging together of the family members or it may bring deterioration of family responsibility and affection within the home as Stead testifies was true in the depression of the 1890's.[29]

The depression of 1930 on account of the recent development of scientific research in family experience was more carefully studied from the family viewpoint than had been true of former periods of panic and unemployment. The most significant fact, and this, of course, would be anticipated by any student of the family, was that the depression like any other difficulty encountered by individual families tested affection, loyalty,

---

[27] Bossard, J. H. S., *Social Change and Social Problems*, pp. 237–238.

[28] *Trends in Public Assistance*, 1933–1939, Bureau Report No. 8, Social Security Board, pp. 6–7.

[29] Stead, W. T., *If Christ Came to Chicago*, p. 133.

endurance, and adaptability. The successfully integrated family withstood misfortune without domestic deterioration while the badly organized family became more so.[30] In his study Angell found that the ability to adjust to new circumstances exceeded integration in importance as a means of protecting the family from injury due to the lessening of income. When great stress was placed upon material values, the lowering of the standard of living proved more disturbing than in homes where material welfare was less emphasized. Angell classified the fifty families he studied as belonging to eight types, ranging from the highly integrated and highly adaptable to the completely unintegrated and unadaptable families.[31] There were three principal conditions that hampered adaptability: a materialistic philosophy of life, conventionalism in family mores, and an attitude of irresponsibility in one or both parents.

The consequences of the 1930 depression emphasized the individual composition of every family. Only as each person in a household group is brought into the picture can there be any adequate understanding of the meaning of unemployment and the necessity of accepting relief. Children, and especially adolescents, were affected not only by the loss of material resources but also by their own and their parents' psychic reactions. Family members sharing the same situation revealed great differences in character traits. As has always been true when relief has been made a governmental function, the depression of 1930 revealed its risk in loss of initiative and self-confidence.

The fact that families on relief had a higher birth rate than other classes of the population attracted considerable public attention. We do not have, however, studies of the fertility of these families before and after their accepting relief which would demonstrate whether governmental aid stimulated reproduction. We do know that these families represented the high fertility group. In part the apparent influence of relief may be explained by the fact that the larger families and those with infants or those expecting a child would be likely to need relief and their condition would attract attention and bring them help.[32]

---

[30] Angell, Robert C., *The Family Encounters the Depression*, pp. 260–262.
[31] *Ibid.*, pp. 14–15.
[32] *The Problems of a Changing Population*, National Resources Committee, May, 1938, p. 139.

World War I.   The first World War profoundly affected American thinking and practices, and its influence on marriage and family life appeared early in the conflict. Its effects were unique, but not on account of the seriousness of the conflict, the numbers engaged, or the suffering that ensued. There have been similar experiences from these points of view in the extensive and prolonged conflicts of the past, notably during the Roman conquest of the civilized world and the era of Napoleon. The uniqueness of World War I appeared in the revelation it brought of the interrelation of nations as a consequence of the development of science and the international havoc bound to follow a conflict in which the deadly powers of recent scientific inventions were employed, draining from every nation engaged all its possible resources. The disturbance that followed the war was unprecedented in its revelation of the strength and sensitiveness of international relationship. Its effect upon the family was not so much to be found in the broken homes, careless war marriages, or any immediate effect upon marriages, the birth rate, or child mortality, as in the widespread cynicism and pessimism which appeared when time drew aside the curtain and allowed people everywhere, with eyes freed from the distortions of propaganda, to see the futility of their incomparable suffering. The recoil appeared in every part of social experience, and marriage and the family did not escape. It added to the strain they were already receiving from the normal changes of modern civilization.

World War I had its social assets as well as liabilities. Among these was the part it played in advancing the status of women. It acted, as did the Civil War, as a means of opening up new opportunities to women, especially in industry, increased their experience in organizing public activities, gave them a larger social freedom, and to some extent stimulated among younger women more radical ideas regarding marriage. Women were quick to make use of the new advantages that war conditions provided for them, and as a consequence they were that much nearer equality with males.

Causes of agitation for Woman's Rights.   In the history of the American family the agitation for Woman's Rights holds a significant place. The leaders in the movement were anxious to gain more than suffrage for woman, but until this was finally granted they held to it as their immediate goal.

The demand for greater political and social opportunity for woman was an inevitable product of the evolution of modern civilization, but the trend away from female subordination was stimulated by the Industrial Revolution. Although this radical change in the form of production was attended with such suffering among the working classes that it appeared destructive of the old-time home life of these people, in the end it brought about conditions that made the denial of woman suffrage increasingly unjust. When the woman, whether married or single, went outside the home to take her place in the factory as a competitor with men for a daily wage, it became clear that she was handicapped by the fact that she had no vote. This discrimination was plainly seen in England, once the male workers had been given the franchise. In the American colonies women landowners were theoretically entitled to the suffrage, but the legal and social status of woman was too well established as inferior to that of man to permit woman suffrage to become a reality. Even male suffrage was undemocratic, being governed by religious and property qualifications.

When the Constitution of the United States was adopted and the several states regulated the process of voting, the suffrage was definitely placed on a male basis. Soon slight modifications occurred, as, for example, the permission granted widows in Kentucky to vote on educational matters. As has been said, the frontier as it moved farther and farther westward developed a civilization freer from tradition and more open-minded with reference to the political rights of women.

Along with the industrial changes which had made woman a competitor of man's for the means of earning a livelihood, there went also a still greater tendency toward opening up to women political rights. Gradually women obtained more and more opportunity to continue their education. As they broke through tradition at this point and were admitted into high schools and finally into colleges and professional schools on equal terms with men, the political discrimination against women grew more and more indefensible. It was the educated women who led in the fight, although it was obvious that the working women had more to gain by the privilege of registering their will through suffrage.

Slavery agitation early became allied with the Woman's Rights movement. Women who took part in the attack upon slavery were also leaders in the drive for their own enfranchisement. The experience that they obtained in organizing against slavery and to some extent speaking against it on the public platform gave them splendid preparation for work on the other reform of such significance to themselves. On the whole, those interested in Woman's Rights joined heartily in efforts for social reform such as the abolition of the saloon and the doing away with slavery. Many other women actively fought those committed to woman suffrage, but the Anti-Suffrage party was greatly handicapped because it seemed that by antagonizing the leaders engaged in the struggle for Woman's Rights they became the party defending the exploitations that the others were attacking. Thus they grew less and less influential as a result of their apparent conservatism and willingness to let social conditions reman as they were.

As the mountain and Pacific states one by one granted suffrage to women for state elections, the political leverage exercised by the women engaged in agitation for a federal woman suffrage law grew greater. Neither of the dominant political parties wanted to antagonize the women voters of the western states. As the leaders of the two parties temporized with the growing agitation for complete suffrage for women, the industrial and educational and social influences that led toward women's full political rights gradually increased the number of thinking people who saw that eventually political rights could not be maintained on a sex basis.

Then came World War I and, as in England, the part that women took in the ordeal gave them a reasonable ground for demanding what no longer could be denied without clear evidence of prejudice. The modern suffragists who adopted an aggressive program pushed to the utmost the opportunity the war brought them. Finally President Wilson reversed his former attitude that suffrage for women should come only through state legislation, and recommended a federal law; the amendment which had twice passed the House of Representatives was voted June 4, 1919, by the Senate, and by the end of the year twenty-two states had ratified it. Thirty-six states were necessary, and the number was completed by Tennessee's accepting the amendment in August, 1920. Wyoming had granted state suffrage in 1869, Colorado in 1893, Idaho and Utah in 1896, Washington in 1910, California in 1911, Arizona, Nevada, Kansas, and Oregon in 1912, South Dakota in 1913, and Montana in 1914. It is clear that the Far West was most ready to act upon the logic of the changing social conditions of American women.

The idea of woman suffrage made headway most slowly in the southern states. Indeed, when the amendment was finally ratified it had been adopted by only two border states, Kentucky and Tennessee. Nell Battle Lewis gives the following reasons for the southern attitude toward the idea of woman suffrage. The initial movement for woman suffrage had come about in the North and had been related to antislavery agitation. This alienated the interest of the South prior to the Civil War, and after that event everything of northern origin was anathema to southern leadership. Slavery also perpetuated the idea of inequality, thus naturally antagonizing the idea of extending the right of suffrage to women. The chivalry that grew up as a defense reaction to the conventional attitude of men toward the Negro woman tended to put a glamour over the southern white woman that made it difficult for her to agitate for or even to desire opportunity to enter politics. The leadership of southern women during the war and the more trying period of reconstruction that followed, and in other realms than politics from that time to this, demonstrates that the slow progress of woman suffrage in the southern states was in no degree due to the lack of potential political leadership among the women of that section.[33]

Advantages expected from suffrage. The advocates of woman suffrage argued for the change because of its advantage both for women and for the state. It was claimed by many that woman's voting would be more rational than that of man because she entered the political arena free from the traditions that limited the insight of man. It was also urged that woman's practical interest in family matters, especially those having to do with children, would bring to the government an element hitherto lacking because of its exclusively male character.

---

[33] *Raleigh News and Observer*, May 3, 1925.

Mothers could be depended upon to press forward the needs of children.

So far as women were concerned, they expected to help themselves by changing laws that discriminated against them, opening up greater educational opportunities and having means by which the government could be made sensitive to the desires and needs of women, especially the working women.

Evils prophesied from woman suffrage. It is interesting and even rather startling to look back at the arguments advanced against suffrage. One of the favorite statements was that suffrage would ruin the home. Much was made of the possibility, which in the minds of the opponents of the suffrage seemed to be a certainty, that wives would have different political commitments from those of their husbands, thus leading to a division of the family. The increasing trend toward a democratic home was ignored by those who made this attack; they assumed that the family would be shattered unless it remained upon a foundation of man's dominance. It was also said that woman would be unsexed by her political activities; just what was meant by this was always difficult to determine. It was a sentimental attack upon the kind of woman that social conditions were inevitably producing; the protected and segregated woman was conceived of as normal. Any variation from this pattern was pronounced an unsexed specimen.

It was also claimed that politics would grow increasingly emotional and sentimental as a result of the appearance of women among the voters. This argument was based upon the common notion that women were more emotional and more given to sentiment than were men. It was prophesied by some that out of the voting of women would develop a sex antagonism between men and women. A Woman's Party would arise that would fight the interests and wishes of men. It is disconcerting to read from so careful an interpreter of history as Francis Parkman these dire predictions regarding the mischievous effects of woman suffrage:

Neither Congress, nor the States, nor the united voice of the whole people could permanently change the essential relations of the sexes. Universal female suffrage, even if decreed, would undo itself in time; but the attempt to establish it would work deplorable mischief. The question is whether the persistency of a few agitators shall plunge us blindfold into the most reckless of all experiments; whether we shall adopt this supreme device for developing the defects of women, and demolish their real power to build an ugly mockery instead. For the sake of womanhood, let us hope not. In spite of the effect on the popular mind of the incessant repetition of a few trite fallacies, and in spite of the squeamishness that prevents the vast majority averse to the movement from uttering a word against it, let us trust that the good sense of the American people will vindicate itself against this most unnatural and pestilent revolution. In the full and normal development of womanhood lie the best interests of the world. Let us labor earnestly for it; and, that we may not labor in vain, let us save women from the barren perturbations of American politics. Let us respect them; and, that we may do so, let us pray for deliverance from female suffrage.[34]

The results of woman suffrage. The most surprising thing about the voting of women has been the little difference that it has seemed to make in our political life. The disturbances prophesied failed to develop. At first it appeared merely that the number of voters had been greatly increased. As time passed, however, it became clear that woman had gained considerably in her progress toward social equality. The government did show a larger interest in matters that pertained to the home. The politician became more sensitive to woman's attitudes on social questions. Prohibition as a national policy was an illustration of the influence of women upon legislation, for women were much more committed to the prohibition policy than were men. They are also more solidly against commercialized prostitution. In such movements woman's power was felt before she had the vote, but her suffrage gave her greater opportunity to express her convictions in a way that carries political pressure.

Women are quite conscious that they have not yet obtained full social opportunity. Agitations for changes in the legal and economic status for women still continue. Attempts, for example, to make the salaries for men and women in corresponding positions in our public schools the same attest this effort on the part of women to reach full equality. Their attack upon the discrimination exercised by educational policy which discharges women who marry, while taking no notice at all of the marriage of males, is another testimony of the demand of women for complete equality.

---

[34] Pamphlet issued sometime between 1876 and 1880.

Those who expected women to be little influenced by the existing political parties were disappointed, for, if women came into politics free from former entanglements, they were easily brought into line and for the most part are at present allied to one of the dominant parties. It is not at all demonstrated yet, however, that eventually women may not bring into politics the pressure of a sex party which will transcend the less significant alignments of the old parties.

The most discouraging thing regarding the suffrage of women has been the considerable number of women who have not exercised their right of suffrage and who have had practically no interest in political matters. It must not be forgotten that many males take the same attitude. Indeed one of our recent Presidents did not care enough about practical politics to vote, so the records show, in the presidential election previous to his own. Even if the suffrage is not exercised by women to the extent that was expected by those who led in the agitation for the franchise, the fact that they can vote if they will has no small political significance, which in the long run is bound to be for their advantage. It is not possible to trace clearly any effect on the home that has come out of suffrage, except that it has tended to strengthen the trend, inevitable in any case, toward a family firmly established on a democratic basis, with the inequalities of the paternal type of home life pushed aside.

Contemporary movements.   What is known as the Woman's Movement did not come to an end with the granting of equal suffrage. There were and there still are various forms of discrimination in favor of men. With the coming of woman suffrage there were also new responsibilities for women. The Woman's Movement of today branches in two directions. On the one hand we find organized effort to induce women to meet their civic obligations and to accept leadership in all kinds of educational and social undertakings. Working with this purpose are the National Federation and local organizations of women's clubs and the League of Women Voters. Although women, before they were given the vote, were performing a magnificent social service through their organizations, their attainment of suffrage increased their power and gave their efforts greater effectiveness.

Suffrage also stimulated agitation attacking the discriminations against women. The most radical reaction to woman's social and political inferiority was taken by the National Woman's Party, which was formed in 1913 and is at present the organization which is most distinctively feministic. Some of the objectives of the present-day feminist movement are: the acceptance of the single standard for men and women, a clearer recognition of an absolute equality in marriage, the removal of all discrimination in education that limits women on account of their sex, a still greater financial independence for all women, the elimination in the education of the girl of the handicap imposed by traditions of physical and social inequality.

Attacks are also made upon woman's legal and political handicaps that have been carried over from the home life of the past. Some of the legal reforms women are demanding are: the guardianship control of children by mothers without discrimination in favor of fathers, the abolition of the idea of the husband as the legal head of the household, a legal residence apart from the husband when the woman finds this separation necessary or desirable, increased legal freedom for wives in business transactions, the removal of all legal discriminations against women in matters that have to do with sex, modification of court decisions so as to give women absolute legal equality with men. In short, women persist in their agitation for a nearer approach to an equality with men. With reference to goal and methods there are differences of opinion among leaders in the contemporary Woman's Movement. All recognize the necessity of educating public opinion, but the National Woman's Party stresses the need of an amendment to the Constitution giving women more substantial equality, while the League of Women Voters directs its effort to the winning of civic reforms by the improvement of the legislation of the individual states.

World War II.   The second World War was the most disturbing event in the history of domestic experience in the United States. It was a psychic and social earthquake that in varying degrees affected every home. It shook every aspect of American life. Its consequences still continue and, as is generally realized, will appear for many years to come. In comparison with the results the war brought along other lines, the family appeared relatively immune. Nevertheless, it profoundly felt the crisis and from a long-time point of view historians of the future may regard what the war did to family life as significant as any of its consequences. It is much too soon for final judgment. Many of its immediate effects are obvious. For example, following Pearl Harbor there was an increase in the marriage rate which during the month after the attack was 50 per cent greater than in the corresponding month in 1940 and 1939.[35] Many of these marriages were aborted by the husband's leaving for military service, since the living together of the husband and the wife was frequently only for a few weeks or even days, too brief a union to constitute a normal start of family life. It is estimated that during the first five months of the war there were some 600,000 marriages in the United States, one-fourth of which were those of war brides, or about 1,000 each day.[36] Some months before the breaking out of hostilities, marriages began to increase in the United States. In 1940 there were 127,000 more than in the preceding year.[37] A similar trend had appeared in many of the European countries. This was the result of a general feeling that war was probable and of the various economic and social changes that accompanied preparation for national defense. The enactment of the Selective Service Act in September, 1940, was one of the most important of these influences. After the declaration of the war the influence of migration to war-industry cities became apparent, especially to those where there was great expansion of industry, of which Los Angeles is an example, because of its aircraft production. It is reasonable to assume that part of this increase in the marriage rate came from the desire to find in marriage compensation for the widespread feeling of insecurity, especially among older youth. The motives of war brides ranged over a large territory from those who felt patriotic in identifying themselves through marriage with a soldier in the great conflict to the considerable number that were influenced by the allowances and pensions that were available to the wives of soldiers.

This increase in marriages was associated with a similar rise in the birth rate. In 1942 it reached the highest point in recent years, 20.9, which meant more than three million babies.

---

[35] Ogburn, William F., "Marriages, Births and Divorces," *The Annals of the American Academy of Political and Social Science*, Vol. 229, p. 21.

[36] *Ibid.*, p. 22.

[37] *Ibid.*, p. 26.

This was in part due to the increase of births among young mothers who had recently married. Later, because of the absence of their husbands, there was a drop in the rate of reproduction among this younger group.[38] Some other important immediate results of the war were the increase in the standard of living, and in saving, especially among the lower-income groups, a result of the high wages paid in war industries. There was widespread migration of families, especially from the open country and small villages to cities producing great quantities of war material. Many mothers of young children left home for war work. In 1944 it was estimated that two million such women were thus employed.[39] Although it was announced early in the war by the administration that the war meant sacrifice for all and the conflict was not to bring to any group a raise in the standard of living, there was in fact considerable advance among wage earners of the low economic classes and a relative decrease among white-collar workers and members of the middle class on fixed incomes or salaries. As the war proceeded, evidence accumulated of a considerable amount of incompatibility among the war marriages and it became evident that this would continue and bring an increase in the divorce rate, as was true during the years following the first World War.

The effects of the war on the family did not appear only in the liabilities that occurred. There was also an increase in family unity, a new awakening to the values and satisfactions of home life, greater tolerance between members of the family, more of the spirit of sacrifice, and the development of willingness to recognize the meaning of kinship ties and to give aid to those family members who suffered hardships or were in great trouble.

The war and the family. Many American families even in their structure suffered temporary mutilation or final fracture as the result of the absence or death of one or more of the family members. Until caution was taken to prevent repetition of such an occurrence, some families lost all their sons in one catastrophe. Great strain was placed upon some of the war brides who almost immediately after marriage found themselves lonely as their husbands went overseas. They were given a taste of the

---

[38] *Statistical Bulletin*, Metropolitan Life Insurance Company, Vol. 24, No. 8, pp. 4–6.

[39] Zucker, Henry L., "Parents of Latch-key Children," *The Annals of the American Academy of Political and Social Science*, Vol. 236, p. 44.

satisfactions of marriage, and then the opportunity for normal fellowship was snatched from them. In some instances they soon became widows because their husbands were reported dead. One result of the quick loss of marital relationships was a considerable increase in promiscuity among these war brides who under ordinary circumstances would never have dreamed of breaking their marriage vows, indeed, would not have had the enticements their situation brought about.

A multitude of families, who under peace conditions could have developed compatibility because they would have encountered only minor stresses, were placed under great strain which tested to the limit the ability of the family members to adjust to the trying circumstances. Some families were undermined by becoming rich through the war. Although the government made constant effort to draw off much of the increased earnings of war workers in the form of saving, there were many families who were hurt by their sudden prosperity. Especially was this true of older youth who often found themselves earning more than their parents ever had. Among these families enriched by the war, this feeling of prosperity was of course relative to previous earnings. Some indulged in an orgy of spending which brought dismay to any thoughtful observer who visited large department stores and saw the prices of luxury goods and the reckless purchases. In contrast to this group who profited from the war were teachers, public officials, clerks, stenographers, and other white-collar workers, who struggled with increasing prices with no or little addition to their incomes. The greater portion of these families belonged to the middle class, and possibly the injury the war brought this group may in the years to come prove to be one of the most dire of the end consequences of the great conflict.

The nervous strain of the war was felt by the civilian population on a scale perhaps of greater intensity than ever before experienced. Older youth who expected to be called to service endured great uncertainty during their waiting period. Others were left with feelings of inferiority because they were found unfit to enter the armed forces. Especially was this true if they were rejected because of emotional instability rather than physical incapacity.

One of the ills associated with the war was the loss of morale

at home and the effect of revealing this through correspondence
with men overseas. The most disastrous of these disturbances of
family origin was the demand of wives at home for divorces from
their distant husbands. Next to this was the suspicion of a considerable number of soldiers that their wives at home were unfaithful. In some cases the birth of a baby demonstrated that
what the husband feared was true. It seems reasonable to assume
that part of this anxiety came from the fact that the soldier himself brought about in his association with wives of other fighting
men what he thought might be true of his own spouse.

The adolescent.   Some of the effects of the war on American youth have already been noticed. Even though young people
could not escape from the effects of the war, there were many of
them who were not greatly disturbed. The absence of the father
or his death in many cases did not bring the emotional disturbance that one might have expected. Much depended upon the
temperament of the child. The employment of both parents, the
earning of large wages, the social restlessness and feelings of insecurity, the opportunities of the war economy in encouraging
adventure and various forms of delinquency were among the
chief causes of the problems the war brought American youth.
The teen-age girl was especially victimized, as she responded to
the pressure put upon her to indulge in sex intercourse with
older men, especially soldiers and sailors. The increase in this
type of delinquency was unprecedented in the United States,
especially among those who were in the early teens, as the
soldiers and sailors in great measure transferred their seeking of
sexual indulgence from the prostitute to the young girl who,
although promiscuous, was in no sense a member of the ancient
profession.[40] Only with the passing of time will it become clear
what has been the effect of this loosening of the sex code among
younger youth upon the moral practices of American people
and the stability of family life.

The war tended to increase the demand of young people
for freedom and to bring them into conflict with parents who
were unprepared to meet the shift in the social circumstances
which provided greater opportunity for the independence of

[40] Groves, Ernest R., and Groves, Gladys H., "The Social Background of
Wartime Adolescents," *The Annals of the American Academy of Political and
Social Science,* Vol. 236, p. 30.

youth and stimulated their normal desire to feel themselves on their own.[41] Conditions during the war demonstrated that the conventional code no longer can safely rest upon the negative program which emphasizes the danger of venereal disease and unwanted pregnancy. The new freedom that industrial and family conditions brought young people gave them opportunity to show their feeling of confidence that modern science provides security against venereal disease and undesired pregnancy.

The child.   Evidence accumulated during the war from schools, social agencies, the police, and the courts that children were neglected in homes where both parents worked or where the mother was employed and the father in service. The attempt to cope with this problem through the Emergency Child Care facilities is discussed in a later chapter. Helpful as was this program there were a multitude of families who either made no use of the service or were in localities where it was not to be had. Even when children were well protected they were sensitive in their reactions to the emotional strain expressed by their elders. Anna Freud, from her experience in English nursery work, tells us that young children, although relatively indifferent to the absence of their fathers, were completely unable to accept the fact of their father's death if this happened. Their expression of this was not only pathetic; it was also revealing as to their need of a feeling of security that depended upon their belief that their fathers would come back to them.[42] If, as present evidence indicates, the possessing or the losing of a sense of security in early childhood contributes significantly to the emotional character of adult life, only when these war children mature will the sizableness of one of the important penalties of World War II be disclosed. Since such children number millions and are scattered all over the globe, their misfortunes prophesy much future suffering and instability.

The New York State Board of Social Welfare, after careful study of the effects of the war upon the children of that state, summarized the situation in the following revealing statement, a description which in greater or less degree describes conditions in every state and most communities throughout the nation.

---

[41] Bossard, James H. S., "Family Backgrounds of Wartime Adolescents," *The Annals of the American Academy of Political and Social Science,* Vol. 236, p. 38.

[42] Freud, Anna, *Infants Without Families,* pp. 107–8.

Children in school: inattentive, unsettled; restlessness and fatigue, tardiness and absence, working over hours.

Employment of children: late-hour jobs; misuse of wages.

Work certificates: tremendous increases; jobs as worth-while substitute for schooling; desire to earn money.

Younger children: misdirected energies of seven-, eight- and nine-year-olds; younger children are stealing; boy-gangs of nine- to twelve-year-olds; delinquency average age drops from sixteen to eleven; twelve- to thirteen-year-olds want a real part in war effort; girl-gangs of eleven- to fourteen-year-olds imitate older groups; meal-ticket children.

Older children, fourteen to sixteen years: busy parents relax supervision, children on streets, commercial recreation; part-time jobs; insecurity of draft-age boy reflected in younger boys; lax morals, drinking, language, unwise spending of allowances and wages; seek role in the war; girls under sixteen frequenting places of cheap amusement; number in trouble increasing out of proportion to boys' cases; promiscuous conduct of runaway girls.

Older adolescents: face much greater responsibilities—home, job, draft, marriage; resistance to parental authority; more money, freedom—shift from peacetime to wartime moral code.

Older girls: frustrated by increasing absence of boys; no part in vital, exciting events; concerned about normal marriage and family outlets; sharp increase in number of young prostitutes and institutional commitments for serious cases, including venereal infections and pregnancies; high school venereal rates up 20 per cent, increase in unmarried mothers, age level up; girls and soldiers.

Older boys: demands for physical fitness and pre-service programs, fourteen- to eighteen-year-olds; loss of natural leaders to the draft; few boys left in upper classes of high schools; vocational high school needs; boys over eighteen associate with older men and older girls; "chucking morals."

Children's opportunities: to serve their country, the positive side of the war emergency.

Children's attitudes: desire to help win the war; realistic education sought; their place in the postwar world.[43]

---

[43] *The Effects of the War on Children*, New York State Board of Social Welfare, p. 54.

Part II

Psychological Aspects of American Family Experience

Chapter 8

EMOTIONAL ASPECTS
OF FAMILY LIFE

FOREWORD. There can be no satisfactory interpretation of human behavior that does not make basic the unity of the normal personality. In order, however, to analyze and describe human activity concretely and with a measure of detail, it proves an advantage to abstract from this totality its three aspects: emotion, thought, and will. The significance of the first, as it is related to domestic experience, is the theme of this chapter. Science in very recent years has gained a considerable knowledge of the emotional side of human nature; especially has this been true of the physiological background of emotions. Here the greatest advance has come from an increasing understanding of the contributions of the endocrine glands. This is a two-way influence, since in addition to the endocrines directly affecting emotions, a situation having intense emotional meaning realized in thought reacts on the endocrine system and this becomes a part of the total affect expressed in fear, anger, or some other emotion. An illustration of this is the disturbance of digestion because of fear, conflict, or some other emotionally stirring experience. Family relationship means the interaction of the total personalities in contact. In interpreting this, however, it is helpful again to reduce the totality of this relationship by distinguishing three psychic elements, and this fact explains the title of this chapter.

The family arena. The family is unrivaled as a source of emotional experience and as an outlet for its expression. Both marriage and parenthood bring forth a new vitalizing of previous emotional traits. Likewise the child, when he enters the family, finds himself in a characteristic emotional environment

206 THE CONTEMPORARY AMERICAN FAMILY

to which his own reactions, particularly during the first and formative years, are chiefly emotional in character. No other human relationship so begets emotion and gives it direction. This has always been a recognized feature of family life. The rare privacy of the home, the constant and close and frank contact, the inevitable clashing of interests, and the large meaning each member of the family finds in the happenings within the home, all work together to intensify individual emotions. As a consequence, the adjustments within the home are largely emotional.

The wealth of emotional experience originating through family associations is psychically and socially advantageous in that it provides opportunity for individual growth and satisfaction. The family, including marriage, is unrivaled in the emotional value it offers developing personality, and its contribution is a basic influence in the life career, especially in its incentives, for the majority of men and women. It cannot, however, provide this opportunity for character making without at the same time making possible various kinds of emotional aberrations. It does not seem strange that this should be true when it is realized that there are contrary obligations that go with parenthood. The parent needs to give the child for his wholesome development attention, tenderness, and love-response, but also in order to prevent later emotional maladjustment must prepare for the breaking of this special relationship. The child also for his adult welfare demands security from the parent, and then as he grows older needs gradually to draw away from this attachment and eventually become an independent individual. Thus what is first needful and easily accomplished and usually mutually satisfying requires in time a reversal. What was once accomplished in the animal life by the fading of an instinct has to come about in a self-conscious association, but, unless it is accomplished without creating conflict and bringing guilt, the relationship which was at first advantageous becomes a peril in the emotional experience of the parent or child or both. This drift from emotional soundness can be so gradual as not to awaken either victim to what is happening. This hazard of childhood and parenthood has to be recognized in any analysis of the emotional characteristics and consequences of family experience, but this portrayal of an inherent risk associated with home life must not give the impression that the emotional ties between the parent and child are necessarily dangerous, making impossible a normal, wholesome character development. Although the maladjustments need to be understood, they should be recognized as departures and exceptions from what can be, and in most instances is, the basic source of good preparation for life. The relationship of parent and child like any other that is intensely emotional can become perilous, but nothing can be more frustrating, especially to the child, than the withholding of this love-responsiveness by the parent. The child's welfare is secured not by sterilizing parental affection but by making it mature and responsible.

Although the emotional hazards of the parent-child relationship can rightly be described as inherent because of the possibility of affection leading to retardation, fixation, conflict, and the like, it is most important that a student of the family recognize in this problem a cultural relativity. Social conditions increase or lessen the dangers involved in the parent-child association. For example, a situation that would become in our country for most young people a source of trouble would in Japan appear normal. We can see this in what in Japan would be a perfectly proper dominance of the mother-in-law over the wife and a continuation of the mother-son fixation, whereas, within the American background such a situation would bring humiliation, conflict, and frustration to the American wife.

This relativity goes beyond mere national culture, although it appears most vividly as we contrast national groups. It is also related to class, religious, educational, and economic backgrounds. The Jewish code, for example, can affect the emotional career of the parent and child somewhat differently than would the Gentile. Parents with many children are likely to escape the testing that comes to those who have only one child. The career of Joseph, however, guards us against generalizations that acknowledge no exceptions. The mother who has a slight attachment or who has varied interests is likely to escape the ordeal that would come to the opposite type of parent who concentrates entirely on the offspring, making him, as we sometimes say, her whole life. Obviously, the unhappily married woman and the widow have greater danger of holding too closely to the child and unconsciously hampering his independent development than have those who are more fortunate.

The analysis that follows assumes a contemporary American background. Our historic trend toward emphasizing individuality, the freedom we permit the adolescent, social pressure which appears from many quarters enhancing the independence of young people, the leisure provided many American women as compared with their forebears or those who in other countries have greater economic struggle thrust upon them are conditions that we take for granted when we discuss the emotional maladjustments that do occur in American homes.

Family relationship a social integration.   The family has often been defined as a social microcosm. It is the greater society in miniature form. It has, however, its peculiarities, and these in part come from this very fact of scaling down and thereby intensifying the area of contact. Family experience requires of the individual, as does social life in general, a social integration for the achievement of good adjustment. Ordinarily the maturing process largely consists of a willingness of the individual to see clearly his circumstances, to accept those that cannot be changed, and to adjust himself to his situation.

This program for integration holds also of the family, but it offers in its restricted field special difficulties, particularly at the beginning of marriage. The facts that confront each member, the situations each faces, appear less objective, less rigid, than those of ordinary life, because they are the result of the other person's dispositions, desires, and reactions. The association, therefore, is seldom merely the learning to know and to accept conditions. There is nearly always a maneuvering for personal status, for changes in the personality or behavior of the other member of the union. Much of the tension immediately developing into incompatibility in married life comes from this mutual maneuvering. It nearly always has a double strategy, each attempting to establish his preconceived role in the comradeship while at the same time leading the other to adopt the role already assumed by husband or wife to be good for the other. The fact that this maneuvering may be largely unconscious, or may be interpreted by both in terms of unselfishness, in no degree lessens its significance or removes the possibility of tension. A stereotyped family experience such as we find in primitive society tends to discourage this while the more fluid modern family stimulates it.

The difference between the past and present appears in greater degree in the reactions of women than of men. The reason for this is obvious and appears from various angles throughout this text. In the past the role of woman has been in great degree interpreted as something fixed by biological necessity. Her life has been regarded as largely determined by instinct. This has been the feeling of both man and woman, the latter taking for her ideal to a great extent a conception of her social function which was man-made. The evolution of the psychic life of men and women has culminated among many women not only in a consciousness of the urge of their own individuality but in a realization that they cannot hope to approach the ideal held for them by the modern man unless they are able to play a different role than that which most men assume to be their proper one and can obtain a means of self-expression not provided for by masculine convention.

As a result the maneuvering of the modern type of woman in the effort to provide an adjustment in accord with her inclinations and standards, while at the same time not antagonizing the just demands of the man, may easily come to seem to the husband an unwillingness to enter team play or a portrayal of restlessness which is likely to become an obstacle to domestic compatibility. As a matter of fact, the insistence of woman on an adjustment on a higher level than that required when her role was interpreted as biological and instinctive is logical, and struggle for its achievement determines the final happiness of both the man and the woman. A great part of our social thinking as related to marriage and family experience is still based upon the old order of things and fails to recognize that woman has out-traveled any purely biological determining of her life, in the same way that man has. Her individuality has come to have the same meaning, the same wide outlook, and the same insistence upon personal satisfaction as his.

Marriage becomes a success, not through compromising masculine and feminine characteristics, but by consolidating the interests of man and woman in a co-operation that provides individuality for both persons. The part each plays in the mutual enterprise may not be identical, but there is no difference between them in the need of finding in their experiences the attainment of individuality and the sense of social achievement.

In so far as domestic experience for either of them becomes a blunting of self-expression, the seed of mutual discontent is planted. It is not that woman, as a result of modern conditions, has been made a competitor with or an imitator of man, but rather that her life, like his, has grown in demands beyond those belonging strictly to biological existence, and she can no more happily tolerate restriction of her life on its highest levels than can he. Her awakening has been more sudden while his has been a more gradual development. But now both of them are more distinctively modern, in the sense that they are a greater distance from the mere primitive and physical stages, than they are distinctive because one is a man and the other a woman.

The qualities of sex have not been thrown aside, but they have been subordinated and built into a larger life-outlook than could possibly rest upon male or female traits. As a consequence, for the woman to surrender her new demands as a token of domestic docility means dropping to a lower level of experience out of accord with all the other conditions of modern life and, however satisfying she may be to her husband, she has then no hope of being his copartner. For the man or woman to fail to seek adjustment on the plane characteristic of modern culture, even though here it may be more complicated than on lower levels, is to miss the real meaning of present-day domestic adjustment.

Although class differences show themselves in the form which this problem takes, the need of adjustment is felt in all classes whenever the man and woman are exposed to the influences of contemporary American life. Aside from any basic difference in reaction to family life of man and woman, due to unlike biological structure, the fact that each has from childhood been subjected to a conditioning process which distinguishes between the social program for the man and for the woman would produce, once they enter marriage, a divergent outlook leading toward emotional incompatibility. In estimating the possibilities of this recoil, it must be remembered that during the process of growth the girl may have frequently felt emotional protest against the restrictions forced upon her by social attitudes and conventions, while the boy may have been made to feel that his masculine soundness depends upon his maintaining the social distinctions that he has seen enforced during childhood and youth. This situation of husband and wife, so provocative of tension, cannot be considered merely a conflict between the woman's unwillingness to become a housekeeper and a mother and the husband's insistence that only as she accepts these roles can family life be normal. The family task that confronts the wife at marriage easily appears to her a culmination of a long-time frustration. Her discontent or confusion may come from the discord of two opposing processes of social conditioning. One has given her the same stimulation leading to demands for individuality and self-expression that has developed in the boy his characteristic attitudes, while the other has attemped to build in her domestic ideals that are essentially different in psychic and social characteristics from those belonging to the male.

In a somewhat similar fashion freedom, opportunities, and tendencies toward sophistication in   modern culture exaggerate the inevitable tension between   parent, who has come to give the child a fixed role in the   family, and the child, who, as he moves toward adolescence and final independence, feels pressure to break away from the family conditions—conditions which to him appear as discrimination while to the parent they represent the ideal, to the achievement of which every effort of the family should be directed.

Since marriage seems a fresh start, there always appears some measure of maneuvering as mutual adjustment proceeds. Immediately there is revelation of the intensely emotional nature of this settlement of status and of the great opportunity the domestic relationship provides for the expression of the major psychiatric mechanisms we employ as a means of describing emotional experience.

Suppression.   It appears in the family life of some that adjustment is actually from the beginning viewed by one or both members of the union as a program of suppression. There is, of course, in family association as in every other human contact, some incidental surrendering of desire; but this normally is thought of, if it becomes conscious at all, as a means to an end. It is otherwise when the entire relationship comes to mean to one of the two persons an aggressive and persistent suppression through the encroachment of the conscious or unconscious desires of the other.

Although there is always the temptation to personify this

experience and regard it as something inflicted by the other member of the union, it occasionally takes a different form. Perhaps then it is more accurately described as repression. Family experience has been made to seem, through some cause that has operated in the past, synonymous with sacrifice and self-restriction. Apparently there are families that transmit through contact of parent and child this notion of domestic experience, and with marriage and with parenthood there comes forth the idea of self-repression either as a solemn obligation or as an unescapable penalty. Home life is defined not by its usual and normal self-expression but by its occasional and abnormal sacrifice. Sex is most often chosen as the chief challenge of this policy of repression, with the result that the entire purpose of marriage is lost through conflict, emotional hostility, and the self-deception that follows inner protest. The husband or wife while under the power of these impulses cannot set aside such handicaps born of his or her past experience, and they may seem deliberate attempts to suppress the individuality of the marital partner.

CASE OF A. K.

Some months after his marriage A. K. developed a neurosis severe enough to make it necessary for him temporarily to retire from his profession. His wife had frankly told him before his marriage of her emotional commitment to another man and the intimacy that resulted. At the time he appeared unconcerned, stating that what had happened occurred before his own friendship and that it meant nothing to him. Soon after the marriage he became so obviously unhappy and disturbed that his physician advised him to take an extended vacation, and his wife finally persuaded him to seek the help of an experienced psychoanalyist. She had been advised to do this by a family counselor. After a considerable treatment the basic difficulty of the husband's life came to the surface. Although he had boasted of his preference for the modern type of woman, he had chosen his wife knowing that she was that type, one who held an advanced university degree and had demonstrated considerable talent in the field of art in which she was interested; emotionally he sought the kind of wife his mother had been to her husband. He desired attention and catering when it was just not possible in his own home life, instead of realizing that his own emotional maturity was not equal to the circumstances of the situation in which he had deliberately placed himself. He chose as the explanation of his unhappiness an unwillingness to penetrate his self-deception and reveal to himself that only by giving up his conception of a wife could he achieve any measure of domestic content. The demand he made of his wife was a product of childhood and youth and was so heavily imbedded in his philosophy of life that it became necessary to ask of the wife some sacrifice of her independence and intellectual adequacy. She was willing to surrender some of her greater maturities and to assume in greater measure the role he had expected of her, while at the same time he made sincere effort to act upon what intellectually he had decreed for himself. Harmony was restored and the neurosis ended by this program. His reaction for what had happened before his marriage disappeared.

Rationalization. Whenever there is an opening for emotional reaction there appears the tendency to rationalize. Conditions of domestic relationship invite this common mechanism as a means of squaring personality defects with conscience. Conduct is freed from self-reproach by being made to harmonize with cultural standards even though to accomplish this, self-deception has to be practiced. Motives and attitudes are dressed up until they are made to appear just what they are not. Ordinarily this attempt at counterfeit tricks only him who carries it out, but even if the hypocrisy is not detected by the other members of the family, their resentment is not lessened. The mere fact that they see selfishness assuming the garb of generosity renders them all the more hostile to demands which if truthfully stated they would resent. In no human contact is there larger opportunity for self-seeking to attempt concealment of its real nature by assuming conscientious motives.

In a recent incompatibility that eventually led to divorce, one of the bitter complaints of the wife was that however selfish the demands of her husband, they were always justified as obligations of his conscience from which there was no escape. This giving of a false coloring to what clearly came from self-centered desire irritated her even more than the exploitations to which she felt herself subjected.

In addition to the tendency to rationalize conduct within the family circle, there has been a large amount of social rationalization on the part of men in the effort to maintain woman's *status quo* while at the same time justifying the discrimination this has meant against women. An example of this is the edict of the school superintendent on a board of education reflecing the masculine tradition that the woman who marries resign her position as a schoolteacher. The insistence that woman's place is within the home has often been an attempt at rationalization in the effort to subordinate women socially while at the same time squaring such attitudes with conscience.

Case of D. M.

D. M. has always been an interfering member of the M. family. She has been quick to decide the obligations of her brothers and sisters, always having impressive arguments on why they should do what she personally prefers. This constant tendency found its supreme expression in the demands she made of an older sister that she be given control of a child that had been left an orphan at the time of a brother's death. The reasons she advanced were all for the welfare of the child and her sister. The latter was too nervous to take over such a responsibility. She also did not have the necessary knowledge of what the mother had wished in the training of her son. This was in spite of the fact that the brother before dying had requested the older sister to care for the child. D. M. advanced a multitude of explanations as to why the child's welfare required that he be brought up by her rather than the other aunt. It was, however, apparent to all but herself that the basic incentive was her unwillingness to see her nephew under the influence of the member of the family whom she had constantly and hopelessly tried to dominate. She had slight interest in the child; her chief drive was for the opportunity to manage his life. Failing to accomplish her purpose, she had gone so far as to insist that her sister was too sick to accept the obligation and too unsound mentally. Failing in her purpose to get control of the boy, she proceeded to broadcast the weaknesses, faults, and bad behavior she found in the child, who actually was a well-adjusted boy. This incident was only one of similar concealments of motives on her part, since she was able always in rare measure to make any desire of hers a solemn obligation of the moral law, especially if it forced something unpleasant upon a relative or a friend.

Identification. Identification is another emotional mechanism frequently found in family experience. The husband or wife has entered marriage with a life so fixed upon a parent as to allow no free individuality. This does not necessarily mean that the relationship of parent and child is one of affection, for, on the contrary, it may be that hate has existed between them.

It is rather that the child has never been able to get out of the clutches of the parent's personality. As a result, the child is left with the feeling of inner insecurity, and the possibility of two opposite types of reaction, each of which as expressed in the continuous contact of domestic relationship will defeat wholesome adjustment. Sometimes the identification is with a weaker member of the same sex, leading on the part of the child to a persistent sense of inferiority. On the other hand, identification may be with a member of the opposite sex who holds for the child a position of dominance. In such experiences identification makes it impossible for the child to break away even though he eventually marries.

Matrimony may be chosen as a means of escape, but it will prove futile until the character of the individual is itself emotionally reconstructed. In this latter type of reaction there will be chronic desire to maneuver the other member of the union into a status of subordination. So long as identification persists, there is constant risk of any happening becoming a symbol of the inferiority that is felt or an invitation to attempt to put the husband or wife in his or her proper place. Whichever way the emotion turns, it clouds issues and withdraws the attention from the objective problems occurring in family association.

Case of B. M.

For years before her marriage and ever since, B. M. has identified herself with her mother. The latter has been a dissatisfied wife who always believed that her marriage made it impossible for her to succeed in one of the arts. Although she possesses some talent, she has given no evidence that she would ever have made a successful career along the line of her interest. Nevertheless, she has always insisted that her marriage blocked her self-expression. Her only child, B. M., took the side of the mother in the incompatibility between the parents, which reached intensity about the time the child was old enough to realize how unhappy her home was. B. M. took over the ambition of her mother and it was understood that she would get the training that her mother's marriage made impossible and carry on a career that would bring prestige to both of them. Her mother at the time of her daughter's marriage had achieved semi-invalidism and was constantly seeking help from doctors. The daughter took this seriously and more than ever blamed her father for the mother's misfortunes. In spite of the fact that her mother had discouraged marriage, B. M. did fall in love. As soon as she was married, however, it became apparent that she was repeating in her own home the discontent that had been so obvious in her mother's reaction to life. She gave up her art lessons, insisting that her marriage made it impossible for her to hope to carry on the career for which she had planned. Soon she imitated her mother in her insistence that she also was not well. Her mother's invalidism had not created any serious economic problem because of the income of her husband, but in the case of B. M. the circumstances were different. Her husband was forced into debt, and his reaction to his unhappy spouse was not the docile and patient endurance of his father-in-law. Instead he charged the wife with having ruined his happiness and was éven discerning enough to see that her close relation with her mother was at least one of the reasons for their incompatibility. Finally, after three years of their living together, he was released by divorce from his matrimonial failure, and his one-time wife returned to her mother.

Projection.   Projection also appears within family interaction. It is born of the effort to escape from chafing self-reproach. Emotional conflict is avoided by the practice of blaming others for one's own fault. It is a method of compensation. Those who hold to high ideals while at the same time revealing serious weakness of disposition are most liable to find a way of escape from self-criticism by projecting upon someone else their own flaws of character. It has long been recognized that people tend to be hard on those who have the same faults as themselves. For example, a New Hampshire judge who drank heavily and was frequently so intoxicated as to be incapable of properly holding court was notoriously severe with persons who came before him charged with drunkenness. It was as if he found in the severe punishment of others a relief from his own feeling of guilt.

The family as a group may be made the victim of projection, or some member of the family may be selected. Thus the inefficient and unsuccessful husband may accuse the family as a whole of extravagance that causes his failure, or some individual of the family may be selected for the blame.

The troubles that have come to one family circle vividly illustrate this. The head of the household is a clergyman of high ideals but with very patent faults. As soon as his daughter was engaged he began a constant sniping at the young man's faults. Eventually he brought about the breaking of the engagement, soon to find that this had not only alienated his daughter but had become an influence leading to the neurosis which she soon developed. At a later time, when the young woman had recovered, she remarked emphatically that she would never again tolerate such tactics on the part of her father. She states that what seems strangest to her was that the faults he had found in her lover were those which all his friends recognized as the chief defects of his own character. This was, of course, natural on the part of a man who was ever on the lookout for an emotional scapegoat upon whom he could put the sins that he did not dare to recognize within himself. The privacy, the intimacy, the frankness of the home afford an unrivaled opportunity for the getting rid of inner conflict through projection.

Case of L. D.

L. D. has revealed an astonishing amount of jealousy which has greatly increased during recent months. His wife states, and he does not deny the fact, that he is constantly charging her with showing interest in other men. L. D. says that it is impossible for her to go anywhere without his questioning her as to where she went and what she did as soon as she returned. She has found it necessary to abandon all her previous male friends, but even though she has as a result largely isolated herself socially she has not allayed his suspicions. In private conference, after he has been forced to acknowledge that he had never found any basis for his extreme jealousy, he admits dissatisfaction with his marriage and finally confesses that he has become fond of his secretary and would like to have a divorce and marry her, but, because of moral scruples and a realization that the fault is his not his wife's, he has not been able to take even the first step toward a divorce. He has not disclosed his change of interest to either woman and admits that it would be a shocking surprise to both of them were he to tell the truth. Meanwhile, it is apparent, even to himself, that he is projecting on his wife his own cravings and protecting himself from a guilt feeling by his unjustified suspicions of her conduct.

Regression. Any situation that involves progressive emotional growth becomes a temptation for some individuals to return to an earlier and less exacting condition. This going backward from painful demands brought forth through the need of adjusting to new experiences is known as regression. Domestic fellowship invites this type of emotional immaturity and as a consequence there are those who, upon becoming conscious of the obligations brought to them by marriage and by parenthood, attempt to escape these conditions by an emotional return to some earlier status.

Marriage cannot avoid this making of new demands upon those who unite their lives, because it cannot be a static relationship. It offers opportunity for advancement in emotional development, but the individual may shy away, finding the cost of maturity emotionally too great. There may be unwillingness to accept the conditions of progress, once they are realized, a reluctance to give up the more pleasurable situation of the past. One of the common illustrations of regression is the woman's attitude toward pregnancy. Foreseeing what the coming of the child will mean, she may retreat from motherhood through fear of the physical danger of childbirth, unwillingness to abandon the freedom she has so long enjoyed, a belief that the having of a child may lessen her physical attractiveness, or the dread that the child will divide the affection that is now entirely concentrated on her. Realizing that the safest protection against pregnancy is to go back as far as possible to the courtship situation, or to her premarriage program, she becomes emotionally estranged from the normal fellowship of marriage. Invalidism is a common method of forcing the husband to consent to this withdrawal. Another favorite reaction is to assume a frigidity which will tend to establish the domestic relationship on interests far removed from those that carry risk of an unwanted child.

There are, of course, many occasions when regression is only partial or fails to accomplish the purpose in the mind of the husband or the wife attempting it. For example, in spite of the wife's program, adopted as a means of protecting herself from pregnancy, she may have a child. Immediately a new type of problem may arise. The attitude she persistently takes toward the child may prove disastrous to his emotional development. In spite of the mother's undertaking the duties of his nurture and care, his realization as he grows older of his mother's fundamental hostility may lead to a feeling of insecurity on his part and later to an emotional conflict. Trouble may also come from another quarter. The mother may become dissociated because emotionally she cannot commit herself to the task that her child has brought her, nor can she be easy of conscience in any open neglect. There may also develop an incompatibility between husband and wife because one detects in the other this inherent unwillingness to take over the responsibilities that parenthood has brought.

Regression has a special appeal for those who feel frustrated in their will-to-power craving. For example, a woman who, as a wife, appears in her thinking to have lost the position she held in her husband's regard before the marriage, naturally looks longingly back to the courtship situation. Her maneuvering may become an attempt to re-establish the more satisfying premarriage relationship. The illustrations of regression are clearest in the case of the woman, but this does not mean that husbands never accept this way of escape from unpleasant family situations.

CASE OF B. N.

Mr. and Mrs. B. N. face a difficult problem of adjustment. The fact is more obvious to the wife than to the husband and it is she who has insisted that they visit a marriage counselor. They are both intelligent, well-meaning persons, and although their affection has been greatly strained during their six years of marriage there can be no question of the sincerity of their love. The problem essentially is the lack of companionship which the wife feels in her association with her husband. She says he was different during courtship but that since their marriage he sinks into himself when they are together and denies her the fellowship she has the right to expect. He agrees with her criticism but explains that he was shy and lonely and unhappy in childhood and that it seems impossible for him to be naturally companionable. He admits that during courtship he succeeded better in accomplishing this than he has since marriage. He thinks that his wife should be satisfied because she knows that he loves her and seeks to do the best he can for her and their one child. When she demonstrates in any outward way her love for him, he withdraws as by an irresistible impulse and just cannot make the response that her type of individual finds so natural. He makes an effort, but this only hurts her all the more because it seems so clearly an attempt to do what is expected of him rather than what he really wishes. For some reason, which doubtless would be understood only through a prolonged psychoanalysis, he retreats to childhood and does not respond frankly to his wife's affection. His work, in which he is highly successful, seems to be

the refuge he has found from this habit of regressing to the behavior that was characteristic of him during boyhood and of which
he became painfully conscious during adolescence. He admits that
he is a disappointing husband but believes that to ask him to change
is a demand so unnatural to his personality as to be an impossibility. He is reluctant to talk about his childhood although willing
to explain in general terms that the influences of his early life led
him to live emotionally within himself. He cannot explain how he
was able during courtship to act so differently but claims that he
was acting a part because it seemed necessary to win his wife and
that it is too much to expect that he will continue in marriage a
behavior so alien to his true self.

Fixation.   Fixation is one of the most common of emotional difficulties in the family experience. It is the consequence
of a previous conditioning of the child by one of the parents. The
individual has been influenced in the formative years to make an
unbreakable attachment to the mother or to the father. There
may be any one of three reactions, each leading to personal unhappiness. There may be such reluctance to leave the parent or
the parent's ideal as to make marrying impossible. Marriage
may take place but the choice of the mate be entirely dominated
by the desire to find in some other human being a prototype of
the parent on whom the individual has become an emotional
parasite. There may be marriage followed by a constant endeavor of the individual suffering from the fixation to remain
true to the father or mother, with the consequence that adjustment instead of being directed toward the relationship with the
husband or wife becomes a hopeless struggle to find in matrimony the means of carrying on a fixation characteristic of childhood. The insistence that parents come to live with the newly
married couple is frequently born of the desire to repeat the
environmental conditions experienced before marriage. As a
consequence, the parents become to the other member of the
union an obstruction to happiness, and an attitude of hostility
develops which all the more complicates the unfortunate domestic situation. Fixation often shows itself in the very first days of
marriage and starts a rift which only widens as the days pass.

As Sears [1] has pointed out, the significance of fixation appears in the detrimental effect it has on social growth and as an

---

[1] Sears, Robert R., *Survey of Objective Studies on Psychoanalytic Concepts.*

inducement to regression. When, for example, a spouse makes unsatisfactory adjustment to his or her partner on account of a fixation on a parent, the strength of the original adhesion is increased by the frustration which results. On the other hand, successful adaptation to the new opportunity for affection and intimacy offered by marriage lessens previous liability. Frequently the early days of marriage are decisive because either the spouse immediately withdraws from the challenge of the new relationship or starts an emotional competition which as it develops and produces its satisfactions leads the man or woman to give in proper proportion emotional responsiveness to the parent and to the spouse.

Case of M. J.

M. J. has had throughout her marriage such a fixation on her father that it has been evident to everyone who has come to know her. Whatever the topic of conversation she soon turns it towards something connected with her father. She is apt, even to a casual acquaintance and in the presence of her husband, to contrast him unfavorably with her father. There is, in fact, nothing to justify this, for although her father was a good man he was in no way remarkable. Her husband has had greater training and during the early period of his marriage was more successful in his profession than was the father in his vocation. The father is dead, but the emotional meaning that he has for his daughter has been increased rather than diminished by his passing. The wife's constant harping upon the virtues of the father has led to a secret estrangement of the husband, and this apparently has been the cause of the husband's decreased efficiency in his business. This has so worried some of his friends that he has been persuaded to seek counsel and as a result of an interview has persuaded the wife to talk over with the counselor what she regards as her marriage problems. Her interview turned chiefly into a eulogy of the father and a criticism of the husband. She refused to take any blame for the increasing incompatibility she herself had come to recognize. Instead she used this as her chief argument for the necessity of the husband's trying to emulate the personality of her father. The husband does not appear strong enough to withstand the attack constantly being made upon him, and the prognosis of this marriage, unless some new condition arises, is not hopeful.

Dissociation. Marriage provides a peculiar form of disintegration of behavior as a consequence of emotional dissociation.

Commonly it appears in the man through his having linked the physical side of marriage with an outcast type of woman who stands in contrast with a different sort, worthy of respect and symbolizing the maternal. Having built in his premarriage days an ethical code that assumes this distinction in women, he finds with the coming of matrimony a division of sentiment regarding his wife according to whether he thinks of her as a physical or an affectionate mate. Similarly, the woman who has been led through childhood teaching to idealize the second and to debase the first of these two aspects of marriage finds in matrimony a distinct cleavage of emotional attitudes. The consequences of this inner division may take the form of such serious objection to marital relationship as to become from the beginning a basic incompatibility. Sometimes the domestic discord brings the unfortunate husband or wife to some kind of neurosis. Often, fortunately, domestic experience becomes the schoolmaster, and integration is achieved by changing the earlier notion and bringing together the two complementary aspects of marriage.

CASE OF R. E.

The mental illness of R. E. which culminated in her suicide was too complex either to be fully understood or to be interpreted as the consequences only of her domestic unhappiness. There is some evidence that there was a basic hereditary unsoundness, but it is equally clear that her disappointment as a wife had a considerable part in the bringing about of the neurosis from which she suffered. Any woman would have reacted against the cold-blooded motivation that led her husband to ask her to marry him. After her death he confessed that he felt that he could not go on so well in his profession unmarried and that he chose his wife because of all the women he knew she was the least undesirable. The first disclosure of her dissatisfaction was to a friend of her husband, who was also a counselor. She illustrated her husband's indifference by various examples of his unconcern, even when one of their children was seriously ill and she had no person to help her care for him other than her husband. This confession was followed a year or two later by her expression of anxiety over the behavior of one of her children. This adolescent had gotten in such serious difficulty that under different economic circumstances it might have led to his commitment to a reform school. The trouble that had occurred disturbed the husband as well as the wife since he felt that it endangered his professional standing. Following the successful solution of this problem—the adolescent growing up to make a good adjustment to life—the unhappiness of the wife soon showed itself again. It became apparent that she was in conflict, blaming herself for disloyalty as she admitted to herself the antagonism and bitterness that she began to have for her husband. The disturbance of her inner life increased rapidly, and soon she herself as well as her husband recognized the need of the help of a specialist. The problem was turned over to a competent psychiatrist, but before he had made headway in his effort to help her by psychoanalysis, her malady had reached the point that required her commitment. She deliberately planned the ending of her life, and finally succeeded.

Fantasy.   Marriage, by the great appeal it makes to human emotions, provides an unrivaled means of retreat from the undesired facts of life. Beginning with the courtship itself there is built up in the mind of husband or wife, or both, an elaborate fantasy which is justified as idealism. The first attack that is made upon this elaboration of fancy is regarded as hostile to the relationship. As a rule such an attack coming from the realities of life is twisted so as to seem a result of the partner's unworthiness. Then the marriage relationship is viewed as a betrayal of the earlier expression of love. Marriage may have been primarily sought as a refuge from hard circumstances, and the moment it appears that the attempt to escape the hardships, the limitations, and the responsibilities of life is futile, there is intense rebellion. Matrimony or parenthood is blamed for shattering the defense against the realities of life, which in the mind of the victim appears as justifiable idealism. If the turning to fantasy is born of the desire to be rid of inferiority feeling, any domestic experience which shatters protection is reacted against with all the emotion belonging to the original inferiority feeling. This explains why husbands and wives react so violently to criticism from each other, which, coming from someone else, would be counted trivial.

The illusive element in all human experience has been commented upon by philosophers since the days of the Greek thinkers, but marriage has been singled out by them as the most vivid illustration of the inevitable disappointment that comes to one who is forced to bring his hope of happiness in contact with the given facts of actual life. Poetry, fiction, and most especially the small talk of the sophisticated adult who prides himself upon his practicality is replete with the idea that disappointment in marriage is axiomatic.

Much of this is the product of a sensible interpretation of common happenings. Men and women do enter marriage with expectations of perfect happiness furnished by an imagination that, driven by the powerful flow of emotions and unrestrained by experience, pictures a state of bliss that nothing human could satisfy. Disillusionment in such cases is bound to come, not as the result of a serious deception in the relationship itself but simply because fancy must at last surrender to fact. Such experiences occur constantly as the individual travels forward from childhood and tries in one way and another to fulfill his cravings. The happy husband and wife look back upon these earlier adjustments with a tender sympathy but with no sense of having been betrayed by false hopes. The fact is that more was gained by the ordeal than was lost.

This transition from love-making to marriage does hold an element of danger and becomes for some married couples a cause of psychological incompatibility. The appeal of courtship for some persons lies almost wholly in its fantasy. They insist upon remaining in an atmosphere that gives them the luxury of the daydream. If the husband or wife becomes the instrument by which such a person is brought back to reality or even pushed toward it, at once upon the head of the ill-fated partner in matrimony falls the blame for having spoiled marriage. The daydreamer who has carried on from childhood the habit of castle-building is the kind of person who cannot make the adjustment from courtship to family responsibility required by wholesome marriage. Any attempt to bring the family life into accord with actual circumstances is resented, and the other member of the matrimonial alliance is chided with bitterness for lack of affection.

It is necessary in such cases to notice that any other relationship involving responsibility and adjustment to obligations would have revealed the character defect just as did marriage. Marriage tempts such persons because courtship offers an exceptional chance for the daydreamer's revels, and they accept marriage as a means of prolonging this delightful experience. These daydreamers detect the ordeal awaiting them in other relationships and either refuse to enter or else try to protect themselves from the rude awakening which they always dread. Marriage is not justly charged with having misled the type of person whose whole life is a pilgrimage in deceit.

The woman who declares that marriage offers nothing except the pleasures of courtship and of the wedding confesses her inability to pass into a mature family relationship, and her statement that marriage is a failure is actually a confession of an infantile character that forbids a genuine trial of marriage.

Marriage is by its nature a testing undertaking, since those who are trying to escape adult responsibilities and those who are unable to pass the examination are naturally more likely to blame their partners than to accept criticism for their own failure. Thus it comes about that family life is at times marked almost at its beginning by the unwillingness of husband or wife to accept a normal, sincere commitment to the tasks of married life.

The problem of fantasy in domestic experience is complicated by the fact that many do lose their original momentum and allow high hopes to fade away and be replaced by dull routine. They rationalize their failure by proclaiming that their attitude at the opening of marriage was merely a sort of hothouse fantasy which could not be expected to withstand the hardships of everyday living. All the idealism and thought of another's welfare that some individuals ever experience in any large way appears in courtship. After marriage these persons flatten out and settle down to a Main Street humdrum that blankets all the hopes of their finer-grained spouse. Protest against making marriage a deadening routine is not evidence of a daydreamer's hostility to the meeting of life squarely, but of a discernment of the tragedy of allowing the finer attitudes of early marriage to evaporate.

A wife or husband who sees that the family has sunk through the other's indifference into an endless round of toil or social dissipation has a just cause for feeling cheated. It is difficult to become reconciled to the draining of any experience of all its human values, but impossible to see a relationship that opens with the promise characteristic of the beginning of marriage fade into dull or even coarse routine without profound resentment. Courtship can at times stir into temporary flame what appears to be noble passion, but due to thinness of personality the fire soon dies down. Even if the attitude was genuine during courtship, it appears wilful deceit to the other member of the new family who feels victimized by the marriage partner's pretenses.

Good adjustment in marriage escapes both persistent fantasy and disillusionment; the past is not remembered as a glimpse of paradise, and the present is not regarded as largely barren of value.

Case of M. H. R.

Miss R. is a chronic victim of daydreaming. The imaginary world in which she spent much of her time during childhood was carried over into adolescence. Her make-believe, even when she had reached the twenties, was at times a worry to her parents and at other times appeared to amuse them. She began to carry on an imaginary courtship. A year or two later this became a more substantial fixation on different men with whom she happened to be associated. The significant fact, however, was that these always were married men and that her interest was expressed under such circumstances that there could be no reciprocity of expression. She was merely enjoying a new kind of fantasy, an emotional commitment that carried with it no responsibility. Meanwhile, younger men came and went who might have been genuine lovers, but toward them she presented a barrier, for though she was physically attractive, economically independent, well educated in a conventional sense, and undoubtedly could have married, she never allowed her romantic attachments to stray toward anyone that might have forced upon her any acceptance of the realities of life. After a decade or two of this kind of play acting she turned to her final fantasy and wrapped herself up in fictions and ideas, all of occult character, that barricaded her against the obligations and responsibilities of ordinary life. Aside from this clinging to fantasy throughout her career, she disclosed no oddity or social unsoundness.

The nervous housewife.   The emotional maladjustments of family life are encouraged by the reaction of some women to the vocational liabilities of housekeeping. The dangers from this source unfortunately do not show themselves clearly at the beginning of most marriages when the wife takes over the responsibilities of homemaking. Indeed, on the contrary, for a time the new type of work may appear more interesting and seem to offer the wife more self-expression than was true of any previous employment outside her parent's home. This is the result of having opportunity in starting housekeeping to make decisions and carry out preferences and ambitions as she begins building a home of her own. The furnishing of the house, cooking of meals, and similar activities provide a sense of achievement which is not lessened by her knowledge that she is increasing the comforts and satisfaction of her husband as well as herself. It is only when the new adventure has changed to a repetitious routine that the hazards begin to show themselves. These are enhanced by the conditions of her work. This has impressively been described by Abraham Myerson,[2] who points out that, in spite of verbal dignifying, a great part of the tasks of the housewife is menial with little opportunity for a feeling of prestige. In addition, a woman works usually in isolation, and if she previously has had the opportunities of a highly gregarious vocation she reacts from the monotony that cannot be avoided. The moment she begins to feel dissatisfied she may turn toward daydreaming or reverie for relief, but this will only intensify her rebellion against the reality to which she has to return.

It is also of no small consequence that her work must be carried on within the same environment where she experiences her husband-wife relationship. The man goes from his home and returns to it; the advantage of this appears whenever we consider the disadvantages of the man who tries to work at home, as, for example, the author. It is generally found that he must in some way isolate himself from the household life or better still transfer his literary workshop altogether outside the house. The home environment may mean refuge and comfort to the man, while to his wife it suggests only home duties. This in itself can become emotionally disturbing if the husband will not cooperate in helping her rid herself of this sense of housekeeping responsibilities by out-of-the-home activities. It may not be true that the wife works harder than the man. The more penetrating question is whether what she does creates greater tension. The answer frequently has to be based upon whether she feels balked in her self-expression or has the satisfaction of personal achievement.

The noncompetitive character of household work creates another liability, and this in turn is greatly determined by the

<hr>

[2] Myerson, Abraham, *The Nervous Housewife*.

wife's previous career and the effect it has had during the building of her personality. Nervousness, a term for a mild type of neurosis, can easily become the means of emotional escape from the disheartening domestic situation while bringing her a measure of protection, sense of dominance, and an outlet for imagined or actual inattention. It may also carry her into the forefront of the domestic relationship and even provide an opportunity to develop a feeling of importance. In the case of the nervous housewife it is easy to blame either her or her husband. This attempt to explain what has occurred by the egoistic traits of one or the other is superficial in that it does not recognize that whether one or both are at fault the basic fact is that the individual is a victim of previous bad training for life, with an inability to handle the environmental stresses and that he or she may not be able to control former habit traits, at least to the extent that is necessary to remove the hazards of housekeeping; and therefore re-education, the reshaping of a life philosophy, offers the only hope of lessening the tension which is finding an outlet through some sort of neurotic reaction.

The total situation. Although we are tempted in the analysis of domestic experience to see in any interpretation of maladjustment, emotional in origin, an explanation based upon a particular fault of personality or an environmental causation, or both, this exposition is logical rather than psychological and exaggerates the importance of something which has contributed to the difficulty rather than determined it. Always it is the total situation that counts. It is because of this that we find a condition which appears to be the cause of marriage failure in one case being surmounted in another, even eventually cementing all the more strongly the mutual affection of the husband and wife. The two situations are not the same even when the trouble-making influence seems similar. Difference comes to the surface when the totality of the situation is recognized. Experience demonstrates that the successful relationship between the spouses and between the parents and children is not decided by propitious circumstances or the opposite. Success may be favored or made more difficult by an auspicious or adverse influence. The final outcome is the consequence of emotional reaction in its totality, and were it not so, there would be no meaning in the marriage troth and the mutual pledges of the spouses for better or for worse. Marriage-family relationship in such circumstances would be secure only as it thrived on good fortune. In counseling people in domestic trouble, it is especially important to keep in mind that the effort to get at causation and solution both require recognizing the total situation in an emotional interaction that is both concrete and unique.

The protective and therapeutic functions of family life. Their profoundness, their intimacy, and the demands made of them for security, comfort, compensation, and self-realization expose both marriage and family life to the hazards of emotional excesses. The most important of these have been dealt with in the preceding pages of this chapter. They need to be understood bcause they then can be successfully guarded against. These maladjustments are faulty growths of what rightly developed would be wholesome human impulses. As they affect emotional adjustment they are like the riotous cell that becomes a cancer and destroys the physical soundness of the body. They are not normal products of family life but the consequences of the misusing of the resources marriage and the family provide for the achievement of emotional satisfaction. Unless this is kept in mind, the student is left with a distorted and depressing impression of American domestic experience.

In a later chapter which discusses the successful family, emphasis is placed upon the values potentially present in the fellowship of the home. There is need, however, in this treatment of the emotional aspects of family life to emphasize the protective and even therapeutic services of both marriage and the family for the human individual. Elsewhere, in some detail, the senior author has portrayed the family as both the nursery and chief support of man and his culture. "The social functions that belong to the family give it the key position in the program of social adaptation which decided the survival of each civilization just as the physical and psychic adjustment determines the life-career of each individual."[3] It is most important that the reader appreciate the significance of the contributions the family usually makes to the emotional maturing and stability of the individual. We ask more of the home than of our other interests and, as a rule, it provides us with the most important

[3] Groves, Ernest R., *The Family and its Social Functions*, p. 594.

of our character-making influences. Much of this material that contributes to the building of our personalities is so matter of fact, a product of intimate association, that we are unaware of its dominance or its value. This unobtrusiveness adds all the more to the power the family life has. In relation to our emotional life both marriage and the family, if they function normally, protect from frustration, encourage maturity, and in great disturbance prove themselves profoundly therapeutic. Illustrations of this are commonplace. The exceptions attract attention, since what is more usual we ordinarily take for granted. The physician, or specialist, or ministerial counselor who is called upon to give help to someone face to face with an emotional crisis knows that no stronger ally can be found for the one in trouble than an affectionate and understanding home. Since many of these most terrific emotional upheavals are themselves connected with a family situation, it is found that either establishing another home by marriage or reconstructing the disturbing relationship so that the family functions properly is the best way of restoring security and dissolving conflict.

Never has there been such a massive revelation of the efficacy of the family in restoring confidence for those who have felt that the very worth-whileness of life has been annihilated than during and following World War II. This strengthening power of family ties has been impressive everywhere among people who have suffered great misfortunes because of the conflict. Without doubt, the reader of this book through his ordinary contacts of life has become familiar with illustrations of the protective and therapeutic influences of family relationships. The following examples briefly summarize such contributions.

C. W. was a Congregational minister, extraordinarily sincere and occasionally audacious and untactful, but always human and friendly in his attitudes toward others. He married, and the intense affection that appeared on his face at the wedding never faltered, although for nearly two decades his wife's illness brought him constant anxiety and hardships far beyond the ordinary. For ten years his wife lived an uneventful life, exercising a constructive influence that greatly enhanced her husband's development and self-discipline. Then she fell ill with an incurable malady which made her an invalid and sentenced her to a wheel chair from which she was unable to move herself. He had never served other than rural churches, and his income was too small for him to employ either a nurse or someone to help him with the housework. He took over the care of his wife and learned to keep house, but the revealing fact was his ability to maintain this program for two decades without ever showing any weariness or resentment. Indeed, he had none, and he found delight in expressing with a patient courage his affection. He endured his daily caretaking, and the thought that it was difficult or praiseworthy never entered his mind. Thirty years of devotion finally came to an end with her death. His followed within the year.

S. F. Y. Miss Y. became a campus leader in one of our large universities, winning the respect of all who knew her. After graduation she trained for social work where she has had a successful career. Her father and mother were divorced when she was a small child, and her mother became an alcoholic who in a fit of depression took her own life. The divorce occurred so early that the child hardly knew her father, who lived in a distant part of the United States. She, however, corresponded with him. Following her mother's death, which occurred when she was still in high school, she began to drink herself and was placed in a private school. Here, according to opportunity, especially during vacation, she carried on a wild life which included living for a time in New York with a married man. Then two new influences entered her life. "I had dinner with my father. I hadn't seen him at all for a long time, and I discovered a real person. It was so futile and rather hopeless to realize that always my father and mother had loved each other but that environmental circumstances had licked them both. Soon after, I met a junior at Harvard, and within a short time we were engaged. There was nothing sordid about this affair. He was a clean-cut boy with high ideals. I was not yet ready to trust my feelings. I lacked confidence in my outlook on life. Nevertheless, there was a definite change that year. I had come into the world of values—decency, love, respect—and they were important in releasing me from my past frame of mind and in the reshaping of it. The following Christmas, to test myself, I went to New York and met the married man with whom I had previously played around and who had repeatedly asked me to come. I stayed in the same hotel with him, and in a day I knew the kind of person I had become could not be prostituted by the kind of person I had been and I knew definitely that I could no longer be drawn back into that futile life, and that was a big step forward. I want to marry someone who is adventurous along the line of social justice, doing something for the practical alleviation of society's ills. There have been three such people in the last two years, one of whom I am very fond of, but I can't marry without love. I want all that goes with marriage. I have knocked around enough to know what I do want. I am in no hurry for it, even though it is a large part of my make-up if I could find the right person. Fortunately, I have other channels for my outlet which will be satisfactory until I find the right person. And if I don't, they will give me a fairly complete life. And this story has a happy ending. My father and I have become very good friends through our letters. This summer for the first time in five years I am going home to have the fun of knowing him for a few brief weeks."

T. M. When a little child, too young to remember the details, she was assaulted by a seventeen-year-old boy. A similar attempt was later made by the director of a summer camp. During adolescence she had to fight her way out of several unpleasant situations. It is apparent, however, that her fellowship with her aunt and her feeling toward her father and her sense of security from what she learned of her parents' love provided a bulwark against the unpleasant situations. "When I was a year old my mother died. Until I was four my sister and brother and I lived with my father, who hired various housekeepers to take care of us in the day. This was not a very satisfactory arrangement, and because of that and also because of financial difficulties we went to live with my mother's sister. The little I know of my mother's and father's married life seems to indicate that they were very happy. They married late, both being about thirty-five. I was born when my mother was forty-nine. Of course, I remember nothing about her, but I have heard my aunt say many times that she believed Daddy loved Mother as much the day he died as he did the day they were married. Aunt E. has never married, and I've heard it said that it is very difficult to grow up normally with an unmarried woman. I admit that sometimes I rather missed not having a real honest-to-goodness mother and father; that is, I really sometimes envied my friends who did. But I don't think my personality is warped because of it. Aunt E. has never shunned men. She was in love once, many years ago, and although she never told me so I think she has kept him in her heart these many years. They were engaged to be married when he died of typhoid fever. And recently I have realized more than ever, as you will see later on in my story, what a wonderful person she is.

"I used to tell lies—not stories like most children tell but real lies. They didn't come from my imagination and I didn't believe they were true. I wasn't even sorry I had told them after I'd been caught up with. I just wished nobody had found out they weren't true. Now I realize that probably many of my difficulties came from the fact that I never felt quite secure. I remember my whole family telling me that I didn't even bear a family resemblance to any of them. I'd lie awake nights and think maybe I'd been adopted. I'd always have the feeling that I didn't exactly belong, not even to my friends. But as I grew older I mastered this feeling of inferiority or whatever it was, and I grew to be a very happy person. But right then I made up my mind that I was going to have children of my own and never let them feel as I did.

"My attitude toward marriage is that of the normal young girl towards marriage. Perhaps I expect too much, but who wouldn't with T. You may tell me that is the wrong way to look at it, but I feel as if we have seen each other in the most difficult circumstances and I think we both know each other's faults as well as it is possible to know them before we are married. We have always been willing to make concessions to each other, and I see no reason to think we'll stop suddenly as soon as we are married. I think we can work out our problems, and if we find that we don't, we will take them to someone who can help us. I hope we won't have any trouble, but I'm glad I've found out that people do so I'll know what to do if we do have trouble. We're both planning to take physical exams before the wedding."

B. M. M. Here we see the family influence giving guidance and support as the young woman with greater maturity finds herself obliged to break an engagement which has lost its promise. "My environment was always the most pleasant imaginable. My father is a college professor; therefore, we were neither wealthy nor poor. I have never been at a loss for something to do . . . a thing my father will not tolerate. I used to read very much, but I was mostly occupied with my music—piano and cello. I was never terribly social minded, although I have always enjoyed the company of others and have never failed to make a friendship where I wanted to. But I have always gotten the most pleasure out of the things I could do myself, since I was brought up with this intention on the part of my parents . . . that I should always have a wealth of things within me to enjoy.

"My sister married when I was eleven, and for the past nine years her married life has had an immense effect upon my outlook and attitudes. As an onlooker, I have learned volumes in the art of patience, self-control, tolerance, and diplomacy in marriage. She has a little girl two years old who has the most beautiful disposition of any child I know, which I am sure is the result of the qualities mentioned above along with the perfect harmony of her environment. I have consciously trained myself in my relations with everybody in order to achieve such happy relations in marriage with a minimum of difficulty and conflict.

"I met him in August, 1939, and last summer we became engaged. We had a wonderful time while we were going together . . . a fact which I argued compensated me for the contacts and experience I missed at the time. As long as I had a better time with him and enjoyed his company more than that of anyone else, I saw no reason for not spending my time with him. My family took him in completely, and I was as sure and happy as I thought it possible to be. Our physical relation to each other was not a very difficult problem.

"Then about three weeks ago a lot of things happened. I began to realize that I was rationalizing concerning a good many things and began to feel more and more that there was the possibility of making a mistake in spite of the abundance of time I had had to make up my mind. During all this unsettled time I met W. R., thirty-one years old, with whom I went out when B. H. was not here. We got along together amazingly well, especially considering that we were from different parts of the country and did not have common friends or background to fall back on for conversation or entertainment. We had spent many innocent, gay times together when I began to realize that I was having entirely too good a time under the circumstances of my being engaged to be married.

"I spent a great deal of time trying to think the whole thing through before I finally went to my family with my problem. My mother was quite upset because of her devotion to B. H. and because I had allowed things to progress so far before becoming doubtful. I tried to explain that the feeling of apprehension and uncertainty had come even before W. R. and that his part was in accentuating this feeling. I may have been rationalizing even then, but all this is still too recent for me to analyze clearly. At any rate, my father was very stabilizing and advised me to let things work themselves out for awhile and emphasized the wisdom of keeping my own counsel.

"I finally realized that in order to be fair not only to myself but to B. H. the engagement had to be broken. And so, not quite three weeks ago, I summoned all my courage and common sense and explained everything as well as I could to him. It was not pleasant, but it was with a minimum of bitterness, and I was more than relieved to have him know my feelings. I know he was made very unhappy, and I was miserable at having done so with the knowledge that I could blame no one but myself and that I alone was responsible.

"In the past two weeks, however, I have become increasingly confident that I acted wisely, for I have had time to think reflectively without pressure. Practically we would have gotten along beautifully, but aesthetically we were opposed. My music meant nothing to him except in so far as it pleased me, and our religious ideas were quite different also. But even these arguments do not keep me from seeing that it was an unfortunate occurrence which made a good many people unhappy. My one consolation is that it happened when it did, and also that assurance that one's future life is one thing to be utterly honest in considering.

"W. R. has been a great pleasure to me. He has known the whole situation all along and has been very understanding and helpful and I am sure that it is not just because it is naturally in his interest to be so. I am extremely fond of him, but having learned the hard way I shall be more than cautious and deliberate, especially since I might be more than normally susceptible after my emotional turmoil."

Chapter 9

BEHAVIOR ASPECTS OF
FAMILY LIFE

FOREWORD. There is a great amount of activity that takes place in the home which although of great value as household routine lacks the special significance found in the responses to relationship that are discussed in this chapter. This does not deny the usefulness of such behavior, because it is indispensable to the comfort and security of the family members; it is, however, as a rule, essentially impersonal even though it may be rooted in a basic devotion. What it does not have is the emotional content of a different kind of family interaction. The latter takes on meaning and immediately is distinguished from labor such as that of the janitor or the housekeeper or the cook or the laundry worker and becomes a behavior expression of family intimacy. This sort of behavior may be either emotionally caused or emotionally stimulating, or both. It has significance for its author and also for other members of the family in so far as it is recognized by them and brings forth reaction. Any conduct, however trivial, can become a vehicle for the expression of emotional reactions. In the analysis of behavior a distinction has to be made between behavior as an objective and as a subjective fact; the latter is frequently plural since the practice may have a meaning to the person responsible for it and a different meaning to the others who are conscious of it. Much of this behavior tends to become, as is later stated in this chapter, habitual; especially is this true where incompatibility develops in an ever deepening pattern. A great portion of this behavior aspect, when it finds advantageous expression in family life, does not become stereotyped, so that we have an ever changing

236

drama as the various members of the family respond in their contacts one to another. In the adults, as one would expect, the tendency is toward a large amount of repercussions in conduct, disclosing the emotional consequences of the individual's pre-marriage life, especially his childhood experience. The child, on the other hand, expresses an originating conduct in the process of building personality and social patterns which he, likewise in later adulthood, will tend to give vent to as he assumes family responsibility.

Personality and domestic interaction. Domestic behavior can be interpreted in so wide a meaning as to include a very great part of the activity connected with the family. Even the individual's vocational interests, because they are a means of support, can be drawn within the concept of domestic behavior. In this chapter, the term "behavior aspects of family life" is used in a more restricted, specific sense. It seeks to describe the significant activities that have to do with the relationship of marriage or of the home. These are necessarily influenced by personality backgrounds and especially the previous emotional career of the individual, but they are expressions of personality brought forth through the association which constitutes the substance of marriage or family life. Although these two categories of domestic behavior blend once children come into the home, analysis is easier and clearer if they are distinguished.

To do full justice to the meaning of domestic behavior it is necessary to go beyond the mere interactions as they represent immediate response at a definite time and recognize motivations which gather their strength because they look toward the future and include the goals which are causal incentives. These are not one but many. Not always are they conscious; indeed in some degree it is safe to say that they are usually too deeply rooted emotionally in the average life to be fully conscious. The distant goals of desire may not be the immediate incitements to action but rather the final motivations that the philosophically inclined would seek to discover; nevertheless, these cravings are potent in stimulating conduct because they are underlying desires. Unfortunately, in many instances this quest for future fulfill-ment of personality yearning loses vitality early and fades away, but even when this happens habit life as it appears in domestic routine usually secures the family, enforced as it is by the pressure born of the previous social background of the individual and the conventions of American culture.

Family life provides a special field for human behavior; it does not add to the personality any fundamentally new equipment nor does it lead to a re-creation of the individual's characteristic disposition. It merely furnishes opportunity for a reconstruction of interests and demands self-expression in activities that are in part new and in part continued from the past, but with new meaning. This is true even of sex, which superficially seems often to come into existence through marriage. Recent science agrees that even this form of domestic interaction is not the spontaneous awakening it seems. It is an experience to which each personality brings a past that has a determining influence on the behavior. Parenthood also, aside from minor changes of physiological character as the result of pregnancy, childbirth, nursing, and the like in the case of the woman, merely offers a new outlet for self-expression, and this has been anticipated in some degree through the child's identification with one or both parents and through play; it does not remake the character of either mother or father. Ordinarily the personality of those entering domestic interaction is not only conditioned by preceding experience but from an emotional point of view is more heavily conditioned than is true of other lines of activity.

Even to the most thoughtless, entrance upon marriage appears as a considerable break from past experience, and it is this that makes matrimony seem something unique. What actually happens is that the new types of activities and reclustering of interests bring on a new level a renewal of earlier influences, so that past patterns of behavior are carried over into new forms of interaction and are intensified. In this process each personality becomes an environment to the other, a source of stimuli that are highly emotional in quality. This is true of all relationships that lead to interaction, but the family constitutes a special type that has its distinguishing features. To the extent that either member of the family grows indifferent to the attitudes and reactions of the other, there is emotional removal from the family relationship. Thus indifference insulates from stimulus and response and contracts the range of domestic interaction. On the other hand, strong emotion flowing forth from past conditioning may intensify at some point the interaction until the experience dominates all other contacts, finally determining for one or both of those reacting to the other the meaning of these relationships.

The mutuality of this interaction needs emphasis. Even though one of those in the domestic drama takes a leading role and dominates the others, he who overtops the rest nevertheless reacts causally to them. Since each adult concerned comes to the relationship laden with past experiences and whatever psychic consequences these may have brought, there has to be an adjustment of the emotional predispositions of all who are linked together in domestic contact. To picture this mutual reaction as merely a clashing of different emotional backgrounds and incentives misinterprets the situation. This is one side of the reaction and the one that gets most attention because it reveals the causation of much domestic incompatibility. The other aspect is even more significant, constituting an emotional accommodation which is profoundly therapeutic in that it brings troublesome incentives into proper proportion and, what is more important, permits an emotional enrichment of both persons as each reacts to the other, because in a measure each vicariously shares the other's experience. It is unfortunate when the interpreter gets the false impression that everything of an emotional nature that happens in childhood is a liability in later adult life. On the contrary, the results of early experience are for most individuals their indispensable preparation for the adult career.

Domestic interaction a rehearsal. For the adult members of the family, and progressively for the children as they move away from the earlier stage of infancy, the family experience is repetitious. It gets in large proportion its meaning from the recurrence of activities and emotional reactions. The child builds a domestic disposition,[1] while the adult expresses and possibly attempts to reconstruct a domestic disposition previously established. With marriage the interactions of husband and wife take on a double aspect. These reactions are truly objective and are attempts to adjust to the realities of their situation, but they are also in faint or great degree subjective in that the existing facts are biased by the interpretations issuing

---

[1] Krueger, E. T., and Reckless, W. C., *Social Psychology*, pp. 21–22.

out of previous family experience. There is, of course, great variation between individuals as to the proportion of attention given to the past and present, and there may be such a difference between the reactions of husband and of wife as to constitute from the beginning of their union a cause of misunderstanding and incompatibility. The emphasis upon the earlier home life may be such as to make domestic experience for either husband or wife or both a straining of existing facts in the effort to force them to conform to the domestic prototype of childhood. Under such circumstances the interaction, instead of being a genuine effort at adjustment, becomes an attempt of the one holding to an idealized past to coerce the conduct of the other until it fits into the picture carried over from the past.

To the extent that earlier home life persists as an influence upon present behavior, it leads to two opposite reactions. One, and this is the more common, becomes a struggle to reproduce and idealize the past. The unwillingness of the married partner to assume the role put upon him, or any inability of response which appears as an obstacle to this resurrection of earlier experience, is looked upon as a fault of personality, a refusal to provide the happiness promised in courtship.

Case of M. H.

Mrs. M. H. in an extraordinary manner illustrated the feeling of a wife disappointed because it proved impossible for her to have during her marriage the continuation of conditions such as had prevailed in courtship. Most reluctantly she took over the responsibility of housekeeping, and later she became a mother. Although she fulfilled her duties with reasonable efficiency, she constantly revealed inner discontent. Not only did she chide her husband in the presence of neighbors and friends for, as she said, changing after marriage; she even more pointedly showed her preference for the conditions that had prevailed during courtship in her conversation with her women friends. Her marriage was essentially disillusionment; this did not mean that she had any particular grievance against her husband or any serious criticism. She thought of him as like all men. As soon as the wife was won, all the romance was thrown overboard and the entire spirit of courtship lost. Marriage was a sort of punishment, or at least penalty, for having accepted the pleasures of courtship. The wedding day was to her the climax of her life. At that moment she began to come down from the peak of emotional satisfaction and she urged her younger friends to carry on courtship as long as possible and warned them of the inevitable disappointment marriage would bring.

The opposite reaction appears in the endeavor to use the new domestic relationship to repudiate the old. In this case earlier bitterness, disillusionment, emotional conflict, and dissatisfaction lead to the desire to shut out of the present anything suggestive of the past or at least any condition which, as it appeared in former family life, was a cause of contention or a source of unhappiness. Although the attempts to reproduce and to repudiate past family life represent opposite domestic programs, it does not follow that the behavior of husband and wife, even when it leads chiefly toward one or the other of these purposes, is consistent. More often both reactions appear in the same individual who at the same time is attempting to find in present circumstances opportunity to revive the past and to divest himself of its persisting irritation.

This intrusion of past experience which obstructs objective adjustment must not be confused with the wholesome desire to learn from past experience how best to manage new problems. In the first reaction the individual carries the present back into the past and, instead of reacting to existing circumstances, seeks to find the means of retreating for emotional content from an existing domestic interaction to one that has substance only in memory. In the other reaction attention is directed toward existing facts, and the earlier happenings and reactions influence a program that seeks to deal with the realities that present themselves. In the one case the goal of effort is fictitious, planted in the past that cannot actually be made to live again, while in the other there is an endeavor to deal adequately with the present and there is a seeking after some form of objective adjustment.

In the latter case there is large opportunity for differences of opinion, differences of emphasis, and differences in desires, all complicating domestic interaction even when there is a firm purpose to face the actual problems of personal and social adjustment; but when one or both members of the union make use of present circumstances as the means of reproducing or repudiating the past merely to satisfy cravings usually infantile in character, confusion, separation, antagonism, and reproach are inevitable. The relationship may continue, for there may be motives that prevent an absolute break, but the distinctive feature of the association will be disorganization.

Interaction within the family framework. The interactions that appear within the family are, as we have seen, the product of normal human impulses. The family merely provides a special setting, a peculiar framework. This consists of a relationship, which, like other associations, has characteristic features. Even these are not exclusive to the family association as distinguishing features, for they appear in other close social contacts; but as compared with friendship, business partnership, and the like, these conditions that influence behavior are in the family essential to the relationship and have a constancy and form a synthesis not found in other associations.

Cooley was the first to emphasize family relationship as maintaining a constant, face-to-face association which distinguishes it from other associations that are partial and intermittent. His stress of its primary character was justified. Although it does not possess this feature exclusively,[2] it does, as a rule, have a greater amount of this kind of contact than is found in the other types of primary contact which he mentions—the playground of children and the neighborhood or community grouping of elders. It is not merely that in the family people are more often in relationship and over a longer period of time; they are likewise franker and more intimate. There is enough difference between the home and other primary associations to give the family its distinction as the most primary of all contact relationships.

It speaks well for the family and especially for marriage that this sharing of emotional expression to an extent rarely experienced in other associations is so generally successful. Of all the contacts that can be thought of as compulsory, in the sense that the family can be so described, no other achieves anything like the success that can be credited to the home. The same statement can be made of marriage when it is compared with other voluntary associations. The child without choice is born into a family, and from it he generally gets enough good training to permit him to become socially normal in his later adult relationships. Marriage is entered by personal pref-

---

[2] Cooley, Charles, *Social Organization,* p. 24.

erence, and, although in the United States its divorce rate is high, there can be little doubt that if other associations such as business partnership, friendship, selection of a roommate, and other self-chosen relationships could be broken only by something similar to a divorce, such public acknowledgment of failure would be much higher than the court record of the collapse of matrimonial unions. The most primary association is not only emotionally most significant; it is likewise emotionally most successful.

The lag between the progress of the personality toward greater maturity and the imperfect expression of this behavior because of a retardation coming from previous practices is not only a general retardation but also particular, opening the individual to the charge of inconsistency. This happens because behavior does not change equally at all points. The movement instead is similar to that which occurs on the battlefield. The line of behavior goes forward much more rapidly at one point than at some other where greater resistance has to be met. It is therefore nonfactual and unrealistic to suppose that domestic behavior is in all its aspects a consistent reflection of the individual's emotional maturity. For example, it is not uncommon to find that in the realm of sex adjustment, for reasons that are explained by family and social background, the individual meets problems less maturely than when adaptation and reconstruction of conduct are demanded at some other point of domestic relationship.

Likewise, there has to be recognition of the complicating influence of an extraordinary situation that perhaps can be best described as catastrophic. These exceptional experiences can of course be used to measure the genuineness of the maturity that is supposed to have taken place. Such appraisal is, however, unfair, because it does not do justice to the general tenor of the individual's career and does not consider the sudden and temporary departure from his usual attitude toward life. For example, a practising medical specialist who certainly as a rule was most objective and factual in the routine of his practice and household was for a moment thrown off balance when in the midst of a consultation word came to him that his infant son had just swallowed an open safety pin. The emotionalism clearly revealed when he was first shocked by the information did not prevent him from meeting somewhat later the challenge of making good use of his professional skill in removing the pin. In explaining his reaction in the spirit of apology some days later he said how many times he had known this accident to prove fatal. This background has to be taken into account when his first emotional reaction is used as a test of the stability and maturity of the doctor. Can he be rightly judged by the immediate effect of an accident which had more meaning to him because of his professional insight than would be true of most parents or by his later recovery that permitted him to deal adequately and successfully with the situation and withdraw the pin from the throat of the child? Domestic life is replete with less dramatic but similar experiences that demonstrate that the general trend rather than episodic occurrences provides the best evidence of the degree of maturity achieved by those reacting to difficult situations. In this judgment, the importance of temperament, that is, the nervous and endocrine basic structure of the person, must also have its proper recognition. Emotional growth is as individual as every other human experience and can be justly valued only when it is related to the total personality, including its environmental history and present situation.

Behavior with constant personal implications. Behavior in the family is potentially charged with emotional significance due to the fact that whatever is said or done may in addition to its first meaning have a secondary significance as expression of the feeling of one individual toward another. This reflection of attitude is commonly in other associations either absent or has a minor meaning in the contact, except when there is a definite expression of sympathy or repulsion, usually deliberate, which draws attention because it is an unusual exhibition of feeling. Not so with family reactions, since, however innocent they may be in form, they convey to husband, wife, or child a statement of nearness or withdrawal, of criticism or approval. The inference that is made from words spoken and acts performed, the tone of voice, or even facial expression may be a misinterpretation, the result of the mental or emotional state of the observer. There is also the greatest opportunity for exaggeration of slight expressions of attitude, so that they become to the interpreter distorted with false meaning. The husband, wife, or child sensitive to the actual or imagined portrayal of personal attitudes on the part of some member of the family may, by the response given, bring forth in the other a new or a stronger response. Although this possibility of conveying emotional significance is rarely absent from behavior within the family, there are conditions that lead to supersensitiveness of interpretation.

In the early days of marriage, when interactions are directed toward a mutual adjustment in the new social situation, every sort of behavior is to both husband and wife highly colored with emotion. This provides invitation for suspicion, jealousy, insecurity, discontent, disappointment, and even nervous fatigue to seize upon some slight occurrence and magnify it out of all proportion. Such upheavals were of course possible also in the earlier courtship, but with commitment to marriage there is usually a more exacting scrutiny based upon the feeling that the mate has finally committed himself to an undertaking and that any apparent change in feeling represents the desire to retreat. Likewise, whenever incompatibility arises between husband and wife, there is unusual quickness to react to the supposed expression of feeling of the other member of the union. Even when there has been a settlement of difference of opinion and the period of tension passes, there may still remain the liability of excessive response to the behavior of the other person. In the child we find that any sort of emotional conflict leads to keen attention to the behavior of the other members of the family in the effort to discover possible revelations of personal attitude.

Time usually wears away any excessive sensitiveness of husband, wife, or child to the emotional suggestions accompanying family interaction, but whenever there is a drawing apart, there is a progressive trend in the opposite direction. Personality defects and immaturities, as they issue in supersensitiveness, jealousy, inferiority feeling, chronic depression, fear, and guilt, awaken the previous disposition to infer blame, hostility, and distrust in the most neutral acts of family associates. Behavior which out of the family would be unheeded or passed over quickly is so interpreted as to lead to a volcanic expression of emotion or to sullen resentment, according to the disposition of the individual.

Behavior within narrow area. A second characteristic of behavior within the family is that it appears in a relatively narrow area. According to our purpose of emphasis, we may think of the family as the household, or the individual members composing it, or the domestic interests that concern husband, wife, and children, but all three conceptions present a diminutive field for activity which stands in contrast with the scope permitted to out-of-the-family behavior. It is not true normally that the family is walled in, for the family as a unit and its members as individuals maintain other relationships, but the interactions that take place within the domestic circle are confined to the area of common interests. Matters that have to do with out-of-the-family situations, if they be brought within the domestic circle, are regarded according to their significance to the family, and when decisions are made by any member of the family which seem important to the others, these decisions are approved or antagonized on the basis of family expediency.

Concentration on family affairs is still expected of the conventional married woman to a degree that the mores do not demand of the married man. Although most American women take for granted that marriage means for them greater commitment to the family than that required of men, many of them resent the amount of difference that actually appears in the matrimonial experience. Here we still find evidence of lag in the masculine notion of what is the desirable program for marriage and the family. Either husband or wife may react to the other's ambitions outside the family if these seem to be regarded as independent values not pursued as a means of contributing to the family. The out-of-the-home activities are thought of as rivals to affection, and it is this that has led to the belief of some writers that domestic happiness antagonizes public service. The family is regarded as a sharp competitor of nondomestic behavior, resenting any interests which seem likely to turn attention from itself.

CASE OF B. C.

The jealousy of a husband or wife of someone who is thought of as a rival has been so often portrayed in literature that there is danger that this be regarded as the only serious expression of the emotion in domestic relations. There is another source of jealousy which takes second place and deserves more attention in the analysis of family incompatibilities than is generally received. That is jealousy of one spouse for the out-of-the-family activities of the other. Most commonly it is the wife's jealousy of the husband's concentration on his work.

Mrs. B. C. illustrated this form of jealousy in an extreme degree. Her husband in World War II was placed in a position of administrative responsibility that took every ounce of energy he was able to give to it. The work he did contributed to the war effort in a large way, since the product of his factory was indispensable for the production of one of the weapons of the Allied Nations. It was not strange that under these circumstances he took his responsibility seriously. One result was a lessening of his social life. When he came home from work his preference was to be quiet, rest in his chair, and read. This program, however, brought criticism from the wife, who interpreted it as a failure to contribute to her happiness. She realized the weight of the task he had to carry, but even so she felt that when he came home he ought to have left energy for the social life she herself so enjoyed. She contrasted him with other men of her acquaintance who in her opinion were more just to their wives. Her feeling toward the situation was clearly one of jealousy. It was not the loss of his former interest in parties and the like that bothered her so much as the fact that she was faced with a competitor and could no longer regard herself as standing first in the interests of her husband. She refused to take into account the emergency situation, although she readily acknowledged that she understood how important his work was. Emotionally she was jealous upon finding that she could not change his attitude and force him to place his business in second place. She finally decided to get a divorce. It was apparent that to her the contest was one that had to be thought of in terms of being first or second. To the husband this classification seemed needless and false. From his point of view the wife lost the greatest opportunity of sharing with him in his service to his country. Although he was shocked by her decision to go her way, he finally reconciled himself to the acceptance of the fact that her attitude revealed a character fault which sooner or later would have brought them both unhappiness.

The fact that family behavior seems to have a peculiar concentration does not justify the idea that it is trivial in character. The confinement of conduct within the realm of domestic interest deepens its meaning so that it becomes the more emotionally significant. Nor is family concentration inherently antisocial. On the contrary, it is the means by which most men and women are made conscious of out-of-the-family responsibilities and obligations and led into sympathy with the needs of others. It is

easy to see that the child needs the family for experiences preparatory to later life; in the same way, adults require an intense,
concentrated fellowship as a basis for the understanding of those
with whom they have contact in their associations out of the
home.

Nothing brings out so clearly the concentration of family
experience as a description of the close contact of family members. The husband and wife, for example, are partners who in
the characteristic American family experience occupy the same
house, rarely being away from one another for more than the
working day, eat constantly at the same table, usually sleep in the
same room and often in the same bed, frequently go together to
any outside entertainment, and rarely are friendly in the absence
of the spouse with any person of the opposite sex, and maintain
throughout this continuous association financial partnership.
Such an interweaving of the interests of two individuals is rarely
found outside family experience.

Behavior with underground pressure.   Family behavior is
not alone in having hidden and distant sources of motivation,
but no human conduct more reveals the influences born of the
past and unconscious to the individual. This feature of family
adjustment has already been discussed from a different angle,
but here there is need of stressing this unconscious feature. As
we have seen, it is not uncommon for the man or woman to
attempt in the second home to imitate or to repudiate the first,
but in addition to this there are innumerable interactions in domestic fellowship that take their direction from the subterranean
pressure of the past. The hidden springs may lie far back even
in the earliest days of childhood, but they have not ceased their
flowing. The past goes forward as domestic experience develops,
but for the most part it works in concealment. Domestic interaction provides rare opportunity for past frustrations, wishes,
fantasies, fears, and conflicts to reappear. The emotional quality and the concentration characteristic of family experience
provide fertile soil for the sprouting of these seeds of the past.
Through the acts and counteracts of domestic fellowship there
run incessantly prejudices and antagonisms born of earlier experiences, adding strength and giving direction to these most
intimate expressions of personality. It must not be forgotten,

however, that out of the past may also come influences that make for wholesome character.

Behavior tends toward fixed patterns. Behavior in the family, in common with all human conduct that can be classified as characteristic of a definite social institution, tends toward fixed patterns. The child's realization of the meaning of the family comes chiefly through the pictures he is given from time to time of the roles he is expected to assume and of those that are being followed by his parents. Courtship for the adolescent not only provides a role for the boy and for the girl but also brings into sight on the distant horizon hazy but impressive goals supposed to belong to marriage. Again, as the man and woman pass through the wedding entrance into the new relationship of matrimony, they carry with them rather definite ideas of the role each intends to play in the association and of that which each expects the mate to undertake.

These roles reveal the influence of individual experiences of childhood, class, educational status, church teaching, community, and section, but it is rare for these various contributions not to be synthesized into an ideal of behavior which to each individual is stamped with social approval. These roles are made up of specific patterns of behavior which are regarded as both desirable and obligatory. They are backward-facing and frequently are so far out of accord with immediate needs as to constitute a serious social lag.

Adjustment in marriage, especially at the first, is in part the defining, changing, compromising, and assuming of the wife's role and of the husband's role. With the coming of the child the same process of adjustment is repeated. Following both these decisions of behavior programs comes a series of minor adjustments with the possibility at any time of conflict and the necessity of another settlement. A part of the energy and insight required for the adjustment of each personality to that of the other is actually spent in a harmonizing of preconceived patterns of behavior. There may be, and often is, a great difference between the ideals that the husband and the wife bring to marriage, and this may prove more difficult to compromise than the other personality traits.

If at any time new adjustment to life is required, as, for

example, when there is removal from one social environment to another distinctly different, there has to be as a part of this process of adaptation the breaking of the patterns to which each member of the family has become accustomed. Likewise, if for any reason either husband or wife repudiates, modifies, or protests his or her former role, the matrimonial program is thrown into confusion, and there has to be a fresh settlement if the relationship is to prosper.

Some of these readjustments are inevitable, but they may be made so gradually as not to lead to disturbance. Reconstruction of family patterns is normally required by the growth of children. As the child increases in age, there comes an awakening of his emotional and intellectual life which forbids the continuation of family patterns adjusted to former circumstances. In the same way, the child, through contact with out-of-the-family attitudes and experiences, so changes as to be out of harmony with the role that has been given him in the family. The child cannot change his role unless the parent also changes his, and this easily may lead to a contest, the one struggling to force new patterns on the family as the other attempts to maintain the old. There may also be changes as the result of poverty, wealth, unemployment, illness, death, and removal from one locality to another that force a reconstruction of the family program. New situations of this kind invite tension within the family when opposition to the changing of familiar roles develops. Although protest is more likely to come from the parents, it may be the child who proves unwilling to abandon some pleasurable role for a more exacting one placed before him. Tension likewise may appear in the husband-wife relationship as one or both members of the union may refuse to surrender roles that have become habitual. Thus the tendency of family behavior to develop into fixed patterns complicates adjustment to circumstances and to persons. Instead of adaptation being made to the facts of the environment, attention is withdrawn in the task of compromising family goals of subjective origin.

In any case the close association of family contact would lead toward the establishment of general patterns of behavior. Family life could not otherwise have substance or continuity, and in so far as the patterns are made up from adaptation to immediate circumstances rather than drawn ready-made from the past, the family functions efficiently.

Behavior which requires co-operation. Family behavior is distinguished by the fact that it so often requires co-operation. This is not an exclusive feature of family behavior, but in domestic interaction it appears in marked degree. It originates in the fundamental fact that the two sexes stand in a complementary relationship and that the association of parent and child under modern conditions has become also emotionally complementary. It is in the interaction of sex character of husband and wife that this appears most clearly, but it also commonly appears in family finances, the care of children, and at times in family recreation and household management. In the parent-child relationship it shows itself in mutual need of each other. This we see on the one side in exaggerated form in the child's fixation on a parent, but a similar extreme is found in the parent's clinging to the child for emotional support and satisfaction. Both of these exaggerations, which are looked upon as social abnormalities, call attention to the fundamental fact that normally in the relationship of the modern child and parent there is an element of mutual need which makes their association, although in an unlike way, complementary, as is that of husband and wife.

Whenever the behavior of an individual requires for its successful functioning considerable co-operation from some other person, there is a possibility of any one of three different adjustments, and in family life through frequent repetition one of these tends to become a habit. The husband or wife may utilize the resources of the other, thus making one the means by which the other achieves success. In large measure this has been the program forced upon women by the social conditions during the dominance of the patriarchal type of family life. Secondly, there may be a struggle on the part of husband or wife to suppress the desires of the other that he or she may be brought to a subordination that will make the first program feasible. This is the situation at present when the dominating type of male with strong patriarchal prejudices marries a woman of modern trend and finds that she cannot be made a means to his purposes until she is led to accept his marriage ideals. The third reaction is one that is essentially co-operative. This is the program of team play in which neither has the habit of assuming dominance over the other. Even sex loses its former tradition of masculine ascendancy and becomes a co-operative experience. This third type of complementary adjustment is the program toward which present American family life tends.

Conditions that influence family association.   An analysis of a family situation, however admirably done as a case study, always bears to the changing home experience much the same relation that a photograph does to the living person. We can by painstaking investigation obtain a clear-cut description of home conditions at a given time, but our study is no sooner finished than new developments begin.

One of the influences that is constantly showing itself in the home is the effect of ages. The mere growing up of children and the growing older of parents modifies the family behavior and demands of all new adjustments in their interrelated conduct.

It is, of course, literally impossible for any parent to give two children of different ages the same treatment or to provide each with the same environment. The difference in age produces an essential unlikeness in their home experience. The older child and the younger child as a rule react upon each other in ways characteristic of their age roles. If the positions of the children in their association are the reverse of what their ages would suggest, the fact that the older is subservient adds all the more significance to the dominance of the other so that the influence of the age difference does not disappear.

A child is prone to criticize his parents for dealing with his brothers and sisters differently from the way they treat him. Putting aside the variations in dispositions, the mere age differences would lead parents to handle the children in ways that would invoke comparisons. A child, for example, who has an older brother has been influenced by the relationship to an extent that forces his parents to recognize this fact and give him somewhat different treatment than his brother at the same age, for the latter had no older brother's contacts to modify his conduct.

In judging the variations of parents in dealing with their brothers and sisters, children are not only unable to appreciate the distinctions that must be made by a wise parent, but their memories carry too much emotional reaction to their own former experiences to make them safe critics. A definite prohibition that led to considerable emotional protest on the part of the child is remembered, and if the parent in his program of management of a brother or sister appears more lenient, much feeling arises, for there is no realization of the differing circumstances which may fully justify what seems to be a change of policy.

It is often minor experiences, easily forgotten by the parent, that attach to themselves the most emotion in the child's memory. The child reacts to an experience not in proportion to its actual importance but according to the way he felt at the time, and this feeling is the product of all the conditions that influenced his responses. The purely subjective elements of such an occurrence have much to do with the child's attitude, but it is a rare parent that senses this and a rarer child that can be made to appreciate it.

The family that contains growing children is always in the process of adjustment to the interactions that contain an age element. The children in their contacts are in frequent strain, both conscious and unconscious; one child is attempting to arise from the limitations set by another because of advantage in age, and the older is endeavoring to continue the former status or at least is finding difficulty in accepting the fact that the other is demanding more opportunity for self-determination. It is folly in so complex a situation to separate family life into hard and fast types and to assume that there is the one-child and the two-child and the three-child home, each with definite characteristics.

Out of any family life there comes, through the interactions, a concrete situation which in spite of change may at least for a time have fairly discernible features, but the family life that emerges is no automatic product of a one-child or a two-child home. For example, a child may shut himself from his brother's or sister's interferences and may be protected in his social isolation so as to have in abundance the mischievous results that are associated with the only-child status. On the other hand a one-child home does not necessarily or inevitably produce a spoiled child whose disposition reveals the evils of lack of competition and contact. The risks of the one-child home are certainly great, but a wise parent who senses the dangers may bring a lone child to maturity with all the traits of a well-developed personality.

The effect of age upon the parents is a matter too important to be forgotten. Parents are altered by their going on in years, and this is reflected in their interactions with their children. Grandparents are prone to react in characteristic ways, not just because they are grandparents but because their age-attitudes show in their dealings with children as in their other reactions to life. Children detect the difference in parents as they change through the adding on of years, and they respond in accord with their personal feelings. It is not only that the parents are older but rather that they are older and also modified more by the addition of life experiences. Here as elsewhere the exact differences are too concrete and individual to be satisfactorily generalized. One parent grows closer to child experience as he gets older; another goes farther away. One gets greater insight, while another becomes the more blinded by prejudices and less able to adjust to changing circumstances as he increases his years of living.

Case of R. M. C.

The case of R. M. C. was that of a young woman in college who had been brought into a clashing with her home that had caused her not only to make low grades but led her to wish to go to work. The trouble chiefly resulted from the continuous criticism of her grandfather and her mother. The former's attitude was merely an illustration of the antagonistic attitude many develop as they grow bitter with becoming old. In the mother's case it was an unsympathetic interpretation of the problems of modern youth, plus an eagerness to maintain control of her child and enforce a code of behavior that the mother preferred. The young woman had left college and returned to her home. She had been given a medical examination which revealed nothing abnormal. Following this she had visited in a distant city a psychiatrist who could find nothing wrong with her but who advised the mother to place the daughter in an institution for at least a week's observation, whereupon the girl was brought to a family counselor. The mother having been invited to leave, the girl asked that she be hypnotized by him. When questioned as to her motives she said that she felt sure in hypnosis she would be able to tell what was the matter with her. Thereupon the counselor answered, "You know perfectly well what the trouble is, but you are unwilling, because it seems disloyal, to tell me what has been making your trouble. Since you are not going to be hypnotized and in that way have the truth drawn from you, the sooner you tell me what you have to say, the quicker we will be able to solve this problem." She then revealed the emotional disturbance that was coming chiefly from her mother's attitude toward her. An effort was made to give the mother a measure of self-understanding, and the daughter was helped to see that she must be strong enough to develop her independent life without feeling guilt or emotionally blaming her mother for the latter's unfortunate but deeply rooted tendency toward criticism. The girl went back to college and applied herself successfully to her work, graduated, and later married, with no return of emotional conflict.

The family and maturity. If the influence of the family is judged by its significance for the individual's growth emotionally, its value is best seen in the contribution it makes to maturity through the behavior of its members. In estimating this, there has to be recognition of the relativity involved. Maturity is not a final goal achieved by those especially fortunate but rather the evidence of a trend which is characteristic of normal family interaction. The progress of the child is so apparent that as a rule it is easy to see the functioning of the home. The adult's change is not so quickly revealing. The desirable progress toward a more mature activity and the product of an advancing emotional growth must never be interpreted to mean that the individual marriage cannot be successful on a level of maturity lower than that which is ideal. The adaptation that satisfactory adjustment requires includes the possibility of comradeship on the plane of maturity each person has reached. Incompatibility can arise on account of the irritation of one spouse because of the lack of maturity of the other. Likewise—and it is easy to forget this—immature individuals may adversely react to qualities in the other that are the product of a much greater maturity. On the other hand, compatibility in another case may be basically established in spite of great differences in the attainment of maturity between the two individuals.

From a social viewpoint emotional maturity is desirable, especially in the parent who is thereby more helpful to the growing child, but so far as the individuals themselves are concerned their measure of maturity represents a personality trait which leads to behavior to which the other, also expressing his degree of maturity, reacts. Whether happiness is in proportion to their maturity is a question leading to profound philosophic controversy. The answer—and it requires a definition of the meaning of happiness—must recognize the significance of quality even in such a human experience as that of happiness.

Behavior and maturity.　In the analysis of character, behavior is not a perfect index of maturity. The progress in self-development can run ahead of its expression in any considerable quantity of action, because the latter is a product of habit and the increased growth of personality does not immediately show itself in all of the ordinary everyday behavior. The change taking place within is a more faithful portrayal of the personality because it discloses the trend toward future realization, while the behavior that seems inconsistent is a product of past experience, developed at a time when maturity had been less achieved. Greater maturity also may appear as protest against practices that were formerly acceptable. Indeed, the first inkling of the increasing maturity may show itself in a struggle against what previously had been taken as a matter of course. Emotional development always means repudiation of behavior rooted in personality when it functioned on a lower level of growth.

This lag of personality appears in domestic interaction. The meaning of such behavior cannot be found merely by an objective appraisal. Safe as this measurement is when an action is valued socially, it is not thoroughly revealing when we seek to get the significance of the behavior as an index of the person responsible. We are more concerned in the latter appraisal with the tendency than with the immediate attainment. Thus it is not to be expected that the newly married are secure because they are physically or emotionally matured but rather on account of the good start they have made in the line of progress along which they are moving together toward greater growth of character. The value of interchangeableness in this movement can hardly be overemphasized. They are mutually maturing as each responds to the other. It is in this potential maturity that we find the promise of the individual marriage. Emotional maturity is not a finality in the domestic career but rather a characteristic momentum which draws strength as it moves on to more and more success. If behavior cannot keep up, it is because inner changes in the personality go forward more rapidly. This inward development is certain to bring an eventual advance in conduct in spite of any temporary lag between inner development and outward behavior.

Chapter 10

PERSONALITY GROWTH AND FAMILY EXPERIENCE

FOREWORD. The purpose of this chapter is to emphasize the importance of the family as it contributes to the growth of the individual personality. Not only is the family's influence fundamental; it is also inevitable, since the child's physical survival depends upon the protective function of the family.[1] In the process of meeting this responsibility of child nurture, the family also takes over to some degree what Bernard has so carefully classified as the affectional and the socializing functions. Even were no deliberate attempts made to give the child anything besides the care needed for his physical welfare, in the doing of this the parental service becomes an influence which stimulates the development of the child's personality. As a rule, there is a conscious attempt to direct the child, a product of the interest and social characteristics of the adult who maintains contact with the child. Therefore, this chapter deals with the most potent social force in the transmitting of the cultural transmission so as to provide the security of society. This is accomplished by the effect of the family on the individual's personality.

In the chapters on the behavior and the emotional aspects of family experience, we were dealing with the expression of personality traits resulting from the influences of the home. In this chapter our problem is to analyze these influences as they operate to construct personality. The two preceding chapters interpreted adult character in its interaction within family fellowship. Behind the conduct and emotions of adult members of the household were the individual childhood careers of each,

---

[1] Bernard, Jessie, *American Family Behavior*, Ch. 2.

absolutely unique, and determining both the conduct and the emotion. No one marries or becomes a parent without this causal background which alone explains the meaning of the domestic experience. Science has made rapid headway in recent years in the understanding of this building of the personality of the child. The more we have learned of human behavior, the more clearly we have come to realize the unrivaled power of the home to shape personality.

The family and the prevailing culture. Although each family is a distinct nucleus of interacting individuals, unique in the content of its relationships, it has its being in a cultural setting which it shares with other families having similar individual traits. Because of this social environment within which it functions, the family derives much of its content from its setting. This experience common to associated families is largely taken for granted, but when it becomes conscious it is grouped about some symbolic appellation which expresses the meaning it has emotionally. This can best be understood as an idealized standard of conduct which is pressed upon the growing child from the first days of his self-consciousness, and in the conventional American family he is expected increasingly to meet its demands and accept its implications. His good behavior as a family member rests upon his conforming to this cultural obligation.

Since there are, however, several such centers of interest in the average family, the child frequently has to establish a compartment program of behavior, and the difficulty forced upon him appears as soon as we define some of these subdivisions of the greater cultural composite. There may be the so-called race grouping. This will be significant if there are two readily distinguishable anthropological types. Another common division is that of religion, which usually includes also the individual church or churches attended. Another is nation. This has come to be a source of emotional reactions largely out of accord with the global cultural environment in which at present all people are placed. Another grouping can best be described as social conventions, including the purposes and actions generally approved by the social group with whom the family maintains contact. This in practice may mean bringing into the family shifting standards of behavior, each approved by the associates of individual members of the household. The conventions are especially forced upon the child because there is a feeling on the part of the parents that they lose face when their children violate the behavior that has come to mean to the family socially approved conduct.

Since so much that controls family behavior comes from the past and represents the force of tradition rather than a realistic adjustment to the environmental demands of the moment, reformers, social workers, and the like, who attempt either to advance cultural standards or improve the life of individual families, come to regard this cultural backwardness in domestic standards as their chief obstacle. In American culture the rights given families both by law and by conventional thought and feeling may hamper action considered necessary for the welfare of a child or less often the wife or the husband in a family that is considered a menace but which escapes outside interference because its behavior is protected by the idea of the inviolability of the home.

As was true of Plato, most of the assaults made upon the family as a social institution have been directed at its irresponsibility as a transmitter of culture. This indictment has met with little response in the United States, since the integrity of the family and its essential wholesomeness has been thus far a basic premise of American conventional thinking. In the nineteenth century, however, there were considerable attempts to reshape domestic behavior through community organizations that were essentially communistic in spirit. Robert Owens' colony at New Harmony, Indiana, and the Oneida Community in New York were perhaps the best known. Most of these were short-lived. Since the domestic innovations attracted most attention, their failure tended to strengthen popular confidence in the American family.

Adult influence unescapable.   Those who distrust the social efficiency of the family resent its power, but it is universally recognized that the child cannot be brought up in a social vacuum. He not only is helpless without the care and protection of the adult; he also requires an emotional attachment in order to have the sense of security that his life requires. These necessary responsibilities could of course be delegated to some other organization than that of our present family, but the relationship of the child and the organization would still have the dependency-and-guardianship qualities which permit the family in so large a degree to determine the behavior patterns and emotional reactions of the developing child.

Even from the early days of infancy more is required than mere physical care by the adult. In the same way that the body of the child makes demands of the parent, the emotional life requires the attention of older people, but in a more complex way than is required for the satisfying of physical needs. Experience has made it plain that the child has to have emotional security as certainly as food, sleep, and cleanliness. Emotionally the child needs a relationship into which he may extend his roots just as surely as the plant must have its soil, and it is through his contact with the personality of the adult that the child obtains this means of emotional growth.

The family provides an artificial (that is, in the meaning of Lester Ward's concept, telic), adult-made environment, which, under wholesome conditions, is as favorable to the personality requirements of the child as it is an advantage along physical lines in the child's struggle for survival. Although this environment is at least in part made up of deliberate attempts by the parents to influence the child, much of it is unconscious and unrecognized by them. To realize fully what they give the child, parents must have an objective self-understanding rarely found in any sort of human relationship, for a very large part of the germinal influences coming forth from the child's environment are the personalities of the adults with whom he has contact. The power of the family cannot be correctly estimated unless it be remembered that its effectiveness is profoundly increased by its freedom from antagonizing influences. At the beginning of the child's life, it possesses very nearly if not altogether a monopoly of control of the conditions that direct the child's life. It exercises over the unformed character a pure influence in the sense that William James described the original never-before-experienced pure sensations. The sensory experience, however, can be had but once, since the memory of the occurrence will give a different quality to the repetition of the stimulus. This is not true in family experience, for repetition will the more thoroughly establish the monopolistic impression. By the time the child, as a result of his growth, comes in contact with influences contrary to those of the family environment, emotional and behavior patterns have become habits that resist influences at variance with his family experience.

It is true that this conditioning may take a negative form, making the child's attitudes contrary to the parent's wishes, and hostile to similar conditioning from whatever quarter it comes. This reaction, however, becomes as rigid a background and is clearly as much a family product as when the child, as is usually true, reflects traits characteristic of the parents.

The mother in the conventional family carries her personality into the life of the child by becoming frequently associated in his experience with pleasure. She provides the first bit of the world which he explores. His interests in the very first days of infancy are purely physical, and she becomes the source of his satisfactions. The normal relationship of the two includes nursing, and it is through his finding in her the means of satisfying physical hunger that she enters his personality. Undoubtedly there is a reciprocal significance in this relationship which strengthens the emotional attachment of the mother to the child. As the child's development proceeds, his consciousness of his surroundings widens and his comfort-needs multiply. The meaning of this source of pleasure, which through his mother comes and goes, increases, and by the time she is objectified as something outside himself, he has come to look upon her as existing for the sole purpose of giving him satisfaction.

In a similar way, but ordinarily at a slower pace, the child comes to react to his father's personality. There is not as a rule in this relationship, as is true of that with the mother, the insistence of the survival-need for comfort-giving attention. As the child orients himself to the personality of the other parent, he may respond to it as pleasure-giving or pain-causing, according to the impression the father makes upon him.

Since the child has already established a pleasurable rapport with the mother, he has a basis for comparison and may resent differences. The mere fact that the father has during the earliest part of the child's life furnished so little of pleasurable experience to the infant puts him at a disadvantage, so that if later he comes to seem to the child unsympathetic, inattentive, or hostile, an emotional pattern of antagonism may start. The significance of the mother's advantage appears when one considers how different would be the emotional introduction to family experience for the child if he were nursed by both parents. It need not be that the father lacks interest in his son; any failure to show his affection, or to show it so that it is appreciated by the child, will make possible alienation. This explains the desirability of the father's very early actively attempting to rival the mother and to prevent the fixation that may so easily become the root of later emotional immaturity.

As the child departs from infancy and his personality begins to take shape, the strongest influences that enter his character still come from the personalities of his mother and his father. We have no reason to assume that the emotional traits that develop are exclusively the product of these family contacts, for we know that emotional expression is in part a product of body-state, particularly of the endocrine glands, and from this quarter there are undoubtedly influences of structural character that are transmitted by inheritance. Assuming the substrata of potential trends of emotional behavior, those that reach expression are brought forth by the operation of environmental influences upon original capacity, and are chiefly the result of family contacts. We have no method at present of determining in any individual the proportion of influences that shape emotion coming from the outside as compared with the importance of inner propensities. It is, however, to the former source of influences that we have to direct the effort of control, and of these we know more.

Emotional security through belonging to the family. It would be difficult to exaggerate the importance of the family to the child, because as it normally functions it gives him the security which he needs as a foundation for the building of emotional soundness. It is not too much to say that the absolute knowledge of the child that he occupies a unique place in the family is the most important environmental fact in his life.[2] Experience in World War II demonstrated that the child's most successful protection from the psychic shock of that conflict was found in making him feel that the family would hold together whatever happened.[3] It was therefore not the loss of the house through bombing but the mutilation or destruction of the family which brought the greatest hazards to a surviving child. It

[2] Leonard, E. M., Miles, L. E., and Van der Kar, C., *The Child at Home and School,* p. 148.

[3] Wolf, Anna W. M., *Our Children Face War,* p. 14.

has become an axiom among informed parents that the first duty of the family, once physical wants have been taken care of, is to give the child a sense of security that comes through well-expressed affection.[4] Indeed it may seem that this is so obvious that it needs no emphasis, but we cannot dismiss this basic contribution of the child-parent relationship because it has been so constantly interpreted by the literature dealing with the problems of childhood. We have too many illustrations of failure to provide this family ministration through emotional neglect and of the later consequences this brings in adult frustrations to permit our assuming that this need of security is a certainty in American family relationships.

This sense of belonging, which has now become a prerequisite for wholesome emotional development, provided in the primitive period the basis and incentives which, taking advantage of the physical lengthening of infancy, carried the prehistoric family forward in the evolution that separated it from the distinctive animal mother-offspring relationship.[5] The original survival functioning of attachment has been carried forward and enriched and now provides opportunity for an emotional contribution not possible in the relationship of the less nervously endowed animals.

This need of the young child for emotional security is now generally recognized even if not always practiced in the normal American home, but it still can be said that there is much less realization of the security which the older child needs for his best development as he passes through the tumultuous period of adolescence. Then, reacting to the most disturbing of body changes since the day of his birth as he attempts passage out of childhood into a new type of gregarious adjustment, he is subject to doubts, fears, conflicts, guilt-feeling, inner tension, and the like which demand for his best development a continuing assurance of family fellowship. He does not want nor can he safely have the same kind of a belonging he possessed during his childhood period. He is now switching to the independence prerequisite for adult maturity, but as he achieves a new status in his relationship he needs a sure feeling which includes a higher type of emotional security. When his home conditions

---

[4] Faegre, Marion L., and Anderson, John E., *Child Care and Training.*

[5] Groves, E. R., *The Family and Its Social Functions,* pp. 75–76.

force him to strive for adult independence through the sacrifice of a sense of belonging to the family, he is forced into conflict and his parents become the greatest emotional liabilities of his environment.

One of the disasters of the American home comes when the parents with no understanding of the impulses operating in the adolescent seek to continue the program of control which has prevailed during childhood. There may even be an attempt at greater control because of the parents' realization of the social dangers the previous lack of discipline now makes possible.[6] The attempt to perpetuate childhood relationships represents the extreme of one dangerous parental policy, while the effort to carry out the policy of completely abandoning the child is the opposite and equally hazardous. His preparation for adult responsibility demands a release from parental oversight but not a withdrawal which takes away the adolescent's feeling of emotional security. Difficult as he finds his self-expression, it reveals an intense craving for the continuation of a love security but not one that requires of him that he surrender his cravings for independence and his widening of interest and acquaintanceship. Nothing makes the family during adolescence so useful as the child moves toward adult life as a well-secured fellowship developed during the previous years of childhood, an understanding relationship which can be taken for granted and which does not include any desire on the part of the parent to make use of this to hold the child from the enlarging life which now so profoundly attracts him.

There is need of some clear recognition by both parent and child during the latter's adolescence that a new relationship between the two has become necessary and for the advantage of both. Perhaps some formal method of expressing this change is incompatible with the spirit of American family life, but it would be well if in some way the adolescent could be made aware of the parents' realizing what has happened and the demand this makes upon the child. One of the authors attempted to accomplish this by the following letter to his sixteen-year-old daughter then at college.

---

[6] Schwartz, Louis Adrian, *An Interpretation of the Emotional Needs of the Adolescent.*

DEAR CATHERINE,

You must not be influenced in your consideration of the invitation from the sorority by your thought that Mother or I wish you to join. We want you to meet your problems without asking yourself what our desires would be. You have been prepared to meet life by yourself, and we do not want to entangle you by the emotional checks on your freedom that affection often brings about. It is more important that you not only make your own decisions but also that you feel in doing so that this self-responsibility is our fundamental request of you. Long-distance control is futile. Everyone has to act for himself, but many are torn asunder in their inner life by forever attempting to satisfy the supposed desires of someone of whom they are fond.

We want you to be happy and useful, but we are much too wise to try to make you happy or useful in our way. We have tried to follow the ideals of our time. We are confident you will choose to follow those of your day. You can count on our understanding and sympathy, but your career is in your own hands so far as the decision of your parents can determine it. Since babyhood you have been trained for this test. We have tried to meet our responsibilities. We must now accept the verdict upon our understanding that your experience with life will render. The greatest assistance we can now give you is to withdraw and let you face the ordeal unencumbered. If you wish advice, we shall at any time give it. If you feel that you have failed, remember we shall be eager to share your confidence and consider with you the experience.

With confidence,

DADDY

Hazards of the American family. In the study of the American family and in any effort directed toward its conservation, the hazards of our domestic experience have to be recognized. Even parents who conscientiously seek to lead the child's growth toward emotional soundness and social wholesomeness reveal that the relationship between them and their offspring offers subtle temptations for the exploiting of their own concealed weaknesses. This fact is constantly forced upon the attention of those who in child-guidance clinics and similar organizations attempt to deal with the so-called problem-children. Impressive as this evidence of parental misguidance is, it represents a small fraction of the mischievous influence of undiscerning parents. It is surprising to find that in some of these homes where needless trouble has been brought into the life of the developing child there has been an awareness of the contribution of the recent science of child study and even some effort, at least on the part of the mother, to familiarize herself with the principles of good child training. The attempt to put these into practice has been frustrated by an emotional concealment on the part of the parent of motivations that supposedly are designed to further the child's growth of independent character but which actually are a means of satisfying parental ambition or expiating conflict, frustration, guilt, or some similar chronic inward maladjustment of the parent himself.

The great majority of homes, however, are untouched at present by the science of child study, and in so far as there is any attempt at a conscious program of discipline or direction of the child it is based upon tradition, conventions, and the personal experiences of one or both of the parents. The complacency of such parents is amazing. It testifies to the neglect that the family as a social institution still receives in American education. Men and women who are eager to gain information when they attempt to raise flowers or vegetables or to keep poultry, dogs, or canary birds take over the responsibilities of parenthood without the slightest effort to become familiar with the principles of child development and the care of the offspring whose welfare supposedly is their supreme desire in life. This incapacity of many American families because of parental ignorance both shows up the power of the family and emphasizes its proper function and also makes clear the need in our present cultural situation of educating for marriage and family life. The occasional example of the inability of a mother to make good use of the principles of child study in her practices reveals the desirability of her gaining greater knowledge and especially her receiving it earlier in her career. Although parental failure as a rule is chiefly charged to the mother, oftener than one might suppose, the trouble comes from the father's being destitute of any understanding of the science of child development and therefore blocking or neutralizing the better training efforts of the mother.

Education, even when it is presented effectively and as early as the high school period, cannot be expected to protect parents who are victims of genuine psychiatric unsoundness of person-

ality from succumbing to the temptations provided by the role
of parenthood. The great majority of potential parents, however, could be prepared to give their children safe guidance if
the American public recognized in its educational practices the
enormous social tasks given over to the American family. Surely
this preparation, which alone justifies any human being having
the great portion of determining control over another's life now
possessed by parents as they maintain contact with the developing child, should not be regarded as desirable only for the
mother. Since the child is being influenced by both parents, both
need adequate training for their responsibility. Fortunately, we
have evidence, even though it comes from a limited number of
fathers, that they respond to any opportunity given for the study
of the science of child guidance as do mothers once they are led
to see the value of understanding the growth of child life. The
system of an adequate educational program for marriage and
for parenthood will be discussed in the fourth part of this text.

Growth of personality.   As we watch the development of
the growing child, we see it taking place simultaneously along
four different lines: the physical, intellectual, emotional, and
social. It is, perhaps, better to think of these as different aspects
of an undivided growth since they are so interdependent and in-
separable. It is easy to detect the dominance of family influence
in directing all four. The physical growth and health of the
child, aside from the contributions of inheritance, are clearly determined by the intelligence and resources of the family. From
this point of view the survival rates of infancy become an index
of the family efficiency of different classes and of different nationalities, and in the same cultural group of different communities. This influence upon physical growth coming from the family must not be thought of in contrast with personality growth
along other lines, since it is a fundamental element in the total
character of the individual.

The family's contribution to intellectual growth is based
primarily upon the same two qualities of intelligence and resources, but the demands made of the parent are more exacting.
Aside from occasional emergencies, the physical care of the child
is rather largely a routine. This can be taught a mother by a
friend or some social agency. Thus a program which is based
upon intelligent understanding of the child may be gathered

from some other source and carried out by the family so that the needs of the child are well met. In case of emergency, the parents may turn to a superior intelligence so that the child will not suffer from their lack of knowledge.

In the case of intellectual growth, the power of the family to help or injure the child in his development comes more largely from the personal background and dispositions of the father and mother. At least this is true in the earliest and most important years of the child's life. At a later time the family is supplemented and possibly outrivaled by the school. The significance of the intellectual qualities possessed by the parents as an incentive to good intellectual growth of personality in the child undoubtedly appears in the record of distinguished families whose members for generations have achieved distinction. To regard such a record as merely evidence of sound biological heredity is to overlook the decisive part played by family contact in bringing to expression the original endowment of children.

When we turn to the problem of emotional growth of personality, we find the situation different. It is now not the intelligence, in the ordinary sense of the word, nor the resources of the family that determine the help or injury that the child receives from his family association. It is rather the nervous soundness and emotional maturity of the mother and to a lesser extent of the father that decide the value to the child of his family fellowship. Neuropathic weakness in either parent will come to the surface in the intimacies of the family group and will become for the child a conditioning influence. In the same way, any emotional immaturity, whether essentially of nervous or social origin, will discolor the family background from which the child must draw in his earliest years the experiences that form his emotional character.

Parents are not likely to recognize their limitations along emotional lines in the same way that they become conscious of physical or intellectual limitations. It is the habit of every individual to protect his emotional faults even from his own criticism, and as a consequence the emotional hazards of a parent are rarely recognized by the person concerned. Outsiders also do not see these problems so clearly as those of a physical or intellectual character, in part because they are most plainly revealed only in the privacy and intimacy of family contact, and in part because they are more subtle. It is obvious that the dangers of family fellowship along the lines of emotional influence on the child are more serious and more difficult to handle than the physical or intellectual, and it is from this quarter that the severest criticism of family influence is coming from those who regard it as a menace to child life.

The social growth of the child's personality is likewise at first chiefly in the hands of parents. Here also native intelligence and family resources, including those resulting from favorable economic circumstances, have a relatively small part in determining the character of the influences. The significance of the parents is largely decided by the contact they maintain with the child and by the standards of social behavior to which they have become accustomed. At a later period of the child's life the neighborhood enters to compete with the family both in the contacts it provides and in the standards it represents. But since at the beginning the child's fellowship is almost exclusively with the parents, he gets from them social attitudes and practices in accord with their life patterns.

In their social policies, also, families are not so likely to seek counsel from outside sources as they are when dealing with the first two sorts of personality problems. When the older child, who has gone beyond the most impressionable years of infancy, begins to show in his social contacts unwanted behavior, the parent, because of pride, anxiety, and mere bewilderment, may seek help from the specialist, and, as we shall later see in another discussion, the child-guidance clinic has in the larger cities of America come to perform just such service as these troubled parents seek. When there are no such resources for the parent or for some reason he is unwilling to seek such help, knowing that it exists, he may choose some individual, minister, teacher, doctor, or relative as counselor. Unfortunately, it is rarely that parents go for such assistance when building up a preventive program. It is only after the horse is stolen that they lock the door.

Although it is possible and necessary to distinguish each of these four processes of personality growth, it leads to a misconception of what takes place in the life of the child if any one is regarded as independent. They are so intertwined that they exist as separate elements only in our thought. Actually each is modified by and modifies all the others. A common illustration is inferiority feeling born of some organic defect. As Alfred Adler has demonstrated, the child may so react to such an experience as to show in his adult character a chronic emotional reaction which dominates all social contact and makes use of the thought-processes only to maintain and defend the compensatory life-program.

The good start. Necessarily, whatever happens at the commencement of a pattern of behavior has a far-reaching effect upon later conduct. First in importance of these new activities is, perhaps, that which provides the nutriment necessary for the child's existence, once he is independent of his mother's body. It may seem strange to find in the child's nursing experience any lasting significance, but that is merely because there is failure to realize the nervous complexity and emotional features of the child's food-getting. Nursing is more than a mere method of the child's satisfying hunger. It is for him a profoundly pleasurable experience if only his nervous-muscular behavior pattern be established successfully. The outcome is not entirely decided by the soundness of the equipment of his organism, since the mother also contributes to the result. From her side may arise complications such as the inadequacy of her milk supply or some structural handicap which hinders the baby's effort to become satisfied. The failure to nurse properly, an insufficient nutrition, or a continuous frustrating of the attempt to establish the necessary rhythmic movement, may from the beginning make the nursing experience for the child emotionally irritating.

Such a start, when his life is simple in content and its mood is established exclusively by organic satisfaction, has a conditioning effect that carries over from the experience itself into other activity. Somewhat later a similar crisis appears when the mother attempts to wean the child. Again more is involved than merely food habits, important as these will prove in later behavior. These are but two of the many starting points of patterns of behavior which, although simple at the beginning, contribute to the building of a characteristic life-program as the earliest emotional reactions are taken over and associated with the more complex habits that develop after infancy. Nursing and weaning are spectacular respresentatives of a group of original activities which on account of freshness and the meager content of consciousness have great emotional intensity and give direction to the expanding personality of the child.

Dangers of growth. The personality growth of the child is intermittent as well as diverse. At times progress seems rapid along some particular line, at other times slow, or perhaps entirely lacking. Much of this change of tempo is seasonable, going forward with a pace that is accelerated or slowed down by the environmental circumstances and the demands put upon the child as he tries to adjust to them.

Since growing up means leaving the pleasant usually and the familiar always, the child's attitude is likely to be inconsistent. He is led at one time to desire to grow up while at another time he desires not to grow up, and sometimes he feels the pull of these opposite directions so intensely that he can hardly make clear even to himself the stronger impulse. This reluctance to go forward into unknown social experience easily becomes an emotional obstruction to growth, even an insurmountable obstacle to some particular form of development.

There is considerable individual variation between children in their growth of personality due to both biologic and social causes. The latter are chiefly a product of family condition. These differences must be kept in mind in any effort to arrive at the maturing rate of the child. Always the child's emotional development is estimated in relation to the physical, intellectual, and social level of his experience.

For the building of emotional independence and security it is necessary for the child to realize that he is emotionally advancing as he grows older. This knowledge is gained through self-control and a feeling of resourcefulness as he meets the demands of his environment, especially of the social group, without family support and guidance. As he advances in maturity, the interference and protection of the parents lessen. When this is not the policy of the adults who furnish his home environment, he can go forward emotionally only by detaching himself from the unhealthy family dominance, and rarely can this be accomplished without a conflict that hurts his personality. Parents can and do become obstacles to their children's wholesome development with very little overt opposition. They need only make overattractive the parent-child status already established or exaggerate the difficulties that face the child as he advances.

The eagerness of the child to cling to infantile patterns adds force to anything the parents do or fail to do in the carrying out of a policy of holding back the child's emotional growth. The latter's recoil from the more exacting conditions that appear as he moves toward greater self-responsibility easily turns him backward to the security he has enjoyed in earlier relations with his parents. He naturally finds in his mother in most cases the refuge from life which he seeks.

This proneness to retreat to the infantile type of mother-child relationship explains why such harm comes from attempting to motivate the conduct of the child by making it a demonstration of his affection for his mother. Such an appeal for proof of love of mother destroys the objective meaning of good adjustment, making it difficult for the child through his experience to find the true consequences of conduct and to achieve that sense of self-mastery which is required for emotional progress. The child may follow the request of his mother that he may enjoy her favor, or he may go contrary to her wishes as a means of attracting her attention, and thus renew the concentration that she formerly gave him in his earlier days of helplessness. The ideals that are held before him are so tied with mother-love and child-dependency that the harder he struggles to be good in parental estimation, the farther he gets from the prudential self-discipline which alone provides a sound basis for emotional reaction.

Family influence on emotional patterns.   Once the basic emotional reactions have awakened in the life of the child they respond to the influences of the family as they become well-organized, characteristic types of emotional response. Love, hate, fear, jealousy, self-confidence, and inferiority feeling are some of the emotional patterns which we soon discover in process during the first three years of the child's life.

Love and hate, fear and confidence, anger and sympathy are three combinations of contrasting emotions that we find appearing as early as the first year of consciousness. These reactions are at first directed toward both things and people, since the child has no basis for discrimination. He therefore is as likely to hit the door or throw down the cup in anger as he is to attempt to strike his playmate who has aroused his hostility. He assigns to some thing or person blame for his subjective feeling and attempts to punish for his pain the object of his wrath. His parents are no exception, and as a consequence his attitude toward them is not consistently one of love, or pleasurable attitude, or of hate, or disagreeable attitude. He reacts to them according to whether the experience for which he holds them responsible is one that pleases or displeases him. Not only does this lead to alternating and opposing emotional responses but also to a simultaneous inconsistency, or ambivalency, because he feels toward the parent both love and hate as he attends to one or the other of the actions for which he holds the parent responsible. His picture of the parent becomes confused because it contains things he likes and things he does not like.

It is not difficult for the family to stimulate hate reaction in the child. Excessive harshness, unsympathetic criticism, severe punishment, persistent nagging are some of the ways in which hate is made predominant in the life reaction of children. Fear may come either from failure to give the child a sense of security or from the contagious influence of a parent who also suffers from fear. Jealousy appears so easily as to be almost a natural impulse of the young child. We see most clearly the awakening of jealousy by family experience in the reaction of the child who feels that his relationship with the parent has been destroyed or menaced by the coming of a brother or sister. Always in these interactions within the family circle there is risk of immaturity on the part of the parent or emotional incompatibility between the parents becoming a cause of emotional difficulty in the child.

The child's reaction in hate, fear, or jealousy is bad enough in itself without the addition of the trouble that comes when it is badly handled by the parent. The use of force drives the child forward toward the fear from which he recoils. Recourse to punishment as the means of destroying anger or hate, denial of parental approval on account of the child's jealousy, only complicates the emotional situation and makes it the more difficult for him to leave his immaturity. Often the child struggling with his own emotional weakness receives from the parent a cruel emotional attack instead of the necessary insight, sympathy, and guidance. Especially is this likely to happen when the parent discovers in his offspring some emotional fault which the adult has never been able to conquer in his own life. A parent who has lost out in his struggle for self-mastery, through failure to mature emotionally, suffers a second defeat as he re-acts with panic to the reappearance of his problem in his child.

The meaning of adolescence. Greater progress has been made in revealing to American parents the meaning of child-hood than in interpreting adolescence. The absolute necessity of the child's having adult attention, his apparent helplessness, the constant emphasis on the effect of childhood experiences as it shows itself in later adult life has led thoughtful parents, espe-cially mothers, to attempt to minister to the child's needs in the light of insight gained from the pediatrician, psychiatrist, and the mental hygienist. The adolescent has been relatively neg-lected. In medicine, for example, this period of great body change is a sort of no man's land, and only from the endocrine point of view do we find any considerable recognition among medical specialists of the meaning of the adolescent period in the life-span of the individual.

The average parent is surprised and frequently baffled when the adolescent first begins to reveal his characteristic traits. These reactions far too often are considered problems rather than normal reactions to be expected during what is usually the most tumultuous period of life subsequent to the throes of birth. The ordeal of the adolescent is, of course, increased or lessened by his social situation, especially within his family.

The reconstruction of the body as it shows itself in the early stages of adolescence is obvious to any observer. Adults are so accustomed to what happens that they tend to think of the development that occurs as a mere growth similar to that which has been going on from the days of infancy. It is, however, a genuine reconstruction of the organism, the taking on of a new function, the consequence of inner changes chiefly endo-crine in origin. The pituitary gland takes the lead in this, but its contribution is allied with that coming from the endocrine functioning of the ovaries or the testicles. Not only are chemical, metabolic, nervous, and peripheral changes inaugurated but along with them emotional disturbances. Likewise, at the same time, as a result of this adolescent reshaping of the organism, new impulses naturally appear leading to a needful readjust-ment in the relationship between the adolescent and his adult associates, especially his family members.

Although medicine and social conventions do not adequately recognize the meaning of the adolescent reconstruction of personality, it is a critical period.[7] In this respect it is similar to infancy and can be justly described as a kind of new birth. It deserves adequate medical supervision, and a physical examination including the endocrine functioning should be commonplace in our health program at this time just as is the periodic examination of the infant during his first months. Parents should be informed of the deeper significance of this first change of life which is far more consequential as a rule than the later changes of the climacteric. Sympathy comes with understanding.

The task of the adolescent.   The child at puberty faces emotionally something similar to his physical experience. Just as the body develops into its adult form, so the personality assumes the characteristics that will be continued throughout life. The testing of emotional immaturity is inescapable. Either the child will safely remove himself from emotional dependency on the parent and the family and assume self-direction, or he will fail to make this passage from childhood to adult responsibility and forever afterward, unless later he is especially helped in breaking away from his parasitic support, fail to reach emotional maturity. The emotional changes that normally go along with adolescence are less noticeable than those taking place in body structure, but they are equally indispensable to the proper growth of personality.

The family, through the influences it has brought the child during the preceding years, helps or hinders the boy or girl upon whom has been thrust the adolescent task of achieving an independent self-life. The family, through its policy at this period, also helps or hinders the efforts of the child to pass out of the tutelage of the family without emotional conflict and without bitterness and to build his life on a higher emotional level. Failure to accomplish this means trouble for himself and for others also when at a later time marriage or parenthood brings new demands for emotional maturity.

Adolescent conflict.   The policy of the family can become the cause of immediate emotional conflict in the adolescent which may be acute or chronic. On the other hand, conflict may be avoided or at least greatly minimized but at the cost of con-

---

[7] Hamblen, E. C., "Adolescence and the Climacteric," ch. 11, in *Understanding Marriage and the Family*.

tinuing an out-of-season relationship between mother and son, or father and daughter. In this way, however, conflict may be merely postponed. It may also prove true at a later time that instead of the coming of conflict there is an inability to proceed in a normal heterosexual fashion in adjustment to life. The condition in the family responsible for these malformations of personality can be understood by examining the development of mother-fixation in the son. The career of the girl may be blighted in a similar fashion through a fixation on the father.

The most common danger that the boy meets in his development of affection is the risk of permanently fixing his love upon his mother in such a way as to make it difficult for him to go through the succeeding experiences. This possibility has long and universally been recognized. For example, savage initiation rites, as practised among various primitive peoples, attempt to sever the relationship of mother and boy, and in case the boy fails to pass successfully through the ordeal his association with the women may be held responsible, and ever afterward he is considered as belonging with the women of the tribe rather than with the men.

There are many different ways by which the child may be hindered in his efforts to pass out of the dominant mother-fixation of his earlier period of childhood. His mother may continue year after year to treat him with the same lavishness of affection that was his right as an infant. She may use her hold upon him to make him prejudiced against any new competing interest. She may prolong his early helplessness until his dependence upon her becomes so habitual that it continues even up into and through his adult period. Even her death may not release him since he then reacts to her memory as if she were still with him. She may shower him with such affection that she becomes all-satisfying and he feels no need of any other. Teachers of boys occasionally find young men of high school age receiving from their mother infantile attention and affection and responding in such a way as to make their emotional maturing impossible.

The mother may hamper the child, especially when he starts to transfer his regard from her to some other individual, often the father. This may be a conscious process or one of which the mother is unaware. The father is discounted and his value for the child concealed. This attitude of the mother may have for its motive deep selfishness or lack of confidence in the father. It may, of course, be both. In that case she uses the apparent failures of the father to protect herself from the withdrawal of the boy's supreme regard.

The family as a continuous socializing process.   The power of the family to construct character comes from its having, at the very beginning of infancy, opportunity to set in motion influences that give the child his first social experiences. The baby, just as soon as he begins to express his impulses in activities, comes in contact with the environment of the home. He is forced into a relationship with persons who are able and determined to interfere with his behavior. It is this thwarting of his impulses that introduces him into social experience. In his attempt not to do those things that he has found productive of unpleasant social consequences, the young child finds compensation for the desires he has to check by dwelling upon his wish to please those from whom his satisfactions and affection come. His control of behavior that is frowned on by his elders is made possible by building up these compensatory wishes.[8] With the origin of the desire to do the forbidden thing, there arises also, in addition to the thought of punishment, the wish to win social approval and to continue in a relationship of affectionate fellowship by being obedient. By this process of building compensations for perverse cravings, the child enters into a sense of the meaning of relationship and in the conflict and conquest of antagonistic motives he becomes consciously social.

The home not only begins this process of socialization for the child who experiences normal family life; it also continues the process for a long period, for most persons throughout life. The motives of right and wrong, the first social patterns of behavior, are embedded in the life at the level of early experience where family influences are predominant, but upon these foundation-experiences all the later attitudes of the personality rest. It is fortunately contrary to fact to say that the personality is necessarily constructed in harmony with these first compensatory reactions, for in that case the power of the family would become a social tyranny forbidding the possibility of progress.

It is true that, varying with the individual, each person con-

---

[8] Kempf, E. J., *Psychopathology*, p. 77.

tinues through life to react to social situations somewhat in accord with these first impressions. The family contribution seldom if ever becomes merely a past experience continued as a memory, but for most people at least it remains a continuous influence and, on account of the tenacious emotions that cling to these first impressions of the home, is constantly bringing about the very same struggle between conflicting wishes that characterized in early childhood the original socializing process.

Thus the family influence as a socializing force remains present in greater or less degree for all persons, and is not permitted to become emotionally a mere happening of the past. Many of the social struggles of life, the tragedies of personality, are the product of this power of the home to keep its influence alive throughout the social career of the individual. It is not strange that attacks are made upon the family by those, often themselves reacting slavishly to family influences that they cannot shake off, who blame the home for inflicting this emotional servitude which so frequently distorts judgment and robs people of the ability to follow without misgivings mature convictions when they are contrary to the early teaching of the home. They declare that the home ties to the individual a weight of prejudice which he drags after him as he goes on in life. The home obtains its influence from the fact that it starts the socializing process, and if this were begun in some other institution the results of these first happenings in the social life of the child would show themselves in equally persistent emotional attitudes.

The home not only begins the socializing experiences of the child; it continues to contribute to his later social development, for compensatory wishes are constructed by the adult as they were by the child, and the home remains for most men and women a chief source of compensatory motives. Parents die, the other family members separate, but the home as a relationship, the home as a means of crushing excessive individualism and awakening social attitudes, persists. Emotionally the home never passes.

Domestic happiness. The terms most commonly used to describe marriage success or failure are the words "happy" and "unhappy." This habit of appraising marriage relationships from the viewpoint of the pleasure principle is frequently criticized. Happiness as a goal for either marriage or the family is regarded as unworthy and immature. Nevertheless, the American practice of estimating marriage and family success, especially the former, in the terminology of the pleasure principle persists. It is in accord with the spirit of American culture since this emphasis stresses the individual's own experience and reaction. This is natural in a relationship which finds its security in the meaning it has for those within the domestic fellowship. It has to be subjective on account of the emphasis on personal motivation our conventional attitude toward marriage encourages. As the critics insist, this judgment does not evaluate either the marriage or the family from the objective or social point of view. For this reason happiness can be neither a perfect nor a final measurement of the qualities of matrimonial or domestic relationships. However, this does not lessen the meaning such an appraisal has as a recognition of that drive toward expectancy which functions in domestic relationships or the significance of the words happy or unhappy as a means of disclosing the degree of satisfaction the individual finds as he experiences the realities of his marriage or his family life.

It would be most strange if such intensely emotional contacts as are provided by marriage and the family did not bring to those concerned reactions in accord with the pain-pleasure principle of organic response. Although satisfaction is described by subjective evaluation, this does not mean that the experience is self-contained. On the contrary, there is an implicit recognition of the contribution made by the others who belong within the relationship; even erotic satisfaction normally demands a relationship of two individuals, although from necessity the satisfaction it brings can directly be experienced only subjectively.[9]

It would be wrong also to suppose that the words "happy" or "unhappy" represent a static appraisal. There cannot be normally a stationary standard of domestic relationship. The fellowship goes forward or retreats, and if attempt is made to describe its immediate meaning it is natural for the individual to attempt comparison and to affirm that the relationship is more or less happy than was formerly true. Thus common terminology, although it lacks precision and provides no means of ob-

---

[9] Wells, Frederick L., *Pleasure and Behavior,* p. 93.

jective measurement, does reveal in the domestic relationship that human drive which has so frequently been interpreted by the philosophically inclined as the illusiveness of life.

There could be no greater error in analysis of personality growth within the family experience than to suppose that a flaw, even serious in character in the functioning of the individual family, necessarily brings disaster. The home is not like a manufacturing plant in which some faulty operation ruins its entire product. Human nature is too complex for such a simple causal determination of character. The question of effect is always concrete and factual and is demonstrated only by finding in the character of the victim of bad family influence the consequence that has been presumed. This may easily be found or it may appear not to have occurred. The reason for its not happening, or not in the proportion one would expect, is the significance of the original personality, in large measure a hereditary product, and the effect on the child of the other influences also entering his life. The home does not have a monopoly of influences nor does any one member of the family completely dominate, and, most significant of all, no one characteristic of the family has absolute sway over the child's developing character. These facts work both ways so that neither a pronounced evil nor excellence appearing in the individual home becomes decisive as it operates as a stimulus in the life of the growing child. The general and persistent influence of the family as a totality rather than one striking feature is most apt to set the course of family influence.

Part III

Social Problems of the American Family

Chapter 11

SOCIOLOGICAL ASPECTS OF FAMILY LIFE

FOREWORD. In order to appreciate the social significance of the family, the student needs to detach himself from his personal family experience and his observation of contemporary family life as he has been brought in contact with it and conceive of the family as an institution in interaction with the total social environment. Thus, although family life proceeds within an individual grouping, particular families possessing in common certain characteristics and reacting to a special environment can be classified. In this way family experience falls within cultural divisions that the student may regard as somewhat similar to the biological classification of species. Everywhere we find taboo, tradition, convention, and, in our country, common and statutory law regulating marriage and family activities and relationships. The familial institution, therefore, is very like the legal corporation. It is a generalized organization possessing qualities and functions that can be described, although when we seek to discover family life in operation we are concerned with something concrete and unique.

Necessarily, since the family is an association of persons continuously adjusting to a physical and social environment, it cannot remain static. It is ever changing. The degree and momentum of change, however, greatly vary, usually being relative to the environmental changes affecting it. Sometimes, as was true of the Oneida Community, the family separates itself as much as possible from the existing cultural surroundings and produces its own environment. However much it seeks to isolate itself from the prevailing conditions, it does not have complete success. The Essenes of Palestine are an example of this inability completely to control sociological conditions by means of self-imposed isolation. In the study of American contemporary family life the student finds that the family in our time reveals many rapid changes, because the environment in which it is placed is constantly and rapidly changing. This makes our family unstable. It can give the student the impression of deterioration and insecurity. This changing family life is, however, the price that has to be paid for the effort to adjust to contemporary circumstances. Although mere evidence of change does not demonstrate that proper adjustment is being made, an unchanging family would be proof that the institution was failing to function and was deteriorating, since it cannot maintain its usefulness in isolation but must maintain vitality as a social organization by sensitivity to environmental conditions which include physical, economic, and social changes. These reactions, which may be basically either docile or aggressive responses, are regarded by the sociologists as problems. The discussion of them should not give the student the feeling of pessimism since they do not involve the survival but rather the functioning of the family. If the family were uninfluenced by these rapid changes so characteristic of our time and especially of American culture, its future as an institution would be dark indeed. The family, like all products of life, must maintain itself by struggle, and it is the business of the sociologist to point out the difficulties it has as it seeks to fulfill its purposes as it reacts to the prevailing cultural situation.

What has changed?   Of all the social changes that have been brought forth by the machine age, none have been so impressive to the American as that which has taken place in the family. This does not prove that the family has been most profoundly influenced, but it does show that people generally have been most conscious of what has taken place within the family. On the surface it might at first appear that there has been no serious change. The youth of America commonly court, marry, keep house, have children, and carry on the same major activities that have been associated with domestic life from our first settlement. It is in the manner in which these are undertaken that we see chiefly the evidence of change. There is also a difference in the proportion of attention which these features of domestic life now receive as compared with the past, and in the motives which impel American men and women to enter upon the family enterprise. We shall also find a greater variation in the attitudes of people concerning marriage and parenthood than used to be true. In short, although there has not been for the great majority of Americans any change in the fundamental structure or form of family experience, there is hardly any family which does not reveal results that have come from recent social changes.

It is the family as a mode of behavior that has changed. This is the result of what has happened to the people who make up our family groups. From this point of view there is nothing strange in the fact that we now have a conventional family life considerably unlike that characteristic of the United States in past periods. The family life has from the beginning been changing, and for the same reason that it is still showing variation. It is the life of the people that has changed, and the family experience as a portion of the individual's total way of living also must change.

The present situation of American family life was not only to be expected; it was inevitable. The only way the family could have withstood the influences coming from every quarter and have remained unchanged in the midst of a rapid-moving civilization would have been for the men and women who make up the families to have continued their former way of living within the family and their former way of thinking about the family while at the same time changing their habits and thoughts and sentiments along all other lines of social experience. Such a power to resist at one point the influences of contemporary life while sharing a civilization never so fluid as at present is possessed by few. Even those who have been successful in walling out influences that would change domestic experience have only succeeded temporarily in creating artificial situations socially most dangerous for the other members of the families which they have commanded.

From the days of Plato it has been recognized by students of the family that the institution tends to be conservative. This is a characteristic of the family interpreted through its sentiments, ideas, and ideals rather than from its practices. Changes in behavior are forced upon the family as a consequence of outside circumstances. These departures from the past, frequently inconsistent with the beliefs that are held concerning proper family life, do not disturb the thought patterns that have become parental possessions. There may be resistance to the new and a clinging to the past, often idealized, but this opposition to change lacks the emotional intensity that comes from any direct attack on the conventional concepts of the family as an institution. Many of the recent changes that have modified the functioning of the family have been made gradually in the effort to accomplish purposes and obtain satisfactions under the conditions to which the family has been exposed. Attention has been directed to outward goals rather than to the inward variation in family practices. Because of this, much of the adjustment of the family to modern life has come about indirectly, only slightly forcing reconstruction of the traditional concepts built upon earlier circumstances. There have been changes in thinking and these are discussed in later paragraphs. These new ideas have not been directed toward the family as an institution, except by those few interested in domestic reform, but have resulted from pressure of the prevailing intellectual environment.

The family has not so much changed as it has had change forced upon it. It is in transition because civilization itself is in transition. The mere fact of change in family experience does not mean deterioration any more than it signifies necessarily the strengthening or elevating of domestic experience. So much has happened in human experience outside the family that it is inevitable that something must change within. This fact of rapid change in our ways of living and acting has become so obvious that nothing is more commonly recognized. The consequences of this revolution in the manner of living for all of us in the midst of it are but dimly realized, however, and in no part of our experience is this so true as in that pertaining to the family. Any attempt to establish the family pattern in accord with the sentiment generated in the childhood experiences of the past is futile in the face of the multitude of radical departures that the machine civilization has brought in our physical, material, economic, and social activities.

Although it is along this avenue that the most important influences for change have come to the family, there has been another line of approach which also needs recognition. People have come to think differently and here also we find the fruits of modern civilization. This change, although not so spectacular as those just described, and not so significant for the family, lays bare most clearly the confusion that accompanies our present transition. Man depends upon his concepts, his traditions, his methods of intellectual attack, and his convictions as the means of stabilizing his career and controlling his behavior. But the same influences that have operated to present him with new problems of adjustment have also undermined his confidence in his resources of thought. Wherever there is the dominance of modern civilization, this is the intellectual situation of many men and women. Nothing social escapes these influences, but to no other institution do they bring the confusion and uncertainty that comes to the family.

These changes in the habit of thinking have been in part a product of the machine. As applied science has changed the material circumstances of people, it has necessarily forced upon them new ideas and new mental attitudes as they have reacted to their personal circumstances. In addition to this unescapable influence, there has also been the deliberate policy of modern society to extend educational facilities widely, with the consequence in the United States that there has been a decline in illiteracy, a marked increase in institutions established for primary, secondary, and higher education, and through newspapers, magazines, libraries, extension courses, lectures, the radio, and a multitude of other agencies an unparalleled popular distribution of information and ideas. None of these has exerted greater influence than the movies. The individual finds himself bombarded from every quarter with intellectual stimuli that forbid the narrow, stereotyped routine-thinking that in all previous periods has been characteristic of the mass of the people. Whatever its faults, the educational program of the United States has succeeded in comparison with the past in enlarging the thought-content of the average man and woman, and has removed the sharp distinction between the aristocracy of learning and mass ignorance.

The inevitable consequence of this absolutely new social achievement has been a shattering of all forms of stereotyped intellectual conventions. The patriarchal family system, undermined by the other social and economic results of machine industry, has especially responded to this popularizing of education. Every feature of family life has revealed the strain of this breaking down of long established fundamental patterns of thought. Nowhere has the confusion been so great as in the parent-child relationship. The necessary dependency of the child upon the parent during the first years of childhood has permitted parents to start the patriarchal scheme of control, with the result that later, as the child attempts to adjust himself to the prevailing social situation, the established family policy becomes an obstruction and the parent and child are driven into conflict, the significance of which neither can understand. The husband-wife relationship provides opportunity for a similar collision between those attempting to hold as much as possible to the patriarchal family program and those attempting to escape from it. Complicating all individual reactions to family situations is the heightening of individual expectation, the intolerance of hard circumstances, and the demand for pleasure, leisure, prestige, and self-expression, for among the first fruits of the popularizing of education has been a new aggressiveness in claiming satisfaction from life. Since the family appears more the product of wilful, personal decisions than do other social relationships, more demands are made of it than of the others and less tolerance is shown toward the dissatisfactions for which it is held responsible.

Influences for change. Time brings change in social realms but only when it leads to the amassing of new experiences. So long as culture remains, generation after generation, merely repetitious, duration does not bring change. In the last century, and especially since the opening of the twentieth century, new experience has rapidly accumulated, forcing reconstruction on all social institutions. As we have seen, this has dislodged the patriarchal family which has had vogue throughout the historic period.

Our present situation, however, cannot be understood as merely the reaction to the periodic accumulation of new experience which throughout human history has from time to time forced the reorganization of social practices and the reinterpretation of social values. Our time has had thrown upon it unfamiliar as well as new experiences. This necessity of meeting new conditions, for which there had been no previous preparation, has happened before but never to the extent that characterizes the present. There are three influences operating upon the

American family that are not only new but radically different, and for the social mastery of which past American history gives no clue.

The first of these, and the most fundamental, has been the effects of applied science. In addition to the economic changes science has brought, there have been three consequences of a social character that are clearly influencing the present American family. One of these is the lifting of the general standard of living, especially as expressed in the increase of leisure and the spreading of the desire for luxury.[1] This advance in material productiveness and the increased stimulation of desire, largely through advertising, has not only injected economic strain within the family, with the possibility of differences of opinion, dissension, and dissatisfaction, but has also created a life-attitude which has led many individuals to value marriage and the family merely as a means of self-gratification. In comparison with the usual reaction in times past, there has developed a new family disposition. This permeates in varying degree the entire American people. There has been no attempt to single out the family, but rather domestic life in all its aspects has been drawn into a life-program that has become accepted as the standard for all experience. Possibly this has led to greater instability in family contacts than in other social experiences, but if so, this has come about not from the desire to discriminate against the family but because tension in home relationship appears so distinctly personal.

Another result that has come from the social influences of applied science on the family has been the heightening of the competitive pressure, the popularizing of the desire for material satisfactions made possible by mass production. The stimulation of personal ambition through the removal of class distinctions and the insecurity of vocation and income that accompanies the technological advance have contributed to the tenseness of economic and social activities so characteristic of modern society and particularly of American life.

A third influence that science has brought to the family has been the perfecting and popularizing of contraception. While this is not something new in the sense that there has been in the

---

[1] Sumner, W. G., and Keller, A. G., *The Science of Society*, Vol. 3, pp. 2090–2095.

past no effort to discover some satisfactory method of birth control, it is new in its high degree of efficacy and in its wide appeal. No discovery of science is affecting family life so much as the improvement and the dissemination of the techniques of birth control. Although what we now have, when competently used, is usually reliable, it is the common opinion of specialists that the future will bring an improved technique.[2]

Urbanization. A second social change of major importance in its effect on the family is the increasing dominance of urban culture. City life is of course not new, but the manner in which the culture brought forth by great cities is spread through the land is something that has not occurred before, because there was not available the efficient means of transportation and communication that modern science has made possible. The recent unparalleled growth of cities in the United States has thus doubly affected family life. The concentration of population has operated upon marriage and domestic experience among those living within the cities or their immediate environment, and in general thus far has added to the instability of domestic life. It has limited the opportunity of many to experience courtship and to find a mate, and has increased the proportion of childless families, encouraged a relatively low birth rate, stimulated the mobility of family life, made possible the decision not to marry, influenced standards within the family, and provided anonymity which has influenced sex morality. It also has established in its strongest form the pleasure philosophy previously discussed.[3]

The significance of the city for family life cannot be found merely in the results that come from massing together a great number of human beings. In modern civilization a city is more than a concentrated population; it is the place where applied science develops most and dominates most, so that, setting aside the inhabitants themselves, the presence in the city of the most recent and most pregnant creations of applied science would give it the cultural dominance denied cities in the past. This cultural influence is of course not confined to the city proper

---

[2] Himes, N. E., "Birth Control in Historical and Clinical Perspective," *The Annals of the American Academy of Political and Social Science,* Vol. 160, p. 64.

[3] Carpenter, N., *Sociology of City Life,* p. 231.

but includes the metropolitan area. Sociologically the transmission of urban culture does not depend on actual adjacency since modern methods of communication, especially the automobile and airplane, make it increasingly true that the city worker can dwell at a distance, and in greater or less degree thereby become a carrier of urban life to the village and country, an effective medium by which the city extends its cultural sway.

The influence of the American city is not confined to those who belong to it geographically, because it represents the supreme expression of machine culture. It enforces its characteristics more or less upon people everywhere, and its styles, standards, behavior, codes, ideas, fads, and passions influence the domestic situation of the entire country.

World Wars I and II. The third major departure that has appeared in recent civilization of importance to the family was World Wars I and II. These also were unique, but not on account of the seriousness of the conflict, the numbers engaged, or the suffering that ensued. There have been similar experiences from these points of view in the extensive and prolonged conflicts of the past, notably during the Roman conquest of the civilized world and the era of Napoleon. The uniqueness of the World Wars appeared in the revelation they brought of the interrelation of nations as a consequence of the development of science, and the international havoc bound to follow a conflict in which the deadly powers of recent scientific inventions were employed, draining from every nation engaged all its possible resources. The disturbance that followed the wars was unprecedented in its revelation of the strength and sensitiveness of international relationship. Its effect upon the family was not so much to be found in the broken homes, careless war marriages, or any immediate effect upon marriages, the birth rate, or child mortality, as in the widespread cynicism and pessimism which appeared when time drew aside the curtain and allowed people everywhere, with eyes freed from the distortions of propaganda, to see the futility of their incomparable suffering. The recoil appeared in every part of social experience, and marriage and the family did not escape. It added to the strain they were already receiving from the normal changes of modern civilization.

Wars accelerate change. They force the giving up of tradition, even the setting aside of moral values, and make many people familiar with attitudes and customs of which previously they had had no knowledge. Modern wars are increasingly contests in material production and discoveries and inventions in science that can be used to destroy human life. This was so true of World War II that it was a unique experience and one that brought both to the victors as well as the conquered social and psychic disturbances never before associated with warfare. Great courage, sacrifice, and hardship on the part of a vast multitude did not prevent for many a profound sense of moral confusion, fatalistic attitudes, and loss of confidence in former values and ways of life. This not only brought about maladjustments for a multitude who found themselves facing new conditions but robbed of the self-reliance they needed to reshape their manner of living. The situation was so unlike that to which the American people had become accustomed in the prewar years that it now seems remarkable that so many families went through the ordeal successfully.

The aftermath of the war was for many individuals and households a greater strain than the war itself. For some persons the return to former occupations and manner of life either appeared or proved impossible. Others who were eager to get back to their life before the war found that, in spite of their idealizing this during their separation from it, they could not adjust to what previously had seemed a most satisfactory situation. Either conditions had changed or when put to the trial these men and women were no longer in accord with former practices or ideas. There were men and women who from service in the armed forces or from their experiences in war industry were unwilling to return to the family life they had willingly accepted before the war. One of the most significant of their changed ways of living appeared in their new sexual attitudes and behavior. The sexual consequences of warfare have always had scant attention in the history of human conflicts,[4] but the breaking of the conventional code, the freeing and intensifying of physical passion are as certain products of war as the losses of property, the diseases, wounds, and deaths.

With the ending of the war there were the familiar prod-

---

[4] Hirschfeld, Magnus, *The Sexual History of the World War* (World War I).

ucts of a long, hard struggle: moral let-down, loss of morale, a sense of futility and disillusionment, and most especially discontent and restlessness.

In the press and in books so much was said of the difficulty the fighting men faced in returning to normal life that it seemed to suggest that the struggle had created a multitude of psychopaths. This fortunately soon proved an exaggeration. Too little was made of the changes in the thinking and behavior of a part of the population that had no part in overseas fighting. It was the unexpected differences that the veteran encountered as he gladly cast off war habits in his former social and home environment that frequently explained maladjustment rather than his experiences in the armed forces. Divorces, as was expected, increased with the ending of the war. Those who had married recklessly or adventurously, who had been married for a brief time and then separated, and those who had never in any serious sense been married at all were naturally quick to feel dissatisfaction and to ask for freedom. Men who had been unfaithful to their wives and, even more, wives who had been disloyal to their husbands were sued for divorce. In other homes, as a result of the war and its after effects of division, restlessness, incompatibility or loss of affection, the prewar happiness disappeared and in its place came emotional separation even when for some reason no attempt was made to get a divorce. No catastrophe is so great an ordeal for domestic life as modern warfare, and unless it is discarded as an anachronism too consequential to be longer endured, family life cannot be made secure however much its interests are fostered by intelligent conserving programs. World peace has become the most urgent of all needs for family welfare.

Changed status of women and sex.   Among the clear and important changes that have occurred recently in the American family, the new status of women is perhaps the most prominent. This has chiefly resulted from woman's greater economic independence, but the significance of the new situation is not exclusively economic. This greater opportunity for self-expression on the part of women, in combination with the breaking down of sex taboo and the more common commitment of Americans in marriage to a pleasure program, has led to a new interpreting of the sex life of women.

Naturally, so recent a revolution as that which has followed the collapse of the conspiracy of silence, which had been maintained in regard to the serious discussion of sex from the beginning of the ascetic trend in early Christianity, and which was strengthened by later Puritanism, has brought confusion and in the minds of many an exaggeration of the importance of sex. After granting that American mass psychology has in recent years revealed the human temptation to go from one extreme to another, it remains true that a new emphasis on the sex needs of women, in the light of their greater economic independence, our better understanding through science of the meaning of sex, and our greater insistence in accord with the disposition of the modern American upon marital satisfaction for both the woman and the man was both logical and inevitable. In any case, this is what has happened, and it has naturally added to the instability of the modern family. The patriarchal axiom that all women were divided into two classes, one made up of ladies who had no thought of sex and the other of women of loose character who deserved no respect, an interpretation which denied the biological needs of the one and dehumanized the other, no longer enjoys its former vogue. As a consequence prostitution is disappearing, while at the same time women are insisting that their sex life receive in marriage equal consideration with that of men. Increasingly there comes from women protest against a double standard of morals which assumes that the male has the greater sex need and therefore the right to formulate the sex code in accord with masculine impulses. This attack on an age-long discrimination has the support of the majority of the men who as scientists have studied human sex.

The most substantial influence leading toward an adequate recognition of the sexual needs of women is coming from the field of medicine, especially psychiatry and endocrinology. The sex life of the individual in the light of present scientific insight can no longer be regarded merely as a problem of morals. It involves the total personality, particularly emotional and nervous well being, and concerns the woman equally with the man. The sexual impulse of the individual is one index of physical maturity, vigor, health, deterioration, and disease. It not only expresses these organic conditions but also contributes to them both physically and emotionally. Among humans it demands more than a physical fulfillment. It thus becomes a source, at

least in part, of romance, spiritual achievement, and the peculiar comradeship made possible through happy marriage. As
recognition of the positive values inherent in wholesome sex
life has progressed, it has become increasingly impossible to
interpret sex as of less significance to women than to men. Since
women have the major role in reproduction, it surely would
have been a strange oversight of nature to have given the female
organism less potential sex endowment than that possessed by
the male. Science, so long limited by taboo, has in recent years
discovered that it is not poverty of sexual resources but complexity and the emotionalizing of the impulse which in the past
have made many women seem meagerly endowed and in the
present have produced the emotional mutilation which explains
the frigid woman.

This changing concept of woman's sexual nature has not
come without a degree of disturbance reflected in the social code
which women accept as their pattern for behavior. The greatest
departure from the code of the recent past most naturally appeared in the conduct of the unmarried young woman. The extent to which the conventional code demanding continence of
the female before marriage has been repudiated by American
young women cannot be known with accuracy because of its
nature. There are those who proclaim their freedom but who
do not carry their words into actions. There are others who conceal their practices and outwardly conform to the program of
continence. Still others keep the letter of the code but not its
spirit, drawing the line only at the final expression of sexual
stimulation. The situation is greatly exaggerated by some
writers, as it is minimized by others. The meaning of the changing attitude is not found merely in the number of those young
women who no longer follow the conventional code but also
in the two significant facts that the change is occurring largely in
the middle class and expresses in great measure the shifting of
personal conviction. This changing of attitude is sociologically
more significant than the behavior itself. Evidence of this growing demand for premarital sex freedom for young unmarried
women appears within the college groups as well as among
other youth.[5]

The experienced marriage counselor soon discovers the

---

[5] Bromley, Dorothy, and Britten, Florence, *Youth and Sex*, pp. 4–5.

danger of oversimplifying the sexual problems of the unmarried woman. Her adjustment can never safely be regarded as merely a question of satisfying one of the strongest of the body appetites even though from the viewpoint of the matured organism sexual fulfillment seems desirable. The least frustrating conduct must be one which meets the needs of the total personality. Human sex has had its specific evolution from the animal and from the primitive, and especially for women has gained emotional and psychic increments that cannot safely be disregarded in any decision of behavior. A considerable part of the extramarital sexual relationships of young American women are motivated, not by the desire to escape organic tension, but to gain or hold favor with the male who is sought as a means of fulfilling urges that go far beyond physical intimacy. Sexual freedom thus becomes an expediency in the case of many. When this is not true, the question arises as to what results originating in the higher demands of comradeship between the male and female are likely to follow the young woman's transitory and relatively indifferent use of the male as a means of sexual satisfaction. This does not mean that sexual fulfillment is not a biological asset for the mature girl but rather that its values must be considered in the light of all the young woman demands of life. The burden of adolescence is not so much repression as unfulfillment. The former is undesirable as a consequence of feelings of restraint, but the greater menace is what may happen to the young woman who reaches out for the satisfactions of life and who fails to achieve a fulfillment which includes sexual satisfaction but emphasizes the fellowship of affection. Meanwhile, it is evident that unlike what has been true in other historic periods when premarital sexual freedom of the unmarried woman was conventional, especially during engagement, no protective code has developed which assures the acceptance by men of their responsibility in cases of unwanted pregnancy.

Throughout American history, as has been true of every people in every age so far as we know, young people have been conscious of their sex problems, and some of them have acted contrary to the conventional program. In the past, however, the approved pattern of behavior has been clear and firmly established socially. The individuals who departed from it realized that they were transgressors, and according to their temperaments and ideals they reacted with guilt-feeling. The unconventional young woman could maintain her social standing only by concealment. Once her conduct became known, she was a marked person who found it difficult to re-establish herself socially. So far as the American youth are concerned, this situation is no longer true. Whatever the individual girl's standards and practices may be, she rarely becomes aggressive in attempting to enforce premarital chastity upon her associates. No longer does the girl subscribe to the one-time taboo of sex, expressing her normal interest and curiosity through subterfuge. Instead, she generally meets her problems with an unprecedented frankness. The popularizing of birth control and the increasing confidence that venereal infection can be prevented have taken away two strong obstacles that formerly checked the personal inclination of some girls toward sexual relationships.

It would be a mistake, however, to regard the young woman's situation as due merely to the pressure of strong impulse on the one side and the restraining code on the other. As Baber [6] points out, American youth are not only made aware of the legitimate importance and value of sex as a human endowment, they are bombarded constantly by stimulations that come from the commercial exploitation of sex interest. They encounter it constantly. Advertisements, movies, books, and the pulp magazines as well as serious literature either openly or by skillful suggestion force attention upon the sexual impulse. As a result, many American youth are made conscious of an impulse expressing itself through normal development but one that has been artificially reinforced through clever exploitation as the hands of those who have become expert in doing this. As Folsom states, evidence is overwhelming that there has been a recent, rapid increase in nonvirginity at marriage. Terman, in his 1938 study, found that the percentage of premarital intercourse was approximately 60 per cent for men and 37 per cent for women. Bromley and Britten gave 52 per cent for men and 25 per cent for women.[7]

Using Terman's findings concerning the decrease of virginity at marriage between the generations of those born in 1880

---

[6] Baber, R. E., *Marriage and the Family*, p. 57.

[7] Folsom, Joseph K., *The Family and Democratic Society*, p. 546; Terman, Lewis M., *Psychological Factors in Marital Happiness*, p. 320; and Bromley, Dorothy, and Britten, Florence, *op. cit.*, p. 289.

and 1910, the Harts constructed a graph showing that if the trend were to continue virginity at marriage would disappear for men born after 1925 and for women born after 1935.[8] In interpreting this study, it is needful to keep in mind that social trends are rarely consistent, since through their progress obstructing influences are usually brought into action. This is especially true of movements that are in conflict with the mores, even of a minority, and especially when they are contrary to the teaching of orthodox contemporary religious leadership.

Obviously, a marital program that recognizes the sex rights of both husband and wife is more exacting than the former program, providing more opportunity for personal dissatisfaction. The new attitude particularly increases the responsibilities of men, who are expected to have insight, consideration, and a sense of justice which in the past was rarely assumed by American husbands.

The pleasure-attitude commonly taken toward marriage by both men and women has been partly expressed through this new emphasis upon sex. Naturally it has led to the making of successful marriage more difficult, particularly since the majority of the younger American men and women are less responsive to any form of social coercion that attempts to keep in a marital relationship those who have for any reason grown dissatisfied and have come to see the failure of their matrimonial hopes. It is also true that the breaking of the former taboo on sex has made possible for these younger men and women a healthier attitude toward marital relationship and to a greater extent than ever in the past has made possible through the gaining of information a better preparation for the experience of marriage.

Changes in attitude toward marriage. Present American culture is characterized by a realistic attitude. Idealism still finds a following, but relatively a greater proportion of the people than formerly have a sophisticated suspicion of abstract goals of conduct and prefer to define their motives in terms of personal desire. Particularly do we find evidence of this change on the part of many youths in their attitude toward marriage and toward parenthood. They are more likely to deny, ignore, or accept with reservation the authority of religious teaching in so far as this attempts to enforce the traditions and ideas concerning marriage and the family which in the past have been generally approved even if not consistently followed. The influences that have brought confusion to the domestic experience have operated upon religious faith. Church dogma is going through the same transitional disturbance that appears in all things related to matrimony.

The Church has in the past considerably failed to command the behavior of those who were without the will to practice its idealism, but, as a rule, its moral authority, even by those who failed to keep its preachments, was not called into question. It is at this point that we discover the significance of the change that is adding to present matrimonial instability. The ideals interpreted by religious leadership no longer meet with such general acquiescence, and the doctrines of the churches regarding marriage, divorce, and sex ethics fail to establish, in the proportion that previously has been true in American history, the standards of conduct. For instance, there is greater insistence upon the right of private judgment even when there is no disposition in any overt way to challenge the authority of the churches.

There appear, as is always true in such a social situation, three groups that deserve, on account of their characteristic reaction, to be designated as the radicals, conservatives, and liberals. The first seeks to be rid of past traditions and to rebuild the purposes of marriage in accord with present trends. The conservatives resist cultural changes in so far as they have to do with matters concerning marriage and the family, insisting that the general matrimonial unrest, the high divorce rate, the falling birth rate, and lax sex standards are the results of drifting from firm anchorage and following the winds of selfishness and physical passion. The liberal group attempts to scrutinize without prejudice both the past and present as related to marriage, and leans heavily upon scientific investigation for discrimination in the effort to reconstruct the marriage program. This group believes that only by the most objective and unbiased examination of matrimonial experience can marriage and the family become adjusted to modern life.

Structure versus function.   For purposes of analysis, distinction can be made between changes in the structure of the family and in its functions. The first has to do with the composition of the institution, the other with its activity. Changes in the one modify the other. This is most apparent when we consider family structure. First of all, there is the question whether there are or are not children. It was Dr. Knight's awareness of the difference between the functioning of these two kinds of family life that led him to coin the term "companionate" for the family that chose to remain childless. The popularizing of birth control, leading to practices that are rapidly becoming an American social trait, has made possible the family without children whose function is radically unlike that home in which husband and wife are parents.

The increasing attention given by medical specialists to problems of infertility indicates, however, that a considerable portion of the families without children result from failure to reproduce rather than from desire not to have children. The lower rate of childbirth in the cities compared to that of the rural area is to some degree the consequence of the conditions of modern life, the tension so apparent in the competitive life of urban people being a marked feature. There are also differences in motivations and in attitudes that tend to give greater encouragement to childbearing in the country than in the city.[9] Likewise, similar differences influence the birth rates of urban groups as appears in the net rate of reproduction of the various classes according to their socioeconomic status, the most privileged standing lowest.[10]

The age of parents, the distribution of the children by age, and especially their number, are structural characteristics that also affect family functioning. A decided lessening of the size of the American family is one of the clearest of structural changes. There has been a striking decrease from the colonial days when the average family had eight children. The home in which there were no children was rare enough at that time to attract attention. This decline in births is in accord with what has generally been true among peoples who have shared western culture. A nation's growth is affected both by the birth rate and the death rate. The decrease of the first has reduced the size of the American family, while that of the second has affected

---

[9] Thompson, W. S., *Population Problems*, pp. 207–210.
[10] Kiser, C. V., *Group Differences in Urban Fertility*, p. 247.

the quality of the population, increasing the proportion of the aged. The family unit as defined by the United States Census for its statistical compilation includes all persons living together in the same household and nobody else. The size of the American family averaged for the entire country has been 5.6 in 1850, 4.7 in 1900, 4.5 in 1910, 4.3 in 1920, 4.1 in 1930. Preliminary data indicate that the 1940 Census will report the family unit 3.8. At the time of the first census in 1790, nearly one in every ten families had ten or more members, while now less than one in fifty is of this size.[11] Although the median size of the American family in 1930 was 3.4 persons, the modal type consisting of two persons represented only 23.4 per cent of the total families. The majority of these consisted of a husband-wife relationship, although some represented a parent-one-child relationship.[12] It is obvious that the quality of family life is largely determined by its composition; for example, a home without a child, the one-child family, and the family of ten or more children each has its distinctive characteristics. The first is denied any of the activities that are associated with parenthood, the second is forced to concentrate attention on the one offspring, while the third provides a variegated association of child-to-child contacts as well as those of parents and child.

The conditions that influence the child during his formative years are too complex to permit causal interpretation wholly dependent upon the size of the family. There is, of course, special opportunity in the small family for the overprotection of the child by the parents. There is, however, no convincing evidence that the one child in a family because of his situation is more likely to experience mental frustration or develop social delinquency. The atmosphere of the family, the character of the interaction of parents and child are too important to make the mere size of the family decisive in the building of the child's character. The family of one or two children, however, necessarily functions differently than one of five or more. The quantity of family life, that is, the mass experience of the household members, in the former case is more concentrated, more limited, and can easily be more intense. The story of

---

[11] Parten, Mildred, and Reeves, Ruby, "Size and Composition of American Families," *American Sociological Review*, Vol. 2, p. 638.

[12] *Ibid.*, p. 639.

Joseph cautions us in assuming that favoritism and jealousy are consequences derived from the composition of the family.

Change in functions of the family.   Not only has the family lost a considerable portion of its former economic and personal functions; its social or institutional functions also have decreased. This is so pronounced that it is generally recognized and is considered by all students of the family one of the most significant things that has happened to the modern family. Not merely has the family generally surrendered many of the productive activities it formerly possessed; but even as a consuming or directing organization it has given to other agencies some of its one-time responsibilities. A list of its losses is impressive. Of course, the functioning of individual families varies considerably, but to a great extent in our present culture we find that the family has largely distributed to other agencies these activities that once it accepted as its own without question: the processing of food, especially baking, canning, and other preserving; the care of the sick; the providing of recreation, including reading; the carrying on of the religious education of children; and the assuming of the responsibilities of childbirth, which commonly are given over to the hospital. Child nurture and education, once the foremost social responsibility of the family, are being delegated increasingly to schools, kindergartens, child-guidance clinics, recreational organizations, summer camps, nursery schools, settlements, churches, and philanthropic clubs and organizations.

Even though the family keeps but a remnant of its former functions, it receives criticism from every quarter from those who charge it with inefficiency in the activities it still attempts to perform, while others are dismayed at the rapid loss of family responsibility and the length to which the community and its various specialized organizations have gone in taking over the tasks once belonging to the family. Some are impatient and see in the power the family still exercises over young life the chief obstacle to social progress. Parents sensitive to the present situation are in doubt as to their duties when they see the social patterns which seemed in their childhood so well established crumbling away with the farming out of one activity after another to organizations which appear to prosper in the degree that the family weakens. There are, however, other parents who would recoil from having children if they were denied opportunity to limit their parental responsibilities. For the most part the competition the family receives has grown without intent on the part of the organizations that are taking over what used to belong to the family. They have developed out of the needs of children and as a means of furnishing equipment, technique, and privileges that ordinary parents working by themselves have no means of giving to their children.

Change in family security. An impressive change has occurred in the feeling of family insecurity. Thus far there has developed no serious disposition to destroy the family organization and to transfer its services to any institution or combination of agencies to be maintained and managed by the state. There are writers who advocate some sort of public organization rather like our homes for orphans and defectives, but this program appears more an effort to draw attention to the failure of the American family as interpreted by its critics than a serious advocacy of a new form of domestic adjustment. In any case, this is the impression the agitation makes on most of those who in this country take any interest in the ideas advocated, which they regard as theoretic rather than feasible solutions for present family difficulties.

On the other hand, those within the family feel quite generally an insecurity which is chiefly economic and most pronounced in what may be roughly called the middle class. It is particularly in regard to the children that this sense of family insecurity arises, and unquestionably it is beginning already to influence the birth rate and will, unless in some manner lessened, affect it in the near future more than at present. There is also an underlying, half-conscious feeling of uncertainty in the minds of individual parents as to whether they are performing their parental duties efficiently and whether they are qualified to take over such obligations. Thus lack of the confidence that formerly supported parents as they felt sure that they at least knew what they ought to do gathers about the family in spite of the fact that no proposed substitute makes at present any serious appeal to most Americans. The applause radical ideals get often expresses the desire of certain unconventional individuals for social support of their personal practices rather than genuine conversion to the schemes advocated.

The security of the family as an institution. The family in some form is one of the social institutions which we find in every culture of which we have knowledge. It has apparently the most important place in the extending of human control and the enrichment of value which has come by the establishment and extension of the social order. Like other institutions it constitutes an organization that carries on among a group of specially related persons, relatively definite and persistent, systematic and socially approved practices. It provides for its members the means of fulfilling human needs that in some degree demand commitment to an intimate association. It accomplishes these functions in many ways. Some of its activities occur within the group as the various members in their reactions one to the other contribute to what we commonly think of as home life. The maintenance of the individual family unit requires also functions by the members that, although they bring advantage to the family, are directed outward toward the physical or social environment. As the family functions in these two directions, it also contributes to the enrichment and the stability of the total cultural possessions of the society to which the family belongs. The sociologist attempts to trace and evaluate these three-sided activities of the family. Jessie Bernard in considerable detail has classified these as reproductive, protective, socializing, and affection-giving types of functions and has estimated the degree of adequacy of the American family along these four lines.[13]

A great part of the functioning of the family can be brought under the concept of security. This is especially true of the part the individual family plays in the maintenance of the social order.[14] Likewise, disorganization expressed in the cultural environment and that appearing within the family are reciprocal in their influences, each affecting the other. This fact raises the question, how far recent social changes jeopardize the security of the family as a social institution. It is evident that if the family were destitute of functions, if all its activities were surrendered to other social agencies, if its peculiar satisfactions were obtained without family organization, the institution itself would be devoid of social service. Thus far every culture has

---

[13] Bernard, Jessie, *American Family Behavior*, p. 106.
[14] Elmer, M. C., *The Sociology of the Family*, Ch. 5.

found it necessary to continue the domestic institution, although rarely, at least in any self-conscious, critically minded social order, have the activities of the family appeared so flawless as to escape censure. Social acquiescence cannot lessen the liabilities of the failures of the family as a social institution, although this may lead to an erroneous feeling as to its security. The American family like its predecessors has been given activities that are indispensable for human survival. These services with their emphasis on highly developed human values must be concentrated in one or more social organizations. Thus far the peculiar inherent qualities of family relationships have led to the consignment of these interests chiefly to the family group. Changes in the physical and social environment, that is, in material and cultural conditions, call for new adjustments as the institution attempts to ensure these basic human wants. This adaptation to the prevailing conditions may mean surrendering in some measure previously possessed responsibility.

The division of labor given over to the family is both a product of and an actuation within the evolutionary process as it concerns humans, and it therefore has the support of the cultural achievement man has made.[15] Rapid social changes, although they force the reshaping of family life and the modifying of family activities and as a consequence cause some amount of disorganization, cannot disturb the sociological significance of the family as an institution unless culture repudiates its own development and turns the social evolution of man toward a radically different direction than that which in the past has established the societies of which we have knowledge.

International insecurity and the family. Throughout the world among intelligent people there is a feeling of international insecurity which in its spread and intensity is without parallel in human history. It expresses a conviction that at last modern science in its development of the atomic bomb has reached a potential destructiveness which places in the hands of ambitious, shortsighted, socially irresponsible heads of governments the starting of a warfare which will test the very survival of the human race.

This feeling of helplessness on account of the death-giving forces of nature now disclosed by scientific research cuts deeper

---

[15] Groves, E. R., *The Family and Its Social Functions*, p. 558.

than even this awareness of international peril. It leads emotionally to a feeling of cosmic insecurity. The energy provided by nature which can now be turned against human well-being seems too great a possession for a moral universe, too tempting to cruel, despotic, or mentally unsound human beings. In somewhat the same manner, the discovery of the Western new world swept away in Europe long-established conceptions, but that mental upheaval gave forth a stimulating ferment to the thinking of the time, while the present advance in the scientific frontier leaves men and women blanketed in their outlook as they become aware of their unexpected, unprecedented peril. They realize that human leadership has not commonly reached the level of social maturity which makes such power as the use of atomic energy a safe possession. Especially does this seem true in a period when there is also great clashing of class, race, and nationalistic feelings and violently opposed ideologies. In contrast with this hazard, the dangers of family disorganization appear incidental problems in the social changing of orderly progress. What the final meaning this slipping of human anchorage will have for domestic experience only time can reveal. For the moment the home seems in contrast a center of assurance and hopefulness.

The marriage situation.   The marriage situation is somewhat different. The attacks made by the critics of marriage have been more vigorous, and there has been greater willingness on the part of individuals to attempt some substitute scheme. Among the ultramodern groups and chiefly in the larger cities there are found experiments that attempt to accomplish sex adjustment, in times past the prerogative of married life, by some other method than the orthodox marriage. The proportion of such experiments can be easily exaggerated and apparently has been by advocates of new types of sex adjustment. The following are the most common of the new experiments: (1) a frankly chosen premarriage promiscuity in which neither man nor woman assumes any responsibility for the other or makes any exclusive claims; (2) a private exclusive relationship without legal sanction and regarded as temporary in character; (3) a private exclusive relationship without legal sanction but considered as a permanent commitment; (4) a trial marriage relationship without legal sanction, looking toward final permanency but carrying with it the right of either person to separate at will from the other; (5) a secret legal marriage, with the idea that either person in case of dissatisfaction has the right without objection from the other to seek divorce; (6) a legal marriage with the idea that it carries no restriction on the sex conduct of either husband or wife but permits both to regard out-of-home sex relationships as a personal right; (7) orthodox marriage except that it is entered upon with the agreement that there shall be no children born to the couple (a) for a period of time, or (b) ever during the union.

Even when such experiments are attempted, the motive for entering upon them is more often the desire to work out some temporary satisfying method of sex adjustment during the delay of marriage on account of economic insecurity or lack of confidence that the right life partner has been found, than a conviction that orthodox marriage should be supplanted. These attempts to discover some feasible premarriage adjustment reveal the strain that youth feels in this transitional period.

The established code of familial ethics has never in America prevented a considerable amount of unconventional behavior. The significance of the new situation lies not in the present unorthodox conduct of individuals but in the rather general feeling of youth that social standards are themselves in confusion.

The social situation in which many young men and women, especially of the middle class, find themselves is unfavorable to early marriage, and postponement tempts some to a program of expediency as a temporary substitute, a solution which would of course get scant consideration were the conventional code unshaken. It is not loss of confidence in marriage as the ideal relationship in the majority of cases but the unwillingness to accept the strain of delayed or frustrated hopes that is antagonizing the institution of matrimony. In the same way, the social situation of many who are married keeps them from accepting parenthood or from assuming it early and at the most favorable time.

The important thing to recognize is the distance we have already traveled from the frontier situation when social conditions encouraged early marriage and early parenthood. Programs that rival marriage are being advocated and to some degree practiced because they appear to offer a practical way out of a social situation that would rarely arise in a culture, like that of colonial America, favorable to matrimony. Unless social conditions change and again so encourage marriage that it will have no aggressive competition from other adjustment schemes, the present situation will continue. None of the programs that are being advanced are new, for in times past they have been either practiced or advocated, but their discussion is revealing a social tension which is distinctly new in American life.

Marriage does not have the support that has come to the family through the culturizing of one of the strongest of human instincts. From the purely sociological point of view, marriage is not indispensable to the maintenance of society even though experience has demonstrated that the formalizing and defining of the relationship of the male and the female which constitute marriage is highly desirable. Because of this expediency marriage in some form is found in all the cultures that have developed within the historic period. The monogamic form of marriage, which has been most approved socially and is therefore generally the conventional type, has always incurred competition from other relationships even though these have been outlawed and thereby discouraged. It is therefore to be expected in a period of rapid social change that marriage, and especially the monogamic status, will reveal greater disorganization than the family.

In its normal functioning, marriage loses a measure of significance as the husband and wife become parents and their relationship to one another is incorporated in the greater fellowship of the family. There are numerous exceptions to this usual development even when marriage issues into parenthood. The more emphasis the marriage relationship itself retains, the more open it is to the disturbances that come not only from social changes but also from the life-changes of the individuals concerned. Thus, for example, an early marriage may shrink in value because of the aging and perhaps the maturing of one or both spouses. If physical passion has had an almost exclusive part in bringing about such a marriage, the risk of this is the greater. In the United States, especially since the beginning of the century, marriage experience has felt the force of the most rapid of cultural changes and although the various conserving programs can minimize the disorganization that appears in matrimony, the impact of disturbances coming from the environment explains many of the situations that lead to the failure of individuals in marriage. Society can conceal these or refuse to dissolve the marriages of those who wish to be released from their one-time commitment, but such policies cannot protect the marriage relationship from the environmental assault. The most promising program is found in efforts to prepare youth for marriage, to help them in their choice of mate, and to provide for them counseling service both as a means of assisting them in making the early adjustments of marriage and dealing with the later problems that so frequently arise in marriage and family life.

In a realm where personal patterns of behavior are so tenacious, whatever change the future may bring in marriage or family structure will be likely to come through the gradual process of adaptation to new conditions rather than by revolution through mass action. This provides opportunity for a social planning, a cultural telesis, that will strengthen the position of both marriage and parenthood as the norms of social experience. Meanwhile, the present situation invites the exploitation of the more adventurous and discontented of the women by men who utilize the opportunity for self-seeking pleasure offered by the prevailing restlessness and confusion, with no serious intention of playing fair with their partners, who run the greater risk of social and physical penalties as a consequence of unconventional conduct.

Loss of family viewpoint in social leadership. Throughout our history as a nation until recently, family experience has been basic in our social thinking, our practices, and our sense of values. The family had first place as an educational influence preparing the child for life, and this assignment of responsibility was taken as a matter of course. The representative, one might say the normal, adult felt strongly his family relationships, and his domestic behavior more than anything else fixed his reputation. His virtues and ambitions centered about his family, as likewise did his vices. The family was not exclusive as either motive or ideal; it certainly was not usually an ostentatious or even self-conscious interest. Nevertheless, although the significance of the family was taken as a matter of course, its influence was so thoroughly absorbed during early life as to make it dominant in social thinking.

This family outlook upon life was open to the criticism that it was often selfish and always limited. Indeed, social concern did need to go beyond the family, but the important thing to notice is the naturalness of using the intimacy of family life, its concreteness and responsiveness as the means of gaining the needed insight to extend sympathy, purpose, and even reform to the greater out-of-the-family area. Even the social planner in order to be realistic needs the background of frank, intimate association, with its person-to-person responsiveness which the family group uniquely provides. It is interesting to notice how, in contrast with our times, social idealism in the middle of the last century took a family form leading to the use of the domestic mold for the shaping of a new community order. It is an illustration of the tendency to accept the family institution as a sort of social tutor and interpreter of fundamental values.

This situation, in which our social problems were chiefly seen within the domestic background, has largely changed. This is most true of those who have assumed social leadership. The domestic philosophy of life has given way and has been replaced by an attitude that comes from thinking chiefly from the viewpoint of group experience.

Mass experience is more impressive. End-results, expressed in group achievements, are stressed. As the manufacturer thinks of products and not of workers, so the social planner concentrates on social goals, accomplishments in his field that are the equivalent of the material things of the industrialist, and assumes that his reforms will automatically and necessarily advance the individual and increase his satisfactions.

There is little realization of the fact that the sense of personal consequence which the true parent cultivates in the child collides with a civilization that appears to make the individual meaningless. The social planner thus ignores the most frustrating of our social coercions. The ordinary men and women who become conscious of this clashing—and the sensitive and thoughtful person is most affected—react in various ways. The underlying motive of a common recoil is the desire to salvage values needed to give living a worth-while purpose. Too frequently this is stigmatized by psychiatrists who assume that the individual should learn to adapt himself to whatever environmental conditions happen to exist. The fact that he has had inner reality which also makes just claims is apt to be ignored. The great majority of those who feel the distance between family experience and the social life which modern culture forces upon the adult suffer disillusionment. The meaning life has had is snatched from them, and they are left with an emptiness that prepares them to follow any enticing or aggressive crusader who is clever with the psychology of collecting followers or directing discontent by giving the individual a sense of partnership in some passion-driven enterprise.

The nonexploiting leaders enlist in a more conserving program. Their social thinking, however, and especially their planning are directed by an underlying concentration on mass purposes. This, as a method of industrial production, works wonderfully, giving us things at the lowest possible cost. Even in this field it robs the processes themselves of intrinsic meaning to most workers. Social programs must assume the task of meeting the human needs of those concerned. It is easy, under the pressure of a culture that along so many lines submerges the individual in the mass, to be satisfied with impersonal end-results, which, when analyzed, seem to mean making even social idealism materialistic. It is the philosophy of things, the confidence that happiness and security can be advanced by multiplying material resources and distributing them better. Desirable as this is, it is but half of what has to be done to advance social welfare. Impersonal, mass-conceived goals are enticing, but they become illusions when regarded as ends rather than means.

The antidote to impersonal, mass-dominated feeling and thinking is the sort of experience that the average family by the mere fact of its living together produces. The proper use of our materialistic achievement could enable home life to be all the more efficient in maintaining the balance between satisfactions that have to be obtained inwardly through human affectionate contacts and those forthcoming from our increasing skill in manipulating our physical environment. This two-fronted advance is achieved by a portion of American families.

Chapter 12

COURTSHIP

FOREWORD. The term "courtship" covers a considerable diversity of behavior. It represents something that not only reaches far back in human history but has its prelude in behavior that we find among many of the lower animals. Among them its purpose is exclusively biologic, since it permits a selective influence in mating; among humans, although it is basically similar, psychic and social motivation consciously predominates. The form that courtship takes reflects the prevailing culture, especially as it has to do with the conventions that establish the status of the man and the woman. Then it becomes not only the means of choosing a mate but also a relationship that influences the conditions of marriage.

The trend in this country has been unmistakably toward a code of courtship that has inclined toward giving woman an approach to social equality with men. This trend has become a part of a movement which is a major trait of the cultural evolution in the United States. Although courtship problems are impressively individual, as the college student encounters them, they can be better understood whatever form they take during the premarriage career for the man or the woman if they are interpreted from the viewpoint of their function in determining and maturing the individual's choice of mate. Since the student is apt to be very close to the prevailing courtship problems and generally personally concerned in understanding and meeting them, it is desirable that the instructor encourage discussion during the class period.

Animal courtship. Courtship is found in the higher groups of animals and has been given much attention by natural historians and zoologists. The term, however, applies to behavior so different on this lower instinctive level from what it now means among humans, that perhaps it is misleading. Among the animals it takes the form of display of colors, spreading of wings, dancing, circling about, making fantastic movements, singing, and various kinds of body contact. It is not carried on by organisms that lack a nervous system or sensory organs. In animal behavior we find courtship assuming two distinct functions. With some, and this is the more common, it is chiefly related to the act of mating and has to do with the arousing of the instinct of sex. This aspect of animal courtship in a higher and more elaborate form appears in the experience of men and women as a feature of marital adjustment. The other aspect of animal courtship more nearly resembles the significance of the term as we apply it to human experience, and its purpose is the selection of a mate. The two types of animal courtship are not exclusive, but even when they coexist, one may clearly predominate.

Among the birds courtship appears in a highly developed form. Anyone familiar with bird life has seen in the pairing season the male wooing the female in a way suggestive of modern human courtship. The male tries to attract the attention of the female by strutting, display of feathers, flying about, and uttering cries; the female assumes a more passive role, but when he shows discouragement she at once changes her disposition and incites him to new interest. And among the invertebrata the courtship antics of the male fiddler crab are especially interesting. In the breeding season the mature male may be seen swinging about his claw to attract the attention of the female as she passes by. Another curious form of courtship appears among the moths when the male attracts the female by scent thrown from his legs. Among the bees the queen's single nuptial flight swiftly directed toward the sky becomes an effective means of selection as she is pursued by a troop of drones, mating only with the individual that first reaches her.

There is often a combative element in animal courtship, especially among the higher animals, where two males fiercely contend for the possession of the female, not uncommonly in her presence. The struggle acts as a selective process, for in most cases the more vital animal becomes victor and transmits his qualities to the next generation. It apparently also acts as a sex stimulus, at least for the female. In modern human courtship this element of combativeness also appears, but ordinarily it takes the form of rivalry and the conventions keep it within bounds and restrict its expression.

Courtship among primitive people.   There are such differences among preliterate peoples that it is difficult to make an adequate generalization. Much depends upon the meaning given the term courtship, for as a rule among primitive people it is far removed from the practices characteristic of modern men and women. Only the experienced anthropologist, who is thoroughly familiar with the everyday life of a tribe, is in a position to interpret courtship customs. Even when the mores antagonize the romantic element, it is not necessarily true that this is altogether absent in the attachments that develop between young men and women.[1] The forms that courtship takes are in such contrast to modern practices that it is easy, according to an investigator's attitude, to read into their behavior more resemblance to contemporary experiences than exists, or, on the other hand, to deny a genuine likeness through failure to understand the significance of unfamiliar courtship procedure. From the data that we now have in regard to the courtship practices of primitive people, it appears that sometimes the woman has, as in modern life, a real choice of mate. A savage Besisi in Kuala Langat on the Malay Peninsula, when asked how a man would speak to a woman he wanted to marry, and who was willing to accept him, replied by giving the following dialogue:

Man.—Are you willing to take me, say?

Woman.—What mean you? I merely follow you. How can I refuse?

Man.—I wish that too.

Woman.—How can I refuse? It is the man with whom it rests. I merely follow you, since I am but a woman. As I am a woman, I merely follow you.

Man.—If that is truth, so be it. I will be father and mother to you, rest assured.

Woman.—What mean you? I follow you for a single day, but not for long.

Man.—That is also my desire.

---

[1] Malinowski, B., *Sexual Life of Savages*, Vol. 2, p. 314.

Woman.—If you are savage, overbearing, harsh-spoken, if you are like that, if you are like a hornet, I shall be unable to endure it beyond tomorrow.[2]

Folsom has brought out vividly the contrast between the American family system and that of the natives of the Trobriand Islands who live just northeast of Australia.[3] His interpretation is based upon data reported by Malinowski in his *Sexual Life of Savages*. The author's dual classification reveals clearly the fact that courtship reflects the structure and functioning of the family system as a whole and therefore that its meaning cannot be found when courtship behavior is isolated and its problems not related to the totality of the domestic conventions and practices.

A similar contrast can be worked out between the American and any other primitive system, provided the latter has been reported by some anthropological investigator in sufficient detail. However, it would be a misconception to suppose that primitive courtship follows a general pattern which stands in contrast to the conventional code of the United States. Instead, the systems of preliterate peoples, like our own, are unique, so that a detailed contrast can also be made between the courtship behavior patterns of any two systems of primitive people.

It also is not safe to generalize with the assumption that the primitive code is in all respects backward as compared with our own. In the study of the Kimberley tribes to which reference has already been made,[4] we find there is a recognized procedure in courtship which permits either the man or the woman to take the initiative. By so simple a procedure as sending a gift of tobacco to a boy the girl may announce her interest in the male of her choice, and if he responds courtship starts. The orthodox code assumes that marriage is the result of a betrothal arranged by the two sets of parents either when the boy and girl are infants or after puberty. There is, however, among these people at present a trend toward boys and girls having a series of affairs ending in their making their own choice of mate as a prelude to permanent marriage. The woman's opportunity to

---

[2] Skeat, W. W., and Blagden, C. O., *Pagan Races of the Malay Peninsula*, Vol. 2, p. 69.

[3] Folsom, Joseph K., *The Family and Democratic Society*, pp. 1–39.

[4] Kaberry, Phyllis M., *The Aboriginal Woman*, p. 111.

initiate courtship without any subterfuge reveals a courtship convention toward which we tend in America but which in an open and frank manner we have not yet attained. It is reported [5] of the natives of Torres Straits Islands that it is considered bad form for the male to attempt to initiate courtship. First advances are regarded as the prerogative of the woman. The man may anoint himself with scent and otherwise indicate that he is ready to exchange bracelets with the girl of his choice, the first step in avowed courtship, but even when this has happened he is expected to go no farther until she sends him a gift of food, which is an indication on her part that she is beginning to contemplate marrying him.

In any discussion of the courtship practices of primitive peoples it is necessary to keep in mind how such traditions and folkways are being changed as a result of contact with western civilization. Frequently there is greater instability in customs than is found even in our own country where machine culture and modern transportation facilities have broken down isolation and social inventions have disturbed the habits of people. It is therefore necessary in any description of primitive courtship practices to raise the question, how much they are in transition because the natives have been influenced by western ways and are being forced to make adaptations to the social changes taking place. Professor Schapera in his *Married Life in an African Tribe* gives us an interesting example of this passing of traditional practices and the coming in its place of modern courtship. According to the former custom, marriages were arranged by the parents, and among the Kgatla [6] not only were marriages permitted on a far wider range of relationship than we find customary in most primitive and civilized societies but also the marriage of first cousins was considered highly desirable. It was felt that the mating of relatives who knew each other well and therefore tended to be more tolerant of one another would have greater chances of success than the union of young people who were comparative strangers. It was also regarded an advantage to bind together even more closely the two families, since this would increase their harmony and co-operation. However, it was not true that all marriages within this tribe were those of

[5] Joyce, T. Athol, and Thomas, N. W., *Women of All Nations,* p. 12.
[6] *Op. cit.,* p. 41.

cousins. In fact, there were far less such matings than the strength of the social tradition would suggest. Since there might not be suitable first cousins, a wife was sought from more distant relatives. There were more marriages of this type than those of first cousins, but even so the majority of the matings were of persons not actually related.

Although the old ways persisted and it was fairly common to find parents arranging marriages for their children, the author reports that it was becoming much more usual for the son to take an active part, and only after he had selected his wife did he ask his parents to conduct the formal negotiations with her family. It was also becoming more and more common for the parents of the girl to consult her in the matter and abide by her wishes. This change revealed the breaking down of former parental control as a result of the influence of Christianity, school education, the greater freedom of children, and the abandonment of old initiation ceremonies which had enforced the authority of the parents.

The periodic migration of the young men to European centers for employment also weakened former parental dictation. One of the consequences of this change in courtship conditions has been a new freedom among both boys and girls expressed in premarriage sexual relations. Formerly considerable social pressure was imposed to keep an unmarried girl at least chaste, but in recent days parents complain of the decay of morality. There are few Kgatla women, let alone men, who are virgins when they finally marry.[7] Sexual adventure not only has a prominent place in the life of the young Kgatla; it also strongly affects courtship. The men put a greater emphasis on qualities of physical charm in their selection of mates. Although the individual preferences vary, the trend is toward a girl very light in color, firmly built, the slim one having very little erotic appeal. Facial beauty has less attraction than body form, but there seems to be considerable preference for oval features, large eyes, slender nose, and thin lips.[8] The Kgatla male is attracted by physical charm; he also seeks additional qualities in his wife similar to those that in the former conventional code were considered desirable by his parents. He shies away from the lazy, garrulous,

---

[7] *Ibid.*, p. 45.
[8] *Ibid.*, p. 46.

and quarrelsome girl. The girl also has her idea of what is desirable in the husband. Industry and the ability to work are considered valuable assets.

The refinement of courtship practices. Courtship as it now exists in modern life is both an enlargement and a refining of such means of sexual attraction as we find among the higher animals and in primitive society. It is a special form of the evolution which has brought man forward to his present complexity of living. Just as the emotional life of man has been elaborated along other lines, so this portion relating to mating and reproduction has expanded and become enriched in marriage. Physical passion has neither been eliminated nor smothered, but it has been stretched far beyond its original significance by being incorporated in the emotional complexity which we know as romantic love. In its present form it is a comparatively modern achievement, historically, appearing from the eleventh century onward. Functioning both as a means of selection and as a physical and psychic stimulus, it has grown in accord with the general expansion of human experience, taking on qualities of fellowship that make it one of the most intense and determining events of the life career.

Courtship as it has developed in western civilization and especially in the United States represents an idealization of biologic urges and characteristically starts in early adolescence. The meaning this has for the individual and the expression given to it are consequences of both social and personal backgrounds. For example, it is obvious that the shy person who becomes over-self-conscious is handicapped even though he shares with those more fortunate the same social conventions. Many writers have called attention to the problem of modern youth that results from the body development that brings physical preparedness for marriage before there is sufficient maturity and economic security to justify matrimony. This time interval, during which biologic change runs ahead of readiness for marriage along other lines, offers opportunity which the adolescent uses in various practices relating to courtship. Daydreaming is one; another may be described as an experimental adventure in comradeship with the other sex. In spite of this being commonly stigmatized as puppy love, it has an educational function and prepares for a later, more matured type of courtship. Although it is not difficult to uncover the contribution adolescent idealization may make to a later feeling of disillusionment in marriage, the value of this premarriage experience lies in developing expectation and thereby giving greater meaning to the adult relationship of matrimony. The possibility in individual cases of backward looking because courtship seems more meaningful than marriage is the negative side of this experience which in most cases tends to elevate and enlarge marriage by the demands made of it.

The motive of love. The basis of American courtship is the love motive. It has become so dominant in our culture that it not only overshadows other motives for marriage but has become such a characteristic national trait that its supremacy in courtship is taken for granted. Although we share our stress of the love motive with other peoples, nowhere has it been more firmly established as the commanding reason for entering marriage. Its position, however, is in considerable measure a cultural rationalization. Whenever the appeal in courtship leads a member of one sex to become attached to another with the expectation of marriage, this commitment will be described as falling in love. Seldom will this not be true of any association before marriage which in a genuine sense may be described as courtship. In second marriages occurring at a higher age level than that of youth other motivations appear, but rarely does this happen during the adolescent period of courtship. The idea of falling in love is enforced by our culture through myriad forms of suggestion. Literature with its love story, the theater with its conventional theme of conflict problems of love, and especially the movies that find their greatest appeal, at least to the adolescent, through portrayal of the falling-in-love romance are the most effective supporters of this incentive to marriage, aside from the folkway transmission which is passed from person to person.

Nevertheless, when any attempt is made to analyze just what is meant by falling in love it soon appears that the experience is complex and vague rather than simple and clear cut. The chief difficulty is to distinguish falling in love from the passion drive. Since the young person may fall in love a number of times with very different types of persons and a final romance that leads to marriage frequently discloses in time no substantial basis of mutual happiness, it is apparent that the term describes a fixation of the mating impulse rather than an explanation and justification of the choice of mate.

In spite of the ambiguity of the falling-in-love motive as a cause of the mutual attachment for young men and women, it has been predominant in determining the spirit of courtship and in establishing the ideal of marriage. It makes the supreme test of both experiences an individualistic appraisal. The significance of marriage to society and to the families of the spouses becomes secondary. This individualistic emphasis is the most characteristic feature of American courtship and marriage conventions. The contribution of marriage to social security is in the feeling and thinking of the average American subordinated to the emotional appeal which commands the courtship experience. There is, therefore, little of that sense of the importance of the marriage to the related families which has been so characteristic of the remarkably strong French family, with the exception of a contrary emphasis of a family alliance through marriage found among American orthodox Jews. The high divorce rate in this country is related to this individualistic aspect of the mating ideal. Not only does falling in love provide the proper incentive for marriage, but the passing of this emotional attraction furnishes the conventional justification for the breaking of ties even when this can become effective in law only by subterfuge. If emotional disillusionment arises before habit establishes sufficient incentive for a less romantic but more mature life-partnership, separation or divorce frequently follows.

The incompatibility which the law rarely recognizes as sufficient grounds for divorce but which is in fact usually the true explanation frequently signifies, when analyzed, the loss of the sort of emotional attachment the term "falling in love" tries to express. This, in some cases, means little more than the kind of passion attraction Casanova experienced and which he knew would die through its own satisfaction. Thus, as he affirms, mere passion destroys its own offspring. If the marriage incentive does not develop beyond a temporary concentration of passion, it is still considered falling in love, even though it only means quickly departing from one spouse and electing another with no regard for the number of times the marriage venture has failed. Although such a marriage career is deplored, the conventional reaction assumes the propriety of the love motive. Its fickleness is recognized, but its right to determine the marriage career is unquestioned and contrary to the characteristic French attitude that the security of the family must be maintained without regard to the presence or absence of a romantic, emotional ecstacy between the spouses in their marriage relationship.

It is apparent that there is a subjective element associated with the term love which makes it difficult to define or describe so highly individual an experience as falling in love. It is, like taste and color, dependent for its significance upon personal response, but it brings certain emotional reactions that can be objectively stated. It disturbs ordinary routine, creates a new life spirit which includes in some degree a feeling of animation and of elevation. In short, it has the markings of a peculiar sort of self-intoxication, but in spite of this similarity in the emotional upheaval it brings it remains in its deeper substance one of the most individualistic of all fundamental life situations. The poets by common consent come nearest to portraying it, but it has also enticed the analytic gifts of a variety of students of human nature. Among the philosophers Schopenhauer stands out as one who recognized the importance of romantic love and who therefore made it a feature of his system of thought. Among the sociologists Lester Ward was among the first to define it as a major socializing impulse and to attempt a classification of the various kinds of love.[9] The author of this text, stressing the psychiatric viewpoint, has distinguished three fundamental love attitudes, and their meaning for courtship and for marriage: the narcissistic, the dependency, and the maturely heterosexual type.[10] At considerable length, Bernard discusses the nature of love and recognizes three basic levels or aspects: the physiological, psychological, and the sociological.[11] Her analysis is one of the most complete and illuminating yet written. Another excellent exposition of love as an experience and relationship including biologic and psychiatric aspects appears in Folsom's *The Family and Democratic Society*.[12]

These various discussions show the experience of love as too composite to be justly portrayed by the expression "falling

[9] Ward, Lester, *Pure Sociology*, p. 378.
[10] Groves, Ernest R., *Marriage*, pp. 47–48.
[11] Bernard, Jessie, *American Family Behavior*, pp. 385–390.
[12] *Op. cit.*, Ch. 11.

in love," for it is a special type of reaction. What really happens is that one enters into a peculiar emotional experience which provides opportunity for the love aspect to develop and to function as a unique man-woman affection but which does not necessarily bring this fruition. It is a cultural achievement recognized and enhanced by conventional American thinking, and although, therefore, of the utmost importance as a part of courtship experience, it does not necessarily bring forth or demonstrate the permanent commitment required for successful marriage.

Meaning of courtship for woman. Courtship has a special meaning for woman, since the form it takes depends upon the social status which she enjoys. So long as she remains mere property or is assigned in marriage by some person or system that takes no account of her personal preferences, courtship is impossible. To the degree that she moves away from such social discrimination and approaches a measure of individuality, opportunity is provided for a higher relationship of the man and woman which requires his wooing her. On the one level she has no self-decision, on the other she has a will that must be respected. Although the importance of this evolutionary change is clear, it is easy to see that there is not in the history of human mating the distinct demarcation we might expect to find. While romantic courtship is usually dated as appearing in the eleventh century of European culture, through the influence of the troubadours, human mating is not absolutely of one type before and of another type since that period. Even in the higher animals there are clear cases of the male's attempt to woo the female and her rejection of his advances. This is one of the perplexities associated with the mating of highly bred domestic animals.

During the long period of woman's social limitation, the conditions that denied her the individuality required for courtship also deprived man of the emotional experiences necessary for this higher method of gaining a mate. Once selection became mutual, the realization of the emotional need of love-response grew, among both men and women, as well as a keener development of personal preferences. As human life becomes more enriched in emotional values, the momentum toward mutual selection in the mating of man and woman will carry courtship still farther toward an equality code of conduct.

It must be recognized that our courtship code has, like any other, its peculiar difficulties. One of them appears when a woman comes to feel that she is not attractive to men and is therefore not likely to be courted unless she herself finds some way to stimulate attention. Her way of escape from a state of affairs which not only offers little chance of marriage but which, and this is perhaps even more significant, denies her the feeling of proper self-respect, is the most hazardous role she could choose in her association with men. A much experienced person, an impressive young widow for example, has the insight to deal with young men so shrewdly as not to create the masculine reaction which generally comes when a man feels himself being pursued. The result is that however fictitious or substantial the original handicap may have been, the woman's effort to attract men, her greater aggression, brings still more self-consciousness and the feeling of inadequacy. On the other hand, she knows full well that unless she exerts herself in some manner she is not likely ever to receive attention because this already has been true.

It is a trying dilemma for the adolescent, though for many it may be basically fictitious and self-created or prove only to be temporary. There is plenty of evidence that the courtship pattern even among higher animals sometimes involves retreat of the female as a stimulus to the pursuit of the male. It is equally clear that this program is not in accord with the social influences that now mold the impulses of women who have been exposed to higher education and an environment that encourages independence and freedom. As has already been noted, we find in the courtship practices of some primitive peoples a reversal of the orthodox trend, permitting the woman to take a more aggressive role in courtship. It therefore cannot be said that the human is so bound to the animal pattern that at this point there can be no escape from what creates a consequential inequality of women as compared with men. On the other hand, there can be no doubt that most men run away from the pursuing female.

Courtship and modern marriage. Courtship in contemporary society is no mere doorway through which one enters marriage. Its function is basic in the maintenance of an emotionally satisfying type of marriage. If it were possible, as some theories have advocated, to substitute a socially manipulated method of selection in human mating in place of our present courtship, the personal values of marriage would correspond-ingly shrink. It is obvious that the lessening of the romance of courtship would increase marriage compatibility, but only by removing from the experience of matrimony the significance that human evolution has brought it. It would mean reversing the historic process, emptying marriage of much of that which has made the experience humanly distinctive and appealing. Mating would, of course, continue, but it would become an emotionally barren association.

The romantic impulse is not only linked with American marriage ideology; it is also a product of western culture. It is therefore held responsible by some for much of the evils and tragedies appearing in the life of western people. One of the most forceful of these attacks on modern romance has been made by Denis de Rougemont.[13] He believes that the cultivation of passionate love started in Europe as a reaction to Christianity, especially to its doctrine of marriage, by people who were pagan in spirit either by natural disposition or by inheritance. Using the Tristan myth of the Provencal poetry as his starting place, he traces the development of the "cult of passion" through the Catharist group; Spanish mysticism; chivalry; the writings of Petrarch, Cervantes, and Rousseau; the music of Wagner; the French Revolution to its contemporary expression in modern social disorganization. He even regards a transplanting of pas-sion into politics [14] as responsible for the growth of intense na-tionalism, finally bringing about World War II. Passion not being able to find its most appropriate expression in the indi-vidual relationships of the sexes obtained another theater. It is possible, he writes, that the global contest which began in Sep-tember, 1939, will wipe out the problem of passion which an artificial civilization had created.[15]

The basic idea of the author is that the modern world idealizes not the satisfactions of love but its unsatisfied passion. The ancient world regarded the frenzy of love as an emotional unsoundness rather than exalting it as western culture has done. From his viewpoint, the Christian Church and especially Puri-tanism made the romantic complex virtuous by a repressive pro-

---

[13] De Rougemont, Denis, *Love in the Western World.*
[14] *Ibid.,* pp. 251–256.
[15] *Ibid.,* p. 255.

gram directed against sex. This led to a separation between sexual feelings and the tender emotion. Another result was the attempt to elevate woman by proclaiming her virtuous through her negation of sex and placing extreme value on feminine chastity. This tended toward the creating of two types of women, the matron and the prostitute as defined by Otto Weininger.[16]

American courtship conventions, a cultural species of the western development, like all other codes, are open to criticism, revealing defects in character and unsocial immaturity, but they need to be dealt with by a program of more intelligent preparation for marriage rather than the attempt to dehumanize passion and to regard marriage as a gamble of impulses that forbid foresight any considerable role in the choice of a mate. Telling young people that their choice must always be arbitrary and that in entering marriage they commit themselves to bear the consequences of a blind choice, whether these turn out well or ill, binds the genuine function of romance, making it—to paraphrase Dean Swift, a temporary possession of being well deceived—an irrational drive toward a life adventure which is entered upon not with hope but through ignorance of its disappointments. Courtship is regarded as a mere adolescent fantasy which has no content and contributes nothing beyond itself. This interpretation of marriage as an obligation binds the individual blindly to accepting consequences that can not be foreseen rather than providing a relationship which offers human nature the supreme opportunity to seek fulfillment through intimate fellowship.

Conjugal settlement. Courtship carries the spirit of the explorer who enters new territory; marriage, that of the pioneer who attempts its settlement. Marriage necessarily becomes a period of readjustment and this includes a reorganization of the motives and emotions of courtship as well as a mutual adaptation of the husband and wife. Although marriage, when it develops successfully, is less turbulent than courtship, it offers greater and more varied satisfactions. The ties that link husband and wife are more numerous and stronger than those that bind lovers, but the attachment is more serene and makes its progress through a practical expression of the spirit of co-operation.

In the development that takes place the monogamic in-

---

16 Groves, E. R., *The Family and Its Social Functions*, pp. 505–506.

centive is rarely absent. There is evidence of the craving of each one for a unique relationship that can fulfill the desire for intimate and mutual response. As the passage is made from the romantic expectations of the earlier period to this challenging experience of greater maturity, three trends in individual reaction soon appear, sometimes almost immediately with the new status of marriage. In the adjustment to matrimonial conditions some persons start toward more substantial happiness, some begin to learn to tolerate disillusionment for economic, social, or other reasons outside the personal satisfactions of the relationship itself, while others begin the conflicts that foreshadow later separation.

The circumstances that confront the spouses can be described objectively as adverse or propitious, but the outcome cannot rightly be interpreted as an example of environmental predestination. Again the entire situation must be held responsible for either failure or success, and in this the inherent propensities and capabilities of both individuals play a decisive role. In spite of the very significant influence of the childhood background, this premarriage career cannot safely be regarded as determining the adjustment. Here as in the therapeutic reconstruction of the neurotically inclined person influences may operate, as, for example, the insight given by the domestic counselor, and an alteration in the responses of the interacting personalities may take place. This recovery of the original attraction toward and need of the other becomes a familiar happening in the experience of the marriage counselor and of the psychiatrist dealing with the deeper neurotic dispositions which find expression in domestic discontent. The reshaping of the emotional propensity may however come from an event rather than a person. This event has been a favorite motivation of the domestic novel. The person in trouble is of course tempted to regard his maladjustment as a consequence of a wrong choice of mate, but divorce and a second marriage frequently give evidence that the basic problem is the victim's personality traits which as long as they remain unchanged forbid matrimonial satisfaction. Analysis may disclose that the choice of mate is itself a futile attempt to substitute for the needful inner reconstruction. Until this is accomplished, mating may aggravate the fault of the character which superficially it may appear to cause. On the other hand, it is impossible to know how often the interactions of marriage and family association become an educative process which modifies the original predispositions which already existed but perhaps were not recognized by either of the spouses as matrimonial liabilities.

American courtship. There have been great changes in the form of courtship during the historic era, and at the present time the variations between nations and even sections of the same nation are considerable. In our own country the history of courtship shows marked changes and the evolution is still going on. Recent changes in American courtship practices have been brought about by the same influences that have operated upon marriage and the family. Among these the greater economic independence of women, the wider spread of education, increased urbanization, and cultural innovations such as the automobile have been foremost. The general trend has been toward greater frankness between the two sexes, more freedom, and a larger degree of initiative on the part of women. Just now the tendency is unmistakably toward permitting the woman to have a more open part in the courtship without meeting social disapproval. She has always had a larger place than appears on the surface, but she is now more free to exercise openly and frankly prerogatives that in the past were supposed to be primarily man's and which formerly she assumed with safety only when she was skillful in concealing her leading part.

No observing student needs to be told that we do not have in this country any consistent general pattern of courtship behavior. Instead we find a degree of variation revealing differences in family background and parental attitudes of class, religion, section, and especially national groups appearing in the effort of immigrants of the first generation to continue the conventions with which they were familiar in the old country. None of these groupings, however, maintain for any length of time an isolated, self-contained code unresponsive to the generally accepted conventions.

On the other hand, we do find evidence of a general pattern which appears to be characteristic but from which there are degrees of variation. These differences complicate courtship and, even more, later marriage adjustment. In spite of the differences that reveal the influence of individual and social background, the general trend toward a greater freedom of youth and self-determination in courtship practices is unmistakable.

Among us today courtship may be said to have three purposes: first, it provides opportunity for the getting acquainted of the two persons; second, it permits their testing; and, finally, it allows their interest in each other to be developed to the point of preparation for marriage.

Getting acquainted. The element of chase which has so large a place in animal courtship shows itself in human courtship primarily in the process by which the individual who takes the more active part wins the attention of the other. What we call flirtation is a mild form of courting, and adolescents are always potentially ready to enter upon the exciting experience of courting or being courted. Certainly the normal adolescent boy or girl finds the opposite sex the most interesting thing in the world and needs little opportunity to start courting. The daydreams of adolescent girls have been studied more carefully than those of boys. We find, as we would expect, that in their daydreaming girls are for the most part reveling in pleasant imaginings that have to do with either love or social prestige. Even the second type of daydream is likely to be more or less related to thoughts of the other sex, since the coveted success is either the starting point of winning a boy's regard or the imaginary delight is exhibited before the applauding male.[17]

We have no reason to suppose that the boy is less given to concentration on the subject of girls and courting when he indulges in daydreams, but he may less often play with his imagination because of his more active life. Being free to engage more openly than the girl in aggressive courtship, he does not need to hide his interests in fiction, as must the girl, of whom social convention expects a more passive part in courtship.

It is the woman's part to attract the attention of the male, and in this sense she is often the instigator of the courtship. Here is rooted the enormous control that fashion has over the dress of the woman, particularly the young woman. Those who know the working girl bear testimony to the fact that she will endure a great deal of physical discomfort and sometimes actual privation in order to have the necessary funds to spend on clothes

[17] Pruette, L., "What's Happening in the Daydreams of the Adolescent Girl," *Social Hygiene*, Vol. 10, No. 10, pp. 419–424.

that give her a fair chance in competing with her acquaintances for the favor of a man. At least in the adolescent period the male is influenced by the dress of the girl and her conformity to the prevailing style of adornment.

Some girls become adept in winning attention, and often the intense pleasure they obtain leads them to an arrested form of courtship so that they do not pass from the first stages and to the surprise of observers they finally do not marry at all. As soon as the courtship begins to be too serious they break it off, frequently using jealousy as the means, and then without loss of time they start another experience.

A young girl of this sort was noticeable during a summer filled with flirtations because of the unusual form in which her skill showed itself. She picked up an acquaintance with a rather unattractive girl, her opposite in coloring, taste in dressing, and degree of vivacity. The flirt stuck closely to her drab friend and accepted no invitation that did not include both girls. Thus she cleverly placed herself against a background where she always excelled in contrast to the inferiority of appearance and attractiveness of the other girl. The latter was no loser since she had pleasures that would not have come to her otherwise and she felt no grievance. Whether the man-hunting girl had consciously worked out her program or fallen into it more or less by accident, she clung to it tenaciously because it so well served her double purpose of exciting the ardor of men and preventing the development of their courtship beyond the point where it gave her a sense of dominance.

Winning the attention of the candidate for courtship is only the first part of the girl's role; she must also incite pursuit. If she is the leading spirit in the affair, it is usually necessary for her to conceal this fact lest the man lose interest and turn aside. He craves dominance and the social stage is set for him to have the leading part. It may be only in appearance that he is in the foremost position, but while this situation complicates the girl's courting, it also tends to make her more skilled in the art of retreat that subtly beckons.

The girl must also know the opportune time for the ending of the pursuit by becoming "the steady," the favored one from among those who were competing for the lover's attention. If she surrenders too soon, the courtship runs risk of anticlimax;

indeed, the man not infrequently loses his zest as a wooer and in time the relationship breaks off. It is equally true that if he is kept too long on the hooks of indecision he may become discouraged and turn his eyes elsewhere so that he is captured by a rival. Commonly held to be a matter of intuition, it must really be observation and thought which enables the girl to know just when to bring the courtship to its climax.

Opportunities for courtship.   There cannot be courtship without social conditions that make it possible. As many observers have pointed out, the working classes are most hampered. Often the girl cannot invite her friend to her own home on account of its crowded condition or its poverty. Students of this problem criticize the regulations of parks and other public places that would naturally be used for courtship if there were no prohibitions. Indeed, these regulations are exceedingly difficult to enforce because there is such great temptation on the part of the young to evade them and it is difficult even for the police to draw the line between what is proper and what is not allowed. When one notices the way many adults who have left their courting days behind them react to any expression of attraction between young people, one doubts whether, as Emerson once said, "All the world loves a lover."

The menace of the automobile is, in part at least, due to the inability of a multitude of city workers to get a reasonable chance for courtship. The great isolation that the automobile permits both makes it a favored choice for courting and leads, as does nothing else, to the incitement of vice. Not only does the automobile provide privacy, it also brings about anonymity. Thus there is temptation to exploit the girl who is not consciously accepting danger, but only embracing an opportunity, as she supposes, for legitimate courtship. Society must take a reasonable attitude toward courtship. Our churches, particularly those that serve young people who live in congested quarters, should more frequently than they do provide opportunity for courtship.

The advantage that the owner of an automobile has explains in part the stealing of automobiles, many of which are later returned to their owners or left where they are likely to be found by the police. The newspapers from time to time record the tragic end of a joy ride which was taken in a stolen

machine, and since these disastrous endings must be a small proportion of the total number of such adventures there can be
little doubt that the desire for courtship is one of the motives
for the borrowing of automobiles without permission. College
officials, for example, know that individuals who would not
ordinarily appropriate another's property have not hesitated to
go off in an automobile which they have surreptitiously taken
from somebody else's garage, as a means of getting girls to join
a party obviously planned for flirtation or courtship.

Although there have been considerable changes during this
century in American courtship practices, these have not prevented a lag in the adjusting of our method of mate selection
to the prevailing social conditions. Since we cannot have recourse to the professional matchmaker who has had so important a role in the choice of a mate in China and Japan and even
in this country among orthodox Jews nor to the parental negotiations which have served the same function in France, improvement of courtship in the United States must come from
greater and wiser preparing for the experience on the part of
the parent, more realization of the relation of courtship opportunity and behavior to the later marriage career by our youth,
and especially a more planned and intelligent program for
courtship on the part of society. The changes that are desirable
are already in process, but they have not kept pace with the
modern needs of American youth, especially women. It is undesirable to have so much masculine dominance in courtship as
now exists, and the fact that this is in large measure fictitious
does not lessen the desirability of a franker acceptance of the
equality of women with men in everything that pertains to
choice of mate. The necessity of the woman's carrying on her
leadership by subtle and hidden aggressiveness is not only a
handicap and a possible obstruction of later happiness but this
deceit also discriminates against the more open or less sophisticated young woman. The lessening of the male's ascendancy in
courtship can come only from the passing of the influences that
have led to it. These are primarily economic and social and in
the past have enforced an actual inferiority of women in cultural status. Not only is there now a disposition on the part of
many men to hold to the past but likewise is this true of more
women. The latter cultivate what is to them most pleasing and

what seems to them the only proper and effective appeal for the attention of men, but their attitudes and actions help to perpetuate their own inequality and work to their disadvantage. In some measure the explanation of their behavior must be found in the influence of their parents, and especially their mothers, who have given them a backward rather than a modern conception of the function of courtship. Parents can contribute to a more intelligent program not only by a more conscious recognition of the need of both their boys and girls being prepared for a normal adolescent experience but also by bringing this preparedness in greater accord with the present near-equality of men and women in the United States.

The greater need of facilities for meeting young men and young women is widely recognized. Especially in the cities there is at present a considerable social neglect of the means for that association of young people of similar background which is prerequisite to courtship, even though such organizations as the Y.M.C.A., the Y.W.C.A., and the churches and neighborhood organizations are beginning to realize the omission and to attempt in their programs to offer more opportunity for the meeting of young men and women. There is still a great lack of favorable conditions for the normal, wholesome meeting of young men and women, especially in the later period of adolescence when they are in the mood to find a mate and establish their own home.

The segregated college especially needs to recognize that its educational program is not in accord with American tradition and that, however desirable it may be for individual men and women, it hampers during the appropriate period of youth the natural meeting of its students with members of the opposite sex and therefore it should accept responsibility for encouraging and providing proper conditions for courtship experience. No college can function in the American way with a policy that aims at a mere protective arrest of adolescence. Such a program will not be acceptable to any men's or women's college which regards seriously its contribution to preparation for adult life. This the forward-looking segregated colleges, especially junior colleges, realize and their constructive attitude they incorporate in their social-life program.

The difficulty of young people's meeting in the cities under conditions favorable to courtship has led to various attempts to provide more normal conditions through special organizations. However genuine the motives of such organizations, it is found in practice difficult to keep them free from the dangers of exploitation.[18] Thus far there appears to be greater promise in a more socialized program for youth on the part of social and religious organizations than by the creating of a special introducing service whether it is frankly commercial or carried on as a nonprofit enterprise. This, however, does not lessen the significance of these experiments nor does it prove that such a courtship program cannot in the future help solve a growing failure in the American provision for mate selection.

A lawyer of experience, impressed through his work with young people by the present difficulties of young people living in the cities in finding advantageous conditions for courtship, has suggested that the government inaugurate an introduction service.[19] This governmental agency would function as a clearing center. The young person interested would file a request to meet at some designated place a member of the opposite sex having certain desired qualifications and of the right age. In response to this request the director of the local agency would suggest the names of several persons apparently fulfilling the qualifications sought. Thus candidates for marriage isolated by environmental situations could be given contacts similar to those naturally developed by the association of young people in a small community. The lack of courtship opportunity now experienced by many youths in the city would be avoided. The introductory service would be in the hands of publicly responsible officials and exploitation would be reduced to the minimum. This suggestion, so contrary to the American folkways of the past, sounds too radical for adoption in the immediate future. Its author, however, impressively uncovers one of the liabilities of American social conditions, and in time it may seem as reasonable for the government to function in the effort to assist mate selection as at present through the public health program.

---

[18] Social Service, started in 1941 in Newark, New Jersey, as a means of introducing like-minded unmarried men and women reveals the difficulties of such an organization.

[19] Gross, Elmer U., *Meet Your Mate the Modern Way*. Privately printed in Milwaukee, Wisconsin.

Meanwhile, Mr. Gross suggests that such a governmental service be conceived as a means of solving the problems of youth not only in our cities but wherever there is individual or social isolation. A young man or woman living in a rural community where there appears to be no suitable mate of similar background would be furnished the means of becoming acquainted with suitable candidates for marriage outside the boundaries of the neighborhood or community.

Propinquity and courtship. In spite of the growing mobility of our population, the propinquity of childhood and youth appears to have remained a fairly constant factor in the marriage choices among a group of Vassar graduates. Three groups of alumni, 1869–71, 1904–09, and 1925–31, were studied —150 in all. It was found that 26 per cent of the respondents married men they had known from childhood and that this proportion had remained practically constant from the 1870's to the 1940's. In only 10 per cent of the two older groups, and 13 per cent of the youngest group, was the acquaintance made through "work or study." Meetings in church work declined from 14 per cent in the 1870's to 4 per cent and then 2 per cent in the last years. The remaining cases were meetings through friends, Vassar and otherwise, and social visits. They made up more than half of the total, and increased from 46 per cent in the '70's to 58 per cent and then 60 per cent. The role of Vassar social connections (included within this last type) dropped from 18 per cent of all cases to 4 per cent and then came back to 11 per cent, a result which may be of no particular significance because of the small number of cases. In general, it appears that the great bulk of Vassar marriages continued to be made through social and residential rather than vocational situations.[20]

We are indebted to Bossard [21] for information concerning the influence of residential propinquity in the selecting of a mate. Based on a study of 5,000 marriages taking place in Philadelphia he found that 17.18 per cent of those applying for marriage licenses, or one out of every six couples, lived less than a block from each other. About one out of four, or 23.26 per cent lived within two blocks or less of each other, while a third of

---

[20] From a study made by Frances Mitchell, of Vassar. Quoted by permission.
[21] Bossard, James H. S., *Marriage and the Child*, pp. 80–82.

the couples, 33.58 per cent lived within five blocks or less from each other. In but 17.8 per cent of the marriages did one of the two people reside outside the city, and from the record it was not known how many of these had previously lived in Philadelphia. The author from his study concludes that the percentage of marriages decreased steadily and markedly as the distance between the residences of the contracting parties increased.

A study by Davie and Reeves of marriages taking place in New Haven [22] revealed that the proportion of couples whose premarital address had been less than three blocks apart was greater for Philadelphia than for New Haven. Dr. W. A. Anderson conducted a similar investigation of a farming county in western New York, Genesee, and tabulated the birth places of the husbands and wives who on the average had started their family life twenty to twenty-five years previously, when of course transportation was more difficult than at present. Of these 584 families whose husbands reported the township where they then lived as their place of birth, it appeared that in 34 per cent of the cases both the wife and husband were born in the township where they then resided. In 32 per cent of the cases the wife was born in a bordering township; thus 66 per cent of these men and women came from the same or a neighboring township. In the case of more than 1,000 husbands who were born in Genesee County, it was found that 62 per cent were married to women of the same county and that 23 per cent of the spouses lived in adjoining counties.

The effect of occupational propinquity has also been investigated. Marvin in a study of 49,000 cases in Philadelphia found that 2.8 times as many marriages occurred within the occupations as would have occurred from pure chance.[23] For the foreign group there were two times as many and for the mixed group 2.5. There were differences in occupations. In textiles it was 9.3, in printing 8.4, while in retail trade it was only 1.2 and clerical work 1.8. A supplementary study made of the marriage selections of Bryn Mawr alumnae showed that 90 per cent of them were married to college graduates and 60 per cent to men in professions. Of the ten women entering medicine seven had

[22] *Ibid.*, p. 88.
[23] Marvin, D. M., "Occupational Propinquity as a Factor in Marriage Selection," *Publications American Statistical Association*, Vol. 16, pp. 131–150.

married doctors. There was also evidence of the same trend of women marrying men in the same profession in education, social work, and music.

Baber has stressed the importance of isolation as an influence in increasing the effect of propinquity. He uses the ocean voyage as an example of a rapid development of mutual interest which may in so short a time as a fortnight even put an end to the commitments of former engagements.[24] He also gives testimony through personal experience of the effect of isolation in stimulating a mutual attraction of such persons as missionaries stationed in isolated foreign communities where they have little opportunity to meet and marry members of the opposite sex having similar background.[25]

The advantage of coeducational association as a means of selecting a mate has become a commonplace observation. It offers in the relationship of the sexes an opportunity for frank and natural acquaintanceship which easily moves on to a mutual commitment. Conditions are not, however, propitious for all. The necessity of a proportion of the men postponing the thought of marriage decreases the chances of the coeducational girl getting a mate from her everyday campus associates. There is also evidence of a disposition among some of the men to prefer finding a mate from those who have had less education and who therefore, so far as an academic career is concerned, are inferior to the men. Any teacher in a coeducational institution has known individual men who most strongly express their unwillingness to consider marrying a "coed" even when they are quite willing to date her and to show her marked attention. This prejudice does not always persist, but, on the other hand, it does operate in a proportion of cases to discourage "coed" engagements and marriage. Among other men there is a different reaction. For them distant pastures always appear greener, and therefore in their serious interests they are attracted to women in other institutions even when these are coeducational, as is true of their own. The author over a period of years has had intimate knowledge of the marriage career of a considerable number of men and women who came to know each other at a coeducational institution. He has been impressed with the

---

[24] Baber, R. E., *Marriage and the Family*, p. 159.
[25] *Ibid.*

high percentage of success both in their marriage and family adjustment that appears to have been true of these men and women.

The social situation of those seeking higher education, their going to a coeducational or segregated college, does not have the significance it would were it not customary for the average boy and girl from very early childhood to play with and see much of the opposite sex. In no modern culture has there been greater freedom between boys and girls, and, as a result, only in unusual instances of physical or social isolation is there lack of this background of mutual acquaintance which is so necessary for the proper working of the American code of courtship. Generally by the time a man or woman enters college there have been, especially during the earlier period of adolescence, experiences which encourage a natural, frank relationship which proves advantageous in the more serious later comradeship prerequisite to the selecting of a life mate. Burgess and Cottrell report from their study that those men who have had several women friends before marriage are more likely to succeed and the same is true of women who have had several or many men friends.[26] Terman, on the contrary, states that his data suggest that marital happiness has no consistent relation with the amount of association with the opposite sex during adolescence.[27] His questionnaire required the individual reporting to estimate the quantity of adolescent association he had had with members of the opposite sex. Thus the judgment made was necessarily subjective and relative. For courtship purposes the significant fact is not the quantity of childhood and early adolescent contact of boys and girls but whether a natural, frank attitude toward such comradeship has been developed. The conventions of mate selection in this country assume a very great degree of social freedom among youth in their premarriage association with one another, and without this our system of courtship could not function.

A recent study of premarital residential propinquity in New Haven[28] discloses, as one would expect, that there is a

[26] Burgess, Ernest W., and Cottrell, Leonard S., Jr., *Predicting Success or Failure in Marriage*, pp. 128–131.

[27] Terman, Lewis M., *Psychological Factors in Marital Happiness*, p. 259.

[28] Kennedy, Ruby Jo Reeves, "Premarital Residential Propinquity and Ethnic Endogamy," *American Journal of Sociology*, Vol. 48, p. 580.

marked tendency toward ethnic endogamy. This was found particularly true of Negroes, Jews, and Italians. In this investigation it was found that in the vast majority of cases the two attracting parties were of the same race, nationality, religion, and socio-economic status. In a special analysis of sixty-three marriages in New Haven [29] in 1940 between couples residing in unlike ecological areas more than half (58.8 per cent) were persons of similar cultural background; it was true of all the Jewish marriages, 80 per cent of the Italians, and 77 per cent of the British Americans. Although there was a slight increase of marriages between persons who were spatially not living in the same neighborhood (2 per cent), nevertheless, as compared with 1931, the data indicated that there was a tendency toward a cultural propinquity among those who married.

Problems of courtship.   Courtship during the period of pursuit is notorious for its financial temptation. The man often spends beyond his resources in order that he may win or hold the interest of the girl. He is expected to "treat" her, as a rule, although there is an increasing disposition, which should be encouraged, for the girl to insist upon paying her own way. The income of the two is so nearly equal in many cases that the man is no better able than the girl to finance all the entertainments that they are likely to attend. A young girl sometimes breaks off an association with a young man in whom she had been interested because he is too sensible to spend beyond his means or in such a way as to hamper his business or educational progress. Such a girl indicts the man for niggardliness when an actual investigation has proved that the man was supporting a relative, paying up his college expenses, or in some other way exercising the judgment or generosity that prophesied well for his stability as a future marriage partner.

The woman likewise is tempted to spend too much money on dress. The judgment of a man, particularly in the late adolescent period, is exceedingly superficial, and he is far more likely to be interested in a girl who overspends, if she outdresses her competitors, than in one who has the good sense not to live beyond her earnings.

Petting.   It is impossible to consider modern courtship without frankly handling the problem of petting. Petting is a

---

[29] *Ibid.,* p. 584.

revival of customs of the past which have permitted great freedom in courtship and stands in contrast with the conventional regime of the recent period of chaperonage. To some extent it is nothing new, except that it is a familiarity more commonly allowed than in the last few generations, when it was countenanced only after courtship had passed out of its first stages and was close to actual marriage.

The exacting girl of high standards finds herself today, according to her own testimony, face to face with a serious dilemma. If she permits the freedom a man frequently expects, she risks self-respect and is unhappy. If, on the other hand, she maintains her customary behavior, she may be considered aloof and uninteresting and quickly dropped. Just how far this is a serious problem in the actual courtship of our youth one cannot know. It must be a problem of some size or it would not be brought up so often in conference by the modern girl.

In considering a situation which admittedly contains risk we must appreciate its origin. The increased frankness of men and women, their more open courtship, their greater sophistication, and the larger freedom of their period would naturally issue in a situation involving risk. The dangers of petting must not blind us to the impossibility of forcing the behavior of young men and women in their courtship back to the more restrained conventions of a decade ago. Moreover, it must be frankly confessed that the change is not so great as it appears, since it is in part only a more open expression of what was largely prevalent in courtship in the past. Parents who realize the seriousness of this problem will prepare their children for the ordeal of adolescence before it comes. The parents of the boy need to give most attention to teaching the safeguarding of the newer freedom in modern courtship.

No problem of adolescence discloses greater individual differences than this one of petting. As a result we find a great variety of circumstances whenever we investigate this type of adolescent love-making. It is not uncommon to find the girl responding to the wishes of the boy, not because this is in accord with her own preference, but because she has the desire to do as he wishes in order that she may enjoy him otherwise. If she gives in to something that she either dislikes or believes wrong, it may be merely because this appears to be a necessary price for his attention. The girl may be willing to pet with one boy and not with another; the latter may be a person whom she values more. Sometimes it is the girl who takes the lead. We find boys who pet with one girl and not with another and perhaps have greater fondness for the second. Occasionally the boy loses interest in the girl as soon as petting between them has occurred, while in other instances the boy ceases to go around with a girl who refuses to pet.

Greater differences exist between individuals who in the earlier and even the later stages of adolescence regard petting as improper; even, among some, kissing leads to a considerable amount of anxiety, conflict, and guilt. It is not strange under such circumstances that young people inherently ethical ask information and guidance from those who have the reputation of being sympathetic and understanding in their attitudes toward the problems of modern youth.[30] Emily Post has said that in polite society there is no petting. She pronounces such practices as cheap, promiscuous, and vulgar.[31] The facts as gathered by Bromley and Britten in their conscientious and careful study challenge this statement.[32] There are, of course, gradations in petting behavior. It seems safe to say that in some form it has persisted in American folkways. Delay of marriage, adolescent freedom, temporary isolation, and anonymity made possible by the automobile have tremendously increased sex play among American youth. The discussion of petting is confused by the different meaning this term has for individuals, and the fact that whereas in one case it is essentially a sublimating experience, in another it is passion-stimulating. The parent rightly wishes to discourage this practice, realizing its hazards. On the other hand, as Floyd Dell has pointed out, although it does bring danger, and needs to be kept within bounds by a self-disciplining idealism, nevertheless, it can play a part in the maturing of the heterosexual attitude.[33] His interpretation, however, cannot be taken to mean that petting in some form in the early

---

[30] Butterfield, Oliver M., *Love Problems of the Adolescent*, Ch. 3.

[31] Post, Emily, *Etiquette*, p. 297.

[32] Bromley, Dorothy D., and Britten, Florence H., *Youth and Sex*, pp. 141–143.

[33] Dell, Floyd, "Why They Pet," *The Parents Magazine*, Vol. 11, No. 10.

period of adolescence is absolutely indispensable to the maturing of heterosexual interest but rather that some mild form of elemental physical interest is likely to occur and that this does, in fact, frequently function as a maturing influence.

Courtship could proceed on a purely friendship basis void of tension and free from some of its hazards if the sex impulse of youth would remain quiescent until on a certain day and hour, authorized by law, it would emerge and bring the two concerned into a special fellowship. This cannot be because courtship itself is a maturing life experience, a development in a social relationship which is directly related to the body changes that have taken place or are in process. The association of young people can be limited and guarded by strict chaperonage, but the hazard of this is an artificial contact which gives little opportunity for the testing of the mutual attraction. This fact is generally recognized by a conventional acceptance of a double standard of sex practices which gives the male freedom as a compensation for the restrictions that make his sexual drive all the more self-conscious.

No courtship policy can be in accord with American attitudes that chiefly seeks to protect the association of young people with no regard to the aftereffects of the program as they influence marriage adjustment. Young people do need to know the strength of physical passion, the ease with which it can be aroused, the danger of turning courtship into a means of obtaining sex pleasures along lines termed secondary in the terminology of the scientist. When this last habit becomes a practice, it does at times prove after marriage to have arrested the sexual development, making later mature adjustment difficult, though rarely impossible. Unwanted pregnancy sometimes follows unrestrained petting, usually because of ignorance concerning the rapid and undesired development physical passion can take when open to intense stimulation and a false confidence in contraceptive measures assumed to be adequate protection. Conflict and guilt are, however, the common problems that come from petting. These result in part from the confusion of ideas to which American youth at present are exposed. The best protection from the risks of petting is found in an understanding of the nature and purpose of the sexual endowment, the cultivation of social interests, companionableness, self-discipline, and commitment to a firmly established code of responsibility.

In spite of the apparent knowledge of the sophisticated modern girl, concrete cases demonstrate that she is far less able to protect herself than is usually supposed. Her ignorance is startling, for she assumes the attitude of one thoroughly informed regarding matters of sex.

A recent case which resulted in the pregnancy and hurried marriage of a college graduate forcefully illustrates the situation. Such terms as birth control were mere abstractions in this girl's vocabulary and she asserted that the majority of her college mates like herself attempted to convey the impression that they were very knowing regarding physical sex when as a matter of fact they were both curious and ignorant. Anyone who knows the effort the modern girl makes to get information concerning sex realizes that men are often deceived when they assume that their partner in petting is well informed and able to protect herself from serious risk. Some boys know no more than their girl friends, although like them they think themselves well informed, as is occasionally revealed by a study of cases of illegitimacy. There is often just enough knowledge to give a sense of false security in intimacies that would not be permitted if their risk were clearly understood.

Courtship as a test. There is necessarily, even when it is unconscious, an element of make-believe in courtship. One who is trying to impress his personality upon another is led to some deception. All highly emotional experiences make it hard for literal fact to emerge from the coloring of heightened susceptibilities, but courtship stands out as the most liable of all human experiences to take on the atmosphere of fiction. In the grip of so powerful an emotion as comes when courtship settles into what is popularly called love, it is impossible even for the person concerned to know what is genuine and what is exaggerated, for this emotional experience has the power to magnify the self and give a substance to the finer qualities of the personality that was absent previously.

All the changes that come with the intense affection expressed in courtship cannot therefore be charged up to the dramatic or the deceptive element of courtship. It seems almost out of the question for these two highly wrought individuals to be frank with one another; yet in order that there shall be a reasonable amount of real knowledge that can serve as a basis for determining the wisdom of marriage, courtship sooner or later takes on a testing function and the fictitious is partially separated from the qualities that are characteristic of the person.

This provision for the getting acquainted of the two persons in a way that will give them some clue as to the advisability of going on with their marriage plans or finally separating before they take that step is one of the most important functions of modern courtship. That it may accomplish its purpose the courtship must be of sufficient duration to permit the emotional attitudes to settle themselves somewhat. On the other hand, a very long courtship or engagement tends to exaggerate differences, and little by little, there being no final commitment, a schism occurs and the marriage is repeatedly postponed until it does not occur at all.

If courtship elates the two individuals enamoured of one another, they must have an opportunity to come down from their superlevel and see life without distortion. This can seldom be entirely brought about during courtship, and herein are to be found the dangers that underlie the transition from courtship to marriage. The sharp break that for some individuals occurs so early in matrimony between the spirit of courtship and the actualities of marriage brings out the fact that each experience must be understood in relation to the other. Courtship and marriage do not stand alone as social relationships requiring emotional adjustment. In a milder degree those entering a business or profession commonly pass through a similar experience as they leave the period when imagination was in control and encounter the realities of their chosen vocation. Usually their reactions are less rapid, less emotional, and more influenced by serious motives than are those of the bride and the groom.

The development of courtship. Considering courtship as it has to do with society, we find that it contains three distinct processes when it has a normal development. It stimulates sex attraction even though the physical element be absent from consciousness. There is also a sublimation of this sex element, and in this way the physical side of the attraction is largely kept from consciousness. As a consequence, we have an idealization which is the most remarkable part of courtship and which makes this particular human relationship the favored topic of the literary artist. Human nature never reaches greater heights of unselfishness or appreciation of another's character, so far as the emotions are concerned, although most persons happily married realize that they tread higher ranges of experience, but without such intense emotional upheaval.

Anticlimax is the obvious danger ever present in courtship. A common statement gives emphasis to this fact. "Man," it is said, "thinks of courtship as a means to an end; woman, as an end in itself." In so far as there is this difference between men and women, it is doubtful whether it is based on inherited peculiarities that accompany sex; it is rather that the woman clings to the courtship because marriage so seldom gives her the social opportunity to transfer her interests satisfactorily. The man as a competitor in the world of affairs is forced not only to make a quick departure from the intense emotional relation of courtship but to concentrate his interests in dealing with the obligations he cannot escape.

It follows, therefore, that the woman is more likely to sense the anticlimax when the days of courtship are ended by the beginning of marriage responsibilities. Perhaps she blames the man's ambition in his business or even imputes to a lack of sincere affection the change which she meets with dismay. The conventional pictures of literature and small talk encourage this attitude in a woman by building up within her the impression that as soon as a man's courtship fervor begins to wane, her power is dwindling and the most interesting period of her life is ended; in the same way she has also been led to think that when practical interests have a large place in married life and the emotional tone of courtship and the honeymoon is lowered, the marriage has slipped from its original high plane of poetic idealism and henceforth must travel on the lower level of material advantage. It may take some years for the woman to come to the realization that her conception of higher and lower was a sentimental mixing of terms due to her immaturity of judgment, since the relationship of the young couple is of greatest social value when it ceases to be predominantly self-centered.

We have reason to suppose that the modern girl has a better understanding of the true situation than had her mother. If there is to be wholesome married life, the courtship must pass on and change its spirit by becoming a part of the calmer and more satisfying experiences of happy married life. Many a woman who does not see this at first soon discovers it; others suffer acutely in their futile attempt to continue courtship beyond its season.

It would be an advantage for the comfortable development of the marriage relation if this necessary transformation from courtship to marriage fellowship were more commonly appreciated by men so that they could more satisfactorily do their part to help the young bride look forward rather than backward as she feels the emotions of courtship ebbing away. It is false counsel to advise a young man to keep the spirit of courtship, for the new relationship makes the old incompatible, but it is good judgment on the part of every man to make his wife feel that she is not taken too much for granted and treated with an irritating certainty which was never present during courtship. It is well for both husband and wife, as a means of protecting themselves from a too matter-of-fact contact, for each to have a degree of privacy of thought and action as well as the opportunity for self-expression that was natural during courtship. One of the baneful results of marriage is a transfusion of both personalities that is so complete as to sink their association to a humdrum level. On the other hand, the attitude in marriage that shuts doors in one's mind to the access of the partner can be a dividing practice that sacrifices a more nearly complete companionship to a false seeking of individualism.

The parental role.   It would be an error to assume that because the adolescent is largely free to make his own choice of mate the attitude of the parent plays no part in the final decision. On the contrary, parental influence may be the dominant factor in the final choice. This influence may be positive or negative in the sense that the parent may favor it in any way he can or instead may attempt to block it. In the latter case, the choice may not be a genuine one because the basic motive easily under such circumstances may become the desire of the adolescent to break away from his family. The domineering parent is the one type most likely to retard the natural development of his child and therefore also to attempt to control the courtship experiences of the adolescent. This antagonistic role of the parent may accomplish just the opposite to what is intended. Going farther one may find that the attitude of a parent toward marriage or the situation the child discovered in the relationship of his father and mother may be the decisive influence over adolescent courtship behavior and the attitude toward marrying.

This parental influence during courtship is likely to be underestimated by those greatly impressed by the recent changes in family life which have tended to lessen the former rigid authority and control of the child by the parent. The emotional ties between parent and child, however, have not been dissolved, even though the freedom of the latter has been greatly increased by recent cultural trends. The parent, therefore, still has opportunity to influence his child along many lines which find expression in courtship practices, attitudes, and choice of mate. It is of course difficult to get statistical insight as to the extent to which parents in individual cases have directly or indirectly affected the child along courtship lines. In a recent effort to gather this information, it was found that among seventy-five unmarried college students 49.1 per cent of the males admitted that their father had tried in one way or another to influence them in courtship, and 79.4 per cent made the same assertion concerning their mothers. It is interesting to find, as one would have expected, that the females answering the same question reported greater effort of their parents to influence them; in the case of fathers it was 68.7 per cent, and in the case of their mothers 97.1 per cent.[34] Interesting as such an attempt at tabulation is, the reader must remember that we are asking of those who make such returns a question which may lead to the very core of personal relationship of parent and child. It requires an objective self-knowledge which frequently may be concealed by the intensity of the emotional interaction of parent and child.

---

[34] Bates, Alan, "Parental Roles in Courtship," *Social Forces*, Vol. 20, No. 4, pp. 483–486.

As the article points out, one basic motivation of parents who attempt to interfere with courtship is their unwillingness to accept the fact that the child has matured into an independence which prophesies that he will soon break home ties. To some parents this comes as a shock and there is profound resistance to this approaching maturity, and therefore an attempt is made to retard the child's choice of mate. This is always defended by reasoning that attempts to conceal the motive of the parent. Indeed, the parent himself may not know the true cause of his reactions.

Chapter 13

MARRIAGE

FOREWORD.   There is no experience in life in which preparation and insight prove more advantageous than in marriage. In order to be useful, however, this preparedness has to be practical, disclosing the difficulties as well as the satisfactions that face those entering and continuing the marital relationship. Information cannot remove the liabilities of selfish or false conceptions of the meaning of marriage. Knowledge does, however, help those who enter marriage in a spirit of love and with the sincere desire to make their marriage a mutual fulfillment of personality needs. Marriage represents the highest form of psychosexual relationship possible between humans. It makes constant demands on the two individuals sharing the supreme expression of fellowship. It demands much in sacrifice and sound discipline but offers more than it costs in a comradeship that is unrivaled. The purpose of this chapter is to acquaint the student with marriage conditions as we now find them in the United States and also to stress the most common problems facing the young person looking forward to marriage.

The purpose of marriage.   Marriage is a union of a man and a woman sanctioned by society and usually entered upon by some sort of ceremony. It has existed as far back as our knowledge extends and in an elementary form is suggested by the male-female relationship among some of the higher animals. Marriage, as we know it, is a social institution although based on biologic urges leading to mating. The history of marriage demonstrates that it has taken every conceivable form. The trend, however, especially in the historic period of western civilization has unmistakably been toward the union of one man and one woman in a lifetime commitment. This monogamic relationship with very few exceptions, of which the Oneida community is an example, has been the conventional type of marriage authorized by law and approved by social conventions. It has been based on the impulse of most of those who have married to possess in a unique sense the personality of another including, as a rule, a monopoly of the sex interests and responses of the other. Over a considerable period of time this zest for monogamic commitment weakens in the marriage career of a minority being replaced by the feeling of insufficiency and monotony, but even among these who are ill fitted for a monogamic career it is seldom that at the time of entrance upon marriage there is any wavering in the impulse to give one's self fully to the other and to receive from him or her an equal return in love and loyalty.

The state from expediency recognizes marriage even though it is maintained on a lower level than a love fellowship, for by definition the law considers marriage as being merely a civil contract differing from other contracts only in that it is not revocable or dissoluble at the will of those making it.[1] Legally marriage embodies a contract giving each spouse an exclusive sexual and love possession of the other, and they who enter upon it assume a status established by statutory law or court decisions which in great measure defines the legal meaning of their relationship. The law reflects the social conviction that this special relationship of a man and a woman requires legal definitions and statements of privileges and responsibilities in the effort to protect the welfare of society.

Marriage because of its legal meaning has been interpreted by some as primarily a licensing of sexual relationships into which men and women are forced by a terrific drive of physiological origin and led to make vows that commit them to future but vaguely understood responsibilities. This is known as the mousetrap theory of marriage.[2]

When we study the actual marital life of men and women, we find very great diversity of experience. The plane upon which an individual marriage flourishes is basically decided by the personalities of the two joined together and the effect one has on the other. It is easy to say that true marriage precludes

---

[1] Madden, Joseph W., and Compton, William R., *Cases and Materials on Domestic Relations,* p. 79.

[2] Binkley, Robert C. and Frances W., *What is Right with Marriage,* p. 7.

the possibility of obtaining satisfaction on a low level but demands lofty moral achievement.[3] No definition of marriage,
however, is acceptable which rules out the multitude of unions
that never reach this high ground. It is safer to insist that the
ideal marriage is creative and not essentially pleasure-fulfilling
but demands growth of character and as a rule, like life itself,
brings the necessity of discipline, sacrifice, and suffering. This
idealistic portrayal of the purpose of marriage may be proclaimed as the only truly creative union, but in fact it is necessary to recognize that marriages on lower levels also are productive as they influence personality and bring about their own
characteristic development of personality.

Marriage trends in the United States.   The increase in the
divorce rate in the United States has attracted more attention
than the fact that there is also an increase in the marriage rate.
Marriage registration for the entire country began in 1887.
Since then the crude marriage rate has been increasing. It was
8.7 in a thousand population in 1887, 9.3 in 1905, and from
that time has been about 10 per cent. This increase has to be
interpreted in the light of shifts in class and age distribution,
since this, in the grouping of the total population, may reveal
the cause of the increase. There have been two major changes
of this sort. Because of the falling birth rate, there has been
a smaller proportion in the population of unmarried youth,
while the increase of the length of life has led to a larger proportion of older people. Ogburn found that there was between
1890 and 1920 an increase of 4.6 per cent in the percentage of the
population who were married, and that of this number 3.1 per
cent was accounted for by increase in the age of the population
and a consequence of the declining birth rate.[4] From his investigations he drew the following conclusions:

Regarding the influence of various factors on marriage the
conclusions are as follows:

The age distribution of the population is a powerful factor
affecting the percentage married. Middle-aged and older persons are
found married in larger percentages than young persons or very old
persons.

---

[3] Keyserling, Hermann, and Others, *The Book of Marriage,* p. 21.
[4] Ogburn, W. F., "Factors Affecting the Marital Condition of the Population,"
Publications of the American Sociological Society, Vol. 18, pp. 58–59.

The greater the number of men in proportion to the number of women, the larger the percentage married, up to a point well beyond the equality in numbers of the sexes. As the excess of men becomes very large, the percentage married decreases.

The composition of our population as to race and nativity also affects the percentage married. The influence of immigrants is to increase the percentage married, largely because of their age distribution and of the American-born children of immigrants to decrease it. The influences of the native whites of native parents and of the negroes are very nearly the same.

The effect of cities is to decrease marriage.

Manufacturing cities as compared with trading cities have on the average slightly larger percentages married, this influence operating partly through the sex ratio.

The employment of women seems to postpone and to slightly discourage marriage.

Certain evidence indicates that the probable influence of birth control is to increase marriage slightly, particularly among the young.

The relation of income to marriage is complex. Business prosperity greatly increases marriage. The more rapidly growing cities have slightly larger percentages married. Cities with larger percentages making income-tax returns have on the average slightly smaller percentages married.[5]

Based on the Fifteenth Census evidence of marriage trends is shown in the two tables given here and on the following page:

TABLE I [6]

MARITAL STATUS OF MALES AND FEMALES FIFTEEN YEARS OF AGE
AND OVER IN THE UNITED STATES, 1930

MARITAL STATUS	MALES		FEMALES	
	Number	Percentage	Number	Percentage
Single....................	14,953,712	34.1	11,306,653	26.4
Married...................	26,327,109	60.0	26,170,756	61.1
Widowed.................	2,025,036	4.6	4,734,207	11.1
Divorced.................	489,478	1.1	573,148	1.3
Unknown................	85,686	0.2	52,385	0.1
Total.................	43,881,021	100.0	42,837,149	100.0

[5] *Ibid.*

[6] Fifteenth Census of the United States, 1930, *Population,* Vol. 2, General Report, Government Printing Office, 1933, p. 837.

TABLE II [7]

MARITAL STATUS OF MALES AND FEMALES FIFTEEN YEARS OF AGE AND OVER IN THE UNITED STATES FOR 1910, 1920, AND 1930

(Percentage Distribution)

MARITAL STATUS	MALES			FEMALES		
	1910	1920	1930	1910	1920	1930
Single and unknown.	39.2	35.4	34.3	29.9	27.5	26.5
Married............	55.8	59.2	60.0	58.9	60.6	61.1
Widowed..........	4.5	4.8	4.6	10.6	11.1	11.1
Divorced.........	0.5	0.6	1.1	0.6	0.8	1.3
Total..........	100.0	100.0	100.0	100.0	100.0	100.0

The marriage rate is necessarily influenced by the ratio of the sexes. On the one hand, we normally have about 105 males born to 100 females, while, on the other, the death rate tends to be slightly greater for the boy than the girl. In the United States there have been differences in this ratio in various sections of the country. The distribution has been affected also by immigration, since more males come to the country than females.

MALES PER 1,000 FEMALES IN THE TOTAL POPULATION OF THE UNITED STATES, ACCORDING TO BROAD GEOGRAPHIC DIVISIONS, FROM 1850 TO 1940 [8]

Year	Total United States	New England, Middle Atlantic, and South Atlantic States	East North Central and East South Central States	West North Central and West South Central States	Mountain and Pacific Coast States
1940	1,007	988	1,011	1,015	1,057
1930	1,025	999	1,030	1,038	1,095
1920	1,040	1,008	1,043	1,060	1,146
1910	1,060	1,019	1,047	1,087	1,289
1900	1,044	1,000	1,038	1,085	1,281
1890	1,050	995	1,042	1,099	1,419
1880	1,036	976	1,036	1,106	1,534
1870	1,022	972	1,030	1,092	1,597
1860	1,047	993	1,064	1,116	2,135
1850	1,043	1,009	1,062	1,118	2,789

[7] *Ibid.*

[8] Metropolitan Life Insurance Company, *Statistical Bulletin*, Vol. 23, No. 10, p. 4.

World War II, as did World War I, stimulated the marriage rate during the early period. The following chart [9] shows how quickly marriages were encouraged by conscription and by the defense programs initiated in July, 1940.

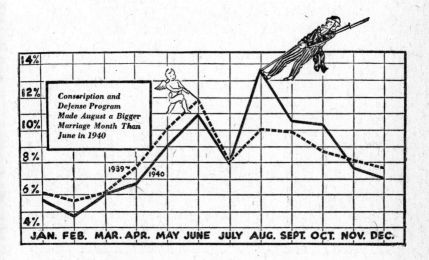

Conscription and Defense Program Made August a Bigger Marriage Month Than June in 1940

Marriage age.   It is obvious that the age of marriage has a direct influence on the birth rate. Data selected from 22 states and the District of Columbia, giving the situation in 1940, disclosed that among the whites half the babies born had mothers younger than 26 and only one-tenth had mothers older than 35 years. For those entering marriage for the first time, the average age for men was 26.7 and for women 23.6.[10] The marriage rate for women reached its peak in the 20–24-years period. These constitute about one-fifth of all those who married in the course of the year, while from the same age group come only a little more than one-ninth of the men who marry. The peak of the marriage age for men was between 25 and 29 years. After 25 the man had a greater probability of marrying than had a woman, and as his age increased his chances of marrying declined much less rapidly than was true in the case of women.

[9] *The Jewelers' Circular-Keystone*, Feb., 1941.
[10] Metropolitan Life Insurance Company, *Statistical Bulletin*, Vol. 24, No. 5, p. 3. Quoted by permission.

This is brought out by the following table which also shows sectional differences: [11]

PERSONS MARRYING PER 1,000 SINGLE, WIDOWED, OR DIVORCED, ACCORDING TO SEX AND AGE, IN THE NORTHERN, SOUTHERN, AND WESTERN AREAS OF THE UNITED STATES, 1940 *

AGE GROUP	MALES				FEMALES			
	Total	North	South	West	Total	North	South	West
15 and over	64.8	64.2	89.2	44.1	63.8	62.6	84.1	48.0
15–19	5.5	4.8	9.2	5.1	47.9	40.4	81.8	49.7
20–24	117.8	111.5	173.4	92.0	184.4	178.0	243.7	158.5
25–29	169.7	174.4	199.3	116.1	151.1	151.5	169.4	124.0
30–34	124.8	128.0	164.7	75.0	88.6	86.8	113.1	68.6
35–39	81.1	80.2	130.2	46.1	51.5	49.8	70.0	38.1
40–44	53.7	52.3	93.3	30.8	31.3	30.7	41.1	22.9
45–49	39.2	37.3	78.6	21.3	20.1	20.0	24.8	15.5
50–54	27.2	25.9	54.0	16.0	11.8	11.8	13.7	9.8
55–59	21.3	20.4	42.2	13.2	7.1	7.1	8.5	6.0
60–69	12.9	11.6	26.0	9.4	2.9	2.8	3.3	3.1
70–79	4.7	3.9	9.9	5.1	.7	.6	.8	.9
80 and over	1.1	.8	2.5	1.3	.1	.1	.1	.1

* Northern States: Conn., Maine, Mass., Mich., Nebr., N. H., N. J., N. Y., Pa., R. I., S. Dak., Vt., and Wis. Southern States: Ala., Del., D. C., Fla., Md., and Va. Western States: Calif., Idaho, Oreg., and Utah.

In 1940 54 per cent of the white men 20–34 years of age were married and 68 per cent of the women of the same age. Divorced persons constituted 1.3 per cent of the white males and 1.7 per cent of the white females in 1940. The corresponding proportions for 1890 were only 0.2 per cent and 0.4 per cent. The proportion of widowers in the white male population 15 years old and over increased regularly with age up to about 40 per cent in the oldest age group, 75 years and over. The proportion of widows in the white female populations was consistently higher at each age than the corresponding proportion of widowers; in the age group 75 years and over, more than 70 per cent of the white females were widowed.[12]

The table on the next page gives the marital situation of whites for states and large cities:

[11] *Ibid.*, p. 4.
[12] Sixteenth Census of the United States, 1940, *Population*, Series P–15, No. 7.

PER CENT OF CHANGE, FROM 1941 TO 1942, IN MARRIAGE LICENSES ISSUED IN AMERICAN CITIES OF 100,000 OR MORE INHABITANTS (JANUARY THROUGH NOVEMBER OF EACH YEAR) [13]

City	Per cent Increase (+) or Decrease (−)	City	Per cent Increase (+) or Decrease (−)	City	Per cent Increase (+) or Decrease (−)
All cities	+ *1.01*	*East North Central*	− *5.2*	Richmond, Va.	+ 24.3
		Akron, Ohio *	− 6.9	Charlotte, N. C.*	+ 36.2
New England	− *3.5*	Canton, Ohio *	− 20.2	Atlanta, Ga.*	+ 27.7
Boston, Mass.	− 2.2	Cincinnati, Ohio	¶	Jacksonville, Fla.*	+ 70.0
Cambridge, Mass.	− 5.8	Cleveland, Ohio *	− .3	Miami, Fla.*	+ 50.3
Fall River, Mass.	− 22.0	Columbus, Ohio *	− .5	Tampa, Fla.*	+ 78.6
Lowell, Mass.	− 26.0	Dayton, Ohio *	− 6.0		
New Bedford, Mass.	− 12.2	Toledo, Ohio *	− 32.2	*East South Central*	+ *6.7*
Somerville, Mass.	+ 1.9	Youngstown, Ohio *.	− 27.4	Louisville, Ky.*	+ 36.2
Springfield, Mass.	− 9.5	Fort Wayne, Ind.*	+ 3.3	Chattanooga, Tenn.*	− 31.0
Worcester, Mass.	− 12.5	Gary, Ind.*	− 4.4	Knoxville, Tenn.*.	− 19.5
Providence, R. I.*§	− 3.2	Indianapolis, Ind.	¶	Memphis, Tenn.*.	− 52.1
Bridgeport, Conn.	+ 16.7	South Bend, Ind.*	+ 9.5	Nashville, Tenn.	¶
Hartford, Conn.‡	+ 19.7	Chicago, Ill.*	− 4.8	Birmingham, Ala.*.	+ 14.7
New Haven, Conn.	+ 1.0	Peoria, Ill.*	− 17.2		
		Detroit, Mich.*	+ 5.8	*West South Central*	+ *40.7*
Middle Atlantic	− *2.6*	Flint, Mich.*	− 1.8	New Orleans, La.	+ 42.3
Albany, N. Y.	+ 16.0	Grand Rapids, Mich.*	− 10.3	Oklahoma City,	
Buffalo, N. Y.	− 11.9	Milwaukee, Wis.‡	− 13.3	Okla.*	+ 51.1
New York, N. Y.	− 6.3			Tulsa, Okla.*	+ 32.3
Rochester, N. Y.	− 7.7	*West North Central*	+ *13.2*	Dallas, Tex.*	+ 22.6
Syracuse, N. Y.	− 8.2	Duluth, Minn.*	− 14.7	Fort Worth, Tex.*.	+ 26.7
Utica, N. Y.	− 2.6	Minneapolis, Minn.*	+ 8.6	Houston, Tex.*	+ 31.8
Yonkers, N. Y.	− 2.6	St. Paul, Minn.*	+ 6.4	San Antonio, Tex.*.	+ 72.5
Camden, N. J.	+ 7.3	Des Moines, Iowa *.	− 27.1		
Elizabeth, N. J.‡	− .9	Kansas City, Mo.*	+ 31.6	*Mountain and Pacific*	+ *51.7*
Jersey City, N. J.*§	+ 12.1	St. Louis, Mo.	¶	Denver, Colo.	+ 35.0
Newark, N. J.	+ 8.6	Omaha, Nebr.*	+ 17.1	Salt Lake City, Utah*	+ 4.2
Paterson, N. J.	− .7	Kansas City, Kans.*.	+ 19.4	Seattle, Wash.*	+ 66.7
Trenton, N. J.	+ 8.3	Wichita, Kans.*	+ 39.3	Spokane, Wash.*	+ 5.0
Erie, Pa.*	+ 3.6			Tacoma, Wash.*	+105.8
Philadelphia, Pa.	+ 8.4	*South Atlantic*	+ *35.7*	Portland, Oreg.*.	+ 18.4
Pittsburgh, Pa.*	− 3.1	Wilmington, Del.*.	+ 13.7	Los Angeles, Calif.*†	+ 35.1
Reading, Pa.*	− .1	Baltimore, Md.	+ 25.0	Oakland, Calif.*.	+ 51.6
Scranton, Pa.	¶	Washington, D. C.	+ 46.3	Sacramento, Calif.*.	+ 84.9
		Norfolk, Va.	¶	San Diego, Calif.*.	+176.1
				San Francisco, Calif.	+ 75.9

* The per cent change in this case relates to the county in which the city is located.
§ January to October.   ‡ The per cent of change is based on the marriages performed.
† Includes the city of Long Beach.   ¶ The report had not been received at the time of going to press.

Delay of marriage.

Western culture assumes that marriage shall take place later than physiological maturity. This delay between physiological readiness and entrance upon the marriage career provides a significant opportunity for the prolonging of education and thereby contributes to the maintenance of high cultural standards. Changes that announce the coming of the reproductive function are more noticeable in the

[13] Metropolitan Life Insurance Company, *Statistical Bulletin,* Vol. 23, No. 12, p. 6. Quoted by permission.

woman than the man. It is necessary, however, to recognize that
this changing is not sudden but proceeds over a period of time
and that between the menarche, the first appearance of menstruation, and full adolescent structure of body there is an
interval during which the maturing development continues.
Even when the structural changes suggest complete maturity
there is evidence that so far as the functioning of the body is
concerned there is not as a rule a completion of the conditions
necessary for the reproductive career. Thus we have for varying
lengths of time after menarche a physiological sterility which is
likely to shorten progressively as the outset of the menarche is
delayed.[14] Temperature, environment, race, and heredity all
influence the coming of maturity. In the United States the average age of girls at menarche is 13.5 years.

During the period between the first occurrence of adolescent changes and final body maturity, there appears as a rule a
new interest in members of the opposite sex and the development in some degree of courtship. Even though this eventually
moves toward the selecting of a mate, it is in its earlier period
an attraction which characteristically flourishes as comradeship.
This experience is both educational and maturing. It is lengthened, and for many young men and young women, and from a
physiological viewpoint, unnaturally lengthened, by the American tradition that a man should be able to support his wife
and potential family before he marries. The meaning of this
responsibility varies with class and family background.

Since the opportunity to obtain economic security differs
in city and country and in various sections of the United States,
this requirement for the acquiring of family support for marriage influences American youth differently. If the adolescent
male can as readily as the adult man earn a living in accord
with the standards prevailing in the group to which he belongs,
there need be no delay. The inclination and decision to marry
lead at once to marriage. These differences in economic readiness for marriage appear in the folkways of the various classes
and influence the degree of delay normally expected. As a consequence, when higher education is sought by the young man
and young woman, the delay is greater and the problems of
later courtship more numerous and troublesome. Parental sub-

---

[14] Hamblen, E. C., *Facts for Childless Couples,* pp. 91–92.

sidy is advocated as a solution for this having to wait to be married, but it is obvious that only in a minority of cases are parents of the middle class in a position to provide the needed help, especially if they have several other children to educate.

The legislation of the states fixing the legal age of marriage has been influenced both by the environmental differences and the traditional folkways, the tendency being in the northern and western states to require a higher age than in the southern states. The general trend, however, is toward requiring a higher age than was common in the colonial and pioneering period. Public opinion has reacted strongly against a few spectacular marriages of children obviously only entering adolescence and in no condition to choose a mate or to assume the functions of a wife. In 1938 Vernier reports with satisfaction that there has been legislation in six jurisdictions requiring a higher age before a binding marriage can be contracted. According to the common law, the male of fourteen and the female of twelve could contract a legal marriage. By 1938 only five jurisdictions permitted so low an age requirement. The highest minimum is found in New Hampshire, twenty years for males and eighteen years for females. According to the common law those who were over the minimum age required could marry without getting the consent of parents or guardians. This has been changed in all American jurisdictions, and now, in addition to the minors having reached the age of consent, they must formally obtain also the consent of parents or guardian. Although the law-makers wish to discourage child marriages, they are even more reluctant to invalidate a marriage actually consummated, so that the penalty for a marriage contracted without the consent of parents or guardian by a minor is a fine placed upon the marriage licenser rather than the declaration that the union is automatically annulled. Nonage is a common ground for annulment through proceedings brought by the party under age, the parent or guardian, the minor's next friend, and in one state the injured party, in another the district attorney.[15] Minnesota, however, has declared a marriage by male or female under fifteen null and void without any legal proceedings.

The legislative situation in the United States, as it concerns itself with the qualifications for marriage, changes every

---

[15] Vernier, *op. cit.*, Vol. 1, p. 251.

year. The data given is significant only in that it shows the trend, which is unmistakably toward not only raising the age requirement where it has been close to the common law principle but also toward safeguarding marriage by advancing the requirements for a marriage license. There is reason to believe that progress is retarded, however, by considerable laxity in administering the laws that regulate marriage. Improvement is not encouraged by the fact that the official who issues licenses may receive a fee rather than a salary for his services or that fees may constitute for him an additional income supplementing a low salary.[16] Careless and even illegal marriages are frequently not discouraged because the marrying parties choose commercially inclined clergymen or authorized civil officials to perform the ceremony. Although all American religious denominations in recent years have sought to lift their standards, they have not been able to get all of their clergy to assume their needful moral responsibility for the youth that come to be married. There are also "marrying parsons" who maintain their legal right to officiate though not genuine ministers of any reputable denomination, but there is a tendency which will surely become more marked to legislate these commercially minded officiants out of what is now for many of them a profitable racket. The Catholic Church is conspicuous because of the regulations it imposes on the priests who solemnize marriages and the strictness with which these are enforced. Intelligent investigations of the right of the two persons to marry is a responsibility placed upon the priest which even had he the inclination he cannot escape.[17]

Delay of marriage and frustration. It is obvious that frequently individuals who wish to marry and who are fully competent to establish a family are obliged to postpone marriage because of their lack of economic security or for some other reason. This is especially true when the man seeks to enter a profession that requires a long preparation, as, for example, in the case of the doctor, or which—and again this is likely to happen to the physician—demands several years of activity before there can be an income sufficient to justify mar-

---

[16] Richmond, Mary E., and Hall, Fred S., *Marriage and the State,* p. 80.

[17] Swift, Arthur L., "The Role of Religious Institutions and Community Control." *Publications of the American Sociological Society,* Vol. 26, pp. 178–179.

riage. Many solutions have been suggested to meet this type of problem. Charles Eliot, formerly president of Harvard University, believed that education should proceed more rapidly and that men should enter their professional career sooner. In the case of the medical profession, the tendency has been in the opposite direction due to the ever increasing quantity of knowledge within the science, acquaintance with which is considered prerequisite to entering practice.

Marriage and frustration. Delay of marriage, whether it be based upon home, economic, or educational conditions, brings those who feel the necessity of setting aside any thought of marrying or, if engaged, the obligation of postponing marriage, very personal and individual problems. These are in essence the frustration of a strong and normal desire, and no discussion of marriage delay is factual that does not recognize that this frustration includes in most cases sexual aspects. Marriage is society's provision for the normal and acceptable expression of the sex drive, a product of the biologic constitution of both male and female. It would, however, be erroneous to assume that sexual expectation always takes, even among the engaged, such form as to bring conscious and considerable sexual stress. The actual situation which a couple face who find that they must postpone the thought of marriage is, along this line as along all others, individual and conditioned by circumstances. Rarely would the marriage counselor advise matrimony merely because of such biologic frustration. The reasons for delay under the circumstances may be compelling and after marriage would continue as a cause of frustration, even perhaps increasing the stress by originating marital incompatibility.

Incompatibility. The basic cause of the stress may not be physical drive but the need of assurance and this would be increased by marriage that brought new or greater strain.[18] How well sexual abstinence can be endured by the individual is determined by many influences varying with the culture and the psychic and physical make-up of the person. Sexual frustration cannot be torn away from the total personality and dealt with as a purely physiological strain. We oversimplify the problem of physical frustration when we forget the highly complex

---

[18] Horney, Karen, *The Neurotic Personality of Our Time,* p. 158.

symbolic structure that is built upon the primary sex function.[19] The problem of marriage delay, therefore, has to be interpreted in the light of the full meaning of the frustration.

Motives for marriage are many, but the one that predominates in most instances is the desire for complete fellowship with the chosen mate. Since this association can be disturbed by environmental conditions such as lack of sufficient
income, the delay of marriage until the untoward situation
changes may be the lesser of two evils and therefore wisely
chosen. But even if approved by mutual judgment this does
not prevent conflict between desire and decision with frustration as a result. Marriage is likely not to be a solution unless
along with it can go a changed situation.

Selection of a mate. The selecting of a mate is apt to
seem a self-conscious preference and one guaranteed by the
intensity of the attraction. Although it is probable that any
selection has a measure of justification, matrimonial experience
drives home the fact that the choice, however strong the mutual
feeling may be, too frequently proves a mistake when tested for
any length of time in a husband-and-wife relationship. These
matrimonial failures uncover the nature of the test marriage
brings.

The basis of the marriage choice is the personality needs
of the individual. These are numerous and not necessarily
harmonious, since they are the outcropping of the total personality, involving the entire life career up to that time, and to
expect them to be fully understood presupposes a knowledge
rarely, if ever, attained. The question, therefore, is whether the
mate selected does in fact offer sufficient fulfillment of the individual's need to permit a continuous creative life fellowship.
Since it is normally a mutual selection of the two persons concerned, the demands of each on the other require at least sufficient fulfillment to make the relationship a going concern. It
is evident that any disposition toward an experimental relationship tends to magnify whatever measure of nonfulfillment the
marriage brings to either spouse. Thus the questioning spirit
itself elevates whatever failure of fulfillment there may be while
minimizing the successful responses of the man and woman
to the demands each makes of the other. It is this fact that

---

[19] Angyal, Andras, *Foundations for the Science of Personality*, p. 212.

gives force to the contention of those who believe marriage should represent a final commitment, with separation the limit of escape from whatever consequences marriage brings. Fulfillment is both the test and the promise of marriage. It is experienced on the highest level of physical and spiritual relationships. The demands it brings, each of the other, are not time-anchored, because there is both a continuous and a changing requirement, the original asking and giving of the spouses being modified through their intimate living together as husband and wife. Success comes from the ability of each to recognize the other's demands and to accept them and in some degree to meet them. Failure brings incompatibility, a topic to be discussed in a later chapter.

The psychoanalyst sees behind this basic urge for completement through fellowship with another person vestiges of childhood tendencies, and the character of these unconscious cravings determines the expectancy of the individual in marriage and the probability of his success or failure in his reactions to the needs of the other. Thus the individual may enter marriage burdened by infantile longings, and, although his choice has been influenced by the appeal his spouse made in courtship as the indispensable answer to his personality cravings, he may be disillusioned in the complexity of marriage relationships and throw on his spouse the blame for a disappointment basically rooted in his own personality defects. The possible range of this faulty preparedness not only for marriage but for life is tremendous and its complications many. The causal influence of marriage itself needs to be recognized as a part of this totality of disposition in the role of husband or wife. Marriage offers great educational opportunity for moving the individual toward greater maturity, and, since the choice of mate was made as an answer to personality needs, there is from the beginning a basis for development unless growth requires complete repudiation of infantile traits too stubbornly built in the personality for marital relationship to make reconstruction possible.

There are, as one would expect of so emotionally charged a relationship as marriage, unconscious ego traits which find expression in the husband-wife association that rightly are defined as pathological. They belong to the literature of the abnormal and are not related to marriage except as its privacy and intimacy provide exceptional opportunity for their appearance. Aside from these that concern only a small and mentally diseased group, there are persons possessing ego traits that can prove mischievous in the marriage relationship. Overpowering demands for domination and complete possession of the spouse, chronic jealousy, or a persistent craving of vindictiveness, whatever its origin, are among the most common of these ego-driven motivations that strangle love. These are personality flaws brought forth by the intimacies of marriage that can only be uprooted by the re-education of the individual responsible. In milder form similar dispositions are more common, and even when they do not destroy compatibility they make the union more difficult and less satisfying. Love and a degree of self-understanding can eradicate them or so redeem them as to make them of little consequence.

The nature of marriage problems. There are two types of marriage problems. One, although it greatly concerns the relationship of the husband and wife, is not exclusively related to their fellowship. An illustration of this is the subject of finances. This may be not only a great problem in its effect on the husband and wife but even the most influential of all in determining their attitudes toward one another. Nevertheless, this type of problem directly concerns all members of a family. For the sake of clarity it seems best in this text to consider problems of this kind in the other chapters where they naturally appear and are dealt with from the family viewpoint. The second type of problems, although they may have profound significance for the family as a whole, are distinctly matters that have to do with the personal relationship of husband and wife. These are the problems that properly belong in this chapter's discussion. These, in turn, can be separated into premarriage and marriage problems.

Marriage expectation. The individual who enters marriage brings with him a considerable amount of conditioning experience which has much to do with his matrimonial career. This is summarized by the term "marriage expectation," a product of cultural background and personal happenings. The core of this conditioning material can best be described as the masculine or feminine complex. Emotional attitudes gather about the individual's being a male and not a female, or a female and not a male. Thus there are both positive and negative reactions included in this complex. Since western culture stresses the prerogatives of the male, it is not uncommon for the man to have an underlying feeling of superiority or for the woman to have gathered from her childhood period onward envy of or protest against this masculine assumption. The psychoanalytic interpretation of this difference between the man and the woman emphasizes the emotional reactions, disappointment, superiority, hate, and revenge, which from time to time the woman may feel as she is made to realize the advantages of the male. This school of thought finds in the physical distinctions of the male the symbol of the woman's body deficiency, and her efforts to surmount these handicaps are described as the compensation complex. Although a woman's recoil from the assumptions of masculine role revealed through her husband's attitudes and actions may take many forms, it is in her sex relations that she has her most effective opportunity for rebuking him or giving herself the satisfaction of a superior power. To accomplish this compensation she may even go so far as to develop a frigidity.[20] In this way she attains a dominance which at heart she prefers to the satisfaction of a good adjustment. Her program can be deliberate,[21] but even in such instances the original decision to make an attack on the husband through their sex relationship may pass out of memory and continue as unconscious motivation. As a rule the woman never realizes the manner of her protest against the masculine role and regrets her frigidity, the cause of which she does not understand. The sex dissatisfaction which comes to her in her marriage career will, however, add even more emotional recoil against the feminine role which she may regard as imposed upon her by society, or by nature, or most likely by both.

The complications that come because western culture has not yet been able to establish full equality of the sexes are not confined to any one aspect of the husband-wife relationship. There is, therefore, no greater, more necessary, or more consequential adjustment in each individual than that which comes from the conventional attitudes expressed in the masculine and

---

[20] Hitschmann, Edward, and Bergler, Edmund, *Frigidity in Women*, p. 5.
[21] Prince, Morton, *The Unconscious*, pp. 462–466.

feminine complexes. Each person's basic expectations in marriage are in accord with his or her fundamental attitude toward being a woman or being a man and are chiefly colored by what each conceives to be the rightful role of the other and his or her own prerogatives. It is in this marriage anticipation that we find the most common source of trouble in the various sorts of mixed marriages. Persons who have had different racial backgrounds, different social and class environments, or unlike religious teaching concerning the rights and obligations of men and of women must find a solution for a profound difference in what they expect marriage to mean through their mutual value to one another; since their task requires a compromising of deeply established standards and a reconstruction of ideals, they may fail in their love, and incompatibility results.

Feminine versus masculine. Marriage as a relationship possible only to individuals of opposite sex raises the question, what differences are there that can rightly be described as belonging to the masculine and the feminine personality. Since the contrast of the sexes is the most spectacular of all distinctions between human beings and is based upon biologic distinction both in structure and in function, it is natural that both in philosophic discussion and scientific investigation much attention has been given to a definition of the essential differences of the two sexes. Plato,[22] Schopenhauer, Weininger, Ellis, and Hinkle are some of those who have attempted to discover the meaning of feminine and masculine personality by philosophic analysis. The investigations that have been carried through to throw light on the meaning of sex difference are myriad, chiefly in the field of biology, psychiatry, psychology, and sociology.

In spite of the interest of recent science in the difference between the sexes, there are many aspects of the problem that still remain subjects of controversy. The major issue is whether man and woman in their social and psychic traits are biologically determined or are products of cultural influences. The falseness of the one-time assumption of woman's intellectual infe-

---

[22] See Plato's *Republic;* Schopenhauer's *The World as Will and Idea;* Weininger, Otto, *Sex and Character;* Ellis, Havelock, *Man and Woman;* and Hinkle, Beatrice, *The Recreating of the Individual,* Ch. 6.

riority [23] appears settled, although there are those who insist
that she lacks man's creative ability. If this inferiority does
exist, there still remains the question whether it is due to innate deficiencies or to the division of labor between the sexes
and the social hardships women experience.[24]

Since marriage is a union of opposite sexes, the question
naturally arises, how greatly do the unlikenesses of man and
woman complicate its success? The emotional and endocrine
differences are obvious. The woman's different and major role
in reproduction also has to be recognized and its consequences
as they appear in the career of motherhood.[25] These biological
characteristics are interpreted by some writers as the essence of
the marriage problem.[26] The experienced marriage counselor
soon discovers that the great variations in marriage characteristics are individual rather than sexual. Men differ from men and
women from women too greatly, when tested by their capacity
to adjust to the physical, emotional, and social aspects of married life, to make possible an interpretation of this relationship
as an attempt to compromise the inherent dispositions of two
different types of human beings. Common peculiarities of behavior in the purely physical relationship may be assumed. In
this sphere the degree of biological and cultural determination
is, however, open to argument, but even here the impulses and
attitudes that the individuals have developed through their
environmental contacts are more decisive as they hamper or
favor marital success. In discussion of masculine and feminine
traits it is necessary to keep in mind that these are variable between both individuals and cultural environments. Much of
the behavior of both man and woman as they attempt to build
their domestic fellowship is the result of the roles that each, as
a result of family and social influences, has been led to accept
as desirable conduct. The cultural setting [27] in which they have
been placed in their formative years thus decides what they
believe are the masculine and feminine patterns, and each in

---

[23] Scheinfeld, Amram, *Women and Men*, p. 306.
[24] Schmalhausen, Samuel, and Calverton, V. F., *Woman's Coming of Age*,
p. 31.
[25] See for a discussion of this Helene Deutsch, *Psychology of Woman*, Vol. 2.
[26] Van de Velde, Theodore, *Sex Hostility in Marriage*, p. 34.
[27] Mead, Margaret, *Sex and Temperament*, pp. xvii–xviii.

the light of this conceives what is proper for himself and for his spouse.

Psychic aspects of marital maladjustment. The sexual mating of animals escapes the subtleties of human union because of the absence or meagerness of what in the life of men and women constitutes the psychic side of sex. This means that a narrow interpretation of human sex maladjustment, reducing the problems to mere structural adequacy or physical technique, so sidesteps one of the two sources of trouble as to be misleading and mischievous. A quantity of marital maladjustments results from the extension of sex and its alliance with self-consciousness. These hazards of human mating are in large measure one expression of that expansion of brain and endocrine which Crile has so forcefully interpreted as both the human organism's equipment for civilization and its strain.[28] This development, which provides the higher evolution of men and women as compared with other animal life, not only influences sex when this is extracted and taken by itself but also incorporates the functioning of sex, so that it becomes a substantial part of intellectual and emotional experience.

A favorite description of sex that attempts to deny this extension appears in the common habit of talking about it or thinking about it as the animal passion. A moment's thought of the sex complications associated even with legal, affectionate marriage makes clear how far human sex experience has traveled from the animal passion out of which the instinct has developed. Not only has sex expanded along with the increase of psychic life among humans; it has also possessed characteristics which distinguish it from the experience of animals. These have come from self-consciousness, the qualitative change that has appeared in human life as a consequence of a quantitative, evolutionary development of nervous equipment. Once self-consciousness arose in the ongoing of organic development, so significant and compelling a human drive as that of sex could not fail to express itself in new and more complicated forms on this highest level of human experience, and, as a consequence, sex conduct became a composite, containing every sort of intellectual and emotional reaction reflecting the prevailing social, religious, and moral standards and concepts.

---

[28] Crile, George, *Diseases Peculiar to Civilized Man,* pp. 24–25.

It therefore becomes necessary to interpret sex maladjustments, whether they appear in the single or the married-life
career, as by-products of this psychologizing of the fundamental
organic drive. The enrichment of the psychic life of humans
provides a superior memory and imagination that not only
increase the qualitative meaning of human sex relations but
bring to them potential inhibitions, obstructions, dissatisfactions, and even recoils that variegate as well as complicate
human sex adjustment. The memory easily furnishes content
that may be worked over by self-consciousness in feelings of
guilt. The imagination likewise offers its contribution to the
building up of anxiety. These are prominent penalties of the
psychic complexity of human sex experience, but merely to
signalize them would mean leaving out of account the vast
amount of troublesome disturbances in the realm of sex that
come to life when we go searching into specific, individual sex
difficulties. Inferiority feeling, jealousy, masochistic or sadistic
impulses, sex antagonism, shame, suspicion, and fear are other
sorts of conflicts to which both memory and imagination contribute. Even our attempts to tag the happenings with such
descriptive terms usually artificially limits the nature of the
trouble. What we really find in our analysis is a character trait
and a situation that may be catalogued for emphasis under
some one suggestive concept but which can seldom be explained by the choice of any one diagnostic term. For therapeutic purposes, it may not matter that we stress one of the
many contributing factors, because in dealing with it we soon
are confronted with the other influences that also have helped
in creating the problem. Undoubtedly, parents make a great
amount of unnecessary trouble for their children as they grow
toward an attempted sex maturity by giving them in infancy
and childhood and even in youth an inadequate or at times
unwholesome training.

Even if the hazards of traditional-mindedness, ignorance,
or insincerity were eliminated, one could not expect that this
would entirely take away in such a complex culture as ours all
influences that complicate the functioning of sex. The fact that
the stress of growing up into adult sex relationships is so little
in evidence in some simple society can only encourage us to
do all we can to lessen tensions that develop in the sex careers

of modern men and women. To do as well as primitive folks we would need to empty ourselves not only of the artificial and the irrational obstructions but also of the inherent difficulties born of the enrichment of individual life and its response to conflicting stimuli. We can throw off the burden of an unintelligent preparation for marriage, but we cannot return to a simplicity of social organization. Instead, our activities, to have any degree of promise, must be directed toward still more maturing of the individual that he may be equal to the burdens put upon him in all his relationships, including sex, by the civilization to which he belongs. To look backward to the easier task of simpler people is mere wishful thinking, a covering up of the unescapable complexities of modern sexual adjustments and sex attitudes. Sex invites within its sphere the expression of any emotional disturbances or conflict, wherever or however they originate.

The stress that sex has come to have in the conscious program of the individual, even though it has been accepted only in a sublimated and disguised form, has led to expectations that complicate life adjustment and particularly sex adjustment. Most young persons make their heaviest wagers in their expectations of drawing the satisfactions that romance has so highly colored. Undoubtedly modern men and women, especially the latter, do more often win effective marital adjustment than when mutual expectation was less strong. Nevertheless, so much is at stake that any considerable failure easily leads to domestic discontent and eventual separation or some promiscuous solution of the disappointing relationship. Frequently sex satisfaction is interpreted as something surely possessed if only one has knowledge of the necessary technique. Even sophisticated youth frequently fail to see that the training that comes from knowledge and experience in the realm of sex is only part of the resources required for successful marital adjustment. Over a long period of time there is needed also the adequacy that can come only from an efficient personality, independent of sex. Sex experience, therefore, cannot be isolated from the total contacts of two human beings attempting to make satisfactory life adjustment. Immaturities, defects of personality, sooner or later are drawn into the sexual relationship where they may abort happiness even though both persons are familiar with the principles of efficient marital technique. There is no way by which modern marriage can escape the strain, the reconstructions, and at times the tragedies that belong to the sex experience, because these are so substantially related to the character of the individuals concerned. This means that the adjustment is never general, determined by the individuals' possessing or not having certain virtues, but rather that it is the concrete testing of the possibility of the two persons, different as they are because of their own peculiar characteristics, achieving emotional unity in a relationship that modern life is tending to consider too significant as a cause of the successes or failures of marriage.

Sex in its most narrow physical sense is like the burning of cellophane, a quick, intense flame which quickly disappears. To bring substance into even the physical relationship, there must be satisfaction of the urge to be desired. Skilled technique [29] cannot by itself give permanence to the relationship even when it is merely physical; there must also be a reciprocity of emotions. Indeed the exclusively physical adjustment otherwise is meager and therefore illusive. Commonly this need of reinforcement of sex passion is considered a characteristic of women, since in their case it is usually more evident; but in fact it is a human demand, and when lacking in marriage there is no certainty that it will be less frustrating for the husband than the wife.

The most serious of all sex problems are the frigidity of women and the impotency of men. The causes of frigidity are many, ranking from the purely physical to the purely psychic. The highly cultured woman seems more subject to the latter. The motives may be conscious or unconscious. They may stem from the past, especially from childhood, or originate in the marriage association itself. The woman may protest against her husband's apparently exclusively sexual interest in her or his reactions may give her a disgust that leads her to smother her body responses until she robs herself of the capacity of response. This reaction may be due to her own prudish attitudes, a result of wrong teaching. It may be the result of the wife's suspicion that she is regarded only as a sexual instrument.

---

[29] Reik, Theodor, *Psychology of Sex Relations*, pp. 202–203.

Desire may battle her determination to be indifferent and then even desire, although backed by strong, normal body impulses, becomes impotent. Often frigidity is not really a sex problem but a notification sexually announced that the union is incomplete, vexing, or victimized by faulty developments of personality of one or both spouses. In such cases, good adjustment can come only if the basic impediments to fellowship and love are removed. In one case, the husband sought from his physician some drug to render his wife passionate. Had he succeeded in solving his wife's difficulty on a purely physical basis, he would surely have found that the estrangement at the bottom of the relationship would have become all the greater. In one incompatibility when a physician taught the husband a skilled technique that made the wife passionate against her will, one of the authors as counselor had to recognize the development of such intense hatred in the wife, who felt that she could no longer command her own body, that he had finally to accept the necessity of the wife's getting a divorce. The alternative was such that even the husband became convinced that immediate separation was necessary. Impotency in the male is the product of physical or psychic causes, or the mixture of both, similar to those that bring frigidity to the woman.

Medical aspects of marital maladjustment.[30] There are many conditions of physical origin that bring about marital maladjustment, some rare and others relatively common. Many of these are easier to diagnose than to treat successfully. The chief physical causes of trouble are physiological, neurological, and anatomical defects and diseases. Disease may decrease or destroy potency, create mental aversion to intercourse, or even destroy sexual vigor. The most trouble-making of the diseases are the venereal, syphilis and gonorrhea, and chancroid and granuloma inguinale and other debilitating diseases which lessen desire or interfere with the sex act. There are some diseases such as leukemia which may bring about excessive sex passion. Tuberculosis may separate the spouses or lead to such invalidism as to put an end to marital relations. There may be

---

[30] Stanford, W. R., "Medical Aspects of Marital Incompatibility," *Social Forces.* Vol. 16, No. 3. The discussion of the text has been influenced by this article.

incompatibility as a result of great differences in the sex desire of the spouses—this at times is basically a problem of endocrinology of the person who seems oversexed or undersexed. Nervous spasm arising from the physical or psychological shock of the wife at the beginning of marriage may lead to the development of vaginisimus. An incompatibility may result from anatomical sex differences or abnormalities of the spouses. Sometimes there is an infantile development of some part of the sex equipment, as, for example, there may be only the vagina of childhood or an otherwise imperfect one. Various mental diseases, both organic and functional, may hamper marital adjustment or make it impossible. The functional disturbances are most numerous. Maladjustment may occur because one of the spouses is basically homosexual and should therefore never have married. Various difficulties originate in psychopathic impulses, of which sadism is an example in the male and masochism in the female.

The value of the premarriage examination in preparation for marriage, to be discussed later, becomes apparent in any discussion of the physical aspects of marital maladjustment. Since, however, the sources of trouble cannot always be anticipated but may show themselves only in the marriage career, the first step in the handling of any problem of marital maladjustment is an attempt at diagnosis by a physician who is thoroughly competent to handle problems of sex. The question seldom is who is to blame but rather what is the trouble and how can it be remedied. Lifetime tragedies as a consequence of physical incompatibility sometimes result through failure to seek the advice of the physician or to follow treatment prescribed. Instead of turning to the resources of science, many of these unhappily married men and women through ignorance are content to blame the other spouse for an assumed fault or, in the spirit of fatalism and sacrifice, to endure what it is wrongly supposed cannot be changed.

The marriage counselor becomes familiar with marriage tragedies that could easily have been prevented if preceding marriage there had been a consultation with a specialist and a physical examination. The B. G.'s illustrate this. Married twelve years, their incompatibility has become such that it is dangerous for them to live together. There is even external evidence of the serious nervous condition of both and of their violent antagonism. Although college graduates, they married without much understanding of the physical aspect of marriage. To accomplish complete sex adjustment, it was necessary for the wife to have a minor operation so simple as hardly to deserve the term operation. Because of the unusual thickness of her hymen, neither she nor her husband ever had normal intercourse. The consequence was a gradual development of aversion on the part of the husband which when their minister explained the nature of the impediment turned to disgust and hatred. Then too late the wife did go to a surgeon, who quickly removed the physical obstruction to their union. The husband felt that the wife had purposely concealed her handicap, or at least he used this idea as a rationalization of his bitter feeling toward her, and refused to attempt a readjustment. The attitude of the woman also was not one that gave much promise of a more satisfying relationship. The tension between them indicated the need of an immediate separation. This was soon followed by the husband's insistence on divorce.

The experiences of the A. G.'s are exactly opposite. They met at a midwestern university, he a graduate student, she a junior. Soon after he obtained his Doctor's degree they married. As an undergraduate he had taken a course in marriage that dealt frankly with marriage problems. Some days before their marriage these young people both sought a conference with the instructor of this course, and this was followed by an examination in preparation for marriage given by a specialist well known to each of them. When they started housekeeping, they met the difficulties of living on the small salary of an instructor without tension. He advanced rapidly in his career, his ability and training being magnificently supported by the co-operation and good judgment of the wife. Now he is well established in his profession at one of the most respected of our large western state universities. The home of these young people with their three young children is representative of the highest type of American culture, and they believe their good start was in part their intelligent effort to prepare for marriage as they would have for any other important life career.

The wedding. The wedding may well be considered the ceremony that either ends courtship or commences marriage, for it does both. It is usually to a large extent a family observance, and so many considerations enter into its performance that the prospective bride and groom are seldom entirely free to arrange it according to their choice. There are decided advantages in a simple wedding, since it frees the bride from fatigue and worry and the groom from nervous embarrassment just at the critical starting point of their new life together. For people who are not wealthy the wedding should also be inexpensive, for financial difficulties are only too likely to cause strain during the early part of married life when the cost of equipping a new home is coupled with lack of skill in the technique of household budgeting. The only risk connected with the simpler wedding is that the bride may be sensitive to the conventions which make the wedding in itself so important in a woman's life, and in later years will regret the simplicity of the occasion.

The present movement toward a greater equality of the sexes is influencing the wedding ceremony in a far more significant way than the omission of the bride's promise to obey her husband. The wedding is taking a more reasonable place in the matrimonial program, and it is this perhaps that explains the tendency, which apparently is on the increase, for the young people to cut themselves away from all the difficulties of the wedding ceremony as a family social event by quietly slipping to some other locality and getting married with the utmost simplicity. Although the press reports this as an elopement, it is, of course, nothing of the sort, but an effort to avoid the ordeal of the wedding which in times past was thought of as the great climax of a woman's career, and in our more normal period is considered merely the legalizing of a relationship which points forward, rather than an event of great significance in itself.

The honeymoon. The honeymoon is a distinctly modern invention and one of the most advantageous of all that have to do with marriage. Its actual purpose is to give the newly married a propitious start in their new relationship with an opportunity to transfer safely from the atmosphere of courtship to the realities of marriage. This is the easier done if travel, a new environment, or something that removes them from their wonted associations accompanies the change of status. The honeymoon, because it does constitute a transition from court-ship attitudes to those of marriage, has a decided significance that may color the entire afterlife of the married couple. It is here that anticlimax is felt by the woman who lingers as long as possible in the delights of courtship.

The honeymoon program sometimes in itself menaces the wholesome start of marriage. The wedding may leave one or both life partners tired, nervous, and supersensitive. The travel that conventionally goes with the honeymoon may be unduly prolonged so that it results in excessive fatigue. There may be also financial worry on the part of the man, for people who, like railroad ticket agents, know the honeymoon program of persons in moderate circumstances tell us that frequently trips are undertaken that are too expensive, and sometimes have to be shortened at the last moment because of a shortage of funds. In contrast with the mistakes of such couples, we have the opposite risk of the wealthy who extend the honeymoon to great lengths or give it an abnormal testing by some such experience as a cruise around the world in a yacht. This tears the two people from their accustomed environment for too long a time, depriving them of their usual pleasures and at the same time forcing them to depend exclusively on each other for companionship until the association becomes monotonous and irritating.

Familiarity with the origin of family difficulties of a seri-ous character teaches one that a considerable percentage of separations start during the honeymoon experience. This is often due to the nervousness and fatigue of one or both mem-bers of the newly founded family. Incidents and remarks that would otherwise receive little attention are magnified out of all proportion by the almost hysterical individual, and from that moment a wedge enters the union and gradually forces asunder the couple.

How far such a honeymoon experience goes is well illus-trated by a case reported by Morton Prince. XYZ had her feel-ings hurt seriously on the first night of her honeymoon. It happened that her husband went down into the hotel lobby where he met some political acquaintance and became greatly interested in a political discussion. Strange as it may seem, he forgot his waiting bride, and when a few hours later he returned to her and explained what had happened she was not only terribly hurt but also angry and determined, to use her own words, that she "would be hanged if" she would show any response to his affection. The result was that she became a victim of a neurotic dissociation which completely ruined her marriage by producing a state of long-lasting asexuality.[31]

Kinds of honeymoon. There are various kinds of honeymoon, but the conventional short travel trip is exceedingly common. Anyone who goes about much is familiar with the couple who start their journey with a send-off from their friends that advertises what perhaps needs no announcement since the self-consciousness of the young couple would in itself attract attention. The honeymooners soon become aware of the interest of curious fellow travelers, and all in all they have a bad beginning for the kind of transition into marriage their interests demand. It would be a great advantage if it became a matter of wedding ethics to allow the bridal couple to slip off quietly without the horseplay that is always annoying and sometimes goes to dangerous lengths.

It is encouraging to notice the growth of the unconventional honeymoon. The automobile trip escapes all the ostentatiousness of the steamboat or railroad journey. There is some tendency also toward camping trips, and for those qualified to enjoy a semiprimitive life such a honeymoon is ideal. An owner of a cottage beautifully located in the mountain section of one of our eastern states advertises his most attractive summer place for honeymooners, and it is constantly occupied by the type of people who appreciate wild nature. Bridal couples who have a touch of the vagabond spirit are quite likely in these days to take a walking trip for their honeymoon. Anything that avoids publicity is an advantage, for experience in dealing with family difficulties reveals the frequency of wedding-journey strain as the primary cause of estrangement in couples that were destined otherwise to a happy married life. The honeymoon is not a trip for the pleasure of traveling; it is a social convention which has come about as a means of providing favorable conditions for the transition from courtship to wedlock. It has its serious side as a preparation for successful marriage.

---

[31] Prince, Morton, *op. cit.*, pp. 462–467.

Spiritual theories of love. Belief in the sacramental meaning of marriage carries with it a spiritual theory of love. This from the Catholic viewpoint has recently been interpreted to show marriage as a wonderful union of two persons in love, and through love [32] instituting a fellowship which finds its fundamental, objective reason for being in a supreme expression of mutual affection distinguishable even from the ties that bind in friendship and in parent-child relationship. This exposition recognizes three relationships: sensual attraction and passion, conjugal love and its fulfillment through marriage, and the spiritualizing of the union as a sacrament. The conjugal love is thus distinguishable from the love of friends or the love of parents and children not merely because of its inclusion of the sexual, as is too often thought, but on account of the unique, mutual giving of one to another, completely and ultimately including the entire personality of both persons. Therefore conjugal love leads to a community of response where two persons become a closed union, the reciprocity of love existing only between them. It is an I-thou relationship which through fulfillment in marriage progresses beyond itself until it becomes or includes a unique relation with Jesus. This love can come only to a man and a woman since it cannot be experienced in any fellowship between members of the same sex, not because of mere biological differences but because each sex has a unique capacity for complementing the other. Being in love is clearly distinguishable from sensual desire. Only in the former is there that fusion of personalities which justifies the statement that they shall be two in one flesh. Conjugal love attains a new status through marriage and one which represents such a surrendering of one personality to the other that it cannot be duplicated while both live. Therefore it is essentially permanent. Conjugal love does not fade into friendship but advances through supernatural configuration so that marriage is completed in a communion with God, thus taking on the character of a religious vow. It is not an insurance for happiness but a life commitment through the conviction of two persons that their union includes their eternal welfare.

The Protestant concept is well stated in the following:

---

[32] Von Hildebrand, Dietrich, *Marriage.*

The Christian conception of marriage has been stated by Christ himself in beautiful and sensitive words. He speaks of how "He which made them at the beginning made them male and female," and quotes the words, "for this cause shall a man leave his father and mother, and shall cleave to his wife." The man and woman in marriage become one flesh, that is to say, the union is organic and it is God who unites them, which means that it is a profound biological-spiritual experience which comes out of the depths of life. The union is permanent: "What therefore God hath joined together, let no man put asunder." The Mosaic law which permitted a man to divorce his wife with no recourse for her is abrogated: "Moses because of the hardness of your hearts suffered you to put away your wives: but from the beginning it was not so."

In this sort of marriage the two become not merely "one flesh" but one in spirit, for the highest values of marriage are in the realm of personality. In Christian marriage the meeting of all the needs of personality and the enhancement of delicate mutual regard must be sought. At the same time the welfare of society must be loyally promoted through the home.

In the broadest sense we need to see that these relationships between the sexes are not only of the greatest importance for society but are also related to a larger moral order. They become linked with faith in God, with sacrifice for others, and with the higher ideals of mankind. Human loyalty and religious faith tend to persist or perish together in the heart. The very fabric not only of our outward culture but of our philosophy of life is woven together with respect for family relationships and a belief in the inherent worth of love.

. . . .

Young people . . . hold as the ideal a type of life in marriage which, while naturally and consciously grounded in a complementary physical relationship, at the same time contributes to that development of personality which is the end and aim of the Christian religion. Thus marriage is not only to be life-long in duration but its fellowships are to permeate to the height and breadth and depth of personal experience. . . .

Such a conception of marriage is sound and should be preserved at whatever cost. Young people are not deceived when they experience profound emotions and visions of mutual devotion. These are not meant to pass, but to persist, to find expression in new forms, and to glorify life.[33]

---

[33] Commission on Marriage and the Home of the Federal Council of the Churches of Christ in America, *Christian Marriage* (pamphlet), pp. 4–6.

Rabbi Goldstein has stated the Jewish ideal:

Marriage, in other words, Judaism teaches, rests upon morals as well as upon mores. It is for this reason that the deepest distress in marriage comes not from biologic defects, nor psychological differences, nor economic hardships, nor legal disputes, but from a violation of ethical principles and a betrayal of spiritual ideals. Marriage at its highest, and who would have it less than this, is a spiritual relationship sanctioned by society and sanctified by religion.[34]

---

[34] Goldstein, Sidney E., *The Meaning of Marriage and the Foundations of the Family*, p. 12.

Chapter 14

THE ARRESTED FAMILY

FOREWORD. The type of family which is the chief theme of this chapter is not new, but it is modern in the sense that recent discoveries have increased the ability of those who prefer it to carry out their intentions. It is generally recognized as a family life which is lacking in one of the essential functions of the institution—parenthood—and therefore in need of a different interpretation than the more common family of parents and children. It has appeared in other cultural periods and has been regarded by social thinkers as a serious problem because of its popularity. The chief reasons for this have been the facts that it influenced the birth rate and thus affected population growth and also denied men and women the personal satisfactions of fellowship and educational influences that come through the association of the parent and the child. As it has lessened the birth rate, it has been frowned upon by those who have felt that the security of a nation depended upon the quantity of its population. In the United States this type of family, herewith described as the arrested family, represents a definite program, at least when it is deliberately chosen, based upon a domestic philosophy which is positive in its implications and expectations. In this chapter both the self-chosen and the unwanted childless family are discussed.

Family experience not static. Individual families show great variation in the way their family life shapes itself. Instead of going forward in accord with common social practices, an individual family may be arrested in its development. In American culture personal inclination, biological conditions, or social circumstances may block the normal program of family growth.

The first two of these influences appear especially in the family life that is arrested because of childlessness, and the third predominates in the retarded or backward family. The first type of family is so common and distinctive in modern culture that it has been given the term "companionate" to distinguish it from the more orthodox form of family experience.

The companionate. The term "companionate" first appeared in an article written by Dr. M. M. Knight of Barnard College, published in the *Journal of Social Hygiene*, May, 1924. The expression was at once incorporated into the technical vocabulary used by scientists in the discussion of family problems. Doctor Knight has hit upon a happy word to describe a modern variation from the historic type of family. It was recognized by all serious students of the family that many married couples were attempting a relationship consciously based upon a program of pleasure and mutual advantage which deliberately sought to sidestep all possible social responsibilities, particularly those connected with the having and rearing of children. Marriages of this sort were clearly in contrast with the orthodox family, and for clarity of discussion a distinguishing term for the modern variant from the family was needed.

With the introduction of the term it became apparent that even the companionate could be broken up into different types. According to Doctor Knight's statement, "we may call the state of lawful wedlock, entered into solely for companionship, and not contributing children to society, the 'companionate,' using the term 'family' in its true historical sense, as the institution for regulating reproduction, early education, property inheritance, and some other things." [1]

A later conception of the companionate added the idea that the union was of temporary character, and that those who entered upon it should be allowed to choose for themselves divorce and remarriage, but only after some delay and conformably to regulations. [2]

In the discussions that followed the introduction of the term companionate, it became evident that some of the advocates of the new relationship stressed as its distinguishing mark the fact that it rested on a contract between the two persons

---

[1] *Loc. cit.*, p. 258.

[2] Kirkpatrick, E. A., *Journal of Social Hygiene,* Vol. 10, p. 473.

concerned, which, even if its registration was required by the state, did not entail the assumption of permanency or the social responsibilities belonging to legalized marriage.

It is evident that the common characteristic of these different ideas of the meanings of the companionate is the deliberate intent of those entering upon it to escape children and all possible social responsibilities. It is with this meaning that the word companionate is used in this text.

In the discussion following the introduction of the term companionate a widespread misconception arose as to its meaning. The companionate marriage is merely a childless union. It is not a marriage in which the husband and wife assume the right of divorce by mutual consent. It is not a trial marriage undertaken with an experimental purpose. Those maintaining the companionate, if married at all, are married with the same legal responsibilities that belong to all who enter matrimony in the state where they reside. The opportunity of maintaining a companionate, offered by modern contraception, provides the possibility of various forms of temporary or trial marriages, since otherwise they would be so likely to lead to parenthood that they would be rarely accepted or advocated. The term companionate, however, does not signify any unorthodox or illegal type of marriage. It is a special kind of family rather than a peculiar form of marriage. Dr. Knight, the originator of the term, believes that on account of the looseness with which it has been used by propagandists it must be stricken from the vocabulary of the social scientist.[3]

The term "arrested family" brings out the social meaning of this childless family as the word "companionate" emphasized the motive of the childless marriage. Although it is necessary to recognize, as the description companionate does, that this special kind of marriage relationship is frequently deliberately chosen, it would be misleading to forget that many of these homes in which children do not appear are not intentionally childless but, on the contrary, represent a frustration of the parental impulse. The arrest of the normal development of family life is the same in both instances. Failure to have children in the home denies to the spouses the opportunity of

---

[3] *Encyclopædia of the Social Sciences,* Vol. 4, p. 115.

making their marriage spread over a wider area that belongs to the normal type of family relationship. The term arrested family therefore seems more descriptive of the essential meaning of this special type of marriage relationship, and, since there is need of some word to depict a type of family life much too common in the United States, that designation has been chosen for discussion of the childless marriage.

The social significance of the arrested family. The companionate is an attempt at an arrested type of family life. There have always been married couples who have had no children; in the past this has been thought of as a defective family life. Because of physiological conditions such as the sterility of one or both members of the marriage partnership due at times to venereal disease, children were not born, a situation which, from the point of view of the orthodox family, has been looked upon as a misfortune. In the program of the arrested family a similar situation, differently produced, becomes desirable for the success of the relationship.

An understanding of the motives that lead to the establishment of the arrested family requires an analysis of the social conditions influencing family life. These conditions are discussed elsewhere in this text, especially in Chapter 11. The companionate is a social product and can be interpreted satisfactorily only if it is looked upon from the point of view of the general social situation and the conditions that are operating upon men and women in these days.

It is clear that economic motives play a large part in the factors that encourage the establishment of the arrested family. It is equally apparent that the arrested family as a conscious program rests upon the widespread confidence that science has at last obtained control of the birth processes so that those who desire can enter marriage with the certainty that children will not be born. Although accidental parenthood happens in individual cases, the careful use of contraceptives by those who have been given an adequate technique by a competent physician generally permits the companionate program for those who wish it. The science of birth control has at least reached an efficiency that encourages those to marry who are unwilling to be parents and offers them reasonable assurance that their decision to remain childless can be carried out.

Birth control and the arrested family. The term "birth control" was introduced to the American vocabulary by Margaret Sanger during the second decade of the twentieth century. The expression is misleading and is gradually being superseded by the word "contraception" which more accurately expresses what is meant. Francis Place (1774–1854), who is generally regarded as the founder of the modern contraceptive movement, had used the term "family limitation." As a result of the agitation pioneered by Mrs. Sanger and the popularizing of interest in contraception, this term was replaced by birth control, and now through a shifting of emphasis, it is being again used to describe the term "planned parenthood," the object of the voluntary motherhood movement. The voluntary, arrested family has become possible through the development of modern contraceptive methods and the diffusion of knowledge concerning them.

The idea of preventing conception is not new. On the contrary, it is very old and is found even among preliterate people.[4] Among savage peoples a great variety of contraceptive methods, some magical and useless and others with some degree of effectiveness, were employed along with infanticide and abortion as attempts to restrict population because of a limited food supply. The organized effort to popularize contraceptive methods in this country was started during the period 1828–1832 by Robert Dale Owen and Charles Knowlton. Owen wrote *Moral Physiology,* a brief and plain treatise on population, and it was published in 1830. By the time of the author's death in 1877, seventy-five thousand copies had been sold. Knowlton, a Massachusetts physician, brought out anonymously *Fruits of Philosophy* in 1832. The immediate popularity of these books demonstrates that already there was in this country an unorganized interest in the prevention of conception. From our colonial beginning there had been attempts at contraceptive practices, the knowledge of which had been given through person-to-person communication, on the folkway level, and by 1800 these had become widespread in western culture.[5]

The significant thing, therefore, about the modern contra-

---

[4] Himes, Norman, *A Medical History of Contraception,* Ch. 1.
[5] *Ibid.,* p. 210.

ceptive movement has been the greater reliability of its methods, its effective publicity, and the progress it has made in establishing its legality. It has met with resistance largely from religious organizations and especially from the Catholic Church.[6] At present it is unlawful for a physician under any circumstances to give contraceptive information in the states of Connecticut and Massachusetts. In contrast with this, the states of North Carolina and South Carolina have made knowledge of contraceptive methods available through maternal health clinics as part of the public health service.

In practice, contraceptive methods reveal for various reasons a percentage of failure. Therefore, the only absolute prevention of conception known to science is sterilization. Investigations made by birth-control clinics report success ranging to as high as 98 per cent;[7] however, the reliability of such statistical reports is challenged.[8] Not only is there constant improvement in technique, especially in instructing of the patient, but also there are at present experiments, especially with animals, based upon recent medical knowledge of endocrinology and biochemistry, looking toward new methods of contraceptive control.

No knowledge is more potent in social consequences than this increase in the resources of science for the control of conception which so largely leaves to those entering marriage the decision to be or not to be parents. It offers opportunity for planned parenthood and the privilege of marital relationships to those who for conscientious reasons are obligated not to have children, but it also permits men and women for selfish reasons to maintain an arrested family and makes possible an inadequate and menacing population policy. It is moreover a knowledge not confined to the married, and therefore it is also socially significant in so far as it influences the sex code of youth and in this way affects courtship and marriage.

Motives for the arrested family. Although the arrested family is an expression of certain trends in modern social life, there are personal motives of various sorts that influence individuals who enter the new type of relationship. Sometimes the

---

[6] Schmiedeler, Edgar, *Twenty-five Years of Uncontrol.*

[7] Himes, Norman, *Practical Methods of Birth Control*, p. 81.

[8] Pearl, Raymond, *The Natural History of Population*, pp. 85–86.

husband or wife is fearful of the physical dangers of childbirth; occasionally one comes in contact with a situation that is literally a fear complex, often started in early childhood. Familiarity with a case in which the mother has died in giving birth to a child, or the undue stressing of the dangers of maternity by the mother, may arouse in a child a fear tendency which increases with advancing years until the individual in maturity regards pregnancy with literal terror. It may be either the husband or the wife that suffers from the fear complex; rarely, both of them feel the same dread. At other times husband or wife fears having children because of an actual or imagined hereditary trait; of course not all such cases are genuine, for rationalization takes place here frequently, and a reluctance to accept the birth of children is justified by concentrating upon some ancestral defect so as to protect the individual from self-criticism. There are, however, conscientious persons who establish childless families because they feel that their family history does not justify their bringing children into the world.

Chronic illness on the part of the man or woman explains some cases of childless families. A, for example, married a young woman whom he knew to be in the advanced stages of consumption; the disease had appeared during their courtship, and the circumstances were such that there seemed no way to give the woman the rest she needed unless her lover married her. Both of them understood that death was not likely to permit their relationship to continue long. The man entered upon the marriage in the belief that he was doing the only just thing, but it was also clear that for this marriage to issue in the bringing of a child into the world would be a wrong against both mother and child.

Another motive that leads many to attempt the arrested family is professional interest. Newly married couples entering missionary or commercial service in a trying climate may be given medical advice not to have children, at least for several years. Women carrying on an occupation or profession that they believe would be jeopardized by the coming of children may adopt the arrested family as a necessity or, if only for a time, as a temporary expediency. Even though the postponement of children is planned for, rather than a permanent childless family, the result may be childlessness. A typical case is that of Mr.

and Mrs. X, an ambitious young couple who married while they were both working their way through college; the husband continued his professional training for several years, while the wife worked as a stenographer to eke out the money he was able to earn during vacations. Children were out of the question during these years of self-denial, but the moment Mr. X finished his training and accepted his first position the happy couple planned to start raising a family. To their dismay no children came to round out their family circle, and for ten years they deeply regretted the course they had pursued in the beginning of their married life, thinking that earlier they were probably more fertile; then one child was born to them, and with that abnormally small family they had to be content.

Undesired childlessness. It is estimated that at least one in every nine or ten couples is sterile. Even when there was such a spectacular rise in the birth rate as occurred in 1941 this proportion was still true.[9] The reasons for childlessness in general may be divided into three groups of causes. The first, pregnancy wastage, describes impregnations which, although started, do not end in the birth of live children, as a result of disease, accidents, or intentional interference for the purpose of abortion. The second group comes about from the deliberate desire to prevent pregnancy and is made possible by the use of some kind of birth control. There are couples that fall into this classification who assume wrongly that they do not have children because of their use of their professed method of contraception. Since their choice frequently is some method known to be unreliable, investigation having proved it in great measure ineffectual, it is to be presumed that, had children been desired, the absolute or low infertility of the couples would have been discovered. The third grouping represents involuntary sterility. In this category we find the marriages that are forced to remain arrested families contrary to the desire of the spouses. The number of those absolutely sterile is small. More commonly the man or woman or both in such childlessness suffer from a temporary or a permanent low fertility. The conditions that lessen fertility are many, and diagnosis by the medical specialist generally involves careful examination of many possible

---

[9] Hamblen, E. C., *Facts for Childless Couples*, p. 5.

influences. Because of the complexity of infertility, possibly even more on account of the fact that people in general do not understand its prevalence and the present-day resources of science in discovering and treating its causes, and frequently the fatalistic feeling of many of those couples, who fail to make effort to be transferred from the infertile to the fertile class, there is much needless childlessness. Couples who have had two years of sterile mating contrary to their choice should assume that for some reason they suffer from infertility and need medical study and, unless the sterility is absolute, treatment to encourage pregnancy. The age of the couple is, however, significant and if the spouses married late or if after years of having used contraceptive protection against pregnancy they now without success seek children, they should wisely turn over their problem to the specialist after as much as six months of waiting. Unfortunately the general practitioner is not equipped to make the investigations necessary to find the causes operating to prevent fertility, and as a consequence many couples, especially in rural or village communities, remain childless when under competent medical care parenthood could be achieved. Undoubtedly in the future this type of diagnostic service will be made much more available; the low-economic group is likely to benefit first through free clinic service, although it would seem that the problem is most acute among those arrested families that belong to what is roughly classified as the middle class.

One of the good results that come from the medical examination in preparation for marriage, a medical contribution to be discussed in some detail later in this text, is the clearing up of conditions that, uncorrected, would hamper fertilization. This does not mean that ordinarily this examination includes any attempt to test the fertility of the couple but rather that the discovery and treatment of inflammations, malformations, and the like assist not only marital adjustment but also reproduction. Since involuntary childlessness may be explained by the condition of either the husband or wife, or both, it is necessary for them both to be examined and since the husband's degree of fertility is more easily ascertained, proper diagnostic investigations rightly start with him. Recent insight reveals that diet, especially vitamin stimulation, and the functioning of the endocrines have a great and, until lately, little understood effect on reproduction. The significance of malformations; foreign growths, such as tumors; inflammation; obstructions, especially those resulting from untreated gonorrheal infection; and the sterilizing effect of certain diseases, mumps being the most spectacular, have been longer understood. Although science cannot restore fertility if it is once absolutely lost, relative infertility as a rule can be successfully dealt with, but frequently treatment has to be carried on for a considerable period of time.

Agitation for and against birth control has led to a popular exaggeration of the significance of deliberate choice as a cause of the arrested family and a minimizing of unwanted childlessness. Since too often the unwilling parent becomes an undesirable, even a menacing parent, it is evident that the most promising policy in dealing with the deliberately arrested family is to decrease the appeal of the selfish motives which lead fruitful spouses to avoid having children and to increase the desirability of parenthood, and in the case of the undesired childlessness to make more available the resources of science for the removal of conditions that needlessly prevent impregnation and successful pregnancy.

Multiplicity of conditions influencing fertility. The conditions that affect human reproduction are so many that the diagnosis in cases of suspected infertility must be made through the study of the entire individual as a functioning organism. This cannot be confined merely to the body as it operates physiologically. Not only is there need of taking into account heredity but also the environment, including not merely physical circumstances but also economic and social conditions. For example, one influence that clearly affects human reproduction is the frequency of coitus, and this in turn appears to be affected by the means of livelihood. Raymond Pearl in *The Natural History of Population* found the following vocational differences in frequency of coitus per month among those studied, whose ages were 20 to 69 inclusive. The average of absolute frequency for farmers was 12.6, merchants and bankers 10.8, and professional men 8.8. Our present knowledge of the short time the ovum and sperm remain in the female body under conditions that permit fertilization shows the spacing of intercourse to be an important factor influencing the potential reproductivity of the couple.

The strength of the libido has to be taken into account since there is great individual variation, and this in turn influences the frequency of coitus. In a small but careful study of 199 couples during a twelve-year period, Pearl found that it took an average total of 259 copulations to produce a pregnancy. These couples were known not to be infertile and on the contrary were considered by Pearl, from evidence presented, highly fertile. They had never attempted to use contraceptives and their sexual habits were not interfered with except by the illness or the absence of one of the spouses. Their pregnancies and births were accurately recorded. He commented that the relative sterility of the human organism is the marvel rather than its fertility.[10]

The complexity of the causes that influence fertility in the lower animals is impressively illustrated by the experience of Pearl in his attempt to get ordinary wild mice to reproduce themselves. Although after their captivity they continued their sexual activity in an apparently normal manner, it was nearly two years before any reproduced. Once this occurred, however, in the next generation there was no difficulty; they reproduced as naturally as white mice. His experience was duplicated by other investigators. There is abundant evidence that the animal which normally reproduces in its natural environment loses or decreases its fertility if closely confined in captivity.[11]

The marriage program of the past. Ordinarily men and women have not married in order to propagate children; they have merely followed personal impulses and have been led by the natural coming of the child into the more complete and mature form of family life. There have always been marriages consciously planned for the having of children, but such marriages have been rare and certainly not characteristic. The young man and woman in the fervor of courtship have wished each other; and the possible coming of a child, although it may have been in the background of their thoughts, has not often received attention; it has been a remote contingency, a distant fruition but not one that was consciously sought. The difference now is that nature can be thwarted in her attempt to lead marriage to its full development. Those who successfully main-

---

[10] *Op. cit.*, p. 78.
[11] *Ibid.*

tain a childless family are limiting their marriage career so as to protect themselves from the responsibilities that in the past were accepted as a necessary complication of marriage even when they were undesired.

Pleasure basis of the arrested family. The arrested family, in so far as it represents a determined policy to prevent marriage from developing into the orthodox family, is in the majority of cases a program that expresses a craving for personal advantage or the seeking of pleasure. Ambition, professional or social, tempts some to establish an arrested family rather than risk success by assuming the liability of children; but for the most part the arrested family issues from the desire to have the pleasures of comradeship and sex without undertaking the social task nature in the past so often thrust upon even those unwilling to have children, as a consequence of their entering the intimate relationship of marriage. Sex obviously impels toward marriage, but the family is something more than the legalizing of sex attraction. In some of the higher animals and in most human beings sex as an experience naturally leads to parental affection; it is the voluntarily childless family's blocking of this development that makes it an arrested type of family life.

The arrested family has to support itself by one or more of the following motives: the professional or economic advantage of a marriage partnership, the craving for intimate association, or sex pleasure. It is sex, however, that looms large in the arrested family. Although sex is well fitted to drive toward marriage, it is not so satisfactory a basis for perpetuating the marriage status. In the past the decrease of sex attraction has been accompanied by the development of a widening range of common interests and pre-eminently by parental interest in the child, who has drawn forth a new element of common sympathy. Sex thus became incorporated in a larger whole and the orthodox family profited from the combination of interests that held the husband and wife together. The arrested family has a smaller province and in so far as it is predominantly sexual in character it is more likely to dwindle with time than to increase. This explains the influence of children in preventing divorce. In short, the arrested family is a willful attempt to keep marriage on the level of pleasure and expediency by cutting off its normal passage into parenthood.

Education and the arrested family. The popularizing of education and its lengthening, especially for the woman, necessarily favor the establishment of an arrested family. The ambitious woman who wishes to get as complete an educational preparation for life as possible tends not only to delay marriage, but when married is more tempted than was her untrained ancestor to protect herself from the obligations of motherhood in order to continue her mental training. The young woman who has been looking forward for several years to a life of professional activity does not easily reconcile herself to being cut off from these interests and confined to the domain of her mother. She is skeptical about the possibility of swinging the double responsibility of a profession and an old-time home, when she sees how hard it is for an unattached woman to forge ahead in her chosen line because of the prejudices of those in power.

Not only is the trained woman tempted to set up an arrested family rather than a more usual type of married life, but the man who has been educated for a profession finds himself confronted with serious reasons for delay in the coming of children. As a consequence, what may have been planned as a temporary childlessness sometimes becomes a permanent arrested family either because of ensuing sterility or because the couple never reach the point of being ready to assume the parental task until surprised by the fact that for them children have become impossible.

The keen competition which faces the professional person at the beginning of his career makes one who is financially insecure hesitate to undertake the rearing of a family. Thus, though education usually fits the man and woman more adequately for parenthood, at the same time it multiplies the motives that lead to the arrested family and encourages a program of postponement or repudiation of the historic family responsibilities. It is not merely that education, by taking over an increasing amount of time, delays marriage and creates standards that hamper the development of the marriage into its complete form, but also that the attitudes and interests of the young couple are turned away from parenthood and concentrated upon intellectual experience or social opportunity.

The childless family an arrested family. The arrested-family marriage under normal circumstances does not constitute a static association, but it does represent a deliberate effort to prevent the marriage from developing into the parenthood type of family experience. Since an arrested family reflects the motives prominent in the early period of marriage, it naturally stresses the physical aspects of the relationship. This, of course, does not mean that the sex impulse is ever absent from the motives that lead men and women into normal marriage, but the arrested family is a deliberate attempt to hold the marriage on the plane of experience which hitherto has been characteristic of the early period of the historic home. In the past the sex impulse has, by the natural progress of events, led the couple into the higher level of parenthood experience. It is this change, which used to be taken as a matter of course, that those establishing an arrested family desire to avoid. As a consequence their union must derive its stability from sex satisfactions and social advantages. Such a marriage loses the cohesion that comes from the growth of parental interest, and this loss forbids the full development of their relationship. Even though the individuals concerned have never been awakened to any sense of loss, their union represents an effort to block the characteristic unfolding of their powers, and, however satisfying to those involved, it represents not only from the point of view of the state but also of the personality-growth of husband and wife a social arrest. In so far as sex is the predominating motive of union the risk of transitoriness is increased, for where sex attraction is reinforced by the addition of attributes brought out by parental sympathy the home has a deeper and more enduring foundation.

Children an economic liability.   The popularity of the arrested family type of marriage in modern life is partly due to the fact that children seem more and more an economic liability, particularly to men and women of the middle class. Undoubtedly in the past one of the motives leading to parenthood has been the self-interest of parents and has been in some instances consciously mercenary, while in others merely a reflection of a social attitude characteristic of a time when children made a significant contribution to family support and brought parents promise of economic security. These conditions, once natural and necessary on account of the cultural situation, are now neither in accord with the attitude of intelligent parents nor from the viewpoint of public welfare desirable. The worker who looks to his child for economic assistance finds that child labor laws and the constantly advancing requirements of educational preparation are taking away from him the asset he once had in children. Social conditions have become such that for many homes the child is distinctly not a material help in the economic struggle, and therefore it is not strange that the family should react sensitively to this situation and adapt itself by the forming of the arrested family.

It is in the city especially that the child is liable to be an economic burden as well as a social problem. The parent is handicapped even in the renting of a home as compared with his married friend who has remained childless. The parent's ease of mobility is also decreased so that he does not have equal opportunity in quickly changing employment and place of residence in order to raise his income and advance to higher and more desirable business openings.

Public opinion and the arrested family. The arrested family could not occupy its present place of importance in our society were it not for recent changes in public opinion. No satisfactory means can be discovered for the measurement of the pressure of public opinion as exercised in the past in keeping the family in its orthodox form. It is clear that both husband and wife when their union has remained barren have felt that they were somewhat frowned upon by neighbors and friends who were doing the expected thing. The legal stress put upon barrenness is a striking illustration of the way public opinion has regarded parenthood. How far this attitude of public thought has pressed individuals into parenthood undesired we have no way of knowing, but there can be no doubt that it is these changes in public opinion that are giving the arrested family its opportunity. Indeed, in the case of many, the movement of thought has completely reversed, and the coming of the child is regarded as a real misfortune by others who have successfully avoided parenthood.

The new social attitude reveals the temper of modern life as it operates upon the family. As the arrested family program becomes increasingly secure by advances in the technique of contraception it will be apparent that married couples cannot be scolded, tricked, or bribed into parenthood. Society itself must develop conditions that favor the home, or a growing proportion of persons will choose the easier and safer and freer arrested family, preferring to keep their union on the sex and comradeship level rather than undertake the burdens that befall parents.

Mothers by coercion. The task of the mother, as Professor Leta S. Hollingworth showed, is similar to that of the soldier as a contributor to the state. This writer's indictment of social leadership for using the processes of control to induce women to bear children and confine themselves to home duties is justified by the facts. The desire for population has expressed itself in social attitudes that in the past have made the childless woman at least uncomfortable. Professor Hollingworth pointed out that not only have the costs and dangers of childbirth been minimized, but also that the average woman has been led, through the construction of her ideals as well as by art, education, public opinion, belief, and the law, to look upon childbirth as her inevitable destiny without reference to her own personal wishes.

It is not too much to say that in the past there has been a conspiracy against childlessness, which has been built not upon the desire for good homes but rather upon exploitation, mass dominance, and national confidence in the security of a multiplying population. It is no longer possible to manipulate social control to such an extent for the stimulating of births by means of pressure upon women. In the better homes children are not likely to come unwanted. Their appearance must more and more depend upon the sincere wish of both husband and wife for children and a willingness to assume the kind of handicaps that children bring.

The family can compete with the arrested family only by providing for many people a more desirable type of experience. The arrested family will not be lessened by attack. The more complete form of married life can be encouraged by creating social situations that permit it to furnish more adequate satisfaction for most married men and women. Certainly the arrested family is to be a persistent rival of the orthodox family and the family must maintain itself by social superiority. How many unwilling mothers we have had under the former regime can never be known, but it is most fortunate that society has at last progressed to the point where the home with children in it will be, for most of those who establish it, a definite choice. If in the past individuals have been pushed from the level of impulse to the more complete experience of parenthood, in our time they who go beyond the reaches of the arrested family will more often proceed by conscious and deliberate volition.

The social value of the arrested family. It is well that modern youth are not made to choose between living a single life and parenthood. The possibility of the arrested family experience offers a compromise of decided social value. Most of those who recognize the motives that influence people to postpone and refuse marriage will not deny the utility of the arrested family. This new type of marriage relation will induce some to marry who, faced with the probability of becoming parents, would hesitate to enter matrimony. As the social currents are now moving, the reasons that make men and women delay or reject marriage will grow more compelling.

The arrested family is not without its responsibilities. It asks more of human nature than does single life; it contributes to the maturing of personality and the stabilizing of the emotions as well as to a larger sense of public obligation and even to more exacting morals. It is well to remember also in a discussion of the arrested family that those who form it do not always remain steadfast in their program. The experience itself tends toward greater maturity and a finer sense of values, and often those who would not have married without confidence that they could maintain the arrested family voluntarily go beyond this into the more difficult and more satisfying experience of parenthood.

It is especially likely to be true of the woman that not until she has enjoyed several years of the comradeship of married life does she realize the strength of her own longing for children; then, finding that the companionship of her husband is not enough to feed her craving for intimate response, she determines to have children. This maturing of the maternal craving is hastened by the pleasure the woman gets from her arrested family opportunity of mothering her husband. There will always be some for whom the arrested family will act as a prelude to the more complete type of family life. If the childless family is an arrested human relationship, single life for the biologically mature is even more an obstruction of human development. Here again social pressure will be found unavailing except as society brings about conditions that make marriage more desirable and the single life less satisfying.

Legislation.   Legislation can of course affect the growth of the arrested family. Laws and public policies that add to the handicap of parents will automatically act as an encouragement of the easier type of marriage relationship. The influence of legislation upon home life is often practically forgotten by those who pass laws with attention upon certain objectives, which, although desirable in themselves, are obtained by regulations that hamper the having and rearing of children. Our income-tax laws have been written with much more thought of the possibility of easily bringing in the necessary funds with the least disturbance of business than of their effect upon childbirth. Lawmakers will become more conscious of the need of keeping the interests of the home ever in mind in passing legislation that influences family life as the trend toward the arrested family grows more apparent. In the effort more nearly to equalize the social burdens of the orthodox family and the arrested family, legislators must beware of fixing upon the arrested family too great handicaps by the passing of taxation regulations, for it will be easy to induce a more ominous trend toward single life and the avoidance of all marriage by overpenalizing the childless.

A positive program.   The arrested family must be treated as a serious change in family relationships. For many it is to be the desirable, even the conscientious, type of family. The prosperity of the more mature form of family life demands a positive program. It is only by building up the most favorable conditions for wholesome and successful parenthood that society can meet the problems thrust upon it by the coming of the arrested family.

Education, that has done so little specifically to foster family life, must develop its new task with zeal and with skill. Our more thoughtful youth are most emphatic in their demand that they be given instruction that will help them to enter marriage well prepared. Likewise from young mothers of intelligence is coming a request, which has become irresistible, for concrete assistance in dealing wisely with their children. The friends of the family must look to education rather than to legislation or social pressure for the means by which the orthodox family may win its fair share of adherents. The arrested family is itself in no small measure evidence of an inadequate and uninterpretive education which distorts the values of life. If the arrested family reduces the number of families with children, it will at the same time reveal the need of elevating the general level of family life.

The arrested family is not born of new motives in human experience. It would have come in the past if it had been possible and if social conditions had stimulated its development as modern life has done. The right sort of educational preparation for marriage and home life will give the great majority of youth the courage to undertake the full task of homekeeping. It will be seen that the more complete form of relationship calls forth moral qualities that more than compensate for the limitations placed upon the parents by their obligations. It is only in the superficial sense that there is real conflict between parent and child. When Sumner said: "The interests of parents and children are antagonistic; the fact that there are or may be compensations does not affect the primary relation between the two," [12] he was oblivious to the deeper and more significant moral advantages that the child brings the parent.

Out of the field of psychiatry, from those at close quarters with human maladjustment, comes testimony that parenthood, because of the incentive it provides for emotional maturity, needs to be included in the marriage program as a means of educating the character and satisfying the cravings of the normal personality.

No positive program to encourage childbearing among those who possess the conditions for good parenthood yet now avoid children is likely to have much success unless based upon a realistic recognition of the motives that lead to the choice of the arrested family. Among these the economic predominates, being the most common explanation given. This must be dealt with by bringing to these individuals not only a greater sense of economic security but also in many instances a more discriminating sense of the values of life. A second common reason given is fear of the woman's health. Unless there is a recogniz-

[12] *Folkways*, p. 310.

able physical disability, chronic ill health, or disease, this motive for not having children is groundless. The same may be said of a third—fear of the ordeal of childbirth. Another reason given is the belief that the woman will lose her form through the bearing of a child. Adequate prenatal, obstetrical, and postnatal care of the mother is the solution for this. In a recent study of 400 professional men and 300 women [13] the following explanations were reported most frequently for the willingness to have children or to have three, which was generally considered as ideal: (1) to complete the family; (2) to enjoy the children. In this study it was found that this group maintained a family that was smaller than they regarded as ideal, while investigation of those who were on relief revealed that they had families larger than they believed ideal. This study of the professional group shows nothing to indicate the loss of vitality of stock since the time required for conception among the couples in this group was on the average only two or three months.[14] No program to stimulate childbearing among the middle and the professional classes has promise that does not decrease the influence of the feeling of insecurity or of ambition as motives leading to the limiting of the family or the postponement or avoidance of parenthood.

Why are children chosen? Since popular thought assumes that human fertilization has become a matter of choice, the question Why do people have children? naturally arises. Once such an inquiry would have seemed needless, since then it was generally taken for granted that after marriage children as a rule would come whether they were wanted or not. In the majority of contemporary American homes pregnancy still occurs without any deliberation; it is regarded as a normal occurrence of marriage, just as it was a century ago. There is also another large number of families where the coming of children, or at least one child, is an accident, contrary to the expectation of the husband and wife. There are several reasons for these accidental pregnancies, but they come chiefly as a result of the ineffective methods carried on for the prevention of conception or because of faulty technique in using a better method. In

---

[13] Flanagan, John C., *A Study of Psychological Factors Related to Fertility,* Proceedings of the American Philosophical Society, Vol. 80, No. 4, pp. 513–520.

[14] *Ibid.*, p. 523.

addition to these two groups of parents, we have those who have chosen to have children, and it is to them that the question Why do people have children? must be directed.

It is important first of all to recognize how general is the inclination to have children among young people even when they take for granted that the decision lies with them. For example, in teaching large classes of men and women in the course in preparation for marriage at the University of North Carolina during the last twenty years, very rarely have the authors found a student, either man or woman, intending to marry who did not also expect to have children. In the few cases where either the man or the woman had looked forward to a childless home, this has been based upon a conscientious feeling that because of a hazardous heredity they had no right to have children. The great majority of these students have expected to have several children, the most favored number being three. It is of course true that the most sincere and strictly confidential statements of this sort may not, when put to the test, prove to have been a genuine decision. Nevertheless, the strength and uniformity of this attitude is significant, and the evidence at present justifies the belief that when a study is made of the families of these students it will be found that most of them who have not had children have been infertile. It is true that the majority of them have been natives of southeastern states where the birth rate is high, but those coming from the north and west have confessed to a similar family program. The same attitude has been found by others who have questioned American youth, but, although this direct attempt to get the information by the questionnaire method usually employed was not used at North Carolina, the information was volunteered in the student's report on the influences that have built the background for marriage, thus avoiding the element of suggestion which encourages reporting the desire to have children.

The Maryland study [15] conducted for The American Youth Commission is representative of the attempts to get the attitudes of youth toward childbearing by direct questioning. On the basis of statements from 11,707 youths it was found that 84 per cent of the boys and 89 per cent of the girls wanted at least

[15] Bell, Howard M., *Youth Tell Their Story*, p. 36.

one child. The older group, twenty-one to twenty-four years of age, were more desirous of children than those between the ages of sixteen to twenty, suggesting that it was a mature decision rather than a sentimental one.

In any attempt to analyze the motives which induced these young men and women voluntarily to desire later to become parents, it is important to keep in mind the natural tendency for rationalization. Here more than in many major life decisions there is a temptation to announce a desire for parenthood that is emotionally approved even when this is not a commanding impulse which will lead toward seeking pregnancy. Indeed, it is not safe to assume that the real reason why children are chosen or not is clear or conscious. In some instances, the difficulty of bringing about pregnancy has made clear the desire for parenthood, leaving no uncertainty as to the attitude of both the husband and wife. It is important also to recognize that the value of parenthood does not necessarily depend upon the motive that has led to it. Misconception of this fact is the chief reason why we must expect to find considerable rationalization when men and women explain why they chose to have children. Among these will be many who actually became parents through accident but who prefer emotionally, when looking backward, to regard the occurrence as a deliberate choice and for motives that they now approve.

Among the motivations that influence American men and women to seek parenthood are the following: First is the sense of social security. This may or may not include economic security which at an earlier period was one of the most powerful motives leading to parenthood. These men and women find the idea of a childless marriage dissatisfying. To them it represents an unconventional peculiarity, even a frustration. Only through the coming of children do they have the feeling of being safely established in their family life. Another group are influenced by religious motives. The feeling that parenthood represents the fulfillment of an obligation which is divinely sanctioned is found in all religions, with the exception of a few contrary groups such as the Shakers, but it is particularly strong in some Protestants sects, among Jews, and among Catholics. There is a group which can rightly be said to be impelled toward parenthood through the acceptance of social attitudes which they regard as conventional. To them parenthood is a social norm and it is the proper thing for them to seek children. This same type of person in the city often belongs to a group holding the contrary idea that the arrested family is conventional, and therefore they try to avoid having children. There is a small group who change from childlessness to parenthood because of the advice of a physician who believes that pregnancy will prove an advantage to the woman's health. Finally, among the major motivations frequently concealed in the thinking of the parent, is the desire to find through the child self-fulfillment. This motivation, wholesome for the matured and disciplined adult, may be just the opposite when it is an outgrowth of emotional immaturity, in which case rationalization is most prominent. Such a type of person cannot confess even to himself that the wish for children is for purposes of self-centered ambition or compensation.

In a study of 400 members of Princeton classes for the years 1902, 1912, 1913, and 1921, the following reasons were given why children were desired: companionship 82 per cent, perpetuation of the family 66 per cent, the sense of creating and developing a new life 63 per cent, the wish for an ideal relationship between parents 59 per cent, companionship in old age 48 per cent, the meeting of social obligations 40 per cent, desire to be conventional 35 per cent, unwillingness to use any artificial attempt to prevent conception 7 per cent.[16]

Another study brings out the meaning parenthood has for those who have chosen to have children. To some it has brought assurance of a biological fitness which was doubted during adolescence. To others it has afforded the opportunity for a fellowship of love, while to another group the presence of children has been a stabilizing influence. The satisfaction of parenthood to a different group is its comradeship, and to still another it provides opportunity to express personal ambition through the child. These statements bring out, as Bernard has wisely said,[17] the significance of the motives conscious or concealed that have led the parent to have children. These motives may be chiefly self-seeking demands rooted in the personality of the parent

[16] Dennison, Charles P., "Parenthood Attitudes of College Men," *Journal of Heredity*, Vol. 31, p. 528.

[17] Bernard, Jessie, *American Family Behavior*, p. 252.

which easily lead to the exploiting of the child. The true nature, however, of the motive must be found not in the verbal statement of the parent but in the actual practice of the father or mother in association with the child. Parenthood therefore provides means for the expression of personality traits which have taken form in the foundation of the life-period rather than after the birth of the child.

It would be misleading, however, not to recognize the complexity, even the inconsistency, of the motivations that lead to parenthood. Even when there is one clear, convincing explanation why the child was desired, analysis of the parent-child relationship discloses that there are also minor reasons, whether the adult realizes them or not.

Otto Klineberg calls attention to the man's satisfaction through parenthood because it gives proof of his virility. The urologist and the obstetrician have constant testimony of injury to pride that comes from questioning the male's fertility. It is this peculiar vanity that has led in the past so frequently to the examination of the woman first when there has been an investigation of the fertility of the spouses, the man refusing to be examined unless it was first demonstrated that the woman was not at fault; and this in spite of the fact that the examination of the male is simple in comparison with that of the female, and that both are usually somewhat at fault.

The problem of population. It is necessary in discussing the social significance of the arrested family to consider its relation to what is known as the problem of population. The relation between the number of people that must be fed and the food available for their support is a matter of the largest concern to society and one that since the publication of Malthus' famous "Essay on Population" has been much discussed. The great growth in the world's population during the nineteenth century, an increase of approximately 100 per cent, naturally brought forth the question of how long the people of the earth could continue to multiply at such a rate without a necessary decline in the standards of living. In the years before the Civil War the population of the United States increased over one-third of its total population each decade. With this increase of numbers there occurred a noticeable advance in the general standards of living.

During the latter half of the nineteenth century, there was in most European countries and in the United States a decline in the birth rate. In this country immigration has had an important influence upon the increase of population and upon the proportion of native stock. Partly because of economic competition between the natives and the new settlers and in part as a result of other social and economic conditions which would have operated had there been no immigration, the size of the families of native American stock has constantly decreased. This gradual displacement of the original stock by the later arrivals and their offspring is popularly known as our problem of race suicide.

It is clear that the influences which have tended to decrease births in this country have also encouraged the arrested family. From this viewpoint the arrested family may be regarded as one of the preventive checks that work against a too great birth rate. Even if desirable from this larger social outlook, the arrested family may nevertheless constitute, when considered in its domestic aspects, a serious social problem for the home. The fact that it is a means of giving social relief from excessive births does not change its influence upon those who maintain it. It may be both an advantage from the standpoint of population and also an obstacle that prevents many from receiving the full satisfactions of marriage.

The problem of population, however, is not merely one of quantity. The question of the quality of a people is also included, and it is in this fact that the social risk of the popularity of the arrested family is revealed. Many of those who choose to marry and go through life childless are just the people who by inheritance and favorable environment are well fitted to have children and give them a good preparation for life.

The arrested family cannot be treated merely as an effective means of decreasing births; it also is a relationship that influences the distribution of population. It leads a large proportion of those who are gifted and fortunate in material resources to deny themselves children and leaves to those less favored the opportunity to supply in excessive measure the population of the nation.

Adoption.   The only escape from the arrested family for infertile couples comes through the adoption of children. Adoption is not modern, indeed it has been suggested that it is probably as old as humanity itself.[18] It was a common procedure in the earliest historic periods, and it has been practiced among preliterate peoples in the earlier stages of human evolution. In times past adoption has been encouraged for ulterior motives, chiefly to make use of the labor of the child or to perpetuate the family. The humanitarian movement of the nineteenth century emphasized the child's needs and rights so much that it has been called the century of the child. One of the results of this interest in child welfare has been a tightening of the protections, both legal and social, of the adopted child.

Neither the law nor the administrative policies of child-placing agencies make it possible now for anyone who wishes to adopt a child. There has to be fulfillment of definite legal requirements, and in addition, as a rule, those who seek the child must pass a thorough investigation by the representative of some child-placing agency, the organization most likely to have a child for adoption. More and more the former American policy of keeping together orphan children within an asylum until they have reached late adolescence has given way to the child-placing agency which cares for the child for a brief period while giving him a thorough physical and mental examination. There is also a careful investigation of the character of persons asking for a child, their home conditions, and the resources they have for bringing up under adequate physical, educational and moral conditions any child that may be given them. They are not generally permitted to adopt a child immediately, since without fault on the part of either the foster parents or the child the placement may prove unfortunate and therefore a period of trial is wisest for both.

The most important questions that arise when childless couples seek to adopt a child have to do with the physical health and mental soundness of the candidate for adoption. This necessarily brings up the question of the child's inheritance. Since rarely do the adopting parents personally know the father and the mother, they must depend upon the information gathered by the agency. Nothing can be more tragic than for the foster parents to find later that they have legally become responsible

---

[18] Brooks, Lee M. and Evelyn C., *Adventuring in Adoption*, p. 93.

for a defective child. Knowledge of such happenings has come to the authors of this text. A seriously defective child, for his own welfare, as well as that of others, is best placed in an institution. When adoption is contemplated, therefore, it is necessary to seek the assistance of a social agency which accepts public responsibility for child placement and safeguards with modern effectiveness the interests of both the prospective parents and the child.

Illegitimate children naturally furnish the greatest source for adoption, and sometimes the fatherless child falls into the hands of a disreputable organization willing to turn him over to anyone who apparently has financial resources, with little regard to the character of the home to which he goes or the background of the child. Some childless couples, because of delay in getting a child for adoption through the legitimate channels, have been tempted to take a child wherever he may be found, judging his normality by his appearance. Attractiveness, especially in the very early period of infancy, affords no security of physical or mental soundness. The childless couple should realize always that the care with which they are themselves investigated reveals also the attention the agency gives to the heredity and the physical and mental health of the child.

Adoption, even when thoroughly safeguarded, has its own problems. Is it, for example, fair to a child to have him or her adopted—and it is most likely to be a girl—by two maiden women, even if they are conscientious, financially responsible, and efficient? Can they justly take over the bringing up of a child when they cannot provide him with a normal home? The question arises all the more forcefully when it is one unmarried woman who is seeking to adopt a child. Since there are so many husband-and-wife families who want children by adoption, it is always open to question whether an unmarried woman should be permitted to take over control of a child's career. Is it desirable to encourage a family who have but one child, and who, fearing too much concentration of affection upon him, desire to provide competition by adoption of a child? Under such circumstances can they be trusted to be just to the child they adopt?

Occasionally a different kind of problem arises when couples that have been childless for a long time find that they are going to have a child of their own although, having believed that this could not happen, they have already adopted a child. Experience also demonstrates that sometimes, in spite of the strength of the desire for adopting the child, one parent or both is not happy in the new relationship. This is always a greater liability than in the case of one's own child, because it seems as if since adoption was deliberate it should be justified by the satisfactions that it brings. Although adoption by the right persons permits the arrested family to become a normal home, it is not something to be entered upon lightly, even when childlessness is undesired by both husband and wife.

The backward family. The backward family for different reasons than the arrested family also fails to move forward to the experiences characteristic of the culture of its period. Family standards are, of course, relative; and a backward family is one that has failed to keep pace with general progress. Socially it is maladjusted, and as a consequence it does not furnish its members the education or the satisfactions that are enjoyed by more adequate families. The word "backward" always raises the question of degree, but, although there are families on the borderland the classification of which would lead to differences of opinion, there are multitudes of families concerning whose backwardness there would not be question.

Although the term backward suggests retardation and in consequence a failure to adjust to the logical meaning of the situation, it also emphasizes the contemporary character of such a classification. As a rule, a backward family will be regarded as out of step by those passing the indictment. The peculiarity of the family consists in its failure to keep in accord with the changing conventions, that is, the folkways and mores that have domestic influence. Such a family may be indicted for its peculiar quality, but this criticism assumes superiority for what is conventional at the period in comparison with those conventions of the past to which the backward family clings. It is, however, fallacious to regard a mere change as progress and especially when social changes are rapidly occurring to suppose that they are consistently advantageous even when the trend appears undubitably forward to the critical observer. Therefore, the family may be rightly considered backward and may clearly suffer the consequences of such a failure to adjust while there would still be the question whether its practices were inferior to the domestic conventions of the moment reflecting the social environment. Thus, although there is no doubt concerning the existence of the family that can be properly called backward, the description does not determine the quality of the family but merely calls it into question. The term backward is frequently applied to family life in another connotation. It then represents a minority judgment condemning the family that is conventional. This point of view, for example, was illustrated by Charlotte Perkins Gilman who in her time attempted to reform the contemporary family program, criticizing it not because it was out of accord with the prevailing conventions but because it catered to them rather than to the changed situation which was making them backward.

Cultural lag.   One type of family is backward because it maintains traditions that lag behind the general practices of the time and place. Immigrants who have failed to assimilate American culture comprise a large proportion of our inadequate families. Since there are native families who also fail to make normal adjustment in their home life to rapidly changing circumstances, it is not strange that those coming from another country, often with a culture in sharp contrast to that which they find here, have special difficulty in wisely adapting themselves to new conditions. Commonly in the immigrant family the backwardness is enforced by the older members, leading to the various sorts of tension and conflict so familiar to all who come in close contact with the home life of immigrants.

These families are not the only ones that are backward on account of cultural lag. In our cities are families that have migrated from the open country after the parents have reached later life and that reveal disturbances due to the difference in ideals between the older and younger members. Family life offers to those who cling to earlier practices and traditions that have long been hardened into habit the most inviting of all their social experiences as they seek refuge from changes that they find difficult and irritating. As we would expect under such circumstances, there are husbands and fathers who adjust tolerably well to circumstances outside the home, on account of economic necessity, but who do their utmost to hold the family to accustomed ways. In interpreting their attitude one must

keep in mind the fact that the influences of the prevailing culture, as they see it reflected in their children, seem, and often
are, disintegrating.

In any discussion of nonconformity as expressed in family
life it is imperative to keep in mind how individualistic American practices have been. Our cultural atmosphere has invited
nonconformity. There has usually been great tolerance of the
social expression of individuality along all lines. With this national characteristic it is natural that we should find great differences in domestic practices, standards, and ideals. The adjustment of the family is rarely merely that of adaptation to
the immediate social environment. Instead of this we have, as a
rule, the family attempting to adjust to a great and somewhat
inconsistent social complex. Although objectively this deserves
to be called a social lag, subjectively interpreted there is no lag
because adjustment is being made to the culture as it is known
and accepted by the family members.

The endeavor to pass on the quality of the family as an
institution attempting social adjustment involves also the recognition of compartments in our culture. We have sectional, class,
and religious cultural conformities so that a particular family
in its practices may be in accord with the core of culture to
which it is chiefly attached while at variance with the contemporary family of its time and place and thereby revealing a
lag. In such instances it is common to find a considerable difference of attitudes between the parents and the adolescent, the
former leaning toward conforming to the cultural environment
to which they are subjectively annexed, while the younger members reveal a drifting toward the culture with which they are
having constant contact outside the family. This has been vividly illustrated both by immigrant families and by those belonging to a peculiar and primitive religious sect.

The isolated family.   There is another type of backward
family which results from physical or social isolation or from
both. Sometimes the isolation is deliberately chosen, sometimes
it is imposed by the mores, and at other times it comes from
conditions of the physical environment. The family that keeps
to itself illustrates the first; the Negro family in many sections
of our country illustrates the second; and the lighthouse family,
the third. The isolated family which resulted from difficulties

of physical contact has been greatly decreased as a result of modern invention. For example, the keeper of the island lighthouse with his wife and children may not often meet with people, but they can be in radio contact with the neighboring city every day of their life.

Some of the effective influences that have tended in recent years to diminish the family isolated because of physical circumstances have been good roads, the automobile, the radio, spread of public schools and popular education, and especially the movies. Nothing at present in American lives spreads culture so effectively among young people as the movies, since they reach the emotions and appeal to the romantic interest of youth even more than do the schools. In his study of the isolated family, Lee Brooks says that the most important consequences of the physically isolated family appeared in diet, midwifery, age at marriage, ignorance of birth control, and reactions resulting from limitations of religious, educational, and æsthetic experience.[19]

As modern life through the use of inventions sweeps into the one-time backward communities, it is made apparent that this type of arrested family is a victim of circumstances and rarely a product of physical, social, or moral degeneration. Family life fails to go forward with advancing culture because of lack of opportunity to know and use the resources of American civilization.

It is rare indeed now to find in any American communities isolated families. They still exist in the southern Appalachian Mountain area, for example, but they are rapidly disappearing. Cultural isolation is more common. It produces a family that is unadapting because it faces backward or walls itself in from the outside life through commitment to some peculiar social or religious program or because on the other hand it has gone beyond the contemporary social environment into what it regards as the near future and a superior cultural situation. Isolation, as we now find it, is therefore usually not indicative of a limiting physical environment but rather an example of a self-maintained nonconformity.

---

[19] Brooks, Lee M., *A Study of Primary Group Isolation*, p. 236. Unpublished dissertation, on file at the University of North Carolina. Quoted by permission.

Chapter 15

THE BROKEN FAMILY

FOREWORD. When we think of the family, we naturally assume a home of children and two parents. We have already discussed a special type of family in which there are no children. We must now recognize another variation from the normal family—a home that has lost one of the parents or lacks the stability of parental backgrounds which is characteristic of wholesome American home life. A convenient term for these two kinds of families is the "broken family," although it is often used to refer only to the home where there is but one parent. The broken home necessarily encounters special hazards because of its misfortune or limitation. This does not mean that it has to be a badly adjusted or unhappy home. The student, therefore, must keep in mind that these homes that we are considering are domestic situations that require special adjustment lest they become sources of trouble for the personalities involved, especially the children.

Social significance of the broken family. The family broken by the death of one of the parents, by divorce, or separation, or desertion, is unable to carry on its normal functions. In his sample study, which included wives 44 years of age or younger and husbands 49 years of age or younger, Professor Ogburn found that in 1930 there were 14.6 per cent of broken families. Had he studied an older age group the proportion would have been larger. On the other hand, had there been a greater number of rural families, the percentage would have been smaller, since the proportion of broken families appears to be about twice as great in the cities as in the country. In interpreting these statistics it must be kept in mind that a family separated may appear as two.[1] From 1900 to 1930 the number of families broken by death decreased from 7.6 to 4.9 per cent, but during the same term those broken by divorce, annulment, or separation increased from 6.7 to 9.8 per cent.[2]

The family broken by divorce. There are relationships that are broken, even when they have led to considerable intimacy, with little consequence; sometimes those involved feel relief that the association has finally come to an end, sometimes they have a mild regret that it ever started. The family, from its make-up, is an intimacy that cannot issue in a breakdown without risk of untoward results. The dissolving of a marriage through divorce frequently illustrates this. The effect of a given divorce on the lives of the different persons concerned varies in accord with the circumstances, such as the amount of attention the divorce has received and the attitude of neighbors and relatives toward it, the religious background of those formerly united by family ties, the living conditions that are endured or enjoyed after the decree of separation.

It is thought by many that a divorce has little significance for the husband and wife in cases where there are no children or when the children have grown up. This assumption, however, cannot be maintained by anyone familiar with the results of some of our divorces, even when the marriage has been childless. Some of these reactions are indeed morbid, but if the divorce trial has received sensational publicity or if one of the parties concerned is particularly sensitive, or if the road that led to marriage was especially bright with promise, thus making the anticlimax of divorce all the more disappointing, the dissolution of marriage injects bitterness into the personality and at times creates antisocial attitudes. It is doubtful whether any couples who have started marriage with genuine affection are left after their divorce entirely free from scar. Those who seek marriage from purely sexual motives (using sexual in its narrowest meaning, void of the psychic element which idealizes and spiritualizes the more mature attraction) escape most lightly the consequences of divorce.

There are those also—and they must not be forgotten,

---

[1] Ogburn, W. F., *Recent Social Trends in the United States,* Vol. 1, pp. 689–690.

[2] *Ibid.,* p. 690.

though they are in a minority—who look back upon the divorce procedure, for which they were themselves responsible, with deep regret, since divorce as well as marriage can be entered upon without due consideration, under the sway of a fleeting emotion. The conscientious lawyer, who is called upon to give counsel to a husband or wife that is seeking a divorce while under the spell of a temporary fit of anger or resentment or in the midst of an unfinished quarrel, knows how easily reconciliation can be brought about in a number of cases if the effort is tactfully made. It sometimes happens, even while the trial for divorce is proceeding, that the contestants settle their differences, and not always with the assistance of their attorneys. The divorce sought without serious deliberation, in a momentary mood or for superficial reasons, may entirely change the personality and discolor forever the outlook upon life.

Problems of the divorced. The adjustment that those divorced have to make is often not an easy one. The entire program of life has to be reconstructed, and this proves complicated even in those cases in which the divorce is sought that there may be an immediate marriage with some other person. Although public opinion is far more tolerant toward those divorced than was formerly true, rarely does one obtain a divorce without encountering as a consequence some expression of social disapproval or aloofness. In some localities and in some professions this reaction may go so far as to become a genuine hostility. For example, it is rarely possible for a minister to be divorced without seriously injuring, if not ruining, his career. In one's own circle there is bound to be some gossip as soon as knowledge of divorce proceedings becomes public. It is common also to find among one's friends, especially those of the opposite sex, a degree of restraint, or on the part of some men, contempt, in their association with those who have become divorced. The seriousness of these social difficulties varies, of course, with localities and with social groups, but it is seldom that the divorced person is not conscious of a new social situation which requires readjustment to persons and circumstances.

There also has to be personal adaptation that usually involves the emotions. Past ideals must be repudiated and even the memory may be a source of conflict. Then, also, the admission of matrimonial failure usually hurts one's pride, and if the divorce has been contested and has received much publicity, there may be genuine shame. The sensitive person repeatedly shrinks from the explanation so often expected by friends and relatives and from the evidence of a change of attitude on the part of former associates. And always, whatever the inner feeling, there is need of concealment of any emotion that will add force to the gossip or widen the social estrangement.

The economic difficulties brought forward by divorce may prove hard to handle and are seldom anticipated. The wife who has been for several years a housekeeper and has no inviting opportunity in a vocation or profession finds her new economic status extremely hazardous. Even if she has been given alimony, it is only in favored cases that she is as adequately financed as formerly. Sometimes she refuses to take money from her husband, not realizing how difficult she may find the attempt to support herself. She may assume that she can go back to her former occupation, only to discover that the time she has spent as a housewife makes her re-entering employment difficult. The husband who is required to pay alimony may find that after he is divorced his financial problems have grown beyond anything experienced during marriage. If his earning capacity changes, and the divorce itself may bring this about, the alimony fixed by the court's decree when he was in more fortunate circumstances may become a grievous burden. Unless he is wealthy, the man who is obligated to pay alimony is likely to find this difficult if he remarries. When this second union brings children, the problem becomes greater with each increase in his second family, especially if there are minor children who were born during his first marriage. If the man petitions the court for a reconsideration of the amount of alimony decreed, the judge has placed upon him a decision hard to make in fairness to both the former and the present family. The younger children cannot rightly be penalized because their father, already responsible for children by his first marriage, dared for a second time to establish a family. The situation may be complicated by the fact that the first wife may be, for some reason, incapable of bringing in any income herself. She must, therefore, depend upon alimony or charity or public support or some combination of these. Rarely, however, is there any just reason for denying the man she divorced the right to remarry or to have children by his second wife. Social workers have come to know many households where the mother either refuses alimony or receives an inadequate sum, while attempting to maintain her home, bring up her children, and also support them by her meager earnings in some outside employment. Contact with such brave mothers, who, too often, in spite of their heroic struggles cannot give their children adequate support, tempts these social workers to favor the court's granting alimony to an amount which, in fact, would be a penalizing decree, a bar to the re-establishment of family life by the man through remarriage. Even when this seems a just punishment for his misdoings, it is clearly a questionable policy, a misuse of the authority of the court to prevent a marriage which, when looked at from the wider background of public welfare is desirable.[3]

Divorce is likely also to produce a physical stress which was not foreseen. The abrupt ending of the sex side of marriage is sure to bring to young people who are physically normal a protest from the body which is heightened by the emotions associated with its cause. In the case of the death of the mate there is a somewhat similar experience, but mitigated by memories of the past and by a spiritual fellowship maintained through memories and imagination. Those who are divorced have no such influences to help them in their new adjustment to life.

Children of the divorced.   Although divorce may mar adults, it is the children of the divorced who run the greater risk of being hurt. The truth of this is generally recognized, for everybody regards a divorce procedure where children are involved as much more serious than one in which husband and wife are the only interested parties. It is, of course, true that some divorces are obtained primarily because one parent sees that the welfare of the children demands separation from the intolerable conditions of the home as it exists, but in contrast with this are the greater number of parents who for the sake of their children are willing to continue a marriage situation which, were the problem of concern only to themselves, they would at once take to the courts. Recently, for example, a woman obtained a divorce for which she had waited thirty years, believing it better for the children to have a father than

---

[3] Rood, Royal D., *Matrimonial Shoals*, p. 312.

for her to get the relief which she was justified in seeking; therefore, she carried her family burden until her youngest child was well established, when she at once went to the court.

It is impossible to unravel the social factors that influence developing character with a precision that shows how far a home broken by divorce is responsible for delinquency and other forms of youthful failure. We also do not know to what extent the child who has suffered by his parents' divorce receives hurt that carries over into his adult experience and becomes a cause of unhappiness or failure in later life. Although the conditions that influence the life of a child who has grown up in a home broken by divorce are too complicated to be expressed satisfactorily in statistics, there can be no doubt that the divorce of their parents is for many children a real social handicap.

Social workers who deal with juvenile delinquency find divorce or separation constantly recurring, either as the chief cause or as a contributing cause of the child's difficulty. In view of this fact, the state fails in its obligations to child life if it does not attempt, through legislation, to conserve marriage and faithfully safeguard the interests of children in all divorce litigation by the wisest laws it can frame.

The consequences of family desertion are similar to those of divorce, but in the case of the former it is more difficult to trace the causal influence. This comes about because the majority of families deserted have so many unfavorable conditions that work against the welfare of the family group. The poverty that may have preceded the desertion or resulted from it, inefficient housekeeping, bad housing, a vicious neighborhood, intermittent schooling, or the unfavorable reputation of the family may make it impossible to estimate how much social harm comes to the children from the desertion directly and how much their career is warped by other bad influences.

The influence of the break in the home on the child is determined by his reaction to the new domestic situation. It is, therefore, not the physical change but the psychological meaning it has that measures its consequences.[4] Such experience is potentially emotional, since the child is deprived of one

---

[4] *The Adolescent in the Family*, Committee on the Family and Parent Education, White House Conference of Child Health and Protection, Vol. 38, p. 119.

of his relationships from which normally he should draw the feeling of security through the intimate fellowship of affection. The loss of the parent, however, may mean little to the child because he has never been given such an association; therefore, the physical absence of the parent does not disturb him. Indeed, it may, on the contrary, increase his feeling of security, for he may no longer be exposed to such a situation as results when there is constant quarreling between the parents or some other chronic expression of family discord. The consequences of the broken home, as is true in all domestic situations, are never automatic or stereotyped but always individual. The sensitivity of the child and the meaning to him of his former relationship with the parent whom he has now lost decide what happens. The responsibility of the remaining parent is increased. It may be difficult to keep the child from being seriously hurt, but a person of good judgment, self-restraint, and discernment can accomplish the task. The effort may also be therapeutic for the parent who has thrust upon him or her the double role of father and mother. In many cases the step-parent proves to be the happy solution.

In a family broken by divorce, the age of the child tends to influence whatever hazard develops. In the case of the younger child, his feeling of insecurity is likely to stem from a loss of personal belonging. He misses the contact he formerly had and the assurance it brought. In the older child, another element is added—a feeling of social insecurity based upon his belief that the family has suffered a loss of prestige. When one of his parents divorces the other, the adolescent may be hurt chiefly because he develops an inferiority feeling which hampers him in courtship or becomes a distrust, conscious or concealed, which he carries over into his own marriage and which takes away the assurance he needs for successful matrimonial adjustment. His basic motive for marrying may be to recover his onetime confidence, but skepticism, born of his parents' experience, may deny him what he craves and needs.

Families broken by death. No greater tragedy can come to a family than the death of the father or mother, for added to the grief at the parting of the life of the parent beloved, there is in the case of children a broken family of the most serious kind.

Although the surviving parent may double his efforts in his endeavor to make good the loss suffered by the children, in spite of all he or she does, the family circle is at once stripped of its normal atmosphere and the home functions as a broken instrument. There is general agreement that the family that has lost its mother encounters greater trials than if it is the father who has died, for hers is the larger contribution. The father who is left to care for little children because of the death of the mother faces a very difficult problem and one increasingly hard to solve. A generation ago, an unmarried relative offered the commonest and best solution and in cases where there were none to be called upon a housekeeper could usually be had. The new economic opportunities for women have greatly changed this situation; relatives are far less likely to feel it their duty to assume a task that all recognize to be a severe test of character, and efficient housekeepers, at least for men with moderate incomes, are even more scarce than sacrificing relatives.

As a rule, widowers find the only solution of their problem to be a remarriage, but although this gives them an immediate way out of their predicament it is likely to create perplexities that do not exist in the normal unbroken family.

Naturally the man hesitates to remarry and experiments, if he possibly can, with other solutions. His delay in the effort to rebuild a home life heightens the risk involved in bringing a new wife into the household; the children may have been hurt during the period of transition—indeed, the recognition of this fact may be the compelling reason why the father has finally remarried. At any rate, the children have grown older and are more likely, unless they are still very young, to sense the difference between the new regime and the old, which memory idealizes. The burden the new mother assumes is apt to be one which the most courageous woman would instinctively shrink from accepting. As a consequence, the broken family is repaired but may not be cemented into an affectionate unity. If the new wife brings her own children into the family circle, complications are multiplied. In spite of all the hazards incident to such a rebuilding of the home life, many foster mothers succeed wonderfully, and the children suffer nothing that human skill and good purposes in such circumstances can prevent.

Any form of bereavement brings a crisis to the individual family, requiring new adjustment of the remaining members. Former behavior patterns are broken up and new ones constructed. In this attempt to re-establish the family routine there appear, as Eliot has so clearly described in detail, the immediate effects of bereavement and the secondary reactions.[5] In families broken by the death of the mother there is likely to be an aggravating of these conflicts and difficulties of readjustment. In addition to the influences of personal grief there is a new economic situation which by itself, under any circumstances, would create tension.

It is interesting to have from an experienced social worker, acquainted with the problems of the motherless family, the statement that in the following situations the effort to keep the family together is generally unsuccessful: (1) when a paid housekeeper is engaged; (2) when a girl under sixteen is in charge of the family, unless there are only one or two in the family and she is carefully supervised by a relative or some organization; (3) when the man is not exceptionally stable, or when he works irregularly, or drinks; (4) when the children have not had good training in the home during the time the mother was with them.[6]

The step-parent.   We have come to realize from observation that anyone who accepts with understanding the role of a step-parent is a person of courage. The undertaking also is charged with potential difficulties for the child, because it demands a new adjustment. Here, as in the case of the family broken by divorce, the outcome is determined by individual situations, the interaction of the various family members. The step-parent has a large part in its outcome but not necessarily the determining one. The child's reaction may be the decisive fact, or the influence of grandparents or other relatives may play the most important role. Each step-parent situation is unique, but if the child can recover his sense of family unity the remarrying of his father or mother tends to lessen any hurt he may have suffered through the breaking of his former home.

[5] Eliot, Thomas D., "The Bereaved Family," *The Annals of the American Academy of Political and Social Science,* Vol. 160, pp. 184–190.

[6] Clow, Lucia, "Motherless Families," *The Family,* Vol. 9, No. 1, pp. 11–14. Quoted by permission.

He may, however, resent the coming of the step-parent and he is more likely to feel jealousy as he sees the affection of his parent for the new life partner than is true of most children, who in an unbroken home react against the love between the parents which denies them the monopoly of affection which they crave. The step-parent may, however, eventually win the child's confidence and help him to find, in this second home experience, as great or even greater security than in his former family relationships. If, following the divorce or death of the former parent, the remaining mother or father heaped upon the child excessive expression of affection, the step-parent is more apt to encounter the obstacle of jealousy from the child who wishes to retain the exclusive fellowship he has enjoyed since the breaking up of his first home. The younger the child, the easier the task of the step-parent. Every generalization, however, is conditioned by the fact that the significance of a second marriage as it affects any child involved is determined by the totality of the interaction of the family members, including the disposition and the former experience of the child as well as the character, tact, sympathy, and insight of the step-parent.

Families broken by religious differences. Bereavement results in an acute breaking of family life. Serious religious differences within the home bring about a chronic breaking of family unity with the same hazards appearing in the reactions of individuals to the persistent division.

It is a common observation that the marriage of couples brought up under the influence of religions that are widely separated assumes an extra hazard. We do not at present know just how influential religious differences in childhood are in breaking down the unity of family life. A recent investigation made by one of my students of some sixty families that represented marriages of mixed religion, and that were in difficulties of one sort or another great enough to bring them to the attention of a social agency, did not yield any definite conclusion as to how far religious differences operate against successful family life. The study made clear, however, the fact that most of the families were hampered by the differences in religious traditions, so that their unlike faiths were at least contributing causes to the family problem. It was also evident that the interference of relatives who wished the household committed to one of the two churches represented was at times the origin of trouble. The couples studied represented marriages of individuals brought up under the dominance of the fundamentally different religious traditions of the Roman Catholic Church, the Jewish Synagogue, and the Protestant denominations. One experienced in dealing with family discord of religious origin knows that a home where one of the parents is a strong adherent to the Christian Science faith and the other is violently opposed to it produces a most tumultuous type of family discord.

Since morality and idealism are almost universally rooted in religious faith, the home broken by religious dissension can become particularly mischievous in its influence upon the developing character of its young children. Not only do they run risk of losing all respect for religion, but their impressions of moral anarchy as a result of the clashing of their parents' early teaching may rob them of all ethical conviction.

Family broken by racial and cultural differences. The marriage of couples representing two fundamentally different races, even when happy for the individuals concerned, creates social difficulties of the most serious sort for the family, and, in the case of the marriage of a white and black in this country, results in tragedy for the child which makes normal development impossible. The child soon realizes that each parent is outside the fellowship and traditions of the group to which the other belongs. Although by color of skin and social conventions the child may find himself forced to remain within the racial group to which the Negro parent belongs, the influence of the white parent may be predominant in the home, and because of this the child in his attitudes and outlook upon life may be fully committed to the Caucasian group. Under such circumstances only the strongest individual can free himself from a deep sense of social inferiority. From a strictly social point of view, the intermarriage of individuals of races whose differences stand in such sharp contrast as those of Negroes and whites or American and Oriental represents in the United States a matrimonial handicap from which all but the bravest or most thoughtless persons would shrink.

The career of the immigrant in America illustrates the difficulties of a family adjusted to one culture adapting itself to widely different social conditions. The problem created is not merely that which we see in the immigrant who has recently arrived and cannot speak English. The helplessness of the foreigner who speaks another language than ours and has been accustomed to a very unlike social environment may attract our attention because of his need of assistance, but often the adult who has been with us five, ten, or fifteen years and who speaks English and wears American clothes, is, in spite of appearance, so linked in habit and attitude to his former experience as to make him almost as badly adjusted to American civilization as he was the day he landed on our shores.

The tug between the old and the new is bound to show itself to some extent in the atmosphere of the immigrant home. It is, however, the gulf that develops all too commonly between the parents and children that constitutes the graver social problem.

Although the child, to all outward appearance, has become thoroughly American, it is seldom that he has received no injury in his social development because of the antagonistic contact between the culture of his home and that of the school and community life. At school he has been taught one thing and at home another until he finds it difficult to commit himself absolutely to either one of his contending environments. Perhaps he changes his name to one more American in sound and ridicules the customs to which the parents attempt to adhere. What he does brings great pain to his parents, and his regret for their suffering makes him react excessively, even to such an extent that he either denounces things American or stifles his conscience and smothers affection in his determination to escape the marks of his parents' culture. Inconsistency of conduct is the more natural, since the immigrant of the second generation finds it difficult often to hold steadfastly either to his sympathies for American life or to his affectionate regard for the ways of his parents.

If he marries a woman who has been brought up in a home consistently American, the new family may be overshadowed by the tragic conflict of his original family circle. In his attitude toward his wife he may be inconsistent, at times acting in an intolerant manner under the influence of his parents' tradition, at other times being overgenerous in his desire to be characteristically American. It is difficult for him not to show the same division which has been built into his personality in his dealings with his own children. As he senses their difficulties, he feels anew the discord which he suffered in his father's home.

It takes little imagination to picture the handicap of the child of the immigrant who is thus tossed about by two antagonistic emotional currents and to realize why he figures so prominently in the records of the juvenile court. One must not forget in judging his difficulties that he is fortunate if he never has occasion to resent the reaction, at least as he interprets it, of the American portion of his community, an irritation from which he suffers in addition to his family situation.

It is the reactions of the individual family that decide the results of cultural differences, as these two contrasting cases reveal:

Case A

My father was born in Denmark, where he spent his boyhood as a cowboy in the true sense of the word, a barefoot boy who tended cows. His parents inculcated in him the idea that work was holiness for a young boy and that idleness was the very devil. Implicit obedience in every regard was demanded of him, and he grew up under a family regime in which the man was master, the wife a servant, and the children puppets. The ways of his people were stolid and severe, and it is still an enigma to me how my grandmother ever overcame her Danish imperturbability enough to take her family and move to the United States.

My mother had an equally severe and circumscribed upbringing in Sweden so that she, too, was imbued with the strait-laced European notion of family life. She came to this country when she was twenty, having heard that it was the promised land, but she got off to a bad start when she got into a French boarding house in New York and learned to speak French under the impression that it was English.

The Dane and the Swede met in Ohio, and after an unemotional and sexless Nordic courtship they were married and engendered four children within eight years. I, unfortunately, was one of these. If we had been brought up in Sweden or Denmark everything would have been rosy, but the difficulty arose in my parents' attempt to establish a Scandinavian family in the United States.

My brother and I went to Sweden for two years with our mother, and since we learned to talk while we were over there we could not speak English when we started school in this country. Naturally all the children made fun of us; so I immediately became a decided introvert, shunning all associations which might have brought hurt to my newly developed sensitivity. The conflict in the family was strong and of long duration. We were told one thing at home, another thing at school, and still other phases of the same subjects by children acquaintances; so we were in a quandary as to which authority to accept. This conflict of cultures dragged me about so much that I became almost a misanthrope. I began to feel out of place no matter where I was or what I was doing. I was sullen most of the time at home, because my parents were always without reason in their demands. That they asked something or denied something was reason enough for their doing so. If I requested an explanation quite sincerely I was told that a kid had no business questioning his parents. They ruled supreme. And we had to adopt the philosophy, "Ours not to question why; ours but to do and die." I enlarged somewhat on this fatalism and adapted it to: "Mine not to question why; mine but to do as I pleased and to keep my mouth shut about it."

Sex was never explained to us; that was meant to remain a sweet mystery of life. And cards, women, dancing, smoking, drinking, parties, and such were all taboo for life. That explains my later indulgence in all of them. I even lied and cheated and perpetrated petty thieveries to "show them." It is always a pleasure to go beyond restrictions.

The divine-right-of-parents idea in the heads of my mother and father finally caused me to leave home. I had always been amenable to reason, and where there was no attempt to be reasonable I could not stay. The household was always sullen and freighted with disapproval. I would go for weeks without speaking a word to anyone in the family, and we were all thoroughly unhappy most of the time. I hated restriction, and they hated insubordination, so we all hated each other with a sort of undemonstrative gusto.

I have wandered "lonely as a cloud" for several years now, but little as I like to be homeless I prefer it to returning to the situation I endured before. And naturally, feeling thus keenly the failure of the home from which I came, I desire all the more to manage differently in the home which I shall some day establish. With that horrible example always before my mind's eye I should be able to avoid committing the crimes of unreasonableness and outrageous omission of my parents. I feel that the problem in my home could have been solved by education and by a more thorough degree of Americanization. Neither of my parents had even a high-school education, and when they came to this country they consorted with people of their own nationality, bringing a piece of Europe with them instead of leaving it all behind as they might better have. Although I realize the value of culture dissemination, the effect on myself was more deleterious than otherwise.

So this is just another broken family, because my brother, too, left when he had had enough. I may see my parents again sometime or I may not; it makes no difference to me. If I do encounter them accidentally it will be like meeting an old acquaintance who had done you dirt long in the past. We would be frigidly polite if we said anything at all. My chief regrets are that the lack of home life leaves a void in my life, and that I must perforce pay my own bills through school. I may be unfortunately objective about all this, but it is not so of my own volition. This has been a process of mechanical psychological extrusion.

Case B

I am a member of an immigrant family from Germany, although I was only about four years old on arrival in the United States. I have also a sister, now thirteen years of age, who was born in this country. We still speak German with our mother, but English with our father, though Mother can read and write English very well. My father was forced to stay here in 1914 due to international law concerning vessels of warring nations in neutral harbors. In 1916 my mother and I came over merely for a visit and to get away from the distressing conditions for a while, it being thought that the war was almost over.

Now, it so happened that the war continued and we remained in the United States and endured all the terrible war propaganda, which would have been enough to curdle anyone's love for the United States. Yet, there is at the present time in our home not the least trace of conflict. A few years after the war things got toned down and everything worked smoothly.

A few years ago we ceased taking a German newspaper. I joined the Boy Scouts and entered an American high school and university, things which would have been unthought of a few years after the war.

Families broken by moral separation between parents. Separation within the family caused by differences of moral standards becomes a serious obstacle to the wholesome development of children; a moral discord creates a deep cleavage. The parent that resents the vicious conduct and bad reputation of the other parent, who has brought disgrace to the home, is constantly trying to protect the child from following in the evil footsteps. The attempt to save the child from the influence of the bad parent is almost certain to be overdone and by its very excess to attract the attention and perhaps the interest of the young child. The parent who realizes that he is being held up as a horrible example may do his best to combat the teaching of the other parent who is striving to undermine his influence with his own children. In spite of bad conduct he may have the more appealing personality, and knowledge of this fact intensifies the resentment of the righteous parent.

Sooner or later the child as he grows up is certain to receive from some source in his life outside the home disapproval or suspicion which is born of his parent's fault in those cases where the family disgrace is publicly known; in other cases, where the parent's misdoings have been successfully concealed, he is likely to have fear of their possible discovery or to feel that he is not quite honest in keeping from his friends something that might influence their conduct toward him. One young woman in this predicament was forced by her conscience to tell the man to whom she was engaged to be married, shortly before the wedding, of her father's theft, his disappearance, and her adoption by an aunt with the change of her name. Although the confession was received most generously by her lover, her tension and remorse and her questioning whether she had a right to marry became at least contributing causes to a mental condition of which there had been no premonition, but which required her commitment for a considerable period to a hospital for the insane.

So far as parental functioning is concerned, many families deserve to be called broken that, according to our conventional classification, are regarded as normal homes. The child needs not only two parents for his best development; he needs also active fellowship with both of them. This double contact is too often denied. It is not uncommon to hear from young people the statement that their father, less often their mother, meant little to them during their childhood. Sometimes the child, so far as his parent's contribution is concerned, is essentially an emotional orphan, but this is relatively rare among American families. We find it occasionally among the wealthy who farm their children out during most of the year at some boarding school and in the summer at a camp. At the other economic extreme, among the very poor we find households that do not deserve even to be called homes because of the parents' attitude, their drinking, vice, and neglect of all their responsibilities, including, of course, the welfare of their children. This difference is in absolute contrast with the characteristic of a different kind of underprivileged family, where parental feeling, especially in the mother, is exceedingly strong, leading on her part to much struggle and sacrifice in the attempt to do the best possible for the child.

If there are proportionately few American families where both parents are indifferent, there are a great many in which only one parent functions in such a way as to offer to the child the genuine relationship he needs for his proper emotional development and wholesome outlook upon life. It is the father who is more apt to deny the child this needful fellowship. In the legal, even the conventional, aspect, the father may not be open to criticism. He is a good provider and is guilty of no overt cruelty or injustice. He merely turns the child over to the mother, frequently interfering with the child's training only when he inflicts discipline. His failure to provide comradeship for his child renders the home, only in a lesser degree than when he dies or is divorced, incomplete and, in that sense, broken. It is not merely that the child fails to get the sympathy and security which he seeks from one of the two adults closest to him; he is denied also the advantages of intimate association with two different personalities. It is well for him, from his first days of consciousness, to have access to a man and a woman who necessarily reflect different backgrounds. This assures him, as he grows toward maturity, a positive influence which will widen his area of experience and prepare him for the diversities of social life he must later encounter. He is saved from being a one-person's child.

The indifferent parent, who remains aloof from the child, denies himself experiences that would not only enrich his own character but would also add quality to the home itself. This nonfunctioning of the parent is not always his choice. The work he has to do to support the family, the demands made upon him by his professional career, may forbid giving the child the time he would like. Competition, highly developed in our country, does tempt toward crowding out the family and thereby hampers the normal functioning of our most important social institution. This, however, was never less true than at present, and, in most cases, the real explanation of the parent's neglect is lack of will rather than the demands of business or his profession. Those who become slaves to their ambition are most tempted to deny the child their needful contact while perhaps at the same time being in other ways too indulgent. Few Americans have had a more busy, versatile, and responsible life than Theodore Roosevelt, who found time, even when President of the United States, to give bountifully to his children, as his volume of letters to them testifies. A marriage counselor, close to family life, not only becomes impressed with the loss that comes to children when they have parents who emotionally neglect them, but also becomes convinced that in a great many cases the failure of the parents comes from their not realizing the importance, the pleasure, and the easiness of the child-parent comradeship.

Families broken by an absent parent. There are many homes from which husbands because of the nature of their business frequently and for long periods are absent. Although this does not by any means constitute in most cases a broken family, it is occasionally the first cause of a family catastrophe. To a certain extent, family conditions are similar to those where the husband has died. The children are excessively under the influence of the mother and lack the comradeship and insight of the father at times when they are forced to meet a crisis while the father happens to be away. The father, as a result of his lack of comradeship, may not understand his children sufficiently to influence them wisely, while they in turn may miss the intimacy necessary for their affection. If his home-comings are usually marked by punishment inflicted on the children at the request of the wife for their conduct during his absence, he at once becomes to them an intermittent police official whom they may fear but cannot love.

The traveling father, if he faces his handicap squarely, can offset much of the loss due to his absences by corresponding with his children, by generous comradeship at those times when he is at home, and by interesting his children in his own travel and experiences, and when possible by sometimes taking one of his children with him on his travels. When some such program is followed, not only do the children look forward, during his absence, to the father's return, but they will become intimate and confidential immediately after his arrival.

Families in which it is the mother that is often absent are not common, but when they occur they reveal even greater difficulties than those appearing in the homes where the father is often absent. Even this most difficult kind of family situation has been by intelligent handling prevented from breaking down family unity. Such a program is rarely possible unless some relative or efficient and trusted substitute takes over the management of the periodically motherless family.

The family broken by unmarried motherhood.   The child born to an unmarried mother usually experiences from his first days of consciousness the hazards of a special kind of broken home. This, of course, is not true of the child who is removed from his mother and placed through adoption in a family life where he will have both a foster father and mother. Experience has demonstrated that in a large proportion of cases it is for the advantage of the mother to be permitted to keep her child.[7] The child may give to the mother the motivation which she requires for her recovery of interest in life. Also her right to the child seems a just reward for the biologic role she has accepted in bringing him into the world. These advantages for her own rehabilitation do not remove the liability the child faces from not having a father to contribute to his development during his early years. What is even more psychically hazardous is his lack of understanding why he has been denied this association.

The peculiar problems presented by the home broken because of illegitimacy emphasize the fact that the situation of each unmarried mother must be handled, not according to generalizations, but individually, with recognition always that the welfare both of the mother and the child must be considered. The home may not remain broken, for the father of the child and the mother may eventually marry or the mother may marry some other man who is willing to accept the fact that she has given birth to an illegitimate child. The mother may maintain fellowship with her child in the home of her

---

[7] Barrett, Robert S., *The Care of the Unmarried Mother,* Ch. 6.

own parents or other relatives. Least desirable of all, she may have a degree of association with her child, whom she has placed in some sort of boardinghouse. This solution is apt to give the child less security than if he were placed in a foster home with little or no contact with his mother. If the mother can have adequate support from the father of her child, she can provide a home life similar to that of the child whose father has been divorced or who has died. Such support should almost always be sought if the mother has the character and disposition to care adequately for the child and needs economic help, but, if possible, this should be accomplished without publicity.

It is now generally recognized that a forced marriage very rarely proves a desirable solution for the problems of the unmarried mother. The conventional attitude in this country toward illegitimacy has been such as to encourage the forcing of the man responsible into marriage in order to save the child from the disgrace and handicaps of being illegitimate. This program, however, is seldom more than a temporary expediency. Although a means of escaping the penalty of American folkways and mores, it is not likely to provide the child with a normal, unbroken home.

The social disapproval of unmarried parenthood, much more strongly directed against the mother than the father, is a far more serious handicap to the normal development of the child than his being brought up in a home in which there is no father. Some progress toward a more humane and constructive attitude toward illegitimacy has been made in this country, and the advance still continues. This shows itself especially in laws which attempt to improve the status of the illegitimate child and give him greater social protection. These are discussed in Chapter 19.

The family broken by constant migration. A real home requires permanent settlement. This is well illustrated by the family life of the gypsy, which, even when strongly knit together, has been necessarily meager. A wandering family cannot establish the community contacts that form part of the substance of a normal home. In these days we have a new type of gypsy family life in the automobile migrants.

These families, found in greatest abundance in the Far West and the South, and especially in Florida and California, wander about in their cheap cars, frequently, like the gypsies of old, receiving enough from the generous people whom they meet to keep them on their way. They are not, of course, all the same in their characteristics or in the motives of their going about. Some travel in expensive cars, splendidly equipped, because they enjoy the life better than conventional travel, while others take to the car because only so have they hope of satisfying their wanderlust. Although the automobile is not the only means employed by the migratory family, it is the most common. Three other methods of getting about are popular: by a wagon, with its wooden or canvas top; by train, generally at the expense of Chambers of Commerce or charitable agencies; and by hitchhiking. This last is, of course, the favorite locomotion among individual migrants, but it is also habitually chosen by a portion of the migrant families that find it easy to get lifts from kindhearted automobilists who are willing to convey the family group so ostentatiously in need of assistance.

There are all sorts of motives behind the wanderer: restlessness, response to advertising, the lure of the romance of the West and South, expectations of a new start in life, the desire to improve or find health, craving for frontier experience, longing to be rid of conventional habits of life, and pure love of automobile travel.

The family, once it takes on the habit of moving from place to place, rarely escapes a loss of its normal functioning. It becomes broken by its inability to build permanent ties or to accept definite social responsibilities. The child's attachments are so transitory that he is robbed of much of the emotional meaning of home life. The adults, as a consequence of their drifting program, lose whatever social stability they once had. The family also suffers from loss of any considerable habit life, and there is a spirit of irresponsibility that shows itself in all the undertakings of the family through failure to develop normal habits, particularly the habit of steady work on the part of the father. Associations are temporary and contribute little to self-discipline and the learning of the art of living with others.

Want of conveniences, lack of privacy—in short, the meagerness of the home—reduces to the smallest proportion the value of family fellowship. Although the migratory family is in a position to do so little for the children, the latter are likely to suffer the added misfortune of little or no schooling. Not only may the child fail to find in his migratory family the security and character-building influences that belong to the home, but he may also be purposely exploited by his parents or by persons who in some manner have got him in their charge. The following extracts from reports of social agencies dealing with migratory families afford a glimpse of the menace this nomad experience may be to children.

If a family stays long enough for the Compulsory Education Department to get after them, they move on. The children develop a wanderlust and restlessness . . . are much excited at the prospect of moving on to a new place and plainly show the love of adventure which a roving life . . . presents. They work along with their parents in the fields gathering cotton and walnuts, picking berries and fruit. They are considered an asset. . . . It is not infrequent that the parents tell us they could not "make a go of it" without the help of their children. . . . We have been morally certain that couples were not married, and that some of the children did not belong to the group but had been picked up in some unexplainable manner and were being used to provide meal tickets.[8]

The development of the trailer has made possible a more responsible type of migratory family. These mobile homes because of their moving about maintain a limited type of household life but they are not necessarily broken. The majority of people who travel in trailers use them for vacations only. The cost of the trailer and its maintenance are such that most of these mobile homes represent the middle and in some proportion the wealthy class. The greater number of trailer families are composed of a husband and wife. Frequently they have children who·have grown up and who live the conventional, settled life elsewhere. In a recent study, it was found that the average size of the trailer family was 2.5 persons. When small children of school age accompany their parents they usually attend school and therefore their parents are likely to remain for a considerable period in one community. In response to the needs of this higher type of migratory family we have, especially in the North Central section, in Florida, the Pacific Coast, and the Rocky Mountain sections trailer parks. Some of these cater to

---

[8] Buffington, A. A., "Automobile Migrants," *The Family*, Vol. 6, No. 5, p. 151.

families who remain for a considerable period, often an entire season.[9] These families are quite unlike those constantly on the move; they seek inexpensive housing of their own choice and freedom to settle down for a season among congenial people and pleasant conditions.

During World War II the trailer was used to furnish housing in congested, industrial communities. It was a substitute for the apartments and private dwellings which would have been preferred had there been any choice. If these families had children, as was often true, they were hampered for space, but even so they were more fortunate than some who attempted to live in one room or even in tents as some did during the earlier period of the great industrial expansion. This use of the trailer continued after the war on account of the lack of houses in many communities.

It is evident that the increase of leisure, especially of aged people, will encourage the trailer type of home. It is not likely, however, that one-half the population of the United States will be living in automobile trailers within twenty years[10] or even thirty.[11] There is nothing to indicate that half, even, of the aged people will desire the kind of home life characteristic of the trailer, but it will be favored by more people than was true before World War II. Improvements adding to its convenience and attractiveness will encourage more families, especially those made up of elderly men and women, to move with the seasons north and south as they carry on such housekeeping as is possible in the limited space of such mobile housing.

The migrant labor problem includes a family life disturbed by constant going from place to place. Many of these seasonal workers follow the ripening of crops and not only are denied permanent settlement but frequently encounter inadequate housing conditions. The children at best have interrupted school life and lack proper supervision if both parents work, as often happens. Increasing attention has been given to this problem of the migrant laborer and in some communities

[9] Cowgill, Donald O., "The Size of Families," *Mobile Homes: A Study of Trailer Life,* American Council on Public Affairs Monograph, p. 46.

[10] Babson, Roger W., "We'll Soon Be Living on Wheels," *Trailer Travel,* Vol. 1 (January, 1936), No. 1, p. 10. (Reprint from Los Angeles Times.)

[11] Stout, William B., "The New Roll-Your-Home Era," *Trailer Travel,* Vol. 1 (May 1936), No. 3, p. 15.

there has been an improvement as temporary housing has been provided and greater effort has been made to meet the school and health needs of the children.

Families broken by continued unemployment. Social workers have had a long experience with families broken by the unemployment of the head of the household. The world-wide depression, revealed first in its full seriousness in 1929, brought to a large proportion of American families the problems that come with unemployment, failure of family income, and a general feeling of economic insecurity. These experiences placed a strain on families, many of whom had always enjoyed comfortable circumstances, with the consequence that a large number, in spite of public relief, were broken in morale, failing to carry on with success their normal functions. Discipline disappeared, leading to constant friction within the household. The man unable to get work often hid behind a neurotic illness, became depressed with feelings of guilt, or attempted by bullying tactics to win again the prominence in the family given him when he was employed. Families formerly peaceful developed the chronic fault of quarreling. Some husbands and wives, taking refuge in different forms of morbid behavior, added all the more to the burden pressing upon the family. Youth, particularly the boys, sought relief by leaving home, and in great numbers took to hitchhiking or riding the freights.

The depression affected the younger children as seriously, even if with less spectacular results, denying them food, clothing, and medical care necessary for their wholesome growth and hurting them emotionally through the insecurity, restlessness, bitterness, friction, despair, and low standards appearing in the family.

Specialists in economics believe that following the reconstruction period of World War II there is danger of another widespread depression. If this should happen, all the adverse influences that affected family life and marriage during our last depression will doubtless be repeated and more disastrously than ever in the past. There is more awareness of this risk, however, among our social and political leaders and a greater effort to prevent what is primarily a domestic calamity. Unemployment insurance is one of the methods of protecting family life from the consequences of a depression.

Negro broken homes. In the southeast so many Negro wives and mothers are employed in domestic service and therefore absent from their own homes for the greater part of the day, that this absence of both parents from homes in which there are children has become a characteristic trait of much of the Negro family life in that section. Small children, too young to go to school, frequently are cared for by a grandparent or other relative, by a neighbor, or by some other adult or older child who is paid for this service by several working mothers. Older children are largely left to do as they please out of school hours. Even in small villages there is need of some sort of well-regulated day nursery such as is found in cities. The social problems of the older Negro child would be reduced were there more recreational facilities or provision for organized play after school closes. Although opportunities for such recreation are increasing, the situation in many communities is such as to encourage idleness and delinquency. The inadequacy of both the home and the community handicaps these Negro children in comparison with the opportunities provided for the average white child.

During World War II many Negro women went into industries, especially in northern and western cities. This for many was the first nondomestic employment. Although their added income affected favorably the material conditions of family life, the separation of mother and child frequently had a detrimental result, in some cases becoming an influence leading to delinquency.

Families broken by war conditions. World War I and, in a greater degree, World War II led to much broken home life. In many families as a consequence of the first war the father was removed from the home through his chronic invalidism or permanent mental disease. These homes, by necessity, became one-parent households. The same situation was temporarily true in a great many homes during World War II, even though it was generally recognized that fathers of children ought not to be drafted until all able-bodied single men whose work was not absolutely essential to the war effort had been taken. Many fathers volunteered early in the conflict; others later had to be sent into the armed forces in order to fill necessary quotas. The full effect of the war experience as it brought temporarily or permanently broken families cannot be known until the children involved have had time to reveal what the war did to their development.

Social implications of the broken family.   A broken family does not necessarily become unstable or unwholesome, but it does encounter extraordinary hazards, and the outcome of its trying experience depends upon the character of the family members, the former standards and practices of the home, and the amount of assistance it receives when it requires help to meet its ordeal.

When the home has been broken or in any way becomes unstable, it must be dealt with as an individual problem. The social worker who assumes the task of helping the family soon discovers that the family disaster cannot often be treated in isolation. A family breakdown produces social consequences; social conditions outside the home are in large measure the forces that wreck the home.

The broken family, once it becomes disorganized, is difficult to mend. The constructive policy of social service stresses preventive work, for no amount of patching home misfortunes will prevent other families from going wrong. Social strategy requires that we keep in mind the implications of family disorder and encourage every movement that makes for wise ways of living and wholesome character. We shall always have broken families to deal with, but whether we have few or many and handle those we have with much or little success is primarily determined by the soundness of society and the efficiency of its relief organizations.

Chapter 16

THE INCOMPATIBLE FAMILY

FOREWORD. Some students in family courses recoil against discussing such a problem as is the topic of this chapter. They insist that it depresses them and imply that the instruction should present a more favorable picture of family life. In some instances this reaction is basically due to the individual's personal experience in an unhappy home. Even when this is true, it proves to the advantage of the student to discuss frankly the difficulties and failures of family life. Were this not true, however, the interpreter of family relationships would have no choice. Incompatibilities do develop in marriage and family life, and they cannot be pushed aside because there is an unthinking and therefore imprudent romantic disposition which prefers to ignore them. This realistic presentation of domestic incompatibilities, however, does not justify nor does it create a pessimistic attitude toward marriage and the family.

Incompatibility in the family. Incompatibility, like its opposite, good adjustment, is relative. The significance of family discord is measurable by its consequences. In all family life, as in every other intimate human association, there are differences of opinion, occasional tensions, and even downright antagonisms. These experiences of friction may go along with the building and the maintenance of a co-operative fellowship or they may be evidences of failure to establish harmonious relations. The incompatible family reveals itself not through the quantity of dissension but by the effect that these collisions of personalities have upon the character of the family members, their attitudes toward each other, and their satisfaction in their life together. These consequences are determined both by the characteristics of the personalities involved and by their social situation. For example, if such contention is rather common in the set or neighborhood to which the family belongs, the family discord will usually have a smaller effect than when this lack of harmony is very unlike the experiences of friends and neighbors. Particularly does this relativity show itself in the results that come to the child from family incompatibility.

Every human relationship makes a peculiar test of the ability of those entering it to get on together and furnishes its own opportunities for incompatible reactions. Business partners, friends, and lovers have their co-operation tested differently, and when disharmony arises its results are in accord with the characteristic features of the relationship. The family also brings not a general but a specific type of testing. Its peculiarities come chiefly from the constancy and the intimacy of the relationship.

The background of family incompatibility. Family incompatibility is but a special form of social maladjustment, and its diagnosis requires full use of the technique science has developed for the analysis of conduct. Conditions that antagonize efficient behavior operate with peculiar force in so intimate a relation as that provided by the family.

The background of the family incompatibility may be conscious or unconscious. Awareness of the conditions that bring it about does not necessarily add tolerance or sympathy as members of the family react in contact with the individual who is being influenced by his personality make-up or some social causation which is operating upon his disposition and behavior. Instead, he is likely to be blamed for his self-expression, and instead of his character or conduct being regarded as in part the product of causes beyond his control he is held fully responsible for doing what he did as if his traits were deliberate and self-chosen. Frequently his operating background is both conscious and also unconscious. Occasionally the victim himself understands the sources of his difficulty and makes use of his knowledge as an excuse rather than as a means of greater control. An analysis of this cultural background permits clarifying the influences as originating in the personality, in cultural differences, or in social conditions. Most often we find that there is a combination of these sources even when one clearly predominates and chiefly explains the incompatibility.

Since successful marriage or family life depends upon a satisfying adjustment of the persons in association, it is obvious that the chief source of trouble is the personal disposition of one or more of those living together. Each personality is a composite product. It may be that the individual experiences frustration in all or most of his undertakings, or, on the contrary, this may appear only in the marriage or the family relationship or in some major aspect of it or in the interaction with some particular member of the family group. The frustrations that attract most attention are those developing through the contact of the husband and the wife. Not only is the range of possible tensions great, extending over the entire area of domestic relationships, but also there is the greatest variability in degree, ranging from trivial and therefore inconsequential wishing that something was different to such strong protests as to force emotional separation. It is not the nature of the trait that determines the amount of frustration but the meaning it has to the individual reacting against it. Thus the disposition of the two interacting personalities is always involved. If, for example, the husband is the offender, the significance of his self-expression is determined by the reception it receives from the wife. Frustration, therefore, always has a dual causation, but the incompatibility when analyzed to its final causation discloses the basic dispositions of the two individuals interacting adversely. This usually is not the interpretation that the two in the unhappy relationship are likely to make of their predicament. On the contrary, they are most apt to consider their troubles due to certain offenses or omissions even when there is no inclination to blame the individual who is regarded as responsible for what he does or fails to do.

The courtship period is expected to disclose these fundamental character obstructions. The interactions of the man and the woman drawn toward each other during this prelude to marriage are held within a limited area of experience and at a time when realistic thinking and mutual insight are difficult. Even with these handicaps, courtship does prevent many hazardous marriages because during the association frustration appears. Courtship and domestic incompatibility originate from personality differences as well as from personality defects. They

arise because the persons in interaction being what they are
cannot maintain agreeable relationships. Even when the characteristic traits of each personality involved have the determining
decision, the clashing may reflect cultural influences or a social
situation which aggravates potential personality liabilities that
easily become incitements toward maladjustment. Although incompatibility in marriage and family life represents a conflict
of self-expressing personalities, thoroughgoing analysis frequently carries us to the recognition of definite external circumstances that operate causatively on one or more of the
clashing individuals. The importance of these outside influences justifies our distinguishing them even though they assert
themselves through the individual responding to them. This
does not mean that the personality becomes a mere medium for
environmental pressure, a passive instrument victimized by
outside forces, but rather that in the clashing of personalities
analysis discloses that external contributions in some marriage
or family discords are so significant as to stand out prominently.
These may be classified as belonging to a cultural background
or originating from a social situation.

Each personality is a product of cultural assimilation. The
consequence of this is that in marriage or family relationships
trouble comes to those interacting to one another because of
unlike or antagonistic social developments. This assimilation
from the cultural setting is greatest and most potent in the degree that it was gathered in early childhood. Such a cultural
germination is apt to be so thoroughly woven into the personality that the reacting individual is unconscious of the command it has and unaware of its source. Religious belief and
commitment is an illustration. The hazards of a mixed marriage, such as the marriage of a Protestant and a Catholic, come
from this difference in the two backgrounds which have gradually formed over a considerable period during which basic
attitudes toward life have taken shape. It is not merely unlikeness of creed or worship or ideals of conduct but a complexity
of feeling, thinking, and behavior that has been rooted in religious teachings.

Another type of conflict of cultural origin appears in the
concept of the role that has become proper for the man and
that for the woman. Each is a two-faced role because it includes

one's own and that belonging to the mate. An example of this as a potential cause of conflict is the marriage of an oriental and an occidental. We have a vivid picture of this form of incompatibility in Baroness Ishimoto's *Facing Two Ways*.[1] She, although Japanese by birth, became westernized and married a man of her own country who had had a similar experience. In time it appeared that she held to her western reconstruction while he went back to his earlier eastern training, with the consequence of a tragic separation which eventually ended in a divorce.

Another type of cultural background that makes for trouble can be described as status. We have in every cultural group differences that are best defined as those of class. Each group possesses characteristic patterns of behavior, attitudes, and common sentiments. The mating of two personalities who have been shaped by influences of unlike class status have forced upon them greater need for accommodation, that is, tolerance, understanding, and mutual adjustment, than successful marriage usually requires of those of the same class. Not only is this generally recognized but also the fact that this dissimilarity of background does not necessarily command the situation. Such a marriage does not face inevitable failure but rather invites special tension with the decision of relationship finally determined by the personalities of the two interacting persons.

Another type of clashing due to cultural background may be described as the influence of social situation. We have marriages that get into trouble because they force upon one or both persons unfamiliar or unexpected conditions that are resented and may be so distasteful as to bring forth antipathy toward the marriage relationship. An example of this is an incompatibility arising when a woman who has had the advantages of wealth marries a man of meager income and recoils from the changed standard of living which she finds unacceptable. A different illustration is found in the experience of a young woman who having enjoyed the advantages of urban life married a mining engineer and attempted to establish a home in a western mining town where there was no other woman of similar background. She eventually solved her problem by going back east

---

[1] Ishimoto, Baroness Shidzue, *Facing Two Ways*.

with her child, where once every year or so her husband came for a brief visit.

Another type of the influence of social situation comes when there is a marked change in circumstances. Perhaps the husband, a prosperous business man, fails and does not find any other employment that brings him anything approaching his previous income. Another expression of this same causal influence is found when one personality changes through development while the other remains stationary. This happens often enough to be credited with a portion of incompatibilities that strain American marriage relationships. We find illustrations of this when a man engaged to a home-town girl continues his education at the university while she makes no effort toward greater intellectual growth. When later they marry, tension arises after a brief period in many such cases because of the changed situation. One spouse has outgrown the other, and this becomes the cause of a cleavage that increases rapidly once it is realized by either husband or wife or by both.

Incompatibility at the beginning of marriage. The most critical period of marriage, as a rule, is its beginning. No undertaking in life is so influenced in its later course by the conditions of its start as is marriage. There are various reasons for this. The happenings at the commencement of married life are embedded in the emotions in a way that magnifies their importance out of all proportion to the meaning they would have under ordinary circumstances; subsequent events also are apt to take on a coloring due to the memories of the first days of matrimony. The more fatigued, worried, or self-conscious either husband or wife is when passing into marriage through the gateway of the wedding, the greater is the risk of emotional stress with its rapid fluctuations and inconsistencies.

Even when no strong emotional undercurrent exists, the early days of married life are particularly significant, for immediately there commences an attempt to reorganize the lives of the two persons who were previously adjusted to different circumstances and other individuals. Even if the courtship has been unusually long and frank, the new relationship completely changes the interaction of the two personalities and forces a different state of intimacy.

It must not be thought from this that there is a definite

procedure through which husband and wife pass in the readjusting process of the honeymoon. Human nature does not operate by a fixed rule. Some individuals slide with little difficulty into the new relationship. Others have considerable trouble, but once they come to their new understanding all goes well and they remember with a smile their serious efforts to meet problems that as they look backward appear so trivial. Still others appear most fortunate in their ease of adjustment, but the passing of time reveals that they were really only extending courtship into marriage and postponing their inevitable disillusionment. When they finally settle down in grim earnest to meet the problems of living together, it grows increasingly clear that they cannot be happy. Then there are some who at once discover the folly of their marriage, their unfitness for one another, and a cleavage begins immediately and widens with time. Whatever the situation at the beginning of marriage, the current starts flowing toward or away from a successful family life.

The conditions that prevail during courtship determine in marked measure the amount of readjustment that the husband and wife have to make during the early days of marriage. The duration of the courtship, its freedom, its emotional intensity, and its opportunities for association are some of these influencing circumstances. They are not, however, environmental causations that stand apart from the personalities, but they play a great part in the accumulation of courtship influences which affect marriage. The love attraction and response attempt normally to usurp consciousness, thereby pushing aside patterns of behavior and traits of character that later in the intimacy of marriage will once more find expression. The engagement period is expected to lessen the differences between courtship and marriage experience, and this it usually does but not sufficiently to prevent the need of a new, more realistic fellowship after the wedding. The concentration of interest and the idealization associated with falling in love both exclude much of the habit-life belonging to each individual and also bring into being new and compelling attitudes and behavior. Waller [2] goes so far as to describe this as an etherizing of many

---

[2] Waller, Willard, *The Family*, p. 306.

of the important tendencies of both the man and the woman. Whatever analogy we use to interpret what happens, it has to be recognized that during a courtship of any length, and especially once the engagement has been made, basic traits of personality faintly or fully intrude, and frequently the consequence of this is an awareness on the part of one or the other of the lovers that in spite of the emotional attraction marriage is too hazardous to be undertaken.

It is the proper function of the honeymoon to offer a favorable period for transition from the premarriage to the everyday marriage experience. Although it is a culmination of the romantic glow of courtship, it also introduces to the union a new companionship from which the marriage must draw its substance and its stability. The inclination of the newly married to spend their honeymoon away from their accustomed place of living is in accord with the psychic passage each has to make from the highly romantic anticipation to the demands and opportunities of their real routine life together. Courtship may be said to be illusive, but in the same sense that any intense looking forward, the product of the imagination, fails to foretaste the different reactions that come with changed circumstances. This readjustment need not be interpreted to mean that marriage must become an anticlimax. Successful marriage is fulfillment of the drives that led to the expectations but not in the form or with the exactness romance pictured. The happily married have no desire to go back to the fervor of courtship or the thrill of the honeymoon. The craving for this backward retreat is demonstration of the failure of the relationship to go forward and mature. The need of making this adjustment does not indicate a failure that will ensue in incompatibility. On the contrary, unwillingness or inability to reconstruct the association in a more realistic manner does reveal the insecurity of the fellowship, prophesying that once the marriage has to face the actualities of life, dissatisfaction will develop and in time incompatibility.

In some measure readjustment is unescapable as the man and woman enter their new relationship of marriage. Irrespective of what has been true previously, marriage creates an original situation demanding a reshaping of their relationship. This reconstruction may be insufficient because one or both are clinging too much to the premarriage conditions, or it may be inadequate for the routine of life as soon as this is established. Either of these reactions represents in essence a postponement of the needed adjustment, creating the conditions for incompatibility and sooner or later the realities make insistent demands for a more fact-facing adaption. Quarreling can easily come about if one or both of the spouses are determined that the temporary settlement continue. As a rule, successful accommodation develops gradually through a series of adaptations and mutual understandings, and in some degree this is likely to be the history of the entire married life. It is important to recognize that successful marriage requires more than a substantial and realistic adjustment. There is need also that it prove agreeable to both concerned; otherwise, even though it provides a workable program of domestic relationship, it will prove frustrating to the spouse whom it antagonizes. There is no set pattern of behavior which assures success.

In some way, if the marriage is to be satisfying, there must be successful passage from the romantic prelude of marriage to the establishment of a mutual habit, the product of satisfying interaction within their intimate fellowship. When this is not achieved, incompatibility results. In his study of two hundred married persons, Hamilton found that fifty-seven were dissatisfied before the end of the first year, thirty-nine by the end of the second year, and twenty-one more stated that they were unhappy but did not indicate how soon after marriage they became conscious of their incompatibility.[3]

Instruction as to marriage problems cannot prevent this necessary process of adjustment, but a previous understanding of possible difficulties does help to make the transition easier and its dangers fewer. The greater risk of committing some costly mistake falls upon those who have no insight into the testing they are receiving in their attempt to find happiness together.

A mistake in strategy.   A mistake often made in the first steps of homemaking, perhaps more common among those who achieve happiness than among those who fail, is the blunder of taking too seriously some part of the new experience. It is more

---

[3] Hamilton, G. V., *Research in Marriage,* p. 69.

often the bride who comes to grief by too much concern. She has heard much of the need of changing her habits and committing herself thoroughly to the matrimonial venture. Driven by love and influenced by her emotional state of mind, she cuts herself off from all her old ways, interests, friends, and relatives, and ties herself utterly to her new experiences. After a time she finds that she has thrown overboard too much, but not until she has lost associations that she ought to have retained or interests that would have kept her from a morbid concentration upon her home. She regrets the friends she has dismissed, who now have departed from her life because they have been so carelessly treated and have been actually given to understand that they are no longer a very essential part of her world. After a little she looks back to what she threw away, blames the marriage, and assumes that married life requires this breakage. It is well to consider a matrimonial undertaking as a long trip that needs a program which one can find satisfying not merely at the start but for the whole journey.

The mistaken strategy of a newly married wife, which expresses itself in too great concentration on the home and a far more radical departure from her past life than the husband, is the result of an overconcern. She has had pressed upon her from many quarters the necessity of making a new adjustment, and, because of her sense of responsibility and loyalty, she simply goes too far and assumes a program that becomes eventually too thwarting of her personal desire to be acceptable as a long-time course of action. Her mistaken policy results from the fact that her adaptation is subjective rather than objective. Unconsciously she is directing her efforts to fulfilling preconceived ideas rather than meeting the actual circumstances as they arise. As she has looked forward to marriage, she has built up ideals of behavior and has made fulfillment of these a demonstration of her affection. Possibly the husband has a similar program, but whatever their preconceptions may be, marriage brings demand that the adjustment be not an act of sacrificial spirit but an attempt to meet common interests and the realities of their life. Their progress must be built upon their new association rather than upon the daydreaming that preceded marriage.

To reconstruct one's self-expression is not good in itself;

neither is it demanded as a test of the genuineness of affection. Marriage does require new adjustments but only because the individual has been placed in a new situation and therefore must modify the behavior that was developed in adapting to the previous single life. The new settlement cannot be a fixed program of conduct which with little variation will continue throughout the husband-wife relationship. Instead it is a beginning of adjustments that must continue to bring changes from time to time as the domestic environment, including the reactions of both spouses, takes different forms. Marriage brings so ostentatious a break from the individual's past that it is easy to feel that the new adaptation is more final than experience soon reveals it to be. Tension can come from this fact when the program that has been adopted with a generous disregard of former habits and values by the husband or wife appears, because of the effort it has cost, a relationship that deserves to be permanent. Success may be interpreted as a product of complete adjustment to this pattern of behavior that has been accepted but which in fact is in great measure as subjective as were the preconceptions preceding the marriage. Therefore it cannot remain as a life program but can only serve as the beginning of an objectiveness which should become more stable, revealing, and compelling as the marriage career progresses.

Exploitation.   The tendency of either husband or wife to exploit the other is one of the most common and perplexing of marriage difficulties. We can assume that from the start of the homemaking one is a little more sacrificing and affectionate than the other. Being part of the new experience of pleasant intimacy, this is rather pleasant for both, and when it runs rapidly on there is on one side a strong desire to sacrifice and on the other a great willingness to accept the sacrifice. If this lasts for any length of time—and once started it often persists throughout life—the resultant family situation is distinctly bad for both. It has come about naturally enough, but it acts more and more against the family welfare. If it does not last, when the movement swings back to something more normal, there may be on the part of the person who received the sacrifice the feeling that the other's affection has weakened. Experience shows that it is the woman rather than the man that is apt to be too prone to sacrifice. It is therefore the man who suffers most from the fact that he becomes the exploiter. The one who gives, develops, though not so far as judgment is concerned; the other becomes unfair and selfish, even childish.

The making of a well-balanced adjustment is complicated by the fact that there must be on the part of both husband and wife some surrender of their ego, and, of course, in each there is the tendency as a result of previous habit not to give up but to cling to what has been characteristic. Success does not depend upon an equality in self-surrender but rather in the bringing about of such proportionate self-expression and self-denial as will permit satisfactory fellowship and will not create in either the conditions of frustration. It is not, therefore, a question of how much or how little egoistic each is in comparison with the other but rather the reaction of each spouse to the total situation which they develop together.

This establishment of domestic organization takes no account of the detrimental effect it may have on the character of the individual whose self-concentration may be encouraged. We commonly speak of spoiling children, and, although this is an exaggeration, it is a forceful way of stressing the injury to character that can come from catering to a child's self-centered interests. To emphasize a similar damage to personality from one spouse being permitted to exploit the other, we can refer to the spoiled husband or wife who has been hurt from the beginning of marriage by an increasing selfishness. Basically this may be the exploitation of the self-seeking person through ministering to his weaknesses, but for the observer who passes conventional judgment it seems that the generous inclinations of the other spouse are being exploited. In whatever manner the relationship is interpreted, the criticism it receives is an attempt to show that however acceptable the relationship may be it impairs the quality of the marriage. We may even find one spouse welcoming the other's egoistic demands, but in spite of this willingness to accept subserviency the character of the union is lowered. In judging the nature of a marriage, we are concerned not merely with how well adjustment has been made but even more with what has been the effect on the character of both spouses of this adjusting and what has been the emotional reaction of each individual to it. It is in the consequences of this domestic settlement rather than in its failure that the novelist and dramatist find the most profound of the tragedies of love attraction as well as its highest achievement.

Quarrels of husbands and wives.   The matters concerning which husbands and wives quarrel are not necessarily the causes of incompatibility, since they may be merely the occasion for the expression of tension. Some degree of sex incompatibility is rarely absent when husbands and wives constantly quarrel. It may be either the root of their difficulty or a medium through which estrangement is revealed. In the latter case, it may become in turn a cause of still greater alienation. Sex incompatibility may be rooted in physical or psychic conditions, or in a combination of both, and the responsibility may belong to the husband or the wife or both of them.

Finances are another common cause of trouble between husbands and wives. Most often the wife's grievance is the inability of the husband to earn more, and the husband's, his belief that the wife is extravagant. Another common cause of tension is difference of opinion as to how children should be treated. The most frequent form of this is dispute regarding the kind of punishment that should be given the child for disobedience or some other misconduct. A fourth source of conflict, often the underlying motive of quarrels regarding sex, children, and money, is antagonism created by the thought that there has been a decided change since marriage in the attitude of the husband or wife, and the loss of affection. The existence of such a suspicion or conviction as the motivating impulse does not, of course, prove that it is the origin of the difficulty, since it may itself come chiefly from jealousy or some other fault of personality in husband or wife, or in both. In the attempt to get at the meaning of incompatibility, it helps to analyze the background out of which comes dissension rather than the expressions that the quarrels of husband and wife take.

A recent study [4] gives a factual insight into the factors involved in the breakdown and, conversely, in the persistence of the marital union. The source of this material is the letters of three hundred and ninety married women who asked for

---

[4] Ciocco, Antonio, "On Human Social Biology, Disruptive and Cohesive Factors in the Marital Group," *Human Biology*, December, 1938.

advice and assistance as they wrestled with personal marital problems. They sought help from a well-known personal adviser. Letters were received during a three-month period and were one thousand, five hundred in number. Of these three hundred and ninety came from married women who were concerned with difficulties in intramarital relations. The letters received from men who were confronted with the same problems were so few that they did not justify a separate analysis and were therefore excluded from the study. Not only does this correspondence record the sort of problems these women face but also their own idea as to a solution, since in every case they stated what they thought ought to be done and gave their reasons for this decision. The following table gives the chief complaints made by these women.

TABLE I [5]

THE STATED ELEMENTS OF THE MARITAL CONFLICTS
EXPERIENCED BY 390 WOMEN

ELEMENTS OF CONFLICT	WOMEN	
	Number	Percentage
Relative to specific intramarital relations:		
Masculine domination	80	20.5
Affective maladjustment	72	18.5
Nonsupport	28	7.2
Sexual-reproductive disharmony	21	5.4
Relative to husband's extramarital behavior:		
Infidelity	123	31.5
In-laws	36	9.2
Social vices	30	7.7
All elements together	390	100.0

The author found that conflicts due to maladjustment were more commonly reported by younger women and the husband's unfaithfulness by the oldest. The first was the complaint of 42.3 per cent of the women who were younger than 20 years and of only 10 per cent of those who were 40 years or over. On the other hand, unfaithfulness of the husband was charged by 55 per cent of the oldest women and by only 3.8

---

[5] *Ibid.*, p. 559.

per cent of the youngest group. The following table shows the period of duration of the marriages in which the conflicts are reported.

TABLE II [6]

MARRIAGE DURATION AND ELEMENTS OF MARITAL CONFLICT

ELEMENTS OF CONFLICT	MARRIAGE DURATION (IN YEARS)						TOTAL WOMEN	MEAN MARRIAGE DURATION (IN YEARS)
	Under 5		5–14		15 and over			
	Number	Percentage	Number	Percentage	Number	Percentage		
Affective malad- justment......	35	28.5	13	16.7	9	11.5	57	6.7
Masculine domi- nation........	26	21.1	15	19.2	14	17.9	55	8.8
Infidelity........	21	17.1	30	38.5	38	48.7	89	12.4
Nonsupport......	12	9.8	7	9.0	3	3.8	22	7.0
Social vices......	10	8.1	4	5.1	9	11.5	23	10.4
Sexual-reproduc- tive disharmony	10	8.1	3	3.8	3	3.8	16	6.9
In-laws.........	9	7.3	6	7.7	2	2.6	17	6.9
All elements......	123	100.0	78	100.0	78	99.8	279	9.3

The reaction of these women to their incompatibility was classified in this study as shown in the table on page 453.

It is interesting to notice that although all these women were unhappily married and were permitted by law considerable freedom of action in dealing with their incompatibility, over 70 per cent reveal no desire to break their marital ties. Nonsupport appeared as the chief motive for dissolving the marriage, while it is one of the least frequent as a cause of conflict. Disharmony in sexual relations was infrequently given as a source of conflict but it is the third most important complaint in bringing the desire to be separated or divorced from the husband. From this study of conflict the author concludes that the elements that appear least frequently as causes of incompatibility and most often as causes of the breakdown of the marriage tend to be those that are most essential for the preservation of the marital relationship: the husband's role as

[6] Ibid., p. 562.

TABLE III [7]

PERCENTAGE OF WOMEN WITH SPECIFIED OVERT REACTIONS TO STATED ELEMENTS OF MARITAL CONFLICT

ELEMENTS OF CONFLICT	OVERT REACTIONS (PERCENTAGE)					NO. OF WOMEN
	Separation or Divorce		Passive Resignation	Desire to Correct the Situation	Total	
	Effected or Considered Without Reservations	Considered but Discarded for Specified Reasons				
Masculine domination..	18.8	21.3	32.5	27.5	100.1	80
In-laws..............	19.4	5.6	36.1	38.9	100.0	36
Infidelity............	24.4	30.1	21.1	24.4	100.0	123
Affective maladjustment..............	29.2	22.2	18.1	30.6	100.1	72
Sexual-reproductive disharmony........	33.3	14.3	28.6	23.8	100.0	21
Social vices...........	46.7	20.0	6.7	26.7	100.1	30
Nonsupport...........	57.1	10.7	21.4	10.7	99.9	28
All elements.........	28.2	21.6	23.6	26.7	100.1	390

provider, as a sexual partner, as a father, and as a companion.

Grievances, deception. Sometimes an incompatibility is caused by one of the married couple discovering that he or she has been consciously deceived by the other. This may be in regard to something comparatively trivial, which in spite of its unimportance comes to have a separating influence. For example, in one case the family difficulty originated from the wife's discovery that her husband chewed tobacco and had secretly continued the habit throughout courtship. It was a disquieting thought that there had been a determined effort to hide from her something that he knew she would not approve. How far could he be trusted in other matters? She reacted at once to the suggestion of suspicion and for a time it seemed as if her married life would come to a quick end. Pride probably saved her from a public confession of failure, but she never developed genuine confidence in her husband.

[7] *Ibid.*, p. 566.

If the husband or wife becomes careless in dress or in any other habits, there is danger of the mate's becoming irritated and disappointed. What starts as a feeling of disapproval and occasional embarrassment grows by constant association until it finally turns to shame and anger. Perhaps the more careful and ambitious member of the household develops the idea that the bad ways of the other are an obstacle to success for both of them and then hate sets in. Family disasters of this type are not the result of the common transition from courtship, with its element of acting, to the serious tasks of marriage, but rather the product of a moral letting down of character which the more efficient individual resents.

Sexual maladjustment. Since the sexual relationship of the husband and wife stands out prominently among the new adjustments marriage requires, it is not strange that the feeling of disappointment or deception frequently centers in this sphere of association. The adverse reaction of one of the spouses may be due to misinterpretation or to an ignorant or immature attitude toward the physical aspect of married life. On the other hand, the spouse may recoil from this relationship because at the first attempt at readjustment insight was given as to the self-centered, coarse, or even cruel character of the individual who has been accepted as the life partner, It then rightly seems as if one of the spouses had been play acting in courtship, concealing a flaw in the personality which would have destroyed love from the beginning had it been recognized. The spouse in trouble is face to face, before any considerable progress has been made in other lines of adjustment, with a painful dilemma. Must the revelation that has come through sex be accepted as one of the disillusions that are commonly regarded as following marriage and the association continued, robbed of its promise, but as an obligation and a sacrifice? Or should there be immediate repudiation and public acknowledgement of the incompatibility which has so suddenly but drastically appeared?

It is evident that any husband or wife in this predicament is certain to be greatly influenced by earlier teaching, the attitudes and expectations of friends and relatives, the shrinking from public confession of marriage failure, and the ideas that have been established as to what is meant by adjustment in marriage. The social pressure in most instances is strongly toward making the spouse willing to go on with the union even though its zest and hope have largely evaporated. It is apparent also that in this effort to make some workable adjustment to the disillusion the spouse cannot expect any help from the mate who is ordinarily the cause of trouble. If the meaning of the situation could be interpreted to the other spouse, a new adjustment could be had, but the flaw of character which has produced the difficulty is an obstacle to any self-understanding, even if the disillusioned spouse had the courage and the skill to portray clearly and unemotionally the cause of the trouble.

The marriage counselor is bound to recognize the frequency with which this cause of incompatibility between husband and wife appears in the failures of American marriages. He also realizes how difficult it is in most cases to find out which spouse was chiefly to blame for the estrangement which sex maladjustment started. For example, the wife's complaint that the husband was brutish, selfish, and oversexed from the beginning of their marital relationships may be due to her unpreparedness for marriage and misunderstanding of what happened and because of this her turning self-consciousness and awkwardness on his part into lack of tenderness and affection.

It must not be assumed that it is always the woman who feels disillusionment. The following case illustrates a husband's reaction. He was the victim of an incompatibility which lasted many years and which finally had much to do with his development of a neurosis that led to his being placed in an asylum. Upon his return to normal life, he sought counsel and explained how during his marriage he had felt bitterness because of what he regarded as the insincerity and deception of his wife. One night, when they were engaged, as he was helping the woman on with her coat, by accident and without consciousness, he placed his hand upon her breast. She immediately rebuked him with great emotion and upbraided him for his undisciplined expression of passion. He was surprised, shocked, and hurt. Indeed, his feelings were too strong for any attempt at explanation. They married, and then he found that she was much more passionate than himself. He interpreted this, having no doubt an underlying sense of grievance, as deception on her part. Naturally their sexual adjustment was difficult and never fully satisfactory, but his religious background and the kind of work he was doing prevented any thought on his part of separation or divorce. Children came, and family life was maintained in American conventional manner, with the wife never having any inkling as to the inner feelings of the husband. By concealing his incompatibility, he, of course, made it all the more a danger. After his release from the institution when he came for counsel, he expressed his belief that this incompatibility was the real cause of his breakdown. Even if this were an exaggeration, it was clearly true that his experience was in part the cause of his trouble. He was advised to stress the fact that his wife had proved a good mother even if, as he said, she had been a miserable wife, and, although this new attitude did not remove his emotional separation from the wife, it gave him a basis for their life together which prevented any recurrence of his neurosis.

A stimulus of disagreeable thought. It is a common psychological experience for one person to stir up disagreeable ideas in the mind of another. Even plants and animals come to have the power of suggesting the unpleasant to those who in childhood had some unhappy experience with a particular plant or animal. Perhaps certain flowers bring always a spontaneous feeling of repulsion. This is even more frequent in reactions to definite foods, especially when they bring back memory of some illness connected with them. We have habitual likes and dislikes that appear at once when the appropriate stimulus acts upon us. It may be that a person with a certain color of hair or a definite mannerism in walking or talking starts disagreeable feelings in the consciousness of one with whom he comes into contact.

This mental mechanism holds in the close contact of home life, and in this way one individual is said to get on the nerves of another. This is a type of complex-reaction that grows rapidly in continuous association and often the originator of the emotional recoil is utterly oblivious of the influence he generates. At first the feeling of repulsion may have gathered about some one characteristic of the other member of the family, later spreading until the entire personality stimulates the victim adversely.

Mrs. L, the wife of a doctor, has left her home and is planning to get a divorce. Her marriage was for spite. She became angry over a note incorrectly interpreted, written by the young man to whom she was engaged, turned from him and a few months later married a doctor with whom she had meanwhile become acquainted. At first the marriage appeared successful, but after a year trouble began to brew. She complained of habits that annoyed although she had to admit they were rather trivial and balanced by other qualities most desirable. The real situation immediately appeared when she told of her first engagement, her regret that she foolishly broke it off, and declared that the habits of her husband that annoyed her always suggested her first lover since they were just opposite to his ways. Clearly her husband had become an innocent victim of her regrets by stimulating thoughts that she found painful.

Becoming an obstacle.   Another social situation that leads to family incompatibility comes about when the husband or wife seems to the other an obstacle to ambition. The following case illustrates a problem of this kind.

Miss K, the youngest and most spoiled of several children, recently became pregnant. The father of her offspring was a young college student who had still one year of study before graduation. He was as much surprised as the girl when he learned of her predicament and before he could adjust himself to the position in which he was placed, the girl's mother entered the discussion with demands that he marry at once. It is probable that he recognized this as his duty; in fact, there was no reason to suppose that the idea of marriage was not attractive to both young people. The mother of the girl, however, displayed the same emotionalism that was the cause of her having had some serious difficulty with each one of her children. The young man was dragged to the church pastor, threatened with various penalties if he did not consent to immediate marriage; indeed, greater mismanagement could hardly be conceived.

While this was developing, I had been asked by one of the relatives who could view the problem without emotion to give counsel. I pointed out the need of winning the sympathy and stressing the sense of honor of the young husband-to-be so that his quick change of plans might not seem something forced upon him by outside pressure as a form of retaliation. The girl confessed at once that she was the more responsible party in the events that led to her conception. Since she had been given no help in understanding and preparing for marriage by her mother, I decided that the latter was the really responsible person. The mother refused to co-operate in any tactful handling of her future son-in-law but rather enjoyed to the full the opportunity to upbraid both of the young people, especially the man.

The college student was hurled into the marriage ceremony in a most insulting manner, and soon trouble began between the newly married couple. What I prophesied as the most likely thing if the girl's mother continued her dominance soon occurred. The young husband had of course immediately left college "so that he might support his family," to quote the mother, although it would have been entirely feasible for him to have completed his remaining year. He found work in a few months that made it necessary for him to leave the country, and soon he was safe where he could not be brought back for desertion. Were he to return, he would discover that he could easily become legally free, for his wife, a few months after the birth of her child, became pregnant a second time and the offender was one whom she knew only a few hours and never saw a second time.

It is easy to see that in such a case as this the young man, forced out of college into a course of action incited by the desire for revenge rather than by any serious effort to help work out a difficult situation for the best welfare of both young people, would have a sense of grievance and would think of his wife as an obstacle to his ambition. Even assuming that he was justly punished for his unconventional behavior, it is certain that using the girl as an instrument of punishment could only result in developing in him the feeling that she had spoiled his life. By the process of time, through constant suggestion, she became to him the obstacle between him and happiness. Successful marriage was impossible.

Persuading a young college girl to leave her education uncompleted for marriage is always a venturesome experiment. Even when the marriage turns out well, as it fortunately often does, there is a shade of regret that hampers the fellowship of husband and wife. The wife frequently feels that another year or two of delay to enable her to get her degree would have been far wiser. If the hazard created by this short-circuiting of educational preparation were more generally understood, the right sort of man would seldom urge it.

There is greater danger when the man's plans are disrupted by a premature marriage than when this happens to the woman, since in the case of the man this more often means the thwarting of his career. It is, for example, a serious handicap that a couple takes over at marriage if the man leaves college or drops a line of business or moves from some advantageous environment in order to marry. At the time this sacrifice may seem normal, if it contributes to the happiness of the bride, but in after years when it is plain that financial success has been flouted at the time when it was almost within reach, the sacrifice seems foolish and becomes a source of deep regret.

There are myriad ways by which one member of a household comes to be an obstacle to the happiness of the other so that chronic dissatisfaction follows. If there were greater frankness, especially in the first months of marriage, so that this feeling of being hampered would be confessed and talked over freely, many situations that go from bad to worse could be handled rationally at the start, thereby only cementing affection the harder. It is surprising how difficult such confidential discussions are in the relationship of marriage. In business and professional enterprises there is a far greater freedom in squarely facing the beginning of an incompatibility than there is in most homes.

Resentment at transferred mother love. Another difficulty which has to be frankly faced occurs in greater or less degree in most marriages. Few men realize that a woman's affection has at least two emotions, tied together when she marries a man but sooner or later separated when she becomes a mother. One is the wife-attitude and one is the mother-attitude. When she first marries, she thinks of her husband in a double way. He is her husband; he is also her child. With the coming of a baby into the family group, the two attitudes are immediately divided, even though the wife did not herself anticipate this. Once the division has taken place, things can never be as they were before. Another interest has come into the life of the young woman which in some ways rivals her earlier affection; her mother-attitude will now be bestowed where it properly belongs, on the child. It is not uncommon for the husband to react against this change, feeling that his wife has ceased to care for him in the intense way that she did. Then the man will say or do something that shows that although he is fond of the child, its coming means for him that he must take second place.

In some women the mother-attitude may seem more powerful than the wife-attitude; in others the reverse appears true. But the two attitudes need not compete with each other. They were bound together in the beginning of marriage when there was no child to receive the mother affection, and now that there are two distinct objects for the two kinds of affection one attitude has been separated from the other. Whether one is stronger than the other does not matter; the husband must take what is his. If women are deeper in their affection as mothers than as wives, no advantage comes from denying this. Whichever way the balance swings, the family life can go on smoothly as long as the husband cherishes no hurt feelings.

Affection cannot be regarded rightly as if it were a limited amount of substance which if directed toward one person must in the same proportion be taken away from someone else. Instead each love relationship is unique and not necessarily competitive. It is true that a new love will destroy a previous concentration, but even then the former dominant love-relationship may be enriched by taking on a new meaning. When motherhood does reconstruct the husband-wife relationship and trouble follows, it is usually because the husband has taken advantage of the previous concentration and is demanding not love from the wife but a monopoly of her affections. If the change then brings incompatibility, it results chiefly from the husband's failure to readjust to the new situation and not because he has been excluded from his wife's affection. His attempt to force the continuation of the relationship enjoyed before the coming of the child may in time bring estrangement as the wife comes to realize that her spouse is self-centered and immature. Sometimes the real explanation of the husband's reaction is not so much concern with love as it is that his wife has been too much his servant and he now resents her giving, as she must, much attention and time to the care of the child.

There are some women and fewer men who, once they become parents, do transfer their affection until it seems to be almost exclusively the possession of the child. This extreme motherhood reaction illustrates the grain of truth in Weininger's classification of the two types of women: "child-loving and man-loving."

In judging the reaction of husband or wife to the new experience of parenthood, it is important to keep in mind that there always have to be changes in habits and routines and that difficulty or reluctance in making these does not mean that the new fact of motherhood is causing incompatibility. To bring this about, there must be greater resentment than comes from difficulty in modifying behavior because of the new situation.

Jealousy. The great enemy of love is jealousy. When jealousy creeps into the home, love packs up and gets ready to depart, for it cannot thrive under the perpetual tyranny of a jealous spouse. Yet nearly all jealousy is unfounded. It is the culmination of childish habits that have never been cast aside, as the jealous person found it easier to conceal them than to go through the painful process of uprooting them.

Babies demand the exclusive attention of their mother; two-year-olds have been known to slap fiercely at the little baby brother or sister that has taken from them the position of supreme importance in the household; even the child of five is apt to feel pangs of jealousy on hearing the first wail of a newborn infant in the home and realizing that the name and prerogatives of "Baby" are to descend to another. Children tend to be jealous of a brother or sister who receives praise, toys, or privileges that seem more desirable than the ones given to them.

Most of us outgrow our infantile habit of giving way to jealousy, but a few people allow the habit to grow stronger with the passing of years because they suffer from a deep sense of inferiority. These people who are driven into jealousy by their inferiority complex are not necessarily inferior in any way to those with whom they compare themselves, but their lack of self-confidence keeps them ever on the watch for fancied slights and opportunities to indulge in an emotional storm of jealousy.

During courtship the jealous person holds in check his suspicions and tries to act like other adults, but once the marriage knot is firmly tied he goes back to his old ways with a slump, for now he seems bent on making up for the difficult self-control he had to exercise while winning a mate. He may dig up trivial occurrences of the courtship that were supposedly forgotten by both young people and rehearse them until he has worked himself into a jealous rage. At the slightest suggestion of rivalry in the affection of the mate, whether from parent-in-law, work, or social activities, he may bury himself in the depths of bitter jealousy. The other member of the marriage partnership hardly dares to look at the opposite sex, much less show any of the courtesy convention demands. But it makes little difference what is done; jealousy can easily feed itself, and the home life is poisoned by unfounded suspicions.

Jealousy that is not a hangover from childhood may be caused by social suggestions. Literature, scenes from the motion pictures, and the chatter of one's friends make jealousy seem the normal reaction to certain stereotyped situations, thus precluding the unemotional talking over of circumstances the wrong interpretation of which causes hard feelings in both young people. The person whose jealous trend is not of long standing can free himself of the inclination before it becomes an integral part of his disposition, if he has the courage and determination to carry out a long and difficult process of readjustment and can obtain the needed advice from one who understands the mechanism of this vexing adult behavior problem.

Troublemakers.   Family incompatibility may arise from influences that originate in outside sources. Relatives, and particularly mothers-in-law, are notoriously troublesome to the newly married. Even the savages by their taboos may have registered their realization of the problems in family life caused by unwise mothers-in-law. It is a common observation that some of our marriage failures originate in the too great interference of the mother-in-law or the over-dependence of the newly wedded man or woman upon the mother.

The difficulty must be considered in its larger and more significant aspects. The mother-in-law has become a symbol of the natural obstacles that must be met by the new family in its effort to establish itself as an independent unit, free from the surveillance of either of the parent families. The marriage of their child means to parents a breaking away from long-accustomed relationships usually maintained since childhood, while for the young married couple it brings about a new alliance which automatically includes considerable intimacy and therefore has to set earlier associations at arm's length. It is not strange that the mother-in-law, husband, and wife all find a degree of difficulty in establishing the new status.

By far the most strain is felt by the mother-in-law. Not only must she give up her precedence in affection to another, but she must have the insight to see when her help is really needed and when it is far wiser to let the young couple work out their own matrimonial salvation. Her ever-present temptation is to attempt to give the young people the benefit of her experience on every possible occasion, forgetting how hard it is for anyone to profit from the experience of another and how necessary it is that the new home get firmly established on its own initiative.

Recent psychology has explained the inner protest many mothers make against their son's or daughter's becoming independent of early home ties. There are mothers whose whole policy has been that of repressing the personality of their children. They have made use of the strong affection between mother and offspring as a method of holding their child in a subserviency which we are wont to call a mother-fixation. This program of keeping the child dependent has become a settled conspiracy against his maturing to the point of self-reliance and what we think of as typical mother-in-law behavior is merely the continuation of a lifelong policy.

The dominance of the mother is likely to be resented after marriage even when it has been accepted by the child as a matter of course up to this time. It is received with instinctive hostility by the child-in-law, who, unfettered by previous subordination, easily sees the significance of the interference and struggles against it immediately. The contest is accepted by both parties to it as a real trial of strength and in its heat there is risk of a tension developing between the married couple, whose interests are not altogether on the same side. This tension may increase until it forms the basis of a permanent separation of interest between the young folks.

It is not hard to indict the mother-in-law, but the fact is that social conventions are in part responsible for her attitude. In the recent past and even yet in a multitude of cases, in certain sections and in the class of persons who are inadequately trained for life, it is customary for the mother to concentrate upon her children and to develop no serious interests outside her home. This is the program expected of the mother; its acceptance is held to be the mark of an ideal home.

The consequence is that as her children leave her the mother finds herself suddenly stripped of many of the habitual activities that have become by repetition the very substance of her life. Without children to assist, plan for, and protect, her career seems all at once like a ship that has dropped its anchor. As she has gone on in life she has never taken out any insurance in the form of out-of-the-home interests, and the escape of each child leaves her with a greater void. The well-trained mother of the present times sees the cause of this disaster more clearly than did her mother, and she is much more likely to welcome her child's maturity than to try to prevent it. The mother of only one or two children runs a greater risk of encroaching upon their proper field of development, but, if she faces her problem intelligently and with knowledge of its cause, she also may succeed in managing her role without bitterness in herself or damage to her child.

This is much the same problem that the man meets who finds himself forced to give up the control of his business to a younger successor. If the older man has no strong interests outside his business, it has become a proverb that he will fade quickly upon retirement. The mother-in-law's problem is therefore not something primarily belonging to women, but the difficult adjustment that awaits the man or woman who has lived too narrow a life. The mother's solution is complicated by the affection that has developed along with her habit of caring for her child.

Fathers occasionally find the transference of a child, especially a daughter, to another home as severe a testing as do mothers, and thus the father-in-law problem originates. We find aunts, sisters, brothers, and foster parents also testifying by their reactions that the protest against the breaking away from home ties to the beginning of a new home circle is a human weakness rather than a fault characteristic only of mothers-in-law.

It would be easier to make a gradual adjustment satisfactory to each member of the tragic triangular contest if only the son- or daughter-in-law were more patient, cool, and sympathetic. Jealousy flares up quickly, and there is a sharp resentment that all ties with the former home are not instantly cut. It seems like criticism of the marriage itself; actually it is proof of a fondness for home life that sooner or later without inner wrenching of spirit can be transferred from the old to the new family.

Family struggle not incompatibility. It is important to remember that the struggle within the family does not necessarily mean incompatibility, that indeed it may have the opposite result. Families that suffer great hardships, and families that are by circumstances seriously limited, do as a matter of fact build happy family life and according to neighborhood and class standards do attain a satisfactory adjustment. Blanchard and Paynter have given us an investigation which reveals the risk of assuming that on account of poverty, poor health, unemployment, or alcoholism, a family is necessarily made incompatible and unsuitable for children. Their study found that the children of the twenty-three families studied at the request of the Family Society of Philadelphia were fond of their parents and happy in spite of their cravings for more opportunity to play and were at least average children in the wholesomeness of their emotional reactions to life.[8]

Struggle is synonymous with life. It is characteristic of the living organism; likewise, it appears with the social contacts of individuals. Its absence therefore in family life is not to be expected. In the home, as elsewhere in the association of persons, it is the result of action and reaction as the individuals related attempt adjustment to one another. Struggle passes over into incompatibility through its subjective consequences. This feeling of conflict may be temporary, disappearing with changed

---

[8] Blanchard, P., and Paynter, R. H., "Socio-Psychological Status of Children from Marginal Families," *The Family*, Vol. 8, pp. 3–10.

circumstances, or it may be inherent in the personality reacting unfavorably to the family situation. Frequently we find the adolescent illustrating in some degree the former. Occasionally a continuous incompatibility is revealed by the reactions of an aged person who has been forced to accept dependency while living with a son or daughter. The most tragic of the marriage incompatibilities appears when two individuals are tremendously drawn to one another by sexual attraction, although, because of the characteristics of their personalities, they cannot establish for any length of time a mutually satisfactory settlement of the differences that force them apart. Their ordeal must be clearly distinguished from the normal difficulties which young husbands and wives often encounter as they proceed to fuse their personalities into a unity of affection which has no need of excluding the differences of background and traits which they possess as individuals.

Chapter 17

DIVORCE AND DESERTION

FOREWORD. The problems of divorce and desertion have to be included in any discussion of the American family. Not only do they represent failures of our domestic life but also the possibility of their occurrence influences courtship, marriage, and family life. Divorce is as truly an American cultural trait as is marriage. It is the legal provision for release from a bad matrimonial situation. Under certain conditions it may be had in every one of our jurisdictions with the exception of South Carolina. There relief from an intolerable family situation has to be found by some sort of separation or a migratory divorce. The legal purpose of divorce is to end an undesirable family situation as a lesser of two evils. This lawful terminating of the husband-wife relationship provides opportunity for the exploiting of the institution of marriage. This appears chiefly in the many marriages of some divorced persons, a serial polygamy, and in reckless marriages that are frankly experimental because from the start the possibility of divorce as a way out of an unsatisfying relationship is in the thought of one or both of the spouses. Hasty divorces are also too frequently encouraged by commercially motivated lawyers.

Not only is it necessary for a student of American family life to understand the divorce problem, but also it must be assumed that some individuals in any class may face at a later time the question whether to get or not to get a divorce. They need, therefore, an intelligent preparation for the making of what is likely to prove a momentous decision, as well as an understanding of the legal procedure if they do determine to get a divorce.

Modern life and divorce.   The American record of an increasing divorce rate is evidence of the difficulty that individual men and women, subjected to the influences of modern culture, are having in working out in matrimony a satisfying, co-operative fellowship. The high divorce rate now prevailing in the United States discloses that the influences stimulating divorce are coming forth from modern culture and reveal the strain that marriage is meeting wherever there is a free expression of the protest against marriage maladjustment which contemporary conditions of civilization encourage.

The influences that are stimulating the divorce rate are world-wide phenomena and issue forth from the environment of modern man and woman rather than from social conditions distinctly American. The forces that tend to bring about divorce are in some countries checked from expression by repressive legislation or by the influence of the churches that hold to a sacramental interpretation of marriage and refuse to recognize the right of divorce. There is, indeed, unmistakable evidence in all countries reflecting twentieth century culture of the working of social influences that favor divorce. It is, however, the American situation in which we are interested.

The history of divorce in the United States.   Although there was variation among the New England colonies in their attitude toward divorce, the general trend was in harmony with the teachings of early Protestantism; marriage was made a civil contract and the right of legal divorce became a logical deduction. The chief causes of divorce were desertion, cruelty, and adultery. As a rule, the husband and the wife were treated as equals before the law. The southern colonies, on the other hand, under the influence of the teaching of the Church of England, moved in the opposite direction, and absolute divorce was not recognized. The statute books of these southern colonies are void of any reference to the subject of divorce restriction.[1]

In the mother country, ecclesiastical courts had jurisdiction over questions arising from domestic incompatibility. These courts were not established in the southern colonies nor did they turn over jurisdiction concerning the dissolution of marriage to any civil court. It was possible for the husband and

---

[1] Howard, G. E., *A History of Matrimonial Institutions,* Vol. 2, p. 367.

wife to separate by mutual consent, but neither divorce nor legal separation was granted during the colonial period. The middle colonies also were conservative in their attitude toward divorce, their sentiment being more in sympathy with the practice of the southern colonies than with the more liberal policy of their New England neighbors.

NUMBER OF DIVORCES IN EACH YEAR, WITH INCREASE, FOR THE UNITED STATES: 1887 TO 1906, 1916, AND 1922 TO 1931 [2]

Year	Number of Divorces Reported	Increase Over Preceding Year		Year	Number of Divorces Reported	Increase Over Preceding Year	
		Number	Per Cent			Number	Per Cent
1931...	183,664	−7,927	−4.1	1902..	61,480	496	0.8
1930...	191,591	−9,877	−4.9	1901..	60,984	5,233	9.4
1929...	201,468	5,529	2.8	1900..	55,751	4,314	8.4
1928...	195,939	3,902	2.0	1899..	51,437	3,588	7.5
1927...	192,037	11,184	6.2	1898..	47,849	3,150	7.0
1926...	180,853	5,404	3.1	1897..	44,699	1,762	4.1
1925...	175,449	4,497	2.6	1896..	42,937	2,550	6.3
1924...	170,952	5,856	3.5	1895..	40,387	2,819	7.5
1923...	165,096	16,281	10.9	1894..	37,568	100	0.3
1922...	148,815	....	....	1893..	37,468	889	2.4
				1892..	36,579	1,039	2.9
1916...	112,036	....	....	1891..	35,540	2,079	6.2
				1890..	33,461	1,726	5.4
1906...	72,062	4,086	6.0	1889..	31,735	3,066	10.7
1905...	67,976	1,777	2.7	1888..	28,669	750	2.7
1904...	66,199	1,274	2.0	1887..	27,919	....	....
1903...	64,925	3,445	5.6				

In New York during the control of the Dutch, a divorce was occasionally granted by the civil courts. When the English took possession, theoretically the system in vogue in England was established, but since no ecclesiastical courts were appointed to deal with divorce and separation and the power was not granted to any other court, the situation in New York was similar to that of the southern colonies. In Pennsylvania in 1682 a statute was passed which recognized absolute divorce on the ground of adultery. The law became a dead letter because no court was given authority to take over the giving of such a

[2] *Marriage and Divorce 1931*, p. 10 (U. S. Department of Commerce, Bureau of the Census).

divorce. It was possible by legislative act in this colony to obtain a divorce, but there is nothing to suggest that this was a common practice.

NUMBER OF DIVORCES PER 1,000 OF TOTAL POPULATION, AND NUMBER PER 100 MARRIAGES PERFORMED, BY SINGLE YEARS: 1887 TO 1931 [3]

[Divorces estimated for those years printed in italic.]

		DIVORCES					DIVORCES		
YEAR	POPULATION [1]	Number	Per 1,000 of Total Population	Per 100 Marriages Performed [2]	YEAR	POPULATION [1]	Number	Per 1,000 of Total Population	Per 100 Marriages Performed [2]
1931	124,070,000	183,664	1.48	17.3	1906	83,941,510	72,062	0.86	8.2
1930	123,191,000	191,591	1.56	17.0	1905	82,574,105	67,976	0.82	8.2
1929	121,526,429	201,468	1.66	16.3	1904	81,261,856	66,199	0.81	8.2
1928	119,861,607	195,939	1.63	16.6	1903	79,900,389	64,925	0.81	8.0
1927	118,196,785	192,037	1.62	16.0	1902	78,576,436	61,480	0.78	8.0
1926	116,531,963	180,853	1.55	15.0					
1925	114,867,141	175,449	1.53	14.8	1901	77,274,967	60,984	0.79	8.2
1924	113,202,319	170,952	1.51	14.4	1900	75,994,575	55,751	0.73	7.9
1923	111,537,497	165,096	1.48	13.4	1899	74,689,889	51,437	0.69	7.7
1922	109,872,675	148,815	1.35	13.1	1898	73,385,203	47,849	0.65	7.4
					1897	72,080,517	44,699	0.62	7.0
1921	108,207,853	159,580	1.47	13.7					
1920	106,543,031	170,505	1.60	13.4	1896	70,775,831	42,937	0.61	6.8
1919	105,003,065	141,527	1.35	12.3	1895	69,471,145	40,387	0.58	6.5
1918	103,587,955	116,254	1.12	11.6	1894	68,166,458	37,568	0.55	6.4
1917	102,172,845	121,564	1.20	10.6	1893	66,861,772	37,468	0.56	6.2
					1892	65,557,086	36,579	0.56	6.1
1916	100,757,735	[3]114,000	1.13	10.6					
					1891	64,252,400	35,540	0.55	6.0
1915	99,342,625	104,298	1.05	10.4	1890	62,947,714	33,461	0.53	5.9
1914	97,927,516	100,584	1.03	9.8	1889	61,375,603	31,735	0.52	5.7
1913	96,512,407	91,307	0.95	8.9	1888	60,128,957	28,669	0.48	5.4
1912	95,097,298	94,318	0.99	9.4	1887	58,882,310	27,919	0.47	5.5
1911	93,682,189	89,219	0.95	9.3					
1910	92,267,080	83,045	0.90	8.8					
1909	90,691,354	79,671	0.88	8.9					
1908	89,073,360	76,852	0.86	9.0					
1907	87,455,366	76,571	0.88	8.2					

[1] Estimated population as of July 1 of each year. Estimates for years 1920 to 1929, inclusive, revised to conform with the results of the Census of 1930. For years prior to 1907 the population of those counties for which no divorce returns were received is omitted.

[2] For the years prior to 1907 the ratio of divorces to marriages is based on the respective rates per 1,000 of the population rather than on the reported numbers of divorces and marriages, since the latter are not quite complete for these earlier years.

[3] Including estimates of divorces for 95 counties which failed to make returns for 1916.

After the colonies became the United States, any divorce granted was obtained by private statute. This program continued for more than half a century until by legislative statutes the courts were given jurisdiction. Gradually, in those states where divorce was obtainable, laws were passed from time to

[3] *Marriage and Divorce 1931*, p. 12 (U. S. Department of Commerce, Bureau of the Census).

time defining the grounds upon which it could be had. Georgia, Mississippi, and Alabama were among the first to transfer divorce-giving authority from the legislatures to the courts.

During the latter half of the nineteenth century, the general trend of legislation among the various states of the union reflected a more liberal policy concerning divorce, leading to an extension of the legal grounds for divorce. In their divorce policies the states reveal influences of sectional character as well as of historical and traditional origin. The first statistical report dealing with marriage and divorce in the several states, territories, and the District of Columbia was authorized by Congress in 1887 and was submitted two years later by Carroll D. Wright, Commissioner of Labor. It covered the period 1867 to 1886. The second investigation of marriage and divorce covered the twenty-year period 1887 to 1906. Because of World War I the third survey was limited to the year 1916. Beginning with 1922 we have had annual reports until 1932 when national statistics of marriage and divorce through annual reports were discontinued because of the economy program of 1933. In 1940 tentative plans were made for selecting and reporting again on a nation-wide basis statistics of marriage and divorce. With a population of thirty-eight and a half million in 1870, 10,962 divorces were granted.[4] In 1929, having the largest number of divorces thus far, there were 201,468, with a population of 121,-526,429.[5] The table on page 469 gives the number of divorces according to the federal investigation since 1887.

In the table on page 470 the number of divorces is recorded in relation to the population and to the number of marriages performed. In interpreting the statistics of the number of divorces granted in any one year for a hundred marriages performed in the same year, it needs to be recognized that this does not give exactly the percentage of the marriages of that year that are likely to terminate in divorce, since most of the divorces in any single year are of marriages contracted in previous years. "If, therefore, the divorce rate in the United States were to continue to increase, even though not very rapidly, the ratio

---

[4] Groves, E. R., and Ogburn, W. F., *American Marriage and Family Relationships*, p. 346.

[5] *Marriage and Divorce 1931*, p. 12 (U. S. Department of Commerce, Bureau of the Census).

between the divorces and the marriages of a given year would somewhat understate the probability of divorce for the marriages of that year." [6]

Who gets the divorce. The table below shows that more than twice as many wives obtain divorces as do husbands. During the period for which we have statistics, somewhat over two-thirds of the total number of divorces have been granted wives.

DIVORCES CLASSIFIED ACCORDING TO PARTY TO WHOM
GRANTED: 1887 TO 1931 [7]

Year or Period	Total Divorces *	Granted to Husband		Granted to Wife	
		Number	Per Cent	Number	Per Cent
1931................	182,203	49,591	27.2	132,612	72.8
1930................	189,863	52,554	27.7	137,309	72.3
1929................	199,335	57,148	28.7	142,187	71.3
1928................	192,342	55,065	28.6	137,277	71.4
1927................	188,685	54,637	29.0	134,048	71.0
1926................	179,397	52,834	29.5	126,563	70.5
1925................	173,480	52,147	30.1	121,333	69.9
1924................	168,312	52,984	31.5	115,328	68.5
1923................	164,479	52,999	32.2	111,480	67.8
1922................	147,775	47,359	32.0	100,416	68.0
1916................	108,702	33,809	31.1	74,893	68.9
1906................	72,062	23,455	32.5	48,607	67.5
1896................	42,937	14,448	33.6	28,489	66.4
1887–1906..........	945,625	316,149	33.4	629,476	66.6
1897–1906........	593,362	195,547	33.0	397,815	67.0
1887–1896........	352,263	120,602	34.2	231,661	65.8

* Exclusive of divorces for which no detailed statistics were obtained: 1,461 in 1931; 1,728 in 1930; 2,133 in 1929; 3,597 in 1928; 3,352 in 1927; 1,456 in 1926; 1,969 in 1925; 2,640 in 1924; 617 in 1923; 1,040 in 1922; and 3,334 in 1916.

The difference is due largely to the fact that the wife has given her by law a larger number of legal grounds for divorce. Nonsupport, or neglect to provide, one of the common legal causes of divorce on the part of the wife, is an example of this difference since it is seldom a legal ground for divorce on the part of the husband.

Even grounds for divorce that apply equally to husband and wife, from their character, as appears in the case of cruelty,

---

[6] *Marriage and Divorce 1931*, p. 13 (U. S. Department of Commerce, Bureau of the Census).

[7] *Ibid.*, p. 17.

are more common offenses among men than women. It must be
remembered also that the social consequences of certain charges
made the basis for divorce carry more weight for the woman
than for the man, as is true of adultery. In some circles, therefore, the social code demands that the man assume the burden

DIVORCE RATES BY OCCUPATION AND RELIGION [8]

Religious Categories	White-Collar Workers			Laborers			Un-Em-Ployed	Total
	Profes-sional	Propri-etary	Cleri-cal	Skilled	Semi-skilled	Un-skilled		
Total Group								
Rate........	6.80	8.39	10.39	11.60	13.38	7.33	10.48	10.38
Number.....	294	906	1183	1535	725	532	315	5490
Non-Catholic								
Rate........	7.01	6.55	9.89	13.04	12.68	8.81	9.62	10.08
Number.....	214	595	698	828	339	295	156	3125
Catholic								
Rate........	3.13	5.45	1.74	2.40	10.61	1.12	—	3.79
Number.....	32	110	172	208	132	89	49	792
Mixed								
Rate........	5.56	20.55	24.21	16.18	20.51	6.38	5.56	17.42
Number.....	18	73	95	136	78	47	18	465
No Religion								
Rate........	—	—	15.79	25.00	40.00	33.33	33.33	23.91
Number.....	1	12	19	24	15	3	18	92
No Information								
Rate........	10.34	13.79	14.57	10.91	11.18	8.16	14.86	12.01
Number.....	29	116	199	339	161	98	74	1016

of guilt, at least as far as legal procedure is concerned, and the
husband in response to this convention at times protects the
character of his wife by taking the blame when he is entirely
innocent. This masculine code has a definite influence on the
granting of more divorces to women than to men.

A recent study has been made of the differential divorce
rates by occupations. This was based upon 5,811 questionnaires
filled in by students attending public secondary schools in

---

[8] Weeks, H. Ashley, "Differential Divorce Rates by Occupations," *Social Forces*, Vol. 21, No. 3, p. 336.

Spokane, Washington, in 1938. In the fall of 1939, 737 additional questionnaires from students of high school level in the three parochial schools were gathered. It was found that the divorce rates increased progressively from the professional group through the proprietary, clerical, skilled, and semiskilled groups. The unskilled group reverses the trend, possibly on account of the cost of getting a divorce, and shows a lower rate than any group except the professional group. The results of this study appear in the table on page 473.

Burgess and Cottrell in their study report the highest percentages of happiness in marriage among those in the highest economic occupations and the lowest among the laboring classes.[9]

Absolute divorce, limited divorce, and separation. American law at the present time provides for the dissolution of marriage by complete divorce; by partial divorce, which is also known as legal separation; and by annulment. When the term *divorce* is used, it generally means a complete ending of the marriage relationship, or *a vinculo matrimonii*. Limited divorce, or, as it is sometimes called, judicial separation, changes the nature of the relationship but does not dissolve the union. This is known in legal terminology as divorce *a mensa et thoro*, literally translated, from bed and board. This type of divorce appeared in the early days of Christianity and is still the only form recognized by the Roman Catholic Church. This decree of limited divorce places the husband and wife in the position of not being within the marriage fellowship in their relation to each other while to all others they remain as if they were fully married. They have neither the legal rights of the married nor those of single persons. This type of divorce came over to this country from the English ecclesiastical courts.

When married persons live apart, having neither absolute nor limited divorce, their legal status is of course not changed by their separation. As a consequence, problems of a legal nature may arise, and it may seem wise that they enter upon some sort of legal agreement. In 1932 there were ten states that had legislation relating to such separation agreements. These usually

---

[9] Burgess, Ernest W., and Cottrell, Leonard S., *Predicting Success or Failure in Marriage,* p. 138.

refer to questions of support, children, and property. The judicial trend now seems to favor the making of such agreements when husbands and wives who do not seek divorce refuse to live together.[10]

The annulment declares by legal decree that the marriage never existed lawfully, and therefore both persons involved return to the status quo preceding their attempt to marry. Unless there is a statute to the contrary, any child born from such a union is illegitimate.

The grounds for divorce. At present the Federal government has no legislative control of divorce, and therefore authority in this field is under fifty-one American jurisdictions, all but one of which—South Carolina—permit divorce. There is agreement among these regarding one ground only, that of adultery. The eight most common causes recognized are adultery, cruelty, desertion, impotence, conviction for a crime and imprisonment, intoxication, nonsupport, and insanity. In addition, there are thirty-one minor grounds recognized by one or more jurisdictions.[11] The great differences in the states as the grounds prescribed for divorce, the equally great variation in case decisions, and the constant passing of new legislation lead to much confusion and domestic litigation. Only a lawyer well versed in the domestic law of his own state is familiar with the situation one faces when seeking a divorce, except in the state of South Carolina.

All the jurisdictions require the legal residence of the plaintiff at the time he seeks a divorce. The length of time required to establish legal residence varies, and it is this that makes certain states favored by those seeking migratory divorces. The most common requirement is one year. As a rule, the plaintiff must appear in court in person at the time of the divorce trial. In 1939 the effort of Joan Crawford, the movie actress, to obtain a divorce from her husband was denied because she did not appear at the time set for the hearing but instead on that day was enjoying a dinner appointment with her husband in New York. Her lawyer attempted to substitute for her, but the judge of the Los Angeles divorce court refused to go

[10] Vernier, C. G., *American Family Laws*, Vol. 2, pp. 467–471.
[11] *Ibid.*, pp. 4–7.

ahead with the case. Later she had to appear in person before her request for a divorce was granted.[12]

The regulation concerning the procedure by which one spouse gives the other notice that a divorce is desired is determined by statute. Since this procedure is in the hands of the court dealing with the case and the defendant may be out of its jurisdiction, considerable litigation has resulted when proper notice according to the state in which the defendant lives may not have been given, even when the requirements of service have been carried out according to the letter of the law in the state in which the trial takes place. This is but one, and a minor one, of the many reasons why there is uncertainty regarding the validity of a divorce, frequently leaving the spouses married in one state while divorced in another. Family law, particularly in the field of divorce, is the most backward and confused of the various divisions of American law. It has been declared two or three decades behind law dealing with industrial problems.[13] The situation concerning divorce is still further complicated in the United States by questions involving the validity of divorces granted in foreign countries. Mexico and France have been the favorite choices of those seeking foreign jurisdiction as a means of getting a divorce.[14] An interesting illustration of possible complications resulting from the different status of a divorced person who passes from state to state is given through the experience of a fictitious divorced husband who remarried assuming that he had been legally divorced.[15] The bewildered husband, safely married in some states, guilty of bigamy in others, is advised to seek a divorce in Europe, only to find on his return that he and his supposed wife were guilty of having violated the Mann White Slave Act. •

The divorce status of a great many Americans who have received migratory decrees has been greatly confused by two recent decisions of the Supreme Court, each concerned with the same individuals. The first of these decisions—Williams and Hendrix vs. State (1942)—held that the courts of North Caro-

---

[12] Clarke, Helen I., *Social Legislation*, p. 119.

[13] Jacobs, A. C., and Angell, R. C., *A Research in Family Law*, p. 3.

[14] Summers, Lionel M., "The Divorce Laws of Mexico," *Law and Contemporary Problems*, Vol. 2, pp. 310–321; and Bates, Lindell T., "The Divorce of Americans in France," pp. 322–328.

[15] Drummond, Isabelle, *Getting A Divorce*, p. xxxiv.

lina were required to give "full faith and credit" to a divorce that had been granted by a Nevada court. This same case was taken a second time to the Supreme Court by the Attorney-General of North Carolina for a ruling as to whether there had been a genuine domicile in Nevada by the couple, each of whom had been divorced there and had then married each other and had returned to North Carolina. On this second appeal the Supreme Court (1945) decided that six weeks' residence in a motor court was mainly for the purpose of getting a divorce and was not in fact a domicile within the meaning of the law; therefore, the divorce did not need to be recognized by North Carolina. North Carolina was duly bound to recognize a divorce granted by the state of Nevada to its own citizens, but a couple that went to Nevada for six weeks for a divorce and then returned to North Carolina would be regarded as still citizens of North Carolina; therefore, North Carolina need not recognize the legal status decreed in a state in which they were not bona fide citizens.

Anyone familiar with the divorce trial realizes that the legal ground given for divorce is often not the true cause. The reason advanced for the giving of the divorce necessarily is influenced by the law of the state; the real root of the family discord may be one not recognized as a sufficient ground for divorce by the courts, so it becomes necessary to make the plea on the basis of some ground that falls within the statute. It is also true that there is sometimes a disposition on the part of both husband and wife to protect their future by having the complaining party charge a less severe cause for the divorce than what both know to be the real reason.

The table on page 478 shows the trend in the grounds given for divorce from 1927 to 1931.

In a comparison of different states as to the frequency of any definite cause for divorce appearing in statistics, great caution must be observed; even when the same term is used by different states as a ground for divorce, the statutory definition or the legal interpretation with reference to a given cause may so vary as to make misleading any statistical statement with reference to the frequency of the cause studied. There are also cases where the legal ground for divorce as it appears on the court records is itself a result of a family situation too subtle to come under the range of any legal term but which is nevertheless the actual cause of the divorce.

DIVORCES CLASSIFIED ACCORDING TO CAUSE AND PARTY TO WHOM GRANTED, WITH INCREASE: 1927 TO 1931 [16]

CAUSE AND PARTY TO WHOM GRANTED	NUMBER OF DIVORCES [1]					INCREASE [2] 1930 TO 1931		PER CENT OF INCREASE [2]		
	1931	1930	1929	1928	1927	Number	Per Cent	1929 to 1930	1928 to 1929	1927 to 1928
TOTAL DIVORCES										
All causes..........	182,203	189,863	199,335	192,342	188,685	—7,660	—4.0	—4.8	3.6	1.9
Adultery..............	13,661	14,841	16,510	16,217	16,658	—1,180	—8.0	—10.1	1.8	—2.6
Cruelty...............	77,225	79,381	81,284	77,998	77,036	—2,156	—2.7	—2.3	4.2	1.2
Desertion.............	50,893	54,802	59,061	57,996	58,421	—3,909	—7.1	—7.2	1.8	—0.7
Drunkenness..........	2,819	3,168	3,589	3,339	3,216	—349	—11.0	—11.7	7.5	3.8
Neglect to provide.......	7,398	7,718	7,741	7,883	7,840	—320	—4.1	—0.3	—1.8	0.5
Combinations of causes...	14,493	13,795	13,635	12,129	9,267	698	5.1	1.2	12.4	30.9
All other causes [3]........	15,714	16,158	17,515	16,780	16,247	—444	—2.7	—7.8	4.4	3.3
GRANTED TO HUSBAND [4]										
All causes	49,591	52,554	57,148	55,065	54,637	—2,963	—5.6	—8.0	3.8	0.8
Adultery..............	5,348	6,280	7,265	7,309	7,645	—932	—14.8	—13.6	—0.6	—4.4
Cruelty...............	17,373	17,625	18,514	17,350	16,475	—252	—1.4	—4.8	6.7	5.3
Desertion.............	20,800	22,451	24,660	24,177	24,309	—1,651	—7.4	—9.0	2.0	—0.5
Drunkenness..........	206	190	236	241	228	16	8.4	—19.5	—2.1	5.7
Combinations of causes...	1,924	1,813	1,857	1,576	1,475	111	6.1	—2.4	17.8	6.8
All other causes [2]........	3,940	4,195	4,616	4,412	4,505	—255	—6.1	—9.1	4.6	—2.1
GRANTED TO WIFE										
All causes..........	132,612	137,309	142,187	137,277	134,048	—4,697	—3.4	—3.4	3.6	2.4
Adultery..............	8,313	8,561	9,245	8,908	9,013	—248	—2.9	—7.4	3.8	—1.2
Cruelty...............	59,852	61,756	62,770	60,648	60,561	—1,904	—3.1	—1.6	3.5	0.1
Desertion.............	30,093	32,351	34,401	33,819	34,112	—2,258	—7.0	—6.0	1.7	—0.9
Drunkenness..........	2,613	2,978	3,353	3,098	2,988	—365	—12.3	—11.2	8.2	3.7
Neglect to provide.......	7,398	7,718	7,741	7,883	7,840	—320	—4.1	—0.3	—1.8	0.5
Combinations of causes...	12,569	11,982	11,778	10,553	7,792	587	4.9	1.7	11.6	35.4
All other causes [3]........	11,774	11,963	12,899	12,368	11,742	—189	—1.6	—7.3	4.3	5.3

[1] Exclusive of divorces for which no detailed statistics were obtained—1,461 in 1931; 1,728 in 1930; 2,133 in 1929; 3,597 in 1928; and 3,352 in 1927.
[2] A minus sign (—) denotes decrease.
[3] Includes "Cause not reported."
[4] None granted for "Neglect to provide."

We can catalog the reasons for divorce under the legal grounds, the moral causes, or the social situation. It is, however, only when we study the divorce problem as an interaction of two personalities, expressing itself in a definite social situation within the family, that we can gain any considerable scientific insight into the influences that lead toward divorce. Divorce is a conscious recognition of marriage failure and, like any other indication of maladjustment, has many causes.

[16] *Marriage and Divorce 1931*, p. 20 (U. S. Department of Commerce, Bureau of the Census).

Divorce legislation.   Although the evils resulting from the diversity of the legislation of the various states in regard to divorce may easily be exaggerated, there is general agreement as to the desirability of greater uniformity. At first, advocates of divorce reform pleaded for a federal law, a program which required for its success the passage of a constitutional amendment. Because of the practical difficulties involved in getting this amendment, later effort has been directed towards procuring greater uniformity in the laws of the separate states.

There are strong differences of opinion among those interested in conserving the family as to the desirability of a uniform divorce law, whether brought about by federal authority or by the passage of similar statutes in the various states. Not only are there practical difficulties in obtaining uniform divorce legislation by either method, but in addition to this there is danger inherent in the enactment in any state of a law regulating divorce that is not in accord with the general public opinion. Undoubtedly the difference in the divorce rate in various sections of the United States is in part due to differences in the average attitude of the populations concerned, and the trend is not at present toward greater uniformity.[17]

The contrast between the divorce rates of the different sections of the nation is not a mere expression of variation in legislation. Even if we had a federal law, or if the statutes of all the states were essentially the same, we should still have variation because of unlike conditions in the different parts of the country.

There does not appear to be the amount of moving from one state to another having more lax divorce regulations that one would expect of persons seeking matrimonial release, but there is undoubtedly some interstate migration for such a purpose. Apparently there are practical considerations which hamper the movement of those who find the getting of a divorce in their own state difficult. The differences in the legal grounds for divorce in the various states do not, according to Willcox, influence materially the number of divorces granted, but affect chiefly the choice of the ground upon which the divorce is sought.[18]

---

[17] *President Hoover's Research Committee on Social Trends,* Vol. 1, p. 693.
[18] Willcox, Walter F., *The Divorce Problem, A Study in Statistics,* pp. 37–38.

Legislation that encourages divorce is of course a social menace, but drastic legislation has its dangers also. Some advocates of divorce reform undoubtedly seek stringent legislation, but their solution of the divorce problem, if it were attainable, would prove mischievous and intolerable. The friend of the family will remember that it is not the legal opportunity for the getting of divorce, or the desire for such separation, but the family situation that seeks court relief which constitutes the heart of the divorce problem. Howard has well said, "For the wise reformer who would elevate and protect the family, the centre of the problem is marriage and not divorce." [19]

We need the best laws that can be written to conserve family welfare, but any attempt to solve the divorce problem by the mere passing of new laws will be futile. The American divorce record is, from a social point of view, startling and, when one translates it into the disappointment and suffering of individual men and women, pathetic; but its real significance is the revelation it gives of social forces at work that are making marriage success difficult, or—and this side of the problem must not be overlooked—the growing intolerance of low marriage standards or vicious conditions within the home circle. An increase in happy, wholesome marriages is the only permanent solution of our divorce problem, for the divorce is only a product of the family's reflection of widespread social conditions that make matrimonial comradeship between modern men and women more difficult than once it was. Divorce, like crime, is forceful evidence that our civilization is developing to a point of strain where there is special need of strengthening the weakness disclosed by a better use of our social resources to encourage sane ways of living.

Many suggestions for the reform of our divorce laws and practices have been made. In 1906 the National Congress on Uniform Divorce Laws drafted a uniform annulment of marriage and divorce act which was approved in 1907 by the National Conference of Commissioners on Uniform State Laws and was later adopted by three states. In 1930 the same group eliminated nearly all of the earlier act and drew up a drastically different reform program. And again in 1938 the commissioners decided to study the problems anew in order to draft a uniform

---

[19] Howard, G. E., *A History of Matrimonial Institutions*, Vol. 3, p. 223.

code. This committee is still at work. Vernier, who believes that uniformity is still not obtainable except in the distant future, has suggested changes in the provisions of the laws regarding divorce and in the court proceedings. He recommends the adoption of the interlocutory-decree system already in operation in about one-third of the states, the recasting or the total abolition of the divorce defense statutes of all states having such laws, the elimination of the discrimination between sexes now present in about a dozen jurisdictions, and finally the giving to the court of greater discretion in the disposition of the property of divorced parties. This minimum of change in family law he believes would greatly advance the divorce laws of the several states.[20] A different and more radical program has been advanced by Rood.[21] This is the outcome of a "lawyer's tabulated analysis of 270,000 divorces, a study repudiating all accepted theories of causes of metropolitan divorce trends and accusing the law." Writing in 1939 he reports that Wayne County (Detroit) had, since 1915, 100,000 divorces and declares that such a situation not only attacks matrimony; it endangers society itself. The author recommends giving the courts authority to grant divorces without a trial and without publicity when the parties agree to separate. The custody and the support of children and the question of alimony should however be tried in law. With the doing away of divorce litigation there would be no need of the appearing of a "Friend of the Court" or a defense counsel. Instead a "Friend of the Court" should be made a part of the prosecuting attorney's office and should be transferred to the court determining the custody and financial questions for the state in criminal nonsupport cases. He should be required to entitle every such prosecution in the name of the People and against the person prosecuted who should be permitted to have a jury trial. The author indicts the professional social worker for encouraging divorce. He believes in making divorce less desirable but not more difficult. It is his judgment that the divorce situation as it now exists in the United States is destroying the incentive for undertaking marriage as a lifetime relationship.[22]

---

[20] Vernier, *op. cit.*, pp. 7–9.
[21] Rood, Royal D., *Matrimonial Shoals*.
[22] Rood, *op. cit.*

A constructive program for a different legal approach to the divorce problem has recently been advocated based upon the idea that the welfare of the home as a moral institution ought to be the emphasis of the court's procedure and that those seeking a divorce should be dealt with as coming from a sick family. The issue therefore should be: Can anything be done to restore such a family to health, and, if so, how can recovery be brought about? The writer suggests four principles that the court should follow and for which there should be supporting legislation.

1. Divorce should be rather a conciliatory than a contentious proceeding.

2. The parties in interest should include the spouses and the members of the family.

3. The goal should be to work out whatever plan is best for the family as a whole.

4. The divorce court should be supplied with interprofessional personnel, tools, and sanctions to enable it to cope with this most serious of domestic problems.[23]

There is need of a radical change in the point of view of both the laws and the courts concerning divorce. The idea that a divorce should be granted because of the offense of the guilty party needs to be replaced by a factual recognition that the real issue is whether the couple are willing to live together. There should be provision for an attempt first of all to discover the causes of the trouble and then whether reconciliation can be brought about. Not until these efforts fail should divorce be granted.

The institution of marriage deserves more consideration. The individual who again and again seeks a divorce demonstrates that he or she does not have the capacity for the making of a successful marriage, and at some point society should deny such a person the right to marry. Three divorces would appear to be a reasonable limitation. A serial polygamy would seem to be more undermining of the meaning of marriage than a responsible legalized status of plural wives or husbands. Those who marry for a few months and then seek a divorce in order

---

[23] John S. Bradway, "Proposed New Techniques in the Law of Divorce," *Iowa Law Review*, Vol. 28, pp. 256–285.

to have another trial at matrimony are asking society to legalize what is basically a mere sexual excursion.

Migratory divorce.   A migratory divorce is one obtained by evading the divorce laws of the stricter states by establishing a temporary legal residence in some state or country that has a more liberal divorce code. This is the aspect of the divorce situation in the United States that attracts most attention and receives most criticism. Opposition to this means of escape from the restrictions imposed by the more conservative states for the purpose of getting a divorce quickly or easily began with agitation led by the Reverend Samuel W. Dyke and his New England Divorce Reform League. He sought a federal investigation of the divorce problem, and through his efforts an investigation of the divorce evil was made by Congress in 1887 during the administration of President Grover Cleveland and again in 1905 when President Theodore Roosevelt sent a special message to Congress urging that the states pass uniform divorce laws. This resulted in forty-two states or territories being represented in a Congress of Delegates which advocated changes that were enacted later by only three states: Delaware, New Jersey, and Wisconsin. Because of the failure of this approach to the migratory divorce problem, agitation started for an amendment of the constitution permitting Congress to legislate, and since 1923 a proposal for such an amendment has been introduced into Congress yearly.[24] It is interesting that the migratory divorce situation is used as an argument both by those who believe that there should be a more liberal divorce code throughout the country and those who believe that the getting of a divorce should be made difficult as a means of protecting marriage and the family.

Although the number of migratory divorces represents a small proportion of the total number granted, the possibility of removing from a strict jurisdiction to one that tries by its legislation to invite those seeking dissolution of their marriage becomes a symbol of the contention between those who hold opposite attitudes toward divorce. It has been estimated that the migratory divorce is not over three per cent of the total number. It is not even safe to assume that all the litigants who have

[24] Lichtenberger, J. P., *Divorce,* Ch. 8.

recently moved from a conservative to a more liberal jurisdiction are motivated by the desire to get a divorce more quickly or more easily although this is generally true.

It happens that the divorces that attract newspaper publicity on account of the standing or the notoriety of the persons involved are in large proportion migratory divorces. Perhaps these men and women seek divorce more quickly than it could be obtained in the state where they have resided, or maybe they wish to give as grounds for the divorce marital conditions that would not be legally accepted where they have been living. The consequence of this publicity is that popular thinking tends to exaggerate the numerical significance of migratory divorces, leading some who disbelieve in the right of divorce to advocate federal divorce legislation in order to have throughout the country a uniform and more stringent barrier to divorce.

It would, however, be a misinterpretation of the significance of migratory divorces to define their importance on the basis of their ratio to the nonmigratory divorces, even though it is true that the news character of individual migratory divorces explains the interest that people commonly take in this special feature of the divorce problem. There are deeper, more substantial reasons for serious investigation of the migratory divorce problem. To some degree the more liberal states and the foreign countries that provide opportunity for easier divorce serve as social experiments, for it must not be forgotten that, though the purpose of the legislative program may be to invite people to come within the jurisdiction for the purpose of getting a divorce, the same opportunity of divorce is offered to the native citizens. This, by itself, justifies the study of these more liberal divorce policies, even though their significance to the permanent residents may be lessened by the fact that the prevailing mores are less favorable to easy divorce than the laws by themselves would indicate. At least it is clear that the mere existence of a freer opportunity for divorce does not operate to entice people unless reinforced by other social influences that lead people to seek divorce. This fact gives evidence that one can never rationally deal with the divorce problem as something created by legislation, even though here, as elsewhere, laws do have an influence. There is a much more significant reason why the problem of migratory divorces should be studied than that it is an experiment in legislation. The migratory divorce has meaning in that it reveals the need felt by some for different conditions for dealing with failure in domestic relations. The jurisdictions that cater to those seeking a divorce also react upon the status and stability of marriage throughout the country. It is this mores-aspect of the migratory divorce problem that challenges the attention and interest of the student of contemporary social life.

Undoubtedly the offering of the more liberal divorce code has lessened the protest that was bound to come from those who felt most keenly the denial or the restricting of divorce in the more conservative jurisdictions. Since those who have availed themselves of the more liberal provisions for divorce have been so largely persons of wealth and distinction, there has been nothing like the aggressive attacks on the more severe divorce code that would have come had there been no way of escape. This includes not only the ease of getting a divorce but also the grounds for a divorce. People have escaped humiliation and the admission of details of marital failure that seemed greatly to their interest not to bring to the court. Even when they were assured that a divorce could be had in the jurisdiction where they were living, they have frequently felt the advantage of going elsewhere so that divorce could be procured without the rehearsal of experiences that were sure to have considerable publicity. The reluctance of legislators to provide as grounds for divorce the unhappy situation which can best be defined as incompatibility—certainly the most common cause of the desire to be divorced—has added to the attraction of laws that are closer to a frank recognition of this motive than the laws and decisions in jurisdictions that are more conservative.

The mere existence of the opportunity to go elsewhere and get a divorce has acted as a revelation of the strength of desire of a part of our population for easier, quicker, and franker ways of withdrawing from marriage ties. To what extent this has been a stimulus that has tended to liberalize the law in the more conservative sections one cannot know with certainty, but without question it has had an influence. The spectacular migratory divorce cases that have drawn public attention have at least made people generally appreciate the desire for a more liberal divorce program among a portion of our people.

From whatever position we advance to the investigation of migratory divorces, we find that the inherent hazard of marriage and the reluctance of legislation to recognize this in all its aspects has distinct relation to the special problem in which we are interested. Rightly, lawmakers and the law interpreters seek to encourage the stability of family life and to offer nothing that invites people who can live together as married to seek divorce. In so far as this leads to the blocking of ways of escape for those who suffer from marital frustrations, the possibility of migratory divorce becomes a sort of social safety valve. Whatever else may be its significance, the migratory divorce situation challenges both our social and our legal thinking.

Whatever else divorce may be, it is fundamentally the recognition of the hazard of human mating. No one can look at modern life with seeing eyes without recognizing the risk of unhappiness and failure that goes with our institution of marriage. If this were not true there would be no reason for divorce legislation. Unwillingness to provide legislation making possible escape from matrimonial dissatisfaction comes either from callous indifference to human suffering or from the insistence that for the social good the individual must surrender personal inclination and continue marriage responsibilities as an obligation even when affection and compatibility have disappeared from the union. No one who believes in monogamic marriage enjoys this fact of hazard, but there can be no sincere discussion of any divorce problem when there is refusal to face it.

There is always a disposition among those happily married to underestimate the difficulty of bringing two human beings, male and female, into the adjustment necessary along many lines to render their living together even tolerable and, still more, to make it a positive success in fellowship. The law attempts to recognize, in the way that seems best for the group life taken as a whole, this undeniable risk of marriage failure without at the same time so influencing those who enter marriage and those who experience problems that result from their union as to encourage them to accept defeat easily.

It would be false to insist that marriage is becoming less a social enterprise and more personal, because the institution always has its group significance interwoven with its values to individual persons. We can say that as people think about marriage they tend to regard its satisfactions as something indispensable in the security of the union itself. This shift is one of emphasis, but even so it leads to an appraisal of the marriage relationship that invites disappointment and discontent. Where, for example, the economic function of the family as a producing unit has precedence, there is less room for the emotional cravings and reactions, since belonging to the relationship is itself of great value. To the modern man and woman the success and the failure of marriage increasingly hinge upon the emotional significance of the union aside from its other contributions. There are great differences between persons in this respect, but the general trend is unmistakable, and the more open women are to the influences of modern life that are moving them toward social equality with men, the more sensitive they are to any domestic situation that antagonizes the modern trend.

Legislation can define and regulate marriage, but its positive contribution to domestic satisfaction is limited and chiefly indirect. It can do more by insisting upon more adequate preparation for the experience than by refusing to recognize marriage failure where it exists. Legislators have been known to express their conviction that they who enter marriage selfishly and recklessly should be forced to suffer the penalties of their carelessness. Such a conception of the divorce problem is too naive to be taken seriously. Although thoughtful, well-integrated people enter marriage less likely to fail than those who are self-centered, irresponsible, and impetuous, this does not mean that the marriage hazard exists only for those who are socially indifferent. Sometimes marriage failure suggests the principle of amphimixis as we find it in inheritance. The traits of personality that seem sound when taken by themselves become the cause of incompatibility through union.[25]

Alimony. Every American state and territory has some sort of statute authorizing the court in case of divorce to grant financial support to the wife. These provisions reflect the mores that carry back to the most primitive conditions of human society enforcing the husband's duty to support his wife. Alimony in this country is granted whether the divorce be absolute or

---

[25] Noyes, Arthur P., *Modern Clinical Psychiatry*, p. 453.

limited and without regard to whether the wife is complainant or defendant, provided there is no reason to doubt good faith in the bringing of the suit. Most jurisdictions permit the court to grant temporary alimony for her maintenance and suit money permitting her to defend or maintain her action for divorce. In some jurisdictions alimony is allowed to the husband, and in others the court is permitted to award him part of his wife's property.

Alimony in the first place was an attempt to give protection to the woman who left her husband and under the handicap of her sex tried to make her own way in the world. In those days when matrimony was the only vocation for women, it seemed fair that the woman driven from her husband's protection by his misdeeds should receive from him maintenance in proportion to his income as a substitute for the support which he promised her at marriage and which she was now losing through no fault of her own.

In the early history of the American colonies, it was so difficult for either man or wife to be self-supporting without the help of the other that couples who separated were sometimes publicly commanded to take up again their life together, lest either of them become a burden on the community. Often the man was ordered to live with his wife or else give her a definite sum of money, or a certain number of pounds of tobacco or bushels of corn and wheat per year for her maintenance.

Since those days women have gone into competition with men in every kind of industry, and matrimony is no longer ordinarily entered upon as a means of support. We have countless women in this country who can earn more than their husbands. It is even true at times that a wife can find employment when her husband cannot.

So long as women were social dependents with no means of support except wifehood, alimony was not only just but a public necessity. No woman, however cruelly treated, would attempt to get a divorce if this left her financially stranded, a candidate for the almshouse. Without the possibility of alimony, the right of divorce was a mere farce.

The possibility of obtaining alimony if her marriage venture fails is without doubt in the mind of many a woman who is enticed into matrimony by economic ambition. To such a

woman divorce may come to mean freedom from the limitations of marriage without the sacrifice of the financial advantages she sought in marrying. The court decree may furnish her
with an allowance that permits an indulgence in personal luxuries beyond what she enjoyed as wife. The opportunity to get
alimony easily becomes under such circumstances a stimulus to
divorce.

Even when the divorce is sought without mercenary motive, the very fact that the court orders the husband to give a
stated sum to his wife when they have separated for some trivial
reason makes later reconciliation difficult. Encouraged perhaps
by a type of lawyer who fattens on the profits of divorce cases,
the wife who left in a fit of anger may refuse to meet her husband halfway in an effort to forget the past and get a second
start on the road toward marriage happiness. If the prospects of
alimony were ruled out, the professional divorce lawyer would
often be less keen in urging a divorce, knowing that even were
the decree granted, it would not be followed by a series of payments to the wife, a substantial part of which he could expect
to fall eventually into his own hands in the form of fees charged
for his services.

The industrial changes that have increased the economic
independence of women are reflected in an increasing protest
against the granting of alimony in cases where the woman has
no children and is able to maintain herself or when she has
enough property in her own name for self-support. There is
a growing feeling, which has found some expression in judicial
decisions, that alimony should not be made a means of punishing the husband in case of marriage failure or permitted to become a weapon of revenge in the hands of the wife.

There has been such obvious exploitation of alimony, especially in the case of young women marrying wealthy men,
that an aggressive attack on this legal procedure is being made
by some students of law. Alimony is regarded by them as one of
the most lucrative of rackets.[26] Kelso [27] points out that the problem of alimony needs to be looked at from the point of view of
family welfare. It is no longer reasonable to hold that any

[26] Rood, *op. cit.*, p. 125.
[27] Kelso, Robert W., "The Changing Social Setting of Alimony Law," *Law
and Contemporary Problems*, Vol. 6, No. 2, p. 186.

woman who gets a divorce has a right to a continuous subsidy from her husband as if she were damaged by her experience. Instead, the proper question is whether she has grounds for needing a continued support. If she has several children, no property of her own, and no special preparedness for employment, this situation is totally unlike that of the young woman who has no children, or has property, and who can be presumed to look forward to a second marriage. The family need should be the deciding issue, and all questions of guilt or innocency should be disregarded. If a woman receiving money from a former husband remarries, her alimony should at once cease.[28] Changes in the income or earning capacity of the husband justify the reconsideration of the amount of alimony which under different financial circumstances was granted to the wife. Complication arises when the husband who is obligated to support his former family remarries and has children. A realistic approach to this problem has been taken by courts that have permitted a reduction in alimony, declaring that it has become the duty of the courts to see that there is a fair division of the husband's income between the two families.[29] A former husband cannot escape the duty of supporting his children on the grounds that his one-time wife has remarried. The allotment for children, however, is open to reconsideration as the financial circumstances of the father greatly change.[30] In order that the trial judge, who is given wise discretion, may in case of divorce decide rightly the husband's continuing liability for his wife and children, he needs to have greater resources for making an adequate investigation as a basis for his judgment.[31]

Social and psychological effects of alimony. Alimony in the majority of cases perpetuates a relationship passionately undesired with the consequence that the antagonism at the time of divorce continues and is increased.[32] The husband's emotional resentment toward his wife gathers about his obligation to pay alimony. The wife, on the other hand, may be led to

---

[28] *Ibid.,* p. 196.

[29] Shattuck vs. Shattuck, 141 Wash. 600, 251 Pac. 851 (1927).

[30] *Ibid.,* p. 245.

[31] *Ibid.,* p. 248.

[32] Peele, Catherine Groves, "Social and Psychological Effects of the Availability and the Granting of Alimony on the Spouses," *Law and Contemporary Problems,* Vol. 6, No. 2, pp. 283–292.

feel as she receives her alimony checks that she has been ill treated and should justly have more money. There is likely also to be on the part of outsiders who know of the money settlement, especially women, the feeling that the alimony discloses a mercenary motive in the former wife. This is encouraged by the fact that, contrary to what one would expect, alimony is usually granted in cases of divorce and separation to those belonging to the higher economic group. Less often those on the lower level who brought to the marriage nothing more than housekeeping or wage-earning ability obtain alimony.[33]

The emotional reactions of both husbands and wives toward the court's order for alimony are in accord with their character and their attitude toward their former relationship. For example, some women seek alimony in order to have the satisfaction of vengeance; others refuse to take anything from the husband, even when they clearly need aid, because they are determined to be absolutely disconnected from him. These emotional reactions to alimony sometimes prevent reconciliation and remarriage. In other instances the demand for alimony becomes a final barrier to the re-establishment of the union when in a temporary mood the wife starts the divorce proceedings. To remove as much as possible these various emotional hazards associated with alimony, it is desirable to treat the question of alimony as a business matter, the sharing of the mutual resources and responsibilities of the spouses, rather than as tribute exacted from the guilty party or charity taken from one and given to the other because he is a man and she is a woman.

The marriage hazard.   Marriage, like all other human undertakings, has its hazards. The forms and the quantity of failures in matrimonial fellowship are related to the prevailing culture. In a society where divorce is taboo, there will be some other expression of unfortunate and unhappy unions. Whenever divorce is permissible, the number of persons who have recourse to it will be influenced by the effect of the social environment in stimulating personal demands, by individualism, and by emotional stability. Marriage failures may be lessened by decreasing expectation just as the hazards of human mating may be made greater by lifting the standard. As a consequence, the quality of matrimonial experience cannot be determined

---

[33] *Ibid.*, p. 284.

merely by the absence or presence of divorce or by the frequency of divorce. The marriage hazard is always relative to the total social experiences of the group.

In contemporary American life the divorce rate is at best a rough expression of the proportion of marriage failure. It serves better to reveal how many of those who marry in this country fail to obtain enough satisfaction to remain together, than as a means of comparison between the American and other cultural groups. We appear at present to have the largest divorce rate, possibly because we are most sensitive to the industrial and social changes brought forth by machine civilization. Just as the amount of bankruptcy in business reveals the difficulty of commercial success, so the divorce rate gives an inkling of the amount of marriage disaster. All business failures, however, are not recorded through bankruptcy procedures nor are matrimonial incompatibilities always expressed through divorce.

There are marriages that appear from the start impossible of success. There are many that seem to the outside observer more than usually hazardous, while there are others that appear to have all the conditions necessary for happiness. The experience of individuals in marriage proves that hazards exist as a result of conditions that were not foreseen. It helps in the understanding of the significance of divorce to divide marriage hazards into two categories.

Hazards of cultural origin.   Influences of economic and social origin already treated in earlier chapters constitute the hazards of cultural origin. The mere summarizing of them makes clear the greater difficulty of those attempting a modern marriage in comparison with the easier task of those who enter upon marriage in a simpler society. The economic independence of women, their greater self-expression, the breakdown of the patriarchal type of family life, the spread of liberal thought, the democratic ideals, the higher ideals of marriage, the lessened tolerance of matrimonial unhappiness, the diminution of the control processes of primary contact, and the decrease of a coercive public opinion which in times past frowned upon divorce are all social influences that increase the possibility of matrimonial failure.

Hazards of personality origin. In sociological literature much is made of the strain of the marriage institution as it attempts to adapt itself to changing social conditions, but as concrete human experiences, this tension belongs to individual men and women who in their particular matrimonial relationship find it difficult to make satisfactory personal adjustment each with his mate. From this angle the hazards of marriage come forth from the personality of those who marry. Marriage failure becomes a special type of inability to make satisfactory life adjustment. To understand divorces that occur from hazards of personality origin, the same effort has to be made to plumb character that is followed by the scientist who endeavors to understand delinquency, crime, neurotic behavior, and the insanities. Marriage maladjustment presents the same problem of character analysis but expressed in a specific and unique relationship. Modern marriage offers to the well-equipped and wholesomely matured a rare opportunity for happiness, but it also forces upon the men and women who enter matrimony emotionally unsound, infantile in character, an ordeal which lays bare any serious handicaps of personality. The matrimonial experiences which offer the means of happiness to one individual become for a different type the rack of emotional torture.

The divorce racket. It is obvious to anyone familiar with the divorce situation in the United States that there is a commercializing of the marriage hazard to an extent that justifies the term "divorce racket." [34] Not only do we have states frankly rivaling one another in their liberal divorce legislation for the purpose of bringing people into the jurisdiction as money-spenders but also well-organized divorce profiteers who advertise for business. Anyone contemplating a divorce needs only to write to a chamber of commerce in a city within a jurisdiction where easy divorce laws have been enacted to receive by mail information explaining the advantage of going to that particular place and also a list of attorneys ready to serve the prospective divorcee. [35] Thus when temporary dissatisfaction or a quar-

---

[34] Bergeson, Rollo, "The Divorce Mill Advertises," *Law and Contemporary Problems*, Vol. 2, No. 3, p. 348.

[35] *Ibid.*, p. 350.

rel which, given time, might be happily adjusted leads to a request for information from those maintaining a divorce mill, the writer is encouraged to start on a divorce quest which, once begun, proves a serious obstacle to any reconciliation. Those who draw their income as professional divorce attorneys seldom dissuade anyone seeking a divorce. American divorce mills have encountered competition from Cuba and Mexico where the divorce racket has gone so far as to provide for the getting of a divorce by mail. The obtaining of such a divorce does not mean that the decree will be automatically recognized outside the jurisdiction where it was granted. Divorces decreed in foreign countries have therefore contributed additional confusion and grounds for litigation to a situation already replete with legal uncertainties.

The churches and divorce. Both Judaism and Christianity seek to encourage the security of the family and regard divorce as an evil. The Roman Catholic Church has been consistent in maintaining its doctrine of the indissolubility of marriage and its ecclesiastical law does not recognize divorce, although provision is made for the annulling of marriages that from the viewpoint of the church were invalid and also for separation of the spouses. Among all the Protestant churches we find concern for the institution of marriage and the desire to discourage divorce. Aside from this basic attitude, there have been from time to time changes in this attitude toward divorce. Lichtenberger in 1931 said that the policy of the Protestant churches was unmistakably in the direction of greater stringency and that their efforts to lessen the divorce evil had been almost wholly reactionary. On the contrary, at the present time the trend is in the opposite direction. No longer does the leadership of any of the Protestant denominations feel satisfied with merely denouncing divorce. Instead, each of them maintains a program of constructive effort for the purpose of helping those who marry to achieve success. It is also true that the recent trend has been toward a more sympathetic treatment of church members who are divorced.

The present trend can best be illustrated by the Episcopal Church, because it has been the most drastic in its ecclesiastical policy toward divorce. The demand for a more liberal policy has been the most controversial issue in recent general conventions of the church. The following are examples of the changing trend, especially among the laity of the Episcopal Church:

The Committee of the Women's Auxiliary on Marriage and Divorce appointed by the Protestant Episcopal House of Bishops to consider the question of marriage and divorce and present their views to the Commission on Marriage and Divorce, appointed under the resolution of the General Convention of 1937, making their report to the General Convention of 1940, advocated in part: "If a divorced person who has been in communion with this church desires to remarry after a reasonable time and desires, as does the partner of this second marriage, the blessing of the church, this might well be bestowed when the parish priest or a suitable committee are assured, after examination of the circumstances involved, of the genuine desire and purpose of both participants to lead a Christian life." The report in the section discussing "Remarriage of a Divorced Person" held that each case "presents a situation peculiar to itself and must be considered before God on its own individual merits in the light of fundamental principles. But no priest unwilling to perform such a ceremony should be required to do so." Under the heading "Admission to Holy Communion of Persons Remarried After Divorce" the report declared: "The Committee is in complete agreement that persons remarried after divorce should not for that reason be deprived of holy communion. Excommunication is the most serious deprivation that can be inflicted upon a communicant of the church. The Committee believes that the use of such a penalty in these cases is contrary to Christ's teaching of mercy." [36]

The Committee on Marriage of the Protestant Episcopal Diocese of Long Island reported in part as follows: "When a marriage fails, the solution of the difficulties should be Christian. . . . When parents cease to love each other, or when for any cause the marriage has positively failed, children are harmed by the state of constant psychological conflict. In extreme cases the breakup of the home may be necessary. It is hypocritical to condone the continuation of a marriage which no longer approximates Christian marriage. Such a union fulfills only the letter of the law. Divorce, like the surgeon's knife, may be the only cure and honorable Christian solution."

Of remarriages the report continued: "It is only Christian that mercy and forgiveness as well as justice should govern the decision of the church." Failure of marriage does not necessarily mean that a second marriage cannot attain the Christian ideal. "A more suit-

---

[36] *The New York Times,* March 31, 1940.

able partner, better conditions, a lesson learned from past experiences may be all that is required." A remarriage, the report pointed out, may be doubly advisable for the sake of the children.[37]

Emotional reactions to divorce. The ground advanced in the plea for a divorce is likely to be determined by the legal provisions for divorce· in the jurisdiction of residence. Therefore, it gives no clue to the real motive. Even when there has been some specific action that led to the decision to seek a divorce, the appeal to the courts is fundamentally the consequence of a state of mind. Because of this the divorce may merely change outwardly directed clashing to an inner conflict. The emotional disturbance may not disappear even when the person who brought it about has been removed from the husband-and-wife relationship.[38] Bitterness, a sense of futility or the feeling that all security has been lost may result, even though a divorce puts an end to the disappointing fellowship. The quantity of this reaction is of course determined by the personality and previous history of the individual and occurrences and reactions during the marriage association. Since the state of mind is the basic cause of the divorce proceedings, two reactions frequently occur. One is the seeking of the divorce during a temporary upheaval, most often of anger, and after the flood of emotion has subsided there is regret, or at least a questioning whether the divorce ought to have been sought. This is especially true if the welfare of children seems to be involved. Another reaction is to defend one's own action, already rued, by encouraging some other person known not to be entirely happy in marriage also to seek a divorce. Thus may come about what has been suggestively described as psychologically contagious divorce-seeking.

The emotional aftermath of a divorce is likely to be great even among those who can be rightly called normal although sensitive. But for the basically psychopathic the results are certain to be volcanic. Obviously this type is apt to enter marriage again and then, when the second trial has failed, to get another divorce in the effort to solve problems of social adjust-

---

[37] *Ibid.*, September 26, 1940.

[38] Lerman, Phillip R., "Psychopathological Aspects in Emotional Divorce," *Psychoanalytic Review*, Vol. 26, p. 1.

ment that cannot be resolved except by a reconstruction of the personality itself. Lacking self-understanding, the individual turns to divorce with confidence that she knows what is the trouble and the way out, and our legal system has no provision for showing her that she is in no position to trust her self-diagnosis but instead needs psychiatric assistance.

Annulment.   Divorce puts an end to what was a legal marriage; an annulment is the decision of the court that the marriage never legally existed. The grounds for annulment are determined by statute in most states of the union. These carry out the principles of the common law, but in nearly all our states the latter are, by legislative enactments, modified and generally liberalized. Insufficient age to contract marriage, nearness of blood, impotence, use of force, fraud, mental incapacity, and being already married are the common grounds for annulment. The various states and territories differ in their laws regarding annulment just as they do in their divorce legislation. Sometimes the distinction between the two appears to be lost, since in some states divorce is a proper remedy for the ending of a marriage which was from the first illegal.

The annulment of a marriage restores the parties concerned to their former legal status as single persons. This in theory means that any property should be distributed according to the situation before marriage and that the wife does not have any right to maintenance or alimony. Since also there was no genuine marriage, any child born as a consequence of the union is illegitimate unless otherwise protected by statute. In practice there are departures from this theory of annulment in accord with specific provisions in the particular jurisdiction where the annulment is obtained. As a rule, however, according to Vernier, the practical and intelligent policy in dealing with the problems that arise through the annulling of a marriage is subversive to the common law interpretation of annulment.[39]

Legislative changes are as frequent in this field as in that of divorce. A new and much needed ground for annulment is provided by a New York law which allows actions for annulment where one party to the marriage has been incurably insane for five years without requiring that such insanity had

---

[39] Vernier, C. G., *American Family Laws*, Vol. 2, p. 238.

existed at the time of marriage.[40] The following statute from West Virginia also extends the grounds for annulment: Marriages may be annulled for disease; or when either of the parties prior to the marriage, without the knowledge of the other, had been convicted of an infamous offense; or when, at the time of marriage, the wife, without the knowledge of the husband, was with child by some other person than the husband, or when, prior to such marriage, she had been, without the knowledge of the husband, notoriously a prostitute; or when, prior to such marriage, the husband, without the knowledge of the wife, had been notoriously a licentious person. This section implies that any marriage brought about by fraud, force, or coercion may be annulled.[41]

The principles of procedure governing annulment are generally similar to those regulating the suit for divorce. Where there are specific statutes determining the process, we find the same variation between jurisdictions as in the case of divorce. It appears, for example, in the provisions of the laws for bringing the action for annulment to the court. There are also regulations limiting the time during which such action can be sought. The law, for example, may not allow an annulment for nonage, impotence, force, or fraud unless proceedings are started within the time limit fixed by statute. In addition to legislation concerning divorce, legal separation, and annulment, we have laws that deal with the dissolution of marriage. In some jurisdictions, and this seems reasonable and desirable in all the states, a marriage can be dissolved because of the life imprisonment of a spouse. Long continued absence or abandonment can also be recognized as grounds for declaring the marriage dissolved. The general principle is that if a former husband or wife has been absent or not heard from for a certain period, usually five years, the other party may marry without being guilty of bigamy.[42]

Seduction is another problem that has to be dealt with in family law. Many of the jurisdictions and legislations make a bona fide offer of marriage a bar to prosecution for seduction.

[40] Vernier, *op. cit., 1938 Supplement,* pp. 27–28.
[41] *Ibid.,* p. 28.
[42] Vernier, *op. cit.,* Vol. 1, p. 287.

As a consequence, we have the question: Shall a defendant be permitted to escape prosecution by a marriage, then almost immediately leave his wife or by his conduct force her to abandon him? Some of the states have tried to meet this problem by stating that marriage merely suspends the prosecution for seduction, and therefore cruelty or abandonment revives the criminal procedure. Crimes of adultery, fornication, and abduction (although this may have been for the purpose of placing the victim in prostitution), and even rape are in some states permitted to have suspended prosecution if the man marries the woman concerned. Other states have acts which make it impossible to make use of the state of marriage as a defense in prosecution for pandering. Legislation in this field varies from jurisdiction to jurisdiction and changes in the laws are constantly occurring.

Family desertion. Divorce and desertion are family problems that have much in common. On account of this likeness, desertion is commonly called "the poor man's divorce." Although this statement correctly brings out the fact that desertion among the poorer classes is often a substitute for divorce, it is misleading in so far as it conveys the impression that these two forms of family disintegration are the same, except that one is confined exclusively to people of a lower economic status. Desertion is one type of family disintegration, divorce is another; the wealthy, the professional classes, and those socially well established turn for various reasons, when family life becomes unsatisfactory, to the divorce court for relief, while the more mobile unskilled worker, or the individual whose occupation provides great economic freedom, cuts himself away from family difficulties by merely leaving the home and disappearing. There are many reasons why the well-to-do should prefer the use of the legal method of getting free from marital difficulties. In addition to the other social advantages of divorce, it is the customary way of getting freedom in their class and, therefore, in accord with the proprieties. In the professional class divorce frequently carries with it social risks from which the individuals shrink, but to attempt to escape these by family desertion would be ruinous; in some cases it would mean throwing away a professional reputation and giving up all hope of a second start in one's vocation and also legal remarriage. Here also the class code does not include family desertion as a proper means of getting rid of marital difficulties.

There are many motives that tempt the poor in family unhappiness to desert rather than to have the court cut the matrimonial ties. It is, of course, in this country the man who generally deserts. Apparently under other social conditions the woman rather than the man may be tempted to leave the family, for I am told by Dr. Asa Matsuoka, a Japanese graduate student, that it is the woman rather than the man who more often deserts in Japan.

A study of the conscious motives that lead men in the poorer classes to leave their families discloses the fact that desertion is not just an easier and cheaper way of ending matrimony than is offered by divorce. Often the husband seeks not so much to get rid of the family as to become free from an economic burden, from conditions of work that seem intolerable, or from unemployment that appears hopeless. Then the family is not so much repudiated as left behind. The man is consciously seeking not so much a permanent separation from his family as a brief spell of relief from the heavy load he has been carrying or an opportunity to start afresh. To be sure, rationalization is as often found in the motives that lead to desertion as in other lines of conduct where the reasons built into consciousness conceal the deeper desires that bring about the behavior. It is easy for the desertion that starts as a temporary expediency to become a permanent separation, and in many of these cases the men drift into a complete and final severance of family ties rather than deliberately break from the family with a definite decision to seek a divorce.

It is easy for the unskilled or factory worker to pack up and leave a family situation which has become troublesome. Indeed, this procedure is often the line of least resistance, for it seems, and often actually is, easier to go than to stay. Wanderlust and the desire for travel are at times contributory motives, and they may even constitute occasionally the chief cause of desertion. It is this type of desertion that has led the social worker to call desertion "the poor man's vacation from his family," rather than a divorce.

Where the desertion results from a family incompatibility

which in some other class would be likely to end in a divorce, it is easy to understand why so many men prefer leaving their family, to the legal method of separation through the divorce court. They are familiar with desertion, for it is frequent enough in their class to be a matter of common knowledge, and they have little understanding of court procedure, particularly when they are immigrants who are perhaps suspicious of any process that has to do with our legal machinery. Moreover, if they have religious scruples against divorce, they find desertion less antagonizing to their conscience.

Desertion brings out clearly the greater instability of family life in the city as compared with our villages and country places. In addition to the greater difficulty of holding together the family in the city, urban life encourages desertion by its greater mobility, the ease with which one can disappear. The city-dweller has fewer of the face-to-face associations that tend to check the feelings of anonymity and irresponsibility which encourage family desertion.

The earlier treatment of the deserting husband by our social agencies stressed the law. Largely as a result of their effort, legislation directed against nonsupport and desertion has been passed by many of our states. Now that our courts are better prepared to deal adequately with the deserter, the tendency has been to make use of the law only as a last resort. Increasingly it is becoming clear that little headway can be made against the tendency among the poor in our cities to desert their families unless each case is treated as a home problem, complex in character and requiring diagnosis and sympathetic treatment. If rehabilitation of family life is desirable, haling the deserter into court and bringing in the wife as complainant is all too apt to become a hopeless obstacle in the way of any later attempt to re-establish the family life.

Desertion, like divorce, is an expression of the instability of modern family life, and it can be more successfully attacked by efforts to reinforce the family and to procure social conditions that will minister to its health than by regarding desertion as a crime that deserves just punishment. The statistics of family desertion seem to demonstrate that the family agencies at present are making little headway against it, and there is no hope of substantial progress in dealing with this particular product of family instability until greater and more practical effort is made to conserve home life.

Economic results of desertion. The financial consequences of desertion as they affect family life are often greater than those caused by divorce. The husband by going away relieves himself of the obligations of family support that would be likely to be imposed if he and his wife were divorced. Moreover, since desertion is most common among those living on the lower economic levels, the loss of the husband's income is felt immediately. The family survives by a great variety of expediencies. Sometimes savings and credit tide the family over until a new source of income is made possible. The family may take in boarders. If there are older children, they may leave school and go to work. Assistance may come from the wife's or husband's parents, from friends, from the church the family has attended, or from some charitable or public-welfare organization. The family may split apart and the children be distributed to relatives or friends. Sometimes the children may be placed in an institution or better still in a foster home. In some instances the wife takes on a new mate, perhaps before she is legally free from her spouse, and therefore their relationship is illegal.

The desertion of the husband is apt to be first reported to the police and then to some social agency. It is fortunate for the family when some family service association or public welfare organization comes to know of the family's plight. Too often the wife, on account of pride or lack of knowledge of the resources available to her for assistance, attempts to carry the family load herself. Only when she becomes ill or can no longer find sufficient employment do the police or any social service organization hear of the desertion. Occasionally it is the wife who deserts. When this happens, it is nearly always true that she has fallen in love with another man. This is likely to end in the husband's divorcing her. Among deserting husbands we find two groups which need to be distinguished from the characteristic type. One is made up of husbands who come and go. They suddenly disappear from their home and after months or even years they reappear. In a short time the same thing happens again. They are known as "repeaters." The other group is made up of husbands who leave home when their wives become pregnant. The repeaters and the pregnancy deserters are most likely to attempt through a third person to keep informed of what happens in their former home. Sometimes they send money back to the family, with or without giving the wife knowledge of their whereabouts. It is apparent that wanderlust as well as dissatisfaction with marriage or family life influences desertion.

Chapter 18

THE FAMILY ITSELF A PROBLEM

FOREWORD. The purpose of this chapter is to provide opportunity for the student to consider and discuss the most important of the criticisms that have been made of marriage and the family in so far as they are reflected in the thinking of people in this country. The family and marriage are both human institutions revealing weaknesses, failures, and even serious tragedies. The hazard of marriage has become a conventional realization among Americans and the dangers of parenthood an axiom among the scientists who study and deal with human behavior. Domestic and marital disasters generally are regarded as a consequence of the faults of the individuals concerned, but there is a small group of critics who insist that the trouble comes from the faulty character of our two domestic institutions themselves. Not content with indictment, members of this group advance programs for dealing with mating and with parenthood. The former social interest is more frequently attacked than the other, because experience with institutions has not given many confidence that, however well organized, they can function as satisfactorily as do parents in the bringing up of children. No course in the American family does justly by its students if it denies them an opportunity to examine and discuss the most significant or the most influential of the various assaults that have been recently made on marriage and the family. Youth normally has the impulse to examine critically what most adults have come to accept as a matter of course. It is not surprising that this finds expression, at least among some young people, as they contemplate marriage or attempt to ap-

504

praise the family life which they recognize has had a command-ing influence in their own experience.

Indictment of the family. In order to have a true picture of the situation of the American family, there must be recognition of the fact that in the minds of some the family itself has become a major social problem. These critics of the family believe that it is failing as a social institution and needs such thorough changing as to become a new type of organization. This judgment is so contrary to the traditions of American civilization that its demonstration would bring about the most revolutionary cultural change in our history.

Those who have this idea usually believe that we are drifting into a radical reconstruction of marriage and the family and that the event will be near at hand before many people have become aware of what is happening. There is a stronger belief that this will come to marriage rather than to the family in the stricter sense, but it is generally felt that the remaking of the conditions of the former will inevitably dislodge the present conventional family as a social institution.

The period is one of social scrutiny and every social organization and convention is receiving criticism. Not one is so secure as not to be under attack as an obstacle to progress. Thus far, government, industry, religion, and education are receiving a severer bombardment than is either marriage or the family. This, of course, does not prove that the latter are more secure, for it may be, as some insist, that the tenacity of our cultural habits is protecting marriage and the family from criticism and merely delaying the reconstruction that is bound to take place.

It would be misleading to assume that the present scrutiny of the family is something absolutely new in human thinking. On the contrary, we find as far back as Plato an attitude toward the Athenian family which suggests that of the modern critic, and between the days of the great Greek philosopher and the present there have been from one direction or another various assaults upon the family as a social institution, in the belief that the type of family then conventional demanded fundamental, structural reshaping. This has been true even in this country as the Mormons, the Oneida Community, the Shakers, and others have tried to work out a family organization superior to that receiving general approval.

It would be strange in this period of cultural transition, when no social trait can appeal to the past as a means of escaping searching examination, if marriage and the family were given a special exemption. In any case the family has not been made an exception even though thus far it has been dealt with leniently by most of its critics. No social institution functions perfectly and the practicing family has always been open to criticism for fault in some form.

This pointing out of inefficiency in family life is not what is meant by the reaction of those who believe that the family is itself a major social problem. They recognize that any social institution will reveal in its concrete expression inadequacies, for it is not an abstraction but an organization of human nature in action. Those who have lost confidence in the conventional marriage and family of American culture insist that our present domestic difficulties are coming not from imperfections of individual men and women but from the archaic character of the family structure itself. They point to the changes in family function, changes that cannot be denied, and insist that these alterations in the quantity of family activity along various lines prophesy the appearance sooner or later of differences of quality which will mean nothing less than the remaking of the structure of the family. They regard the social support the family is still receiving as an obstacle to clear thinking that retards the coming of the new family which they consider desperately needed.

The basis of criticism. The indictment of the family by those who consider that it is an inadequate social institution is greatly influenced by the recent developments in the sciences that have to do with human behavior. This gives the modern criticism of the family a distinction in comparison with that in the past, since the latter came chiefly out of philosophic speculation. Behind the recent attacks on the family is a considerable quantity of factual material collected from psychology, psychiatry, sociology, and psychoanalysis which reveals the inefficiency of individual families.

The specialists in these different fields of science are impressed by the social incompetency of many of the families that they have investigated and, as one would expect, a portion of these experts have become convinced that some change is radically needed in domestic and parenthood relations. Among these workers are some of the severest critics of the American family, but for the most part the attack on the institution comes from agitators and reformers who make use of material which has been gathered by the scientists in dealing with the consequences of maladjustments in marriage and the parent-child association.

The disposition to analyze the problems of character defect and not to be content with descriptions of faulty behavior such as selfishness, jealousy, sensitiveness, delinquency, and the like tends to a critical appraising of family influence in a way and to a degree unknown in the past. Instead of trying to fix blame, there is an effort to analyze the situation, to uncover the influences that have operated to make the individual selfish, jealous, sensitive, or unsocial. As soon as this is undertaken, it is usually found that family influence has been the root of the difficulty. In the desire to prevent such occurrences, specialists have produced an impressive literature which has had more popular reading than is generally true of scientific material. The result is that not only does the critic of the family find himself free to make use of the great quantity of findings that illustrate faulty family life, but he also addresses an audience that already has been impressed by the same material from which he draws his ammunition.

Mental hygiene has done much to popularize the consequences of family failure in the effort to prevent social maladjustment and emotional conflict. The purpose of the mental hygienist has been to give husband, wife, and parent understanding of their problems as a means of prevention, but, as is always true under such circumstances, his revelation of family incompetency has often impressed a portion of his readers and listeners more than have the principles of conduct that he has tried to enforce.

It is in the work of the child guidance clinics that mental hygiene has come closest to the faulty functioning of the family. At the start, these organizations focused their therapeutic endeavor upon the child only to discover shortly that, as a rule, the problem-child who came to them for analysis and guidance was the product of an unwholesome family situation. The consequence of this was an overemphasis of the power of the parent, particularly the mother, to determine the destiny of the child. The experience of those working in this therapeutic field has led away from a concentration upon either the problem-child or the problem-parent [1] toward an appreciation of the complexity of the child's development in which the parents have a most important influence but rather as guides than persons possessing such control as to permit them to mould the child. In place of such determination the parent-child relationship is regarded as an unique fellowship of two individuals in which the child as well as the parent needs to be an active participant.

There can be no doubt that the more thoughtful part of the American population has been made conscious of and sensitive to the dangers of family experience. Some parents have become panicky toward their responsibilities to their children while other men and women, apparently with sincerity, refuse to enter parenthood because they dread its obligations. Such persons lend a willing ear to those who preach the need of saving children from the risk of parents by organizing an institution that can take over the functions of child training which always have been a major part of family life.

This exaggeration of the responsibility of the parent, especially the mother, and the confidence in her almightiness came from the misinterpretation of the influence of normal parenthood that developed in the earlier period of the child-guidance clinic, when attention was directed away from the problem-child to the problem-parent and any serious mishap in the development of the former was charged against the latter. It is not strange that some sensitive, conscientious parents, believing that they determined the life-career of any child born to them, either hesitated to assume such tremendous responsibility or, in the attempt to take over the task they believed assigned to them, became dangerous to the growing child by magnifying their commission. As a result of this taking themselves too seriously, they, with the best of intent, overstrained their parental relationship and then, failing to accomplish their ideal, became afflicted with guilt-feeling. This sense of failure increased the unwholesomeness of their family program.

---

[1] Allen, Frederick H., *Psychotherapy With Children*, pp. 11–12.

Science has dislodged the home from its safe refuge in sentiment and has forced it to come under an impartial investigation, and the result has been a disclosure of the bad functioning of both the family and marriage, which has weakened the confidence of many in regard to the social value of these institutions. It is to be expected that the attack on the home and marriage will become even more aggressive as new information is gathered regarding the social evils that are products of unwise home life, and as the reformer learns from actual experience how difficult it is to change unwholesome family life or to remove from the personality injury that has been received from harmful contacts within the home circle.

The recent advances in the social sciences that throw light upon human conduct make it necessary that we enlarge our ideas of family failure. From the point of view of mental hygiene, the bad home is not merely the place of low standards, poverty, obvious brutality, or discord. Family life that runs smoothly, yields a fair share of happiness to its members, and outwardly shows no evidence of disturbances may contain, as we now know because of our better understanding of the problems of conduct, conditions inherently mischievous that prohibit normal personal development and distort emotional behavior to such an extent that good social character becomes impossible.

Formerly, the distinction between the good and bad homes lay on the surface and was patent to all observers. Now that science has made a beginning in its study of family life, we have to include in our list of bad homes many that in former days were considered markedly good. The problem has become complicated by our new knowledge, and the differences between the homes that function well and those that function to the detriment of personal and social welfare have become more subtle. Naturally, the first phase of this change is a growing skepticism as to the social value of marriage and the home.

Every period has its favorite scapegoat, and during the first quarter of the twentieth century this role fell to the family, at least in the United States. This assertion does not minimize the force of criticism directed by the scientists against inadequate family experience, but it does emphasize the need of proportion lest we transfer to the institution the emotional blame-fixing impulse which we have learned to restrain when dealing with individuals.

In any case the family is no independent fountain of influence, a sort of first cause of social trouble, but merely a special relationship of persons and one that is in constant interaction with all other social institutions and persons with which it has contact. Powerful as is the family, its responsibilities are nevertheless limited, for it does not possess a monopoly of the influences that shape the character of the child or that operate upon the adult. Moreover, much of the malpractice of the family as a social institution is the expression, in intimate association, of character faults that reflect the weakness of social culture as a whole rather than simply that of the family. It may be that the family must change and even change radically, but it is reasonable to assume that no mere reshaping of the family or finding of a substitute for it will reorganize civilization and eliminate the possibilities of maladjustments. At least there must be social reconstruction outside the family as well as within, and surely the first means lessening the risk that science reveals in the functioning at present of individual families.

Literature and family failures.   One of the favorite topics of modern literature is marriage incompatibility and family tragedy. The coming of romantic marriage and the individualism characteristic of modern life would in themselves turn the novel and the play to an inspection and portrayal of familial experience, but, in addition to these influences of social evolution, the searching of human conduct that has gone on in science has also inspired the literary artist. The result of this stimulation from science appears most clearly in the so-called psychological novels which are sometimes so psychoanalytic in character as to seem more an attempt at dissection of character through the use of the terminology of the specialist than an expression of creative art. Even the novel and the play which steer away from this extreme disclose the familiarity of the author with the exploration of human behavior recently made by science.

If the contributions of the psychological and sociological sciences were negligible, deserving scant attention from the novelist and the playwright, our cultural situation would in itself tend to develop in literature the interest in marriage and family disaster which is now so apparent. The significance of romantic love, the cravings and the clashes of persons which come forth in the intimacy of the family, and the disturbance and restlessness that gather about matrimony and parenthood in this period of transitional culture would necessarily be reflected in literature. Since these are the major emotional experiences at the present time, they invite the skill of the portrayer of the dramatic.

There is no uniformity of attitude or general agreement as to necessary reforms among the multitude of writers who have used the novel to discuss family problems. The most common element in this material, which is so varied in both content and form, is the portrayal of the failure of the family as an institution in its effort to satisfy human desire. As one would naturally suppose, the novelist is more skillful in his criticism of family life than he is when he presents suggestions for reform.

The description and analysis of marriage difficulties provide an easier task for the writer than the presentation of a program for the reconstruction of the family. The novelist is, of course, not to be criticized because he makes a better critic than reformer, for the interpretation of human experience offers more dramatic opportunity than the effort to direct human behavior. Nevertheless, the student of the family who turns to modern literature for assistance in finding clear pathways through present family difficulties into a more satisfactory home life is bound to be disappointed. What modern literature does give is a realization of the great variety of unhappy home life in our modern social world and the different ways in which family troubles come about. Fiction, as expressed both in the novel and the play, proves helpful to the student of the family by the concreteness with which it portrays the basic difficulties of maladjustment and the values procurable through the fellowship of husband and wife, and parent and child. Marriage and family are so frequently the theme of the novel and the play as to make domestic problems seem omnipresent in occidental fiction. In the Appendix of this book a selection of representative novels and plays emphasizing domestic experience has been listed to encourage analysis of family situations on the part of the student and class discussions of various types of marriage and parenthood problems.

Any attempt to estimate justly the significance of this literary presentation of the tragedies of marriage and the home must take into account the temperament of the writer. The literary artist is apt to be a person who is supersensitive to the faults and irritations of the family experience. He is also, because of his gift, a person who has a vivid appreciation of the ideal and an intolerance in dealing with the hard circumstances of everyday realities. He obtains personal relief from what is, by his portrayal of what he would wish to have true. What becomes for him a means of releasing his emotions acts to the reader as a stimulus and to some extent encourages matrimonial restlessness and impatience in dealing with the problems of the modern home.

It is well also for the modern student of the family who turns to literature for insight into the matrimonial restlessness of today to remember that the writer himself is sometimes a victim of personal experiences and that he finds emotional relief in generalizing regarding home conditions on the basis of the happenings of his own childhood or the dissatisfactions that have come to him through marriage or parenthood.

In the literature that is characteristic of our times, we also find a greater and franker attention given to problems of sex, especially as they have to do with matrimonial happiness. This feature in the recent novels also reflects changes in our social culture. As the taboo with reference to sex has largely broken down and as science has come to have a larger understanding of the significance of sex as an influence upon human behavior, literature has naturally tended toward greater and more conscious use of sex as a motive in literary creation.

From the days of Daniel Defoe and Samuel Richardson the sex motive has been prominent in English and American literature. By the eighteenth century writers—for example, in the novels of Fielding and Smollett and the writings of Sterne—sex is exploited, but in a way that seems coarser in comparison with the more subtle treatment it receives in most modern literature. The difference is that the earlier break from taboo showed itself in a portrayal of the strength of human passion, while at the present time writers lay bare the significance and the intricacy of the sex impulse.

There has been an advance in sophistication which shows

itself when any characteristic product of modern literature is put in contrast with the pioneering fiction of the eighteenth century. Science has been exploring human sex life and has found it complex beyond the dream of the writer before the epoch-making work of Freud.

In its efforts to make use of the material newly furnished by science which reveals the social significance of sex, modern fiction more than any other influence has lessened the power of taboo and has made it possible for the student of the family, in his discussion of home problems, to deal justly with sex as a causal influence in both marriage and family experience. Among the twentieth-century novelists representating the group of writers who have shown unusual skill in dissecting family experience and uncovering the incompatibilities and tragedies of the home are Robert Herrick, W. L. George, Sinclair Lewis, Sherwood Anderson, D. H. Lawrence, Zona Gale, Willa Cather, Dorothy Canfield Fisher, Samuel Butler, Floyd Dell, Pearl Buck, Theodore Dreiser, and William Saroyan. Another popular literary form for the expression of present-day skepticism regarding the home and marriage is the short story, especially among the younger writers, who are naturally most sensitive to the prevailing criticism of the family.

Human interest in family failure. Any radical criticism of the family or any disclosure of family tragedy always has news value. This explains the space given in newspapers and magazines to spectacular divorce cases, domestic scandals, and radical theories of marriage and the family.

This material on a wider stage has an appeal similar to that of gossip in the small community. It is interesting because it caters to a certain type of curiosity and satisfies a primitive love of the dramatic. Doubtless it has had some social significance as a cultural influence but one that can be easily exaggerated. It has contributed to the breaking of the taboo of sex and has had a part in creating a general tolerance of divorce. It is reasonable to assume also that it has added somewhat to the general restlessness and feeling of insecurity prevalent in the field of domestic relations. To regard it, however, as evidence of the passing of the family is to take it too seriously and to forget that the normal and the usual is devoid of news value.

The contribution of the newspaper and magazine does not take merely a destructive or critical form. Even greater space is given to the popular but serious discussion of parenthood problems, diet, household management, and medical information that concern the family. Much space also is given over to discussions of matrimonial adjustment, but to a lesser degree this takes cognizance of present scientific information. The higher type of literary magazines such as *Harper's, The American Mercury, The Atlantic Monthly,* and others present frequently a more critical and thoroughgoing presentation of some phase of family experience. Editors are expected to have an accurate knowledge of public interest and their policies demonstrate that they believe more readers are interested in meeting the problems of family life than in the sordid domestic disasters.

On the whole, the publicity the family receives in our current literature stimulates the desire for higher standards of family experience and more satisfying adjustment in marriage. Although articles appear that interpret the disorganization of the modern family and, less often, that advocate the reconstruction of the family as a social institution, the trend of these discussions is toward condemnation of inadequate family practices and suggestions for their improvement rather than a pleading for the replacement of the family as a social institution.

The motion picture. The movies have had a decided influence, especially among young people, in building attitudes toward marriage and the family, but for the most part this has been an enforcement of romantic ideals. To some extent domestic tragedies have been portrayed, but this usually has come about when some popular book has been adapted for the screen. Even in these cases, as a rule, what was the major theme of the book has been played down and replaced by a more cheerful emphasis of romance. Although the movies have had a widespread and very great influence in breaking down taboos, their contribution to criticism of marriage or family life has been meagre. They have exploited to the full sexual attraction by adroit suggestion, but they cannot be given credit for helping to promote more intelligent attitudes toward sex or better preparation for marriage. This same appraisal can be made of a host of magazines of wide circulation among young people which put in popular form discussions of sex or of romance.

Radical program. The most aggressive attack upon the family as a social institution is coming from those committed to some sort of social revolution. They belong to no one school of thought and are not united in the solutions they offer for the reconstruction of family life. Some attack the family as the root of special privilege, believing that society needs to change the status of private property and cannot accomplish this without dissolving the present family as a social institution.

Others are more impressed by the risk of the family as a source of archaic tradition giving support to cultural traits which in their opinion are retarding progress. Still others believe that there is need of a freer relationship of the sexes and consider monogamic marriage the chief obstacle to bringing this about. They are persuaded that any change such as they desire in the matrimonial code will require the reshaping of the family. Some are interested in lessening the influence of family life upon children and giving over to specialists in charge of state organizations much of the responsibility now in the hands of parents. These are the chief items that appear in programs for the replacement of the family as a social institution and they are presented in different combinations and with much variation in detail. .

As a rule, we find, as is to be expected, more denunciation of family failure coming from its aggressive critics than definite programs for its replacement. The following are the most common proposals set forth by writers in the United States for the reconstructing of the family: (1) a freer sex code; (2) trial marriage; (3) easier divorce, often taking the form of advocacy of mutual consent as the method; (4) limiting the marriage and family obligations to a definite duration, after which the relationship becomes dissolved; (5) farming out the care of children to state institutions and greatly decreasing the rights as well as the powers of parenthood.

Although the first four of these would influence the stability of the family and the character of domestic experience, it is only the last one that strikes at the integrity of the family as we now have it and, by cutting off its activities, replaces it by a different sort of organization. Some would entirely dissolve the family as an educational agency for children after the manner advocated by Plato, while others are content greatly to lessen its activities. This was attempted with considerable success by Nazi Germany.

Some who advocate restricting the responsibilities of the family for the care of children do not seek to destroy the institution but to increase its efficiency and to free it from ulterior motives. These reformers are persuaded that much of what the family now does for the child can be better accomplished by other agencies and that what we now know as the family should be chiefly a husband-wife relationship expressing a mutual commitment of affection. They would change the form of family experience by lessening the child-parenthood aspects, but only for the purpose of establishing higher standards of child nurture and making more prominent the love motive of marriage.

Emotional criticism.   There are attacks upon marriage and the home which find expression in writing, addresses, and conversation that are both radical and emotional. The constant attendant at forums is familiar with the questions and statements that members of the audience inject at any opportunity without reference to the topic under discussion, which express an emotional radicalism that seldom has any positive program for social reconstruction. As some tirade against industry, government, or religion, in order to give vent to personal discontent and tension, so others inveigh against the family as a means of escape from inner unhappiness.

This type of radicalism must not be mistaken for that which is essentially intellectual and represents genuine, impersonal doubts of the adaptability of the orthodox home to modern life. The emotional type of radical, though he may wear the cloak of a reformer, is actually reacting against family tragedy or matrimonial unrest. His attack is self-projection and is to be considered a confession, unconsciously made, rather than a skepticism that deserves serious consideration. Radicalism of this sort constitutes a problem for the psychiatrist, not for the sociologist.

Some critics of parents.   One of the by-products of behaviorism, as introduced by John B. Watson, was a criticism of American parents based upon their inability to meet adequately their responsibilities. The spirit of this criticism appears in the dedication of Watson's *Psychological Care of Infant and Child* when he writes "dedicated to the first mother who brings up a happy child." The author warns mothers of the dangers of their love, the temptation it brings to pet their child which may inflict a never healing wound, making infancy and adolescence a nightmare, and finally spoiling the adult in both his vocation and attempt to achieve marital happiness.[2] The book, however, was not merely denunciation or warning but also a plea for a more sensible scientifically based program of preparation for life and especially for marriage. The author in his forward-looking insists that every college and university have a department of sex education for students during their eighteenth, nineteenth, and twentieth year. This should include instruction in sex and the prevalence and dangers of venereal disease and should be open to both men and women.[3]

A book that appeared the preceding year (1927) also reveals the critical attitude that was becoming prevalent at that time, when emphasis was being placed on the responsibilities and the faults of parents. *Parents on Probation,* by Miriam Van Waters, discloses by its title the trend then prevailing in this country among those who were impressed by the problems that were being charged to the family's failures in its educational function. In Chapter Fourteen the author discusses nineteen ways of being a bad parent.

Freudianism, especially through its theory of the Oedipus Complex,[4] added force to the censure the family was receiving as a social institution. Although this hypothesis became modified in time,[5] its first emphasis on the inherent jealousy of the father by the son offered a new point of attack for the critics of the conventional relationship of parent and child. The tendency at first was not only to universalize the child's impulse to become jealous of the parent of the same sex but also to regard it as an unescapable flaw of human nature rather than as a problem which when it arose in the family constellation needed to be understood and intelligently handled.

---

[2] Watson, John B., *Psychological Care of Infant and Child*, p. 87.
[3] *Ibid.*, p. 182.
[4] Coriat, Isador H., *The Meaning of Dreams*, pp. 127–130.
[5] Allen, Frederick H., *Psychotherapy With Children*, Ch. 2.

Some critics of marriage.   Marriage has had much greater criticism than has parenthood. It has been recognized by most writers on the family that there is no satisfactory substitute for fathers and mothers in the nurture and training of children; on the other hand, since marriage is a convention for the control of the mating impulse and has taken different forms in various periods and groups of people, it offers fertile field for experimentation and improvement. Charlotte Perkins Gilman (1860–1935) a brilliant and persuasive lecturer, agitated against the dependence and lack of freedom of the conventional American woman who married. Her most important book was *Woman and Economics*. She insisted that there was no need of motherhood making such a demand as convention assumes, and, because modern industry had taken so much away from the household routine, women after marriage should continue their interest in vocational and professional careers. Although her fiery assaults on the narrowness and monotony experienced by many housewives met with considerable popular response, she proved a better critic than reformer. There were three obstacles to the practicing of what she preached. Many wives had no ambition for out-of-the-home activities but were content with homemaking and child rearing and were at least as free from monotony and dependency as were their husbands in their earning of a livelihood. There was nothing like the amount of the stripping of the family of its functions that Mrs. Gilman supposed. Finally society did not accept the wiping out of the division of labor between men and women that her argument assumed. Her real contribution was in awakening millions to the need of reform in homemaking practices and ideals.

More constructive efforts to improve the role of the married woman were made by Anna Garlin Spencer, whose greatest influence along this line resulted from her *Woman's Share in Social Culture,* which appeared in 1912. Another contribution especially uncovering the problems faced by the woman who married and attempted to continue an out-of-the-home vocation was made by Alice Beale Parsons in her *Woman's Dilemma,* published in 1926. These three authors are representative of the recognition that began to be general among students of the family in the early period of the twentieth century, that the new opportunities brought women by their advance in social status and their greater economic and vocational independence were disturbing to the conventional ideal of the home and the family and were forcing many thoughtful women to choose between marriage and the continuation of a career made possible by their education and development of talent.

From Sweden came a voice that brought into question the prevailing American mores as they had to do with marriage and family life. Ellen Key (1849–1926), who had already written *The Century of the Child* and *The Woman's Movement*, brought out in 1911 in an English edition *Love and Marriage*. She advocated a reconstruction of ideas about marriage that would distinguish between the right to love and the obligation to have children, and that would accept love as the ground of marriage with the legal right to withdraw from marriage whenever a husband or wife found that affection had disappeared. This, carried into practice, meant divorce by mutual consent.

A controversy in the United States which centered about the notion of a temporary or experimental marriage for youth resulted from the publication of *The Companionate Marriage* (1927), written by Ben Lindsey, at that time Judge of the Juvenile Court of Denver, Colorado. Lindsey's discussion had two chief ideas, the popularizing of modern contraceptives and the social approval of divorce by mutual consent. In order to meet the problem of a growing sex freedom among youth, he advocated a marriage which would permit sexual relations within the period of storm and stress, with the understanding that children were not to be born, but which later could be dissolved at the request of either the man or woman. Unfortunately for clear thinking, Judge Lindsey took over the term "the companionate" which had been previously added to the sociologist's vocabulary by Knight [6] in order to clarify the peculiar character of the marriage that did not have children. The consequence of the use of this concept for what was in fact trial marriage, or at least temporary marriage, brought about a confusion of terminology which led Dr. Knight to express the opinion that the term "companionate" had become useless to the social thinker. Lindsey's program made little progress because there was no disposition on the part of youth to seek a

---

[6] Knight, Melvin M., "Companionate Marriage," *Encyclopedia of the Social Sciences*, Vol. 4, p. 115.

temporary or trial marriage, but the discussion itself was welcomed by many young people who made use of it to justify sexual relations that they had no desire to legalize. Although they sought freedom in their personal contacts, they had no wish, once love inclined them toward marriage, for any provisional mating.

Bertrand and Dora Russell writing independently advocated free love, the former in *Marriage and Morals* (1929) and the latter in *The Right to be Happy* (1927). A more effective argument against the exclusiveness of monogamic marriage had been advanced earlier by Edward Carpenter's *Love's Coming of Age* (12th edition, 1923). Although this book appeared in London, it was widely read in other countries, including the United States, and is still the most penetrating criticism of monogamic marriage yet written. The general influence of much of the writing of Havelock Ellis encouraged doubt concerning the functioning of the conventional marriage. Now that we know the tragic failure of his own married life this influence is understandable.[7]

An earlier English writer, James Hinton,[8] certainly influenced Ellis, and probably Carpenter, although his theories were little known in this country. Impressed by the existence of prostitution and by the domestic unhappiness of many husbands and wives, he began in 1870 to advocate a new moral code for the sexual conduct of men and women. It was his belief that good as monogamy is, ideally considered, society had arrived at it too soon as a legal or universal form with the result that the coercive marriage relationship calls into being more licentiousness than would be possible under an open polygny or polyandry. His solution, somewhat vague, through the vehement and often mystic style of the author, was a new type of polygamy, insisted on by the woman and designed to turn the passion of the male from prostitutes. Whether equal freedom for self-directed, out-of-marriage relationships was to be granted women when they likewise were driven by passion is not made clear.

Psychoanalysis and especially the writings of Sigmund Freud brought forth considerable skepticism as to the success of both parenthood and marriage. The probing of the inner

---

[7] Ellis, Havelock, *My Life*, Part Seven.
[8] Ellis, Havelock, *James Hinton*, p. 124.

experience of neurotic individuals that sought help through analysis necessarily revealed and emphasized the failures of the two relationships in life ordinarily most emotionally significant, childhood and marriage.

The attack on marriage as it reached its height in the third decade of the twentieth century is represented best by V. F. Calverton's *The Bankruptcy of Marriage* (1928). This marshals the various weaknesses that had become apparent in the conventional sex code and marriage. The skepticism of the book in regard to marriage as an institution appears in the titles of some of its chapters: "The Social Background of Our Moral Chaos," "The Decay of Modern Marriage," "Abortion and the Bankruptcy of the Old Morals," "Illegitimacy and Revolt," "The New Morality in Germany," "Revolutionary Chaos and Change."

This bombardment which both marriage and the family were receiving from many quarters disturbed confidence in these two institutions even among some of the serious students of family and marriage experience, as the literature of the period reveals. An illustration of this reaction which impressed the authors of this text was the statement in conversation by the editor of one of our most influential serious magazines, "Marriage is hopelessly on the rocks." This conviction was held in spite of the fact that the speaker's own marriage and family life were highly successful. He was answered that what was happening at the moment down at City Hall demonstrated that marriage was still the commanding ideal of modern youth, an expectation that had not in the slightest been undermined by the current pessimism being expressed in literature.[9]

The question of values. Marriage through the centuries has taken many forms. The support of our monogamic type must come from its offering to human nature the highest values that can be drawn from the mating impulse. It is true, as Briffault states, that the mores, including religious conventions, buttress present conventions. Society, so far as we know, has always insisted upon control of sexual relations, thereby in some form developing the institution of marriage. This necessarily has meant that the mores—and here religion has always been dominant—have been the basic source of control. It is

---

[9] For authors' position at this time see *Marriage Crisis,* by E. R. Groves (1928).

clear, however, that this has not meant that change could not occur but rather that society has never consented to a purely individualistic code of behavior, since it has always been conscious of the values involved. A support that comes from the mores is not because of its source precarious as an emotional enforcement, smothering the native impulses of man or woman; on the other hand, its coercive strength does not eliminate the testing that is intelligently decisive, namely: Does monogamic marriage offer human nature its inherent satisfactions and the family its greatest security? It cannot be, as Briffault suggests, simply the question of personal versus social interests. What starts as a mere value-seeking of the individual immediately takes on social character, irrespective of the existence of property or children. An experimental or temporary commitment, a merely private arrangement, becomes, because of its meaning to and effect upon the individual concerned, socially consequential. No one can live unto himself in this field more than elsewhere. Mutual approval of departures from the prevailing code of the mores is not sufficient; the practice must withstand the test of being universalized.

The values that have been lodged with marriage are not confined to the transmission of a name or property or the legalizing of children, nor is the interest of society limited to the licensing of sexual relations and the avoiding of unwanted parenthood. The home is as indispensable to the survival of society as is mating to the going on of the race. With all its liabilities as a human organization for the living together of man and woman, irrespective of whether this leads to an orthodox family or the arrested family, it is a needful social structure and the only orderly way of dealing on the human level with the basic division of the sexes. Marriage offers to the individual opportunity for happiness, but its purpose transcends the giving of happiness. Because of this, only in moments of social anarchy when there is a breaking down of coercive influences do we find mating temporarily treated as an individual venture.

The world-wide trend at present in Western culture and to a less extent in the Orient has been toward standardizing monogamic marriage. This type of marriage has been vulnerable to attack because circumstances conspire to deny so many, especially women, a fair chance to marry and because there is so large a proportion of matrimonial failures in part due to lack of social concern in providing favorable social conditions for success and the factual preparation youth now needs for the experience. In the United States, although conventional thinking upholds the monogamic idea, there is in contemporary practices a trend toward greater freedom in premarriage sexual relations and to some degree an attempt to continue similar practices after marriage, provided the husband-wife fellowship is not disturbed, a condition which, in this country, experience proves to be exceedingly difficult to fulfill.

Limitation of family reform.   In the future, as in the past, children will be born and it will fall upon adults to take care of them. Whatever may befall the child after birth, his entrance into life must continue to be through biological parenthood. This fact of reproduction will always prove itself a stubborn obstacle to any attempt to abolish the parent-child relationship. It will be found also, whenever experiment is attempted, that the adult protection required by the child will, in whatever form it is offered, present problems. There is no short cut that can carry the child into maturity without passing through the contacts with human nature that are always potentially hazardous.

This fact cannot be used to protect the family from criticism, but it does disclose the complications involved in any attempt to abolish the family as a social institution. The family cannot escape the test of social adequacy, but neither can any substitute. What Edward Carpenter, one of the severest critics of marriage, once said about the institution of matrimony is even more true of the family. Although we wish to reduce the natural tragedies of family relationship by removing every influence that tends to create artificial difficulty, still we must recognize that, short of the millennium, these consequences of failure in the adult-child relationship will always be with us, and no form of family institution or absence of institution will, by itself, rid us of them.[10]

Functional reconstruction of the family.   The problems resulting from the faulty functioning of the family do not necessarily demonstrate the need of abolishing the family as a

---

[10] *Love's Coming of Age,* pp. 110–111.

social institution or radically changing its structure. These evidences of family failure may indicate the necessity of functional changes and improvement. That this is their meaning is the conviction of the authors of this text.

Any attempt to build a program for the better functioning of the family under conditions of modern life reveals the impossibility of dealing with the family as a thing apart, since it is interrelated with all the other constituents of our culture. The family should not be conceived as a docile instrument whose efficiency is found merely in the way it caters to cultural demands. Throughout social evolution the family has maintained values which from time to time have challenged cultural changes.

The tenacity of the family in this period of cultural confusion and transition suggests that the family needs to play a positive part in our revamping of society and should influence social conditions as surely as it should be influenced by them. Modern men and women require for their greatest happiness and maturity better family life rather than no family life. In any concrete effort to lift family functioning to higher standards there is need of a double program, the improving not only of the family itself but also of the conditions that operate upon it from the outside. There is no quick, simple, expedient program of reform, but rather it is the larger use and better organization of the resources gathered from the study of many problems of human behavior that promise the most substantial progress. These different approaches to the conservation of the family are considered in detail in the following chapters.

Part IV

Specialized Programs for the Conservation of the American Family

Chapter 19

THE LEGAL APPROACH

FOREWORD. There is no better way for the student of American marriage and family life to gather insight than through the most important of the specialized approaches to the study of domestic problems. One of these is the legal. It is most often the first choice of those who seek some method of advancing family welfare. This attempt to depend upon laws to correct social difficulties is characteristic of the American people who have both too much confidence in this means of social reform and too often the tendency to become complacent once legislation has been passed.

The student of this text is likely to be aware of this American habit of exaggerating the power of law to correct social ills. This knowledge should not lead, however, to an underestimating of the influence of laws and court decisions upon the functioning of marriage and the family. In considering what legislation can do, the student becomes conscious of its necessary limitations.

It is, of course, apparent that no chapter in a college text can do more than introduce the reader to the most significant of the interests that are affected by the law of domestic relations. The legal aspects of divorce and alimony have already been treated in Chapter 17. The topics that have been chosen for discussion here are those most helpful in giving the student a realization of the meaning and complexity of the legal aspects of both marriage and family experience. The chapter attempts to impress the reader with the fact that in this area, as elsewhere, there is no promise in seeking a static ideal, but rather that domestic law like all other legal enactments needs to retain the spirit of continuous adaptation to changing environmental conditions while maintaining with constancy faith in the social usefulness, human appeal, and possibility of fulfillment of marriage and the family as they function in contemporary American life. The influence of law on marriage and the family is not confined to the decisions and statutes that specifically treat domestic relations. These are the concern of the lawyer in his professional practice, but the student should recognize the even larger influence on the well-being of marriage and the family of legislation which, although not specifically directed toward domestic matters, nevertheless affects them greatly. Marriage and the family are so sensitive to social conditions that many of the enactments and decisions of the courts either antagonize or strengthen the home. This larger meaning of the legal approaches to the problems of marriage and the family is illustrated in the following chapters of the text, especially in the discussion of problems that fall within the fields of eugenics and euthenics.

Legislation can neither establish wholesome family life nor in any large measure prevent the opposite kind of home, but it clearly has an influence that encourages or hampers successful marriage and family life. Undoubtedly any program that seeks to advance domestic experience and to make family life personally more satisfying and socially more profitable must include not only an effort to direct the laws especially applicable to the family but must also give attention to all other legislation that has indirect significance for marriage and the family. The power of law to further the interests of the American family is limited, but its contribution to the conservation of the family cannot safely be ignored.

An adequate use of our legal resources demands a public opinion that is in sympathy with the purposes of the laws, an honest and efficient administration of the laws that are passed and a willingness to make the legal changes necessary to permit the family and marriage to adapt themselves to human needs and progressive social conditions. In the past the laity has been too much concentrated on divorce, neglecting not only the more important concern of the law in establishing and regulating marriage but also a great quantity of legislation and court decisions that indirectly influence the family.

Legal regulation of marriage. One of the first evidences of the part the law plays in American domestic relations appears in the state regulations concerning entrance upon marriage. A portion of these have to do with the physical aspects of marriage. One requirement that has long been recognized is that there must be physical capacity to consummate marriage. The law provides for an annulment of a marriage in case there was physical impotency at the time it was contracted. Marriage unconsummated because of physical incapacity is rendered voidable. American law, however, does not, as is true often in the regulations of primitive society and in the legislation of earlier civilization, make ability to propagate the test of a valid marriage.

Early in the history of English law, impotence was recognized as one of the grounds for the annulment of marriage, jurisdiction being given to the Ecclesiastical Courts. In this country, since there were no such courts, authority to annul for this and other disabilities, such as lack of consent, nonage, insanity, and fraud, was exercised by Courts of Equity. Thirty-four states and Alaska have legislation dealing with impotency as it affects the validity or voidability of marriage.[1] These laws tend to be uniform, providing for the annulling of a marriage when either of the parties "shall be incapable from physical causes of entering in the married state." Some of them raise the issue of curability. For instance, a recent West Virginia amendment declares that if any marriage be solemnized when either of the parties "is incapable because of natural or incurable impotency of body of entering into the marriage state, it shall be void from the time they are so declared by decree of nullity."[2] New Hampshire authorizes divorce when there has been for three years refusal to cohabit. If the parties are able to have sexual intercourse, the legal requirement for valid marriage is fulfilled. Vernier tells us that, strictly speaking, impotency does not, except possibly in the states of Georgia and North Carolina, mean that marriage is prohibited, but merely that if the parties concerned so desire, physical incapacity can be used as grounds for divorce or annulment. Thus it becomes possible for those who have become impotent through age to contract marriage if

---

[1] Vernier, C. G., *American Family Laws*, Vol. 2, p. 38.
[2] Vernier, *op. cit., 1938 Supplement*, p. 23.

this is their choice.[3] This also, of course, means in practice that
many marriages that developed into an incompatibility on account of impotency or unwillingness to cohabitate end in divorces that are sought on some other ground than what is really
the cause of trouble.

In the legislation concerned with this aspect of physical
fitness for marriage there is a reluctance to recognize the significance of the actual situation of the married parties at a
later time than that of their entrance upon marriage, and we
find qualifications such as that marriages between persons either
of whom is at the time physically impotent shall be void (North
Carolina) or that a marriage is voidable where either party was
physically and incurably impotent, provided the party making
the application was ignorant of such impotency or incapacity at
the time of marriage.[4] The principle embedded in these various
laws is that marriage requires a physical qualification and makes
physical demands without which it cannot justly be held to
have been established. It is, however, clear from human experience that incapacity at a later time, excluding the years
in which it is reasonable to assume the passing of sex vitality,
is equally incompatible with genuine marriage and may be as
destructive of marital fellowship as it would have been at the
beginning.

The legal conservation of marriage must inevitably include a clearer recognition that the continuing of a physical
inability or unwillingness to meet the physical marital responsibilities becomes, if such be the desire of the capable member, a
just ground for dissolving a union which has in fact ceased to
exist. So long as this provision is withheld by legislation, divorce will be sought by many through a legal subterfuge or by
a deliberate attempt to qualify for a divorce by an offense which
the law recognizes. The present reluctance to recognize with
frankness and clarity, in the legal theory, the sexual basis of
marriage is due to fear that this might encourage separation
and divorce. Undoubtedly that would prove true if at the same
time there were not also greater effort to increase the physical
compatibility of those married. In the past, when the economic
significance of marriage was great, even primary, marriage sta-

---

[3] Vernier, *op. cit.*, Vol. 1, p. 197.
[4] *Ibid.*, pp. 197–198.

bility was less influenced by the success or failure of marital adjustment, especially since the man, whose interest predominated, found through the double standard a way of escape from sexual dissatisfaction without sacrificing the comforts and economic advantages of family life.

Already there are a few statutory enactments [5] that reveal this trend toward a recognition of other physical prerequisites, not only for the beginning but for the continuing of the marriage relationship, a legal evolution that is both logical and socially most desirable. Hawaii provides for divorce in the case of the contraction of the disease of leprosy; Illinois, when the other spouse has been infected with a communicable venereal disease; Kentucky, in the event of the contracting of any loathsome disease after marriage; Maine, Massachusetts, Mississippi, North Dakota, and Rhode Island, in case of a gross and confirmed drug habit; Alabama, if the husband becomes an habitual user of drugs.[6] By a Hawaiian law passed in 1935, the habitual excessive use of opium, morphine, or any other drug, continued for a period of one year, becomes a ground for divorce.[7]

The influences that give impetus to this legal trend toward safeguarding from physical menace, not only the entrance to, but also the experience of marriage itself, come from several social changes that are certain to grow more forceful with time. Science is making clearer the dangers of such diseases as syphilis and gonorrhea and at the same time is increasing its curative skill so that the persistence of infectious conditions must in the future appear willful neglect and as serious an assault on the physical welfare of the spouse as any deliberate method of injury. There is also every reason to suppose that the attack on these and other infectious diseases will be more and more aggressive and that therapeutic diagnosis will become routine.

One of the most important contributions American statutory law has been making in recent years to family welfare has come about through legislation requiring premarital examina-

---

[5] The various statements in this chapter concerning existing laws should be considered suggestive examples only, since in order to keep them accurate it would be necessary to maintain continuous legal research to revise this chapter at least once a year.

[6] Vernier, *op. cit.*, Vol. 2, pp. 66–71.

[7] Vernier, *op. cit.*, *1938 Supplement*, p. 46.

tion for venereal disease and forbidding marriage to those who are infectious. This law has usually been directed against syphilis because of the difficulty of diagnosing gonorrhea and especially the uncertainty of its cure, but in many states this disease also falls within the provisions of the statute. In 1945, only twelve American jurisdictions had no laws requiring premarriage examination. Four had inadequate laws.[8] New York strengthened previous requirements by the kind of enactment that seems likely soon to be prerequisite for a marriage license in all of the American jurisdictions. The statement of the physician making such tests "shall include the name and address of the applicant; a statement that a serological test for syphilis was performed; the date on which the specimen was taken; and the name and location of the laboratory in which such test was made." The physician's statement must accompany the application for a marriage license. The bill provides, however, that the result of the serological test shall not be included in such statement but that a detailed report of the laboratory test when positive shall be filed with the local health authorities and held in "absolute confidence" and not open to inspection by the public.

The Hawaiian law which permits divorce for leprosy but permits the courts to decree, if it seems just, the support of the divorced leper, points the way to a legal interpretation of marital relationship which appears to be in accord even now with the attitude of many judges. Examples of this are the granting of such decisions as a divorce in Pennsylvania on the ground that the communicating of a loathsome disease by the husband to the wife is an indignity and on the ground that incurable venereal disease endangers health and life. Louisiana interprets the communicating of a venereal disease as cruelty, and Michigan authorizes a limited divorce on the ground that communicating venereal disease to the wife is cruelty.[8] On the other hand, there are more literal interpretations, less in accord with public feeling, that hark back to the earlier ideas of marriage. An example of this is the North Carolina decision that the communication of an infectious disease to the wife by the husband was not cruelty.[9]

---

[8] Vonderlehr, R. H., and Heller, J. R., *The Control of Venereal Disease*, p. 71.
[9] Drummond, I., *Getting a Divorce*, pp. 106, 290, 308, 350, 366, and 396.

It is reasonable to attempt through legal barriers to prevent the marriage of diseased persons when such unions clearly carry risk to the health of the individuals who enter them, to the children that may be born, and to society itself. But similar conditions arising after marriage may in fact prove equally injurious if the afflicted spouse refuses adequate treatment, and it is in accord with public interest, when these perilous conditions are unmistakably present, to dissolve a marriage that under similar circumstances it would be illegal to establish.

Common-law marriages. There is need of legislation abolishing common-law marriages. The situation that leads to a common-law marriage means to most people the living together of a man and woman in adultery, but where such marriages are recognized as valid by the state, the individuals concerned are as much married as those who, having obtained their license to marry according to law, have celebrated their union by a church or civil wedding. To create a binding common-law marriage, most courts require "present consent followed by cohabitation" or an assumption of the marital relationship. This usually means entering marriage by the pathway of fornication or unlawful sexual intercourse, and by thereafter agreeing to continue cohabitation the couple have created a common-law marriage.

It has been held by some that in England a marriage contracted without the presence of an ordained clergyman was never regarded as legal by the common law. According to Pollock, an English authority, this opinion "is now regarded by most competent scholars to be without any real historical foundation." [10] In England proper, Scotland and Ireland being excluded, marriage by mutual consent without lawful authorization was made illegal in 1753.

In America this form of marriage has in the past been held valid on the basis of the common law in the majority of the states. Only recently have the states begun expressly to repudiate such marriages, and even when by statute there had been set up definite and detailed regulations regarding the licensing and solemnizing of marriage, the court decisions have held that informal marriages ignoring these provisions were nevertheless

[10] Pollock, F., *First Book on Jurisprudence*, p. 328.

according to the common law valid. This one-time conventional legal position is well expressed by the following extract from an American decision.

In fine, in every shape in which the question has been presented to the courts of common law in personal actions, or in relation to personal matters, a marriage in fact has been deemed valid. A contrary doctrine, in this country, would be attended with the most mischievous consequences. The statute prescribing the mode of celebrating the rites of matrimony requires that when either party is under the age of twenty-one, the consent of the parent or guardian shall be given in person or in writing; that bond and security shall be given before license can be issued; that license shall be issued only by the clerk of the county where the female party resides; and that no clergyman who has not previously obtained testimonials for that purpose from the county court, shall celebrate the rites of matrimony. A compliance with the whole of these particulars is necessary to render the marriage conformable to the statute; and a failure to comply with any one of them would render it but a marriage in fact; and if a marriage in fact be void, many of the marriages of the country would be so, for there are many in which there has been a failure, either intentionally or otherwise, to comply with some one or more of the formalities presented by the statute. A doctrine which would thus tend to vitiate a great proportion of the marriages of the country would result in incalculable evils, and cannot be admitted to be correct.[11]

In this same decision appears the theory of the law.

Marriage is nothing but a contract; and to render it valid, it is only necessary, upon the principles of natural law, that the parties should be able to contract—willing to contract, and should actually contract. A marriage thus made without further ceremony was, according to the simplicity of the ancient common law, deemed valid to all purposes and such continued to be the law of England until the time of Pope Innocent the Third, when the ceremony of celebrating matrimony in *facie ecclesiae* was first introduced into that country. That ceremony, however, though introduced by the usurpation of the church, was afterwards recognized to a certain extent by the common law; and it would have been idle for the law to have recognized the ceremony without attaching to it any legal consequence. It was therefore held, that to constitute a *marriage de jure,*

---

11 Madden, J. W., *Cases on Domestic Relations,* p. 556. (Dumaresly vs. Fishly. Court of Appeals of Kentucky, 1821. 3 A. K. Marsh. 368.)

and render it valid to every purpose, it must be celebrated in the church. But a marriage contracted without that ceremony was, nevertheless, a marriage in fact and was still deemed valid to most purposes.[12]

The confusion in the United States regarding the status of common-law marriage is so great that there has been disagreement between authorities who have attempted to classify the position of the various states. These variations of interpretation are only in part to be accounted for by the different periods in which the compilations were made. From time to time modifications of the common law are made by statutes so that until the meaning of these changes has been tested there is uncertainty as to the attitude the courts will take toward what on the basis of earlier decisions would or would not be a valid marriage. Jacobs writing in 1931 considers that neither the statutory laws nor court decisions established the validity of common-law marriages in the following states in 1931: Arizona, Arkansas, California, Connecticut, Delaware, Illinois, Kentucky, Louisiana, Maine, Maryland, Massachusetts, Missouri, Nebraska, New Hampshire, North Carolina, North Dakota, Oregon, Tennessee, Utah, Vermont, Virginia, Washington, West Virginia, and Wisconsin. Writing in the same year, Drummond declares that there are seven states that make common-law marriages illegal: Arkansas, Arizona, Idaho, North Carolina, Vermont, Washington, and West Virginia.[13] Kansas declares them a crime but recognizes them civilly. New Hampshire requires for recognition that they shall have continued for at least three years. In Oregon there must be a year's cohabitation. South Dakota, by statute, demands consummation as a prerequisite to the marriage.[14] Vernier, also, writing in 1931, declares that only three states—Arizona, Illinois, and Missouri—unconditionally enact that common-law marriages shall be null and void, while Alaska, Connecticut, Kentucky, Louisiana, Nebraska, and Utah less clearly disposed of the validity of these marriages by declaring that marriages contracted without proper solemnization are null and void.[15] That there were in 1945 twenty-five states in which

---

[12] *Ibid.,* pp. 554–555.
[13] Jacobs, Albert C., *A Research in Family Law.*
[14] Drummond, I., *op. cit.,* pp. 27, 44.
[15] *Op. cit.,* Vol. 1, p. 104.

the common-law marriage was valid demonstrates how folkways expressed in law lag behind changed social conditions. When the frontier existed and isolation made conventional marriage difficult, there was a genuine need of common-law marriages. The unwillingness of legislators to force children born outside orthodox wedlock to be stigmatized as bastards also leads to a reluctance to remove the legality of common-law marriages. The constant confusion that exists at present because of the differing laws and decisions in the various American jurisdictions is well illustrated by a complicated problem that had to be decided by the United States Supreme Court. Without it many couples would have had to delay marriage a year or more, waiting for the proper religious or civil official to arrive.

The case came before the court because of the necessity of interpreting the will of Nicholas Travers of Washington, D. C., as it affected the selling of certain real estate in the city. Travers had died leaving four sons and three daughters. One son, James, was a native of the District of Columbia and while with Sophia V. Grayson, a native of West Virginia, went through some sort of marriage ceremony in Alexandria, Virginia. Although the statutes of Virginia provide that every marriage shall be solemnized by an authorized person, it also affirms that no marriage shall be adjudged void because the ceremony has been performed by someone lacking proper authority, provided that in other respects the marriage is lawful and consummated with a full belief on the part of the persons so married or either of them that they have been normally joined in marriage. The husband and wife shortly left Virginia to reside in New Jersey, where they continued to live together as husband and wife. Still later they moved to Maryland, where they purchased a farm. Sixteen years later this was sold because of the husband's poor health, and they returned to New Jersey, where they lived together until the death of Mr. Travers. During the years they continuously cohabitated as husband and wife, they acted as if they were lawfully married, and there is no proof that anyone doubted that they were legally husband and wife. Some five years after the woman began living with Mr. Travers, he told her that they were as surely married as if they had been married by a priest or a minister. In his will he recognized Sophia Virginia Travers as his wife, and the court had to decide whether when James died the woman with whom he had been living

MARRIAGE LAWS AS OF JANUARY 1, 1945
(Information furnished by Women's Bureau, U. S. Department of Labor.)

State	Minimum Marriage Age Specified in Law		Common Law Marriages Are Valid	Prohibit Marriage of Those with Transmissible Disease in Infectious Stage	Physical Examination and Blood Test for Male and Female			Waiting Period	
	Male	Female			Date of Enactment	(a)	Scope of Laboratory Test	Before Issuance of License	After Issuance of License
Alabama	17	14	★	....	(b)	15 da.	(g)	....	....
Arizona	18	16	....	....	....	....	..	....	....
Arkansas	18	16	....	....	....	....	..	....	....
California	18	16	....	....	1939	30 da.	(e)	3 da.	....
Colorado	18	18	★	....	1939	30 da.	(e)	....	....
Connecticut	16	16	....	....	1935	40 da.	(e)	5 da.	....
Delaware	18	16	....	★	....	....	..	....	★ k
Florida	18	16	★	....	....	....	..	....	....
Georgia	17	14	★	....	....	....	..	5 da.	....
Idaho	14 d	12 d	★	....	1943	30 da.	(e)	....	....
Illinois	18	16	....	....	1939	15 da.	(g)	....	....
Indiana	18	16	★	....	1939	30 da.	(e)	....	....
Iowa	16	14	★	....	1941	20 da.	(e)	....	....
Kansas	18	16	★	....	....	....	..	....	....
Kentucky	16	14	....	....	1940	15 da.	(e)	....	....
Louisiana	18	16	....	....	(i)	....	..	....	....
Maine	16	16	★	★	1941	(e)	..	5 da.	....
Maryland	18	16	....	....	....	....	..	2 da.	....
Massachusetts	18	16	....	....	1943	30 da.	(e)	5 da.	....
Michigan	18	16	★	....	1939	30 da.	(g)	5 da.	....
Minnesota	18	16	....	....	....	....	..	5 da.	....
Mississippi	14 d	12 d	★	....	....	....	..	5 da.	....
Missouri	15	15	....	....	1943	15 da.	(e)	....	....
Montana	18	16	★	....	....	....	..	....	....
Nebraska	18	16	....	★	....	....	..	....	....
Nevada	18	16	....	....	....	....	..	....	....
New Hampshire	14	13	....	....	1937	30 da.	(e)	5 da.	....
New Jersey	14 d	12 d	....	....	1938	30 da.	(e)	2 da.	★
New Mexico	18	16	....	....	....	....	..	....	....
New York	16	14	....	....	1938 f	30 da.	(e)	3 da.	★
North Carolina	16	16	....	....	1941	30 da.	(e)	....	....
North Dakota	18	15	....	....	1939	30 da.	(e)	....	....
Ohio	18	16	★	....	1941	30 da.	(e)	5 da.	....
Oklahoma	18	15	★	★	....	....	..	....	....
Oregon	18	15	....	....	1937	10 da.	(h)	3 da.	....
Pennsylvania	16	16	★	....	1939	30 da.	(e)	3 da.	....
Rhode Island	18	16	★	....	1938	40 da.	(e)	....	★
South Carolina	18	14	★	....	....	....	..	....	....
South Dakota	18	15	★	....	1939	20 da.	(e)	....	....
Tennessee	16	16	★	....	1939	30 da.	(g)	3 da.	....
Texas	16	14	★	....	(j)	....	..	....	....
Utah	16	14	....	★	1941	....	(e)	....	....
Vermont	18	16	....	★	1941	30 da.	..	....	★
Virginia	18	16	....	....	1940	30 da.	(e)	....	....
Washington	14 d	12 d	....	★	....	....	..	3 da.	....
West Virginia	18	16	....	....	1939	30 da.	(e)	3 da.	....
Wisconsin	18	15	....	....	1939	15 da.	(e)	5 da.	....
Wyoming	18	16	★	....	1943	30 da.	(g)	....	....

a Time allowed between date of examination and issuance of license.
b In 1919 law adopted applying to male only; laboratory test authorized but not required.
c Syphilis.
d Common-law marriage age.
e Syphilis and other venereal diseases.
f Amended in 1939.
g Venereal diseases.
h Syphilis and gonorrhea.
i In 1924 law adopted applying to male only; laboratory test authorized but not required.
j In 1929 law adopted applying to male only; no provision as to laboratory test.
k 24 hrs., residents; 96 hrs., non-residents.

was in fact his legal wife. The majority opinion is in part as follows:

Naturally, the first inquiry must have reference to what occurred at Alexandria, Virginia, in 1865, when as the woman supposed—in good faith, we think—that there was a real, valid marriage between her and James Travers. But we will assume for the purposes of this case only that that marriage was not a valid one under the laws of Virginia. . . . We will also assume, but only for the purposes of the present decision and because of the earnest contentions of the appellants, that cohabitation in Maryland, as husband and wife, for more than fifteen years, and the recognition of that relation in the communities where they resided in that state, did not entitle James Travers and the woman Sophia to be regarded in that state as lawfully husband and wife. We make this assumption also because it appears here that James Travers and Sophia V. Grayson did not become husband and wife in virtue of any religious ceremony, and because it has been decided by the court of appeals of Maryland that in that state "there cannot be a valid marriage without a religious ceremony," although "a marriage may be competently proved without the testimony of witnesses who were present at the ceremony. . . ." That court also said in the same case: "The law has wisely provided that marriage may be proved by general reputation, cohabitation, and acknowledgment; when these exist, it will be inferred that a religious ceremony has taken place; and this proof will not be invalidated because evidence cannot be obtained of the time, place, and manner of the celebration of the marriage. . . . 'Where parties live together ostensibly as man and wife, demeaning themselves toward each other as such, and are received into society and treated by their friends and relatives as having and being entitled to that status, the law will, in favor of morality and decency, presume that they have been legally married. . . .' "

This brings us to consider what were the relations of these parties after selling the Maryland farm and after taking up their residence in New Jersey in 1883. That their cohabitation, as husband and wife, after 1865 and while they lived in Maryland, continued without change after they became domiciled in New Jersey and up to the death of James Travers, and that they held themselves out in New Jersey as lawfully husband and wife, and were recognized in the community as sustaining that relation, is manifest from all the evidence and circumstances. It is impossible to explain their conduct towards each other while living in New Jersey upon any other theory than that they regarded each other as legally holding the matrimonial relation of husband and wife. It is true that no witness proves express words signifying an actual agreement or contract between the parties to live together as husband and wife. No witness heard them say, in words, in the presence of each other, "We have agreed to take each other as husband and wife, and live together as such." But their conduct towards each other, from the time they left Alexandria, in 1865, up to the death of James Travers, in 1883, admits of no other interpretation than that they had agreed, from the outset, to be husband and wife. And that agreement, so far as this record shows, was faithfully kept up to the death of James Travers. When it is remembered that James Travers assured the woman Sophia that they were as much married as if they had been married by a priest or minister; that in his mortgage of 1867 she is described as his wife; that in the holographic will of 1881 he recognized her as his wife; that in his last will, made at his domicile in New Jersey, he referred to her as his wife, and devised by that will property to her while she remained his widow and did not contract another marriage; and that he made her sole executrix of his will, describing her as his wife, when these facts are supplemented by the fact that they lived together, without intermission, in good faith and openly, for more than eighteen years as husband and wife, nothing more is needed to show that he and the woman had mutually agreed to sustain the relation of husband and wife. Under the evidence in the cause they are to be held as having prior to the death of James Travers agreed *per verba de praesenti* to become husband and wife. . . .

We are of the opinion that even if the alleged marriage would have been regarded as invalid in Virginia for want of license, had the parties remained there, and invalid in Maryland for want of a religious ceremony, had they remained in that state, it was to be deemed a valid marriage in New Jersey, after James Travers and the woman Sophia, as husband and wife, took up their permanent residence there and lived together in that relation, continuously, in good faith, and openly, up to the death of Travers, being regarded by themselves and in the community as husband and wife. Their conduct towards each other in the eye of the public, while in New Jersey, taken in connection with their previous association, was equivalent, in law, to a declaration by each that they did, and during their lives were to, occupy the relation of husband and wife. Such a declaration was as effective to establish the status of marriage in New Jersey as if it had been made in words of the present tense after they became domiciled in that state.

Justice Holmes gave the dissenting opinion in part as follows:

I feel some doubts in this case which I think that I ought to state. I understand it to be assumed, as it must be admitted, that James Travers and Sophia V. Grayson lived together for many years, calling themselves man and wife, when they were not man and wife, and probably knew they were not man and wife. This condition of things lasted from 1865, the time of the pretended marriage in Virginia, to which their cohabitation referred for its justification, until 1883, the year of James Travers' death. So long as they lived in Maryland, that is, until some time in 1883, if they had attempted to make their union more legitimate by simple mutual agreement they could not have done it. Therefore, the instances of James Travers calling Sophia his wife during that period may be laid on one side. Just before he died, Travers moved to New Jersey and there made his will. As in Maryland, he spoke of his wife in that instrument, and, as I understand it, the decision that he was married must rest wholly on this recognition and the fact that in New Jersey a marriage may be made without the intervention of a magistrate. I do not see how these facts can be enough. Habit and repute might be evidence of a marriage when unexplained. But they must be evidence of a contract, however informal, to have any effect. When an apellation shown to have been used for nearly eighteen years with conscious want of justification continues to be used for the last month of lifetime, I do not see how the fact that the parties have crossed a state line can make that last month's use evidence that in that last moment the parties made a contract which then, for the first time, they could have made in this way. It is imperative that a contract should have been made in New Jersey. Therefore, even if both parties had supposed that they were married, instead of knowing the contrary, it would not have mattered. To live in New Jersey and think you are married does not constitute a marriage by the law of that state. If there were nothing else in the case it might be evidence of marriage, but, on these facts, the belief, if it was entertained, referred to the original inadequate ground. A void contract is not made over again or validated by being acted upon at a time when a valid contract could be made. When a void contract is acted upon, the remedy, when there is one, is not on the contract, but upon a quasi-contract, for a *quantum meruit*. There is no such alternative when a marriage fails.[16]

There is an impressive unanimity among students of the subject that the common-law marriage should be abolished. This is the position of the American Bar Association, the Com-

---

[16] Madden, J. W., and Compton, W. R., *Cases on Domestic Relations*, pp. 800–804.

mission on Uniform State Laws, and of most sociologists and students of law. In addition to the legal tangle the present situation involves, there are forceful social motives for doing away with this unconventional type of marriage.

The common-law union debases conventional marriage and encourages deceit and vice. The state certainly has the moral obligation of protecting the institution of matrimony from exploitation by the indifferent and by those who wish to enter marriage under cover because for some reason they wish to escape the responsibilities of a publicly acclaimed union, although as a matter of fact the couples living together in common-law marriage do not usually regard themselves as married and generally do not intend to live together permanently. So long as common-law marriage is recognized, there is opportunity for blackmail and for a woman who has been mistress of a man to claim after his death a share of his property as his legal wife. It is also true that when the court decides that there has been a common-law marriage, a later union of one of the two concerned is rendered bigamous, and if any children have been born they become illegitimate.

Child marriages. According to the common law a male had to be fourteen years of age and a female twelve in order to make a binding contract of marriage. By 1944 this had been changed by all but five of the states of the union by laws requiring higher ages than these. The common-law restriction is, of course, out of accord with our prevailing culture and our ideas of the meaning of matrimonial responsibility. In addition to the listing of the minimum age for marriage by statutory provision, there is in all our states the requirement that minors, even if they are within the age period for the contracting of matrimony, obtain from parents or guardians consent to marry. A plurality of the states now require that the male be eighteen and the female sixteen years of age prior to marriage. New Hampshire enacted the highest age requirement, eighteen years for girls and twenty years for boys, although for special causes judicial permission for a marriage may be obtained when a female is thirteen and the male fourteen.

In the practical administration of the existing laws we find even greater diversity among the states. There is also laxity in many localities in the enforcing of laws relating to the marriageable age, and misstatements concerning their age are frequently made by one or both of the parties applying for a license to marry. When the consent of the parents or guardians is necessary because of the age of those seeking to enter matrimony, many parents show little insight or sense of responsibility respecting the child marriage. The children in some cases forge the names of their parents to written statements of consent, and by means of this false document obtain their marriage license.

Richmond and Hall, in 1925, after a careful study of the problem of married children, estimated that in this country there were 343,000 women and girls who began their married life as child brides within the last thirty-six years.[17] In 1930 according to census records there were 4,241 girls married under fifteen years and 761 boys married under fifteen. In 1940, data collected for twenty-seven states gave 428 girls married between the ages of ten and fourteen and 3 boys married between the ages of ten and fourteen. Recently there have appeared in American newspapers a few sensational examples of the possibility in some of the Southern states of a child as young as twelve being legally married even without the parents' consent. For example, in 1937, in Tennessee, the court refused the request of a mother to annul the marriage of her twelve-year old daughter to a man thirty-two years of age. The statement of the court as reported by the press was in part as follows: "I believe society, law, and everyone concerned will be better served by the court's refusing to annul this marriage because to annul the marriage would result in turning Geneva out of house and home with no place to go." Obviously what the child needed was the help of a children's agency which would look into and contribute to her needs.[18]

The marriage of the immature is hostile to the prevailing standards of modern culture. Many such marriages are of short duration, are contracted lightly, and reach their logical anticlimax in the divorce court; others are ended by seeking an act of annulment from the court, based on the fact that one or both of the contracting parties were below age when the marriage was performed. When, as is often the case, the man is much

---

[17] *Child Marriages*, p. 57.
[18] Clarke, Helen I., *Social Legislation*, p. 90.

older than the girl he marries, the home is bound to be one of masculine dominance, with the likelihood that the girl's personality will receive little chance for development. Although there is need of greater knowledge concerning the biological aspects of child marriage, Carr-Saunders tells us that such evidence as we now have seems to show that when marriage is consummated at an early age there is a marked tendency for the premature death of the wife from tuberculosis or some other form of respiratory disease or some type of ovarian complication. He also tells us that in India, where the Hindus practice child marriage and Mohammedans do not, fertility is much higher among the latter than among the former.[19]

Efforts to lift the minimum marriage age are complicated by the attitude of the general public regarding illegitimacy. In the popular mind adequate solution of the pregnancy of a young girl is immediate marriage. In spite of this handicap of sentiment, the trend toward the fixing of a minimum age for marriage is unmistakable. It is also true that progress is being made in the improvement of the administration of the laws we now have.

The friend of the family will seek to encourage the coming of the following reforms. In states where the minimum marriageable age is low, it needs to be advanced as rapidly as public opinion will permit until it corresponds with the age at which children are now permitted to leave school in the more progressive states. Eventually the intelligent leadership is bound to insist on eighteen years as a minimum age for the marriage of girls. There is need also of requiring reliable evidence of the age of the contracting parties and the only satisfactory method of bringing this about is by the presentation of the birth certificate when the marriage license is issued. Since parents are not always to be trusted to exercise wisely their power of granting consent for the marriage of a child whose age is below that required by the law, it appears necessary to make some additional provision, such as that of the New Hampshire law, which insists upon the court's consent as well as that of the parents. To reduce the temptation of those in charge of the issuing of licenses, as much as possible, the fee system should be abolished

---

[19] *Population Problems*, p. 104.

and the authorities in charge of the licensing of marriages should be paid a salary. The requirement that both the parties contemplating marriage should appear for the license would also safeguard the home.

Although these reforms and others that are needed are likely to come about gradually, those who have the welfare of the family at heart must bear in mind that this is not a social problem that can be solved merely by legislation. Laws can be passed that will have an educational value, but they must not be far in advance of the prevailing public opinion of the states enacting them. Social strategy demands that the emphasis be primarily at present upon the necessity of educating public opinion. Progressive legislation regarding the marriageable age cannot go far unless there be a more intelligent and reasonable attitude toward the pregnancy of young girls.

Legal right to break engagement.   In order that courtship and engagement shall carry out their needful function, the right to break an engagement without risk of legal action for damages should be recognized by all our jurisdictions. The leadership of New York in recently eliminating action based upon alleged alienation of affections, criminal conversation, seduction, and breach of contract of marriage is based upon recognition that changed circumstances have made former emphasis upon the contractual aspects of the promise to marry an impediment to the freedom of decision that it is the purpose of the engagement to permit. Not only is it contrary to public policy to maintain legal coercions that would influence persons to enter marriage against their will, but the mere threat of action which in most jurisdictions is still possible leads to a pressure essentially blackmail, excessive damages through emotional appeal to juries, and the conception of engagement which denies its proper purpose as a period of probation during which both parties have opportunity of finding one another out and discovering any existing incompatibility of taste or temperament or other characteristics which would make their union undesirable.[20] Unless a reasonable escape from a contemplated marriage is clearly recognized by law, the contractual aspect of marriage as compared with its meaning as an intimate relation-

---

[20] Madden, J. W., and Compton, W. R., *Cases and Materials on Domestic Relations*, p. 38.

ship continues an emphasis contrary to public interest. The New York decision establishing the constitutionality of the statute removing the right to recover damages for breaking the agreement to marry rightly declared that it is not in accord with the welfare either of marriage as an institution or public policy for anyone to be influenced to enter marriage because of threat or danger of an action to recover damages or to be caused the embarrassment and humiliation such an appeal to the court is likely to bring to the individual who no longer wishes to marry.

Abortion.   The desire to control birth is by no means a new thing in the history of mankind; it is the increasing ability to do this by scientific methods that is new, so that the desire to escape children is more often satisfied than formerly. It must not be forgotten, however, that in the distant past abortion has often been used either to prevent the coming of any children or to limit the size of the family. Savage life discloses that the use of abortion for such purposes has had a real social significance.[21]

Nomadic tribes, those living chiefly on meat or fish, and all that do not have a constant supply of soft food, such as milk or grains, that furnish pap for the feeding of young children must allow an interval of several years between the rearing of the several offspring of each woman, since the child is dependent on the mother's milk for from two to six years, according to the living conditions of the people. Infanticide is a common means of thus spacing the children to be brought up; continence, enforced by taboo and aided in some cases by polyandry, is the rule among many peoples; and abortion or mutilation resulting in sterility is practiced in some tribes.

Although these methods of influencing the size of the families were primarily efforts to keep the population from becoming too great for the safety of the group, there is no reason to suppose that individual and family motives played no part. Indeed we are specifically told by one anthropologist that the women of a certain tribe employed abortion to spare themselves the labor of rearing many children.[22]

---

[21] Descamps, "Comment les Conditions de Vie des Sauvages Influencent leur Natalite," *Revue de L'Institut de Sociologie*, Tome I, No. 2, pp. 175, 183; See also Westermarck, *op. cit.*, Vol. 3, pp. 68, 79.

[22] Skeat, W. W., and Blagden, C. O., *Savage Races of the Malay Peninsula*, Vol. 2, p. 23.

Although in the strictly medical sense abortion means the detachment or expulsion or a combination of both of a foetus up to about the twenty-eighth week of development, the term as used by the laity means the wilful and criminal destruction of the foetus. It appears to have been a common practice among the upper classes in both Greece and the Roman Empire but not without opposition. Hippocrates included in his oath for those practicing medicine the words, "I will not give to a woman a pessary to produce abortion." Christianity from the beginning set itself against the pagan tolerance of the practice, regarding it as a sin. Its attitude was well expressed in the second century by Tertullian in these words: "Murder being once for all forbidden we may not destroy even the foetus in the womb. To hinder a birth is merely a speedier homicide; nor does it matter whether you take away a life that is born or destroy one that is coming to birth." [23] The Roman Catholic Church has insisted that "abortion is simply murder, a violation of the precept of God and of the law of nature, 'Thou shalt not kill,' " and has refused to approve even a therapeutic abortion performed by a physician in order to save the life of the mother.[24] This does not mean, however, that a physician is not morally free to prescribe what seems necessary in the effort to cure a disease from which the pregnant woman suffers even though indirectly it may abort the foetus. What is not permissible is a direct effort to destroy the foetus through the choice of attempting to save the life of the mother instead of that of the child. In case of the indirect abortion, it is held that the life of the mother is not endangered by the foetus but by some other condition. If the treatment she requires leads to the expulsion of the immature foetus, this was not the purpose of the treatment but a concomitant result of removing what was likely to cause the woman's death.[25] It is apparent that frequently in the Catholic hospital, especially in case of emergencies, the moral problem as to what is permissible and what is prohibited requires an authoritative decision. Ordinarily this is the responsibility of the chaplain, but sometimes in his absence it falls upon the doctor,

---

[23] Finney, Roy P., *The Story of Motherhood*, p. 294.

[24] Schmiedeler, Edgar, *Encyclopaedia Sexualis* (Victor Robinson edition), p. 100.

[25] Moore, E. R., *The Case Against Birth Control*, p. 50.

the nun in charge of the delivery room, or some other hospital official, and perhaps the patient.[26]

Frequency of abortion. No one can state with authority how many abortions are performed yearly in the United States. There is a considerable difference in the estimations made by those who have specially studied the problem. The number has been placed as high as two million annually, but most authorities believe that this is an exaggeration.[27] Taussig, a conservative student, believes that abortions number about 700,000 in this country yearly. In interpreting the statistics, it must be remembered that there are three types of abortions: spontaneous, those therapeutically induced, and the criminally induced. The last is the most common and the most dangerous. The same author states positively that there are not more than 5,000 deaths from abortion each year in the United States.[28] The uncertainty regarding the number of abortions performed is not only due to the reticence of the women concerned and the effort of concealment on the part of doctors who carry through the operation illegally but also because of inconsistency in the definitions of abortion and in the records reported by physicians. For example, there are without doubt numerous cases in which the woman, believing herself pregnant assumes that she has had an abortion performed, when as a matter of fact she was not carrying a child.[29] The Children's Bureau's study of maternal mortality in fifteen states found that twenty-five per cent of all the deaths from puerperal causes were due to abortion.[30]

It is estimated that at least fifty per cent of induced abortions are criminal. The number of therapeutic abortions is relatively small. The remainder of the total number are spontaneous. The causes of the last are many, such as a sudden fall, defective ovum or sperm, the presence of fibroid tumor in the uterus, or a dietary insufficiency.

The laws against criminal abortion have not been effective. They have only driven the practice underground, and, instead

[26] Gossett, W. B., *What the Public Should Know about Childbirth,* p. 250.

[27] East, Edward M., *Mankind at the Crossroads,* p. 262.

[28] Taussig, Frederick J., *Abortions, Spontaneous and Induced,* p. 26.

[29] *The Abortion Problem,* Proceedings of the National Committee on Maternal Health, p. 28.

[30] "Maternal Mortality in Fifteen States," U. S. Children's Bureau, Publication No. 233, 1934.

of the operation being performed in a hospital under proper conditions, it is usually carried through by an unskilled midwife, the pregnant woman herself, or a physician who, even if skillful, because of the necessity of secrecy does not have the safeguarding provisions that lessen the hazard of the operation when it is performed legally in the hospital for therapeutic purposes. As a consequence, the death rate is notoriously high. It is believed that one-fourth of all the maternal deaths each year are the result of criminal abortion.[31] In addition to this we know that a considerable proportion of these operations bring about sterility or ill health from which the woman never recovers. It is extremely difficult to get legal evidence sufficient to bring about a conviction, except when the abortion has been a clear cause of the death of the woman involved. The general public is usually ignorant or indifferent regarding the dangers associated with the illicit abortions. The consequence is that those responsible for enforcing the law and prosecuting the offenders are often not aggressive in their effort to prevent these illegal operations except when the public is aroused as a result of the death of some victim of the abortionist.

Taussig points out that it is much easier to criticize the present laws against abortion than to suggest a satisfactory constructive substitute. Taking into account the public attitude toward the problem, Taussig thinks that there should be recognition of four principles. First, the health of the mother should be made primary and respect for the unborn foetus as a living organism should be secondary to the consideration of her health. Two, the interest of the family as a whole, including the welfare of the children already born, should have consideration. Three, the law should be free from coercion from religious bias. Four, punishment should be provided for those who seek to profit financially from the practice of abortion. The abortionist shall be subject under this proposed legislative program to imprisonment for not less than six months or more than two years unless the operation has been performed in a licensed hospital by a regular practitioner of medicine after consultation with another such practitioner and for the purpose of preserving the mother's life or health or because of the

---

[31] *The Abortion Problem,* Proceedings of the National Committee on Maternal Health, p. 108.

physical depletion or moral irresponsibility of the mother. The penalty for an abortion performed by someone not a regular practitioner under the conditions previously stated, when the victim dies, should be an imprisonment from two to twenty years. By definition, abortion means to Taussig the attempt to destroy the foetus before it is capable of sustaining life if it is expelled from the body of the woman. If the foetus has reached a later development, any attempt to produce premature birth that leads to the death of the child except in the case of a regular practitioner of medicine and for the purpose of saving the life or the health of the mother or because of serious deformity of the child should be considered manslaughter. The author recognizes the fear of many that the clause "in the case of physical depletion or moral irresponsibility of the mother" will encourage the abuse of the law but he thinks that the requirement that two physicians be held responsible subject to the loss of their licenses will safeguard this provision of the law. He is also convinced that such legislation would put the professional abortionist out of business.

Abortion and birth control. It is held by the advocates of birth control that legal restrictions in the spread of knowledge of adequate contraceptive techniques are the chief cause of criminal abortion, that where the sale of preventives has been made punishable by law, the practice of abortion has increased measurably.[32] On the other hand, it has been affirmed that the recognizing with medical sanction of contraception leads to the belief that if contraception is right the destruction of the result of its failure cannot be wrong.[33] Raymond Pearl in a study of fertility and contraception in New York and Chicago reported that the abortion rate was higher in both cities for the users than for the nonusers of contraception. In a later investigation, based on 25,000 hospital records of white women, he found by grouping the cases economically that the abortion rate was much higher for those practicing contraception than for women who did not among the very poor, the poor, and those in moderate circumstances, but for the well-to-do was slightly lower.[34]

[32] Sanger, Margaret, *Motherhood in Bondage*, p. 395.

[33] Vaughn, Alec W., "Social Aspects of Abortion," *British Medical Journal*, Vol. 1, p. 408.

[34] Pearl, Raymond, "Fertility and Contraception in New York and Chicago," *Journal of the American Medical Association*, Vol. 108, p. 1385.

This statistical assertion that more abortions are performed by those who use contraceptives has been interpreted as merely meaning that of the pregnancies that occur as undesired accidents a larger proportion are aborted than among those people who are willing to become parents. Therefore, among this group who seek to avoid pregnancy, the use of contraceptives leads to fewer abortions than otherwise would happen. Because of this conviction, there are those who believe that the problem of abortion can best be solved by widespread contraceptive information and that this should be part of a state-wide program of abortion control.

Legality of abortion. The legal situation in regard to therapeutic abortion is as confused as are the laws concerning divorce. In every jurisdiction in the United States, statutes have been passed prescribing punishment under certain conditions for anyone that produces an abortion. Sometimes the term abortion is so badly defined as to include premature birth. An example of this is the law of Louisiana which would imprison at hard labor from one to ten years anyone bringing about premature delivery, although this is probably the daily practice of a busy obstetrician according to Taussig.[35] If the child dies after having been delivered alive, the offense becomes murder under the statutes, a penalty obviously impossible to impose. In some states it is still technically illegal to induce abortion even in cases of toxemia when this is the only means of saving the mother. In many states, mainly in the East and South, in spite of the statutory laws prescribing punishment for any person who induces an abortion, principles of the common law applicable to abortion still persist. According to common law it is not an offense for the mother to destroy the foetus before "it has quickened." There is the curious provision that although it is no offense for the mother to induce abortion upon herself, she becomes guilty of criminal conspiracy if she arranges for someone else to bring it about.

States can be grouped in five classes according to their attitude toward therapeutic abortion: permitting no exemptions, allowing exemptions to save the life of the mother, exemptions to save the life of the mother when medically advised, exemp-

---

[35] Taussig, Frederick J., *op. cit.*, p. 428.

tions to save life or preserve the health of the mother when medically advised, permitting abortion whenever deemed necessary by a physician.[36]

The unmarried mother and the illegitimate child. Although more abortions occur among married women who do not wish to have children or who dare not have another, the tragic situation of the unmarried pregnant girl frequently leads her to seek an abortion.[37] After trying every method known to her by hearsay to restart menstruation, she is apt to go from one doctor to another, accompanied by her lover or her mother, asking for an abortion. The physician, knowing that the operation under proper conditions at that time could be performed with a minimum of risk, may wish, especially if she is very young or has been raped, that the law permitted him to relieve her of an ordeal which one experienced specialist considers worse than death, but the professional ethics of the physician give him no choice. He realizes that she will probably continue her quest from office to office until at last she finds a professional abortionist who is likely to be incompetent. Later the first doctor may hear of her death or may be called upon to try to save her life after she has become desperately ill from an infection, the consequence of the conditions under which the operation had to be performed.

At present the unmarried Negro girl in parts of the rural South seldom seeks an abortion. Although this attitude seems likely soon to pass, it throws light on the motive of most of the unmarried mothers who desire abortions. It is the social penalty of her predicament, once it becomes known, that impels her, even at the risk of life, to rid herself of the stigma that will fall upon her and her child. The ordeal she faces comes from a social attitude that is very ancient and one that has been softened in recent years. No longer is a parent free to kill a daughter as was true in early Roman times. No longer must she wear the notorious "A," the theme of Hawthorne's *The Scarlet Letter*, but, nevertheless, the social punishment that she must bear, and usually alone, makes her desperate.

The problem of illegitimacy has been a difficult one for the

---

[36] *Ibid.*, p. 430.

[37] *The Abortion Problem*, Proceedings of the National Committee on Maternal Health, p. 163.

modern lawmaker. He has desired to mitigate the hardships of the unmarried mother and to protect the welfare of her child. At the same time, he is reluctant to make any radical departure from the legislation of the past, repressive in spirit and motivated by the desire to discourage delinquency.

In its attitude toward the illegitimate child, English common law was ruthless. He was a social outlaw with no legal relationship between himself and his mother. Neither parent had the right to his custody, neither parent was responsible for his support, and this naturally added strength to the public antagonism directed toward the unmarried mother, the fruit of whose misdoings thus added to the tax burden, since he was cast upon the parish for support. In the United States the early legal attitude regarding illegitimacy was in accord with that of the English common law. As this was gradually more humanized by English legislation directed toward giving the child more rights as a human being, a corresponding advance was made in this country. These decisions and statutes lessened the severity of early common law by giving the mother the right to custody of the child and imposing upon her the duty of supporting him. The father had no rights of custody and also no responsibility for supporting his offspring. This attempt to protect marriage and to discourage illicit intercourse by punishing the innocent victim of his parents' unlawful relationship seemed just neither to the courts nor to the legislators. Statutes were passed making provision under certain circumstances for the child to be legitimized, to inherit, and to have his support safeguarded, and, when the paternity was admitted or proved, to place upon the father the responsibility for the support of the child.

It is the general attitude of the public toward the unmarried mother and the illegitimate child more than the coercive aspect of the law that upholds the orthodox code and discourages irresponsible sexual relations. Neither influence is effective, however, as a means of preventing illegitimacy, although the former especially punishes the woman. The reason why these penalties have such slight success in dealing with illegitimacy becomes clear when the causes of the problem are considered. First of all, the impulsive nature of sexual desire, once passion is aroused, tends by its nature to force prudential considerations out of the mind. The situation is similar to anger when it reaches the degree that leads to unpremeditated murder. Judgment is pushed aside and not until desire has been satiated has the thought of the possibilities gained entrance into consciousness. How comes it then that the woman who runs such risk allows herself to be put in circumstances that may make her the victim of passion? The answer, in a multitude of cases, is ignorance. She has little knowledge of sex and even less understanding of the strength of passion, whether it be hers or that of the man with whom she is associating. Society that is so keen to punish her for her misdoings is in large measure itself responsible for what happens because of its unwillingness to include sexual information in her education. Both the home and the school through neglect often leave her ill-prepared to deal with the strongest of body appetites. The boy may be in the same predicament. Poverty, bad home conditions, failure of parental affection and control, vice, moral standards of one or both parents, bad environmental conditions, and her own low mentality —all may contribute to the situation that ends in unwanted motherhood. Each case is individual and ordinarily complex. It is evident, however, that punishment of the woman after the deed is done, whether this chastisement is expressed in social attitude or in law, can never play the major role in any preventive program. The legal trend, as a consequence, is toward giving both the mother and the child protection in the effort to lessen the hazards of her misfortune.

It becomes evident as soon as an analysis is made of individual cases of illegitimacy that unwholesome family or environmental influences can not be regarded as specific causes of unwanted motherhood. The family and social conditions may be predisposing, but in the majority of cases any one of them may operate without bringing about illegitimacy. The situation is never so simple that any single explanation, whether it be social or psychological, fully accounts for the undesired pregnancy. It is usual to find in the background of the young girl who has become an unmarried mother such conditions as ignorance, and especially ignorance of sex, poverty, low standards of living, a broken home, failure of family discipline, early sexual trauma, etc.; but on the contrary the same problem may occur in families and social backgrounds of a different type. In these cases, the decisive factor appears to be the product of mechanisms characteristic of the personalities concerned.[38] From this viewpoint such illegitimate motherhood has its psychological background—the urge to get rid of conflicts, including tension in the relationship of the girl and her parents, and to fulfill personality needs.

Since in a majority of these cases even the pregnancy itself is not anticipated, the insight that is sought by the study of the individual case is concerned with explaining how the relationship occurred which led to the pregnancy.[39] From such studies it becomes clear that in a large proportion of cases the occurrence cannot be explained by sexual desire on the part of the girl. Instead, it is not uncommon to find that she had no wish to do what she did for the purpose of obtaining physical satisfaction, that indeed she found the experience unpleasant or even painful. Also, as a rule, there is no permanent attraction toward the boy concerned or any thought even after pregnancy of marrying him when that is possible. Likewise, illegitimacy and promiscuity do not always coexist. The girl's first offense may make her pregnant and she may never become promiscuous. Such adolescent unmarried motherhood has been interpreted as a symptom of a maladjustment clinically intermediate between neurosis and delinquency. In the adolescent, as compared with the adult unmarried group, we find emotional immaturity significant, while in the latter more motivations suggesting feminine psychopathology or a quest for fulfillment through motherhood are found.

Every thoroughgoing study of a group of unmarried mothers reveals the complexity of the influences that led to their misfortunes. An example of this is an investigation of ten very young pregnant girls.[40]

Mary: Pregnant at thirteen, father dead, mother psychotic, and brother epileptic. Intimate with two men. Hostile toward the man she assumed to be the father of her child. Intelligent and responsive and affectionate toward her child, who was later placed in a foster home. Ambitious to finish school.

---

[38] Kasanin, J., and Handschin, S., "Psychodynamic Factors in Illegitimacy," *The American Journal of Orthopsychiatry*, Vol. 2, pp. 66–83.

[39] Clothier, Florence, "Psychological Implications of Unmarried Parenthood," *The American Journal of Orthopsychiatry*, Vol. 13, p. 543.

[40] Bernard, Viola, "Psychodynamics of Unmarried Motherhood in Early Adolescence," *The Nervous Child*, Vol. 4, No. 1, pp. 26–45.

Ruth: Only normal member of a family in which there was intense quarreling between parents. Mother, a chronic beggar, taught Ruth to use every means to get financial help. In accordance with this teaching the child permitted a forty-seven-year-old man to have sex intimacy with her short of intercourse. Later received attention from the young man who made her pregnant at thirteen. The girl expressed neurotic behavior but after treatment graduated with honors from a boarding school at nineteen, supported herself, and two years later entered college.

Jane: Up to the age of five lived with her grandmother, then rejoined the mother she had never known, who was living with a new husband. The girl discovered that she was an illegitimate child. The mother and step-father quarreled constantly. At twelve she was seduced by her step-father. She became pregnant, and then promiscuous, and was pregnant again at sixteen. She finally took a night course in vocational training, obtained and held a job. Is now maintaining a common-law marriage with the man responsible for her second pregnancy.

Beatrice: Became pregnant at fourteen and a half and declared her father was responsible. Girl and her father believed to be emotionally connected because of their reaction to the death of an infant boy of whom they were both very fond. She has now drifted into homosexual relations with a girl friend.

Alice: Pregnant at fifteen and a half after casual relations with a married man. The girl was her father's favorite. He died when she was fourteen. Her pregnancy was interpreted as an attempt to outrival her younger sister in her mother's affections by calling forth sympathy from the mother.

Alma: An intelligent, musically gifted high school girl pregnant shortly after her sixteenth birthday. Trauma resulting from an automobile accident and desire for independence from her family seem to have been influences that encouraged the intimacy that ended in pregnancy. She had no desire to marry the man.

Katherine: Pregnant at fourteen and a half as a result of one intimacy with a young fellow she had known for about three years. Her parents were estranged. Childhood frustration through lack of parental love appears to have been the major influence in this girl's experience.

Elizabeth: Although attractive and popular, felt outrivaled by her twin sister. She reacted to the parental coldness of her father toward her. Parental disapproval of her high school boy friend increased her tensions. Her experimenting in love-making brought about a pregnancy when she was fifteen years and eight months old. The girl responded to psychiatric treatment, finished high school, and entered college, developing finally a basically healthy personality.

Barbara: Pregnant at sixteen. Her parents had been living in a common-law marriage for thirteen years, separating when she was eight. The mother showed favoritism to a younger sister. The girl turned alternately to each parent in an attempt to find emotional security. She finally had sexual intercourse with one of her boy friends to see what it was like. She had no desire to marry the boy as she had no serious interest in him. There is evidence that for a time he represented her father to her. Added to this motivation was an attempt to revolt against maternal control as she entered a sexual relationship against which she had been frequently warned by her mother.

Patricia: An intelligent, normally attractive child whose parents are divorced. The mother has been married three times and divorced, the second marriage being with the girl's father. Until she was twelve she lived with her maternal grandmother whom she hated and who appears to have been cruel to the child. The girl made an unsuccessful effort to run away from home and was placed in a convent. Then between the ages of fifteen and sixteen she went to live with her mother for about a year. The mother treated her indifferently and eventually even showed competitive hostility toward the maturing daughter. The girl idealized the mother in an adolescent fantasy, and then she turned in the opposite direction and dramatized herself as replacing her father in the mother's love. Neither mechanism put an end to her frustrations and inadequate feelings, and impulsively she entered into a sex relationship with a nineteen-year-old boy whom she had met only two or three times. When she became pregnant, her mother shipped her to the father. Their life together became increasingly difficult for both. Eventually the girl worked through her conflicts sufficiently to achieve success as she adjusted herself to real life.[41]

Law and illegitimacy.   The study of individual cases of unmarried motherhood shows that illegitimacy is a problem that cannot be successfully solved by any direct legal attack on the problem. Law, however, has an important role in the social

---

[41] *Ibid.*

program that attempts justly and wisely to deal with the consequences of these unwanted pregnancies. One of the legal contributions has been through statutes providing for the legitimizing of the child born out of wedlock. There are three methods by which such a child may be made legitimate: marriage of the parents after the birth of the child, petition to the court for legitimation of the child if the parents are not married, and by acknowledgment of paternity. Since the law has not generally made clear the conditions of this acknowledgment, the court, as a rule, has to state how this can be accomplished. An Illinois court in 1905 declared that this acknowledgment must be general and public with the father giving evidence that he considers the child his own and wants this fact to be known,[42] that it was his intention to have the child known as legitimate and permitted to inherit. Most statutes provide that the child born out of wedlock becomes legitimate when the parents subsequently marry. Ten states and Hawaii have laws authorizing a change in the birth certificate when the illegitimate child has his status changed. In some states this alteration of the birth certificate can be made at the request of the parents and the presenting of the evidence of their marriage. Statutes of nearly all the states provide for this legitimizing by a subsequent marriage, but a large proportion of laws add as a condition that the father recognize the child as his. Most jurisdictions have moved away from the common-law principle that children born of a marriage which was void from the start are illegitimate, making it possible under certain conditions for children of such a marriage to be legitimate. The most liberal of these statutes declare that children born of a marriage null in law shall nevertheless be legitimate.[43]

As a rule, American statutory law declares the illegitimate child the son of the mother, gives him her domicile, and declares him connected with her by ties of inheritable blood. Nearly all states permit him to inherit from her, and most of them permit her also to inherit from him. Also in some states illegitimate children may inherit from each other through their mother. The most advanced legislation concerning illegitimacy is the laws of Arizona and North Dakota which attempt to pro-

---

[42] Clarke, Helen I., *Social Legislation,* p. 323.
[43] *Ibid.,* p. 325.

vide equal rights for legitimate and illegitimate children. These laws follow legislation enacted in Norway in 1915 which for the first time placed upon the father all the obligations of legal paternity once his paternity status was established. The Arizona law asserts the following:

Every child is the legitimate child of its natural parents and is entitled to support and education as if born in lawful wedlock, except the right to dwelling or a residence with the family of its father, if such father be married. It shall inherit from its natural parents and from their kindred heirs, lineal and collateral, in the same manner as children born in lawful wedlock. This section shall apply to cases where the natural father of any such child is married to one other than the mother of said child, as well as where he is single.[44]

The North Dakota statute is similar. Vernier approves the principle of these laws, believing that once the interest of the reputed father is rightly guarded by proper court proceedings for the establishment of paternity he should be required to accept his share of obligation for the child.[45] A committee of the National Conference of Commissioners on Uniform State Legislation, appointed in 1920 at the request of the United States Children's Bureau, drew up and adopted for recommendation to the several states a uniform illegitimacy act. This dealt with the support of the child, and with some changes it has been enacted by five western states.

The harsh attitude of the common law toward the illegitimate child was rooted in two motives: the desire to protect money and property and to uphold religious and moral ideas. The trend away from this stand has come from an increasing recognition of the rights of the child as an individual and to a lesser extent those of the mother. It reflects a more humane attitude toward unmarried motherhood, a realization of the just claim of the child for opportunity to develop normally and to a lesser extent a conviction that society has itself obligations toward both mother and child. The change has been toward allowing the child to inherit from the mother, fixing the status of the child's relation to the mother as similar to that of the

---

[44] Arizona, Revised Code, Sec. 273 (1928).
[45] Vernier, C. G., *op. cit.*, Vol. 4, p. 155.

legitimate child, giving the child the right to support from the father even to the right of inheriting from him, determining and liberalizing the methods by which the child can become legitimized and paternity can be proved and placing upon the state responsibility through designated agencies for the establishment of paternity and the supervision of the child. These tendencies, largely the product of socially minded lawyers and judges and social workers, continue, enforced by an increasing support from the general public because of a growing conviction that no human life should be victimized, in so far as that can be prevented, by the misdoings of others.

Amount of illegitimacy. Statistics concerning illegitimacy tend to be unreliable on account of the motive of concealment and the desire if possible to have the child recorded as legitimate. There are two methods for finding the rate of illegitimacy. One, the most common, is based upon the proportion of illegitimate births to the total births. The other is the rate of such births per thousand of single, widowed, and divorced women of childbearing age. The Children's Bureau reports on the basis of records from twenty-five state health departments that during April, May, and June of 1942 there were 9,410 illegitimate births compared with 8,081 for the same months of the preceding year, or an increase of 1,329 such births. The percentage of illegitimate births to the total births, however, was 3.3 for 1941 and 3.1 for 1942, the decrease coming from the increase in population and in total live births in many communities. Due to a nine months lag the increase in sexual delinquency among young girls did not show itself in an expected increase in illegitimacy.

Although World War II clearly revealed its disturbing effect on the behavior of adolescents in an increase of delinquency, especially among girls, statisticians were surprised by the fact that the rate of illegitimacy decreased during the first year of the war 8.8 to the lowest recorded proportion since 1931.[46] There is every reason to suppose that the increasing familiarity with birth-control methods among American youth has prevented to some extent the occurrence of unmarried motherhood in spite of the greater sex freedom resulting from

---

[46] *Vital Statistics,* Bureau of the Census, April, 1944, p. 141.

war conditions. The Florence Crittenden Home in Boston stated in its 1942 report that during the first part of the year very few of the fathers of the babies born in the institution were servicemen, but that the number increased so that at the close of the year fifty-one out of the one hundred and sixteen men mentioned as alleged fathers were said to be in service.[47]

Birth certificates and illegitimacy. Birth certificates have become increasingly important. Their significance increased during World War II through the need of individuals to present them in order to meet the requirements of the Federal government and employers. As a result, in the effort to protect those born out of wedlock from embarrassment, some states authorized an abbreviated form of the birth certificate, giving only the name of the child, date, and place of birth. An additional safeguard has been provided by states which refuse to issue copies of the complete birth certificate except to proper applicants and for a proper purpose. Many registration officials, sensitive to the possible hardship to an individual with a public record of birth to an unmarried mother, believe that the fact of legitimacy should not be recorded on a birth certificate and advocate changing the reporting of the parents of a child. By 1942, seven states—California, Maryland, Massachusetts, Nebraska, New Hampshire, New York and Wyoming—had eliminated the question of legitimacy from the birth certificate blank.[48]

Legal status of husband and wife. No problem in law is more difficult than the definition of the legal status and rights of husbands and wives. In no aspect of American law has there been greater change. Women have enjoyed a legal equality with men in but few societies. The English common law placed wives in the control of their husbands both as to person and property. They were under the power of their husbands, whom they were bound to serve and to obey. This definition of the status of the married woman is well expressed in the famous statement made by Justice Blackstone late in the eighteenth century.

---

[47] *Problems Associated with Birth Out of Wedlock,* United States Children's Bureau, p. 7.

[48] *Vital Statistics,* Bureau of the Census, April, 1944, p. 141.

By marriage the husband and wife are one person in law; that is, the very being or legal existence of the woman is suspended during the marriage, or at least is incorporated and consolidated into that of her husband. . . . Upon this principle of a union of person in husband and wife depend almost all the legal rights, duties, and disabilities that either of them acquire by the marriage. . . . For this reason a man cannot grant anything to his wife, or enter into covenant with her; for the grant would be to suppose her separate existence, and to covenant with her would be only to covenant with himself; and therefore it is also generally true that all compacts made between husband and wife when single are voided by the inter-marriage.[49]

Although the spirit of the English common law continued, there was from the beginning a tendency in America to move away from the severity of the English law. This was nourished by the scarcity of women in the early settlements. The changed attitudes found still greater expression in the independence permitted women in all the colonies and in the chivalry that developed in the South. The social position of women was inconsistent with the legal definition of her inferiority and limitations. For example, although the husband was not entitled to inflict permanent injury or death on his wife, he did have the power to chastise her, since in the words of an early commentator "Her will ought to become his will and to make her obedient there unto the common law doth seem to allow him to give her lawful and reasonable chastisement." It is clear that public opinion seldom supported a husband who attempted to exercise such a right. The actual position of women in American social life from the early days of colonial settlement reveals the lag between her status at law and that established by public opinion, and, as a consequence, there began a gradual redefining of the rights of women before the law. The trend was accelerated by frontier conditions and its tempo measurably increased with the settlement of the territory west of the Appalachians and departure both through distance and inclination from the one-time dominant English-rooted seaboard culture.

In interpreting the status of women from the early colonial days onward, there is risk of two opposite exaggerations. One

---

[49] Goodsell, Willystine, *A History of Marriage and the Family,* pp. 359–60.

overemphasizes the significance of the legal discriminations and handicaps that the law in accord with the English legal tradition placed upon her. The other overstresses the significance of those women who, in spite of their legal and social handicaps, carried on a career and achieved a degree of distinction.[50] With reference to the first error, it is important to keep in mind that the folkways and the mores always are more revealing when we attempt to judge social practices than laws or court decisions. There can be no doubt that colonial women and, even more, those whom we call the frontier women enjoyed more freedom and exercised more influence than could rightly be expected from their legal status.[51]

The conditions of American life, in the colonies and later in the Middlewest, and the opportunities thereby given women necessarily forced a departure from the pronouncements of the English common law.[52] The frequency with which women entered economic life, especially when their husbands were away, ill, or dead, made evident the unjustness of the English common law in its definition of the property rights of the husband as compared with the wife.[53] As a result, the shifting of the law toward our more modern point of view, already apparent in England, moved more rapidly in the United States. It was, of course, not a consistent movement. There were differences between the states, the tendency being for the western states to express in law their greater freedom from the tradition brought over from England. However, in each state there were also differences as the law moved forward at one point while remaining stationary at another.

The most advanced definition of the wife's property rights is expressed by the community-property legislation now found in eight states of the union. It exists in many European countries and in other parts of the world and has a Roman-Dutch origin. Women obtained a high legal status in the Roman Empire, and in the colonial period Dutch law was much more liberal with reference to women's rights than the English common law. This more modern attitude was brought to America

---

[50] Dexter, Elizabeth, *Colonial Women of Affairs*.
[51] Bell, Margaret, *Women of the Wilderness*.
[52] Beard, Mary, *America Through Women's Eyes*.
[53] Groves, E. R., *The American Woman*, Chs. 2 and 3.

by the French and Spanish. Their influence led to the Louisiana
Code, while Spain through Mexico contributed to the law in
New Mexico, California, and Texas. Later, community-property
rights were extended to Arizona, Washington, Idaho, Nevada,
and more recently Oklahoma. This system recognizes the mutual rights of husband and wife to property in the acquiring
of which they both have contributed as members of the marriage relationship, and the justice of this is so in accord with
the recent trend toward the social equality of men and women
that it is to be expected that the system of community property
will continue to spread among the states of the union, especially
west of the Mississippi River. These laws, like all others relating to domestic relations when applied to individual situations,
give rise to many issues. There are also great differences in the
details of the laws passed by these states which have accepted
in principle the idea of community property. A comparison of
the law of Louisiana and its interpretation by court decisions
with a more recent and more liberal enactment of Oklahoma
illustrates this variation.[54]

In spite of the great diversity among the states holding to
the general community principle, there is a common tendency
to maintain the following: (1) Property acquired before marriage continues as separate property. (2) The same is true of
property acquired after marriage through gift, devise or descent.
(3) Through rents, issues, or profits of separate property. (4)
Through exchange, purchase, etc. with separate consideration.
(5) Through earnings of husband and wife. (6) Compensations
for injury to person or property become community property,
except in Louisiana and Texas. California and Nevada permit
the wife under certain conditions and by meeting certain prerequisites to enter business on her own and thereby acquire as
her own property what otherwise would belong to the community.[55] The distance between the original concept of English
common law and the community system is perhaps best expressed by the statement of the former that the family is a union
with the husband as its legal representative. The wife's identity
disappeared at marriage, her legal existence being represented

[54] Daggett, Harriet S., "The Oklahoma Community Property Act, a Comparative Study," *The Louisiana Law Review,* Vol. 2, pp. 575–596.
[55] Vernier, C. G., *op. cit.,* Vol. 3, pp. 212–216.

by the husband, to whom she belonged. This original principle of English common law changed through pressure of social conditions both in England and the United States, with an increasing recognition of the rights of the wife as an individual.

The community-property principle conceives the family as a union of two individuals who share in common any property acquired through their living together as equal members of the family organization. The husband in accord with Spanish tradition nevertheless is dominant in this relationship, the wife playing the role of a sort of silent partner, until the marriage ends and the community which they own together is dissolved. The same influences that have lessened the prerogatives of the husband in common law are of course operating in similar manner on the community authority of the husband which the Louisiana Code states as that belonging to the husband "as head and master." Vernier states there is a marked tendency to increase the protection of the wife and to limit the powers of the husband.[56] As a legal principle expressing the spirit of present-day domestic relations the community system is in accord with American social trends even though its application in the states maintaining it may in practice bring no advantage over what is provided by the statutes of other liberal states. The community system offers the logical basis for the evolution of the legal equality of husband and wife, while progress where the English common law has prevailed comes from the moving away from the onetime concept of the family as an organization personified by the husband.

The discussions of this chapter illustrate the progress that has been made and indicate the legal trends that must continue in order to adjust the law to the increasing recognition of the rights of the child, the woman, and the wife as an individual. As advance comes through statutes and decisions, there arises also the need of redefining the position of the husband. In many instances responsibilities were placed upon him because of his authority and legal superiority as the head of the family. As his prerogatives are withdrawn, there is frequent need also of removing liabilities placed upon him as a means of safeguarding the interests of his wife and children. Otherwise, in

[56] *Ibid.*, p. 219.

the shifting from the old to the new legal concept, he may in practice find himself discriminated against by limitations and requirements no longer in accord with the prevailing independence of the wife. The important thing to notice is that the law, as it deals with domestic matters, in order to be in harmony with American cultural changes must accept constant readjustment in the effort to establish the just equality of the man and the woman.

Discrimination, whether it comes from statutory law or from decisions of the courts, is increasingly difficult to defend. This legal trend is in line with the sentiment of American culture, but there is a limit to what law by itself can accomplish. Undoubtedly women still encounter discrimination in education, in professional activities, and in industry, but these are for the most part of conventional origin that harks back to the period when masculine rights were dominant both in the mores and in the law. The present tendency to lessen these limitations of social character will continue. They should be legislated against when possible, but for the most part progress must be made through a greater sense of justice in public thinking.

The present problems of legislation come less from efforts to establish the rights of women and more from attempts to deal justly with the conflicting interests of individual husbands and wives. The principle of legal equality must, to accord with prevailing American sentiment, be the basis of the adjustment of domestic differences.

Juvenile and family courts.   The juvenile court came into being as an American innovation in the legal system designed to deal more justly and constructively with the child offender. Although it represented a radical departure, it was nevertheless the outgrowth of a legal principle recognized in the common law, whereby children under seven lacked the capacity for criminal responsibility and therefore could not be found guilty of a felony. Between seven and fourteen the question of guilty intent was not presumed but had to be demonstrated by evidence. After fourteen the child was regarded as an adult so far as responsibility for crime was concerned. The juvenile court lengthened the period during which, because of his immaturity, the child could be dealt with differently than the adult offender.

The juvenile court also took over and enlarged ideas in relation to the dependent and neglected child already recognized by the equity doctrines of the court. Thus in function the juvenile court was symbolic of the state's fatherhood. This has been most fully expressed in a decision holding the constitutionality of legislation establishing juvenile courts.[57] "To save a child from becoming a criminal, or from continuing in a career of crime, to end in maturer years in public punishment and disgrace, the legislature surely may provide for the salvation of such a child, if its parents or guardian be unable or unwilling to do so, by bringing it into one of the courts of the state without any process at all, for the purpose of subjecting it to the state's guardianship and protection." [58]

In this same decision authority was given to the court to proceed in the spirit of a father to deal with the child as seemed best for his welfare: "nor is the state, when compelled, as *parens patriae*, to take the place of the father for the same purpose, required to adopt any process as a means of placing its hands upon the child to lead it into one of its courts. When the child gets there, and the court, with the power to save it, determines on its salvation, and not its punishment, it is immaterial how it got there. The act simply provides how children who ought to be saved may reach the court to be saved." [59] Thus the juvenile court in accord with the factual knowledge of science was free to recognize the significance of childhood as a formative period in the effort to provide the guidance the child needed as preparation for the social responsibility of an adult.

The greatest significance of the juvenile court came from its freedom to cut away from traditional court procedures in dealing with the child and to make use of the new insight science was bringing as to the meaning of childhood and the consequences of unwholesome environmental conditions. The new point of view soon found expression in the Juvenile Psychopathic Institute, which was established in Chicago in 1910, and the Child Guidance Clinics, which through the pioneer demonstrations under the auspices of the National Committee of Mental Hygiene led to their organization for the study of

---

[57] Commonwealth vs. Fisher, Supreme Court of Pennsylvania, 1905.
[58] Madden, J. W., and Compton, W. R., *Cases on Domestic Relations*, p. 717.
[59] *Ibid.*, p. 718.

problem children and through them their problem parents in many of the American cities.

Illinois is rightly given credit for establishing the first juvenile court. Its origin was the dissatisfaction of many social leaders of Chicago with the treatment being given delinquent children. Children over ten were being arrested, held in police stations, tried in the police courts, usually fined for their offenses, and, if the fine were not paid, sentenced to the city prison. The Chicago Woman's Club as early as 1880 was concerned with various reforms in the attempt to improve conditions in the police stations and jails, and as early as 1892 the Jail Committee of this organization suggested a juvenile court. In 1895 a bill was drafted providing for a separate court for children and a probation staff, but because the club's legal advisers doubted the constitutionality of the proposed measure it was abandoned. The project was not, however, dropped, but instead there was a widening of interest which finally led the Illinois State Conference of Charities in 1898 to appoint a committee which drafted the Illinois Juvenile Court Act. The proposed legislation was supported by the Chicago Bar Association, which appointed a committee which did much to convince the legislature that the bill known as the "Act to Regulate the Treatment and Control of Dependent, Neglected, and Delinquent Children" should be enacted. The following year the law passed.[60] The organization of the Chicago court was fostered by a supporting committee known as the Juvenile Court Committee, of which Miss Julia Lathrop was the first president, with a membership composed of women delegates from various clubs. It became apparent that there was need of a more scientific study of some of the children who came before the court than was possible without the establishing of a special clinic. In 1914, largely through the interest and benevolence of Mrs. William Dummer, the Juvenile Psychopathic Institute was established and William Healy became its director.[61]

Juvenile court legislation is an example of the changed public attitude toward children which has led to a new definition of their legal status. Public officials have been given power

---

[60] *The Child, the Clinic and the Court,* a group of papers published in cooperation with the Wieboldt Foundation, pp. 320–330.

[61] *Ibid.,* pp. 204–214.

to enforce the responsibilities of parents, and the meaning of parental obligation has been enlarged. It has been made possible to separate children from parents who are clearly neglectful, although there is still a tendency in the courts to overemphasize the ties of parenthood and to minimize the neglect or abuse of children aside from physical injury or cruelty. Child-labor laws have limited the rights of parents to profit from the earnings of their children, and the father's responsibility for the support of the family has been enlarged by "the abandonment, nonsupport, and contributing-to-dependency-and-delinquency laws."

Experience revealed the need of a court where the family in all its aspects could be handled, for otherwise the legal problems arising from the effort to deal adequately with a bad family situation had to be scattered among several different courts. Thus came the court of domestic relations which now is often known as the family court. These courts when they first appeared were restricted to a narrower program, having in charge enforcement of family desertion and nonsupport legislation.

The Cincinnati Court of Domestic Relations was perhaps the first to express fully the new attitude toward the family symbolized by the juvenile court. In 1913 it took over the administration of the laws which had led to the establishment of the earlier type of courts of domestic relations, and also the functions of the juvenile court and jurisdiction over divorce and establishment of paternity. This court, under the inspiration of Judge Charles Hoffman, had great influence over the thinking and practices of social workers upon whom so largely falls the decision, in dealing with incompetent and bad families, whether to seek the assistance of a court.

It is the belief of some that the difficulty of administering in one court the laws relating to such diverse aspects of the family will prevent the full consolidation of family legislation under one jurisdiction. This practical difficulty appears particularly in dealing with divorce litigation. Three different types of problems predominate in divorce proceedings, each appearing characteristically in the three economic classes, the wealthy, the middle class, and the poor. The first centers about the distribution of property; the second, the right to the divorce; while the third has to do with provision for family support. Experience may prove that there is risk of so swamping a court that has charge of all the aspects of family relationship, if divorce is included, that the problems of children are slighted.

It is not so important that all family law be administered by one court, as it is that the idea which led to the establishment of the juvenile courts and the courts of domestic relations should be carried forward and made the point of view of all courts dealing with phases of family relationship. This notion, which stands in sharp contrast with the spirit of common law, is that it is the business of the court in dealing with family maladjustment to go beyond the immediate problems presented instead of being content with making a decision in accord with legal routine and tradition. The court should seek to understand the family situation and act in an advisory capacity for the good of all concerned. Only by the development of this legal attitude can the courts become a conserving influence in the realm of domestic relations. Emphasis on this approach seems likely to develop as a result of pressure from modern social conditions, and, although divorce litigation will probably respond last, it also, in dealing with the climax of domestic maladjustment, will seek knowledge of the human situation to determine whether there is hope of reconciliation or whether the divorce is necessary.

Chapter 20

THE BIOLOGIC APPROACH

FOREWORD. The student is likely to come to a consideration of the biologic aspects of family conservation with the feeling that here is an opportunity for a relatively easy and rapid advance. He is apt to regard a eugenic program as scientific defense against many of the human tragedies which he believes have resulted from bad inheritance. Through his own contacts with defective people he has become familiar with very impressive pathological conditions as consequences of bad inheritance. He also has knowledge of the progress that has been achieved in animal breeding and the care that is taken in the mating of individual animals by those engaged in animal husbandry. It seems that only an intelligent attitude toward human reproduction is necessary for eugenic welfare and that this can come once people have an understanding of the significance of heredity. This point of view, natural as it is, does not do justice to the complexity of the causes that affect the human organism, the lack of certainty of hereditary background in the great majority of people, and the conflict of values associated with any attempt to control human breeding. The effort to apply what we do know concerning human inheritance raises issues that are legal and moral and that involve questions of social control. Human genetics is not an exact science in the same sense that is true of the genetics of plants and lower animals. The scientist in the field of human eugenics does not have available the experimental knowledge so easily gained from animals whose traits can be followed through many shorter generations. There is also greater difficulty in separating the influences of the environment from those that come forth from inheritance. Then also there is the troublesome fact that many hereditary consequences do not appear until late in adult life. Therefore, those who die too soon to reveal their traits hide the hereditary influences that otherwise would be apparent.

Public policy regarding human mating is also hampered by the insistence upon individual rights and the rightful recognition of the legislator that too great control of mating will in our culture lead to alternatives that may be equally or even more undesirable socially. Marriage cannot be made an aristocratic opportunity for a few highly favored individuals. The most the eugenist hopes for at present is that the group of persons who are serious victims of bad heredity, either by persuasion or coercion, will abstain from bringing children into the world. As this chapter discloses, even this program goes forward slowly and with considerable opposition. This hostility to eugenics comes from those who feel that the state has no moral right to forbid the individual to reproduce or, and this is much the more significant, from the inertia of public opinion which is either ignorant of eugenic principles or unconvinced that they are important enough to merit recognition in human mating.

Eugenics and euthenics. Eugenics is the science concerned with the improvement of man's hereditary characteristics; euthenics seeks to improve man's environment. It is obvious that both are important and that advancement in one contributes to the success of the other. In specific cases of defectiveness we have situations that clearly come from inheritance, for example hemophilia, or "bleeding." Poverty and crime are frequently illustrations of the influence of environment. Some conditions appear to have their source in both inheritance and environment. Diabetes is a disease that reveals this double causation when it occurs both because of hereditary tendency and such environmental influences as habitual overeating, emotional tension, or excessive strain. The defectiveness of men, women, and children when we attempt diagnosis frequently discloses this combination of unfortunate hereditary and environmental influences, and the apportioning of responsibility cannot be made with exactness.

Euthenics seems to have an easier task. Culture, or man's

social environment, has largely pushed aside the dominance of physical environment so apparent in primitive society. Urbanization and mechanical achievement have led to changes in the competitive processes of survival, so that no longer is there the advantage coming from physical strength, size, speed, and endurance that once were so decisive in the struggle to live. Attention is therefore more willingly given to the improvements that come through the manipulation of environmental conditions. Euthenic improvement can be made more quickly and, since it does not meet with the opposition that comes from any effort to limit the freedom of mating, it also can be made more easily than any eugenic control. Man is not limited in his adaptations to the slower and more cumbrous methods of transmission of biological inheritance as is the lower animal. He has, in addition, intellectual resources that can be passed on by cultural transmission and that are cumulative. Some eugenists see danger in euthenic progress, believing that by protecting the weak and permitting them to survive and propagate the race deteriorates. Human welfare, including conservation of the family, can best come, not by retarding euthenics, but by linking its progress with that of eugenics.[1] Environmental improvement enforces the need of both eugenic ethics and a eugenic program encouraging those who are physically, psychically, and socially fit to have children, and those who appear to have significant hereditary weakness to remain childless.

This chapter seeks to emphasize the value, aside from a general eugenic program, that the biologic approach to marriage and family experience has for the individual. Trouble can come from husbands or wives misunderstanding our present knowledge concerning the problems of human mating. Needless fears may arise from a mistaken idea as to the transmission of traits. A feeling of fatalism, based on one's family background, may lead the individual away from marriage or parenthood when such a policy is not justified by the insight contributed by the recent advances of science. Biologic dogmatism may be accepted as demonstrated facts when it is merely radical opinion disregarding the significance of the environment. This chapter seeks to help those who believe they have personal

---

[1] Fisk, Eugene L., "Is Modern Health Work Dysgenic?" *Eugenics,* Vol. 2, pp. 3–7.

problems that are biologic in character and that need to be settled in the light of our present knowledge of the significance and the limitations of human heredity.

Ancient eugenics. The term "eugenics" is comparatively recent, but the idea is old. It appeared in the ancient world as one of the first attempts to advance human welfare, finding expression in Greek thinking as early as the sixth century before Christ. Infanticide and some of the other savage customs that seem to us cruel appear to have had at times in primitive society some eugenic result, and it is possible that in such cases these practices had, even in that period of human evolution, a vague, pragmatic intent.

In the ancient world Sparta attempted to build a civilization on a eugenic program. Having become dominant over subjected races through physical superiority, the Spartans undertook to maintain their position by control of breeding. They destroyed sick and deformed infants, penalized celibacy, and encouraged marriage within their own group. Plato and Aristotle both revealed an interest in eugenics. Plato, as was true of other writers of the ancient world, believed the explanation of inferior children born to superior parents was incompatibility of ages. This was to be guarded against by rules determining the ages beyond which parents were not to have children. These writers also assumed that the transmission of physical superiority guaranteed a corresponding mental superiority. With the advent of early Christianity, interest in eugenics disappeared, and not until the seventeenth century was there revival of eugenic thinking, when Campanella, apparently influenced by Plato, advocated regulation of human breeding.

Modern eugenics. The word "eugenics" was first used in the nineteenth century by Sir Francis Galton, an Englishman and cousin of Charles Darwin, and with his work began the modern interest in the advancing of human welfare by discovery of the facts of human heredity and more rational control of mating. Because of his genealogical studies he became convinced that intellectual superiority and degeneracy were both inherited, and he sought public support for various eugenic proposals. In 1904 at the University of London a research fellowship in eugenics was started which later developed into the Francis Galton Laboratory of National Eugenics. These investigations were continued and carried ahead by Galton's successor, a former co-worker, Karl Pearson. In 1908 the Eugenics Educational Society was founded, with Galton serving as the first honorary president. His successor in this position was Leonard Darwin, the son of Charles Darwin. Leonard Darwin became internationally known for his contributions to the eugenic movement that developed not only in various parts of Great Britain but also on the continent and in the United States. The Eugenics Educational Society published *The Eugenics Review,* a quarterly that had great influence in promoting the eugenic program. In the United States the pioneer in eugenics was Alexander Graham Bell, the inventor of the telephone. Another early leader was Charles B. Davenport, who, influenced by the development in England, started in 1910 a Department of Genetics at Carnegie Institution, Cold Spring Harbor, Long Island. The American Eugenics Society started in 1926. Another important pioneering organization was the Human Betterment Foundation in California under Paul Popenoe, which has done much to publicize knowledge concerning eugenic sterilization.

From every point of view the eugenics idea has close relation to the family. The major concern of the advocates of eugenics is race improvement, and they consider marriage primarily as a means of regulating human breeding. This larger aspect of eugenics has an indirect significance for the family, but our chief interest is in the effect of eugenics on the family life itself. Any eugenics program in this country must conform to the democratic pattern. It can never be merely an attempt to maintain an optimum population or even to increase the birth rate among the more intellectual or economically secure classes. In order to be in accord with the American tradition it must stress the welfare of the individual family, encouraging social conditions that will lead to the wanting of children in homes that can provide the right sort of environment and from parents whose inheritance gives no indication that they are unfit to have children. Irrespective of the social class in which they can be catalogued, families that are biologically sound and possessing a realization of the meaning of parental responsibility should have children not merely on account of their obligation to contribute to social welfare but because of the value of parenthood for them as a means of fulfilling their needs and obtaining satisfactions. It is useless to indict the social order for self-chosen childlessness when the family policy is based upon an estimation of values that places luxuries and social appearances as more desirable than children. There are, however, many ways by which society can provide resources that will lead those who do wish children to become parents without sacrificing anything essential to family experience.

Significance of genetic inheritance. It is impossible to know with accuracy how many people in this country suffer physical or mental incapacities of hereditary character. Osborn estimates that at least five million suffer to some degree from handicaps that are at least in part the consequences of their genetic constitution. Of this number two million or more have liabilities that are tragic for them and their families and are a costly burden to society.[2] The estimations of Osborn will seem reasonable to most students of the problem. In interpreting the significance of this group of our population, it is necessary to keep in mind two facts when dealing with individual cases. One is that the environmental circumstances frequently have a large place in determining the consequences of a personality's liabilities even when these are due to inheritance. The ignoring of this explains in part the fallacious reasoning that appeared in the studies of the Kallikaks and the Jukes. It has been said that if ever eugenics becomes an exact science the history of the Jukes will be regarded as chemistry now regards alchemy.[3]

A hereditary handicap may become a problem to the individual who nevertheless from the social viewpoint either because of his ability to overcome his misfortune or his capacity along other lines is a social asset. Here there may be a difference of values according to whether we stress the hereditary welfare of the race or the cultural values of society. An individual who, under the program of Plato, would not be allowed to survive may prove an invaluable contributor to social welfare. This, however, may not justify the individual's becoming a parent. Eugenics, at present, has gathered enough actual knowledge for the advocating of strategic principles, but the

---

[2] Osborn, Frederick, *Preface to Eugenics*, p. 29.

[3] Scheinfeld, Amram, *You and Heredity*, p. 365.

application of these to individual families is not so clear. Judgment as to the meaning of hereditary incapacity, even when its origin is certain, must be based on the personality as a whole.[4] As the science of genetics increases and its knowledge of causation is more certain, the significance of hereditary handicap as it influences the progress of the race will become less controversial and the application of the principles of the science to concrete cases will become more certain.

Eugenics, marriage, and parenthood. It is obvious that there is need, in discussing the advantages of eugenics as a means of conserving the American family, of distinguishing between marriage and parenthood. Before the coming of an effective method of contraception and a safe process of sterilization, the only humane means of carrying out the eugenic program lay in control of mating. In practice this meant regulation of marriage, since it had to be assumed that those who married would be likely to have children. Science, in bringing us modern methods of contraception and sterilization, has made possible a more intelligent eugenic program for mating and propagation. The full use, however, of these better methods of race selection awaits the growth of a social and moral attitude, at present possessed only by a minority, which will lead individuals to face definitely and conscientiously the two questions that can now be dealt with independently, whether one is free to marry, and if one marries whether one has the right to bear children.

There can be no doubt that eugenic concern for both marriage and parenthood is making slow progress in the United States. The movement necessarily encounters opposition, in part from the *laissez faire* attitude regarding marriage that has long been characteristic not only of our culture but of all modern civilization. It is interesting to note that the first departure from the notion that marriage is a human right with which the state should interfere as little as possible appeared in this country in the unconventional groups such as the Oneida Community and the Mormons, in both of which there were practices that had distinct eugenic purposes. The business of the state, according to conventional thought, was limited to determining the methods of solemnizing marriage, to recording

---

[4] *A Decade of Progress in Eugenics,* Third International Congress of Eugenics, p. 473.

it, fixing its responsibilities, and deciding, once it had been entered upon, whether the individual might be freed from his matrimonial contract.

Although eugenics emphasizes race welfare, it is likely to make much of its progress through the appeal it has for the man or woman who contemplates marriage or parenthood. The individual facing marriage, knowing his family record, may realize that his entering matrimony brings a special hazard. When he considers his situation intelligently, he is not content merely to know the facts; he must endeavor to discover their significance. This means that he must learn from an authoritative source the probable results that will come from his marriage, so far as its hereditary significance is concerned. Once this information has been gathered, justice demands that it be given over to the person whom he is expecting to marry. It is always difficult for a person in love to deal calmly and objectively with problems of this sort, but as our knowledge of inheritance increases and is more widely distributed, the number of those who can meet this supreme test of affection is increasing. In a case where there is genuine doubt as to whether one has the right to marry, it is exceedingly important that investigation be made of the family record of both the man and the woman, for if there appears to be the same danger of inheritance on both sides there is a double reason why the marriage should not take place.

Marriage is a normal experience for sound individuals and one that usually proves beneficial to both persons. It is not, however, safe to particularize this general fact and to assume that marriage in an individual case will mean improvement of health, will increase nervous stability, and will lessen the liability of expression of bad hereditary traits. Everything depends upon the character of any existing body weakness or disease or mental defect, and upon the significance of the trends of inheritance revealed by the family history.

When the problem includes parenthood, it is even more complex. Again the same routine has to be followed in getting information, facing it squarely, and bringing it to the attention of the other candidate for marriage. The hereditary risks of parenthood are, along certain lines, clearer than those of marriage. Science has obtained a definite knowledge of the proportion of risk of transmission of certain bad hereditary traits, such as Huntington's chorea, so that an impartial investigation of one's heredity may lead to the conclusion that marriage is justifiable but parenthood is not.

It would be most unfair under such circumstances not to give the other person a new choice as to whether he or she wishes to marry and not have children. In some cases the danger may be so great that if marriage takes place it may not be wise to trust birth control, efficient as it is at present when effectively taught, but recourse should be had to sterilization as the only positive assurance that no child will ever come from the union.

Transmission of defectiveness. Popenoe states that at least one-half of all those admitted to hospitals for the insane reveal a history of mental disease or defects among their relatives.[5] An English investigation shows that 40 per cent of the children of the insane themselves become insane.[6] Evidence of the significance of the laws of inheritance for human nature has become the support of the eugenics program. It has a double purpose. It aims to increase the birth rate among individuals superior in hereditary tendencies and to decrease that of the inferior. The first effort is known as positive eugenics and the other as negative. Clearly the second is at present the easier to carry out, and it is along this line that most of our progress in practical eugenics has taken place. The leaders of eugenics advocate the spreading of information so that many victims of bad heredity will voluntarily abstain from parenthood and also the enactment of legislation to prevent the propagating of the unfit who are not willing or who are incapable of avoiding parenthood. Two methods are at present proposed: the segregation and the sterilization of persons who are likely to transmit serious defectiveness, that is, types of abnormality known to be the result of defective heredity passed on from parent to offspring. From the knowledge we have at present, judgments concerning the hazards of mating fall into two classes: one where the certainty of the risk of transmission has been conclusively demonstrated and the other where we deal with probabilities. This distinction is based upon the fact that we have

---

[5] Popenoe, Paul, "Eugenic Sterilization in California," *Journal of Heredity,* Vol. 19, No. 2, p. 73. Quoted by permission.

[6] *Ibid.*, p. 80.

the certainty of transmission in some cases, while in others the family record discloses a potential risk but no one can be sure what will happen to the offspring. In all attempts to anticipate the consequences of a specific mating, the difference between dominant and recessive characters has to be recognized. Very significant information concerning human inheritance has come from the study of identical twins, especially when they have been brought up in different environments. Although Mendel's contribution to the working of heredity is a basic principle, the knowledge upon which genetics rests has gone far beyond his famous laws. The working of human heredity reveals a much greater complexity with at least a dozen important methods of transmission with various combinations and modifications. There are three fundamental forms of genetic behavior—dominant, recessive, and blending—and the working of these is complicated by the various factors that influence the hereditary pattern, of which sex-linked inheritance is one example. The physician comes to know of many hereditary conditions not often recognized by the general public, since many of them are relatively uncommon. He finds the following classification convenient for his purposes: hereditary blood-types; mental disorders; abnormalities of eye, ear, skin, skeleton, and muscles; diatheses and susceptibilities; blood diseases; and cancers. For a clear, useful summary the student should study Laurence Snyder's *Medical Genetics*.

It is apparent that the interpretation of the hereditary background of concern to the thoughtful individual who wishes to become a parent has to be a particular application of genetic knowledge, and evidence of soundness and immunity has to be considered equally with that of liability, abnormality, and suggestibility. An illustration of the significance of immunity, a hereditary factor which the nonspecialist is likely to forget, is given by Davenport, who reports a family record in which approximately half of the members have goiter and the other half do not although they all live in a community where the iodine content of water and soil is so lacking as to encourage the development of the disease. Family eugenics, in any attempt to counsel persons in doubt about becoming parents, demands a detailed analysis of the hereditary background of both prospective parents and an individual interpretation in the light of the general principles of eugenics. It is not a matter for the husband or the wife to decide, for the problem can be safely handled only by a medical specialist or biologist.

In order to have an intelligent attitude toward human inheritance on the part of the general public, there is need of specialists who as a public service will diagnose hereditary backgrounds and predict what is to be expected from a definite mating. At present, the information concerning animal breeding is much more available through the services of agricultural colleges, extension departments, and experimental stations. Certainly there is equal need of authoritative, scientific insight for those who are in doubt as to whether they possess the heredity that gives them the right to bring children into the world. It seems reasonable to expect that the demand for such assistance will increase as people become more familiar with and more concerned about the ever increasing knowledge of the workings of the principles of heredity. This will not come about, however, until there is a better distribution of the facts of eugenic science and a better developed sense of ethical responsibility on the part of potential parents.

Mental diseases.   The problem of heredity which at present most commonly brings worry is that concerned with the significance of some mental disease which has appeared in the family background. This is usually thought of as an insanity, using the legal term for mental incompetence, and the question that troubles the person who is about to marry or to have a child is: Am I destined to the same misfortune or will I transmit this danger to my offspring? A similar anxiety frequently develops in the person who finds himself in love with an individual whose family history reveals some kind of mental disorder. In dealing with such problems it has to be recognized first of all that what we call mental disease is at present less understood than most of our physical diseases. The causation has not been established, as is true of so many of the diseases that come from bacteria or from anatomical or physiological conditions. The definition of most of the mental diseases depends upon the behavior of the victim rather than upon a knowledge of their causal origin.

The difficulty of assigning in proper proportion the influences that come from inheritance and those that are contributed by environment is even greater than in those diseases that we call physical. Naturally there is more controversy concerning what brings about mental disease. Since we do not have the certainty as to causation, as is true of tuberculosis for example, the result is that there are many theories and even various schools of thought. In some mental diseases improvement or even apparent cure takes place in spite of different sorts of treatments. Although there is a great quantity of factual information that the psychiatrists have gathered concerning these various ailments, we do not yet have the understanding of them that medicine has of most physical illnesses. Since there is little opportunity for experimental knowledge in the effort to apportion the hereditary factors, the geneticist must for the most part depend upon statistical analyses of family histories for insight as to the significance of transmission. The results give us certainty on one hand, as appears in the Rh blood type, or considerable confusion, as is found in the contrasting findings and studies of manic-depressive psychoses and epilepsy. This does not mean that the importance of hereditary transmission is denied but rather that the part it plays is in individual cases not so clear as to prevent differences of interpretation.

Although there is need of much more statistical knowledge concerning manic-depressive psychosis, for example, before we can safely apportion the hereditary factors, there is no doubt that inheritance is involved.[7] Snyder asserts that the evidence now available, although limited in quantity, indicates that the disease is the result of an irregular dominant influenced by environmental factors that at present we do not understand.[8] The student will find in the literature attempts to determine mathematically the hazards of the appearance of mental disease in the family background.

Rudin concludes that in the case of one defective parent the following results appear in the offspring. In the case of manic-depressive insanity at least 33 per cent of the children have the same malady and as many more show mental abnormalities. In the case of dementia praecox or schizophrenia 9 to 10 per cent of the children have the same disorder, and those

---

[7] *Eugenic Sterilization,* Committee of the American Neurological Association, p. 112.

[8] Snyder, Laurence H., *Medical Genetics,* p. 28.

having other abnormalities bring the total to 50 per cent of mental pathology. The same rate appears in children of those having genuine epilepsy. From those having hysteria we get 48.61 per cent of mentally and nervously abnormal persons. If both parents have schizophrenia the children are 82 per cent abnormal, and if both the parents are manic depressive the offspring will be 100 per cent abnormal.[9] In view of our limited knowledge, these assertions must be regarded as dogmatic opinion rather than the findings of science. Any decision as to marrying or becoming a parent by those who know that in their family background mental disease has appeared should be made not on the basis of general statements such as Rudin's but on the specific interpretation of the record by a specialist in the field of human heredity. Karl Menninger in *The Human Mind* rightly calls attention to the danger of believing that because structure is so clearly inherited the same is true of the behavior of the personality. When we see similarities in outward appearance between parent and child, it is easy to jump to the conclusion that they are alike in personality characteristics even when there is abundant evidence to contradict this. He goes so far as to say that there is at the present time no reliable scientific evidence that insanity or any common mental disease leading to it is inherited.[10] He is a representative of those stressing the environmental origin of mental difficulty when he states that the schizoid or queer personality results largely, if not entirely, from the attitude and behavior of the parents during the child's formative years.[11]

When a husband and wife are convinced that any child of theirs may be born with a definite hereditary defect because of the family record of one or both, they need knowledge as to the probability of the risk, the degree of the hazard, and the alternative. Each family situation is individual. Macklin illustrates this. A couple, wishing a child but having lost one soon after birth, as did the wife's grandmother, from abnormal bile ducts, asked for counsel. They were advised that the next

---

[9] Rudin, E., "The Significance of Eugenics and Genetics for Mental Hygiene," *Proceedings of the First International Congress on Mental Hygiene,* Vol. 1, pp. 474–475. Quoted by permission.

[10] Pp. 23–25.

[11] *Ibid.,* p. 90.

pregnancy was likely to lead to the same disaster, but since the child would not live to suffer and the pregnancies appeared unlikely to be a hardship, they might wisely gamble if they cared that much for children and could face the emotional strain of losing another child. They did and the next pregnancy resulted in normal twins.[12]

Predicting the outcome of any human mating becomes more certain, the less influence environmental conditions have. For example, the color of the eye is a product of transmission that is utterly independent of environment. Heredity has command and nothing at present can be done to change its decisions. There are, however, a great many hereditary predispositions in which the final result is largely determined by environmental circumstances. Body structure provides an illustration of this. As a result of hereditary predispositions, body characteristics tend toward three types: the slender, the fat, and the intermediate. It is difficult for the first to take on weight and the second to avoid too much weight, but diet, eating habits, and behavior can play a large part in what actually happens to the individual. This effect of environmental conditions is most apparent in the third type where the hereditary tendency is least extreme.[13]

The relationship of environment and heredity which we have recognized in physical characteristics also appears in those we distinguish as mental or personality traits. We have instances in which the consequence of human mating is clear because heredity again has command. This appears, for example, in the rare disease Huntington's chorea, which is one of the most tragic of all inherited maladies. It is believed to have been brought to the United States in the seventeenth century by three brothers who carried the genes that produce the disease. Not until early middle life is there any evidence of the bad inheritance, but at about thirty-five or forty a degeneration begins that rapidly carries the victim to idiocy and death. Any offspring born in such a family has a one-in-two possibility of having the same experience. Science is helpless.

Regarding most of the mental diseases, there is no such certainty. Although the individual may inherit a predisposition

---

[12] Macklin, M. T., pp. 133–134, in *Medical Genetics and Eugenics*, by C. B Davenport and Others.

[13] Bogert, L. Jean, *Diet and Personality*.

toward some sort of abnormality of personality, whether it finds
expression in such a way as to justify the term disease may
depend upon the individual's environmental history. One's
way of life and education have a large place in deciding for
the great majority of persons the intellectual, emotional, and
moral development. Those who lack the endowment for normal life—for example, the idiot—can profit little from whatever opportunity is offered. It seems also that those extraordinarily endowed as geniuses will surmount any environmental
obstacle and in some way reveal their superiority. Although the
investigation of human characteristics thus far demonstrates
that the human organism, like that of lower animals and plants,
is controlled by the same laws of heredity, man's ability to
modify his environment makes possible modifications of
hereditary predispositions, thereby complicating the problems
of human breeding. Differences that appear between individuals even when they become victims of the same malady suggest
that there are hereditary influences that operate, of which we
have little understanding at present. For example, every human
being seems open to the contracting of syphilis when the
conditions necessary for getting it are present. If, however,
the disease runs its course, it will lead to paresis in one
individual, locomotor ataxia in another, and many other disorders—for instance, heart trouble—in other victims, suggesting that there is some hereditary weakness that turns the
disease in one direction rather than another. It seems probable
that the same situation is true of many human ailments,
although there is less reason to assume the influence of predisposition.[14]

Snyder states that people commonly have the following
misconceptions of human heredity: that students of heredity
believe and seek to prove that all human characteristics are the
result of inheritance; that if the characteristic is conditioned
by heredity, environmental influences will have no effect; that
when a hereditary basis is discovered for a pathological condition, medical effort to deal with it ceases; that when a causative
agent is demonstrated for a disease, heredity had no part in its

[14] Webster, Leslie T., "Inborn Resistance to Infectious Disease," *The Scientific Monthly,* Vol. 48, pp. 69–72.

expression; that heredity is used to explain occurrences whenever there is no real knowledge of causation; that nothing can be constitutional unless there is evidence of hereditary influence in the family history (this fallacy comes from forgetting the vast possibilities in the hereditary history of any individual); that there is no difference between congenital and hereditary (an illustration of this is a child's getting syphilis from the mother and then being said to be a victim of hereditary rather than congenital syphilis); that when we do not know how heredity operates to bring about certain conditions, inheritance has no meaning and should be disregarded.[15]

New knowledge concerning human inheritance. The biologic approach to the conservation of marriage and the family emphasizes two important facts that need to be realized by those contemplating marriage or parenthood. The first is that any question that arises concerning human heredity needs to be dealt with as an individual problem by a specialist qualified to interpret family history. The second is that our insight is constantly increasing as a result of the gathering of new knowledge. The recognition of these two facts is of greater practical value than becoming familiar with the abstract principles of human heredity.

Advances in knowledge are constant. They proceed along many lines. The following are cited as illustrations of this progress of genetics. Since 1900 it has been known that there are various blood groups and that this is based upon inheritance. This resulted from the discovery that when the serum of one person was mixed with the red cells of another in some instances agglutination occurred while in others it did not. This was the result of the presence in the individual's blood of a specific antigen for which in the serum of others there was a specific antibody. Based upon this fact, it was found that there are four blood groups, each containing one or both antigens, or neither, designated by the letters A, B, AB, or O. These differences are accounted for by genes. Genes A and B are dominant to gene O but not to each other. These hereditary facts are so well established that they have a practical legal

---

[15] Snyder, Laurence H., *Medical Genetics,* pp. 8–9.

application. In some cases of baby exchange in hospitals it has been found that the child accredited to one couple could not have been born to them but could have been to another who had been thought to have received the wrong baby. In the same way in disputed paternity it is sometimes possible to demonstrate that the accused man could not have been the father of the child.[16]

Recently a new blood factor has been known, one which accounts for a deadly disease that appears occasionally in the newly born child, for which until recently there was no explanation. This is the Rh blood factor. It was discovered through blood serum from the Rhesus monkey. When this was applied to human blood, it appeared that there was another antigen, since the new serum agglutinated the blood of some persons but not that of others. It was finally discovered that about 85 per cent of the white or caucasoid possess this Rh factor or were Rh positive while the rest did not or were Rh negative. In 1941 it was worked out that the disease erythroblastosis occurred only when the child was Rh positive and the mother Rh negative. The theory is that the elements from blood of the child get through the placenta of the mother and this blood difference of mother and child causes antibodies in the mother's blood stream which in turn get into the blood stream of the foetus, thus causing the disease. It has to be treated by a blood transfusion from an Rh-negative individual, who, unlike the mother, does not have Rh antibodies in the blood. It is apparent that science has merely crossed the threshold in this new discovery in genetics.[17]

The brains of living animals, including man, carry on an electrical activity which it is now possible to step up by electronic methods to record pulsations objectively on what is known as a brain wave chart, or electroencephalogram. At present, this new resource for scientific investigation has seemed most useful as a possible means of detecting inherited functional instability of the central nervous system of the apparently normal relatives of epileptics. The investigation of

---

[16] Snyder, Laurence H., op. cit., p. 16; Wiener, A. S., "Heredity and the Lawyer," The Scientific Monthly, Vol. 50, pp. 139–146.

[17] Stamscot, L. H., "The Rh Blood Factor," Scientific Monthly, Vol. 60, pp. 451–454.

brain waves as a means of disclosing constitutional unstable brain activity clinically not apparent is in its infancy.[18]

Another line of genetic investigation of great importance has to do with the endocrines. This has proceeded in various directions, of which the experiments of Charles R. Stockard of the Cornell University Medical College are an impressive example. In his breeding of giants, dwarfs, and monstrosities he demonstrates the interrelation of heredity and environment.[19] Another approach in the same field of endocrinology, which has already yielded some startling practical results in plant culture, has come from the study of hormones. Here, also, science has merely broken into a new field of study, the significance of which for the better understanding of heredity only the future can reveal.[20]

Medical genetics and family welfare. Family welfare demands greater regard for the science of genetics. This aspect of health and disease deserves more attention during the training of the physician than it usually receives. In his premedical instruction he is not likely, even in his biological courses, to gather the information he needs for the interpretation of family history. Later in the medical school he seldom has opportunity to study in any detail medical genetics, although from time to time reference will be made to principles of inheritance in the instruction. The student is too apt to carry from his college courses theories of inheritance rather than specific knowledge of the hereditary factor as it influences health and disease.[21] The consequence is that although the physician, like all natural scientists, places emphasis on the significance of human heredity he lacks adequate detailed understanding of the working of heredity unless through experience and further study he makes up the deficiency of his training.   .

There is even greater need of families realizing the advantage that can come from gathering all the insight possible concerning the family history on both the husband's and the

[18] Löwenbach, Hans, "The Electroencephalogram in Healthy Relatives of Epileptics," Bulletin of Johns Hopkins Hospital, Vol. 65, pp. 125–137.

[19] Stockard, Charles R., *The Physical Basis of Personality*.

[20] Bonner, James, "The Hormones and Vitamins of Plant Growth," *The Scientific Monthly*, Vol. 47, pp. 439–448.

[21] *A Decade of Progress in Eugenics*, The Third International Congress of Eugenics, pp. 157–158.

wife's side. This knowledge will prove of increasing value as the science of eugenics makes it possible to use such information for a family program of preventive medicine or for dealing with illnesses as they develop. Many times this understanding of the family background will enable the physician to remove needless fears, and in times of crisis it may prove a decided asset in treating some serious illness or disability. When we speak of dealing with the total personality, we need to remember that this includes hereditary influences as well as the environmental occurrences that have made the substance of the total personality. The more adequately both are understood, the better equipped the physician is to meet any problem that confronts him.

It is an advantage also to parents in the training of their children to know the family hereditary history. Two extremes must be avoided. One is that of using inheritance as a constant explanation of traits appearing in the child. Such an attitude can be highly suggestive and undoubtedly often leads to the development of characteristics that are assumed to be inherited when they are not. The other mistake is to assume that it is the business of a parent to weed out an inherited tendency when, as a rule, the proper role of the father and the mother is to direct it. The constant danger of conceiving heredity too simply, according to hearsay dogmatism, is very great. It is not to be expected that ordinary parents will be specialists in the field of genetics, but what family welfare requires so far as inheritance is concerned is the disposition on their part to realize the significance of heredity as a causal factor in the life of their offspring and, whenever it seems desirable, to seek from the biological specialist or the competent physician information that will guide them in their dealing with the inborn tendencies of their children. Ideally, it would be helpful if such information was desired by every family. This will not come about, however, until the significance of the biological aspects of family welfare is much more generally understood. Meanwhile, the intelligent family exposed to the present findings of the science of genetics will have the incentive to compile as far as possible a hereditary record of the family backgrounds and to get an authoritative interpretation of their meaning.

Limitation of eugenics.   Important as eugenic breeding is for human welfare, it has its limitations. If every child were an exact duplicate of either parent or a mere synthesis of both, the task of eugenics would be simple. Since, however, the combination of genes that come from the parent is unlike that given to either the mother or the father and, except in identical twins, is different from that received by other children born of the same parent, full control of human breeding would not bring quickly the characteristics regarded as desirable.

Even if it were possible to concentrate upon one trait as the goal of breeding, progress toward it would necessarily be slow. Unquestionably, however, breeding from parents having this wished-for trait would tend toward its establishment in the line of hereditary descent. The children of selected parents would tend toward the characteristic trait, but it would take many generations before it would be fixed in the progeny. As a matter of fact, however, the problem is more complicated because in human breeding, unlike that of animals, there cannot be concentration on any single characteristic, since in a sound policy of human breeding there is need of encouraging the establishment of many different traits, all desirable as a basis for public welfare and for individual happiness.

Social selection.   Since the problems of human breeding are so complicated and there is at present so much that we do not know, it might seem hopeless to attempt to influence the quantity or quality of population. Such a *laissez faire* program ignores the fact that the principle of natural selection still operates and that there are influences coming forth from social conditions that affect both the growth of population and its qualities. The most apparent of these is birth control, the result of the development since the beginning of the nineteenth century of efficient methods of contraception and an ever spreading knowledge of their efficacy. The effect of this, in the opinion of many, has been dysgenic. Restrictive legislation in this country has undoubtedly limited knowledge of effective birth control among the lower economic classes to a much greater degree than among the middle class and the wealthy. Other influences also have operated, such as greater religious opposition, indifference, and inability on account of economic conditions to procure the means of protection. Birth control, moreover, cannot be charged with exclusive responsibility for the dysgenic trends in the growth of American population. Abortion, venereal disease, late marriage, urban life, and various influences coming from an industrial civilization in contrast with the rural and frontier life characteristic of earlier America, appear to have decreased fertility and lessened births. It is reasonable, however, to assume that had there been no legislative restriction hampering the dissemination of knowledge of contraception, the decline in the birth rate among those on the lower economic level would have more nearly approached the decrease we find in the professional class, the better educated, and the well-to-do.

Eugenics as public policy.   At present, only the intelligent and conscientious are concerned with the significance of their inheritance as an influence on marriage and parenthood. This minority slowly increases as public opinion becomes more impressed with the meaning of inheritance in human mating. The reckless, indifferent, and unintelligent ignore the most obvious hereditary hazards and, as a consequence, often bring children into the world that lower social vitality, are a financial burden, and out of proportion to their numbers bring about all sorts of social problems. Such children, if they survive, often become a burden to others and, as specific studies have demonstrated, cost the public an enormous amount of money and an even greater amount of trouble. As the meaning of human inheritance becomes clearer, the obligation of society to protect itself grows more imperative. Interest in this method of social advancement is world-wide, but the United States has thus far led all nations in its eugenics legislation and its practical efforts to prevent the breeding of defective strains. This, however, does not mean that a great deal has been done in this country, for it is only in recent years that there has been much use of sterilization as a means of social protection. Germany, under the Nazis, developed a more radical program but for other than eugenic motives.

Sterilization.   A part of the opposition to the use of sterilization for eugenic purposes comes from misunderstanding as to what it is. It usually signifies the making of the man or woman sterile by a surgical operation that produces no change except the inability to reproduce. It must not be confused with castra-tion, which results in considerable changes in body structure and emotional disposition.

Sterilization means for the man vasectomy, an operation easily and quickly performed, trivial in character, and, with the use of a local anaesthetic, practically painless. Operation in the case of the woman is less simple because it requires deeper entrance into the body. It is known as salpingectomy and con-sists of the cutting of the Fallopian tubes so that the egg cannot pass nor become impregnated. From 1909 to the first of January, 1927, approximately five thousand operations to sterilize men or women were performed in California. There were but four deaths, those of two women from peritonitis and of a man and a woman through the aftereffects of ether. No death occurred after 1920 in any hospital, although more than half of the five thousand operations were performed after that year.[22]

Sterilization legislation. Eugenic sterilization was first le-galized in 1907 in the state of Indiana. Since then there have been many laws passed in various states and considerable litiga-tion regarding them. There has been a disposition on the part of the courts to declare such laws unconstitutional when they have been punitive in purpose, on the basis that they provide for cruel and unusual punishment.

The courts also have insisted that laws authorizing sterili-zation must be so written and administered as not to be class legislation. The tendency has been to consider provisions for sterilizing as an expression of the police power of the state cor-responding to regulations to protect public health, rather than as enactments involving the procedure required in criminal cases. The laws are written to apply to all of the same natural group, without regard to the economic status. It has become the routine, in accord with sound judicial practices, not to authorize sterilization without a proper hearing and without giving the person concerned an opportunity to appeal to a court of higher jurisdiction.

A case involving the legal status of sterilization laws was decided by the Supreme Court of the United States in 1927. The state of Virginia had ordered that the operation of sal-

---

[22] Popenoe, Paul, *Sterilization in California* (Pamphlet), p. 168. Quoted by permission.

pingectomy should be performed on a feeble-minded woman whose mother was feeble-minded and who had an illegitimate feeble-minded child. With one dissenting vote the court declared the law constitutional, the opinion being written by Mr. Justice Holmes, who asserted in part:

We have seen more than once that the public welfare may call upon the best citizens for their lives. It would be strange if it could not call upon those who already sap the strength of the state for these lesser sacrifices, often not felt to be such by those concerned, in order to prevent our being swamped with incompetence. It is better for all the world, if instead of waiting to execute degenerate offspring for crime, or to let them starve for their imbecility, society can prevent those who are manifestly unfit from continuing their kind. The principle that sustains compulsory vaccination is broad enough to cover cutting the Fallopian tubes. Jacobsen vs. Massachusetts, 197 U. S. 11, 49, L. ed. 643, 25 Sup. Ct. Rep. 358, 3 Ann. Cas. 765. Three generations of imbeciles are enough.

But, it is said, however it might be if this reasoning were applied generally, it fails when it is confined to the small number who are in the institutions named and is not applied to the multitude outside. It is the usual last resort of constitutional arguments to point out shortcomings of this sort. But the answer is that the law does all that is needed when it does all that it can, indicates a policy, applies it to all within the lines, and seeks to bring within the lines all similarly situated so far and so fast as its means allow. Of course, so far as the operations enable those who otherwise must be kept confined to be returned to the world, and thus open the asylum to others, the equality aimed at will be more nearly reached.[23]

Sterilization in California.   The state of California has made more use of sterilization for eugenic purposes than any other state of the Union or any nation. California law makes sterilization of an insane or feeble-minded person compulsory if it is the judgment of the medical superintendent of an institution for the insane or feeble-minded that the operation should be performed and if this decision is approved by the director of the State Department of Institutions and by the director of the State Department of Public Health. To avoid any possible litigation, however, it has been the policy of those who have in charge the administration of the law to seek the

[23] Castle, O. H., *The Law and Human Sterilization*, pp. 565–566. (Address.)

written consent of the nearest relatives of the patient, if such were to be found. Usually these have been willing to approve the sterilization. In some cases they refused because they feared that the patient later might become hostile if they authorized the operation. In other cases it appeared useless to seek approval because of their ignorance and illiteracy, while in a few instances, although the relatives objected, it was held necessary for the interest of the patient or the state, or both, to proceed with the operation.

The Human Betterment Foundation of Pasadena, California, has undertaken as one of its projects the study of the effects of this practice of eugenic sterilization in the state. Valuable information has been collected regarding the attitude of patients toward the operation, the behavior of sterilized persons on parole, the effect of sterilization on the marrying of the patients, its influence on the success or failure of such unions, whether sterilization leads to criminality, and other questions that require answer in determining the value of eugenic sterilization as a public policy.

The chart on page 594 shows the sterilizations officially reported from states having a sterilization law up to January 1, 1944.

Although statutes authorizing the state to perform sterilization for eugenic purposes, complying with the requirements of due process of law, avoiding class legislation and applied to individuals, are well established constitutionally, this is not true yet of self-chosen sterilization not performed by the authority of the state. Several states permit sterilization only when the patient himself consents. This is termed in the law voluntary sterilization. Voluntary sterilization in the more restricted sense where the individual himself goes to the surgeon asking that his ability to reproduce be removed by sterilization is in such legal confusion that the physician may be subject to damages for having committed an illegal act even when both husband and wife in writing agreed to the sterilization.[24] Such operations are performed, but, as a rule, the surgeon protects himself on the basis that the sterilization was performed as a

---

[24] Miller, Justin, and Dean, Gordon, "Civil and Criminal Liability of Physicians for Sterilization Operations," *American Bar Association Journal*, Vol. 16, pp. 158–161.

health measure. Although it is likely that when this was done with the patient's and spouse's consent it would not be interpreted by the courts of most states as constituting the crime of mayhem, there is need of the legality of such operations being

STERILIZATIONS OFFICIALLY REPORTED FROM STATES HAVING A STERILIZATION LAW UP TO JANUARY 1, 1944

(Collected and tabulated by Birthright, Inc., Princeton, New Jersey.)

State	Totals				Insane			Feeble-minded			Others		
	Total	Male	Female	1943	Total	Male	Female	Total	Male	Female	Total	Male	Female
Ala.	224	129	95					224	129	95			
Ariz.	20	10	10		20	10	10						
Calif.	17,012	9,005	8,007	459	10,559	5,738	4,821	5,747	2,561	3,186	706	706	
Conn.	488	31	457	31	408	21	387	80	10	70			
Del.	658	342	316	17	278	207	71	355	135	220	25		25
Ga.	287	31	256	97	118	6	112	169	25	144			
Idaho	14	4	10		12	2	10	2	2				
Ind.	1,286	660	626	55	467	249	218	819	411	408			
Iowa	551	170	381	58	295	127	168	231	36	195	25	7	18
Kans.[1]	2,794	1,629	1,165	88	1,929	1,129	800	755	459	296	110	41	69
Me.	218	20	198	1	20	6	14	128	14	114	70		70
Mich.	2,466	606	1,860	78	325	72	253	1,962	495	1,467	179	39	140
Minn.	2,157	478	1,679	46	391	117	274	1,766	361	1,405			
Miss.	546	149	397	4	478	135	343	56	14	42	12		12
Mont.	213	61	152	5	40	17	23	173	44	129			
Neb.	609	286	323	79	143	53	90	466	233	233			
N. H.	492	93	399	24	201	24	177	240	69	171	51		51
N. Y.[2]	42	1	41		41		41				1	1	
N. C.	1,498	343	1,155	152	339	115	224	964	170	794	195	58	137
N. D.	671	235	436	43	328	125	203	312	98	214	31	12	19
Okla.	553	122	431		303	71	232	250	51	199			
Ore.	1,654	645	1,009	57	669	301	368	884	314	570	101	30	71
S. C.	74	8	66	17				74	8	66			
S. D.	646	242	404	3				629	236	393	17	6	11
Utah	379	179	200	69	87	44	43	292	135	157			
Ver.	228	75	153	3	13	1	12	187	65	122	28	9	19
Va.	4,675	1,958	2,717	203	2,704	1,134	1,570	1,971	824	1,147			
Wash.[3]	685	184	501		403	147	256	276	33	243	6	4	2
W. Va.	48	1	47	1	19		19	10		10	19	1	18
Wis.	1,420	261	1,159	48				1,420	261	1,159			
30	42,608	17,958	24,650	1,638	20,590	9,851	10,739	20,442	7,193	13,249	1,576	914	662

[1] One of the six state institutions in Kansas failed to report.

[2] New York's law was declared unconstitutional. Ground of adverse decision was that it denied equal protection of the law, because it did not include those at large as well as those in institutions.

[3] In 1942 the State Supreme Court of Washington declared the law unconstitutional. Ground of decision was technical deficiencies in the act.

Nevada and New Jersey passed sterilization laws that were declared unconstitutional before they were applied.

well enough established so that persons who are aware of serious hereditary liabilities may feel free to protect themselves from the possibility of defective offspring by the only method that science at present knows to be certain.

Moral and religious opposition to sterilization. Sterilization is opposed by those who believe that it is immoral or irreligious to take from the individual his right to propagate in lawful marriage. Sterilization is but one aspect of the eugenics program [25] which they oppose as contrary to what they believe is right. Their solution for clear and severe hereditary liabilities is self-chosen continence. The use of contraceptives as a means of birth control for eugenic reasons is also condemned. The position of Catholic opponents of sterilization has been authoritatively expressed by Pope Pius XI in his Encyclical Letter.

Finally, that pernicious practice must be condemned which closely touches upon the natural right of man to enter matrimony but affects also in a real way the welfare of the offspring. For there are some who, over solicitous for the cause of eugenics, not only give salutary counsel for more certainly procuring the strength and health of the child—which, indeed, is not contrary to right reason—but put eugenics before aims of a higher order, and by public authority wish to prevent from marrying all those whom, even though naturally fit for marriage, they consider, according to the norms and conjectures of their investigations, would, through hereditary transmission, bring forth defective offspring. And more, they wish to legislate to deprive these of that natural faculty by medical action despite their unwillingness; and this they do not propose as an infliction of grave punishment under the authority of the state for a crime committed, nor to prevent future crimes by guilty persons, but against every right and good they wish the civil authority to arrogate to itself a power over a faculty which it never had and can never legitimately possess.

Those who act in this way are at fault in losing sight of the fact that the family is more sacred than the State and that men are begotten not for the earth and for time, but for Heaven and eternity. Although often these individuals are to be dissuaded from entering into matrimony, certainly it is wrong to brand men with the stigma of crime because they contract marriage, on the ground that, despite the fact that they are in every respect capable of matrimony, they will give birth to defective children only, even though they use all care and diligence.[26]

Registration of mental defectives.   Some states have established central registries for mental defectives, where many

[25] Mayer, Joseph, "Eugenics in Roman Catholic Literature," *Eugenics*, Vol. 3.
[26] Pope Pius XI, *Four Great Encyclicals*, pp. 90–96.

thousand individuals are recorded. The advantage of such a state registry as a source of information regarding individual defectives and as a means of knowing the size and character of the problem of the state is so great that eventually it should become a universal policy. Useful as it will prove to the public administrator and the student of human heredity, it is hoped that it will lead to an extension of the idea of recording the individual data necessary in the building of sound eugenic public policy. The real need is a means for the keeping of family records, and until this is done on a large scale eugenics must be greatly limited. The genealogist already demonstrates that family descent can be traced even with the meager records now available. The inclusion in such data of pertinent facts having possible hereditary meaning is a prerequisite to a more rational attitude than we have at present toward mating.

Such a keeping of family histories might seem impracticable, something likely to develop in the far future, if at all, were it not that the advantage of the central registration of defectives will lead toward an enlargement of the scope of the undertaking and the gradual recognition of the value of more complete records. An example of this trend is the growing importance that various public policies have given to the birth certificate in recent years. The mere bringing together of each individual's birth and death certificates would prove useful to those attempting to discover the hereditary probabilities of a particular marriage.

The legal trend.   It might seem that the legislative trend toward greater restriction on eugenic grounds of the right to marry is inconsistent with the drift of public opinion to interpret matrimony as a relationship chiefly of concern to the two persons involved and to show greater liberality in dissolving the ties of union. Rarely does social evolution move forward in one harmonious current, and such is not the situation at the present time in matters pertaining to marriage.

The idea of limiting the right of marriage, however, is not antagonistic to the more pronounced inclination to recognize the inherent hazards of marriage. It represents a special feature in a complexity of changing attitudes, but one that is strengthened by the growing tolerance of public policy toward those persons who have failed to achieve happiness in marriage. The more it is realized that marriage failure is disastrous to those who do not make the grade and that success cannot be expected when those who marry are unfitted for the ordeal, the stronger becomes the conviction that it is socially desirable to keep out of marriage those who are incapable of meeting its responsibilities. One of these, which is clearly of the greatest significance for society, is the bearing and rearing of children, and, as knowledge of eugenics is spread, there is an increasing realization that individuals of unsound heredity ought not to be permitted to experiment with parenthood when the consequence may mean physical or menal suffering for their offspring.

It is not inconsistent with the growing emphasis upon marriage as a means of human satisfaction that every attempt consistent with public policy should be made to prevent unreasonable, that is, unpromising, mating. Thus far science can clearly uncover conditions that interdict marriage only along eugenic lines, and so it is here, as we should expect, that we find the tendency to stiffen the conditions for marriage. If the evidence were equally clear regarding the hazards of individual unions because of psychological or sociological impediments, legislation would reflect this knowledge by additional safeguards against unwise mating.

It appears probable, at least for the immediate future, that American legislation will reflect these two different but not incompatible trends. The legal prerequisites for marriage will grow more severe while at the same time it will become easier for the dissatisfied to be relieved from their social contract. It is true that the common law has enforced the individual's right to marry, but there also has been recognition of the necessity of limiting this right, and no social prohibition has been more stringent than that forbidding incestuous relationship. Eugenics legislation is merely an extension, as a result of new knowledge gathered by science, of this ancient disposition of the law to recognize the stake society has in any individual marriage and to taboo those that are contrary to public policy. "When the people are convinced not only that mental inferiority is inheritable but that it can be detected with certainty in its victims, past records make it appear probable that the law will not lag behind medical science in the protection of future generations." [27]

War and genetics.   War is a chief obstacle to the building of an intelligent eugenics program. In past and simpler cultures the role of war has been such that it cannot justly be given such an indictment. Undoubtedly at times it has by its emphasis upon physical strength played a useful part in the survival process and served human progress. The experiences of World Wars I and II demonstrate that such an appraisal is no longer justified. The extraordinary degree to which war has become mechanized has changed its character and has made it deadly beyond all past imagination. The army and navy need for their operation a superior type of person both in mind and body. Once these men enter the service they encounter the hazard not only of dying prematurely but of finally returning so injured in mind or body as to lessen their fitness for marriage or for parenthood. In addition war tends to discard the weak and defective, leaving them with greater opportunity to breed than otherwise would be true.

Modern war has become total conflict leading to adverse environmental conditions even for the population that is not directly exposed to the furies of the various forms of modern attack. These adverse conditions cannot in the light of our present knowledge of the working together of heredity and environment be thought of as confined merely to the former. For example, susceptibility to tuberculosis that under normal conditions could be handled safely by preventive medicine may result in a lingering disease and final death on account of the scarcity of food, emotional strain, and other untoward conditions, products of total war. There is evidence also that those who have profited from higher education run a greater death risk.[28] Although this group cannot be safely interpreted as eugenically superior merely because they have had college opportunity, it can be said that for the most part they possess a mental endowment that made their educational career possible and that as a group they can be considered of good stock.

---

[27] Chamberlain, J. P., "Eugenics and Limitations of Marriage," *American Bar Association Journal*, Vol. 9, p. 430. Quoted by permission.

[28] *A Decade of Progress in Eugenics,* The Third International Congress of Eugenics, pp. 247–248.

The mere fear of war may be an obstacle to the eugenic program in so far as it stresses increasing population without regard to quality or the general economic and social welfare. No thoroughgoing eugenic policy is likely to develop as a national program unless some effective means of preventing war is established which will give a feeling of international security to all peace-loving people.

The family and mental defectives. Only through close contact with a family that is burdened by a mentally defective individual can one realize how tragic such a situation can be and how abnormal under such circumstances family life becomes. The birth of a feeble-minded child once this is discovered changes the climate of home life, making it abnormal by forcing continuous adaptation to the defective individual. It matters not whether the defectiveness is clearly inherited or whether it is the result of such an accident as cerebral hemorrhage during the birth process. In all its functioning the home must adjust itself to the defectiveness of the child. If there are other children, they also are influenced by the abnormality of their brother or sister. One of the consequences of this contact not to be regarded lightly may be the normal child's feeling of shame and defensive behavior based upon inferiority feeling because of the publicity the misfortune of their family receives. Likewise, it is an injustice often to the child of lower mentality to be in association with his normal brother or sister. Frequently the parents, unable or unwilling to recognize the mental deficiency of their offspring, spend both money and time in the hopeless effort to give the defective child normal capacity.

With rare exceptions, the proper place for the idiot, imbecile, low-grade moron, and the mentally diseased is in an institution. This is as beneficial for the unfortunate individual as it is for the family. How great our dysgenic problems have become is illustrated by the fact that our state institutions are so overcrowded that it is often difficult for parents, even when they are conscious of their problem and willing to have their child placed in a special environment, to get him admitted. Insane adults present a similar problem. Periodically, newspapers recount a tragic occurrence such as sexual murder which results from the irresponsible, mentally deficient person being outside an institution where alone society could have been protected from his mental unsoundness. The financial burden of attempting to provide proper supervision for the feeble-minded and insane is already a major public expense and unless there can be greater progress in the application of eugenic principles, the cost for proper custodial care must increase. Since the state creates no wealth itself, the individual families must assume through taxation this burden that comes in large measure from the reproducing of persons who have bad inheritance. An intelligent society must endeavor through education to increase better understanding of eugenic principles among the general public and also develop among them a more conscientious concern for biologic soundness in human mating or continue to make ever increasing appropriations for the hospitalization of defective individuals.

FOREWORD. No application of science to human need has contributed more to the welfare of the family than preventive medicine. Its greatest accomplishment, however, has been its demonstration of the need of a new and more social outlook on the health problems by both the community and the individual and greater use of the resources now available for the prevention of disease and the increase of physical vigor throughout the general population. There are, at present, needless obstacles to the establishment of a health service commensurate with the resourcefulness of science. The greatest incentive for a more adequate health program is found in family affection, especially in the love of the parent for the child. Medicine in both its preventive and curative aspects affects family life in a multitude of ways. As the student considers the specific advances medicine has made in ministering to the problems relating to marriage and family experience, it is most important to remember that the progress made is cumulative, each accomplishment becoming an incentive for still greater advance. The common tragedies that diphtheria and typhoid fever, for example, once inflicted upon the family now occur so seldom as to attract attention. Such conquests have changed the spirit of medicine and prepared it for the new social program that must come in response to family need and pressure, especially that developing within the middle class.

Public health. So far as family welfare is concerned, the contribution of medicine has been greatest through the public-health program. In accord with the social attitude emphasizing the needs of childhood, the greatest success of the program appears in the decrease of the infancy death rate. The problem of care and protection for the older child has not been so adequately dealt with, although in comparison with conditions previous to the present century there has been immense progress. The difficulty has come through the inability of many families, either from ignorance or insufficient income, to utilize in full the resources now available for the protection against disease and for the building of health. Public opinion is more and more revealing the conviction that modern medicine must be a resource of society itself. As a consequence, the public-health program is constantly expanding, making greater and greater use of the advances of medical knowledge for the development of a more adequate preventive program.

The social program for the employment of the curative services of medicine has relatively lagged, and, as a result, illness, when it comes, falls on the family as an individual burden, crippling the home and frequently creating conditions that invite later trouble in personal relationships or another illness. Since the so-called underprivileged are often administered to as a professional charity on the part of doctors, it is the middle class that largely suffers. It is apparent that the profession of medicine cannot exist if this group is also taken over as a nonpaying obligation, and therefore with such a program the physician would have to be an employee of the state. At present, this solution is opposed almost universally by members of the medical profession and also by most of the laity trying to distribute more adequately medical service to the middle class. The trend at present is toward a co-operative program based upon the principles of insurance.

Taking into account the character of its responsibilities and its opportunities for exploitation, medicine as a profession has a code of ethics unexcelled, and the American physician believes these standards would quickly be undermined if the practice of medicine came under the control of either the State or Federal government, thereby becoming subject to political manipulation and pressure. There has been in the recent past among members of the profession who enjoy positions of great influence and large incomes opposition to co-operative programs designed to meet more nearly the needs of the middle class. The trend of social pressure, however, is unmistakable.

In some manner the resources of modern medicine must be made more available to the middle class, and if the members of the profession refuse to help work out a program that will conserve the interests of both the physician and the general public, reform will be forced through government control.

There are many organizations throughout the nation, especially in cities, attempting to work out practical schemes for the better distribution of medical service and the lessening of expense to the individual family. More progress has been made in taking care of the low-income group than for those in moderate circumstances. An example of this is the Corlears Hook Medical Association which was established in 1940 under the sponsorship of the Medical Society of the County of New York. The funds came from the New York Foundation. In May, 1942, there were 695 families belonging to the Association, each paying twenty-five cents a month with a limit of a dollar for a family. This fee carried the right to unlimited house or office treatment from any doctor in the Association, the patient having the right to choose his own physician and to change to another whenever he wished. The Director of the Association, Dr. Morris A. Brand, states that the monthly fees go entirely to the doctors, and even then they receive only an average remuneration of ninety cents per visit. This is clearly not very profitable for the physician, and at the end of the two-year period the original panel of fifty-eight doctors had shrunk to about half that number. The fee may be looked upon as a sort of bonus for doctors who would otherwise assume their share of charity work with no pay whatsoever. It is obvious that this program, although it has hope as a means of meeting the needs of the low-income group—in this instance averaging about $1,050 per year—offers no hope of solving the middle-class problem.

Another plan also operating in New York City is the Group Health Co-operative, a nonprofit medical service listing 2,500 physicians in all fields of medicine and surgery and offering services to the subscribers at an average cost of $2\frac{1}{2}$¢ per day. The annual fees are $9.60 for an individual, $19.20 for husband and wife, $24.00 per family. It provides medical service in the doctor's office or at the subscriber's home, obstetrical care at home or at any hospital, and medical service while the subscriber is a bed patient at any hospital for any illness not requiring surgical or obstetrical care. However, this program is open only to subscribers whose annual income does not exceed $1,800 for a single person, $2,500 for husband and wife, and $3,000 for a family. If a subscriber has an income exceeding these limits or if he engages a doctor not enrolled in the plan, he does receive a certain credit on his bill, but the doctor may charge an additional fee which the subscriber pays. It is an attempt to place medical service on the same nonprofit basis as hospital care. It provides for group enrollment so that any person under sixty-five years who belongs to an organized group can become a subscriber, and lower rates are provided for those who join as a group.[1]

The greatest progress in programs for co-operative protection from the costs of illness has been made through organizations that on an insurance basis provide for hospital care of persons who are sick. This service has already reached a mature development through various national organizations and now enrolls a large number of subscribers. This type of organization has established its value and in no way has jeopardized the medical profession or the private practice of the physician. It provides a substantial protection for a great multitude of families both in the lower- and the moderate-income-earning groups. It is not, however, a complete solution, because it does not utilize to the full the nonhospital preventive resources of medical science now available for the maintaining and the improving of the health of the individual subscriber.

An example of such organizations is the Hospital Saving Association of North Carolina. It is a nonprofit service association—not an insurance company—that provides essential hospital and medical services through participating hospitals and physicians. In the report to the Board of Trustees, made in 1942, the following reasons for the organization of the Hospital Saving Association were outlined:

(1) To furnish a way for the people, by small periodic payments, to be assured of proper hospital and professional care, so that this protection may prevent each person from becoming medically indigent and therefore increase his morale and assets as a self-sustaining citizen.

---

[1] *The New York Herald-Tribune,* January 11, 1943.

(2) To assist the hospitals by establishing a fund for cash payments for essential services rendered participants, which indirectly lightens the tax burdens involved in the support of these hospitals, thus benefiting the entire community.

(3) To establish, with these ideas in view, a sound public policy, commensurate with good business principles, so that the people, the community, and the profession will be served in a manner that will best accomplish tangible and equitable results for all.

The Hospital Saving Association is one of eighty-eight separate corporations operating in forty-five states, the District of Columbia, five Canadian provinces, and Puerto Rico. These plans form a kind of federation, operating under certain standards set up by the American Hospital Association and are entitled to use the symbol Blue Cross, which is the seal of the American Hospital Association superimposed on a blue cross. This national program has been called by the *Saturday Evening Post,* the "world's outstanding example of co-operative common sense." By 1947 more than 21,000 new subscribers were joining the Blue Cross every working day of the year. Over twenty-one million Americans now enjoy its protection and while Congress debates plans for medical care for the American people, the Blue Cross, the employers, employees, and millions of free-thinking Americans are quietly joining together to get low-cost medical protection under the age-old system for which America is famous, the voluntary system. It does not attempt to provide complete medical coverage. It is seeking to "walk toward," a partial and practical solution—first taking care of catastrophes and then, as the people themselves become more educated to their needs, gradually unfolding into a more elaborate program. Its growth is impressive as typified by the table on page 606.

Venereal diseases.   One of the greatest contributions to human welfare coming from medicine has been the recent progress in the preventing and the treatment of venereal diseases. This has been made possible not only by the new discoveries of science but also through the changed attitude of the general public. In the past, both syphilis and gonorrhea were regarded by most Americans as something so different from other diseases that even the words were taboo in ordinary conversation and in the public press. When references had to be made to them, they were referred to by the blanket designation "social diseases." How greatly the situation has changed appears in the fact that the majority of the states now require a blood test as prerequisite to marriage in order to determine that the indi-

HOSPITAL SAVING ASSOCIATION OF N. C., INC.
YEARLY PROGRESS

HOSPITALIZATION

Year	Members	Admissions	Days	Paid
1936	14,395	541	4,451	$ 17,886.39
1937	36,913	2,326	18,681	76,844.49
1938	83,436	8,345	64,835	267,696.49
1939	123,848	13,484	103,557	431,418.16
1940	137,761	16,087	128,880	521,197.74
1941	166,201	18,590	143,675	577,680.69
1942	181,032	20,065	154,510	635,069.76
1943	212,616	23,664	176,347	777,757.72
1944	233,010	25,437	194,110	857,118.22
May 1, 1945	245,000 +			
Totals		128,539	989,046	$4,162,669.66

SURGERY

Year	Members	Admissions	Paid
1941	5,086	130	$ 3,335.00
1942	23,770	1,346	36,689.00
1943	39,371	2,562	74,058.50
1944	63,717	3,738	113,205.50
Approx. May 1, 1945	83,000		
Totals		7,776	$ 227,288.00
Total Hospitalization and Surgery		136,315	$4,389,957.66

vidual is free from syphilis. It is probable that soon such a law will be enforced in every state in the union. There has been evidence also of a similar change with regard to gonorrhea. Fewer states require a physician's statement of freedom from this disease as a condition for obtaining the marriage license, but the reason for this is the practical difficulty of obtaining the degree of certainty that the test for syphilis provides. The new attitude toward this disease shows itself in the change from regarding it as a temporary unimportant affliction to the realization that it can become as great a menace in its consequences to the individual and to the family as syphilis.

Great credit should be given to Dr. Thomas Parran, Surgeon-General of the United States Public Health Service, for his leadership in the control and elimination of syphilis and gonorrhea. The campaign has advanced on many fronts. Legislation has been enacted chiefly along two lines of protection.[2] The best established are the laws already referred to that require a premarriage testing for syphilis as a prerequisite to marriage. The second attack on the problem has come from the laws requiring prenatal examinations. This makes it necessary for the physician or midwife in attendance upon the pregnant woman to take or cause to be taken specimens of blood for submission to approved laboratories for the testing of syphilis. In addition to the value of these laws as a means of safeguarding marriage and pregnancy, their importance is even greater as a means of educating the public to the seriousness of the diseases of syphilis and gonorrhea. The taboo has been removed, and the public health services have been set free to make their full contribution to the lessening of two of the greatest afflictions families in the past have suffered, diseases which seem likely soon to become as uncommon as typhoid fever.

It is fortunate that the curative resources of medical science have also made almost miraculous advances in the treatment of both syphilis and gonorrhea. The two recently discovered drugs—sulfa compounds and penicillin—as well as the use of fever and rapid-treatment techniques have given the physician resources for cure that in the recent past would have sounded so improbable as to be beyond reasonable expectations. Not long ago the controversy was whether syphilis was ever really cured. Now the question is how quickly and safely in a great majority of cases the disease may be brought to an end. The results of the treatment of gonorrhea have been equally spectacular. This progress does not mean, however, that cure is always easy or in every case successful. There is no reason to suppose that medical science has yet reached the limit in both preventing and curing the two diseases. Already studies

[2] See "Premarital Examination Laws," "Prenatal Examination Laws," *Journal of Social Hygiene*, Vol. 30, pp. 472–478.

in the use of penicillin in early syphilis have so demonstrated the value of the drug as to lead conservative specialists in the field to estimate that 75–80 per cent of cases can now be cured. The chemical advance in the treatment of syphilis and gonorrhea has led to renewed interest in the problem of venereal disease control, as evidenced by such undertakings as the widely publicized community- and county-wide surveys carried on in various cities and counties in Georgia.[3]

Physical examination in preparation for marriage. There has been another contribution not yet so well known or so well established as premarriage testing for syphilis. This new resource, physical examination in preparation for marriage, is medicine's most promising aid to those entering marriage. The idea of a special health service for the married and for those about to be married appears to have found first expression in Austria and Germany after World War I. In 1919 the Berlin Institute for the Study of Sex, a privately supported organization at first, later taken over by the government, opened a consultation center for advice and guidance on sex problems. At Dortmund, in 1923, a marriage consultation center was opened. This was privately supported. In Vienna, in 1922, there was under public control the first matrimonial health consultation center for marriage candidates. This was part of the work of the municipal board of health. Switzerland opened an official marriage consultation center at Zurich in 1929 with a threefold program, advice on problems arising before marriage, during marriage, and in relation to the welfare of the child.[4] The Nazis' preparation for a European war aborted this developing medical service for the conservation of marriage.

In the United States Dr. Robert Latou Dickinson has done most to enlist the interest of the medical profession in the specialized health examination as a preparation for marriage. His writings, charts, models, and manuals [5] have not only been useful tools for the physician but have done much to popularize

---

[3] "Georgia Conducts Mass-Testing VD–TB Survey," *Journal of Social Hygiene,* Vol. 33, No. 1, pp. 34–35.

[4] Kopp, Marie E., "The Development of Marriage Consultation Centers as a New Field of Social Medicine," *American Journal of Obstetrics and Gynecology,* Vol. 26, p. 122.

[5] Dickinson, Robert L., "Premarital Consultation," *Journal of the American Medical Association,* Vol. 117, p. 1687.

the idea among the thoughtful laity of the examination in preparation for marriage. The development in this country thus far has been chiefly through the services of private specialists rather than the clinic form which established itself in central Europe. It is among the college group, especially those who have had adequate instruction in marriage courses, that we find the greatest demand for this examination before marriage in order that any hindrances to good physical adjustment may be discovered and treated. Young people seeking such help are often disappointed because the doctor to whom they go is unfamiliar with the special type of examination sought or is unprepared to give it.[6] Gynecologists are apt to be both capable and interested in the giving of this examination.

It is encouraging to learn that in a recent study of 500 individuals who had such premarriage examinations two-thirds of the couples came together.[7] Undoubtedly this premarital preparing for marriage by means of a medical examination will become a customary part of various types of health services. Gladys Gaylord, Executive Secretary of the Maternal Health Association at Cleveland, Ohio, states on the basis of eight years experience that 666 potential family relationships have received premarital consultations and that this has been probably the most important part of the contribution of the organization.[8] Anyone who becomes familiar with the content of this medical contribution to an intelligent preparing for marriage will be led to the conviction that "here is the beginning of an improved premarital advice service for the next generation, one basically more effective than the service the parents received." [9] Not only will the spread of knowledge of this medical resource for success in marriage make possible the right beginning of the relationship for those taking advantage of their opportunity; it will also encourage recognition in the instruction of our medical schools of the relationship between good sexual adjustment and health and emotional stability.

[6] Warner, Marie P., "The Premarital Medical Consultation," *The Medical Woman's Journal*, Vol. 50, pp. 293–300.

[7] Gaylord, Gladys, "Premarital and Preconceptional Care," *Proceedings of the First American Congress on Obstetrics and Gynecology;* for a description of this examination see E. R. Groves, *Preparation for Marriage.*

[8] *Ibid.*

[9] Stokes, Walter R., "Premarital Medical Service," *Psychiatry*, Vol. 5, p. 369.

Emotional aspects of premarriage preparation. The premarriage consultation, including even the physical examination, has an emotional significance that needs recognition. Because of this there is need of the client's having opportunity to clear up doubts and fears and gain assurance by means of a discussion that brings to the surface feelings and attitudes that might hamper marriage adjustment. Psychic preparation is as important as the physical. Sometimes the two types of service are performed by the medical specialist who does the examination. In other cases the marriage counselor deals with the emotional side of the preparation and the physician gives the physical examination. Once the desire for this premarriage preparation becomes common, in order to save the time of the physician and permit him to concentrate on his specialty, the emotional contribution will be rightly the responsibility of the well-equipped marriage counselor. Dr. Robert L. Dickinson indicts any community that waits to give training in anticipation of marriage until the patterns of individuals are set or are well on the way toward setting into frigidity and impotence, divorce, or in any degree toward promiscuity and homosexuality, as guilty of an indefensible lack of courage and foresight.[10]

At present, the marriage counselor is confronted with the fact that many young people lack the emotional attitude toward the sexual aspect of marriage that is required for wholesome adjustment. Most of these who come for premarital preparedness seek to start aright in marriage and in spite of parental or social misguidance have the disposition to know and to reconstruct wrong feelings and ideas. The premarriage consultation is incomplete if provision is not made for the questions that the man and woman desire to have answered. These are likely to have an emotional content, and they require more from the counselor than the mere giving of information. The way the help is given is more important than the factual information itself. Fear, shame, guilt, and anxiety all need to be brought into the open, if in any degree they exist, and dealt with in such a way that they are not likely to menace the coming marriage. More than this, however, is needed. A positive, forward-looking, confident, eager readiness for marriage should if possible be

---

[10] Dickinson, Robert L., *op. cit.*, pp. 1687–1692.

made one of the results of the preparatory consultation. If the examiner himself is not free from the emotional hazards that forbid intelligent handling of the psychic aspects of marriage, he will best serve his clients by not attempting to discuss their conflicts but turning such problems over to some qualified person. It is to be expected that the busy medical specialist will prefer to deal only with the physical aspects of preparation for marriage.

The counselor during his conference with the client should have the background which will permit him to detect the need of a more serious and lengthy treatment whenever evidence arises in the conversation of lack of normal attitudes toward any aspect of the marriage relationship. As one would expect, knowing the taboo policy concerning sex that our culture has in the past maintained and which in considerable measure still exists, it is the physical aspect of marriage that is most likely to become associated with underlying and often unconscious fears, conflicts, and antagonisms. In a proportion of cases, emotional complexes exist in such strength that they require treatment from the psychiatrist. Unless they are cleared up, they can prevent the adjustment which the marriage needs in order to succeed. Occasionally, also, the counselor in his attempt to deal with the emotional aspects of the marriage preparation discovers a still greater neurotic disturbance which raises the question, whether the client should marry. Under such circumstances, the marriage is unadvised unless and until a psychiatrist has been able to reconstruct the personality and give the individual a fair chance to enter upon the marriage experience. As more and more young people seek the assistance of the counselor, the number of those found to be suffering from serious handicaps will be such that the problem cases coming to the psychiatrist will be far too numerous to justify his giving time to the more ordinary difficulties that can be dealt with by the specialist in the science of marriage.

The counselor will not content himself merely with the effort to discover emotional liabilities already developed but will attempt to prepare the husband and wife for the emotional problems of marriage adjustment that men and women commonly experience, or such obstacles to their future happiness that he may detect as likely to face them at some later period.

In this consultation, care must be taken not to create anxiety or even build up in the minds of either husband or wife the feeling that their approaching marriage will be an ordeal. The conscientious individual is apt to overstress any suggestion of future trouble, and here again the influence of the counselor is likely to be greatly determined by the manner in which his suggestions are made. The interview is, in most instances, itself an emotional experience for the man and the woman, and the counselor can help greatly by draining off this needless but natural tension and replacing it with the spirit of courage and confidence.

Infant and maternal welfare. When Luther Emmett Holt, who has rightly been called a pioneer in a children's century, took his degree in medicine in 1880, one out of every four babies born in New York City died before the end of the year.[11] Between 1880 and 1924, the date of his death, a new science of medicine—pediatrics—came into being, and a new attitude stressing the preventive resources of medicine for the infant and the young child followed. Fortunately, this new departure in the division of medical responsibility was associated and reinforced by better understanding of the hazards of infancy and childhood and a remarkable advance in knowledge and technique. The campaign to lower the death rate of infancy not only enlisted medical men of influence but also a large number of the socially minded laity. An impressive illustration of such a working together in the attempt to reduce one of the great hazards confronting the infant was the crusade for safe milk. Milk, an ideal culture medium for bacteria, was dirty, impure, and badly handled and was also a source of profiteering and political corruption. Although a major food of babies and young children, it was one of the chief causes of their deaths. New York City was the scene of a reform which ended in making milk one of the safest of food products. The first advance came, not in New York, but in Boston through the success of the Walker-Gordon Company in producing quality milk which became known as certified milk. A branch of the company was opened at Princeton, New Jersey, furnishing good milk in New

---

[11] Duffus, R. L., and Holt, L. Emmett, Jr., *L. Emmett Holt*, p. 1.

York City to a limited number of families able to afford it. Nathan Strauss, a philanthropist, realizing the need of providing safe milk for the masses, established a series of milk stations where pasteurized milk was sold at a price the multitude could afford. This service started in 1911, and gradually the public was led to appreciate the value of safe milk through pasteurization. A decade later it was possible to make the pasteurization of milk compulsory as a health regulation. This is but one illustration of the many lines of progress which brought about the most impressive perhaps of the recent successes of preventive medicine.

Thus far the largest gain from preventive medicine has been this saving of the lives of babies and young children. For example, the death rate from diarrhea and enteritis has declined so rapidly since the beginning of the century that in 1942 in the white population the mortality was only 11,815 in comparison with the 160,000 deaths that would have been expected on the basis of the one-time death rate.[12] This success has been due to the public health measures for the protection of water and milk and other food, better knowledge among mothers as to how to care for their infants, and the increasing control by medical science of the principal communicable diseases of childhood. The most spectacular of these conquests has been that of diphtheria. Once the most dreaded scourge of childhood, it has become evidence in most cases of the failure of parents to make use of the protective measures now available. It has been estimated that of the lives being saved by preventive medicine from all causes combined, at least two-fifths are of children under five years of age.[13] The physical examinations and the rejections that occurred as a result of the national draft legislation of World War II demonstrate that much of this progress has been merely the half-winning of the battle. There are those who go so far as to criticize this saving of life as being basically unbiological in causing the survival of the unfit. In the past a considerable number of the children who died early were victims either of communicable diseases or of needless

---

[12] *Statistical Bulletin*, Metropolitan Life Insurance Company, Vol. 25, No. 11, p. 7.

[13] *Ibid.*, p. 8.

dangers encountered during pregnancy, at birth, or immediately following. It has been more difficult to lower the neonatal mortality than that of infants aged two weeks to one year. A part of this difference is explained by the prematurity of many of the infants who subsequently die. The physician is forced to include among the neonatal deaths a group of infants who are really born dead, because extrauterine life was never really established. The fact that there is a temporary heartbeat is taken as evidence of neonatal life, whereas actually it is only a continuation of foetal life. Conservation of these infants' lives must come through the preventing of the precocious birth rather than only by trying to save them after they have been born. The causes of trouble are many and must be met by improvement in the care of the mother during pregnancy and in the delivery technique of midwife and physician.

World War II brought forth two problems of maternal health that had to be recognized and dealt with. One was the protecting of the woman in industry who became pregnant. The great increase of women in industrial occupations, especially those connected with the war, demanded development of a policy for women who became pregnant and for those who had infants. Although each case necessarily had to be treated individually, the following principles needed to be observed both for the welfare of the woman and her child: opportunity for adequate prenatal care; sufficient time off before delivery to prepare her for the time of delivery and to prevent strain during the latter part of the pregnancy (to carry out this program prenatal clinics were required and the informing of the women as to where such services could be obtained); keeping women from the night shift, including the hours from twelve midnight to six-thirty A.M.; preventing their employment more than eight hours a day or more than forty-eight hours a week; giving them at least two ten-minute rest periods during the work shift with opportunity for resting and for securing nourishing food; keeping such women out of occupations that involved heavy lifting or other heavy work, continuous standing or moving, that had a special accident risk, or exposure to toxic substances. Women who had been working in occupations characterized by the dangers described needed to be placed in other work. The desirability of the woman having leave at any time during the pregnancy upon the recommendation of her physician demanded recognition.[14]

In most cases, given sufficient time, the physician can protect the foetus even if the mother has syphilis. It is this fact that makes important the recent legislation in many states of the union requiring a blood test for the pregnant woman. It is a heartening evidence of medicine's increasing conquest of syphilis when maternal clinics can report that the influence of syphilis as a determining factor in foetal and neonatal deaths has almost disappeared.[15] There are of course neonatal deaths and spontaneous abortions as a result of defective sperms or ova. These should be recognized as the result of nature's effort to be rid of unsound organisms. For the most part, however, neonatal deaths are more justly charged to failures of social origin. Only a portion of those now saved in infancy, who but for medical science would have died, can rightly be regarded as raising the issue of the right to survive biologically. Since the human right to live cannot be reduced to the Spartan program of physical strength and vitality, medicine cannot be indicted for saving the lives of infants who without modern care would have died early, but instead medicine must take over a continuing responsibility for helping these survivals attain in great measure normal health and usefulness.

Progress in maternity care. Medical leadership in the United States is committed to a preventive program for maternity care that is certain to be one of the most valuable of all the contributions of medicine to family welfare. Already the science of obstetrics and its application in safeguarding pregnancy and child delivery have gone a great distance since 1843 when Dr. Oliver Wendell Holmes first read his revolutionary paper on "The Contagiousness of Puerperal Fever" before the Boston Society for Medical Improvement. At that time death from childbed fever in the United States was never less than 10 per cent and in some instances as high as 90 per cent. One hundred years later only about three thousand mothers out of two

---

[14] "Standards for Maternity Care and Employment of Mothers in Industry," The Children's Bureau and the Woman's Bureau of the United States Department of Labor.

[15] *Proceedings of the First American Congress on Obstetrics and Gynecology,* p. 216.

million died from this cause, and even that record is now regarded as excessive. Anesthesia in obstetrics came as the result of the courage of Dr. Simpson in administering chloroform four years after Dr. Holmes' paper. Surgical asepsis did not appear until the middle '80's and was late in developing in obstetrics. Such resources as ergot to arrest bleeding after delivery, pituitrin, blood transfusion in case of obstetrical shock, and relatively safe Caesarean deliveries are a few of the very recent resources that, added to X-ray measurement of the pelvis, analysis of urine, and testing of blood pressure, provide the means by which the life of the woman during pregnancy and childbirth and also her subsequent health can be safeguarded.

The maternity care that does full justice to the resources of medical science and the need of family welfare has been defined as resting upon the following principles:

1. Any public program of maternity care and medical care of infants and children should be the joint responsibility of local, State, and Federal governments financed under the grant-in-aid plan from general tax funds.

2. Administrative responsibility should rest with the State departments of health with expenditure of Federal funds under plans approved by the Federal agency given responsibility for the grants.

3. The program should be state-wide in effect and be so organized as to include a network of maternity and pediatric services that will reach out from a few highly organized maternity and pediatric units in hospital and teaching centers to a chain of smaller hospitals and clinics located strategically in medium-sized cities, and thence to the many small local maternity and child-health units in towns and counties and rural areas.

4. Maternity care of good quality should be available under this program to any woman who seeks it, regardless of residence, economic status, race, color, or creed; eligibility should be on the basis of medical need alone: this is surely one aspect of our total medical care program for which there should be no means test.

5. Standards of care should be established by the responsible administrative agencies with the advice of experts in the various professional and technical fields.

6. Employment practices in the case of professional personnel should be determined, first, by the required standards of care and, second, by economy in the expenditure of public funds.

7. Hospital and clinic facilities meeting established standards

of maternity and infant care and care of sick children should be available or easily accessible to every community, rural as well as urban: public institutions should be open to everyone in the community, whether the community or the individual pays: existing voluntary, nonprofit institutions, if used, should meet established standards of financial accounting as well as professional service.

8. The plan for training professional and technical personnel should be a part of the plan for service and reach down from the most highly organized teaching unit to the smallest rural unit.[16]

Although comparison between countries as to their maternal mortality is inconclusive because of the differences in the gathering of statistics, early in the present century it seemed as if the death rate in this country was abnormally high. The situation was such as to attract the attention of many individuals and agencies who from various fronts began to attack the problem of decreasing the mortality rate. This campaign has been highly successful. Prior to 1934 there were between six and seven maternal deaths per thousand live births in the United States per year. Ten years later, in spite of a sharply increased birth rate, a shortage of doctors and nurses and crowded hospitals, the Metropolitan Life Insurance Company announced that based on provisional reports the rate appeared to be just under two per thousand. Added incentive was given the movement to lessen the hazards [17] of childbearing by the report issued by the New York Academy of Medicine on the maternal mortality in New York City. This was a study of all the puerperal deaths from 1930–1932.[18] This investigation demonstrated that two-thirds of the deaths from maternity were due to inadequate or improper care during pregnancy, confinement, and the postnatal period.[19] It was apparent also that a chief cause of this was the ignorance and misinformation among the lay public which led them to neglect the medical services available. It was also true that many of those who did seek adequate care, consulting their physicians frequently when pregnant, did not get proper attention. Another cause of death was the high incidence of

---

[16] Eliot, Martha M., "Design for Tomorrow's Maternity Care," *Briefs, Maternity Center Association*, Vol. 7.

[17] *Statistical Bulletin*, Metropolitan Life Insurance Company, Vol. 24, No. 8, p. 6.

[18] Hooker, Ramson S., *Maternal Mortality in New York City*.

[19] *Ibid.*, p. 213.

operative interference. This included needless Caesarean operations or not performing them until after the woman was worn
out by a long labor.[20] Private and public agencies were awakened to the need of making greater effort to lessen this loss of
life. It was recognized that conditions were as bad or even worse
in other parts of the country than in New York City. The medical standards of obstetrical practice were lifted throughout the
nation and greater emphasis was placed on obstetrical training
by the medical schools. Hospitals also raised their standards.
Both Federal and State governments contributed through maternity and child-hygiene bureaus. Departments of public health
helped to educate pregnant women through nurses who visited
them in their homes—one of the services for the family contributed by the public-health nurse.

The record in the south and southwest shows need of special effort in those areas. The highest maternal death rate is in
the states where the hazards of Negro women, because of environmental conditions, are greater than those of white women.
Not only is the mortality greater among the Negroes, but its decline has been slower than that of the white women. One explanation of this is the fact that while about 97 per cent of the white
women have the services of a physician at birth, only a little
more than half the Negro women are given this care. The
effects of environmental conditions on the death rate of the
newly born infant are too obvious to justify the contention that
in saving the lives of such children we are defeating biological
purposes.

The great gain in the later period of childhood is certainly
in part the result of the control medicine now has over communicable diseases. Although our knowledge of inheritance
does not permit us to separate the deaths of children who succumb because of hereditary weakness when they are attacked
by some disease from those who have normal soundness but are
the victims of misfortune rather than any original handicap, the
saving of the first group emphasizes the fact that values on the
human level cannot be the same as those emphasized by a mere
biological effort to survive. We owe too much to individuals
who have had some degree of physical impediment to permit us

---

[20] *Proceedings of the First American Congress on Obstetrics and Gynecology,*
pp. 14–15.

to take a Spartan attitude toward the hazards of infancy. Instead, the modern disposition is toward depending upon medical science to continue its ministration to children who, without the advantages of modern medicine, might not survive and to help them to go on into maturity, achieving as much of health and vigor as the resources of modern science applied to the individual problem make possible. This policy is the only one that is in accord with the moral and spiritual development attained through the evolution of the family.

Tuberculosis and typhoid fever. The medical conquest of tuberculosis and typhoid are two impressive examples of the relief that comes to the family through the progress of both preventive and curative medicine. Tuberculosis is the most damaging and widespread of all the major infections,[21] although it does not usually develop into a serious, active expression. In the memory of the older readers of this book, it was *a* chief, if not *the* chief burden placed upon the family by a communicable disease. It was generally regarded as having a family origin because it so frequently passed from one member of a family to another. The general attitude toward it was one of fatalism, because it was usually diagnosed only in its advanced stages and was generally fatal. It accounted in 1924 for 9 per cent of all deaths. It not only most often cut down its victims in the life period of greatest usefulness—in the age period between fifteen and sixty where it comprised 30 per cent of all deaths—but it also characteristically produced a long, lingering illness which weighed heavily upon the unfortunate family both emotionally and financially. Soon, in a great many such cases, another member of the family was stricken, often a child or an adolescent who had had contact with the sick person.

It was natural to presume that the disease was hereditary, since it constantly appeared in some families, never in others. Better knowledge completely changed this philosophy. It was discovered that the infection was almost universal, usually attacking the young child, and that the condition the doctors had recognized was as a rule one of the last stages of the disease. When the X ray came, it made possible early diagnosis. Meanwhile, the significance of dire poverty, overwork, and other

---

21 Rosenau, Milton J., *Preventive Medicine and Hygiene*, Sixth Edition, p. 27.

environmental conditions upon the developing of the disease became known. A curative program which gave great hope for all except the most advanced cases was worked out, including sanatorium treatment. The physician also taught the afflicted individual how to protect the other members of the family. The mortality continuously decreased until it became about one-fifth of what it was at the beginning of the century. From 1921 through 1943 the rate of death went down an average of 4 per cent annually. The following chart [22] shows this increasing conquest of one of the once most dreaded of diseases. The graph also suggests what is to be expected in the near future.

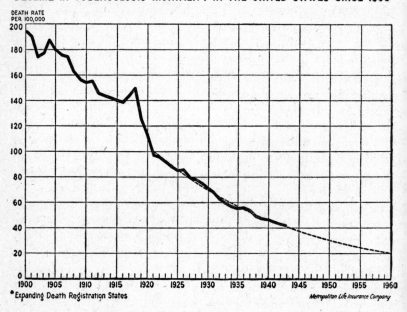

DECLINE IN TUBERCULOSIS MORTALITY IN THE UNITED STATES* SINCE 1900

* Expanding Death Registration States

Metropolitan Life Insurance Company

This progress has carried with it other advances also of great value to the family, including better nutrition through more adequate and better balanced diet; clearing of slum areas; shortening of the working day in industry; better protection in occupations that tend to affect the worker in such ways as to encourage the disease, stonecutting and polishing, for example;

---

[22] Statistical Bulletin, Metropolitan Life Insurance Company, Vol. 26, p. 2.

a widespread use of the X ray for childhood diagnosis; and the periodic health examination.

Typhoid fever is another disease that illustrates the progress of preventive medicine. In the past it weighed heavily upon the family, since even if the patient recovered after a long illness it was months before he could return to work. The prevention of infection through milk and water, the discovery of typhoid carriers, then the finding of a preventive inoculation affording a person security from infection, have reduced this one-time deadly malady, frequently, as some doctors have said, their chief means of support in rural sections, to such a rarity that it is reasonable to expect its eventual, almost total, disappearance. This conquest has also influenced standards of living, enforced improved sanitation, and educated the public to a greater appreciation of the preventive resources of medicine.

These two conquests added to other less marked successes have contributed to the new attitude taken by public opinion toward syphilis and gonorrhea. The recent legislation directed against the two diseases would have been impossible had not a multitude of people become convinced of the effectiveness of preventive medicine.

Gynecological advance.   One of the most apparent traits in American life has been the almost superstitious vogue of patent medicine. European travelers, Charles Dickens, for example, have been so impressed by this fact that it has seemed to them as if nearly every American suffered from dyspepsia or some other self-diagnosed ailment that was dealt with by the taking of a nostrum. This recourse to patent medicine was especially true among women who suffered from what doctors described in the vague terminology of the past as "female weakness." Unfortunately, in a number of cases there was a basis for the belief that something was wrong with the woman. One of the great advances, not only saving the lives of mothers but greatly adding to their physical energy, emotional stability, and domestic security, has come from advances in gynecology. Although there is still much to be done, especially in popularizing the resources science now has for dealing with the special health problems of women, this advance in medical knowledge has already made it possible to eliminate a great amount of the suffering that was wrongly charged up to menstruation and other normal functioning of the female reproductive system.

Gynecological progress has likewise contributed to family welfare by removing the worry based upon false ideas concerning what in popular language was known as "the change of life." Medicine has also brought relief to many who in fact did have some measure of difficulty during this period when the organism is adjusting itself to the disappearance of the power of reproduction. The necessity of periodic examinations at this time has been recognized by the physician and is being more and more understood by the laity. Improved techniques have taken care of minor injuries resulting from childbirth. This has been especially true in the repair operation of the cervix, thus eliminating some of the conditions that in previous times were charged up to female weakness and that were in fact potential sources of serious illness. Periodic examinations are now making it possible to discover most cancers in their early, curable stages.

Frigidity. A great part of the new insight concerning medical problems relating to the role of the woman in reproduction has come from the remarkable, even revolutionary, discoveries in the field of endocrinology. At the beginning of the century, aside from the well-established relationship between thyroid gland deficiency and cretinism, there was little knowledge of what were then termed the ductless glands. There now exists a great and ever growing fund of information based upon experimental investigation that has had immense importance for medical practice. This is especially applicable to problems associated with the female and male roles in reproduction. Endocrinology has thrown new light upon menstruation, the climacteric, and a portion of the cases of frigidity.

Frigidity, or the inability of the woman to be aroused sexually in marriage, is a condition that lessens the value of marriage for many women and frequently becomes the root of an incompatibility that leads to divorce. Frigidity is the result of many different kinds of causes, some physical and some psychic. Each case is individual. In the past, the experience in a large proportion of cases has been met with complacency by physicians who felt helpless in any attempt to change the situation or who feared to create domestic trouble by suggesting to the dissatisfied person that the other spouse was responsible.

Fortunately for the welfare of marriage, recent years have seen a decided change. The physician is more willing to accept the responsibility of diagnosing the incapacity as a medical problem. There are a multitude of possible physical causes which can be catalogued as those due to disease, to anatomical defects, faulty physiological processes, and neurological defects.[23] In addition to these are causes that are psychological, some of which are so serious as rightly to be considered psychiatric. The most common of all causes appears to be the poor sex technique of the husband and the brevity of the period of intercourse due to his quick discharge. Naturally any individual situation may be the product of several influences working together to make trouble.

The causal background of frigidity in women is so complex that unless new knowledge concerning the functioning of the endocrine glands gives the necessary insight, it is impossible after the early stages to uncover the primary or remote origins —they are so many and so diffused.[24] It is a normal condition before puberty and in old age. Freud's belief that the achievement of the biological goal has been delegated to the aggressive man and made independent of the consent of the woman has in the opinion of some a biological basis, since on a low evolutionary level it seems true of the two sexes. Those holding to this point of view believe that in primitive life there is evidence of this same relative superiority of the male.[25] This theory is considered unconvincing by the American medical specialist who explains the greater difficulty of woman as compared with man in her marital adjustment as the consequence of a more complex, sensitive, and diffused endowment than that of the male. There are, however, those who have been led by their practice to believe that many women achieve marriage happiness and remain physically and psychically normal although throughout their marital lives they are frigid.[26] Among the American young women now in their twenties, there is a growing disposition to look forward to physical adjustment in marriage with frankness and expectation, and they are less and less

[23] Stanford, W. R., "Medical Aspects of Marital Incompatibility," *Social Forces*, Vol. 16, p. 401.

[24] Dickinson, R. L., and Beam, Lura, *A Thousand Marriages*, p. 129.

[25] Hitschmann, E., and Bergler, E., *Frigidity in Women*, pp. 1–2.

[26] Novak, Emil, *The Woman Asks the Doctor*, p. 183.

willing to accept frigidity with complacence. The marriage counselor, therefore, becomes familiar with the trouble caused by frigidity in the marriage relationship and the wisdom of preventing it by means of medical and psychic preparation. It is not only the woman who reacts against it, since frequently her situation brings dissatisfaction to the husband.

Frigidity must not be regarded as a permanent state continuing from early marriage to death. Sometimes it develops after a period of successful adjustment. More often it disappears, having been characteristic of the first months of marriage. It can never safely be interpreted as a consequence of conditions belonging exclusively to the woman. Two persons are likely to be involved. At least diagnosis must consider the husband as well as the wife in both the physical and psychic investigations. It is more and more widely held that the effect of frigidity influences the entire personality of the woman, becoming a source of frustrations, conflicts, and aggressive behavior that thwart proper development of personality.[27] It is clear that medical science, in spite of the uncertainties and confusions as to the causations of frigidity in the individual case, increasingly recognizes it as undesirable for the woman's health, and the marriage specialist agrees that in most cases it is an impediment to a fully satisfying marriage.

Frigidity, therefore, cannot be isolated from the total contacts of two human beings attempting to make satisfactory marital adjustment. Immaturities, defects of personality, sooner or later are drawn into the sexual relationship where they may abort happiness even though both persons are familiar with the principles of efficient marital technique. There is no way by which modern marriage can escape the strain, the reconstructions, and, at times, the tragedies that belong to the sex experience, because these are so substantially related to the character of the individuals concerned. This means that the adjustment is never general, determined by the individual's possessing or not having certain virtues, but rather that it is the concrete testing of the possibility of the two persons, different as they are because of their own peculiar characteristics, achieving emotional unity in a relationship that modern life is tending to make supremely decisive in the successes or failures of marriage.

---

[27] Dickinson, R. L., and Beam, Lura, *op. cit.*, p. 129.

The therapeutic problem that faces anyone who tries to help people in trouble in marriage ranges from the simple need of some detailed, practical information or assistance to a thoroughgoing revision of the personality. In the latter case, any effort to help to bring insight is not only difficult but one for which the person in trouble is ill prepared. The incentive necessary to reconstruct the life-spirit is weak or lacking. Instead, a miracle is requested, some quickly given remedy that will operate immediately to remove the sex maladjustment, there being no realization that this is itself a product of a much wider and deeper problem.[28]

Infertility. One of the tragic disappointments of many married people is their failure to have children. In the past there have been commonly two reactions when married couples discover that they seem to be infertile. One has been the acceptance of their sad misfortune, and when this has been true no effort has been made to find out the causes of infertility and to eliminate them. A smaller group have tried to get medical help for their problem, usually assuming that the difficulty originated with the woman. Fortunately, in recent years there has been among the laity better understanding of the meaning of apparent infertility and a greater willingness to seek medical help when the man and wife become convinced that for some reason they lack the capacity to reproduce.

Medical science has also gone forward in its investigations of the causes of infertility and has gathered resources both for diagnosing the problems of the male and the female and for the treatment of the conditions discovered responsible. Sometimes the infertility of one or both spouses is absolute. In many cases, on the contrary, the problem is to increase a low potential fertility and to make reproduction effective.

The contribution of endocrinology to the understanding of hormones has decidedly added to the resources of the medical specialist. Techniques for the examination of both the male and the female in the effort to get at the causes of infertility are more complete than formerly and therefore more helpful for diagnosis.[29] Progress in helping the married achieve satisfactory

[28] Groves, E. R., "The Psychic Side of Marital Maladjustment," *Social Forces,* Vol. 16, pp. 399–400.

[29] Hamblen, E. C., *Facts for Childless Couples,* Chs. 4–5.

sexual adjustment, the better understanding of the significance of diet, especially vitamins as they effect fertility, new attitudes toward venereal diseases and the greater ability of science to deal with them, improved techniques for the elimination of obstacles to fertilization, the control of infections, the willingness of the infertile to seek medical help early are the chief reasons for the progress that is now being made against infertility in marriage. Clinic services are increasing as an aspect of the maternal health program. Involuntary sterility, estimated as affecting about one-tenth of all marriages, is beginning to be recognized as a major social problem, one that must be included among those dealt with by our state and national programs of public health. There now needs to be a realization among married people who wish children and are fit to have them that failure to achieve conception during a six-months period means that they should take their problem to a physician rather than let their disappointment drag on with hope that eventually they may prove fertile.

In recent years there have been a small number of conceptions brought about by artificial insemination. Among the reasons for this method of achieving parenthood have been situations in which the husband was sterile and the wife apparently fertile or those in which the husband had hereditary characteristics which made it seem unwise for him to become a parent. This method of fertilization has been highly successful in the breeding of animals. According to tradition, it was first developed among the Arabs in the fourteenth century in the breeding of horses. It has been applied to humans for 150 years, but not yet has it proved as effective as it is in the practice of animal husbandry. Unless the husband is the potential father, artificial insemination being used because of some condition that prevents the natural method, the procedure raises certain moral and legal issues that have to be clearly recognized and dealt with. Some people, opposed to any artificial insemination except that using the husband's semen, believe that the practice is immoral, a form of adultery. Legally this means of parenthood also brings into question the legitimacy of the offspring. To meet this it is suggested that the physician who arranges for the insemination should not act as the obstetrician but some other doctor who in good faith can state on the birth certificate that the child's father is the husband when in fact, the husband and the wife know, he is not. Popular thought exaggerates the frequency of this method of reproduction and minimizes the difficulties that appear when this method is attempted to bring about a pregnancy.

Planned parenthood. The progress that science has made in gaining control of conception has led to a self-chosen childlessness in some families and to planned parenthood in others. Whatever the advantages of children as a contribution to social welfare and to the development of the personality of the parents, it is a hazard for the individual child to come into any home unwanted. In a considerable number of cases, his appearance leads to a change in parental attitude so that the child is finally welcomed. When this does not occur, he is denied normal home life. It also is no advantage to society to have children born seriously handicapped because their parents were unfit to bring children into the world. It is also clearly undesirable for more children to be born than can be adequately cared for by the individual family. These and other motives, some selfish, some prudential, explain the increasing use of contraceptive methods for the prevention of pregnancy. American social leadership is nearly unanimous in recognizing that there are some families that ought for conscientious reasons to remain childless or to limit the number of children they bring into the world. There are, however, radical differences as to the right way to carry out this program. For Catholics and many Protestants the use of any contraceptive device to limit fertilization raises a moral issue, since such practices violate the principles of their religious faith. The former believe that abstinence is the only absolute control of contraception that can be morally justified. They accept, in addition, what is termed the "natural" method of control based upon an estimate of the individual woman's monthly period of infertility. Although this gives a measure of protection, it is recognized that it often fails as a means of preventing conception, because so many unstable conditions are involved, especially changes in the fertility and infertility rhythm.

A large number of American families regard the more effective control through contraceptive devices morally justified and make use of the most reliable means science provides for the planning of parenthood or by such methods carry out their desire to avoid having children. It is the belief of many obstetricians that our present contraceptive resources can be used to encourage younger married women to bear children and to release older women who already have become the mothers of several children from the continued responsibility of reproduction.[30] Two recent studies, one made on 45,514 consecutive viable deliveries at Johns Hopkins Hospital, the other on 250,000 that occurred during 1936–1938 in New York State exclusive of New York City, arrived at the same conclusions that the first birth carried more hazard than the second or third, while the fourth was about equal to the first. From the fourth childbearing onward, including the eighth, there was an increasing danger to the mother, the eighth child being born with twice the risk of the third. According to the first study, having a ninth baby was 330 per cent more dangerous than having a third, while according to the second investigation, it was 344 per cent more hazardous.[31]

In spite of the disagreement between groups of American people as to the morality of contraceptive methods, and legislation that obstructs the diffusion of contraceptive knowledge, birth-control practices are rapidly becoming an American trait, especially among the younger married men and women. The effort to control conception is not recent but instead is a very ancient attempt. Birth-control practices have been carried on by primitive people as well as by those whose historic records give evidence of their practices.[32] What has happened has been a decided increase in the efficacy of the methods used. Medical science has made possible a new human control of nature's processes that is certain to have great social consequences. As is true of many other significant discoveries, it is likely to be a source of both assets and liabilities, providing for some married couples an intelligent and safe family program while bringing to others the evasion of a responsibility that for the sake of their social maturity they ought to accept. Confidence in contraceptive devices will permit some persons to marry who otherwise would feel obligated to maintain a single life. It will likewise offer

---

[30] Guttmacher, Alan F., "Selective Pregnancy," *Human Fertility*, Vol. 6, No. 2, p. 33.

[31] *Ibid.*, p. 34.

[32] Himes, Norman E., *Medical History of Contraception*, Parts 1, 2, and 3.

opportunity for a sexual freedom based upon the avoiding of pregnancy. It is certain that the popularizing of the knowledge of birth control is forcing the code that has been orthodox among American youth to find its support in positive motives, since fear of both venereal infection and unwanted motherhood, the motives once emphasized, have for a multitude of young people disappeared because of their confidence in the preventive resources recently furnished by science.

There is no reason to believe that the control of fertilization means that most Americans entering marriage will remain childless. On the contrary, it is already apparent that the desire for children is strong among most of those who marry. Galton was opposed to child-labor laws because they would eliminate the profit-motive in childbearing that in his opinion was the only assurance of a normal population growth. Even though his prophecy appears true in individual cases, no social catastrophe resulted from the child-labor legislation. American families practicing birth control are demonstrating that, although a portion of homes are childless by choice, in most families children are desired. In so far as society must maintain itself by self-chosen parenthood, it will have to furnish confidence and incentives to those who wish children. This means providing conditions that make for security in giving birth to the child, in nurturing him, and later in preparing him through education to enter adult life well equipped.

Preventive medicine and adolescence. At present, the life period of adolescence is a medical no man's land. The general practitioner is seldom equipped to deal with this stage of organic development most radical in its changes aside from those appearing at birth and at the climacteric. When disease occurs or a rather general health examination is required such as colleges, summer camps and the like prescribe, the internist does not regard the period as falling within his specialty and the pediatrician also as a rule does not regard so late a development of childhood as belonging to his preventive responsibility. The endocrinologist, however, appreciates the adolescent's special need of the resources of preventive medicine, especially since malfunctioning of endocrine glands at this period may account for later adult troubles, for example, low fertility. Adolescence presents a serious body crisis. The individual should have the advantages of medical supervision by a specialist who takes over the problems of this period and develops the techniques required for a proper preventive medical program. This includes a thoroughgoing physical examination, with special attention to the functioning of the endocrine glands. Likewise, at this time adult marriage should be anticipated by those in charge of the training and guidance of the adolescent, and every effort should be made to build in him an intelligent attitude toward the physical as well as the other aspects of marriage which are already getting his attention.[33]

Medical-school instruction for marriage and the family. Crowded as the curriculum of the medical school now is, there is nevertheless need of finding an entrance for the consideration of marriage and family experience as related to disease. It is generally recognized that with the relative passing of the family physician, there is necessity of emphasizing the total personality of the individual, since specialization tends to develop a compartment approach to the human organism. If the person is to be rightly regarded as an individual both in health and disease, there must be greater recognition of the role of marriage and the family as basic sources of emotional consequences that express themselves in problems that come to the doctor. Useful as the medical social worker is, she cannot, by herself, give marriage and the family the importance they deserve in the background which the physician must understand if he is to diagnose the sick person rather than a disease. There should be definite attention given to the influences of marriage and the family in the training that the doctor gets during his medical school and hospital study in order that he may get the habit of considering what is often a complicating and sometimes the most important cause of illness. Since this curative approach cannot fulfill the necessities of preventive medicine, an understanding of the values of good marital adjustment, the conserving influence of a comfortable home, the contribution to the health program of an intelligent, satisfying marriage comradeship ought to be included in the training that prepares the physician to play his part in helping his client to maintain good mental and physical health. The more progress science and the practice of medicine make in safeguarding health, the more

---

[33] Hamblen, E. C., *Endocrine Gynecology*, p. 93.

certain will appear the importance of domestic experience as a contributing influence and the clearer it will be to the medical man that he has a responsibility to contribute to successful marriage and family life.[34]

Medicine and the aging process.   One of the most obvious trends in American population is the increasing proportion of aged persons. Until recently the high birth rate and the heavy migration made the United States a youthful nation. With the beginning of the present century came a lowering of the birth rate and a drastic restriction on immigration, resulting in a radical increase in the proportion of older persons. At the beginning of the century 4.1 per cent of the total population was over sixty-five, in 1941 the per cent was 6.8, and it was estimated that by 1980 this would increase to 14 per cent, approximately twenty-two million people over sixty-five.[35] The change is influencing the practice of medicine, and, as a consequence, the specialty geriatrics is developing to do for the old what pediatrics has accomplished for the child.

There is a minority, a pessimistic school of thought, which insists that there has been no improvement during recent decades in mortality after sixty. Preventive medicine has been effective in bringing a larger number of persons through childhood, where environmental conditions have been made more favorable than formerly, while the reverse is true for the aged who are finding their life more difficult.[36] It is true that the fruits of preventive medicine have been greatest in the period of childhood and that at present there is an increase in degenerative diseases which science does not as yet handle as successfully as it does the one-time deadly infections of childhood. This situation is a natural consequence of medicine's greater control of the dangers of childhood. More and more it is becoming clear that the preventive program for the aged must largely depend for its effectiveness upon conserving health during early years.[37] Although the aging process brings to medicine

---

[34] Richardson, Henry B., *Patients Have Families*.

[35] *Statistical Bulletin*, Metropolitan Life Insurance Company, Vol. 27, No. 5, p. 1.

[36] Bowerman, Walter, "Centenarians," *Transactions of the Actuarial Society*, Vol. 40, p. 361.

[37] Stanford, W. R., "The Aging Problem and Its Relation to the Earlier Treatment of the Individual," *The Urologic and Cutaneous Review*, Vol. 47, pp. 368–372.

its most discouraging problems, at present this is at least in part due to the slight knowledge science now possesses concerning the phenomena of aging. As Frank suggests, we know little yet as to how the individual man and woman can be protected as they age and, perhaps what is just as important, how much can be demanded of them in order to get the full activity which the welfare of each demands.[38] MacNider, through experimentation with animal organisms, believes that the aging process, even when it expresses itself in what is regarded as disease, is the body's fight to conserve life by its adaptations to existing circumstances.[39]

The attention directed by medical thought to the problems of the aged can lead to one of the science's greatest contributions to family welfare. It is obvious that a change from a rural to an urban way of life has made the presence of aged persons a much greater burden for families living in cities and industrial communities. The housing problem by itself would bring this result. The confinement of many old people and their limited opportunity for out-of-the-house activity adds to their difficulty. Their presence also hampers the privacy of husband and wife. Their restlessness, irritation, or loneliness is reflected back to the family group, frequently adding needless strain. The mere existence of an aged parent occasionally is responsible for a tragic situation such as that of a daughter who gives up marriage or unduly postpones it, or remains childless in marriage because of the financial problems associated with caring for the older person. Conflict and frustration often come into the family through the older person, who may, as a consequence of aging, have personality changes that make living with him very difficult. There may be mental manifestations that create conflict, and it may be questionable whether these are primarily psychogenic, or physiogenic, or a combination of both.[40] Old people feeling insecure frequently become extremely sensitive, ultraconservative, suspicious, domineering, or even given to the making of false accusations. If sick they may strain to the uttermost the family economy and the physical and nervous endur-

[38] Cowdry, E. V., *Problems of Aging*, Foreword, p. xxiv.
[39] MacNider, Wm. de B., "Age, Change, and the Adapted Life," *Science*, Vol. 99, p. 419; and Cowdry, E. V., *op. cit.*, Ch. 25.
[40] Crispell, Raymond, "Degenerative Neuropsychiatric Conditions Due to the Aging Process," *Virginia Medical Monthly*, Vol. 67, p. 670.

ance of whoever takes over their care. In some cases, problems
arise that are evidences of a psychosexual regression, occasionally expressing itself in sexual offenses which the law interprets
as willful crime.

Associated with these tensions appearing in the family
through the presence of the aged is, in many instances, an unwillingness of children to accept the responsibility of aged parents. To some degree there has been a cultural change reflecting
the greater burden that the aged bring to the urban family, as
is evidenced by two consequences: one, the attempt by legislation to make children responsible for their aging parents, something previously accomplished by cultural pressure; and, two,
the attempt to solve the problem of old people by committing
them to institutions. The latter in part explains the fact that
our hospitals for the mentally ill are so crowded with those revealing brain deterioration. People everywhere and in all periods have had to recognize the consequences of old age. Their
cultural attitudes have ranged from the killing of the aged,
through indifference, to extreme care.[41] The economic dependency of the aged has forced in this country the beginning of a
program for their social security. This has become a federal
problem and increasingly also that of the states. These provisions are chiefly a relief for those on the lower economic level
and only slightly a help for the middle class. Pensions, especially as they have developed among industries, are a greater
help to the latter group. By organization and political pressure
the aged have agitated for various schemes in hope of satisfactorily solving their economic needs.

The medical needs of old people have a financial aspect of
great concern to medical leadership. The individual is apt to
require increased help from doctors in the period when he has
least income. This situation, unless adequately met by a policy
developed by medical men, will give momentum to the growing
demand for socialized medicine, the employment of doctors as
government agents.

The problem of security for the aged emphasizes the fact
that in so far as services organized for profit shirk the burden of
accepting their share of responsibility for those of advanced
years the state and nation will be forced to take over increas-

---

[41] Cowdry, E. V., *op. cit.*, p. 87.

ingly and develop a social program supported by public taxation. The policy of one of the largest and most profitable of
accident insurance companies may be used as an illustration.
A policy carried for years automatically ends at the age of
seventy. It is evident that the risks of accidents increase at that
time, but, instead of accepting this liability and prorating the
costs through the preceding years of the company's clients, the
hazard is placed upon the family or upon public or private
charity. The consequence of this policy of withdrawal of insurance when it is most needed will be more and more pressure
for legislation which private enterprise considers socialistic. So
long as these laws are confined to responsibilities the commercial companies wish to escape, they are willingly accepted. The
fact is ignored that any public service once started tends to
spread. The insuring of the aged, therefore, illustrates an issue
of public policy which is becoming increasingly clear. Either
private enterprise must more adequately meet human need or
more and more socialistic programs will replace it. This is what
is now involved in the controversy popularly known as the
socializing of medicine.

Chapter 22

THE MENTAL HYGIENE
APPROACH

FOREWORD. In the mental hygiene approach to the conservation of marriage and the family the student studies the most recent and one of the most promising of all the programs contributing to the security and success of American family life. It is modern because it is the product of the better understanding of human behavior and needs which has been gathered chiefly by the services of psychology and psychiatry. Although it represents a very ancient interest and at present a field of investigation highly controversial, the advance already made in mental hygiene knowledge greatly aids efforts to strengthen and improve family life. Marriage counseling is a most recent attempt to apply this newer insight, and as a profession it is slowly emerging and obtaining recognition. The student will find it in accord with his attitude toward facing marriage realistically and being prepared to use intelligently the resources now possessed by science for dealing with serious marriage problems if and when they arise.

The purpose of mental hygiene. The mental hygiene movement was an original development during the first quarter of the twentieth century, and nothing is more representative of the preventive science of that period. Although its birth can be fixed, since it crystallized as a result of the publication in 1908 of Clifford Beers' book *A Mind That Found Itself*, there were new forces at work in psychology, psychiatry, and sociology that were making inevitable some such attempt to apply the new knowledge of human behavior. The roots of mental hygiene reach backward a long distance, since for many centuries wherever civilization existed there have been thoughtful students of human behavior who attempted to formulate adequate philosophies of life. This interest had increased markedly during the last quarter of the nineteenth century and was evidenced in this country by the writings of William James and G. Stanley Hall, both of whom took an active interest in the mental hygiene movement. An earlier forerunner, who approached the subject from a philosophical background, was the famous educator William T. Harris. Among the many pioneers during the formative years of the mental hygiene movement were Adolph Meyer, who suggested the term "mental hygiene"; William A. White of St. Elizabeth's Hospital, Washington, who from his rich psychiatric experience gave both guidance and inspiration; William H. Welch of Johns Hopkins University, who was able to win the financial support of philanthropists; Thomas W. Salmon, first medical director of the National Committee of Mental Hygiene; Frankwood Williams, who succeeded him and who had most to do with the development of the journal *Mental Hygiene* which perhaps more than anything else interpreted the new interest to the general public.

Mental hygiene was not and is not a new discipline but rather an attempt to unite the insight coming from several sciences attempting to minister to human needs, in a synthetic effort to prevent human suffering that arises from mental causes. At the first, interest in mental disease predominated, but with time there has been an application of mental hygiene to all the major fields of the activities of men, women, and children. Always the emphasis has been upon the utilization of our ever mounting knowledge of human nature so as to decrease personal maladjustments and eliminate their social causes. Mental hygiene has not only made use of information gathered by medicine, neurology, psychology, psychiatry, psychoanalysis, anthropology, sociology, and social-case work, but it also has broadened each one of these divisions of scientific interest and therapeutic service and made each more sensitive to the wider, more catholic attitude of mental hygiene.

No sooner did the mental hygiene point of view emerge than there came a new realization of the strategic place occupied by the family in the mental hygiene program. It was found that family relationships were often prominent in the influences that were responsible for the maladjustment of individuals, even in cases of mental abnormality. It was also found that marriage and parenthood were among the most effective of the allies upon which mental hygiene must depend in any effort to apply its principles to human needs. Mental hygiene has not only studied the family and the individual consequences of domestic and parenthood failures, it has not only used the resources of domestic experience and the impulses of parents for its therapeutic purposes, but it has also developed its own special provisions for dealing with problems of maladjustment, and these have come to have a large place in any program for family reconstruction. In previous discussions in this text, there has been an interpretation of the social conditions that complicate domestic experience and make marriage and parenthood more difficult. These liabilities accompanying the higher standards of twentieth-century living have evoked new help for human needs, and one of the answers of science has been mental hygiene.

Mental hygiene and the family.   Mental hygiene finds the family a going concern of major social importance. Whatever the type of problem that confronts the mental hygienist, he sooner or later finds involved in it some family aspect. Often it concerns a personality defect for which childhood experiences within the family seem chiefly responsible. Occasionally the trouble seems more largely a present tension of family origin or one resulting from the inability to find an outlet for cravings that require family experience for their satisfaction.

As mental hygiene finds the family, it is taprooted in sentiment flowering forth in the most delicate of human adjustments. Although a product of social evolution, it now seems indispensable, for it has been entrusted with fundamental functions. While these are shared by other social organizations much more than they have been in the past, with rare exceptions—such as the Spartan experiment—there is no indication of a substitute for the family as a means of achieving growth of personality and the carrying on of certain essential social services.

Parenthood, through the responsibilities that it brings during the first months of the infant's life, represents a continuation of uterine protection. From the beginning the child has been an individual organism although resident within the mother's body. Now he has been brought forth to the greater hazards of an outside existence, but he still requires a great measure of assistance. This can no longer be provided by the physiological activities of the mother, largely automatic in character, but must come through her deliberate concern and demands, if the child is to be well treated, serious, conscious thought on her part regarding her diet, working schedule, emotional self-control, rest, and other matters that influence the quality and quantity of her milk flow.

The family is more than a means by which the infant's helplessness may receive the necessary care; there is also a new type of service which grows more important as the other decreases in significance. As the child acquires greater independence by moving farther away from the conditions of uterine existence, the family provides a diminutive society which permits the establishment of the child's first contacts with other persons. These are as necessary for the growth of his personality as physical care is for his bodily development. He is led on to independent existence by gradations as his social boundaries extend, and he explores more deeply his relationships with other members of the family. All this, as the history of the orphanage has demonstrated, requires for best results close contact within a small group held together by strong ties of personal interest. Any substitute for the conventional family must of necessity become another sort of family, for children cannot be cared for in a wholesale manner as chickens are hatched in an incubator and reared in a mechanical brooder. This is recognized by the severest critics of present family life, who seek usually merely to displace the parent by the specialist.

It is true that some scientists [1] have indicted the family, and there are those interested in child welfare who look forward to a home life in which the parent will have little or no part. This denunciation of the family is motivated by the desire to find a method of training children for life which will avoid the neglect and the excesses of the wrong type of parent. These failures of the family have impressed the specialists who have been called upon to correct character defects caused by wrong treatment within the home. These reformers recognize the

---

[1] See writings of John B. Watson.

power of the present family but insist that parents cannot be taught to use their opportunity wisely. Necessarily, when any individual home fails to make good use of the influences it exerts upon the growing child, the consequences for the victim of family incompetency are serious and difficult to correct.

The history of mental hygiene is of course brief, but even in so short a time there has been development and, as a result of experience, changes of emphasis. The mature attitude of the mental hygienist at present more justly appreciates the complexity of the family problem, and there is a lessened disposition to charge upon parenthood entire responsibility for the faulty adjustment and undesirable habits of children. Undoubtedly, at first there was a tendency to simplify the family situation and the difficulties of children and explain them as products of personality defects in parents. This was similar to the earlier medical diagnosis that followed the discovery of bacteria. The significance of infection and of hereditary susceptibility, for example, in the case of tuberculosis, was exaggerated. We now know that although the virility and frequency of infection and the strength of native resistance in the individual case have great importance, there are also other influences that are involved in an active case of consumption.

In the same way, the progress of mental hygiene has widened the meaning of causation and led to an interpretation of a multifarious setting in each individual case, in which often the parents appear as much victims of circumstances as the children themselves. There also is less proneness to be satisfied with diagnosis that concentrates upon a descriptive term, such as parental fixation or parental compensation and the like. Not that these emotional reactions have proved untrue or unimportant but rather that they are themselves a description of a relationship rather than a causal or interpretive diagnosis. Everything we know about the child and the parent has led us away from a mechanical treatment of family difficulties according to some formula.

There also is beginning to be a more just realization that it is the nearness of the parent to the child rather than the blood tie that is hazardous and that any adult who is in a constant, familiar, and affectionate relationship with a child may easily become injurious to the latter's growing life. The escape cannot be made by abolishing the association, since it is demanded by the child, and any effort to deny him a particular fellowship proves even more disastrous.

The mental hygienists who deal with problems of children have become expert in locating the failures of individual families. They have gathered from many such cases principles that have preventive value, and the recent trend has been to popularize these in the attempt to help parents. In this work with fathers and mothers, great care must be exercised not to build up in them a feeling of guilt but to lead them to see their mistakes in a more objective manner than ever has been possible in the past. The child specialist takes this attitude, not primarily to spare the feelings of the parent or to protect him from morbid self-accusation, but because such an interpretation squares with the facts and permits fathers and mothers to see the meaning of the total situation which explains the predicament of the child. This new method of handling a problem situation is not only more thoroughgoing but is also more appreciative of the task of the family as a social institution. This viewpoint gives more weight to the difficulties inherent in twentieth-century living and shows more clearly the searching character of the responsibilities assigned to the family.

Mental hygiene and marriage.   There has been the same enlargement of the interpretation of matrimonial maladjustment in mental hygiene that has been true in the diagnosis of family difficulty. From the first, mental hygiene has been forced to recognize in marriage something more than a mere social convention. Marriage has appeared an attempt at emotional security and personality fulfillment which has made it a human quest unrivalled in both the quantity and quality of its demands. It has been looked upon as a human co-operation heavily loaded with desires and expectations, a relationship not only supremely testing of character but one sensitive to all the social forces that operate on modern men and women. It has the romance of an enticing adventure, affording an exceptional chance to exploit inclinations tied up with any tendency to fantasy, while at the same time it forces upon husband and wife the testing of a persistent, intimate, and matter-of-fact association.

To the mental hygienist, marriage successes and failures are determined by the adjustment of personalities, each bringing to the union an original background, a product of previous experience. Each marriage is individual in the problems it presents, and never static. The amount of satisfaction experienced by the husband and by the wife is decided by the determining conditions, including the qualities of character of both in a relationship always dynamic and highly emotional.

The workers in mental hygiene, through analysis of many cases, have come to recognize the most common problems and have built up an effective technique for dealing with these difficulties. Mental hygiene has been led to criticize the conditions that produce the unhappy marriage just as it indicts the family life that destroys the personality of the growing child. On the other hand, through familiarity with human need, mental hygiene has come to recognize the possibilities of conventional marriage as a means of providing incentive for character development and as an intimacy encouraging emotional stability.

Security. The need for emotional security has a large place in the mental hygiene program for both marriage and the family. The necessity that the normal individual feels for the certainty and completeness of emotional response appears early in the life of the child and as the adult matures and lives his active years and passes through senescence lingers to the end. Recognizing from the insight gathered from the several sciences which attempt to uncover motives of human nature that much of the behavior of men and women and children is this seeking for the establishment, for the maintenance, and for the proof of emotional security in the affection of some other person, mental hygiene gives a prominent place to this special problem of adjustment.

It is often easy to detect what the individual wishes and requires, but mental hygiene seeks to go beyond the mere diagnosis. In its effort to help people to attain a greater degree of emotional security, it operates along two different lines. It tries to build in the character of the person a maturity that will withdraw him from refuge in any sort of fantasy and will enable him to face the circumstances of his life, even though they are contrary to his choice. This means an encouragement of self-reliance and the achievement of emotional balance.

Mental hygiene also looks toward the social environment

in the effort to give the individual assistance in the reconstructing of a life program that has become shaken by the feeling of insecurity, and also that social circumstances may not encourage mental abnormality by both stimulating the need of emotional security and denying the means of its being attained.

In both these methods of helping people in trouble and of preventing maladjustment, mental hygiene gives great attention to the family and to marriage. An indispensable function of the family is to provide the child in his earliest years with the certainty of an unchanging affection. Through it alone he can find the needed emotional security. Marriage is recognized as a later attempt under different conditions to accomplish the same end.

Family adjustment. The word "adjustment" frequently appears in the vocabulary of mental hygiene and conveys the viewpoint of the science. Mental hygiene approaches marriage and the family as a special form of adjustment. It looks upon the relationship as a continuing interaction which makes demands upon each person within the association. Anything approaching finality is impossible, and even to attempt to crystallize in permanent form any temporary alignment of persons antagonizes the functioning of that particular family.

Mental hygiene interprets each individual family experience in perspective. It seeks the meaning of any difficulty in the family association or any conflict between husband, wife, and child in the personal history of each member of the group. Mental hygiene assumes as a matter of course the coming of crisis situations, mild or serious in character, since these are to be expected in a continuous adjustment of changing and complex personalities. It recognizes that the significance of these experiences depends upon the ability of those concerned to make adjustment, and also upon the reaction that each person carries from the experience. It becomes necessary in these interpretations to distinguish problems that originate within the family from those that merely find their expression in the family.

Rarely is it found that the giving of understanding in the sense of interpretive information proves sufficient help for those in the throes of maladjustment. If, as is seldom true, the conflict arises from lack of knowledge, enlightenment suffices. As a rule, the crisis situation is a product of emotional patterns, and these are so thoroughly characteristic of each person that adjustment cannot be accomplished unless there is re-education of character. The psychologist and the psychiatrist in recent years have been building a technique for the reconstruction of personality. Mental hygiene makes use of this, stressing prevention by preparing individuals for these inevitable experiences of family contact. Mental hygiene is synthetic and pragmatic in its attempt to apply the material gathered from various schools of psychology, psychiatry, and sociology. Although there are differences of emphasis even among the exponents of mental hygiene, their point of view is catholic rather than partisan, and this brings together in the preventive program individuals who in their special fields are committed more aggressively to a particular point of view.

In attempting to help the individual successfully to adjust to matrimonial or family circumstances, the mental hygienist seeks to utilize the resources of the individual, for new motives must grow out of the self rather than be imposed upon it. Effort is made to draw forth from the personality itself a new incentive and to provide means for initial success. This technique is similar to that used by the specialist attempting to lead his patient away from a neurosis, but our interest is in the application of these principles to marriage and family relationships and in their preventive purpose.

It is clear that the mental hygiene movement is essentially educational in character, an effort to distribute in a popular way the information gathered by the various sciences concerned with human behavior, so as to establish wholesome attitudes that will enable individuals to make successful adjustment. Thus it is similar to physical hygiene, but it ranges over a larger territory of behavior and serves as a means of emphasizing a distinct point of view in various fields of activity. Now we have, for example, mental hygiene in industry, in the school, in religion, and in other special types of human conduct. The major interest, however, is not any of these special forms of personality expression but the individual himself. Nothing more clearly reveals the significance of the family and of marriage than that mental hygiene, through its interest in the problems of the individual, is forced to emphasize the sources of maladjustment and the opportunities of reconstruction provided by family and matrimonial relationships. Of these the first has, of course, greater significance, since it is so often the origin of influences that have determined the personality.

The child guidance clinic.   The child guidance clinic is an outgrowth of mental hygiene, and in any program for the conservation of the family it performs an important function. It is a product of the science of psychiatry but draws a portion of its insight in dealing with children from the other sciences that explore human conduct. It is a clinic designed to diagnose the problems of behavior and of personality arising in children. It concentrates upon the task of assisting children to achieve healthy mental habits. In practice, this means that the clinic has to concern itself with the personality difficulties of parents, since the problem-child is usually a product of a family situation. The child guidance clinic applies the knowledge science has gained concerning the emotional experiences and behavior of children who have become problems to parents, teachers, juvenile judges, and others responsible for children.

A considerable proportion of those treated at the clinic are children sent to it by other welfare agencies that find need of assistance in dealing with difficult families and children. In certain communities this sort of service has been designated a mental hygiene clinic, and the term suggests more adequately what the child guidance clinic has now become.[2]

We date the beginning of the mental-hygiene clinic from the work of Dr. William Healy at the Juvenile Psychopathic Institute in Chicago in 1909. A somewhat similar interest in the mental welfare of children developed at the Boston Psychopathic Hospital, at the Phipps Psychiatric Clinic at Baltimore, and somewhat later at Boston through the work of the Judge Baker Foundation under the leadership of Dr. Healy who had come to it from Chicago.

Although these clinics were the first for children that made use of the resources of psychiatry, psychology, and social work, their point of view was influenced by the fact that they dealt with the delinquent child chiefly, and because of this they differed somewhat from the clinics that became known as child-guidance clinics. These later demonstration clinics were estab-

---

[2] *First International Congress of Mental Hygiene,* Vol. 1, p. 279.

lished in various cities, financed by the Commonwealth Fund
and organized by the National Committee of Mental Hygiene.
Although at first these also emphasized the problems of the
delinquent child, they gradually developed a larger purpose as
their attention shifted from the delinquent child to the child
having trouble in his home and school adjustments.[3] The child
guidance clinic movement developed slowly at first, but during the second decade of the twentieth century this use of the
resources of science for the helping of children in trouble increased rapidly.

As this service for children has multiplied, it has increasingly emphasized prevention and extended its field of interest
as experience has proved that the whole child had to be studied
and treated, since, whatever the immediate problem, his entire
social and personality background was involved.

As the child guidance clinic is usually organized, it includes a director, generally a psychiatrist, and a staff embracing
a psychologist, social workers, stenographers, and other clerical
assistants. Its work has not been restricted merely to the diagnosing and treating of problem-children and their parents. It
conducts educational services in accord with its mental hygiene
purpose and acts as a co-ordinating agency for community organizations engaged in different phases of child welfare work.
It also makes use of its opportunity as a medium for research,
and its contributions have not only influenced its own technique but have had a prominent place in the rapid development of a science of childhood.

The family and marriage clinic.   Another mental hygiene
product is the family clinic. It is similar in purpose and outlook
to the child guidance clinic, but in origin it is broader in its
scope and less intimately connected with psychiatry. The Institute of Family Relations in Los Angeles may be taken as an
example of this type of service for the family, since it was the
first in this country to undertake the work in a specific way.
After two years of preliminary activity, it offered its resources to
the public in 1930 under the directorship of Dr. Paul Popenoe.
It functions by means of a staff composed of social workers,
physicians, and consultants representing various phases of the
science of human behavior.

---

[3] Stephenson, George, and Smith, Geddes, *Child Guidance Clinics,* p. 47.

There are now a number of such organizations, chiefly in the large cities. The following are representative and nationally recognized: Boston: Counseling Service, Lester W. Dearborn, Executive Secretary. Chicago: Association for Family Living, Lester A. Kirkendall, Director. Detroit: Marriage and Family Consultation Service, Advisory Service, Merrill-Palmer School, Robert G. Foster, Director. New York City: Bureau of Marriage Counsel and Education, Inc., Valeria Hopkins Parker, Director; Jewish Institute on Marriage and the Family, Sidney E. Goldstein, Chairman; Marriage Consultation Center, The Community Church, Abraham Stone, Director; Commission on Marriage and the Home, The Federal Council of the Churches of Christ in America, L. Foster Wood, Secretary; Family Guidance Consultation Service, Child Study Association of America, Mrs. Sidonie M. Gruenberg, Director. Cincinnati: Family Consultation Service, Mrs. Anna Budd Ware, Director. Cleveland: Maternal Health Association, Gladys Gaylord, Executive Secretary. Philadelphia: Marriage Council, Mrs. Emily Mudd, Director. Washington, D. C.: Family Life Bureau, National Catholic Welfare Conference, Edgar Schmiedeler, Director. Chapel Hill, North Carolina: Marriage and Family Council, Inc., Gladys H. Groves, Director. San Francisco: Family Relations Center, Henry M. Grant, Executive Director. Los Angeles: American Institute of Family Relations, Paul Popenoe, Director.

Many of the Family Service Societies, formerly Family Social Welfare Associations, provide a consultation service. Once chiefly designed to help the underprivileged, their guidance is beginning to be sought by members of the middle class. There are also many private marriage and family counselors.

In the effort to maintain professional standards and to keep profit-seeking individuals from exploiting those needing help because of family or marriage difficulties, the American Association of Marriage Counselors has been organized. Dealing as he does with difficult and confidential problems, the counselor needs the same professional standards as the physician, but at present there is no legal protection such as has developed in the field of medicine for the clients that seek counsel. In addition to the men and women who may be classified as professional counselors, there are a multitude of persons who because of their profession and their serious interest are prepared as a by-product of their vocations to give counsel. These include physicians, ministers, priests, rabbis, experienced social workers, and specialists in psychiatry, psychology, and sociology.

The development of marriage and family counseling.   It is obvious that the seeking of advice by people in trouble is nothing new. The distinction between this and counsel-giving appears in both the type of problem that is presented and the quality of the service rendered. It is something more than the help attempted by an adviser. The problems are such as not only demand expert judgment but also the giving of enlightenment to the client. This can be accomplished only by one who has gained insight through the scientific study of human behavior. This desire for expert guidance on the part of the adult who is face to face with some sort of problem is a natural result of the progress in spreading the insight concerning human behavior gathered by science in recent years, especially through the popularizing of psychiatric, psychological, and sociological knowledge. The reading public has been immensely interested in literature that has sought to interpret the mechanisms of conduct, and the publicity given psychoanalysis in this country has done more perhaps than any other influence in awakening lay people to an appreciation of the complexity of their own motives and of those with whom they associate. The theory of the unconscious has become widely known and its terminology an accepted part of the educated person's vocabulary.

Mental hygiene has been interpreted by many skillful writers and through popular lecturing, with the result that an increasing number of people having trouble in their family or in marriage have realized the seriousness of their difficulty, the folly of trying to deal with it themselves, or of going to others who, although they may have sympathy, lack the background that counsel-giving requires. These people in trouble because of maladjustments have been made to realize that their own emotional attitudes limit their ability to handle their problem. Recently they have become familiar with a new type of counseling concentrating on marriage difficulties. The publicity concerning this professional service has spread faster than the development of the counseling itself, thus providing an enticing opportunity for the clever but inadequately trained pseudo scientist to announce himself as a marriage counselor. A similar situation developed in the early period of psychoanalysis, but that service had the advantage of involving medical aspects; thus the law could be invoked to maintain professional standards and ethics. The profession of counseling must chiefly, at present, be safeguarded by publicizing the qualifications needed by those who counsel and the hazard that the client faces who goes to the ill-prepared or exploiting advice-giver. It is probable that in some instances even blackmail is the result of such conferences. More often the client is the victim of reckless suggestions.

It is important that the individual in trouble be assured that his confidences will be respected, since one of the conditions for helpful counseling is a feeling of security that enables the individual to be perfectly frank. This in itself in many cases removes tension and so clarifies the situation that the client sees what should be done. It is usually easier to talk without restraint to a professional counselor than to a relative or friend. The emotional aftermath is also different. When an individual relieves emotional tension and confesses frustrations to someone with whom he is intimate, there is frequently a regret that so much has been revealed once the intense emotions have receded. In talking with a close associate or relative, there is also the tendency to indict rather than to explain. This attempt to place blame, although it relieves the feelings, accomplishes little and the professional counselor switches the client away from this, whereas the friend or relative is too apt to encourage it. In the one case, the listener is interested in diagnosis in order to discover what best can be done; in the other, there is either partisanship or unadmitted satisfaction in hearing the sufferer pour out his grievances and distress.

Anyone who is called upon to give counsel has to beware of an attitude of mind that distorts judgment. To be called upon for advice gives a sense of power and a feeling of superiority. When inferiority feeling has been characteristic of the individual or there has been envy previously of the person in trouble, the listener can get a peculiar but unacknowledged satisfaction in the other person's misfortunes, and any advice given will be influenced by this. The professional counselor is safeguarded because he understands the danger of this and is also free of the previous personal relationships that warp the relative's or friend's judgment. Therefore, the professional counselor can be more objective and his suggestions will come out of the situation as he sees it rather than from his own reactions and prejudices. As a rule, a person in trouble who is seeking a solution rather than an opportunity to rehearse grievances has the impulse to go to someone who has experience in marriage and family problems and who is a stranger. This is one of the explanations of the growing demand for marriage and family counseling. The development of this type of service is already creating a need for specialists that is greater than can be met by the existing number of trained experts. The professional counselor needs background comparable to that of the physician. The danger is that popularizing the advantages of the professional counselor in the field of marriage and the family will not only attract the exploiting pseudo scientist but also well-meaning men and women who with little scientific background and the most superficial training will believe themselves prepared to deal with human problems that are inherently complex and to the client, momentous, often the most important happenings in the victim's adult career.

Influences retarding marriage counseling. In spite of this development of confidence in the professional counselor, it is still true that the great majority of American men and women hold to traditions which retard the acceptance of marriage counseling as a profession. There are three common ideas that are hampering the emergence of counseling as a specialty. One is the philosophy which accepts marriage handicaps as unescapable. In theory, few of those who hold this belief would go so far as to state boldly that whatever is in marriage must be endured, but in practice they hold to the idea that marriage must not be regarded as a relationship which should justify itself through human satisfactions but only as a commitment of moral obligation. Human mating has both aspects. The emphasis upon the second as interpreted by some people—most certainly not all—discourages those having marriage trouble from seeking help.

Then there is another line of thinking which considers the disappointments, frustrations, and alienations that appear in individual marriages as evidence of the failure of matrimony as a social relationship. To them it appears futile to attempt to make marriage succeed. Nature tricks the lover, and society adds to the illusory human cravings by its support of a romanticism which pushes youth toward marriage but with the certainty that sooner or later they will feel betrayed by their impossible ideals. These matrimonial skeptics see no hope of conserving marriage through the counseling of experts.

The most effective of the influences impeding the progress of marriage counseling is the impulse of persons in trouble to go to friends, relatives, and others who have no special background for the giving of the advice desired. If people generally, when they find themselves sick, were to seek the help of untrained people instead of that of the physician, the medical profession would be in a situation similar to that which now is true of marriage counseling. As a matter of fact, the physician has developed his high standard of professional ethics through a long social evolution during which for a time he had to compete with those who were giving both diagnosis and treatment without seeking even the meager background of knowledge at that time available. Marriage counseling must necessarily move toward its professional maturity more rapidly than did medicine. Its standing as a reputable service depends upon gaining the confidence of an ever increasing number of people wrestling with marriage problems who will realize the wisdom of going to the specialist rather than to the neighbor, relative, or friend.

Function of the professional counselor. The marriage counselor has a double task at present, and if he can demonstrate his usefulness along these two lines, an increasing number of people will appreciate his value and will then discriminate between the genuine and the pseudoscientific, self-appointed expert. The first of these two responsibilities is to encourage the present trend of our young people, especially those who have had marriage courses in universities, to seek conferences before marriage for the purpose of preventing later problems and for gaining insight for such adjustments as they find needful once they are married. This is a preventive service similar to that which has become so great a contribution to the physician. More and more American youth are coming to understand that successful marriage requires preparedness or the necessity of learning through experiences that are both trying and hazardous. Naturally, the conscientious and informed young person prefers the first method of gaining insight.

It appears reasonable to expect that when marriage counseling becomes well established and generally accepted as a special type of service, young people before they marry will seek the assistance of the counselor, as now, for example, the business man makes a practice of going to the legal or the economic specialist for information that he needs in order to avoid trouble or to be successful in his undertakings. It will also be common to desire the aid of the counselor when any problem arises in marriage which seems to require greater insight than the person himself has. There will be no feeling in such circumstances that the marriage is in jeopardy or that the husband or wife or both could not finally work out their problem but rather that the intelligent procedure is to gain an objective analysis of the difficulty before it gets to a point that threatens their happiness.

In addition to this development of a preventive program, the marriage counselor must give proof of his usefulness by the second and more traditional type of service, the handling of serious marriage incompatibilities. This curative aspect of counseling is at present better understood and therefore more in demand. It cannot be as effective as the other sort of help, because too often the counselor gets the problem only when it has become unendurable and so much estrangement has occurred that reconciliation is impossible. Nevertheless, the marriage counselor must convince people having serious trouble in marriage that in such a situation no friend or relative can be a safe consultant, that an objective point of view is necessary and that the sensible thing is to go to someone who has made the study of marriage problems his specialty. Even when the family must be broken up, the method and spirit of doing this may increase or lessen the tragedy for those concerned.

It is to be expected that the marriage counselor will often be called upon to take over after a minister, doctor, or lawyer has failed to accomplish reconciliation. This transferring of clients grows, and the more members of these other professions gain confidence in the marriage counselor, the more commonly will it occur. The members of other professions who have straightened out their part of a marriage problem will then send their client to a marriage counselor when they feel that he needs help other than that which they are trained to give. The marriage counselor frequently sends his client to a physician or a psychiatrist. The opposite co-operation is equally needed, but the profession of the marriage counselor is not yet so well established that his assistance is always appreciated. It is, however, encouraging that physicians who are called upon to deal with the physical aspects of marriage adjustment are beginning to turn to the marriage counselor as a colleague that can handle aspects of adjustment which the doctor does not wish to take over, indeed which he cannot treat without encroaching upon time which he needs for his medical practice.

Background of the professional counselor. The great distance between the mere giving of advice and the function of the marriage and family counselor is perhaps best brought out by considering the background of science that the latter finds useful in his work. The following lines of study are all desirable, and as counseling matures and establishes itself as a profession with requisite standards these subjects will contribute to the training program of those fitting themselves for clinic or private practice.

1. *Social work.* Knowledge of the principles and techniques of social work, including practice in the handling of cases, is indispensable in the training program of the marriage counselor. As much of this instruction should be provided as the schedule permits.

2. *Anthropology.* The marriage counselor will profit from familiarity with primitive social life not only because it reveals basic human motivations expressed in folkways, mores, myths, and symbols, but also because it encourages an objective interpretation and evaluation of alien cultural backgrounds. This vicariousness in sharing the personal background of the client is desirable in counseling.

3. *Biology.* Knowledge of the essential contributions of biological science brings an appreciation of the meaning and significance of the human organism. The counselor also should recognize the importance of human heredity and the signifi-

cance of the eugenic programs now functioning or advocated for the security and the improvement of the race.

4. *Medicine.* In this field there is need of a course given by various specialists with emphasis on: (1) embryology as it reveals the development of sexual structure; (2) endocrinology, especially as it is related to adolescence, fertility, pregnancy, and the climacteric; (3) child bearing; (4) representative health programs of preventive medicine; and (5) available resources for safeguarding and improving the health of communities and individuals. In this medical course or by allied instruction there should be discussion of human sexology, emphasizing the normal and also giving attention to such abnormal expressions of sex as the counselor is most likely to encounter in his conferences.

5. *Law.* The counselor should not only be acquainted with the principles of domestic law, with special attention to marriage, annulment, and divorce, but also for his own security he requires clear understanding of his professional limitations, that he may not intrude into the field of the lawyer, and of his legal status and liability as a counselor.

6. *Psychiatry* can add to the background of the counselor knowledge of the mechanisms that influence human conduct, of the theories of leading psychoanalytic schools, and some understanding of the principal mental diseases and their characteristic expressions. The marriage counselor should be prepared to recognize mental abnormalities that indicate the need of the counsel of a psychiatrist.

7. *Psychology.* This science furnishes the counselor with an appreciation of the manner in which human personality develops, with emphasis on the significance of the formative period of childhood and youth. The student should also be acquainted with the most common tests given by the professional psychologist, that the counselor may send his client for an examination when this appears desirable.

8. *Sociology* should provide a clear picture of the development of American social life and the common social problems of those who are courting, marry, become parents, or who have given up the idea of marriage. The significance of class and section as they influence attitudes and behavior should be

stressed, since the counselor must always be prepared to take these cultural differences into account.

9. *Religion.* The counselor must have a clear conception of the Catholic, Protestant, and Jewish philosophies of marriage. This material can best be given by a representative of each of these faiths. In counseling there is frequent need of appreciating the significance of the basic religious convictions of the client.

10. *Counseling experience.* The principles of counseling should be taught with opportunities for diagnosis and treatment of representative cases. This instruction, in preparation for counseling, should encourage class discussion and should make the student conscious of any tendencies he may have toward personal prejudices or generalizations in judging the conduct of others. Candidates for counseling, toward the later part of their study, should be permitted to give counsel in dealing with the simpler problems under the guidance of a professional counselor. Since marriage counseling is developing rapidly as one of the important functions of many social and religious organizations, it would seem that the program for training in marriage counseling should include the working out of some sort of student apprenticeship with such organizations as maintain a well-developed counseling service.

The pastor, priest, and rabbi as marriage counselors. In many communities, especially villages and the open country, those having trouble in marriage and in family relationships are most likely to seek the help of their religious leaders. They assume that members of the clergy are prepared to give this guidance. They have come to have confidence in the spiritual leadership of these men, and it is natural for them to ask for advice when they find themselves struggling with domestic problems. They take for granted that their confidences will be respected, and they are inclined to accept the judgment of the leaders they trust for spiritual insight. It is, of course, not true that all clergymen are well prepared by training or by disposition to act as marriage and family counselors or that they have taken enough interest in such ministration to make an effort to prepare themselves for it. At best, for most of them it can only be a by-product of their work. Fortunately, however, there has been of late a marked trend toward accepting such responsibility, with the result that there has been a considerable interest among the clergy of all faiths in the literature of guidance and in discussions of counseling problems. This, at times, has been made a topic of ministerial and other conferences. There also has been introduced in some of the Protestant theological seminaries instruction to prepare the students for this special type of pastoral guidance. There is an even greater demand on the part of the students for such instruction, and the courses now offered, as is true of marriage courses in the colleges, have largely developed to meet the desire of students. This type of instruction is not new in Catholic seminaries, although the teaching now given reflects the influence of psychiatric and social science. The priest has always been looked to as a source of authority whenever there has been need of knowing the teaching of the church concerning marriage and family matters. In order to function, he has had to have preparatory training.

The danger of ministerial counselors who are called upon to give counsel concerning some problem of domestic relations comes from their tendency to conceive it purely as a moral problem and to pronounce judgments that although made with assurance lack the necessary insight on account of their neglect of the contributions of science. Although the clergyman may take a genuine interest in preparing for counseling, his reading may consist so much of literature written by persons of his own prejudices and background that he adds little through his study to his equipment for objective analysis and fact-based guidance. Even when his contribution is helpful, it may be too partial to prove effective. Sometimes, because it is so one-sided, so committed to a moral interpretation of the difficulty, it leads the client away from the causal understanding of the situation which alone provides a way of escape. The ministerial counselor will function best if he realizes his limitations and is quick to detect when his client needs the more expert help of the psychiatrist, physician, or the professional counselor.

The mental hygiene emphasis. A large part of the value coming from mental hygiene is its emphasis upon preventive measures as a means of lessening human maladjustment. Mental hygiene enforces the strategy of prevention in all the professions that deal with human conduct. The mental hygiene aspects of medicine, law, the ministry, teaching, and business are of the most practical importance for the conservation of the family. Undoubtedly, much will be done for the improvement of family life indirectly through concern for the mental hygiene program among men and women in these strategic professions.

The period of indifference to the social conditions affecting family life, with its criticism of family failure and agitation for some panacea for family reform, is over, and instead those interested in family problems are turning with confidence to the mental hygiene approach. The mental hygienist, as he concerns himself with problems of marriage and the family, recognizes that many of these are derivatives of still greater difficulties. He realizes that there is a limit to self-help and also to the usefulness of the professional marriage and family counselor. The victim of mental disease, the individual developing neurosis, or suffering from some sort of nervous malady or something that expresses itself in nervous symptoms requires a psychiatrist, psychoanalyst, or physician. Individuals who are having domestic troubles as a result of a deep-seated inability to deal with life need more than the principles of good adjustment which mental hygiene emphasizes. The professional marriage or family counselor is expected to be alert in discovering those who cannot profit from his services but who need care from psychiatric or medical specialists. Mental hygiene can help most in these more serious maladjustments by creating in the general public better understanding of the meaning of mental disease and an appreciation of the value of the victim's committing himself at once to the ministrations of the appropriate specialist. Any mental malady quickly shows itself in the intimacies of family and married life. For the welfare of all concerned such a source of trouble-making behavior needs discovery and attention. The mental hygienist or the professional marriage and family counselor who encourages men and women to attempt through their own insight to deal with the expressions of a mental disease in the behavior of spouse or child exerts a delaying and even dangerous influence. Mental abnormality often shows itself first in home life. The marriage and family counselor must always be quick to suspect the possibility of this causation behind domestic incompatibility and in any case of doubt get the advice of the proper specialist before going on with his services. In many cases the diagnosis of a psychiatrist must be sought at once.

An adequate life program. Mental hygiene regards the difficulties of marriage and the family chiefly as indications of the inability of individuals to cope with life. With the ever increasing complexity of modern civilization go greater demands that must be met by those who achieve any measure of good adjustment to life. The refinement of the erotic is one of the chief changes of recent culture and, as a consequence, the occasion of much tension. This complicates family adjustment, for not only is it a cause of much maladjustment in marriage, but it also becomes for many the means of appraising success.

Another result of the machine era is the growing delicacy of parental influence. The significance of parenthood is no longer found in its obvious and essential services but rather in the more subtle and intimate attitudes and responses. This means that the influence of the parent upon the child and that of the child upon the parent is such that the essential features of each personality determine the quality and wholesomeness of the relationship.

Under circumstances that are so severely testing of one's fundamental traits of character, the family, because of closeness of contact, cannot avoid providing the freest expression of any inadequacy of personality. This brings to the surface any character weakness resulting from emotional immaturity. Social conditions in the modern world invite the appearance of this insufficiency of personality while at the same time demanding a stability and restraint which the complexities of life make difficult. Emotional immaturity comes from a clinging to lower levels of behavior, an attempt to procure satisfaction without meeting the ordeals that go along with modern culture. The circumstances of personality growth, the background which psychoanalysis attempts to explore, explain this blocking of maturity. The individual has refused to go on emotionally and is seeking happiness in some easier way, but since he cannot prevent his desires and his activities from emerging on a higher plane than that to which he sticks emotionally, he is in constant tension through his inconsistency.

The result is a sensitive egoism that throws all its experiences out of perspective. This signifies more than the development of extreme selfishness. The personality as an organism of adaptation becomes disintegrated and cannot function with success. The greater the failure, the more intense becomes the struggle to put aside truth, especially to conceal the impotency of the self, and instead of turning factward the personality seeks some parasitic release.

In the marriage experience this is likely to mean the finding of a victim upon whom the blame can be heaped for the individual's own faults. Although this method lessens one's emotional protest against his own weakness, it greatly adds to the seriousness of his social maladjustment. His relief is a fiction but the increasing maladjustment is genuine, and the more his problem grows, the greater his need of finding refuge in the notion that he is misunderstood and badly treated. In the parenthood experience the relationship invites the gaining of parasitic relief through substitution. The adult transfers to the child and the latter fixates upon the parent.

In dealing with these aberrations of family fellowship, mental hygiene attempts to establish an adequate program for life. This can be accomplished only as the personality is socialized and matured. Not only must the individual be reformed emotionally, he must be reconciled to the difficulties of adaptation on the higher plane. He must be made more tolerant with himself and more reasonable in his expectations. This requires a reconstruction of the purposes and satisfactions of marriage and of the family.

Since such reshaping is difficult even when it can be accomplished, mental hygiene stresses more and more the building of right attitudes in anticipation of adult experiences, that the individual may be prepared to meet the demands of matrimony and of parenthood. This requires understanding of the meaning of successful family life under modern conditions, and to the consideration of this we turn in our next chapter.

Chapter 23

THE HOME ECONOMICS APPROACH

FOREWORD. The student is likely to bring to the discussion of the economic aspects of family life personal conviction, the product of experience and observation, previous thinking and study. Not only does the individual family function in its own economic background, but the family as an institution adapts itself to the economic system, the prevailing resources and standards, and the established economic background. A thoroughgoing consideration of all the economic facts that indirectly concern the family would turn this discussion away from its present purpose into an interpretation of the science of economics. Here the interest of the student is in those specialized aspects of the science that concern the family. This material includes both the production and consumption processes of the household and constitutes the province of the applied science, home economics. To emphasize this fact the chapter is entitled "The Home Economics Approach."

Family basis of home economics. Although no approach to the conserving of the family is more important than those interests that rightly fall within the domain of home economics, there is still among many well-informed people a minimizing and a misinterpretation of the function of this division of applied science. This largely comes from the early history of home economics when stress was placed upon cooking and sewing as techniques without emphasis upon their meaning for family life. There has been more, however, than a shift in the attitude toward household skills. The science in recent years has firmly established itself as education for home-life activity. It is therefore concerned not only with the problems and processes of household economy; it is a point of view and an accumulation of knowledge needed in the functioning of family life. It is concerned with all the characteristic activity that maintains the cultural quality of the American home. Its central purpose is to prepare for an intelligent, skillful use of the resources for homekeeping, including the material, the psychic, and the social aspects of household economy. Thus it not only endeavors to strengthen the individual home but deals with it as it is related to the community, state and nation. Home economics sees the family not as a social institution, not as an abstract concept, but as a group of individuals bound together by common interests in an intimate, ever changing relationship. As an applied science it draws heavily from other fields of knowledge such as chemistry, biology, psychology, and sociology, integrating its material by the dominant viewpoint of family welfare.

The function of present-day home economics, the need of securing and enriching family life, justifies its becoming a requirement of public education without regard for sex, because public policy, recognizing the value of the home, must consider every boy or girl educated at public expense as a potential candidate for marriage and family membership. Since pupils end their schooling at various periods and, even more, because during the formative years attitudes toward the family can be guided and developed, home economics education in some form should be a part of the instruction of the grades, the secondary schools, and the colleges. Indeed, it is the only department of instruction during the school career where the pupil can be assured that family living will receive the attention it requires.

It is obvious that at present home economics does not have in our educational curricula the place it deserves as the core about which preparation for family life can be developed. This is in part due to the neglect the family still receives in our educational program due to the tradition that the family can take care of itself as was true before urban culture became dominant in the United States. There is, however, another influence that retards proper consideration of family welfare in our instructional program. Home economics is regarded by some administrators, instructors of the subject, and students as a specialty to be emphasized from the professional viewpoint, just as college programs in biology and chemistry tend to be organized for those who are going to major in the subject. Home economics is too much influenced, at least on the college level, by the needs of those students who elect the subject as a professional vocation. In order to be well adjusted to modern life, college graduates, especially if they concentrate outside natural science, have great need of an introductory course related to life experiences in the fields of biology and chemistry. Similar home economics instruction is even more desirable for women specializing in other fields of study, since without a course adapted to their own nonprofessional interest they are denied preparedness for the homemaking that most of them eventually accept as their life career. Investigations by Foster and Wilson have made clear that women do not gather from their general colleges readiness for tasks of homemaking. Indeed, they are likely to carry away from college unfavorable attitudes toward household skills and activities as well as a lack of knowledge of household management.[1] To the degree that this is true, college life becomes an impediment rather than an asset to the woman as she takes over the responsibilities of wifehood and motherhood.

In order to accomplish its purpose, this general course must be not a summary of the science of home economics but an interpretation of its resources for family living. This is true not only in secondary education but in college also. There is genuine need, too, of some sort of instruction in family living adapted to children in the elementary grades. If the family is to be successful as a going concern, its activities and functions should be brought close to the child during his formative years and as a basic interest built into his life development. The human and concrete aspects of home life must, however, have emphasis. On whatever level this instruction is given, the program should rest on a clear realization that what the student needs is not a basis for professional specialization in the field of home economics but an insight that will aid him as he meets the problems of everyday life as they concern marriage and the family.[2] This approach does not preclude during the secondary and college period the different kind of instruction that seeks

[1] Foster, R. G., and Wilson, P., *Women After College*, p. 250.
[2] Bonde, Ruth, "Education for Living," *Journal of Home Economics*, Vol. 36, pp. 327–330.

to interpret the family as an institution and which may be given by either the home economist or the social scientist. The purposes, values, and problems of this special emphasis will be dealt with in the chapter on the educational approach to the conservation of marriage and the family.

Efficient home life. The responsibility for providing preparedness for efficient home life necessarily belongs chiefly to the home economist. She has the training and the background of technical experience and the understanding of values that such instruction must have if it is to be practical and to appeal to the student. In content such courses include the development of skills and the giving of information for the handling of household problems.

This type of course can be definitely linked with home activity and thereby strengthen the ties between the family and the school. On the secondary level care has to be taken that the instruction does not become in the mind of the student a criticism of his or her home life. A course that gives training for household activities has been well described as one belonging to the "doing" departments of the school.[3] It offers opportunities for projects that can be carried out with parental co-operation. Through assignments in cooking, sewing, embroidering, home decoration, music, games, and the like, the home can be enriched but in such a natural, matter-of-course way as to lead to no self-consciousness in the critical sense in either parent or child. These practical projects by using the home of the parents as an allied workshop for the school can easily prepare the child for his own later family life. On the college level such co-operation is more limited and difficult. The college course, however, can profit from an alliance with specially selected homes. Students studying definite problems of family life when husband and wife both work outside the home can get extremely valuable insight by talking with husbands and wives who have made such adjustments. The building of an alliance between schools and homes helps greatly to keep the instruction from seeming artificial and detached from the practical, characteristic activities of the household. These courses naturally emphasize the preparing of the girls, although fortunately similar work for

---

[3] *Education for Family Life,* American Association of School Administrators, p. 120.

boys is appearing in high schools and colleges rather often. Boys are invited now into the course which is chiefly taught from the girl's point of view. Although there is an overlapping of the boys' and girls' needs, there is a growing recognition also either through special courses or specific attention in a course, open to both, of the peculiar household responsibilities belonging to the husband. For example, there are problems of repairs, construction, and maintenance in the average home that are turned over to the man, for which he needs a preparedness he is not likely to get in a conventional course seeking primarily to prepare girls for household skills.

Housekeeping liabilities. In the conventional thinking about marriage there is very little realization of the liabilities of housekeeping. It is commonly assumed that the only problem is the developing of efficiency in household management on the part of the wife. If we are to improve the quality of home life and men and women are to achieve satisfaction from their domestic experiences, there must be a realization of the ways in which household responsibilities can work against real compatibility. The most obvious hazard is rooted in lack of skill and interest on the part of the wife as she tries to keep house. She needs preparedness, a service that can best be provided by the home economist. In addition to instruction for the preparing of the housewife in high school and college, there is a place for short courses in the various communities. These can best be handled by extension departments of our state universities. It is a mistake to assume that this kind of instruction is seldom needed, though rarely does one find a community in the sad plight described by an eminent sociologist in a public address when he affirmed that he knew well a country community where there was not one efficient cook. No one who has traveled in our rural districts is unaware of the great differences between households in their efficiency, including the preparation of food. In the country the problem is likely to be that of breaking away from traditional practices handed on from one family to another, while in the city there is frequently a lack of any kind of housekeeping experience on the part of the girl who turns from employment to the task of caring for her own home.

There are, however, two other liabilities in housekeeping that are not so generally recognized. One of these is the significance of fatigue. The wife constructs her housekeeping program on the basis of what she thinks is expected of her rather than what she can undertake without creating the possibility of too great fatigue. This does not mean that she is merely concerned with the quantity of tasks she assumes. There are also two other factors that have to be taken into account. These are her attitude toward such work and her sense of monotony. The first aspect decides her reaction to what she does. No matter how skillful she may be, if the work gives her a feeling of futility or frustration, perhaps because she compares the repetitious responsibilities with her former, more stimulating activities in some kind of work before marriage, she will develop more fatigue than one would expect from the work itself.

Without doubt the employment of a multitude of husbands is equally lacking in interest, but even so there is a difference. Fatigue developed outside the home may even enhance the domestic fellowship because through this the husband recuperates after the day's work. Such relief is more difficult for the wife since her relaxation must be largely secured, if at all, within the area where she has gathered her fatigue. It is this situation which frequently explains the wife's desire to go somewhere in the evening while her husband is eager to stay at home. If courses in home economics and lectures by home economists are to accomplish what they should in lessening the fatigue that gathers about housekeeping, there must be conscious recognition of this danger. The standards of household management must not be set up as abstract ideals without regard to the emotional reactions toward household toil characteristic of the individual housekeeper. The tired wife is likely to be a discontented and a disappointing wife. One of the clear consequences of chronic fatigue is a lessening of the sexual impulse and especially of the wholehearted response to intercourse that is desirable for the building of the matrimonial unity. Women are blamed for their loss of sex energy, accused of self-chosen frigidity when they are merely revealing a lack of organic vitality expressed in the fading away of sexual desire. Nervous fatigue is probably basically physical. Just as there are reasons to believe that the husband's competitive pressure decreases sexual desire and potency, so the wife from a different cause of fatigue may likewise suffer. In her case, monotony, a result of the nongregarious character of housework as she labors alone in her kitchen, may create a fatigue factor that lessens the quality of her marriage companionship and, if she has children, of her motherhood also.

The home and the house. It is beginning to be recognized that the family of the future must dwell in a more modern, practical sort of house. The architecture of the past does not provide a functional environment for the modern housekeeper. It is not enough to bring in more of the mechanical aids that applied science has produced to lighten the work of the home. In addition, there is need of structural changes that will make possible the full use of mechanical and electrical devices in a building conceived as a place where with economy of effort the family may carry on in comfort, security, and with satisfaction. It is obvious that there are still standing a multitude of houses that would menace any family that attempted to maintain them with their one-time toil-making demands. These houses were adapted to conditions no longer common—large families, servant help, and fewer out-of-the-home interests. The changed architecture has not as a rule caught up with departures along other lines of construction. It is fair to say that dwellings lag behind other functional architecture and that the influence of tradition in homekeeping is the explanation. Instruction in preparation for homemaking can help create the demand for houses better adapted to present-day family needs and also aid in resisting suggestions coming from commercial advertising that lead the housewife to elaborate her activities until the leisure she could have is lost as she attempts to keep up with what she assumes the Joneses do. She follows household fashions with no idea of keeping entertaining and the like as simple and as nonwasteful of energy as possible. Another example of this wastefulness is found in recipes for cooking leading to difficult, time-consuming dishes that add nothing to diet. The welfare of many families is antagonized by forgetting that the average home needs not only economy in the handling of money but even more economy in household activity.

Unless the future brings a radical departure through the development of co-operative and community enterprises that will take over a considerable share of the tasks now carried on by private housekeeping, it will be a mistake to conceive household efficiency as something comparable to that developed in industry. Some well-trained wives who by disposition like to have things systematic and according to a routine forget the necessity in housekeeping of flexibility and adaptability. Doubtless this is one of the explanations of the frustrations that bring tension and hurt domestic compatibility.[4] Likewise trouble can come from women who are so anxious to be good housekeepers that they allow their ambitions for household efficiency to get in the way of their opportunities as wives. Their eagerness as housekeepers can go so far as to ruin domestic fellowship, forcing both husband and children to go outside the home for comradeship, recreation, and contentment. The unmarried home economics instructor, unexperienced in the everyday, ordinary problems of housewives, can easily so stress routine and system as to breed in some students the disposition to fret when they cannot maintain in their housekeeping the ideals they have made their goal.

Among the many improvements that are desirable in house construction are greater privacy and more flexibility if the family is to have a more functional dwelling place. For financial reasons it does not seem likely that the ideal situation of a room for every member of the family, as William McDougall, the psychologist, once advocated, can be achieved, at least in the near future. There can be, however, a greater degree of privacy, especially in sleeping quarters, through sound-proof construction. The providing of this assurance of quiet and privacy will remove a more common source of household tension than is generally realized. One of the causes of the irritation that so easily develops when in-laws live with their children is the loss of privacy, especially in apartments where the walls transmit sounds as if they were made of cardboard. The restraint that such lack of privacy often places upon the relationship of husband and wife becomes in some cases the starting place for marital incompatibility. Various problems connected with the caring for children, especially in city homes, can be greatly lessened by the greater use in building construction of sound-proof materials. If people become aware of the advantages of such privacy-giving construction, the architect and the con-

---

[4] Myerson, Abraham, *The Nervous Housewife.*

tractor will be forced to provide this better type of family dwelling.

The problem of flexibility is a more difficult one, but it also can be accomplished, except in city dwellings, once the idea is firmly established as a family need. Already arrangement for increasing the size of the house as the family grows has been worked out as one of the possibilities of prefabricated construction. There is need of providing for a family's decreasing the size of its dwelling as well as increasing it. As children come it is desirable for family living that the spatial environment of the home also expand. As children grow up and leave, there is equal need of providing for a decrease. Although this idea of flexibility is far from the thought of most families at present, there is no reason to suppose that it will not make headway once its feasibility becomes well demonstrated. It will then be possible both to buy and sell additions without acquiring or disposing of an entire house. The individual family will be able to organize household life in accord with its needs. At present, we often have congestion because of inadequate space in homes where children have come, and we also later have wasted space which can be a considerable burden for aging family members who have seen their children leave home or who have need of reducing the expense and care of housekeeping because of their age and their lessened income. The only means of providing this economy at present is to move into smaller quarters, even though there may be reasons why the present dwelling would be preferred if only it could be made smaller. The oncoming generation should be conditioned in the schools to a more flexible type of dwelling place for the family.

Housekeeping when the wife works. In a minority of homes no adjustment is more consequential than that which makes possible the wife's working outside the home. The social status of woman which gives her opportunity for such employment is discussed in the sociological approach to the conservation of marriage and the family. Here we are concerned with the effect of the wife's working on homemaking. It is obvious that no woman can carry on two jobs at the same time. The most fortunate arrangement is that which permits her to give part-time to each of the two responsibilities. Industry, however, except when under great pressure as of wartime production, does not offer much opportunity for this arrangement. Since, therefore, the employed wife finds that the hours of work outside the home constitute a full day's job, she must either have the assistance of others, limit the amount of housekeeping she assumes, or surrender the effort to maintain home life. The solution may be having a relative take over or living with some other family or at a hotel, abandoning the attempt to carry on an independent household. More often the woman tries one of the following: Housekeeping is reduced as much as possible by living in an apartment and purchasing food that is either cooked or can be quickly and easily prepared, going out for some meals, sending out the laundry, and perhaps hiring someone who will take over part of the housekeeping. Another program is made possible by the husband sharing in the homekeeping. In this case they both accept responsibility for the limited work necessary to maintain their home. Such an arrangement can be carried out most successfully in the city and in an apartment adapted to limited housekeeping.

There is abundant testimony that any of these programs or, what is frequent, their combination in actual practice proves difficult and often becomes a cause of dissatisfaction even to the point of incompatibility. It is likewise true that such an arrangement frequently is brought to an end if the wife becomes pregnant and a mother. On the other hand, there are numerous marriages that could not take place were there not some opportunity for the wife to work. This is not always because of economic pressure. The career woman many times would refuse to marry were it not possible for her to continue her vocational interests. Many of these women work out a different solution and one that is often satisfactory. A third person takes over the housekeeping. This is not without its problems. Not only is it difficult to get women who are qualified and willing to maintain such a home, but the presence of such a person within the household lessens its privacy and its independence. Even when the woman comes in only for the day she is in some measure a family member and one of considerable importance. This latter fact may become irritating to one or both spouses, especially when in order to keep her and make her satisfied the family program has to be considerably adjusted to her wishes.

It would be a mistake, however, to assume that this situation is always undesired because the conventional independent household is generally regarded as the normal choice for family living. Although this is commonly true, there are wives who prefer to turn over to other women the tasks of the home.

The production of war material during World War II very greatly increased the opportunity for women to work outside their homes in both full and part-time employment. Many homes in which there were young children solved the problems arising from the absence of the mother by some older member of the family taking over the supervision of the children. In a great many instances the children were left to care for themselves, and the consequence of this was an occasional tragedy where there was no child old enough to safeguard the brothers and sisters. Both the Federal government and industry recognized the need of providing through day nurseries for the children of mothers who were drawn into industry. The program of the city of Cleveland for the care of the children of working mothers is representative of these efficient efforts to replace inadequate home supervision or the substandard child-care centers which sprang up in the city with a higher type of emergency child-care centers and foster-family day-care programs. At first financed by parents' fees and contributions from the welfare foundations, the Cleveland Foundation, and various gifts, these centers were finally placed on a more substantial basis by the Cleveland Board of Education, receiving a grant under the Lanham Act from the funds of the Federal Works Agency. At that time there were ten centers; in 1944 there were twenty-nine, and all but two were financed through the assistance of federal funds.[5] They provided eight to ten hours' care a day for preschool children and several hours for children of school age. The centers for preschool children opened at 6:30 A.M. and closed at 7 P.M.; and those for school children were open at lunchtime and after school on school days, all day on Saturdays, and during vacation periods. It was impossible to get helpers who were graduates of qualified nursery school training courses or had equivalent training, but the training program had technical supervision which helped to maintain proper standards. The health program was in the hands of a trained public-health

---

[5] *The Child,* Vol. 8, pp. 167–172.

nurse and the food program was in charge of a professional nutritionist. Foster-family day care was designed to provide daytime supervision for children of working mothers in licensed private homes. In Cleveland these were licensed by the state on recommendation of the Emergency Child Care Office.

It was found in Cleveland that mothers generally preferred group care to a foster-family day-care home. This was because of the lower fee, the better trained supervision, and the more impersonal aspect of the center's service. The parent also was influenced by knowing that many other mothers were placing their children in such a group. It seemed that the foster day care was best adapted for children under two, for families of two children where one was in the preschool center, when the mother worked on an irregular or short schedule, for children who should not be in the group because of some special health or emotional problem, or as a substitute for group care when no center had been established. Foster-family day care was more costly to the parent and less so to the community.

There undoubtedly was more emphasis on the prevention of disease, more thought on the building of the health of the child, including correction of defects, than in most of the homes from which the children came. For example, the cooks and the helpers were given a physical examination, including a chest X ray, and instruction in personal cleanliness in the handling of foods. The Cleveland program did not experiment in the twenty-four-hour care of children of working mothers, believing that the man-power situation did not justify disregarding what was considered the best interests of young children.

An interesting by-product of the day care of children was the development of a counseling service to assist parents in planning a successful family life that would include provision for the health and welfare of the child.[6] This counseling had three main purposes: to help parents decide the wisdom of the mother's employment from the point of view of the welfare of the children and the stability of the home, to furnish information as to the resources available in the community for the care and supervision of children of working mothers with attention to the needs of the individual child and the family situation, and to make available directly or through other agencies advice or

---

[6] *The Child*, Vol. 7, pp. 31–34.

assistance regarding problems of development arising from the working of the mother and her absence from the home.

Organized to meet a war need, this service has proved itself too valuable as an assistance to homes with working mothers not to be continued in our industrial communities. Leadership in this welfare work rightly falls to the social worker with a home economics background in the field of child care.

Division of labor and homemaking. One does not have to look backward any great distance to realize how greatly conditions of modern life have changed the activities of the home. Since this must be a continuing adjustment, those who give instruction in the field of marriage and the family must avoid giving the impression that the security of the family as a social institution depends upon household practices that at the moment happen to be conventional. Recognition of this fact is especially important in any discussion of the role of the man and the woman in homemaking. In common law, whether the woman understood this or not, she assumed by her marriage the responsibility for serving her husband as a housewife. It was embedded in the *consortium* which became the right of the husband and included three elements: service, society, and sexual intercourse, each becoming her obligation to the husband throughout her marriage. Thus at law the wife was assumed to consent to a division of labor which appeared necessary for the stability of family life. This assignment of responsibility to the wife for homekeeping rested not upon special instinctive resourcefulness but upon an arrangement determined by culture and which clearly worked to the advantage of husband and wife.

This division of labor, which is still orthodox, is not at all in accord with conditions in many homes where both husband and wife work outside. Even though, as commonly happens, the wife accepts the greater responsibility for homemaking, it is clearly impossible for her to carry on as does the woman who attempts only to keep house. Although the assignment of home management to the wife continues as the conventional division of labor and her task is assumed to be a full time responsibility, it is apparent that we already have many variations from this arrangement and that the exceptions are likely to increase. We already know that successful home life is maintained even when the wife carries on a career or accepts employment under conditions similar to the husband's. Many marriages in which both husband and wife go out to work remain childless. Sometimes this is due to the desire of husband and wife not to make the wife's employment difficult. Sometimes it is the childlessness that explains the desire of the wife to carry on out-of-the-home employment. It is not uncommon for the wife to work until the child comes and then to devote her entire time to homemaking. We have, however, career women and employed women, especially widows, who find a way to provide home life for their children even though they are limited in the time they can give to housekeeping responsibilities. Their success demonstrates the need of recognizing the difference between homemaking and housekeeping. If courses attempting to foster home life are to reflect changing social conditions, some attention must be given to the problems of those who marry and attempt a limited type of housekeeping or even homemaking.

Although such a situation may concern in later life only a minority, even a small number of the pupils, instruction of a general character in preparation for marriage and parenthood should give attention to the problems of those who do attempt to maintain a limited type of family life. It is an advantage to the teacher also to keep in mind the need of these students, since it lessens the danger of the instruction appearing to take for granted a standardized type of family experience. One thing is certain, social changes in the future will affect home life, and any preparation for marriage and the family should encourage flexibility for those who must adjust to various individual circumstances. The class discussion can be used to make two important contributions. One is an awareness on the part of the student of the resources now available for the simplifying of housekeeping. Since housework is not in the obvious way a competitive enterprise, there is a natural tendency for many housewives to place their activities on a stereotyped, routine basis and not to be alert in discovering new methods made possible by improvements and inventions. If the habit of looking for advances in equipment and techniques can be established, it will measurably help those who later must somehow organize homekeeping in such a way as to make it possible for them to carry on outside the home.

It is important also in this preparatory instruction to create the willingness to accept departures from orthodox homemaking when this needs to be done and to change without frustration. Contemporary housekeeping practices must not be so idealized as to give the student the coercive suggestion that the family can be strengthened by attempts to discourage variations from the wife's full-time commitment to the home, because this concentration on homemaking is generally held to be more desirable. The woman who works outside accepts a considerable burden at best, and this can become too heavy and prove a cause of tension if she becomes dissatisfied because she is unable to develop the kind of homemaking that would be her preference. It is not the business of the instructor to become the advocate of the type of homekeeping that she has found most satisfactory for herself.

The situation of children in these unorthodox homes is individual and factual, not to be defined by *a priori* assumptions. It is true that the occupation of the mother may limit her relationship with the child and the latter may suffer loss. Whether this is true will depend upon the actual circumstances, the quality as well as the quantity of comradeship that is maintained by the mother and the child. There may be a slight advantage if the mother's concentration is on housework rather than work outside the home, but only because her presence gives the child a greater sense of security and in cases of emergency the needful attention. If the mother is engrossed in housework the possibility of her neglecting the child is at times as great as if she worked elsewhere. Frequently the housekeeping functions of the mother intrude upon her parenthood services in the same way that this can occur if she works outside the home. The latter type of employment may, as a rule, provide greater difficulties, but even so the significance of the parent-child relationship will be determined by the comradeship that actually develops between them. The habit in the past among the aristocratic classes of England of sending their boy at an early age to what we know as a private school and, in considerable measure, the girl also, although this lessened the amount of fellowship between parent and child, has not given evidence of weakening family ties.

It certainly would be unfortunate if instruction in prepara-

tion for marriage and the family led the student to feel that
inability to maintain the conventional type of housekeeping
makes childlessness, so long as the program lasts, a moral obligation. It would be cruel for instance for a woman left a widow
with children and forced to accept employment outside the
home for their support to feel at a later time that she necessarily neglected them or prevented them from having conditions adequate for normal growth. The experiences of many
such families prove that this cannot be assumed. It would also
be unfortunate to give the girl in her formative years the feeling that the limited type of home is so hazardous that if she
becomes a widow she is led into remarrying merely because this
permits her to stay at home with the children when otherwise
she would have to go out to work. The step-child relationship
also has its hazards, and the widow who feels that above all else
she must remain a housekeeper for the sake of her children may
contract a marriage undesirable for her children because of this
mistaken idea that she cannot be just to the children if she
works away from home.

New discoveries, inventions, and processes, such as the
quick freezing of foods, are changing housekeeping, and these
ever increasing aids and advantages must be kept in mind in
any discussion of the homemaking problems of the wife who
enters outside employment. These resources and the shrinking
of the working day will surely lessen the difficulties experienced
by the employed woman who in the past has attempted to maintain a home. Her housekeeping may have to be modified somewhat in order to adjust to her working, but it may not remain
the exacting, frustrating task it has been in the past for many
such women.

Nutrition.   No part of a course in preparation for homekeeping is more important than that concerned with nutrition.
The American people maintain one of the most expensive of
dietary standards, but this does not mean that all families are
well nourished. Although our country produces the greatest
variety and quantity of wholesome foods yet achieved, there
have been in recent years spectacular statements concerning the
number of Americans who suffer from malnutrition. It has
been asserted, for example, that one-third of our population do
not have food adequate to maintain good health, that less than

one-fourth get a good diet.[7] Various surveys of the diet of individual families have been made and, although these indicate a real need of improving food habits, the nature of the data, its subjective elements, as well as the complexity of the nutritional problem itself, leads to caution in generalizations that attempt to measure the quantity of malnutrition. There is, however, general agreement among students of food problems that irrespective of economic conditions many of our families are not properly nourished. Lack of knowledge, food prejudices, bad dietary habits, and unwillingness to accept new foods are the chief causes of this. It is apparent that these causes of malnutrition can best be eliminated by instruction accompanied by opportunity for new experiences in forming food habits, and that this is likely to be most effective when given to children and youth.

A study which reports the popular knowledge of nutrition in a highly favorable group demonstrates the value of an intellectual background. In this survey the nutritionists, dieticians, and home economists usually had an excellent score of 90–100; doctors and some homemakers, 80–89; dentists followed closely; college students ranged from fair, 60–71, to good, 72–79; clerks, stenographers, unskilled laborers, and high school students made a poor showing, grading below 60 to fair. It was surprising to find that the adults who had had no formal nutrition training but had talked, read, and heard lectures on the subject of nutrition were almost as well informed as college students who had taken courses in nutrition. Five per cent of the persons who scored below 70 were considered not well enough informed on nutrition to make a wise choice of food.[8] The self-chosen diet in a co-operative dormitory of girls at the University of Nebraska reveals clearly the influence of their instruction in nutrition.[9] Although these students were limited in both time and money, they planned and prepared a far more adequate diet than we have reason to suppose is the national average.

---

[7] Carlson, A. J., "Food and Fitness," *Scientific Monthly*, Vol. 55, p. 403.

[8] Kilander, H. F., "The Public's Knowledge of Nutrition," *Journal of Home Economics*, Vol. 36, pp. 78–79.

[9] McMillan, Thelma, and Leverton, Ruth, "The Self-Chosen Diets of College Girls in a Co-operative Dormitory," *Journal of Home Economics*, Vol. 35, pp. 514–518.

Various studies of income reveal that there are a considerable portion of our families that do not earn enough to make an adequate diet possible for their members. Obviously, solution can come only from increasing income or decreasing the cost of food or both.[10] However, even in this group it has been found that a few families, despite the very little money they have to spend for food, do manage to maintain good, low-cost diets.[11] On the other hand, a surprising number of families on higher economic levels fail to provide adequate diet for their members.

Nutrition includes more than merely providing the proper food substances. There is always the problem of preparation, and certainly one of the retardations of American households appears in unskillful cooking. Possibly an even greater inefficiency is disclosed by the low standards of commercial cooking. Any traveler or any individual who frequently eats away from home discovers that often, even when good food material has been selected, it has been made indigestible or robbed of nutritive value by bad cooking. There are, of course, in our cities striking exceptions, for there are organizations functioning on a large scale which furnish excellent food, well cooked and at reasonable prices. In the smaller cities such establishments are more difficult to find, and the average hotel or restaurant catering to the public is notoriously indifferent to the art of cooking.

When one remembers how large a proportion of single men and women must eat at commercial boarding houses, restaurants, and hotels, the significance of faulty cooking for health and efficiency becomes apparent.

There is special need of providing instruction in cooking for inexperienced housewives. Few communities at present would fail to profit in their family life if opportunity were provided for attendance at cooking schools publicly maintained as a part of adult education. The time may come, and more quickly than anyone now anticipates, when most of our food will be commercially prepared and need no home cooking. It may be that private preparation of meals in individual homes

[10] Hambidge, Gove, "Nutrition as a National Problem," *Journal of Home Economics,* Vol. 31, p. 361.

[11] *Ibid.,* p. 364.

will prove uneconomical and will be largely a luxury occasionally enjoyed rather than, as at present, the usual practice. Even under such circumstances, there will be need of greater knowledge of food values, of the wise combining of food elements, and of the art of serving food than is generally possessed at present. Meanwhile, improvement in cooking is a sure way of advancing family happiness and household efficiency. Present standards are wasteful as well as lagging behind most of the household practices that have significance for health.

Malnutrition. Malnutrition is included in the problem of diet but does not, in so far as it is organic in character, concern this discussion. It falls within the field of medicine. The home economist is interested in the discussion of food as it influences nutrition. The body is not, however, merely a receptacle for nutritive material but an organism that carries on a physiological process which when it works badly or imperfectly may bring about malnutrition in spite of the wholesome quality and abundance of the food. It is important, however, to remember that this malfunctioning of the body itself may be the consequence of previous inadequate nourishment. This fact was strikingly emphasized by many who because of the lack of adequate food were in a condition of starvation when the Allies rescued these victims from the German concentration camps in World War II. It was found impossible to feed them properly because the body as a consequence of starvation had lost its power to make use of food. Material injected into the body had to precede the attempt to feed these starved men and women in the normal manner. The home economist recognizes the medical aspects of malnutrition as something outside her province. She also understands that many diseases either originate from an inadequate food intake or are reinforced by insufficient nutrition.

The instruction in nutrition can become a later handicap if the course is taught in the spirit of dogmatic finality. The great variation in diet among the various nations, and to a lesser extent between classes, makes it apparent that people maintain health and efficiency on dietary programs very different from what is customary in this country. The progress that is made in the science of nutrition likewise suggests the need of caution in advocating standards. The senior author recalls not many years ago, before vitamins were discovered, being unable to convince a well-trained home economist that there could be other food values than minerals not measured in calories in spite of the fact that as far back as the childhood of both disputants cod-liver oil had proven itself on an empirical basis to have food property of special value.[12] It is to be expected, especially in the light of the rapid advance in our knowledge of vitamins, that many changes will occur in the science of nutrition and that we are in no position to presume that the diet proper for humans can ever be unchangeably standardized. Instead, the instruction should leave the student with the impression that new dietary facts will be discovered leading even to radical changes from our present knowledge of nutrition.

One of the most important contributions that comes from the discussion of nutrition is the building in the student of a proper attitude toward food. As she supplies the family diet the housewife may be hampered by her food prejudices and those of other members of her household. Those who have been brought up on a low standard of living and have been accustomed to a small choice in their diet are especially liable to aversions which may not only be uneconomical but deny to them as adults a well-balanced food program. Essential food elements may be deficient or absent, lessening vigor both physically and mentally and even predisposing to disease. Care must be taken in interpreting such problems in class discussion not to create in a child disrespect of parental judgment, but nevertheless it becomes an important function of such teaching to release him as much as possible from such prejudices, making him willing to cultivate a taste for new kinds of food. Physiological idiosyncrasies, that is, allergies, have to be recognized. That matter taken care of, the instructor is concerned not only with creating an open mind toward unfamiliar foods but also toward changes in eating habits. Here the task is psychological and has to do with an aspect of human nature that is especially open to the developing of emotional attitudes. The problem is essentially the reconstruction of mental habits, and this fre-

---

[12] For an early eighteenth century illustration of the magic power of fruits, "particularly those of acid kind," to save men dying of scurvy, see Lord Anson's *Voyage round the World,* Everyman's Edition, p. 282.

quently requires insight and skill in dissolving indirectly what often cannot be changed by direct attack.[13]

In this reconstruction of food prejudices and preferences, the instructor finds commercial advertising both an ally and an opponent. On the whole, the suggestions from this source tend to break down tradition and to widen food choices. This does not mean, however, that the changes always indicate better dietary discrimination. It may work the other way, as, for example, when money that should go into the budget for the purchasing of food is drained away in the buying of needless or at least relatively expensive vitamin pills. Frequently those who buy them do not need them and those who need them cannot afford them. Advertising has made the general public conscious of the value of vitamins. It has not, however, stressed the fact that the best source of these essential elements is to be found in foods and not in synthetic drugs.

From time to time there have developed in this country food fads that obtained a considerable following and then after a brief period faded away. They have not been as common as the popularity of well-advertised patent medicines, but they have had a similar vogue. Occasionally they have come from a pioneering effort based upon what has been demonstrated later to be sound dietary principles, but as a rule they are the product of such motives as the desire to be different for purposes of prestige or to exploit human gullibility for profit. Even when they are in accord with some finding of science, they sometimes have been so exaggerated as to throw the food program out of balance. Once in a while they result from lack of discrimination in reading some popular article on diet. They illustrate how easily emotional attitudes can get tied up with appetite, and they stress the need of good judgment in interpreting dietary principles. Even the zeal of an instructor in home economics can be excessive in advocating some particular type of food, however wholesome it may be. For example, recently such a teacher, who constantly was stressing the value of milk until it seemed the one indispensable food element, appeared astonished in a discussion with a medical specialist when she found it impossible to get him to agree with the exaggeration that

---

[13] Selling, Lowell, and Ferraro, Mary, *The Psychology of Diet and Nutrition*, p. 16.

had become the cornerstone of her thinking. The emotional conditioning of appetite, particularly when expressed in the aggressiveness that characterizes food fads, may come from underground motivations that can only be brought into the open by psychoanalysis. Originating in some personal experience, they may be implanted in others through suggestion.

The teacher attempting to interpret the science of nutrition so as to affect in a practical way the eating habits of her class has to keep in mind that not only may she encounter opposition based upon tradition or fashion but also a suspicion that comes from her hearers considering that she herself is a faddist. The psychological basis for food fads explains why so often peculiar religious or social communal groups adopt nonorthodox food programs. These departures from contemporary foods were at times closer to our present nutritional knowledge than were contemporary practices. An example of this was the Shakers' emphasis upon vegetables and fruits. Their placing meat-eaters at a table of their own also illustrates the exaggeration that is so apt to happen when food gets tied up with religious or social crusades.[14]

Food consciousness. So far as nutrition is concerned, the most important contribution that the home economist can make through this general preparatory instruction is to develop a realization of the importance of nutrition and the need of adapting the diet to the special problems of individuals when they arise. This means not only a recognition of the many ways in which good nutrition affects physical, mental, and social welfare but also the necessity of its being adapted to particular body needs when they arise. There are four of these special conditions that deserve emphasis.

One is infant feeding. Here perhaps the greatest dietary progress has occurred. This is because the physician has been forced to give attention to the feeding of infants because diet at this period has so clearly affected survival and health.[15] The fact that so many children have been born in hospitals in recent years and the mother has been taught while there how to feed her infant properly has undoubtedly contributed greatly to the advance that has been made. The advantage of breast feeding

[14] Melcher, M. F., *The Shaker Adventure,* p. 152.
[15] Duffus, R. L., and Holt, L. Emmett, Jr., *L. Emmett Holt,* Ch. 14.

has rightly been emphasized, not only on account of the quality of the mother's milk and the protection it provides for a brief period from some childhood diseases, but also because of the emotional by-products of nursing as experienced by both mother and child.[16] However, it is well recognized by pediatricians that although as a general rule it is best for the mother to nurse the child the decision as to how the baby is to be fed is an individual one and has to be made in the light of all the circumstances concerned. No dietary change has in this country been so radical as that which has occurred in the feeding of infants.

The second special dietary need appears in the feeding of the growing child. Here also much has been accomplished, and at present it seems safe to say that the average American child is better fed than has ever previously been true. This is a time when not only is guidance required in the choice of foods but also in the establishing of good feeding habits. The family program, that is, the practices of other members of the family, undoubtedly has more influence in establishing these habits than anything the parents can say. It is the time when the child needs to be introduced to a variety of wholesome foods and as far as possible to escape prejudices in food selection.

Another period where at present neither science nor practice has yet accomplished very much in dietary reform is the feeding of the aged.[17] The problem here is complicated by the fact that the older person is frequently hostile to change and, unlike the infant and the child, has confirmed food habits and usually the will to express his preferences. Even if in his earlier life he has followed a good food program, body changes now require some alteration in his diet. Unless this can be brought about with the consent or, better still, the co-operation of the aging person, emotional problems may be created that are even greater in their harmful consequences than the following of the previous eating habits. If preparation for this recognizing of the peculiar dietary needs of the aged can be established in early years, when what can be rightly called the "food philosophy" is developing, the task of feeding aged persons could be

---

16 Selling, Lowell, and Ferraro, Mary, *op. cit.*, p. 57.
17 Cowdry, E. V., *Problems of Aging*, pp. 875–877.

measurably lessened. In any case, the student should be made
aware of the special difficulties he may face when he assumes
responsibility for the care of some aged person. Meanwhile, it
is to be expected that science will make considerable headway
in discovering just what foods the aged person requires both
for health and for emotional well-being.[18]

Another situation that is generally well handled concerns
the feeding of the sick. As a rule, during the critical period of
illness the nutritional problem is in the hands of the physician.
In the case of chronic or long-continued diseases, diabetes
being an example of one and tuberculosis of the other, the
dietary program is likewise determined by the physician. When
one looks back to the starvation regime once followed in
typhoid fever or the earlier time when the sick person was
forbidden water, both within the life span of the older readers
of this book, it is apparent that great progress has been made in
the nutrition of the sick person. Our knowledge of vitamins has
immensely added to the resources possessed by the physician
and the nutritionist as they seek to bring the ill back to health.
In many respects revolutionary changes have occurred as a result of laboratory studies and better-controlled experiments in
the effort to discover the relationships between food and various
pathological conditions. Naturally, much of this new insight has
been made a part of the preventive program and dietary control has been made one way of lessening disease. Science has
demonstrated the great complexity of nutrition and the very
great role food plays in the maintenance of body health.

Food incompatibility. Among the various causes and expressions of family incompatibility must be included food conflicts. Occasionally, cultural or childhood food habits become
a source of friction between husband and wife or between
spouse and in-law. Moreover, tension along other lines spreads
over into food preferences, bringing an emotional collision.
The attempt to determine the dietary program may be part
of a persistent struggle for dominance. Dissatisfaction with the
marriage also may lead the wife to attempt to punish the husband by forcing upon him food he does not like or denying
him what he prefers. The wife's confidence that she has better

---

[18] Tuohy, Edward L., "Nutrition for the Aging," *Journal of Home Economics*,
Vol. 37, pp. 260–262.

judgment concerning food may lead her to forget the necessity
of getting his co-operation in the effort to improve the family
diet. She may in good faith fail to realize the strength of his
food prejudices and ignore the psychological problems that his
former food habits may present as she tries to follow good
nutritional principles.

Here, as in other relationships, frequently there is compromise when food contention arises. It is not enough for the
wife to be right; she must also obtain the approval of her
husband if the nutritional program is to succeed. Trouble may
come to her as she attempts to improve the family diet merely
because she seeks to accomplish too much too quickly. Her
problem may be a campaign that cannot be won unless headway is made slowly and the husband becomes gradually adjusted to food choices contrary to his former experience. Sometimes it is the wife who resists the husband's desire for nutritional reform. If she is the cook, she may defeat his purpose
by her failure to prepare properly the food and this can be
an unconscious motivation. Chronic hostility finds in this part
of the housewife's functioning an enticing opportunity to inflict punishment, especially if she cooks different dishes for
herself or depends largely on what she eats between meals for
the satisfaction of her appetite. In like manner, the excellent,
thoughtful cook can lessen the husband's tension along other
lines by the satisfying meals she furnishes him.

The most successful family dietary program will be democratic, respecting the special likes and dislikes of all the members while at the same time buying food in accord with the
available budget and established principles of nutrition. The
authoritative family impressively reveals itself at the dinner
table. Some years ago the author had a vivid illustration of this
when he was a guest in a household where even the older
children had to ask their father to give them such items as
butter which were carefully measured out with no regard for
the child's desire but only the father's notion as to what and
how much they should eat. Since these were children in the
later teens, it was clear that masculine dominance went so far
as to control not the choice of food but its distribution. There
was no economic problem involved; it was merely another
exhibition of the father's authority so firmly established that

it was taken as a matter of course even in the presence of guests.

Education of the consumer. Any unbiased study of the food habits of the American people shows clearly the great need of educating the consumer. Much has been accomplished in recent years, and in bringing this about no one has been more useful than the home economics teacher in the field of nutrition. Here, however, as is true in every field of applied science as it concerns the welfare of people, knowledge has outrun its distribution. The teacher of a general course in preparation for family life has an unexcelled opportunity to help this information gathered by the scientists to reach families that specially need it. The medium through which this is accomplished is often the child. Experienced home economists, however, realize the dangers that can come from the child who on account of his classroom instruction becomes an aggressive reformer determined to change the food pattern of his parents. A safer line of approach is through the mothers, using the instruction given the children as a means of reinforcing what is also said to or demonstrated for the mothers. Indirect suggestion based upon illustrative material is a better strategy than a frontal attack on food habits that the specialist knows are contrary to the science of nutrition.

It is important for the teacher, in whatever way she operates in contact with the homes that need her service, to keep in mind the separation that so often exists between her and those she is trying to influence. If she is a college graduate with special training, this not only removes her from the average housewife but also occasionally leads to impatience on one side and deep-seated prejudice on the other. Perhaps there is nothing carried on in the household that is so emotionally rooted as food habits. Anything that seems to be criticism of family practices, especially if it comes from one who is looked upon with resentment or suspicion, easily arouses hostility. Self pride is involved and tactless attempts to change dietary programs may fail because the teacher does not realize this feeling of distance. She stirs up emotional opposition, making reform needlessly difficult. If the food choices are a part of a clinging to an old-world culture by immigrants who are trying to salvage as much as possible of their family patterns the opportunity for resentment is great. Nevertheless these natural human reactions can be greatly exaggerated. Not only do we know that food habits can be changed, but we have constant evidence of the progress that is being made in dietary reform. This attempt to reach into the homes and influence housewives is shared by the home economist and those skillful in the suggestions of commercial advertising.

The effort to influence household consumers by means of advertising can be both indicted for its detrimental suggestions and praised for contributing to higher standards in the purchasing of food. Therefore, in education for housekeeping, the instructor wishes to establish the basis for discriminating judgment. The intelligent consumer resists misleading advertising and can, as a rule, detect this type of exploitation. Great progress has been made since the beginning of the century through federal and state legislation in protecting the consumer. The Pure Food and Drug Act which prohibited the sale of foods or drugs unfit for human consumption was passed in 1906. Preceding its passage there had been for nearly a quarter of a century a continuous battle to win the support of the public in the passage of such legislation. Foods injurious to the consumer were being sold for profit by various commercial organizations that sought to protect their financial interests. This struggle was only a prelude to what occurred as soon as the bill was signed by President Theodore Roosevelt and responsibility for its enforcement placed in the Bureau of Chemistry under Harvey W. Wiley.[19] We now have considerable legislation, both federal and state, which outlaws injurious foods and drugs and, in the case of the latter, forbids the sale without a physician's prescription of certain drugs which are useful when rightly administered but potentially harmful when indiscriminately used. In addition, there are many regulations authorized by federal, state, and municipal bureaus that attempt to help the consumer by establishing grades of quality not only of food but of clothing. The administering of these laws and regulations is a sizable problem, and there is constant need of an alert public opinion as consumers' and commercial interests collide.

Efforts to protect the consumer must in order to succeed rest upon factual information. It is, therefore, most important

---

[19] Wiley, Harvey W., *An Autobiography*, Ch. 19.

that students in a general course attempting preparedness for household life become familiar with the various agencies that carry on such investigations. Some of these are chiefly concerned with seeing that quality is maintained. Others take over what can be thought of as the strategical investigation as compared with the tactical already mentioned. Knowledge, especially concerning newly introduced foods and drugs, must be gathered by investigation in order that the laws and regulations be adapted to changing circumstances. In addition to this there has to be the popularizing of new foods and new knowledge of nutrition and the introducing of the former to the public. To a great extent this is accomplished by bulletins issued by various departments—federal, state, and municipal—and by magazine articles and newspaper statements. A different means of bringing to the consumer information that will protect his interests is carried on by various organizations such as The Consumers' Research and The Consumers' Union.

The family planning for itself.   No successful program for family advancement can be built on the notion that something needs to be done for the home, for success can be had only to the degree that there is as a part of any social effort a quickening of family function. This has been demonstrated through the evolution of economic relief culminating in the family welfare society. Little can be done for the family that remains an impassive recipient of outside assistance. In order to obtain the co-operation of the home, it has been found that some sort of educational service must go along with any form of poor relief. This principle must be recognized in any attempt to construct a program of family conservation. It is interesting to notice that in so favored a group as was that studied by Ruth Lindquist, all having had several home economics courses in colleges, there was a keen sense of the need of further training along the lines of both homekeeping and child training.[20]

An important item in the contribution of the family itself is the budget. The idea of providing for family expenditures by budgeting developed in the last quarter of the nineteenth century. In recent years much thought has been given to budget making. Minimum budgets have been constructed for the guidance of relief agencies, and analyses have been made of the

---

[20] *The Family in the Present Social Order*, Ch. 6.

proportion of expenditures that should be assigned to food, rent, clothing, education, recreation, savings, and other items by families that, although capable of self-support, need assistance in their spending.

It has come to be recognized that every budget needs to be an interpretation of the situation of an individual family and must have regard to the changing circumstances within the home itself as well as those likely to come about in the external circumstances that influence the family income. The growing up of children, their need of education, the lessening or increasing of the earnings of the head of the family as time passes, the probability of retirement, and the like are examples of the first. Conditions of employment prove for most families a significant illustration of the second. Community facilities for the education of children, ranging from the nursery school to college and the efficiency and completeness of public health work are additional examples of environmental circumstances that have major importance for the intelligent family that attempts to plan a budget not only to meet its expenses but also to furnish an economic strategy for successful home life.

Not only is the budget an efficient method of planning expenditures; it becomes also a practical education in finances and in discrimination, separating imperative needs from the unimportant, and genuine values from the fictitious. The household budget brings together not only the facts necessary for the distribution of income at any definite time but also utilizes past experiences and leads to the consideration of possible emergencies likely to occur in the future. The effort to manage household money with intelligence gives a higher purpose to family expenditures than when there is merely the attempt to pay out of the income debts that have been incurred; and as the second, irresponsible scheme tends to cause tension between the various members of the household as a result of independent expenditures, the first plan strengthens the unity of the family, because the spending is looked at from the point of view of the whole family and becomes an organized cooperative form of family relationship.[21]

Buying.   It is obvious that efficiency in buying is required to carry out successfully any budget. This presents a problem

---

[21] Bigelow, Howard F., *Family Finance*, Ch. 14.

more difficult than appears on the surface. In order to purchase with discrimination, there must not only be a standardizing of goods but also a realization of the household needs. Since there is a persistent, skillful, and elaborate propaganda in the form of advertising for the purpose of stimulating desire and encouraging expenditures beyond actual necessities, and since industry depends to a great extent upon this artificially stimulated buying, widespread conservatism in purchasing restricts the market, and unemployment follows. Thus a wider use of intelligence in budgeting will require readjustment in business so that it will cater to the needs of discriminating customers rather than to those largely at the mercy of the suggestions of advertisers. This is so true that in America buying on installments, which permits purchasing in anticipation of future earnings, has become an essential feature of our economic life, but installment buying was carried to unreasonable extremes before the depression of 1929 and helped to precipitate the break. It had again reached a large volume but was reduced during World War II by specific restrictions under the price control program.

In the recent industrial development in the United States, the consumer has undoubtedly been relatively neglected. Much attention has been given to the building of a selling technique, which functions to encourage uncritical buying. As B. R. Andrews states, "the business world deals too much in opiates for the consumer. The retail buyer needs to keep awake and not allow himself to be exploited by pressure to buy generally." [22]

The lessening of excessive unsatisfying purchasing in the individual family acts, of course, to increase the funds for essentials, but widespread success along this line would mean at present the changing of the market upon which our manufacturing depends. From the point of view of the family, it is desirable that the effectiveness of high-pressure salesmanship be lessened, if not eliminated, and that there be a popularizing of trustworthy information regarding the value of standardized products offered for sale, similar to that which on a small scale is now performed by the consumers' information services.

Consumers' information services provide valuable help for

---

[22] *The Annals of the American Academy of Political and Social Science,* Vol. 143, p. 43. Quoted by permission.

those who do the purchasing for individual families. These organizations seek through investigation to determine the comparative value of standardized food products, textiles, and other articles put on the market for the consuming public. Since they are free from any commercial ties with the producers and manufacturers and have no other motive than the gathering of the facts that concern consumers, their usefulness is increasingly recognized. They gather the information that the homekeeper needs but cannot obtain from personal investigation, since this involves accurate, scientific testing, experiment, and research. Thus the individual family is furnished guidance in buying somewhat similar to that which large corporations maintain for the purchasing of their materials. The consumers' information tests are as objective as possible, but their findings cannot always remove from the consumer the influence of habit and personal preference, especially when there is slight difference of value found between two articles that compete with one another. It is also true that no organization of this sort can keep up with the demands for information from consumers when so many different articles are involved. Likewise the consumers' information devices cannot interpret conditions in the local market of the purchaser.

The progress that has already occurred in the protecting of the consumer justifies the confidence that the gathering of substantial knowledge, the enactment of desirable legislation, and the administration of laws and regulations will continue to advance and increasingly safeguard the consuming public. It is most important that the significance of this be realized by American youth who when they become family members will be alert in supporting the investigators and the public officials whose responsibility it is to lift the consuming standards of American households.[23] No one can do more to accomplish this than the home economist if only she has the opportunity.

Co-operative resources. In the economic activities of the family there is the same need of better co-operative organization that is so clearly true in the field of medicine. More at present is demanded than a reorganization of household activities. The individual family must be reinforced by community resources. We have already discovered the value of the visiting

---

[23] Bigelow, Howard F., *op. cit.,* p. 133.

housekeeper and the visiting nurse, but the first of these operates as yet chiefly in our cities. These two social workers have not only come to the rescue of families in desperate need of service; they have educated their clientele to higher standards of household efficiency. There is need of similar help for mothers who have the responsibility of caring for an infant. All three of these forms of assistance are greatly needed in the average American community.

There seems also to be a place for a different kind of service which can best be described perhaps as that of the household counselor. American sentiment shies away from any idea of inspection, and without a considerable change in our culture there will be unwillingness to accept this in any form of supervision, as a few critics of family management have recommended. On the other hand, there is some recognition of the advantage of an opportunity to talk over family and household problems with a specialist, and if such counseling were offered there would probably be from the beginning, at least in certain city homes, a disposition to make use of this service even by those who would resent the notion of standardization or inspection. Already in some of our larger cities the expert's advice is procurable for parents with problems or for persons facing marital difficulty. The economic and managerial problems would profit from a similar use of expert guidance. Especially would this be helpful in the early years of marriage and parenthood. The giving of counsel for food and clothing programs was carried on during the war and has again appeared in the programs of the experimental family consultation services.

The recreational and artistic interests of the family open up an immense opportunity for community co-operation. Facilities for recreational pleasure, for art appreciation and expression, can be provided under modern circumstances only in a meager form by the individual family. Experience proves that commercial enterprise cannot be expected to offer along these lines all that the family requires for its best development. The Little Theater movement is an illustration of the advantage of a noncommercial co-operative provision for the making up of the deficiencies of the profit-seeking organizations. Even when the latter maintain high standards they require for a complete program some supplementary activity. The old singing school is an illustration of the way in which such a problem was successfully met in former days. The church socials afforded at a later time a different type of group recreation. There is great need of a new emphasis on co-operative art and recreation.

The park, chiefly in cities but also in the country in the case of the national and state mountain and forest park reservations, has become one of our successful pleasure-giving resources. There is much too great a tendency in the average community to depend upon the radio and the movies for entertainment and for art. The economic conservation of the family provides in the United States an almost virgin field for community co-operation. Recreation is a good starting point for this learning through experience of the advantages of neighborhood and community co-operation as a means of providing opportunities beyond the possibility of the average individual family.

Chapter 24

THE EDUCATIONAL APPROACH

FOREWORD. The student will notice that although this chapter is concerned with preparation for family life through an educational program its point of view and emphasis are different from the preceding discussion which so largely fell within the area of the science of home economics. That chapter dealt with household activities and the various skills that contribute to the family maintenance, with stress upon economic interests. Here, the student's attention is turned toward the value of the various kinds of instruction carried on in different age periods by our most important educational agencies for the purpose of preparing parents or children to gain the values of their intimate personal relationships. The chapter discusses the development of this sort of instruction, its potential contributions to family living, and the different kinds of programs that have been taken over by the agencies that have accepted responsibility for their role in the conserving of marriage and the family.

On the college level, the development of this particular approach to the conservation of marriage and the family has been largely due to the demands of students themselves. Especially has this been true of education for marriage, the need of which the students have felt more than that of courses directed toward the more inclusive interests of family life. The insistence of students that a university could not properly say that it prepared for life if it neglected instruction for marriage led to the giving of the first college-credit course in the field of marriage. The same pressure from students explains the introduction of this type of instruction in the curricula of a great

many American colleges and universities. These students also
have well-defined ideas of the kind of instruction that should
be provided. They have always wanted instruction that
grapples with the problems of marriage sincerely and practically and thereby accepts as its purpose the contributing of
insight that can help individuals to meet the adjustments and
achieve the values of marriage. Nothing in the college curriculum has so definitely originated from the desires of students
or has been organized so largely in response to their demands
as the courses in preparation for marriage now fortunately
commonly offered by American colleges and universities.

Value of general education for marriage and family life.
Education must always have a large place in any practical effort
to conserve family life. Even in the simplest societies of primitive people we find informal methods of instruction, enforced
by custom and tradition, that are directed toward the establishment and maintenance of stable family life. The United States
depends for its social security mostly upon education, and few
will question the value of universal public education as an
influence affecting the standards and satisfactions of family
experience. Any form of effective training as it operates in the
formative years contributes to general intelligence and indirectly concerns the family. Social conditions, however, are
demonstrating the need of more specific education, a definite
preparation for marriage and parenthood. Pressure coming
from changes in American civilization, already discussed in an
earlier part of this book, are leading to the development of
instruction along two different but allied lines. The first to
appear, and the one that has at present most attention, is directed toward giving to all parents a better use of the resources
science is contributing for child nurture. A second trend is
development of instruction that chiefly concerns adjustment
within the family. As the psychologists and psychiatrists have
chiefly contributed to the first, the sociologists have had most to
do with the second.

Each of these potential contributions of marriage and the
family is promoted by intelligent preparedness best brought
about by education. The confidence of the American people in
their ability to maintain their way of life and to improve their
choice of a social order rests primarily on their faith in educa-

tion. Criticized as the schools and colleges constantly are for faulty performance, even these attacks assume the premise that education is our most powerful social resource for security and improvement. It is therefore strange reasoning that insists that our most effective means of cultural protection and enrichment cannot include marriage and the family in its program. This skepticism comes largely from two sources: one, the newness of such instruction, at least in any formal, systematic presentation; and two, the resistance of some of the teachers and administrators who have committed themselves to longer established lines of teaching. This opposition, indifference, or doubt, as education for family life seeks to find a chance to function in the educational program, is nothing new. It indicates institutional lag and has appeared with every important innovation that has been made in American education.

The more fundamental skepticism regarding education for marriage and the family is expressed by those who consider the problems that appear in marriage and the family exclusively moral. They explain the maladjustments as the results of blameful personality faults that must have some other solution than education. They disregard the accumulation of insight gathered by science that discloses the significance of early conditioning, and the operation of causal influences that create the difficulties appear to them as moral flaws for which the individuals responsible deserve censure. The end results of wrong training issue into habits and attitudes that do violate moral character, but their prevention rather than the distribution of blame is the only constructive method of dealing with them. Intellectual training alone cannot assure the wholesomeness of personality that successful marriage and home life demand, but it is an effective instrument and one that can be directed by society. The more spiritual qualities that are likewise required in achieving desirable family life demand more than instruction, but they are furthered and not antagonized by teaching that is both inspirational and scientific, as courses in preparation for marriage have to be to fulfill their purpose.

Then there are those who insist that since the past required no education for the family there is no need of such an innovation. Instead of seeing the advantage both to the home and to the school of a co-operative training program, they would place upon parents the entire responsibility for preparation for marriage and the family, ignoring the fact that the majority of the homes have neither the inclination, the resources, nor the insight required. They forget that the better training of the present generation of youth is the most effective method of improving the training of future homes. It is the authors' personal experience that the parents who have done most to prepare their children for marriage and parenthood, especially physicians, psychologists, and the like, are eager to have their foundation work reinforced by college instruction. They recognize that the adolescent is likely to seek some of the information he needs to carry on as husband or wife from some less personal source than his own parents. The high school and college courses provide opportunity for him to gather what he seeks from understanding and trustworthy persons.

The decrease in family functions once monopolized by the home and now to a considerable degree transferred to other agencies as a result of conditions of modern life has been discussed in a preceding chapter. One result has been greater emphasis on the values that come out of the fellowship of husband and wife and parent and child. This aspect of the home, once minor, has been elevated to major importance. Since there is abundant evidence that marriage and parenthood have not lost their appeal for American youth, the need of instruction to help them gather the fruits of the most intimate and demanding of human associations becomes apparent in any effort to conserve the family. Aside from the many studies of the attitudes of American youth toward marriage and the family, each necessarily inviting even the most honest of those giving the information to rationalize in some degree, the almost universal interest of youth in courtship and other practices, including daydreaming that looks toward marriage and the home, attest that most young men and women intend to marry and that also they expect to find in marriage their greatest satisfaction. Feeling as they do, no type of instruction has a greater opportunity to contribute to their life preparation than education for marriage and home life.

Folsom has listed three essential functions most thoughtful persons believe the family will not surrender: the physical reproduction of the race; a minimum of physical care and training of the child in his earliest years; and provision for the fundamental conditions of happiness and mental health through sex fellowship, personal security, and assurance of affection.[1] That there are many families quite willing to farm out to schools and colleges their own responsibility for giving the child information concerning marriage and especially sex cannot be questioned. There is no reason to suppose that these families will meet their obligations if only schools and colleges refuse to give instruction for marriage and family life. The explanations of the failure of these parents to inform their children are many and not always selfishness or indifference. Such parents are not likely to be awakened to their opportunity by a similar refusal on the part of our educational agencies to assume their share of the training program. The hope of getting these parents to function is in providing for them the background they need to give them incentive and confidence. This adult aspect of the preparatory program is considered later in this chapter.

If the needs of youth as they look forward to marriage and family life are to be satisfied, it is necessary that the instruction provided be practical and applicable to family living. The history of the family, the interpretation of the institution as a sociological concept, theories concerning its origins, and such topics have an intellectual interest, and their discussion contributes to a cultural background. Important, however, as such knowledge may be for the professional sociologist, it does not provide the understanding that students electing courses in preparation for marriage and family life expect, nor does it prove of value when later tested by the adjustments that have to be made in life relationships. The title "Marriage and the Family" or either one alone appears to the student an invitation to come and get preparation for what most of them regard as the future source of their greatest happiness or disappointment. The offering of such courses should be looked upon by the instructor as a pledge that the student will not be forced merely to study about the family, learning a mass of details of no significance so far as personal adaptations are concerned, but rather will be given entry into the meaning and values of family life, vicariously as well as through his own intense but

---

[1] Folsom, Joseph K., *Youth, Family and Education,* p. 26.

limited personal experience so that in later years the instruction and the discussions of the class demonstrate their worth. The students do not seek advice-giving any more than they welcome abstractions. They are aware that they need information. This is even more true as they look forward to marriage than in their thought of the family.

They are disappointed by instruction that evades frank discussion of the subjects concerning which they have hearsay knowledge and realize that they ought to have trustworthy information. They are also disappointed in instruction that concentrates upon the immediate campus problems of courtship which the marriage instructor can so easily exploit until there is little time to deal with the more difficult problems that genuine preparation for marriage has to anticipate. This maneuvering brings a reaction quite unlike what happens when the instructor admits frankly that there are marriage topics which he does not feel competent to deal with or that for some reason he is not as free to discuss as he would prefer. Students may wish it otherwise, but they respect the instructor who confesses his limitations. What they do resent, as the marriage counselor knows well through correspondence, is a course in marriage and the family that steers away from the more difficult problems of adjustment and, at least in the thinking of the student, seems to be an evasion. The students rightly ask from instruction in marriage and the family something in addition to useful information.

They welcome objective fact-giving, but they also seek encouraging attitudes from the individual who delivers the instruction. His personal background, not only that he is married but happily married, is significant only as it influences the spirit of the instruction. This explains the inadequacy, even the mischief, of attempting to give preparation for marriage through the incidental discussions of whatever faculty members are inclined from time to time to refer to marriage and family life. These teachers have no assigned responsibility and thus are free to bring forth the cynicism or pessimism or romantic emotionalism that reflects their personal inclinations. They are sometimes even guilty of unwittingly making erroneous statements that conflict with present knowledge. For example, a highly trained, very competent and influential professor in one of the specialties of liberal arts warned his students that no woman should ever permit a fluoroscopic examination to be made of her because it would make her sterile. His authority was accepted by some, and their false idea later became a cause of conflict which was dissolved as soon as they understood the truth concerning the X ray and sterility. No experienced instructor of marriage courses remains long unacquainted with the half-truths, exaggerations, and amazing pronouncements based on personal prejudice that come from irresponsible comments concerning marriage and the family from teachers who have never given serious study to either of these human relationships.

The spirit, what one may call the atmosphere of marriage instruction, has, on account of the nature of the course, much to do with determining the value of the instruction for later years. In the teaching of such subjects as geology or chemistry and the like, we are not primarily concerned with the life-attitudes of the instructor, but youth who come to gather resources for making the adjustments of marriage and the family have the right to ask from their instruction a strengthening of their faith and courage, stimulation and inspiration, as they seek to equip themselves for the gathering of the values that they rightly regard as the richest achievement of human associations.

History of parent education. Tradition and social routine have furnished a sort of parent education from the simplest society onward. Anthropological literature gives in great detail descriptions of the differing folkways and mores of primitive peoples as through initiations, ceremonies, storytelling, taboos, secret societies, and the like they transmit their culture from generation to generation. In the distribution of these practices, beliefs, and sentiments the family, as with us, has a prominent part, and its obligations are enforced by a public opinion alert to laziness, indifference, or inefficiency. The girl receives from her mother not only training in household skills and an introduction to child care but in addition the planting of social attitudes which make her subservient to tradition.[2]

In America there has always been some special effort to

---

[2] For examples see: Dennis, Wayne, *The Hopi Child;* Mead, Margaret, *Growing up in New Guinea;* and Kaberry, Phyllis, *Aboriginal Woman.*

develop among parents the feeling of responsibility for the training of their children. This was at first largely through sermons. The appeal made was often emotional and the task of the parent was usually considered a moral one. In addition to these preachments from the pulpit, lectures, books, and magazine articles provided a medium for incidental treatment of the problems of parents. The most useful instruction of parenthood came as a by-product of home life. In the colonial period and on the frontier, survival required that the children contribute to the support of their homes, and in the doing of this they learned much that they made use of later when they established their own families. As the girl grew up, she was as a rule assigned the care of her younger brothers and sisters until she gained considerable experience in the management of the infant and young child.

By the beginning of the present century, education in the United States had developed vocational instruction along various lines. The complexity of modern life, the specialization required by the individual who would be successful, and the increasing inability of the family, as well as of the conventional curriculum of the school, to provide the specific instruction that certain individuals demanded led to departures in the school system and a revamping of the theory of education. The first instruction that definitely dealt with problems of the home was that of home economics. Its emphasis was at first almost exclusively on activities that had to do with the material interests of home life, such as cooking, sewing, the furnishing and decoration of the house, and household management. With the development of the extension work of our state colleges, the State Departments of Education, and other organizations, the home economics movement reached women who were actually dealing with household problems. Both in the schools and colleges, and in extension classes and public lectures, only occasional reference was given to the problems of parents.

The first serious grappling with parenthood problems appeared in 1888 in New York in the coming together of a small group of mothers to study under the leadership of a progressive teacher the problems of the education of the child. This grew and become The Society for the Study of Child Nature, later the Federation of Child Study, and in 1924 The Child Study

Association of America. Another development of interest in parenthood education resulted in the National Congress of Mothers, which was first organized in 1897. Meanwhile, from various quarters was appearing information of the greatest value to parents, and, at the same time, there was increasing recognition of the difficulties of the parent's task under the prevailing circumstances of modern life. Home economics instruction in both schools and colleges reflected this knowledge coming from the different sciences. Federal grants provided by the Smith-Lever Act in 1914 and the Smith-Hughes Act in 1917 made possible the work of the county home demonstration agents, and the vocational home economics instruction, which, although chiefly concerned with household technique, from the first gave some attention to parenthood problems and laid the foundation for the later service, once the interest in the more human aspects of the family developed.

The large number of organizations that had a part in the development of parent education and the diversity of their contribution indicates how closely the movement was tied up with cultural changes. It was an expression of an increasing conviction that education for life was neglecting its most important obligation. In 1923 Vassar College established its department of euthenics in the effort to offer instruction that would help the woman college graduate meet her social and domestic responsibilities. In 1926 it started its summer session, a coeducational school which with its allied nursery school has been one of the most important centers for motherhood and parental education. The same year California pioneered by establishing a first Bureau of Parental Education in its State Department of Education, thus committing the state to the furnishing of instruction on child development and other allied problems. During the year 1939 there were fifty-three classes in homemaking education in twenty centers carried on under the direction of the State Department of Education in addition to the work carried on as a part of the emergency education program of the W.P.A. The White House Conference in 1930, called by President Hoover, for the first time gave national recognition to all the major problems of the child and the home. The meeting at Washington brought together a large group of specialists representing important approaches to family welfare, and the findings of the conference carried its values to a multitude of thoughtful readers.

Successful efforts to co-ordinate the various lines along which parent education developed came from the work of the National Council of Parent Education founded in 1926 and supported through the years until 1938 by grant of the Laura Spelman Rockefeller Memorial and the General Education Board. One of its useful services was the publication of *Parent Education.* Since 1938 this organization continued on a basis of self-support, finally being merged with the Progressive Education Association which was organized in 1918 and has recently been reorganized.

Another contribution came from the establishment of the first nursery school as a training center for Home Economics girls at Iowa State College of Agriculture and Mechanic Arts. Soon nursery schools became an orthodox feature in college training in home economics. In some instances, fortunately now increasing constantly, similar provision was made for the use of a nursery school or at least the care of an infant as part of the training of girls in the high school. In 1919 the University of Minnesota brought a baby into the home-management house, giving the students a glimpse of a real home in spite of the risk this innovation brought of spoiling the smooth-running household schedule which had become a feature of efficient home-management houses under the control of departments of home economics. This was a fulfillment of Anna Garlin Spencer's suggestion years before that the home-management house would not reach its full function in family education until a complete family of father, mother, and one or more children, including a baby, lived in the house as guests of the students.

The parent-education program. The parent-education program is built upon three strong convictions that have become characteristic of American thinking. These are the value of education as a means of meeting social needs, the importance of recent knowledge concerning the child and the parent made possible through the investigations of science, and the realization that recent economic and social changes require new methods of adaptation and that these distinctly concern family practices. The bringing up of children has always presented problems for the parent, but at present these are more complex, more impressive, and fortunately, also, more understood than ever has been true before. The greater leisure characteristic of American culture has not only brought forward new perplexities for the parent but also has freed the average mother from the excessive burdens characteristic of former times. She now has greater opportunity for observation, a wider background for judgment, and time to invest in meeting the character needs of her child. Even this possibility of doing more for the child carries its hazards, rendering the mother's efforts, when there is unfamiliarity with or indifference to the teachings of science, a source of danger to the developing personality.

In its earliest expression the interest of parents in child training centered about problems. To a very great extent this is the prevailing concern of most parents who enter child-study classes, attend lectures, or read for the purpose of preparing themselves to deal with their children. This emphasis on specific problems is natural, for it is through these that most parents are awakened to the need of better understanding of the science of child care. Nevertheless, the treatment of problems, although an effective introduction to the subject, proves superficial if it does not lead on to a more serious program.

The problems that attract the attention of parents fall into three groups. They have to do with the preparation of the child for future experience, the adjustment of the child within the family at the present time, and the manipulating of the child so as to make him a source of satisfaction to the parent. This third type often appears clearly as soon as the parent attempts to interpret the difficulty he feels in the handling of his child. It is also evident in such cases that what the parent requires is not skill in carrying out his purposes but an absolute reconstruction of his ideal of parenthood which can be made effective only by serious changes in his own personality, and this need the parent seldom realizes because much of his thinking is a rationalization, a means of concealing from himself his own maladjustment and immaturity.

The parent-child relationship is peculiar in that it inherently contains the necessity of the readjustment of emotional weaning, not required in any other human relationship, discussed in Chapter 8. The meaning of this appears when we contrast the function of the parent on the human level with the higher animal who also has the task of nurture. The animal commanded by an instinct, normally intense, maintains a fiercely defended attachment and automatic care which passes when the offspring reaches a period when independent existence is safe. The human mother has to provide a much more complex and demanding administration in which, as a rule, the father assists in lesser degree. The concentration of attention is normally great and affection strong. This relationship with the maturing of the child must gradually give way to an increasing independence on the one side and the lessening of control on the other. For many reasons—and we owe much to psychoanalysis for revealing the emotional obstructions to this wholesome passage out of childhood—both the child and the parent can retard this growth, which requires restraint of affection by the parent and the child's willingness to lose the satisfactions of dependency. This reconstruction of relationship is a normal problem, but the form it takes, the degrees of conflict and frustration, the misunderstanding and emotional estrangement that occur are individual.

The success or failure of the parent in first giving the love the child needs and then the release equally required for normal development cannot be determined until the character of the child takes a final form. Moreover, there also are other influences complicating the child's successful adjustment. The child's ordeal may be in great measure biologic in origin, a product of endocrine changes, since the physical maturing proceeds at the time he is most concerned with the establishing of his emotional integrity.

The task of the home at this childhood period of strategic development is made more difficult also by lack of competitive contact with other families. There is a degree of this rivalry, which is so important in maintaining the efficiency of commercial interests, but it is in great measure based upon trivial comparisons. The child's career at school may be used as an example. Although on the basis of grades one mother may feel successful and another a failure, it is evident that such a test leaves out too much to permit the first mother to be given credit and the second criticism. Indeed, the goals of parents for their children are so greatly different that there is no basis for genuine competition between homes in their training of children. Likewise, we do not have at present, except for homes in great trouble, supervision or other means for an objective interpretation of the mistakes parents are making. Instead we ask them to be self-conscious of their problems and objectives, analyzing their own motives and practices. In any functioning this would prove difficult, but in a relationship involving affection it is especially so.

The disregard of the peculiar difficulties of parent-child relationships, especially that of the mother, explains in part the emphasis upon problems and, from our present viewpoint, the relatively negative approach that was characteristic of the earliest period of interest in parenthood education. Because of this the movement occasionally brought forth opposition, especially from fathers who felt that child study was leading mothers to exaggerate their difficulties and to be suspicious of perfectly wholesome maternal attitudes. This misapplying of the information given in the lectures and discussions of child-study classes did in some instances betray mothers into reactions that created skepticism as to the value of scientific child study. Trouble came also from fathers committed to ideas of discipline and obedience which were anachronistic and out of accord with the life-training the modern child needed. With two parents committed to opposing philosophies of child training, there resulted an inconsistency in family policy which gave critics of the new movement greater confidence that their opposition was justified. Soon discussion of the problem-child became that of the problem-parent, and for a time many clinic specialists were too prone to put upon the mother the responsibility for whatever maladjustment appeared in her child. As is always true in science with greater advance came self-correction until it became generally recognized that child development is exceedingly complex, with the parent usually taking a commanding responsibility but never complete control of all the formative influences that develop the total personality.

Parent education stands alone in the demands it makes on sincerity and self-scrutiny. This difficulty, inherent in the giving of this sort of instruction, enforces all the more the need of parental education. The reactions of mothers and fathers that prove troublesome in arriving at an objective and critical attitude toward their own practices are the bottom-most sources of

their failures as parents. Successful parenthood education, therefore, can never be merely the learning of a special technique in
the handling of children or the gathering of information that
concerns child development. It must also include a large amount
of self-knowledge and self-discipline.

Parenthood is an art. At best, science can only supply the
basis for intelligent practices, leaving to the individual the use
of judgment in adapting these principles to the immediate situation and the need of the individual. The significance of parenthood education is that it seeks to place the practices of the
home, not on tradition which is oblivious to social conditions,
but on the understanding which comes from the knowledge
specialists gather as they study children and their problems.
Family education recognizes that the inevitable changes of social life forbid routine adjustments possible only by perpetuating patterns of conduct that developed under different circumstances. In so far as the home attempts this backward policy,
the child is forced into needless conflicts as he becomes more
and more independent and sensitive to the existing environment.

Parenthood not only demands much of the individual but
also offers satisfactions. In the American culture it is not regarded an insurance against old age or an economic resource
nor is it considered a means of gaining prestige. Each of these
motivations has its emphasis in other cultures. In ours the advantage of being a parent comes chiefly from the growth of character and the satisfactions of fellowship that the responsibility
encourages. The more parenthood is a choice and not a consequence of accident, the more its values need emphasis. In some
cultures the appeal to patriotism is used to increase the bearing
of children. This motive brings little response from American
homes, and it is not likely to prove effective unless there is a
radical change in our social thinking. With us the desire to have
children can be best strengthened by a preparedness that gives
a sense of assurance of successful parenthood. This requires
more than courses of study, for health, economic security, educational opportunity, and other conditions for normal standards
of living are involved. Education for parenthood contributes to
these resources for child care a direct, conscious motivation, the
product of study and discussion.

Parent education is not developing as the function of any single private or public organization. On the contrary, it is being carried on by so many agencies and organizations, and exhibits such a variety of types, that the movement seems at the moment diffusive. Child-study classes independently organized, parent-teacher organizations, social service agencies, churches, public schools, colleges, mental hygiene and social hygiene organizations, and extension classes are some of the forms in which the present parenthood education functions.

There is as much variation in the content of parenthood instruction as in the kinds of agencies that carry on such education. The method of presentation as well as the material is influenced by whether it is preparatory in purpose or is designed to help parents already engaged in child nurture, and also by whether those who are interested in the study are persons of broad or narrow background. Women who are already mothers, especially if they have had limited opportunity educationally, prefer discussions that deal with the various specific problems of which they are conscious and expect definite counsel in the handling of difficulties they consider important in their relations with their child.

Useful as this form of instruction often proves, there is no hope of much being accomplished by such a program if parenthood education becomes fixed at this elementary stage. Obviously, the only way of interesting many mothers in a more serious and valuable type of instruction is to extend and improve the preparatory education for parenthood that can be distributed during the formative years by our schools and colleges.

On the college level much that concerns parenthood has to be anticipated and, as a result, there is rarely the eager interest in such discussions that we find in the child-study classes for mothers and fathers. The college student is as a rule very conscious of the problems of courtship and quite willing to turn attention toward marriage relationships which are already beginning to seem tangible and on the horizon. Even so they are aware from their own experiences how significant the influences of the family are, and it is not difficult for the instruction to tie together home life and marriage expectation and prepare the way for a later intelligent parenthood policy. Courses in the family and marriage or a combination of these two aspects of domestic experience make the student familiar with the resources of which they need to know in their later career as husbands, wives, and parents. Instruction along any one of these three specialties can measurably stimulate the attitudes which perhaps more than all else give the right start in marriage or in parenthood.

On the secondary level, the instruction has to adjust itself to the timely concern of the adolescent boy and girl which for most of them involves their social relationships. They are eager for suggestions that lessen the inferiority feeling or at least the sense of insecurity and the sense of uncertainty so characteristic of their period of growth and which so often explains their expressions of stress and emotional exaggerations that appear to the unthinking adult as fictitious. Once this is recognized, the instructor in the family course has an unrivaled opportunity to win the confidence of the student and lay the groundwork for both a more sympathetic attitude toward their present families and for a successful career later as husband, wife, or parent. Along with such teaching is certain to go a great deal of counseling. The adolescent wants help, but even when there is close fellowship with the parents there is apt to be reluctance to discuss some types of problems at home when there is less hesitation in bringing them to the teacher. A great part of the value in high school courses in the family comes through this counseling. If the instructor is sincerely interested in the problems of youth, he or she will be called upon to give guidance to a degree that is rarely true of any other high school teachers.

The rapid development of interest in parent education during the first quarter of the present century led in this country to an increasing need of some organization that would serve to bring together leaders in the work, who, in spite of the great diversity of activities, had a common interest. In 1925, representatives of thirteen organizations dealing with some phase of parenthood education met together and before adjourning their conference organized the National Council of Parent Education. In the effort to co-ordinate and advance the work for parents, this agency undertook to: "(1) assemble and make available research material for workers in the field; (2) serve as a clearing house for research; (3) suggest qualifications and guide the training of workers; and (4) collect and disseminate educational materials other than research." [3] The service of this organization until it rapidly developed required the full time of a director, a secretary, and an office staff.

Child-development research centers. The effort to study scientifically the development of children was, in part, one of the many expressions of interest in human nature springing up from every quarter of the field of science. Particularly it was an offshoot of the emerging experimental psychology which became an epochal influence in the development of science during the last quarter of the nineteenth century. In this country G. Stanley Hall, one-time president of Clark University, represented in the movement both the prophet and the pioneer. In 1883 he published an important paper entitled "The Content of Children's Minds," and perhaps with that we can date the beginning of the scientific study of children in the United States.

This new sort of interest in children soon branched out in a multitude of directions. For example, Professor Lightner Witmer started at the University of Pennsylvania the study of the retarded child, while Dr. Walter Fernald, in Massachusetts, was investigating the mentality of children on the lowest levels of defectiveness and building a technique for their training. In 1917 the Iowa State Assembly by its appropriation made possible a departure of great significance for the new science of child study through the establishment of the Child Welfare Research Station, under the direction of Bird Baldwin, as a part of the State University. It expressed the conviction of a group of forward-looking people in Iowa that there was need both of gaining better knowledge of children and of distributing it more widely. Its function was to be "the investigation of the best scientific methods of conserving and developing the normal child, the dissemination of the information acquired by such investigation, and the training of students for work in such fields." [4] In view of recent developments, it is interesting that the studies undertaken and published included from the first

---

[3] Bridgman, Ralph P., "Ten Years' Progress in Parent Education," reprinted from *The Annals of the American Academy of Political and Social Science,* September, 1930 (Pub. No. 2420), p. 42. Quoted by permission.

[4] *Ibid.,* p. 39. Quoted by permission.

the physical, the mental, and the emotional aspects of the development of children. Similar organizations have now become an integral part of several of our leading universities in the United States and Canada.

A different sort of contribution to our growing knowledge of the child came from the establishment of the Merrill-Palmer School, in Detroit, in 1920. This was organized to undertake the training of girls for homemaking and parenthood, and in the effort to accomplish its purposes a nursery school was established to provide opportunity for the observation of children and contact with them and to make possible research in the problems of normal children. When the Psycho-clinic was established at Yale, in 1926, it took over the investigation of child development under the direction of Arnold Gesell, who studied with G. Stanley Hall at Clark University. This later became a clinic of child development at Yale School of Medicine, continuing under the same leadership. The child guidance clinics, which were discussed in Chapter 22, influenced greatly both the growth and the development of parenthood education.

The nursery school. No educational happening in this country so reflects the significance of recent social changes as does the growth of the nursery school, and nothing in American education has more potential meaning for the family. Although it was suggested by the development of nursery schools in England, it has taken such a different form and assumed so different a task that it has become an original creation of our own civilization, little suggesting its European origin. Across the Atlantic, the nursery school for the most part functions with the same purposes that were attempted by the infant school of Robert Owen at New Lanark, Scotland, in the early part of the nineteenth century. It seeks to save the underprivileged children during their preschool years from the consequences of poverty, low standards of living, and the slum environment. As a rule, therefore, the English nursery schools are located in the congested sections of the cities and their emphasis is upon the prevention of the defects of health that children from the poorer families had been showing when they entered the elementary school.

In the United States, the nursery school has not been brought forth by pressure of economic conditions but in re-

sponse to the conviction of educators of the need of a preschool
organization for the study of the development of children and
the increasing recognition of intelligent mothers that for their
welfare and that of their children they need the assistance of an
agency that can supplement the home in its service for the preschool child. At first the demand for the nursery school came
from those who from their knowledge of the science of parenthood realized how much parents needed the assistance that the
nursery school could bring them and without which the child
could not gain his rightful share of the benefits of modern science.

Since the nursery school fulfills an increasing need in the
growing life of the child and in the functioning of the American family, there is certain to be a reversal of the direction from
which the incentive for nursery schools has been coming. Demand for the help of the nursery schools will be made more and
more by mothers, at first by those who have had the benefits of
higher education, and particularly in the cities. The power to
appreciate the value of the nursery school as an integral part of
our education is not, however, a product of a special experience
of one class but something inherent in the prevailing civilization. The motive that leads some mothers to seek a method of
partially farming out their children is often indicted as selfishness and in a narrow sense may frequently be so described. Fundamentally, however, the momentum leading to the nursery
school is an outcome of our cultural circumstances. This trend,
at present, is concealed by traditions that still enforce the ideals
adapted to former American family practices. But this lag is
merely affording a much-needed period of experiment, an incu-
bation of technique; it is not holding back the influences that
are spreading the nursery-school idea.

There are leaders in the movement who fear, and with
reason, the democratic development of the nursery school that
will make it an integral part of the public-school system. But
the most they can hope for, unless there shall be a social earthquake that will throw the American family back to earlier and
more primitive conditions, is a breathing time in preparation
for the ordeal that faces the nursery-school movement once it is
popularized.

Undoubtedly the average parent is distrustful of the nursery-school idea. This, however, has happened before in educational innovation, and it has not prevented parents' accepting the new practices when they have been shown to be good for the child or an advantage to the home. The progress of the nursery school in the United States already has proved that it is beneficial to both the modern child and the family. Even indifferent or hostile to the idea as many American parents are at present, it is doubtful whether in any community except perhaps the open country nursery-school facilities can be offered without mothers taking advantage of the new public service more rapidly than the work can be organized.

An obstacle to the development of the nursery school is its cost. The groups of children have to be small, and this necessitates a relatively large teaching overhead. The equipment of playgrounds, the medical preventive work, and the professional skill of those who serve the children all contribute to make it expensive. This fact undoubtedly retards the development of the nursery school and might prevent its becoming a substantial part of the public-school instruction were it not for the steadily increasing pressure for some such service that will accompany the social evolution of the American family. To some extent, the cost of nursery schools will be lessened as they increase. Even more important will be the recognition that much of the costliness of the nursery school is apparent rather than real, that in the long run no social service will prove more economical than this which fulfills the need of the growing child in his most significant years. If public education is ever justified, it is surely when it can accomplish most. The nursery school is an agency for bringing to child and parent in an effective, practical manner the resources of science that are required for wholesome education and that can rarely be provided by an individual family.

By 1932 there were nursery schools in 121 cities of thirty-five states, the District of Columbia, and Hawaii. More than three-fourths of these came into existence after 1925. Children in attendance ranged from two years and eight months to four years and two months, the average age being three years and five months. Altogether there were more than two hundred nursery schools, and already some have been established as part of the public-school system.[5]

The Works Progress Administration, during the depression when Franklin D. Roosevelt was president, established by federal funds local projects known as Federal Nursery Schools. It was left to the local communities to ask for these and to organize them, the government paying the salaries of the teachers. The lack of trained personnel needed for such a quick expansion made necessary the lowering of the standards of the older, well-established nursery schools. The government organizations were known at first as Emergency Nursery Schools and for the most part served low-income families, with emphasis upon complementing the food of the children, thus having a function similar to the original English nursery schools. At the end of 1937 there were about 1,500 such schools with an attendance of 40,000 children. In 1943 there were about 100,000 children in nursery schools. Most of those from underprivileged homes were attending the schools organized by the W.P.A. Those of private or university origin drew their children chiefly from well-to-do homes. The latter type of school particularly emphasized the co-operative relationship with the parents and thereby in various ways contributed to parenthood education.[6]

As part of this service there has been much emphasis upon consultations with parents and frequently research in the behavior of children. Some of the nursery schools have provided opportunity for a parent to observe objectively the conduct of his child, without the knowledge of the child. The schools that were maintained by the W.P.A. were to a greater extent a means of relieving the mother of the care of the child, as was true of the day nurseries discussed in the preceding chapter.

The nursery school does not attempt to be a substitute for the home. Those who administer it realize that the proper functioning of the family is indispensable to its success. What parents are beginning to learn is that without the co-operation of such an organization, their effort to give the child the right preparation for life is frustrated.

Elementary and secondary education for family life. At

---

[5] Davis, M. D., *Nursery Schools, Their Development and Current Practices in the United States* (U. S. Office of Education Bulletin).

[6] Folsom, Joseph K., *op. cit.*, p. 74.

the time that the education of children began in this country to crystallize in our public-school system, the responsibilities of the family for the training of the child were large and the task put upon the school was formal and limited in scope. The social evolution is reversing this situation, constantly enlarging the educational services of the school and lessening those of the family. In this change, there has until recently been relative neglect of the training for family experience which was inherent in the routine of the home at the time when the family was the dominant educational agency. This has not been the conscious intent of educators but has resulted merely from their not recognizing that with the inability of the home to function as formerly, a new type of instruction must be provided by the schools or modern men and women of necessity come to marriage and parenthood inadequately prepared. There has also been the usual lag of well-established social agencies. Educational leaders, however, have become increasingly aware of this need of specific training for family experience.

In the preceding chapter the beginning of a new type of education emphasizing household skills given by the home economist has been discussed. It was natural under the circumstances that the first instruction relating to family interests should be along the line of the household arts, since one of the changes in family life was the lessening of the training girls received from their mothers in cooking, sewing, and household management. As this earliest educational program matured, two changes occurred. The tradition that family-life education was of importance to girls rather than to boys was replaced by a realization that the modern home could be strengthened by giving boys as well as girls preparedness for family living and the recognition that the former responded to instruction that was adapted to their interests. The growth of these courses for boys and men at first developed mainly in the West and the Far West as a consequence of less conservatism and the more apparent need of the instruction because of the predominating rural type of family life. It also became increasingly clear that there must be greater emphasis upon problems of personal relationships, for not only were these close to the interests of the adolescent but also the giving of insight that would enable youth later to gain the values of marriage and family association was one of the most promising of all attempts to conserve marriage and the family.

It is generally recognized that the building of right attitudes toward marriage and the family should begin, as far as the contribution of the schools is concerned, in the elementary grades. The programs for accomplishing this are, however, at present, less developed than on the higher levels. To a great extent, training for family living must in these first grades be a by-product, coming through the interest of teachers of many subjects as they use their opportunity to help children appreciate the meaning of home and to establish habits that later will further their adjustment in marriage and family life. There is need of gaining the co-operation of mothers and of convincing them that they can help this education by permitting and encouraging their young children to take part in household activities, even though the assistance of the child may seem to the mother more of a trouble than a help. The attitudes of both boys and girls toward the various skills and responsibilities associated with homekeeping can be greatly influenced by the mother's attitude. If she is willing to encourage the interest of the child until a degree of efficiency is attained, the child may learn to enjoy the activities of home life which might otherwise seem pure drudgery. The boy who learns to cook, purchase food sensibly, and choose a good diet has an asset that proves both an advantage and a source of satisfaction.

It is often difficult to gain the co-operation of families in the carrying on of this dual preparation for family living adapted to the young child, but in no other way can elementary education contribute to family welfare as it should. If this enlistment of parental support should be generally recognized as a major objective of the school administration, the needful co-operation would be made traditional. At present, the chief lack is a conviction in the school personnel and the parents that this mutual functioning is important enough to be made a primary concern both of the home and the school. In this training, the use and value of money, the use of a budget, experience in buying, and thrift are given special attention. If the child is to have training along these lines, he must be given the practical experience which is difficult to provide unless the home takes some part in the school program.

One of the tasks of the school is to lessen the consequences of the divided, broken, or unhappy home, conditioning the child in such a way as to increase his own hope of success in his later family life. The elementary school effort to conserve family life must be conceived in the most catholic terms as something involving manners, self-discipline, and many other personality characteristics, since these are all significant for the family and get their direction early according to the influences that affect the child.

It is inconsistent for any school administration to attempt to develop education for family life on either the elementary or secondary levels while at the same time retaining an edict that no woman who marries can be a teacher. Such a rule is in itself a disclosure that there is no genuine appreciation of the values of marriage and family life that anyone attempting to strengthen the family needs to have. Parents are apt to discount the leadership of the unmarried woman in any training for family living. Such a prejudice in itself makes the necessary co-operation between the home and the school all the more difficult to achieve and suggests the advantage of assigning married teachers to the courses in the family.

In many high schools, contribution to education for family life has been given in part through courses in social science. Their approach has been different than that developed in the field of home economics. There has been more stress placed on the social problems of the family, especially those that are economic. In some schools there is a still different type of instruction dealing principally with problems of personal adjustment. These can be described as psychological in character, but, as a rule, they are offered by departments of home economics or to a lesser extent social science. There are even a few high schools that are giving preparation for marriage, most often as one part of instruction in preparation for family life but occasionally as a portion of a course in biology.

College and university instruction.   Education for family living and for marriage developed relatively late in American colleges and universities. Even so this type of instruction appeared first in this country and is more firmly established and more common here than elsewhere. The increasing awareness among thoughtful people that the family and marriage were finding it difficult to adjust to the changing social conditions characteristic of the period and were therefore showing considerable disorganization made inevitable their turning to the colleges, the source of much of our social leadership, for the strengthening of the family through education. Those who were concerned with domestic problems were for the most part college graduates, often members of college faculties, teaching either sociology or domestic science. The development that had already taken place in various forms of parenthood education gave support to the college program. Preparation for marriage had, as already has been stated, a different origin. It has continued true that most of the instruction in the field of marriage has been offered in response to the demands of students. Courses in the family are now well secured, and there are very few American colleges that still refuse to give this instruction. Courses in preparation for marriage are less common. It is difficult to discover just how much of this instruction is given, because there are courses entitled "Marriage" which are, in fact, courses in the family, just as there are courses that have titles that do not bring out clearly that they are in the field of marriage.

At the present time, the instruction can be classified along three lines.

(1) *The family.* Because of different emphasis these courses fall into two classes. One type deals largely with the institutional and cultural aspects of the family and does not attempt to contribute very much to practical insight. This type is most likely to be catalogued among the offerings of sociology. Then there is the instruction that features personal relationships in the effort to equip the student for the opportunities of family life through better understanding of its problems and its potential values. This course is generally taught either by sociologists, home economists, or, least often, by psychologists.

(2) *Marriage.* This instruction devotes itself exclusively to the experiences of marriage, and therefore the content of the instruction is drawn from a group of sciences. This course at present is usually given by some instructor in whom the administration has confidence without regard to his particular specialty. Although the development of this instruction has been

slower than that of the family, it has been steady and it is becoming generally accepted as a responsibility that the college owes the student. There is less variation in the content of the course than in discussions of the family, since it is concerned with the problems of the marriage relationship and these are definite and well understood.

(3) *Marriage and the family.* This is a combination course frequently given in answer to the demands of the students for instruction in marriage when for some reason it does not seem expedient to give the students the course they seek. It represents a compromise, sometimes giving very little attention to marriage problems and occasionally, except for its title, being actually a course in the family or a course in marriage.

Nearly all of those who now in our colleges are teaching courses in marriage and the family have not been trained specifically for the giving of this instruction. The growth of the interest, however, is creating the need of a specialty which at present is developing along two lines: training for the teaching of marriage and the family and for counseling. The interest in both of these preparations at the University of North Carolina where credit courses in marriage preparation had their start has led to a graduate program in co-operation with Duke University, emphasizing these aspects of professional service for the conservation of marriage and the family. Graduate programs are developing at other institutions, especially along the lines of parenthood education, for example, at the University of Minnesota and at Columbia University and in marriage counseling at Pennsylvania State College.

National and regional conferences. At the present time, educational efforts to conserve marriage and the family reveal the American trait of excessive organization. The need of the family has been so apparent that a great many of our educational and social organizations have added family conservation to their other activities. The movement would be more fruitful if there were less duplication. An attempt to bring together these various interests is being made through the National Conference of Family Relations started by Paul Sayre in 1937, and its effort to concentrate the widespread interest in family welfare which in 1947 became the National Council on Family Relations has been hampered by the fact that it seems another competing organization. It has especially contributed to the movement by the regional conferences it has organized or supported.

A different kind of approach to the same problem has been the Annual April Conferences for the Conservation of Marriage and the Family at the University of North Carolina, and at North Carolina College, which have been directed by the authors. These conferences originated in answer to the request of those who sought help in starting courses in marriage and later it took over marriage and family counseling. It became the meeting place for specialists who by face-to-face discussion could profit from their experiences as workers in many varied special fields. In order to accomplish this purpose of discussion and to prevent any one section or profession from becoming dominant, attendance has been by invitation and has been limited to 225 because of a conviction that a larger number changed the character of the conference, which is a meeting for the interchange of experience rather than for the delivering of learned papers.

The contribution of the churches.   Throughout the history of the American family there has been evidence of the influence of the churches. During the last fifteen to twenty years this has been growing more distinctly educational as the churches have become more conscious of specific obligations, not only for the maintenance of high standards of family life but also for the eliminating of social conditions that antagonize marriage and the home. There has been a movement away from the dualistic attitude toward sex and marriage which, as it found expression in some of the preachments and attitudes of churches in the past, hampered wholesome marital adjustment and created in some of those attempting to follow these teachings a morbid feeling of guilt and emotional conflict. There has also been a trend away from a negative attack on vice and family disorganization to a positive program looking toward improvement of family experience. This has led to an increasing emphasis on education and a greater attempt to make use of the resources science has made available for the solving and for the preventing of family problems. There has also been recognition of the obligation of the church to youth who at the mating age have need of opportunity for getting acquainted and for courtship.

At present the educational contribution of the churches is functioning along four different lines. There is beginning to be in the theological seminaries an instruction for pastoral work which grapples with the kinds of problems of family relationship that come to the modern clergyman. In the more progressive theological seminaries there is even recognition of the minister's need of becoming acquainted with the mechanisms of human behavior that provide insight and the diagnostic technique required for helping people out of family difficulties. At first, however, these adjustment problems were interpreted in the teaching of the theological seminary as chiefly moral, and the science of behavior coming from psychology and psychiatry as it concerns marriage and family experience was largely ignored or even antagonized. This is becoming less and less true.

Some churches have sponsored or organized study classes for parents. This support of parent education by the churches is most fortunate, for in some communities these parent classes provide the only means by which at this time instruction in marriage and parent education can be given. This adult education, in addition to its influence in the making of sounder ideas of family life, will add its part to those forces that are modernizing religion itself.

A third type of work carried on by the churches is also in the formative period. This has to do with preparation for marriage and is usually designed for those who are engaged or who have just married. At present it takes various forms: lectures, which is the most common type; the distribution of literature by means of a circulating library; and group and personal instruction. This last type, supported by the second, is proving most successful and is rapidly increasing among American churches. This recognition by the churches of their obligation to help prepare people for marriage has become a very important contribution to the conservation of marriage and the family. Briefly, it is a counseling service now increasingly made prerequisite in churches of all faiths before the marriage ceremony.

The fourth contribution of the churches is through provision for clinics. This is confined to the cities thus far, and is frankly experimental in character. It is sometimes maintained by an individual church with a staff of volunteer or paid specialists, and it also takes the form of a co-operative enterprise functioning for several churches. This latter type sometimes results from individual ministers in a locality or belonging to the same denomination in an ecclesiastical administrative unit sending their more difficult family problems to a colleague who is especially interested and skillful in dealing with such problems. There is, of course, no reason for church organizations duplicating the work of marital clinics in localities where they already exist, but in all such family counseling, whatever its foundation, there is need of a moral specialist on the staff of experts, for there is an ethical element in maladjustment just as there is a physical, a mental, and a social aspect.

Among Protestant denominations, the Federal Council of the Churches of Christ in America has offered valuable leadership in these various constructive services for the family. So important has this part of the work of the Council become that at present it requires the full time of an administrator. L. Foster Wood, who holds that position at this time, has described the program of his organization as follows:

1. The collection, dissemination, and creation of literature in this field.

2. The conducting of city-wide conferences in chosen centers.

3. The promotion of classes in summer assemblies of pastors, of laymen, and of youth.

4. The promotion of lectures and courses of study in the schools in which our leaders are trained.

5. The encouragement of the movement to establish family adjustment centers or institutes of family relations.

6. Encouragement of the movement for courts of domestic relations.

7. An influence on the educative processes, not by way of church interference, but by way of inspiration and encouragement.

8. Promoting the placing of good books on marriage and the family in all libraries.

9. An attempt to elevate the standards of the films in portraying matter bearing on marriage and the home.

10. Using the radio and keeping this thing in the air, pleading the cause of better ethical and cultural standards, and better standards of living for all families everywhere, since these are the

nurture centers for humanity and the primary means for the carrying on and improvement of our culture.[7]

A similar form of conserving marriage and the family is maintained by those of the Roman Catholic faith, differing in its teachings in accord with the Church's conception of marriage and family life. The organization that provides leadership is the Catholic National Conference on Family Life of which Edgar Schmiedeler is director. He also has charge of the research in family problems carried on at the Catholic University at Washington, D. C. The Catholic position is more definite than that of the Protestant churches and is authoritatively expressed by the encyclical letters of his Holiness, Pius XI. The Catholic teaching therefore avoids the diversity so marked in the attitudes of the Protestant churches toward marriage and the family. The National Catholic Conference on Family Life publishes the *Catholic Family Monthly* which interprets the Catholic position concerning contemporary domestic problems and also gives spiritual stimulation to its readers. Dr. Schmiedeler and other writers have contributed to the Catholic movement by articles and books, including college and high school texts.

The third major religious faith of the United States, the Jewish, also provides various services for the conserving of marriage and family life and for the interpreting of Jewish domestic traditions. Rabbi Sidney E. Goldstein, Chairman of the Jewish Institute on Marriage and the Family, is nationally recognized for his contributions to education for family life and the interest he has aroused among his fellow believers in various undertakings seeking to strengthen and improve family life. All three of these religious leaders have much in common and through their writings,[8] research, and speaking have added to the resources for the conservation of marriage and the family.

Sex education. The need of giving children information concerning sex, right attitudes toward it, and truthful answers to their questions, usually born of normal curiosity, is now

---

[7] *Journal of Social Hygiene*, Vol. 18, p. 437. Quoted by permission.

[8] See: Sidney E. Goldstein, *The Meaning of Marriage and Foundations of the Family;* Edgar Schmiedeler, *Christian Marriage, an Analysis and Commentary on the Marriage Encyclical;* and L. Foster Wood, *Harmony in Marriage.*

generally recognized. However, parents have less confidence in their ability to meet the child's needs along these lines than along others. This inadequacy has been felt especially concerning the earliest questionings of the child and those occurring in early puberty. Many parents, possibly due to their exaggerating of the importance of technique, have sought the help of others assumed to be better trained than themselves for the giving of instruction in sex. The institutions that have been asked most often to take over this responsibility have been the church and the school, especially the latter.

Leaders in family welfare activities emphasize the importance of the parents' role and by offering courses, or through books, pamphlets, and lectures, have sought to equip parents for their responsibility and to give them courage in the handling of their children's sex problems. As a consequence of this attention, in some instances parents have been overimpressed by the possible difficulties of such training and have been all the more reluctant to attempt the sex education of their children. One reason for this reluctance has been the utterly different background of the parent in his or her childhood which gave sexual interests a peculiar and often morbid coloring which creates embarrassment or at least self-consciousness as the parent starts to answer the questions concerning birth and other aspects of reproduction and the like that so naturally come out of the child's early curiosity. There is, however, among specialists general agreement that the fundamental foundation of the sexual career is laid down early and that normally the parent, usually the mother, can have the most determining influence. The conscientious parent is apt to be aware of two limitations in the effort to meet the needs of the child: inadequate information and lack of a suitable vocabulary. In recent years much has been done, especially through books, to provide parents with these resources, and already it is evident that many children during their formative years are being given more wholesome attitudes toward sex than was true of their parents.

There are differences of judgment about the giving of sex education in the early years of adolescence. There are those who believe that this should be regarded as wholly a parental obligation. There are others who feel that few parents are qualified to undertake such a task and that it should be given to persons especially trained as a part of the school program. The third position puts upon both the home and the school responsibility for preparing youth for normal sexual development. It is felt that the adolescent has need of getting right attitudes from his home and also considerable factual information during adolescence from the educator; the latter is needed in part because the young boy and girl appear reticent and self-conscious in the presence of the parent in discussions of certain aspects of sex which nevertheless they are eager to understand. It is a common practice of parents to substitute for personal discussion some book on sex written for children or youth. Helpful as most of this literature is, those familiar with the problems of young people insist that the child still needs opportunity to talk with some adult who has proper attitudes toward sex and who is well informed.

Experience has demonstrated that the parent accomplishes most in helping the child by not becoming overanxious and by observing the following principles. The child should not be given lectures but should be given informed and progressive enlightenment. What he is told should be made simple, it should be truthful, and it should be clearly presented. As far as possible, the facts given the child should be in answer to his questions or related to personal experience. Advantage should be taken of incidents that are likely to stir up his curiosity and that come out of home and neighborhood happenings. Care should be taken not to get beyond the understanding of the child and not to overwhelm him with needless factual material. Emotional attitudes should be regarded as more important even than correct knowledge. Shame or guilt should never be used in an attempt to control the sex interest of the child. Little good can come from instruction in sex when the relationship between parent and child is unwholesome or the child feels antagonism toward the parent. In giving sex education, the level of development of the child always must be considered, for little profit comes out of information-giving that is not adapted to his stage of maturity. Although in youth there is not the need of the emotional intimate relationship with the informer that is prerequisite to success in the earlier period of childhood, the teacher must have the confidence of his students to be successful. There should be at this later period greater emphasis upon factual material, but the emotional attitudes are still extremely important and largely determined by the teacher.

Extension service. The extension program is chiefly directed by the United States Department of Agriculture, in cooperation with the various state colleges and universities. A large part of this service falls within the division of home economics and especially adapts itself to the needs of village and rural people. Much of it is carried on through the activities of the home demonstration agents. Specialists in such fields as food and nutrition, clothing, home management, child care, household furnishings, health, and parental education, organize local clubs, instruction classes, conferences, lecture programs, and act as a medium for the distribution of all sorts of useful information. The thoroughness and practicality of this extension work is illustrated by the following clothing program carried through in California in 1933. The instruction was divided into these four sections: [9]

Construction, 25 per cent
   Dressmaking, tailoring
   Pattern study
   Cutting, fitting
   Dress form
   Sewing technic
   Sewing-machine use
   Finishes
   Remodeling, mending
   Hat blocking

Health, 25 per cent
   Growth, development
   Personal hygiene
   Shoes and stockings
   Underwear, outerwear
   Foundation garments
   Dry cleaning, laundering
   Infants' clothing
   Children's self-help
   Sleeping garments

Economics, 25 per cent
   Accounts, budgets
   Wardrobe planning
   Better-buying studies
   Hosiery-wearing tests
   Fabric-wearing tests
   Mending, repair
   Made-over clothing
   Moth control
   Dry cleaning, laundering

Esthetics, 25 per cent
   Wardrobe planning
   Dress design
   Applied color
   Personal hygiene
   Good grooming
   Care of clothing
   Spot removal, pressing
   Dry cleaning, laundering
   Storage

---

[9] Dodson, Ethelwyn, "The Clothing Program in California Home Demonstration Work," *Journal of Home Economics*, Vol. 25, No. 1, p. 31. Quoted by permission.

The effectiveness of the country-wide extension service was especially demonstrated during the world-wide depression which began in 1929.

There are other kinds of extension work for the family besides this carried on by the government and the state. Magazines, particularly those appealing to women, and newspapers constantly give space to discussions that have to do with various phases of family experience. Child care has special prominence, as shown by the number of serial syndicated articles appearing in daily newspapers throughout the United States. The radio gives attention to parenthood problems in talks sponsored at times by federal or state agencies, by organizations interested in parental education, and even by commercial firms. Institutes concerned with the problems of marriage and parenthood are held under the auspices of local, state, and national organizations. Such problems likewise appear from time to time as subjects at forum meetings and are often on the programs of religious conferences. There is also in book form an extensive treatment of marriage, the family, and parenthood interests. These books have a wide circulation in individual families as well as through public libraries, besides being much used by study classes. A library of books discussing in a popular and practical way the many phases of parenthood is becoming indispensable to churches, high schools, and child-study organizations.

Significance of education for family life. The large amount of educational resources already in operation dealing directly with family interests is impressive, but without doubt its chief significance is the trend it discloses to turn to education as the economical and profitable way of conserving marriage and parenthood. This confidence in education as it receives direction from the various experiments that are being carried on leads logically toward some sort of public program. Compulsory education for parenthood seems far off to the average American, but there are forces already in operation that suggest this as the ultimate social program. Science as it reveals the consequences of the malpractices of well-meaning parents who are utterly untrained for their great responsibility and ignorant of or indifferent to the science of child life is forcing an issue that society may not always evade. There is little hope of making any considerable progress in human standards and satisfactions unless children have a far better training for life than that given at present in the average home. It is no secret that there have been child specialists who have lost hope of training the majority of parents for parenthood responsibilities and who have prophesied, especially in their frank conversations, the passing in America of the family as a social institution. They look forward to the time, not many decades away, when children will be removed from private families and trained by the state in somewhat the way that Plato advocated.

The alternative is universal training in the art of parenthood so that the private family may continue its historic functions of child nurture without robbing the child of the advantages that science is prepared to give him, if only there is efficiency and insight among those who direct his life. No one assumes that any form of instruction will do away with all social maladjustments and failures, but the evidence is convincing that there is no other instrument quite so successful as education as a means of prevention. Education, to function, must be precise in its application to the family and must be of a practical character. Parenthood is one of the largest, if not the most significant, of all social undertakings, and it requires of those who practice it a preparation and a sense of responsibility that the prevailing *laissez faire* attitude toward the assumption of the power of fatherhood and motherhood forbids. Although not so obvious and not so compelling, there is evidence also that marriage as a form of human experience cannot be expected to meet with much success the tests of modern life unless it becomes customary for those who enter it to receive the educational preparation now fortunately increasingly given by family, church, school, and college.

Chapter 25

THE SUCCESSFUL FAMILY

FOREWORD. With a few extraordinary exceptions, the students who elect courses in the family look forward to marriage and successful home life. As a rule, their motive in choosing such a study is the desire to equip themselves better as husbands or wives and parents. Some of them are hoping to discover why their own parents have been unhappy, and most of them who have this interest seek to understand their own family background in order to avoid the mistakes they feel sure that one or both of their parents committed. As students in these courses look forward to their own domestic career, rarely can any of them imagine their own failure. Nevertheless, they are acquainted with unhappy and broken families and are forced to recognize that some of these individuals who have not been able to attain success have had the best of intent and in many instances are intelligent and mature. It is apparent, therefore, that well-meaning people do not always succeed in marriage and parenthood, and thoughtful youth are confident that if they could understand how this happens they would be sure to prevent the blunders that explain the unsuccessful family.

Studies of successful families. As anyone would expect, the studies that have been made of successful families, based upon information given in answer to questions, have demonstrated that those who come from unhappy homes are less likely to succeed than those who have been brought up in the opposite type of homes. This is similar to what one would also take for granted with reference to the health of parents. We reasonably expect children of healthy parents to be themselves healthy and to have an advantage over children coming from

727

homes where there has been chronic invalidism. From neither of these generalizations do we have a clue to causes but rather an end result. For example, homes of the second generation may not have illnesses characteristic of the first, because the sons and daughters may have the advantage of knowing why their parents were hampered by sickness and may be able to correct some of the causes. The realization of children that their parents were hampered or hurt through ill health that could have been prevented may make them all the more determined not to suffer from the misfortune that came to the parents. In that case, unless it is an unescapable hereditary weakness, the children are more likely to maintain a home in health than is the average family. Even when there is hereditary handicap, a greater concern may largely, if not fully, counteract the liability placed upon them as they go forward through life.

The child from the unsuccessful home likewise has suffered a misfortune but not one that predestines the victim to domestic failure. Again we have the two questions: (1) What was the cause of the unhappy home? (2) What can be done to prevent its repetition in the second generation? It also must be remembered that those who are happy in their married and family life are inclined to see happiness in their own childhood home even more than those who are themselves unhappy tend to interpret a similar failure in the relationship of their parents. In all such backward estimations, the characteristic disposition of the individual colors judgment.

The student who studies the family is supposed to realize that there is no standard experience which is shared by all who maintain successful family life and which explains their good fortune. Those who achieve success are too unlike for this to be true. Their adjustments are highly individual, revealing a wide range in variations. It is evident as soon as close contact is made with their home life that it fulfills their wishes but that it also might never satisfy another family who also have achieved happiness. Satisfaction in marriage and the home is therefore relative, determined by the kind of people who seek it and their ability to construct the sort of home that pleases them. It is in part the result of favorable circumstances, but it is also the reaction of those concerned that makes them seem propitious. Appraisal of success in family life is subject to the considerations involved in any other estimation of human-adjustment values. There are many grounds for judgment, and this has to be reckoned with in making the appraisal. The social worker is likely to find homes that are happy that she disapproves. From her social outlook they are not good families and ought not to be happy.

Later in this chapter, differing aspects of successful family life will be considered. Before pronouncements can be made as to the character of the individual home, the basis of judgment must be clearly determined and also at what period of time in the career of its members will the final appraisal be made. For example, judged by their childhood, the family life of the Earl of Shaftesbury or that of Dorothea Dix can be condemned. However, when the final consequences of such early misfortune are considered from the larger social viewpoint, a contrary estimation seems indicated. One thing is certain, and this is perhaps the most significant fact for the student looking forward to marriage and parenthood. Success, if looked at from the viewpoint of the individual himself, can neither be a complete fulfillment of desire, nor a static consummation, nor the mere satisfaction of the demands that from time to time are added to the original anticipation. Instead, as is true of every other successful life adjustment, it is a continuing, progressive achievement, with much of its satisfaction coming out of its struggle toward an ever increasing adequacy.

Awareness of family disorganization. During the closing quarter of the last century, certain thoughtful men and women, sensitive to social trends and interested in family experience, became conscious that something was happening of fundamental significance in the realm of domestic adjustment. By the end of the first decade of the twentieth century, this group of persons had considerably enlarged, and some of its members were attempting to interest intelligent men and women in the approaching crisis of the family or were seeking to interpret for those already convinced the meaning of the emerging social experience and the best way of meeting it. Among those who had come to have an inkling of the impending changes were Edward Carpenter and James Hinton, in England; Ellen Key, in Sweden; and Charlotte Perkins Gilman and Anna Garlin Spencer, in the United States.

Somewhat later, as has been brought out in the chapter "The Family Itself a Problem," a group of writers representing divergent attitudes, including the Russells, Lindsey, Calverton, Schmalhausen, Keyserling, Wile, the Binkleys, Burgess, Folsom, Schmiedeler, Hart, Waller, and many others, including the authors, drew attention to the disorganization that marriage and family life were revealing under the impact of the rapidly changing social conditions of the twentieth century.

The smug complacency of the period and the strength of the taboo against even the discussion of the conventional practices and ideals relating to the family may perhaps be best illustrated by the fact that Carpenter's *Love's Coming of Age* was published by himself in 1918 after it had been refused in succession by five or six of the best known London publishers. It was generally felt that even questioning the finality of the prevailing family as the climax of domestic evolution was an attack upon the stability of the home and a dangerous expression of social heresy. However, in comparison with the slow way in which new social thinking usually develops, the awakening of the public to the changing situation was rapid. This was due chiefly to three influences: the agitation for woman suffrage, the increasing expression of matrimonial and social discontent by intelligent women, and the increase of divorces. This third factor was the most persuasive, because the statistical facts could not be argued away, and they brought with them a feeling of alarm among those who saw in any considerable instability of the family the certainty of its decay.

Thoughtful people had, of course, been long familiar with the significance of family problems, but this had meant in the past the failures of individual families to live in accord with accepted standards. The bad family was the low, the vicious, and the irresponsible home. Critics of family experience were calling attention to a very different sort of problem, one that appeared to invade the integrity of the family itself. Their interpretations were regarded at first as attacks illustrating the moral deterioration which was responsible in the minds of these defenders of the *status quo* for the weakening of family ideals. There was little recognition of the connection between the family situation and the changing social environment.

Even those most sensitive to the disturbance occurring

within the domestic realm had only slight realization that the family was reflecting external conditions which were soon to force a new alignment of family and marriage experience, that, as the Renaissance and the Reformation had shattered the family form of an earlier period and reshaped it in harmony with its new environment, so a new civilization, chiefly the product of modern industrial influences, was leading the family forward to a new disorganization and eventual reconstruction.

Although women chiefly led in the agitations of the time and were usually the seekers of divorce, there was little disposition to look into the meaning of these facts and to realize that modern civilization was destined to operate chiefly upon marriage and the family through the changing status of woman. In her attitudes and through her opportunities, which she was gaining by a militant aggressiveness from a reluctant social leadership, she was becoming a new type with no counterpart in any of the preceding stages of human culture. Although only a few women in either the United States or Europe apprehended what was taking place, there was an increasing and largely unconscious restlessness. These expressions of discontent indicated how profoundly the status of women was beginning to be disturbed, and it was clear, as some of the pioneers of thought discovered early, that any considerable departure of women from their traditional role must force essential changes in the quality of matrimonial and familial experience. Women were not seeking the new outlook so much as they were being driven toward it. Men were less resisting the demands of the new women than they were unknowing of what was taking place.

The most radical cultural change concerning the status of woman and domestic relationships accompanied the revolution in Russia and the establishment of the Soviet government. Previously Turkey had made the most marked transformation of the status of the sexes in modern history. Woman was released from the traditions that had restricted her to domestic isolation and was free, so far as law could bring this about, to enter commercial and political life in a near-equality with men.[1] The change in woman's position, however, was much greater in Russia. It came later and therefore reflected more forcefully

---

[1] Woodsmall, Ruth F., *Moslem Women Enter a New World.*

modern trends. It was also associated with the economic revolution expressed in the first communistic experiment on a nation-wide basis. Getting married, which had sometimes been difficult, was made easy. Registration was the only requirement. Partners could adopt the surname of either or they could continue their former surnames. It was only necessary to be eighteen years of age, mentally normal, not closely related in blood, and unmarried. The spouses were obligated to inform each other regarding their health. Place of residence was by mutual consent, and if one moved to another locality the other was not legally required to follow. Housekeeping was not the woman's responsibility but a joint obligation. If either partner became incapacitated, the other was required to give support. Any property acquired after marriage belonged to both and if divided was to be shared alike. Divorce was made as easy as marriage. The union could be dissolved by mutual consent.[2]

It was the governmental policy to release women as much as possible from household drudgery and therefore collective cooking as well as nursery care for children was provided. In many ways women were encouraged to enter other than family employment, and in 1935 two-thirds worked outside the home in comparison with about two-fifths in the United States.

This radical reconstruction of family life became governmental policy. Here, as always happens in radical reforms, folkways retarded the program. Many women preferred a private kitchen to a communal eating place. As was to be expected in so extensive a country as Russia, there were within the republic great differences in the degree to which these various attempts to reconstruct family life functioned. There was also misinterpretation of the meaning or purpose of the new laws. The consequence was that a considerable number of the younger generation asserted that sexual relations were purely physiological and not essentially different from drinking water to quench thirst. This theory of free love proved socially disturbing and led to a rebuke from Lenin himself, who is reported to have said in part: "Of course thirst cries out to be quenched. But will a normal person under normal conditions lie down in the dirt on the road and drink from a puddle? Or even from a glass with a rim greasy from many lips? But most

---

[2] Halle, Fannina, *Woman in the Soviet East*, p. 132.

important of all is the social aspect. Drinking water really is an individual concern. Love involves two, and a third, a new life, may come into being. That implies an interest on the part of society, a duty to the community." [3]

Provision was made for abortions secured at government hospitals maintained in accord with modern medical standards. The woman who chose to escape childbirth was free to do so. The number that made this decision was so large that its effect on the population was one cause of the government's later reversing its policy. Divorce also was discouraged and made more difficult. On the other hand, positive measures were taken to recognize the value of family life and to encourage the stability of marriage. The extreme promiscuity of the earlier period lessened. There was no regression, however, as far as the status of woman was concerned. She was even permitted to assume combat service in the Red Army, and in the front ranks during the struggle with Germany in World War II many individual women won distinction, bearing dangers equally with men.

The family crisis during the twentieth century. Influences that we now call the machine culture were doing to the family what we are beginning to realize they did to every aspect of human experience. The family was entering upon an epoch of transition and facing a crisis from which there was no escape except by readjustment in ideals and in functions. The fact that along with this shifting there went an ever increasing divorce rate, more and more domestic restlessness, and eventually even the challenging of the code of conduct as it applied to the relation of the sexes convinced many who had at heart the welfare of the family that society was being menaced by a moral degeneration which must be resisted at all points. As in every great social crisis, stubborn emotion and faulty insight led many to fight on the wrong side, making it all the harder for the family as an institution to make a safe passage through the ordeal which was forced upon it by the compulsions arising from a material environment never before experienced.

This transitional experience of marriage and the family, extravertive in origin, has now prevailed so long and gone so far as to be rather widely realized and for the most part even accepted. This more mature attitude which has resulted from

---
[3] *Ibid.*, p. 113.

our familiarity with a major social feature of our time has
brought forth a new attitude toward the experience, and with
this has gone a new definition of the meaning of the successful
family. There also has developed a new strategy for the helping
of the family in its present disturbance.

Although only the dogmatist insists that he is certain of
the outcome, most friends of the family have become persuaded
of the uselessness of a negative program of repression. Confidence in coercion as a means of recovery has been lost, in part
because it is being recognized that the convictions which alone
give power to regulations and legislation have been widely
destroyed as a result of our changing culture.

The present disposition among those seeking to assist marriage and the family is to find the impulses of human nature
that support these institutions and to make use of them in
strengthening the individual who is attempting to make matrimonial or domestic adaptation. There is understanding that
these resources must be found largely within the personality of
those experiencing matrimonial and family difficulties and not
in some outside force such as law or preachment.

There is also frank recognition of the difficulties of adjustment, and these are regarded less as evidence of fault and more
as consequences of the complexity of domestic relations under
the conditions of modern civilization. Even in the maladjustments that are clearly the result of undisciplined and unintelligent personality, the tendency is to look upon these persons in
trouble more as victims of adverse preparation for their experience than as individuals who are blameworthy. As a consequence of this different attitude toward any family failure,
attention is directed toward the conditions that make for success, and this has permitted a more dynamic program than was
possible in the days when only the defeated family drew attention.

With this change of front there has gone a greater willingness to diagnose the causes of family failure and even more
the desire to find methods of preparing individuals for the
testing they cannot avoid as members of a family and as persons entering matrimony and accepting parenthood. There is,
however, enough lingering of the older attitude, which insisted
upon locating the blame for family disaster, to retard the use

of modern science in helping married people in trouble, but the new understanding is spreading widely and rapidly and releasing in increasing measure the resources of science available for the assisting of those attempting family adjustment.

The prevailing philosophy. The nature of the problem of achieving success in family adjustment cannot be understood without recognition of the prevailing milieu in which the domestic institution has to function. Both marriage and the family encounter a severe testing on account of the emotional attitude and the motivation associated with the dominant pleasure philosophy. This outlook upon life is of course a rough generalization which brings together a great quantity of individual variations. Even though one cannot justly describe the purposes and standards of American family life by a blanket term, the pleasure program is the vogue and established the current milieu of the family.

The efficiency of applied science has led in the occidental world to a popularizing of desire to such an extent that success in any undertaking is defined in terms of satisfaction. Obligations and sacrifice within the family are not swept aside but are driven into the background. The lessening of the economic functioning of the family also tends to make more prominent the purpose of family experience as a means of fulfillment of personal desire.

Thus the family experience becomes a strategic point in the long social battle line of present-day culture. The individual's struggle for happiness, wherever it occurs, has a meaning for the strivings that gather about his family interests. It is equally true that the value he finds in his family relationship is distinctly influenced by his successes and his failures at other points of struggle.

As has often been pointed out, there is a lessening of tolerance of hard circumstances within the family and a proneness to denounce the family experience that seems lacking in pleasure-giving qualities. This attitude, however, is subordinated to a more positive demand that the family justify itself by its satisfactions. Modern youths are less concerned as to how one can retreat from an unhappy marriage or irksome domestic situation and more insistent that the way be opened for them to attain satisfaction. More and more, unless their religion forbids their having a choice, they take for granted that they are not only free but morally obligated to break up any disastrous or disappointing relationship. This is so much a matter of course that it gets scant attention in their program. For them the divorce problem can never be a major issue. They are too thoroughly committed to the pleasure philosophy to recognize any portentous problem in divorce or, if that be against their scruples for religious reasons, in separation. Their thought turns to the question, "How can marriage and family experience be for me and for those I love a success measured in terms of satisfaction?"

This interpretation is of course a derivative of the social atmosphere of the moment, but besides making subjective decisions as to the values of family experience inevitable, it also puts upon the individual the task of constructing a working ratio of demands and possibilities. However far man has been carried in the pleasure economy by our machine civilization, he has not and he cannot, because of his inherent limitations as a finite, discover a fairyland of complete satisfaction. Reality still offers a stubborn barrier to his desires, from which he recoils. Pleasures multiply, but happiness remains an achievement, a product of discrimination and compromise between demands and possibilities.

Since expectation runs high upon entrance to marriage and with the coming of parenthood, these experiences are reluctant to accept the restraint of the self-discipline which alone permits the maturing required for any substantial, permanent satisfaction. Thus marriage and the family cannot cradle the mere pleasure-seeker. They provide no artificial social paradise segregated from life but relationships that range through all the possibilities of human experience. Their success requires growth of personality, and this in process may lead to pain as well as to pleasure and may seem to the individual a repudiation of the promises which made marriage and parenthood and domestic fellowship appear desirable.

A new social adventure.   The study of the past evolution of the family will always be to the student fascinating and suggestive. There is, however, no practical value in trying to relate the present situation of the family with the situation in preceding times. Only of late has woman been given any large amount of free expression of personality, and only more recently has this been true of the child. The man-made family pattern is at an end. Apparently the new order must provide self-expression for man, woman, and child.

Under such unparalleled conditions it is futile to go back to the earlier times for a sense of direction. Realization of this has led to the loss of assurance that seemed so firmly planted with the coming of the doctrine of evolution. The present family is making as original an adaptation to environmental circumstances as did the human family when it first emerged as a social institution. Family success is attainable only on the present cultural level, and this requires a sense of personal achievement and appraisal of circumstances utterly foreign to primitive man and woman. The great quantity of resources applicable to every sort of human experience has led to higher qualitative standards, and in the family experience these lead to most exacting expectations. Each member of the family is both an environment and a person making demands. The more modern the family, the more this is true. No passive program of compromise or subordination can solve so intricate an interaction. There has to be fusion of interest without the feeling of suppression which under the circumstances easily arises.

The tensions of modern domestic experience are in part related to the outside social environment in which the family is embedded, but chiefly they appear within the personality of each family member and require self-adjustment as well as successful interaction with the other members of the family. It is because of this that the family seems so often disappointing to those whose marriage and domestic experience fail. Any inability to cope wisely with the intricacies of modern civilization, any unwillingness to check the tendency to flight from the necessary discipline of human life, shows itself with consequences within the family arena.

Doubtless there have always been problems due to family interaction, at least from the time that human culture reached the level which permitted any considerable degree of self-consciousness and self-expression. Nevertheless, it is clear that in our time problems come that reveal the present difficulties resulting from the lack of self-control and the faulty discrimination of values among those committed to a pleasure-seeking life program. Failures of adjustment, due to such circumstances, call attention to the larger and more fundamental problem that now confronts humanity—the need of learning to make good use of the abundant resources made possible by applied science.

The discipline of hard and meager circumstances has in the past made easier all personal relationships, but it has especially lessened the frictions of domestic interaction. The new order brings more opportunity for tension, but family life must thrive under modern conditions, and success can only be achieved through insight that enables it to build success. In large degree present family insufficiency is rather less a problem than a symptom. That is, it reflects the deeper problem which man through his material conquests has thrust upon himself. The family cannot be protected, as some seem to expect, from the ordeal of modern civilization. It is distinctive merely as a specialized experience; it lies exposed to the same conflicting influences that are testing and reshaping governments, industry, religion, education, and all other forms of social organization.

Emphasis of familial satisfaction. Industry and commerce by advertising and other methods of stimulating desire draw attention to out-of-family satisfactions. These do not necessarily rival or antagonize domestic life. There is need, however, for greater emphasis on those satisfactions that can be gathered through the relationships of marriage and parenthood. Once there was little reason for interpreting the value of domestic experience. The conditions of life were such that it became natural for the majority of American men and women to discover much of their content within the home. The difference between the past and the present is relative. The home never had a monopoly of satisfaction-bringing experiences. Nor was it always true that all who married and had children enjoyed family life. For many it was a burden, for others tolerable. Nevertheless, it was a characteristic of the time that attention turned toward the home, since the social environment tended to stress family life as a source of satisfaction. In these days there has been a reversal of environmental stimulation as it affects the family. Perhaps the best illustration of this is the loss of family recreation and the almost universal trend on the part of youth and many adults toward finding their pleasures outside the home. So great is this that for the protection of teen-aged children in some communities, specially adapted night clubs have been organized by churches and by schools to keep the boys and girls from patronizing unwholesome "joints" and similar hazardous meeting places.

The time has come when there must be definite educational efforts to help young people learn to enjoy home life. The values that can be gathered through fellowship of family members united by affection needs not only to be emphasized but stimulated in the same way that the opportunities for out-of-family enjoyment are now stressed. Strange as it may seem in contrast with the past, modern youth require preparation for enjoying the resources of domestic relationships and for the building of attitudes that will make the home more than a place to sleep and eat and to carry on the activities necessary for existence while they look elsewhere for most of their enjoyments. The two sources of satisfaction should be complementary, and successful family life requires for most men and women a balance of domestic and out-of-family pleasures. Sex alone cannot give long-lasting security to a home that is relatively barren of other means of enjoyment.

The progressive family.   The family as a social institution attempting to meet the demands put upon it and to maintain its integrity is put at a disadvantage through the rapidly changing characer of modern civilization. The cultural current gathers its momentum from the swift transformation occurring in the material portion of man's interest, often amounting along some line of custom to a veritable revolution, and, as a consequence, the rest of man's life, which we distinguish as social in the narrower and more precise sense, is forbidden any stability.

Traditions, attitudes, codes, and institutions may lag behind, but they cannot settle themselves and establish anything more than a transitory adjustment. Material culture goes onward with unprecedented speed, and social experience has no choice but to follow after. So long as this continues, all successful social adjustment must be achieved in passage, and this means an addition to the other strain that is coming from influences of our complex and pleasure-driven civilization. Perhaps our only parallel in human evolution appears in the situation of a relatively simple society when there has been rapid and continuous introduction of a more intricate and advanced culture.

The difficulty of the family in this predicament can be realized only as one pictures the perplexities, the inconsistencies, the compromises, and the periodic settlements of individual families, each differing from every other in the responses it makes to the flood of change that flows into it on the one side and the resisting influences that come forth in a different direction from the less progressive part of the environment as a result of the lag of the mores. The individual family may develop a policy of attempting to hold to the past, but it succeeds in hanging back only in the proportion that it isolates itself from the quickly moving outside world, and at best it cannot maintain a segregation which will bring any considerable relief.

Under present circumstances, family adjustment is a continuous process and rarely does any family achieve a *modus vivendi* that compromises conflicting desires as thoroughly as is possible when adjustment can be had in the clear definitive form characteristic of a slow-moving culture. Even when the family obtains a rest from change and establishes an equilibrium, its program is soon swept aside and the new interactions are as original as if there had been no temporary adjustment. For example, the mere advance of the child in age demands in the American home a frequent recrystallization of family experience merely because in the present order the child plays a more active role than ever was previously true.

No formula for family success.   There can be no formula for family success. The task that confronts any family is too individual, too complicated, and too changeable to profit from any recipe for satisfactory adjustment. At present there is a disposition among some to find in sex technique, or what is called the art of love, a prescription for matrimonial success. Important as the evidence demonstrates sexual adjustment to be for matrimonial happiness, even here there can be no formula that wholly meets the demands within this restricted sphere of domestic interaction. Sex maladjustment is not only both cause and result in the tragedies of marriage, but even sex satisfaction more and more becomes something that requires of the individual an achievement beyond mere physical sex. If a

formula could be written for successful interaction on its physical level, sex as a human experience has become too complex
to find satisfaction on the plane of mere passion.

One can gather from those happy in their family experience statements of prerequisites for marriage or qualities desired, but these are only descriptions of the personal preferences
of individuals and are for the most part rationalizations. They
are clearly not causes of successful family life in the sense that
satisfaction is guaranteed by the possession of any one or any
combination of these desirable traits. They suggest some of the
accomplishments of good family life, but they do not state the
methods for the gaining of such successes. Those confronted
with the necessity of working out some adjustment of a family
character are seldom aided by a catalog of domestic virtues, and
rarely does conviction of the value of these objectives afford
insight in dealing with a concrete problem of family relationships. What is meat for one family often proves poison for
another.

To attempt to find family success by cataloging the essential virtues is not only of little worth for diagnosis; it also
harks back to the prescientific outlook and thus distracts attention from the more effective methods of dealing with family
problems. There is undoubtedly a moral significance in all
family maladjustment, and no one would deny that character
traits have much to do with deciding a family career. Merely,
however, to list desirable personality characteristics provides
no clue as to how any individual may attain wholesome family
life but substitutes preachment for specific analysis. For example, the family member may be condemned for selfishness,
for jealousy, or for the lack of pluck to succeed, but after these
indictments have been placed there is no greater understanding
as to why the individual has failed under family testing or
what must be done to bring him hope of success. This explains
why the oncoming generation gives such scant attention to any
list of qualities prerequisite for family success.

Statistical studies. Studies have been undertaken to discover the proportion of happy and unhappy marriages. In one
of the earliest of these, made by Katharine Davis in 1929, 1,000
married women, including 691 college graduates, were asked
the question: "Is your marriage a happy one?" Eight hundred

and seventy-two declared themselves happy.[4] The same year a more detailed and careful investigation was made by G. V. Hamilton through interviews using a list of questions. His findings were based upon the answers given by 200 spouses. From the data gathered, he found 29 men and 21 women expressing a relatively high degree of satisfaction; 22 men and 24 women, a fair degree; 13 men and 14 women showing considerable dissatisfaction; 36 men and 41 women, a high degree of dissatisfaction.[5] A similar investigation was made by Terman. His material came from 792 husbands and wives who were willing to give information concerning their marital situation. Eighty-three per cent of the husbands and 85 per cent of the wives considered their marriages at a point of happiness superior to the average. Less than 5 per cent of the men and less than 6 per cent of the women thought their marriages below a norm.[6] Other experts, E. W. Burgess and Leonard Cottrell, with the co-operation of 526 couples, made a statistical study as a basis for predicting failure or success in marriage. Distributing some 7,000 questionnaires, they received 1,900 replies, of which 526 were such as could be used in carrying out the investigation. Sixty-three per cent of these men and women considered their marriage happier than the average. The happiness ratings were as follows: 42.6 per cent very happy, 20.5 per cent happy, 14.4 per cent average, 13.5 per cent unhappy, 8 per cent very unhappy, 1 per cent no reply.[7] In 1931 a medical study made by Robert L. Dickinson and Lura Beam resulted in less optimistic findings. In this investigation emphasis was placed upon sexual adjustment. Three hundred and ninety-three of these women, living with husbands, stated that they had no complaint of any kind, while 375 admitted that they did have problems that they were willing to discuss with the doctor. Since 275 of these women were diagnosed as suffering from some sort of sexual problem, the high percentage of those seeking medical help was not surprising.[8]

All of these studies are based upon expressed opinions.

[4] Davis, Katharine B., *Factors in the Sex Life of 2,200 Women*, p. 39.

[5] Hamilton, G. V., *A Research in Marriage*, p. 532.

[6] Terman, Lewis M., *Psychological Factors in Marriage Happiness*, p. 75.

[7] Burgess, E. W., and Cottrell, Leonard, *Predicting Success or Failure in Marriage*, p. 33.

[8] Dickinson, R. L., and Beam, Lura, *A Thousand Marriages*, p. 11.

The subjective nature of their material therefore has to be recognized. Findings are buttressed by various correlations. Jessie Bernard charted a summary of these tests showing the proportion of cases that may be said to function successfully through affection. The range was from 87 per cent to 58.6 per cent.[9] All of these investigations, aside from their statistical evaluation of marital happiness, something which they recognize as difficult to define, are open inherently to the risk of rationalization in some degree. They are, however, valuable to the student of the family even though based upon the judgment of those providing the material. This is especially true of the Burgess and Cottrell investigation which reveals various conditions that correlate with the statements concerning marital failure and success. Like the prediction of the death rate upon which life insurance rests, the findings are useful for group appraisals and must not be regarded as causal determinations applicable to the individual. Like the mortality tables of life insurance, they also are subject to the conserving influences, when there is at least reason to believe that a proposed marriage is laden with a liability. For example, one would expect a child brought up by parents who have been happy in their married life to have, as the studies show, greater probability of himself being happy when he marries. Those, however, who have experienced the opposite condition in their early childhood profit greatly from knowing that this is true. The Burgess and Cottrell contribution is priceless to them in helping them guard against possible risk to their marriage success. Their foreknowledge of their possible injury can give them an insight and a determination to succeed that can be expected to bring them greater than average happiness in marriage.

Mere maintenance not enough.   Statistically, family failures can be enumerated by bringing together divorces and separations. There is a sense, meager though it is in content, in which families that have survived dissolution may be counted successful. The mere maintenance of the family, however, is not evidence of the kind of success we usually mean when we speak of a well-adjusted family group. It has become so commonplace to estimate success or failure in the family relationship by the individual's attitude and reaction to his experiences that no one

[9] Bernard, Jessie, *American Family Behavior*, p. 103.

considers any family successful merely because it does not suffer a breakdown.

There can be no doubt that there are in this country a great many families that fail in addition to those recorded through public confession by divorce or separation. We all know families seriously maladjusted that for some ulterior reason do not break up. There is, at least among our youth, little disposition to estimate the success of the family in other terms than its satisfactions and consequences for the individual. The more the family concentrates upon affection as its major purpose and the less it performs an economic or social function, the more exacting will be this test of success.

Objective standards. Marriage and the family cannot be standardized. If these experiences were merely means to an end, precise methods of carrying on necessary human activities and nothing more, objective standards could be formulated showing degrees of efficiency. Such ideals can be described even under present circumstances, but no one regards these as affording insight in dealing with the more difficult and determining issues of family life. Marriage and parenthood have become more and more personal quests, adventures that are chiefly significant because of the meaning they have for those engaged in them, rather than through their utility.

It is apparent also that the period when the family can function to any great extent as a means of coercing human nature into a socially approved pattern is at an end. For both adult and child the experience cannot be predominantly coercive without being made so distasteful as to become to the individual, chafing under compulsion, a failure. Marriage and the family are being organized as vehicles of satisfaction. To admit this is not to conceive the purposes of the family in any infantile fashion. Success is unattainable along any path that leads to immaturity, for the satisfaction that fulfills the needs of the modern man and woman must be substantial. To describe it as mere pleasure-seeking or self-gratification is to misrepresent its essential craving. There is need of a mature form of fellowship with another personality as certainly as there is the necessity of self-development and self-expression. It is the exacting quality of the conditions that permit success within the family rather than the pitching of desire at a low level that is making domestic relationships difficult.

Subjective standards—the husband.   The new order is destructive of the historic attitude which men have taken toward women, and a new masculine role is in process. The culture of the past has operated to subordinate woman to man. In so far as modern conditions have tended to release women from masculine dominance, it has become apparent how artificial woman's place has been and how impossible it is becoming to maintain a family that attempts to carry on the former conventions. It is at this point that the most critical processes of transference are taking place. It is likewise here that we find the greatest tension and the most frequent explanation of marriage and family failure.

It is not merely that woman is changing; she is also changing man. Each is operating upon the other to produce a different type of social being and one that requires adjustments totally unlike those which were required in the past for the making of a successful family. The masculine family is at an end, but it is not so clear what is to be the new type of family which is being built upon mutual co-operation of husband and wife free from the sex discrimination of the past.

The wife.   The modern woman's hunger for individuality expresses her confusion in our present period of transition. Man has carried his demands for affection to the point where satisfaction can be approximated only by the development of the new woman. She has been forced to become conscious of the necessity of changes which he has less appreciated. Since the transformation has chiefly been realized by her, she has had greater consciousness of the difficulties of adjustment to life, and especially of adjustment through family experience.

The force of modern culture strikes individual women with differing degrees of strength, and there is, of course, great variation in the reaction of individual women. The trend, however, is unmistakable. Success in marriage and in family life can be had only as the relationship brings satisfaction, and for most women this means greater opportunity for self-expression than ever has been true in the past or is yet common. This magnifies the purpose of marriage and elevates the character of family experience. Success comes not from making the family a means to an end, as was true when its function was largely economic; the family has become an end in itself and one that is essentially the development and satisfaction of personality. If success is realized, it has to be by at least a partial fulfillment of the individual's union with another self. The woman has become less a helpmate, and more a comrade in an adventure which proves hopeless unless it is a reciprocity not so much in services as in responses.

The child.   The child likewise is emerging as an independent personality within the modern family. His status has enlarged, and parenthood, as a consequence, has become more difficult. If he finds the family atmosphere coercive, he considers his relationship a failure in proportion to the extent that his consciousness of self has been developed. How far this better way of looking at the meaning of the child will change the functioning of the family only time can reveal. The trend, however, is clear. The child is being admitted more and more to a family fellowship which achieves success to the degree that each member realizes satisfaction. For him as for the adult the security of the family rests upon the opportunity it provides for fulfillment, but in his case this is complicated by the fact that he is a more rapidly changing personality than his parents and more susceptible to the conflicting stimuli that come forth from the modern social environment.

Under such conditions success is inconceivable as a static ideal or by any mechanical prescription. To be wholesome and satisfying, the family has to be as dynamic as modern life itself and must always be incomplete and promising rather than something final. Such a conception antagonizes those who insist upon a precise formula for the gaining of family success. The family has become a specialized relationship that offers exceptional opportunity under the conditions of modern life for the intensive cultivating and satisfying of strong human desires as well as for the carrying on of fundamental social services.

The security of the family.   It has been repeatedly pointed out by investigators that the present-day American family is undergoing a decline. This is largely a readjustment of functions and reveals that the family has a smaller social purpose than formerly. It is surrendering activities that once were not only its prerogative but that also established its dominance as a social institution. Under such circumstances, it is natural that the question arises, "What of its future?"

Along with this lessening of the field of the family as a social organization, there appears from a different quarter an enlargement, and apparently its security must increasingly come from its usefulness in this new undertaking. It is easy to exaggerate the meaning of this change in the family, since what now has come to have great significance was never entirely absent in the past. In a period of transition such as ours there is a tendency to overstate what is rather more a different emphasis than a stripping of the family of all that it used to do and a putting upon it of an original function.

When the risk of this exaggeration is recognized, it still remains true that the values coming out of family experience are being interpreted in their meaning for personal relationship rather than from their utility in a social enterprise. It is not strange that such a shift should be alarming to those who assume that the family must always find its security in the same sort of activities that it has long carried on as a social institution. Direct values issuing from the association of the family itself are, however, as substantial a basis for the future family as have been the predominant indirect services in the past. Possibly the new values are more difficult to achieve; certainly under present circumstances they seem so, but this does not indicate disintegration of the family but merely the seriousness of its modern task.

How much of the prevailing disorganization of the American family is a necessary liability of complex civilization and how far it is temporary failure to adjust the family program to present needs time alone can reveal. At least the evidence is unmistakable that the family is not only going through a transition but is having a difficult passage.

It is possible to contrast sharply the family of the present and of the past and to see in the new emphasis upon personal satisfactions in marriage, parenthood, and family relationships a trend alien to the function of the family as a social institution. This reaction fails to recognize that these values, experienced and appraised by individuals, are indirectly social and may give the family as strong a security as its economic functions, for example, did in the past.

It is now commonplace to insist that the immature find marriage and the family difficult and disappointing. This does not mean that individual families thrive only as they are established by those who have completed personality growth, but rather that the family to be successful demands of its members ability to develop toward maturity. The test the family now puts on those who demand satisfaction of cravings that have become in the modern world the deepest of human nature uncovers the present social significance of the family and the basis for its security. The family is a satisfying organization to the degree that it is a socializing experience. It is not a storehouse of happiness to which the individual is given access; it can only provide an opportunity and an incentive for the achieving of the emotional maturity which alone makes possible the integration of the individual personality. Upon the accomplishment of this, society depends not only for its social soundness but even for its very existence. The family is as safe as civilization itself.

Suggestions for individual success in marriage and the family. College students who have studied marriage and the family are not likely to doubt the security of either of these fundamental human relationships. The future of each of these social institutions seems to them assured. The students' feelings of uncertainty are more likely to be concerned with their own careers. They are too aware of individual families that have failed and of the increasing divorce rate not to wonder sometimes whether they will themselves achieve marriage and family success. The authors, having had for many years, through counseling service, confidential knowledge both of failures and successes, have become convinced that much depends upon the personal program adopted for and actually practiced in marriage. Herewith they summarize the procedures that have from their experience the most promise of bringing an increasing happiness and success in marriage and family life.

1. Intelligent preparation is necessary. Rarely do they fail who seriously try to prepare themselves for the personal re-

sponsibilities and opportunities of marriage. Thought has to be given to the demands of the relationship and information gathered concerning its problems and opportunities. This getting ready can best be accomplished calmly in the spirit of confidence without the strain of those who overemphasize the consequences of mistakes. Passion, romance, daydreaming, the intensity of falling in love cannot provide a secure preparation for marriage. They are not obstacles, however, if they are allied to an intelligent effort to become realistically equipped for the experience.

2. In such a program, from the beginning the great importance of health should be recognized. This means that before marriage a special medical examination which will reveal any possible handicap will be sought from some physician competent to carry through this service. This will be true of both the man and the woman and periodically a general physical checkup will be had. It is true that chronic illnesses have not been able in some instances to destroy married happiness. The Robert Brownings and Wendell Phillips are impressive examples of successful marriages despite ill health. Nevertheless, in planning for marriage, the advantage of safeguarding physical and mental health should be recognized and the maintenance of a sound health program made a continuous, conscious policy of both husband and wife. This will include the effort not only to escape disease but to maintain energy at its highest level. To accomplish this, some men and some women must curb ambition and avoid overfatigue. For many this is no small task, for American life invites behavior that leads to tension and the dissipation of energy successful marriage needs. This health program will include the sex life. The sexual impulse is influenced by the conditions of the body and contributes to its well-being. It is an index of body vitality and one of the first physical functions to suffer from overdraft of nervous energy.[10] Sex should be accepted as an asset of great value, and any problem connected with it should be dealt with quickly, frankly, and in the light of scientific knowledge. If necessary, eroticism should be either cultivated or, in some cases, it should be disciplined and restrained. A satisfactory sex life should be achieved by both the man and the woman. This expression of

---

[10] Walker, Kenneth, and Strauss, Eric B., *Sexual Disorders in the Male*, p. 51.

fellowship should be maintained as long as a conserving health program permits.

3. It should be realized by both husband and wife that a continuous adjustment is required to make marriage and family life a success. In accomplishing this, the interests of all parties involved must be considered in the spirit of equality. No program that sacrifices the well-being of one in order to fulfill the demands of the other should be tolerated. The compromising of mine and thine should be avoided as much as possible, the emphasis being placed upon the "our" of family relationship. Differences of personality should be accepted and stress put upon the possessions that are common or those that are complementary. The right to privacy and to interests that the spouse does not share, the right to remain an individual needs to be respected by both husband and wife and they in turn owe a similar obligation to their child.

4. There can be no successful separation of family life and out-of-family life as far as character is concerned, although there can be a concentration of interest that is not emphasized in the fellowship of husband and wife. For some spouses this policy works best, while for others the husband keeps intimate contact with domestic affairs, and the wife does likewise in his out-of-family work. The spirit of adventure that is felt, as a rule, at the beginning of marriage can be kept vigorous throughout the life career. Any static goal will lead to a petering out of the zest for life which strengthens marriage and invigorates all activity. The acquisitive impulse which leads to money grasping frequently chokes marriage. Contrarily, it is often the outward expression of a relationship already dead. Great wealth accompanied with interest in doing things and a desire to be useful has given us some of the highest types of family in the United States. On the other hand, it is not always true that love flies out of the window as poverty stalks through the door. The very poor, in spite of their hardship, maintain, more often than people suppose, as social workers will testify, a magnificent and affectionate family life. Nevertheless, the most auspicious economic condition for the successful family is one in which income provides the genuine necessities and the luxuries that commonly belong to the standard of living to which Americans are accustomed and which they take for granted. If the husband

or both spouses commit themselves to the accumulation of wealth as their supreme desire, the values of their family life ordinarily shrink.

5. No one reaches high levels in domestic experience who has lost his faith in ideals. The form this necessary confidence in the worth-whileness of human experience takes varies greatly. Most commonly it is rooted in religious belief. Sometimes its source is what can best be described as humanism. Much more rarely it gathers nourishment from a dominant artistic outlook on life, the philosophic approach that Hegel would call "the beautiful." The important thing is its genuineness and its actual functioning as the test of values. The mere acceptance of dogma and tradition or a docile following of convention is barren as an asset to the family.

6. The will to permanency in marriage greatly contributes to success.[11] In consultation with those who have had serious problems in their marriage and family life, especially those contemplating divorce, the conviction of the authors has been that most of these men and women started marriage reasonably hopeful that they would be successful. In spite of some initial mistakes, there was no unescapable cause of failure. Looking backward, it is not difficult to detect what the blunders were and why the marriage developed trouble. A smaller number of these cases indicated a lack either of basis for congeniality or the still more serious handicap of one or both of the spouses not being well adapted to monogamic marriage. A considerable number of the latter would probably have succeeded if their code could have been that of some parts and classes in continental Europe.

Through conferences with those entering marriage, the experienced counselor comes to have a confidence in many of these young people which makes him feel that there is certainty in the case of most of them that they will achieve happiness and success. The attitude they take, the preparedness they make, and the kind of persons they are give the counselor assurance of their ability to handle whatever problem arises. It is the experience of the authors that this expectation thus far has never proved faulty.

[11] Spaulding, Clarence A. (Editor), *Twenty-Four Views of Marriage*, Ch. 3.

The practice of adjusting. One of the safeguards of marriage is the cultivation of the habit of adjusting. This is much more conducive to happiness than the striving to attain some generalized virtue, desirable as that may be. One of the most stressed of these virtues in the popular literature is maturity, and rightly so, since it is a most desirable achievement in personality development. Nevertheless, the ability to adjust is more important, since maturity is relative and also inconsistently expressed. Tension comes into marriage frequently not from immaturity *per se* but from too great differences in maturity between husband and wife and inability to adjust to these. If one is very mature and the other only slightly so, trouble is more likely than if neither are much matured. There is also always the question How is the immaturity expressed? since rarely do we find a person mature in all respects. If there is mutual attraction, affection, and the ability to tolerate differences in maturity, both husband and wife can find success in marriage. The marriage experience of Disraeli is a striking example of this. The attempt of husband or wife to change the other greatly is frequently deadly in its effect on the marriage fellowship. The cultivation of a facility in adjusting to differences in the spouse, on the contrary, invigorates the fellowship of husband and wife.

Children. Those who have a good inheritance and are willing to develop the values of parenthood will find happiness and enrichment in having children. As a rule, it is an advantage to begin having children in the second year of marriage, or if some temporary condition such as economic struggle indicates postponement parenthood should be sought as soon thereafter as the situation permits. The risk of waiting for economic security should be recognized. Financial struggle, unless it is very great, does not justify not having children. If there is reason to suspect low fertility and an examination of husband and wife proves that this exists for one or both, an attempt to bring about pregnancy should be made within the first months of marriage.

Marriage and the career wife. When the wife follows a career, marriage is usually more difficult for her and for the husband than with the more common division of labor between the spouses. For the woman who wishes to follow a profession or business and has prepared herself for it, it is just that she have the opportunity to go on with her lifework so long as this continues to be her choice. Since she cannot succeed unless her husband co-operates, at least not without spoiling her marriage, there needs to be before the marriage a sincere acceptance of her decision by her husband. The possibility of his developing inferiority feeling should be recognized by both and guarded against from the start. From time to time in such a marriage there will be the necessity for new adjustments, and these should be faced with frankness by both husband and wife. The woman's contribution to marriage and parenthood is too much taken for granted to bring her social prestige, even though its significance makes it as deserving of recognition as any out-of-family success. Since there are, however, women who have an ambition that drives them to make use of their talent in the same ways as men, their happiness requires a marriage fellowship that permits them to maintain a career. Their choice of mate must therefore be highly selective or failure in marriage is almost certain.

The promise of marriage and parenthood. Marriage and parenthood can be the source of the greatest satisfactions in life. The marriage counselor is most impressed, not by the failures that lead to divorce, but by the needless petering out of the relationship and the meager achieving of the values that potentially belong to marriage and parenthood but which through lack of domestic development are never realized.

Appendix A
LITERATURE ILLUSTRATING FAMILY EXPERIENCES

FICTION

Anderson, S., *Dark Laughter.*
Banning, M. C., *Mixed Marriage.*
Beede, L., *Prairie Women.*
Bentley, P., *Inheritance.*
Buck, P., *Dragon Seed.*
Buck, P., *The Good Earth.*
Butler, S., *The Way of All Flesh.*
Campbell, L. B., *These Are My Jewels.*
Carroll, G. H., *As the Earth Turns.*
Cather, W. S., *The Professor's House.*
Cather, W. S., *Shadows on the Rock.*
Clear, G. F., *The Years That Crown.*
Comstock, H. T., *Penelope's Web.*
Deeping, W., *Kitty.*
Deeping, W., *Sorrell and Son.*
Dell, F., *Moon Calf.*
Dreiser, T., *An American Tragedy.*
Eichler, L., *Stillborn.*
Ferber, E., *Cimarron.*
Fisher, D. C., *The Bent Twig.*
Fisher, D. C., *The Deepening Stream.*
Fisher, D. C., *Her Son's Wife.*
Fisher, D. C., *The Home-Maker.*
Glasgow, Ellen, *Barren Ground.*
Glaspell, S., *Brook Evans.*
Graham, Gwethalyn, *Earth and High Heaven.*
Green, P., *The Laughing Pioneer.*
Hannum, A. P., *Thursday April.*
Herrick, R., *The End of Desire.*
Herrick, R., *The Healer.*

Hersey, John, *A Bell for Adano.*
Heyward, DuBose, *Mamba's Daughters.*
Hughes, Langston, *Not Without Laughter.*
Hull, H., *Heat Lightning.*
Hurston, Zora Neale, *Their Eyes Were Watching God.*
Hyde, R., *Young Family.*
Jameson, Storm, *The Other Side.*
Jarrett, C., *Night Over Fitch's Pond.*
Joseph, D., *October's Child.*
Lamande, A., *Dorette.*
Lawrence, D. H., *Kangaroo.*
Leader, P., *And No Birds Sing.*
Leech, M., *The Feathered Nest.*
Lewisohn, L., *The Island Within.*
Meller, Sidney, *Roots in the Sky.*
Mitchell, Margaret, *Gone With the Wind.*
Norris, C. G., *Seed: A Novel of Birth Control.*
Pagano, Jo, *Golden Wedding.*
Peterkin, J., *Bright Skin.*
Peterkin, J., *Scarlet Sister Mary.*
Pinsky, D., *The Generations of Noah Edon.*
Poole, E., *His Second Wife.*
Priestley, J. B., *Angel Pavement.*
Rawlings, Marjorie Kinnan, *The Yearling.*
Roberts, E. M., *The Great Meadow.*
Rolvaag, O. E., *Giants in the Earth.*
Rolvaag, O. E., *Their Father's God.*
Royde-Smith, N. G., *In the Wood.*
Rudd, J., *Wives and Mothers.*
St. Martin, Thad, *Madame Toussaint's Wedding Day.*
Sherriff, R. C., *The Fortnight in September.*
Steele, W. D., *Meat.*
Steinbeck, John, *The Grapes of Wrath.*
Stern, E. G., *A Marriage Was Made.*
Storm, L., *Seven Daughters.*
Suckow, R., *The Bonney Family.*
Swinnerton, F., *A Brood of Ducklings.*
Trites, W. B., *Paterfamilias.*
Wassermann, J., *Wedlock.*
Waugh, A., *Three Score and Ten.*
Weaver, J. V. A., *Her Knight Comes Riding.*
Wharton, E., *The Children.*
White, N. G., *This, My House.*
Wilder, I., *Mother and Four.*

Wiley, J., *Queer Street*.
Wilson, M., *The Kenworthys*.
Wolfe, Thomas, *Look Homeward, Angel*.

PLAYS

Akins, Zoe, *The Old Maid*.
Andreyers, L., *He Who Gets Slapped*.
Barrie, J. M., *Mary Rose*.
Beach, L., *Ann Vroome*.
Beach, L., *The Goose Hangs High*.
Besier, R., *The Barretts of Wimpole Street*.
Boothe, Clare, *The Women*.
Caldwell, Erskine, *Tobacco Road*.
Colton, J., and Randolph, C., *Rain*.
Connelly, Marc, *The Green Pastures*.
Crothers, Rachel, *Nice People*.
Dave, C., *A Bill of Divorcement*.
Davis, O., *Icebound*.
Ervine, St. John, *John Ferguson*.
Fisher, D. C., *Lavender Ladies*.
Galsworthy, J., *A Family Man*.
Glaspell, S., *Alison's House*.
Goodrich, A. F., and Palmer, R. A., *Caponsacchi*.
Green, Paul, and Wright, Richard, *Native Son*.
Heyward, DuBose, *Porgy and Bess*.
Howard, S., *The Silver Cord*.
Hughes, H., *Hell-Bent for Heaven*.
Ibsen, H., *A Doll's House*.
Ibsen, H., *Ghosts*.
Ibsen, H., *A Pillar of Society*.
Kaufman, G. S., and Connelly, M. C., *To the Ladies*.
Maeterlinck, M., *Monna Vanno*.
Maugham, S., *The Circle*.
Nichols, Anne, *Abie's Irish Rose*.
O'Neill, E. G., *Beyond the Horizon*.
O'Neill, E. G., *Desire Under the Elms*.
O'Neill, E. G., *Strange Interlude*.
Steinbeck, John, *Of Mice and Men*.
Wharton, Edith, *Ethan Frome*.
Wilde, O., *A Woman of No Importance*.
Williams, J. L., *Why Marry?*
Williams, J. L., *Why Not?*

BIOGRAPHY AND AUTOBIOGRAPHY
(With emphasis upon childhood experience.)

Adams, H., *The Education of Henry Adams*.

Anderson, S., *Tar: A Midwest Childhood*.

Baker, C. H. (ed.), *Diary and Letters of Josephine Preston Peabody*.

Baker, R. S., *Life and Letters of Woodrow Wilson*.

Barnes, C., *Life and Letters of John Burroughs*, Ch. 2.

Barnett, S. A., *Canon Barnett, His Life, Work and Friends*.

Brandes, G. M. C., *Reminiscences of My Childhood and Youth*, pp. 1–163.

Brown, P. H., *The Youth of Goethe*, Ch. 1.

Burroughs, J., *My Boyhood*.

Carossa, H. (Scott, A. N., tr.), *A Childhood*.

Chase, M. E., *A Goodly Heritage*.

Clark, Sir E., *Benjamin Disraeli*, Part 1.

Cotton, E. H., *Life of Charles W. Eliot*, Ch. 2.

Cushing, H., *The Life of Sir William Osler*, Chs. 1 and 2.

Daniels, Josephus, *Tar Heel Editor*.

Darrow, C., *Story of My Life*, Chs. 2 and 3.

Dreiser, T., *Dawn*.

Elliott, M. H., *Three Generations*, Chs. 1–8.

Ellis, Havelock, *My Life*.

Ferber, Edna, *A Peculiar Treasure*.

Freeman, Douglas, *Robert E. Lee*.

Freud, S. (Paul, E. C., tr.), *A Young Girl's Diary*.

Gordon, G. A., *My Education and Religion*, Chs. 3–6.

Gorky, M., *My Childhood*.

Hall, G. S., *Life and Confessions of a Psychologist*, Ch. 3.

Helm, MacKinley, *Angel Mo' and Her Son, Roland Hayes*.

Holt, Rackham, *George Washington Carver*.

Hudson, W. H., *Far Away and Long Ago*.

Hurston, Zora Neale, *Dust Tracks in the Road*.

Huxley, L., *Life and Letters of Thomas Henry Huxley*, Ch. 1.

James, H. R., *Mary Wollstonecraft*.

Johnson, G. W., *Andrew Jackson, A Hero in Homespun*, Chs. 1 and 2.

Johnson, James Weldon, *Along This Way*.

Lagerlof, Selma, *Marbacka*.

Morris, L., *The Rebellious Puritan; Portrait of Mr. Hawthorne*, pp. 3–44.

Morrow. H. W., *The Father of Little Women*.

Palmer, G. H., *Life of Alice Freeman Palmer*.

Parker, C. S., *An American Idyll; The Life of Carleton H. Parker*.

Percy, Alexander, *Lanterns on the Levee; Recollections of a Planter's Son*.

Pollitt, J., *Life of Emily Dickinson*, Chs. 1, 3, and 4.

Pruette, L., *G. Stanley Hall; A Biography of a Mind*, Ch. 1.

Ravenel, Mrs. H. H., *Eliza Pinckney*.

Roosevelt, T., *Diaries of Boyhood and Youth*.

Sanborn, F. B., *The Life of Henry David Thoreau*, Ch. 2.

Sandburg, C., *Abraham Lincoln—The Prairie Years*, Chs. 1–30.

Spencer, H., *An Autobiography*, Part I, Chs. 1 and 2.

Stuart, Jesse, *Beyond Dark Hills; A Personal Story*.

Van de Water, V. B. T., *The Heart of a Child*.

Wallas, G., *Life of Francis Place*, Ch. 1.

Waln, N., *The House of Exile*.

Webb, B., *My Apprenticeship*, Chs. 1 and 2.

Wright, Richard, *Black Boy*.

Appendix B
TOPICS FOR REPORTS AND REFERENCES

CHAPTER 1

SOCIAL SIGNIFICANCE OF THE FAMILY

SUBJECTS FOR REPORTS

1. Family life among the higher animals.
2. The evolution of the mother-offspring relationship.
3. Plato's criticism of the family.
4. The infancy period and the transmission of culture.
5. The family as it reacts to social changes.

REFERENCES
Books

Bernard, Jessie, *American Family Behavior*, Chs. 1 and 2.
Dell, Floyd, *Love in the Machine Age*.
Elmer, M. C., *The Sociology of the Family*, Ch. 1.
Groves, E. R., *The Family and Its Social Functions*, Chs. 1 and 7.
Groves, E. R., and Brooks, L. M., *Readings in the Family*, Ch. 1.
Groves, Gladys H., *Marriage and Family Life*, Ch. 1.
Lindquist, Ruth, *The Family in the Present Social Order*.
Messer, M. B., *The Family in the Making*, Ch. 1.
Nimkoff, M. F., *The Family*, Ch. 1.
Parsons, E. C., *The Family*, pp. 20–25.

Articles

Colcord, J. C., "Strengths of Family Life," *The Family*, Vol. 11, pp. 211–216.

Frank, L. K., "The Family as a Cultural Agent," *Living,* Vol. 2, No. 1, pp. 16–19.

Goldstein, S. E., "The Family as a Dynamic Factor in American Society," *Living,* Vol. 2, No. 1, pp. 8–11.

Ogburn, W. F., "The Family and Its Functions," *Recent Social Trends.*

Sumner, William G., "The Family and Social Change," *American Journal of Sociology,* Vol. 14, pp. 577–591.

Taylor, C. G., "The Sociology of Family Life," *Journal of Home Economics,* Vol. 29, pp. 512–516.

Thompson, Warren S., "The Family as a Unit of Survival," *Social Forces,* Vol. 7, pp. 141–144.

Truxal, A. G., "The Present Status of the American Family," *Journal of Home Economics,* Vol. 24, pp. 773–781.

CHAPTER 2

THE STUDY OF THE FAMILY

SUBJECTS FOR REPORTS

1. Major problems in the study of the family.
2. Illustrations of the questionnaire method in the study of the family.
3. The interview as a means of getting information concerning family life.
4. The case method of study of the family.
5. Psychoanalysis and family research.

REFERENCES

Books

Bernard, Jessie, *American Family Behavior,* Chs. 3, 4, and 5.

Burgess, E. W., and Cottrell, L. S., Jr., *Predicting Success or Failure in Marriage.*

Burgess, E. W., and Locke, H. J., *The Family,* Appendix A.

Drummond, L. W., *Youth and Instruction in Marriage and Family Living.*

Hagood, M. J., *Mothers of the South.*

Hamilton, G. W., *A Research in Marriage.*

Lundberg, George A., *Social Research.*

Odum, Howard, and Jocher, K., *An Introduction to Social Research.*

Richmond, Mary, *Social Diagnosis,* Ch. 7.

Rockwood, Lemo D., *Teaching Family Relationships in the High School.*

Sowers, Ray V., and Mullen, John W., (eds.), *Understanding Marriage and the Family,* Chs. 14 and 15.

Terman, L. M., *Psychological Factors in Marital Happiness.*

Webb, Sidney, and Webb, Beatrice, *Methods of Social Study.*

Articles

Alexander, F. D., "Family Life in a Rural Community," *Social Forces,* Vol. 18, pp. 392–402.

Day, George M., "The Family in Soviet Russia," *Social Forces,* Vol. 16, pp. 556–561.

Groves, E. R., "The First Credit Course in Preparation for Family Living," *Marriage and Family Living,* Vol. 3, No. 3, pp. 7–8.

Hart, Hornell, and Bowne, Henrietta, "Divorce, Depression, and War," *Social Forces,* Vol. 22, pp. 190–194.

Jocher, Katharine, "The Case Method in Social Research," *Social Forces,* Vol. 7, pp. 203–211.

Jocher, Katharine, "Methods of Research in Studying the Family," *Family,* Vol. 9, pp. 80–85.

King, Charles E., "The Negro Maternal Family, A Product of an Economic and a Cultural System," *Social Forces,* Vol. 24, pp. 100–104.

Malcove, Lillian, "Margaret E. Fries' Research in Problems of Infancy and Childhood," *The Psychoanalytic Study of the Child,* Vol. 1, pp. 405–414.

Ogburn, W. F., "Marriages, Births and Divorces," *Annals of the American Academy of Political and Social Sciences,* Vol. 229, pp. 20–29.

Parten, Mildred, "A Statistical Analysis of the Modern Family," *Annals of the American Academy of Political and Social Science,* Vol. 160, pp. 29–37.

Sanderson, E., Foster, Dwight, and Foster, Robert G., "Sociological Case Study of Farm Families," *The Family,* Vol. 11, pp. 107–114.

Shaw, Clifford R., "Case Study Methods," *Publications of the American Sociological Society,* Vol. 21, pp. 149–157.

Sheffield, Ada E., "The Situation or the Unit of Family Case Work," *Social Forces,* Vol. 9, pp. 465–474.

Thompson, W. S., "Adolescents According to the Census," *Annals of the American Academy of Political and Social Science,* Vol. 230, pp. 17–25.

CHAPTER 3

THE PRIMITIVE FAMILY

Subjects for Reports

1. The contribution of Malinowski.
2. Westermarck's theory of monogamy.
3. The marriage system of a chosen group of primitives.
4. Social significance of exogamy.
5. Levirate and the Old Testament.
6. Family life in a chosen tribe of American Indians.

References

Books

Baber, R. E., *Marriage and the Family,* Ch. 2.

Benedict, Ruth, *Patterns of Culture,* Ch. 5.

Crawley, Ernest, *The Mystic Rose.*

Dennis, Wayne, *The Hopi Child.*

DuBois, Cora, *The People of Alor.*

Folsom, J. K., *The Family and Democratic Society,* Ch. 1.

Freud, Sigmund, *Totem and Taboo.*

Goldenweiser, Alexander, *Early Civilization,* Ch. 3.

Goodsell, Willystine, *A History of Marriage and the Family,* Ch. 1.

Goodsell, Willystine, *Problems of the Family,* Ch. 1.

Hill, R., and Becker, H., (eds.), *Marriage and the Family,* Ch. 3.

Hobhouse, L. T., and others, *The Material Culture and Social Institutions of the Simpler Peoples,* Ch. 3.

Kaberry, P. M., *Aboriginal Woman.*

Knight, M. M., Peters, I. L., and Blanchard, Phyllis, *Taboo and Genetics.*

Malinowski, Bronislaw, *The Father in Primitive Psychology.*

Mason, O. T., *Woman's Share in Primitive Culture.*

Mead, Margaret, *Coming of Age in Samoa.*

Mead, Margaret, *Growing Up in New Guinea.*

Mead, Margaret, *Sex and Temperament.*

Nimkoff, M. F., *The Family,* Ch. 3.

Parsons, E. C., *The Family,* Ch. 12.

Schapera, I., *Married Life in an African Tribe.*

Sieber, S. A., and Mueller, F. H., *The Social Life of Primitive Man*, Ch. 25.

Simmons, Leo W., *The Role of the Aged in Primitive Society*.

Unwin, J. D., *Sex and Culture*.

Articles

Erikson, E. H., "Childhood and Tradition in Two American Indian Tribes," *The Psychoanalytic Study of the Child*, pp. 319–350.

Groves, E. R., "Adolescent Strain and Social Pressure," *Social Forces*, Vol. 7, pp. 243–250.

Hallowell, A. I., "Psychic Stresses and Cultural Patterns," *American Journal of Psychology*, Vol. 92, pp. 291–310.

Mead, Margaret, "Contrasts and Comparisons from Primitive Society," *Annals of the American Academy of Political and Social Science*, Vol. 160, pp. 23–28.

Spencer, D. M., "The Composition of the Family as a Factor in the Behavior of Children in Fijian Society," *Sociometry*, Vol. 2, pp. 47–55.

CHAPTER 4

THE PATRIARCHAL FAMILY

Subjects for Reports

1. Illustrations of the patriarchal family in the evolution of American culture.
2. The religious basis of the Hebrew family.
3. Woman's status among the Greeks.
4. The decay of the family during the decline of Rome.
5. Causes of the criticism of Roman family life by the early Christian fathers.
6. Cases of patriarchal family life in the United States.

References

Books

Abrahams, Israel, *Jewish Family Life in the Middle Ages*.

Aristotle, *Nichomachean Ethics*.

Aristotle, *Politics*.

Baron, S. W., *A Social and Religious History of the Jews.*
Brav, S. R., *Jewish Family Solidarity.*
Cohen, E., *Women in Jewish Law and Life.*
Cohen, Israel, *Jewish Life in Modern Times.*
Cross, E. B., *The Hebrew Family.*
Goodsell, Willystine, *A History of Marriage and the Family,* Chs. 2, 3, and 4.
Goodsell, Willystine, *Problems of the Family,* Ch. 2.
Groves, E. R., and Brooks, L. M., *Readings in the Family,* Ch. 3.
Hill, H., and Becker, H., (eds.), *Marriage and the Family,* Ch. 4.
Kiefer, Otto, *Sexual Life in Ancient Rome.*
La Croix, Paul, *History of Prostitution,* Vol. 1.
Parsons, E. C., *The Family,* Ch. 13.
Plato, *Republic.*
Sait, Una B., *New Horizons for the Family,* Ch. 3.
Wise, Stephen, *Child Versus Parent.*

CHAPTER 5

THE EUROPEAN BACKGROUND OF THE AMERICAN FAMILY

SUBJECTS FOR REPORTS

1. The teaching of asceticism as a Christian ideal.
2. The Renaissance and family life.
3. Luther's attitude toward marriage and family life.
4. English ecclesiastical courts.
5. English common-law principles as related to family life.
6. Asceticism as a religious ideal outside Christianity.

REFERENCES

Books

Abram, A., *English Life and Manners in the Later Middle Ages.*
Ante Nicene Christian Library.
Bradley, R. M., *The English Housewife in the Seventeenth and Eighteenth Centuries.*
Calhoun, A. W., *A Social History of the American Family,* Chs. 1 and 2.

Coulton, G. G., *Life in the Middle Ages,* Vol. 1, pp. 225–6, Vol. 3, pp. 114–115.

De Rougement, Denis, *Love in the Western World.*

Folsom, J. K., *The Family and Democratic Society,* pp. 85–96.

Goodsell, Willystine, *A History of Marriage and the Family,* Chs. 6, 7, and 8.

Goodsell, Willystine, *Problems of the Family,* Ch. 6.

Groves, E. R., *Christianity and the Family.*

Groves, E. R., and Brooks, L. M., *Readings in the Family,* Ch. 4.

Howard, George E., *A History of Matrimonial Institutions,* Vol. 2, pp. 73–120.

Lenski, G. E., *Marriage in the Lutheran Church.*

St. Augustine, *Letters,* Vol. 1.

Zimmerman, C. C., and Frampton, M. E., *Family and Society,* Ch. 6.

Articles

Miller, Nathan, "The European Heritage of the American Family," *Annals of the American Academy of Political and Social Science,* Vol. 160, pp. 1–6.

CHAPTER 6

THE COLONIAL AND FRONTIER AMERICAN FAMILY

SUBJECTS FOR REPORTS

1. Family life in the Southern colonies before the Revolutionary War.
2. Family life in New England before the Revolutionary War.
3. Review of the letters of Abigail Adams.
4. Vocational opportunities of colonial women.
5. Review of Samuel Sewall's diary.
6. Patterns of frontier family life.

REFERENCES

Books

Adams, Charles F., Jr., (ed.), *Familiar Letters of John Adams and his Wife Abigail Adams.*

Baber, R. E., *Marriage and the Family,* Ch. 4.

Bell, Margaret, *Women of the Wilderness.*

Calhoun, A. W., *A Social History of the American Family*, Vol. 1, Ch. 3–20, Vol. 2, Ch. 8.

Cranford, Mary C., *Social Life in Old New England*.

Dexter, E. A., *Colonial Women of Affairs*.

Gaines, F. P., *The Southern Plantation*.

Goodsell, Willystine, *A History of Marriage and the Family*, Ch. 9.

Groves, E. R., and Brooks, L. M., *Readings in the Family*, Ch. 5.

Earle, A. M., *Home Life in Colonial Times*.

Hill, R., and Becker, H., *Marriage and the Family*, Ch. 5.

Johnson, G. G., *Ante Bellum North Carolina*, Ch. 8.

Odum, H. W., *An American Epoch*, Ch. 5.

Roosevelt, Theodore, *Winning of the West*.

Sewall, Samuel, *Diary*.

Shaw, A. H., *The Story of a Pioneer*.

Spruill, J. C., *Woman's Life and Work in the Southern Colonies*, Chs. 7 and 8.

Turner, F. J., *The Frontier in American History*, Ch. 13.

Wertenbaker, T. J., *The First Americans*.

Wharton, A. H., *Colonial Days and Dames*.

Winthrop, John, *Winthrop's Journal*.

Articles

Calhoun, A. W., "The Early American Family," *Annals of the American Academy of Political and Social Science*, Vol. 160, pp. 7–12.

CHAPTER 7

THE MODERN AMERICAN FAMILY

SUBJECTS FOR REPORTS

1. Review of Mary R. Beard's *America Through Women's Eyes*, Chapter 4, "Machine Industry and Plantation."
2. Life of Elizabeth Cady Stanton.
3. The career of Jane Addams.
4. World War I as it affected domestic relationships.
5. Family life within the Oneida Community.
6. The domestic life of the Shakers.
7. The child and World War II.

REFERENCES

Books

Beard, Mary R., *America Through Women's Eyes.*

Bernhard, Dorothy L., and Others, *The Effects of the War on Children.*

Burgess, E. W., and Locke, H. J., *The Family,* Ch. 21.

Calhoun, A. W., *A Social History of the American Family,* Vol. 2, Chs. 9–14.

Cavan, R. S., *The Family,* Ch. 1.

Folsom, J. K., *Plan for Marriage,* Ch. 9.

Foster, R. G., *Marriage and Family Relationships,* Ch. 18.

Freud, Anna, and Burlingham, Dorothy, *Infants without Families.*

Gilman, C. P., *The Living of Charlotte Perkins Gilman.*

Goodsell, Willystine, *A History of Marriage and the Family,* Chs. 11 and 12.

Goodsell, Willystine, *Problems of the Family,* Part 2.

Groves, E. R., *The American Woman,* Chs. 2, 3, 8, 9, and 10.

Groves, E. R., *The Family and its Social Functions,* Ch. 18.

Keyserling, C. H., *The Book of Marriage,* pp. 216–243.

Leopold, *Robert Dale Owen,* Part 2.

Melcher, M. F., *The Shaker Adventure.*

Molkin, Richard, *Marriage, Morals and War.*

Nimkoff, M. F., *The Family,* Ch. 5.

Noyes, G. W., *The Putney Community.*

Noyes, G. W., *Religious Experience of John Humphrey Noyes.*

Parker, R. A., *A Yankee Saint, John Humphrey Noyes.*

Parsons, A. B., *Woman's Dilemma.*

Parsons, E. C., *The Family,* Ch. 14.

Schneider, H. W., and Lawton, George, *A Prophet and a Pilgrim.*

Stern, M. B., *The Life of Margaret Fuller.*

Articles

Allen, Frederick H., "Dynamics of Roles as Determined in the Structure of the Family," *American Journal of Orthopsychiatry,* Vol. 12, pp. 127–134.

Anderson, Nels, "The Mormon Family," *American Sociological Review,* Vol. 2, pp. 601–608.

Baber, R. E., "Marriage and the Family After the War," *Annals of the American Academy of Political and Social Science,* Vol. 229, pp. 164–195.

Bender, Lauretta, and Frosch, John, "Children's Reactions to War," *American Journal of Orthopsychiatry,* Vol. 12, pp. 571–586.

Boothe, Viva, "Gainfully Employed Women in the Family," *Annals of the American Academy of Political and Social Science*, Vol. 160, pp. 75–85.

Bossard, J. H. S., "Family Problems in Wartime," *Psychiatry*, Vol. 7, pp. 65–72.

Burgess, Ernest W., "The Effect of War on the American Family," *The American Journal of Sociology*, Vol. 48, pp. 343–352.

Folsom, J. K., "Changing Values in Sex and Family Relations," *American Sociological Review*, Vol. 2, pp. 717–726.

Gardner, G. E., "The Family in a World at War," *Mental Hygiene*, Vol. 20, pp. 50–57.

Gardner, G. E., "Sex Behavior of Adolescents in Wartime," *Annals of the American Academy of Political and Social Science*, Vol. 236, pp. 60–66.

Goodsell, Willystine, "The American Family in the Nineteenth Century," *Annals of the American Academy of Political and Social Science*, Vol. 160, pp. 13–22.

Groves, E. R., and Groves, Gladys H., "The Social Background of Wartime Adolescents," *Annals of the American Academy of Political and Social Science*, Vol. 230, pp. 26–32.

Levy, David M. (chairman), "The War and Family Life," *American Journal of Orthopsychiatry*, Vol. 15, pp. 140–152.

Lichtenberger, J. P., "The Changing Family in a Changing World," *Mental Hygiene*, Vol. 17, pp. 573–589.

McDonagh, Edward, and McDonagh, Louise, "War Anxieties of Soldiers and their Wives," *Social Forces*, Vol. 24, pp. 195–200.

Newcomb, Theodore, "Recent Changes in Attitudes Toward Sex and Marriage," *American Sociological Review*, Vol. 2, pp. 659–667.

Panunzio, Constantine, "War and Marriage," *Social Forces*, Vol. 21, pp. 442–445.

Thompson, Clara, "Cultural Pressure in the Psychology of Women," *Psychiatry*, Vol. 5, pp. 331–339.

Thompson, Clara, "The Role of Women in this Culture," *Psychiatry*, Vol. 4, pp. 1–8.

Wieman, Regina W., "The Part of Religion in Child Guidance," *The Journal of Home Economics*, Vol. 35, pp. 336–338.

Wolfe, Z. S., "Readjustment of the Child in the Postwar Era," *American Journal of Orthopsychiatry*, Vol. 15, pp. 529–531.

Zilboorg, Gregory, "Masculine and Feminine," *Psychiatry*, Vol. 7, pp. 256–296.

CHAPTER 8

EMOTIONAL ASPECTS OF FAMILY LIFE

SUBJECTS FOR REPORTS

1. The origin of guilt feeling in children.
2. The causes of parent-fixation.
3. Family incentives to emotional conflict.
4. Review of Myerson's *Nervous Housewife.*
5. The emotional training of the child as a preparation for marriage and parenthood.

REFERENCES
Books

Bernard, Jessie, *American Family Behavior,* Ch. 10.
Burgess, E. W., and Locke, H. J., *The Family,* Ch. 10.
Flügel, J. C., *The Psycho-Analytic Study of the Family,* Chs. 2 and 11.
Folsom, J. K., *The Family and Democratic Society,* Ch. 11.
Groves, E. R., *The Family and Its Social Functions,* Ch. 14.
Groves, E. R., and Brooks, L. M., *Readings in the Family,* Ch. 7.
Hart, Hornell, and Hart, E. B., *Personality and the Family,* Ch. 14.
Levy, David M., *Maternal Overprotection,* Chs. 3 and 4.

Articles

Ebaugh, Cameron D., "Consciously or Unconsciously," *Social Forces,* Vol. 17, pp. 405–410.
Gelerd, E. R., "Observations on Temper Tantrums in Children," *American Journal of Orthopsychiatry,* Vol. 15, pp. 238–246.
Goldfarb, William, "Psychological Privation in Infancy and Subsequent," *American Journal of Orthopsychiatry,* Vol. 15, pp. 247–255.
Gregg, A. B., "The Problem of the Parent in Child Analysis," *Psychiatry,* Vol. 3, pp. 539–543.
Groves, E. R., "The Child's Need of Parental Patterns," *Child Study,* Vol. 9, pp. 224–226.
Levy, David M., "Release Therapy in Young Children," *Psychiatry,* Vol. 1, pp. 387–390.

McLean, Helen, "The Emotional Background of Marital Difficulties," *American Sociological Review,* Vol. 6, pp. 384–388.

Nimkoff, Meyer F., "Parent-Child Intimacy: An Introductory Study," *Social Forces,* Vol. 7, pp. 244–249.

Reimer, M. D., "Loving Versus Spoiling Children," *Mental Hygiene,* Vol. 24, pp. 79–81.

Silberpennig, Judith, "Mother Types Encountered in Child Guidance Clinics," *American Journal of Orthopsychiatry,* Vol. 11, pp. 474–484.

Taylor, Louise, "The Social Adjustment of the Only Child," *The American Journal of Sociology,* Vol. 51, pp. 227–232.

Ward, Anne, "The Only Child: A Study of One Hundred Only Children Referred to a Child Guidance Clinic," *Smith College Studies in Social Work,* Vol. 1, No. 1, pp. 41–65.

Young, Kimball, "Parent-Child Relationships: Projection of Ambition," *The Family,* Vol. 3, pp. 67–73.

Zoohey, C. B., "Customary Stresses and Strains of Adolescence," *Annals of the American Academy of Political and Social Sciences,* Vol. 236, pp. 136–144.

CHAPTER 9

BEHAVIOR ASPECTS OF FAMILY LIFE

SUBJECTS FOR REPORTS

1. Review of Cooley's *Social Organization.*
2. Motivations that lead to domestic aggression.
3. Imitation and the conditioning of behavior.
4. The family as the origin of social prejudices and social justice.
5. Childhood experience as a cause of incompatibility between husband and wife.

REFERENCES

Books

Bernard, Jessie, *American Family Behavior,* Ch. 11.
Burgess, E. W., and Locke, H. J., *The Family,* Ch. 8.
Flügel, J. C., *The Psychoanalytic Study of the Family,* Ch. 19.
Goodsell, Willystine, *Problems of the Family,* Ch. 19.

Groves, E. R., *The Family and its Social Functions,* Ch. 13.

Groves, E. R., and Brooks, L. M., *Readings in the Family,* Ch. 10.

Groves, Gladys H., *Marriage and Family Life,* Ch. 14.

Levy, David M., *Maternal Overprotection,* Ch. 5.

Schmiedeler, Edgar, *An Introductory Study of the Family,* Ch. 12.

Articles

Axelrod, P. L., and Others, "An Experiment in Group Therapy with Shy Adolescent Girls," *American Journal of Orthopsychiatry,* Vol. 14, pp. 616–627.

Bender, Lauretta, and Vogel, B. Frank, "Imaginary Companions of Children," *American Journal of Orthopsychiatry,* Vol. 11, pp. 48–55.

Bonney, Merl E., "Parents as the Makers of Social Deviates," *Social Forces,* Vol. 20, pp. 77–87.

Brown, Fred, "An Experimental Study of Parent Attitudes and their Effect upon Child Adjustments," *American Journal of Orthopsychiatry,* Vol. 12, pp. 224–230.

Green, Arnold W., "The Middle-Class Male Child and Neurosis," *American Sociological Review,* Vol. 11, pp. 31–41.

Hacker, T. J., and Geleerd, E. R., "Freedom and Authority in Adolescence," *American Journal of Orthopsychiatry,* Vol. 15, pp. 621–630.

Hirschberg, Rudolf, "Placement of Maladjusted Children in a Controlled Environment," *American Journal of Orthopsychiatry,* Vol. 11, pp. 304–319.

Levy, John, "The Impact of Cultural Form upon Children's Behavior," *Mental Hygiene,* Vol. 16, pp. 208–220.

Nimkoff, M. F., "The Relation of Parental Dominance to Parent-Child Conflict," *Social Forces,* Vol. 9, pp. 559–563.

Witmer, Helen L., "The Influence of Parental Attitudes in the Social Adjustment of the Individual," *American Sociological Review,* Vol. 2, pp. 756–763.

CHAPTER 10

PERSONALITY GROWTH AND FAMILY EXPERIENCE

SUBJECTS FOR REPORTS

1. Domestic readjustments demanded by the coming of a second child.

2. The effects on family patterns of the changing experiences of the growing child.
3. The social hazards of adolescence.
4. The influence of a happy home on the growth of a child.
5. The value of affection as stimulus to normal child development.

REFERENCES

Books

Bernard, Jessie, *American Family Behavior*, Ch. 14.
Burgess, E. W., and Locke, H. J., *The Family*, Ch. 7.
Deutsch, Helene, *The Psychology of Women*, Chs. 1–3.
Elmer, M. C., *The Sociology of the Family*, Ch. 24.
Flügel, J. C., *The Psychoanalytic Study of the Family*, Ch. 5.
Folsom, J. K., *The Family and Democratic Society*, Ch. 10.
Groves, E. R., *The Family and Its Social Functions*, Ch. 5.
Groves, Gladys H., *Marriage and Family Life*, Chs. 5, 6, and 7.
Hart, Hornell, and Hart, E. B., *Personality and the Family*, Ch. 15.
Hill, R., and Becker, H., *Marriage and the Family*, Ch. 20.
Hunt, J. McV. (ed.), *Personality and the Behavior Disorders*, Vol. 2, Chs. 20, 21, 22, and 23.
Jordan, H. M., *You and Marriage*, Ch. 4.
Levy, David M., *Maternal Overprotection*, Ch. 6.
Nimkoff, M. F., *The Family*, Ch. 9.
Sowers, Ray, and Mullen, John (eds.), *Understanding Marriage and the Family*, Ch. 2.
Waller, Willard, *The Family*, Ch. 3.

Articles

Barker, R. H., "The Effect of an Unsatisfactory Relationship Brother to Brother on the Development of Personality," *Social Forces*, Vol. 9, pp. 85–91.
Crichton-Miller, H., "The Significance of Parental Responsibility," *Mental Hygiene*, Vol. 21, pp. 8–16.
Emery, E. Van Norman, "A Biological Perspective for Education during Periods of Social Change," *Mental Hygiene*, Vol. 22, pp. 177–192.
Finesinger, J. E., "The Needs of Youth," *Psychiatry*, Vol. 7, pp. 45–57.
Frank, Lawrence, "Freedom for the Personality," *Psychiatry*, Vol. 3, pp. 341–349.
Gesell, Arnold, "The Protection of Early Mental Growth," *American Journal of Orthopsychiatry*, Vol. 11, pp. 498–502.

Gildea, M. C. L., "The Modern American Family," *Mental Hygiene,* Vol. 27, pp. 43–54.

Hartwell, S. W., "Adult Adjustments and Non-Adjustments in Relation to Their Effects Upon Children," *Mental Hygiene,* Vol. 16, pp. 598–609.

Murphy, L. B., "Personality Development of a Boy from Age Two to Seven," *American Journal of Orthopsychiatry,* Vol. 14, pp. 10–20.

Nicholson, Marian B., "Developmental Difficulties in Children under Three," *American Journal of Orthopsychiatry,* Vol. 13, pp. 45–52.

Thorner, Isidor, "Sociological Aspects of Affectional Frustration," *Psychiatry,* Vol. 6, pp. 157–173.

CHAPTER 11

THE SOCIOLOGICAL ASPECTS OF FAMILY LIFE

SUBJECTS FOR REPORTS

The contributions to our knowledge of the family made by the following sociologists:

1. Auguste Comte
2. Frederic Le Play
3. Lester Ward
4. William G. Sumner
5. Charles Cooley

REFERENCES

Books

Angell, R. C., *The Family Encounters the Depression.*

Bossard, J. H. S., and Boll, E. S., *Family Situations.*

Bossard, J. H. S., *Marriage and the Child.*

Burgess, E. W., and Locke, H. J., *The Family,* Ch. 11.

Duvall, Evelyn M., and Hill, Reuben, *When You Marry,* Ch. 19.

Elmer, M. C., *The Sociology of the Family,* Ch. 18.

Groves, E. R., *The Family and Its Social Functions,* pp. 520–529.

Groves, E. R., and Groves, Catherine, *Dynamic Mental Hygiene,* Ch. 7.

Hart, Hornell, and Hart, E. B., *Personality and the Family*, Ch. 9.

Hill, R., and Becker, H., (eds.), *Marriage and the Family*, Ch. 24.

Pratt, G. K., *Soldier to Civilian*.

Sowers, Ray, and Mullen, John, *Understanding Marriage and the Family*, Chs. 1 and 13.

Articles

Bossard, J. H. S., "Family Problems in War Time," *Psychiatry*, Vol. 7, pp. 65–72.

Chisholm, G. B., and Hincks, C. M., "The Soldier's Return," *Psychiatry*, Vol. 8, pp. 107–113.

Foster, Robert G., "Marriage During Crises," *The Journal of Home Economics*, Vol. 35, pp. 329–332.

Frank, Lawrence K., "The Family as a Cultural Agent," *Living*, Vol. 2, No. 1, pp. 16–19.

Gardner, G. E., "Sex Behavior of Adolescents in War Time," *Annals of American Academy of Political and Social Science*, Vol. 236, pp. 60–66.

Groves, E. R., and Groves, G. H., "The Social Background of War-time Adolescents," *Annals of American Academy of Political and Social Science*, Vol. 236, pp. 26–32.

Jennings, H. S., "From Amoeba Up," *Survey Graphic*, Vol. 12, pp. 272–276.

King, C. E., "The Negro Maternal Family: A Product of an Economic and Cultural System,"*Social Forces*, Vol. 24, pp. 100–104.

McDonagh, E., and McDonagh, Louise, "War Anxieties of Soldiers and Their Wives," *Social Forces*, Vol. 24, pp. 195–200.

Plant, J. S., "Social Significance of War Impact on Adolescents," *Annals of American Academy of Political and Social Science*, Vol. 236, pp. 1–8.

Williams, M. J., "A Socio-Economic Analysis of the Functions and Attitudes of Wartime Youth," *Social Forces*, Vol. 24, pp. 200–210.

CHAPTER 12

COURTSHIP

SUBJECTS FOR REPORTS

1. The movies as an influence on American courtship ideals and practices.

2. Lester Ward on the kinds of love.
3. Recent changes in American courtship.
4. The woman's role in modern American courtship.
5. Residential propinquity and choice of mate.
6. Suggested reforms in American courtship patterns.

REFERENCES

Books

Baber, R. E., *Marriage and the Family,* Chs. 6 and 7.

Bernard, Jessie, *American Family Behavior,* Chs. 15 and 16.

Bowman, H. A., *Marriage for Moderns,* Ch. 8.

Burgess, E. W., and Locke, H. J., *The Family,* Chs. 12 and 13.

Butterfield, O. M., *Love Problems of Adolescence.*

Cavan, R. S., *The Family,* Ch. 4.

Duvall, Evelyn M., and Hill, Reuben, *When You Get Married,* Chs. 3–5.

Folsom, J. K., *The Family and Democratic Society,* Ch. 16.

Folsom, J. K., *Plan for Marriage,* Ch. 5.

Foster, R. G., *Marriage and Family Relationships,* Part 2.

Gross, Elmer U., *Meet Your Mate the Modern Way.*

Groves, E. R., *Marriage,* Chs. 4 and 5.

Groves, Gladys H., *Marriage and Family Life,* Ch. 10.

Hill, H., and Becker, R., *Marriage and the Family,* Ch. 8.

Jordan, H. M., *You and Marriage,* Ch. 2.

Parker, Valeria H., *For Mothers and Daughters,* Chs. 6 and 7.

Sladen, F. J. (ed), *Psychiatry and the War,* pp. 184–194.

Waller, Willard, *The Family,* Chs. 9, 10, and 11.

Articles

Bates, Alan, "Parental Roles in Courtship," *Social Forces,* Vol. 20, pp. 483–486.

Carpenter, Niles, "Courtship Practices and Contemporary Social Change in America," *Annals of the American Academy of Political and Social Science,* Vol. 160, pp. 38–44.

Cuber, J. F., "Changing Courtship and Marriage Customs," *Annals of the American Academy of Political and Social Science,* Vol. 229, pp. 30–38.

Groves, E. R., "Courtship and Marriage," *Mental Hygiene,* Vol. 18, pp. 26–39.

Groves, E. R., "Sex Adjustment of College Men and Women," *Journal of Educational Sociology,* Vol. 8, pp. 353–360.

Hill, Reuben, "Campus Values in Mate Selection," *Journal of Home Economics,* Vol. 37, pp. 554–558.

Kirkpatrick, Clifford, and Caplow, Theodore, "Courtship in a Group of Minnesota Students," *American Journal of Sociology,* Vol. 51. pp. 114–125.

Kirkpatrick, Clifford, and Caplow, Theodore, "Emotional Trends in Courtship Experience of College Students as Expressed by Graphs with Some Observations on Methodological Implications," *American Sociological Review,* Vol. 10, pp. 619–625.

Landis, P. H., "Control of the Romantic Impulse Through Education," *School and Society,* Vol. 44, pp. 212–215.

Landis, P. H., and Day, K. H., "Education as a Factor in Mate Selection," *American Sociological Review,* Vol. 10, pp. 558–563.

Popenoe, Paul, "Mate Selection," *American Sociological Review,* Vol. 2, pp. 734–743.

Popenoe, Paul, and Neptune, D. W., "Acquaintance and Betrothal," *Social Forces,* Vol. 16, pp. 552–555.

Waller, Willard, "The Rating and Dating Complex," *American Sociological Review,* Vol. 2, pp. 727–734.

CHAPTER 13

MARRIAGE

SUBJECTS FOR REPORTS

1. Common engagement problems.
2. Guilt-feeling and premarriage confessions.
3. Factors in successful marital adjustment.
4. Premarriage counseling.
5. The contribution of Robert L. Dickinson to the medical examination in preparation for marriage.

REFERENCES

Books

Baber, R. E., *Marriage and the Family,* Chs. 8 and 9.
Bernard, Jessie, *American Family Behavior,* Chs. 17–20.
Binkley, R. C., and Binkley, F. W., *What is Right with Marriage.*

Bowman, H. A., *Marriage for Moderns*, Chs. 2 and 12.

Bromley, D. D., and Britten, F. H., *Youth and Sex*.

Burgess, E. W., and Locke, H. J., *The Family*, Chs. 14 and 15.

Cavan, R. S., *The Family*, Ch. 5.

Deutsch, Helene, *The Psychology of Women*, Vol. 1, Chs. 5–7.

Dickerson, R. E., *So Youth May Know*.

Dickinson, R. L., and Beam, Lura, *The Single Woman*, Part 2.

Duvall, Evelyn M., and Hill, Reuben, *When You Get Married*, Ch. 9.

Folsom, J. K., *The Family and Democratic Society*, Chs. 12 and 13.

Folsom, J. K., *Plan for Marriage*, Ch. 2.

Goldstein, Sidney E., *The Meaning of Marriage and the Foundations of the Family*.

Goodsell, Willystine, *Problems of the Family*, Ch. 18.

Groves, E. R., *Marriage*, Ch. 2.

Groves, E. R., *Preparation for Marriage*, Ch. 1.

Groves, Gladys H., *Marriage and Family Life*, Chs. 9 and 17.

Hartson, L. D., "Marriage Records of Alumnae for the First Century of a Co-educational College," *Eugenical News*, Vol. 25, pp. 41–44.

Hill, R., and Becker, H., *Marriage and the Family*, Chs. 14 and 15.

Hinsie, L. E., *The Person in the Body*, Chs. 5, 7, and 10.

Hirschfeld, Magnus, *The Sexual History of the World War*.

Kahn, Fritz, *Our Sex Life*.

Keyserling, C. H., *The Book of Marriage*.

Kirkendall, L. A., *Sex Adjustments of Young Men*.

Landis, Carney, *Sex in Development*.

Landis, P. H., "Rural-Urban Migration and the Marriage Rate— An Hypothesis," *American Sociological Review*, Vol. 11, pp. 155–158.

Laton, A. D., and Bailey, E. W., *Sex Responsiveness, Mating, and Reproduction*.

Macmillan, A. T., *What Is Christian Marriage?*

Nimkoff, M. F., *The Family*, Ch. 10.

Reik, Theodor, *Psychology of Sex Relations*.

Rockwood, Lemo D., and Ford, M. E. N., *Youth, Marriage and Parenthood*.

Sherrill, L. J., *Family and Church*, Ch. 5.

Strain, F. B., *New Patterns in Sex Teaching*.

Strain, F. B., *Sex Guidance in Family Life Education*.

Unwin, J. D., *Sex and Culture*.

Walker, Kenneth, and Strauss, E. B., *Sexual Disorders in the Male*.

Waller, Willard, *The Family*, Part 3.

Weiss, Edward, and English, O. S., *Psychosomatic Medicine*, pp. 588–589, 592–595, 600–604.

Articles

Baber, R. E., "A Study of 325 Mixed Marriages," *American Sociological Review*, Vol. 2, pp. 705–716.

Conn, J. H., "Sex Attitudes and Sex Awareness in the Young Child," *Child Study*, Vol. 16, pp. 86–87 and 106–107.

Dooley, Lucile, "The Genesis of Psychological Sex Differences," *Psychiatry*, Vol. 1, pp. 181–195.

Frankenthal, Kate, "The Role of Sex in Modern Society," *Psychiatry*, Vol. 8, pp. 19–25.

Herschberger, Ruth, "Sexual Differences and Character Trends," *Psychiatry*, Vol. 6, pp. 301–305.

Hunt, Thomas C., "Occupational Status and Marriage Selection," *American Sociological Review*, Vol. 5, pp. 495–504.

Kennedy, R. J. R., "Premarital Residential Propinquity and Ethnic Endogamy," *American Journal of Sociology*, Vol. 48, pp. 580–584.

Kirkpatrick, Clifford, "Techniques of Marital Adjustment," *Annals of the American Academy of Political and Social Science*, Vol. 160, pp. 178–183.

Lamson, Herbert D., "Marriage of Coeds to Fellow Students," *Marriage and Family Living*, Vol. 8, pp. 27–28.

Lastrucci, C. L., "A Reconsideration of the So-called Sex Instinct," *Social Forces*, Vol. 21, pp. 215–217.

Nelson, Lowry, "Intermarriage Among Nationality Groups in a Rural Area in Minnesota," *American Journal of Sociology*, Vol. 48, pp. 585–592.

Nimkoff, M. F., "Occupational Factors and Marriage," *American Journal of Sociology*, Vol. 49, pp. 248–254.

Popenoe, Paul, "A Study of 738 Elopements," *American Sociological Review*, Ch. 3, pp. 47–53.

Ramsey, Glenn V., "The Sex Information of Younger Boys," *American Journal of Orthopsychiatry*, Vol. 13, pp. 347–352.

Rice, Stuart A., "Undergraduate Attitudes Toward Marriage and Children," *Mental Hygiene*, Vol. 13, pp. 788–793.

Rogers, Ethel, "One Hundred Juvenile Marriages," *Social Forces*, Vol. 13, pp. 409–414.

Tomasic, Dinko, "Personality Development and the Dinaric Warriors," *Psychiatry*, Vol. 8, pp. 473–480.

Waggoner, R. W., and Boyd, David A., Jr., "Juvenile Aberrant Sexual Behavior," *American Journal of Orthopsychiatry*, Vol. 11, pp. 275–291.

CHAPTER 14

THE ARRESTED FAMILY

Subjects for Reports

1. The history of Knight's companionate theory of the family.
2. The medical diagnosis of infertility.
3. Recent progress in the treatment of unwanted childlessness.
4. The birth-control movement in the United States.
5. Programs for encouraging childbearing.
6. Problems in child adoption.
7. Arguments for and against birth control.

References

Books

Berkow, S. G., *Childless.*
Brooks, L. M., and Brooks, E. C., *Adventuring in Adoption.*
Blanchard, Phyllis, and Manasses, C., *New Girls for Old,* Ch. 18.
Calverton, V. F., *The Bankruptcy of Marriage,* Ch. 7.
Groves, E. R., *The Drifting Home,* Ch. 5.
Hamblen, E. C., *Facts for Childless Couples.*
Hotchkiss, R. S., *Fertility in Men.*
Lindsey, B. B., and Evans, W., *The Companionate Marriage.*
Meaker, S. R., *Human Sterility.*
Pearl, Raymond, *The Natural History of Population,* Chs. 2, 3, 4 and 5.
Prentice, C. S., *An Adopted Child Looks at Adoption.*
Reed, Ruth, *The Modern Family,* Ch. 18.
Siegler, S. L., *Fertility in Women.*
Spaulding, C. A. (ed.), *Twenty-four Views of Marriage,* Ch. 15.

Articles

Clothier, Florence, "The Psychology of the Adopted Child," *Mental Hygiene,* Vol. 27, pp. 222–230.
Cottrell, J., and Leonard, S., "Research in Causes of Variation in Fertility, Social Psychological Aspects," *American Sociological Review,* Vol. 2, pp. 678–685.
Jaffe, A. J., "Urbanization and Fertility," *American Journal of Sociology,* Vol. 48, pp. 48–60.

Kirkpatrick, E. A., "Render Unto Caesar," *Journal of Social Hygiene*, Vol. 10, No. 8, pp. 461–473.

Kiser, C. V., and Whelpton, P. K., "Sociological and Psychological Factors Affecting Fertility," *Milbank Quarterly*, Vol. 22, pp. 61–94.

Knight, M. M., "The Companionate and the Family," *Journal of Social Hygiene*, Vol. 10, pp. 256–267.

Parten, Mildred, and Reeves, R. J., "Size and Composition of American Families," *American Sociological Review*, Vol. 2, pp. 638–649.

Pearl, Raymond, "Pregnancy Rates and Coitus Rates," *Human Biology*, Vol. 12, pp. 545–548.

Popenoe, P., "Family or Companionate?" *Journal of Social Hygiene*, Vol. 11, pp. 129–138.

Popenoe, P., "Motivation of Childless Marriages," *Journal of Heredity*, Vol. 27, pp. 467–472.

Stix, R. K., "Research in Causes of Variation in Fertility: Medical Aspects," *American Sociological Review*, Vol. 2, pp. 668–677.

Whelpton, P. K., and Kiser, C. V., "Social and Psychological Factors Affecting Fertility; Developing the Schedules and Choosing the Type of Couples and Area to be Studied," *Milbank Quarterly*, Vol. 23, pp. 386–409.

Wires, E. M., "The Foster Child and Separation," *Mental Hygiene*, Vol. 30, pp. 250–256.

Woofter, T. J., Jr., "Size of Family in Relation to Family Income and Age of Family Head," *American Sociological Review*, Vol. 9, pp. 678–684.

CHAPTER 15

THE BROKEN FAMILY

SUBJECTS FOR REPORTS

1. The contribution of Thomas Eliot to an understanding of the problems of the bereaved family.
2. Trailer family life.
3. Problems of Catholic and Protestant mixed marriages.
4. Problems of Jewish and Gentile mixed marriages.
5. The only child.

References

Books

Barrett, R. S., *The Care of the Unmarried Mother.*

Burgess, E. W., and Locke, H. J., *The Family,* Chs. 19 and 20.

Cavan, R. S., *The Family,* Chs. 10 and 11.

Colcord, Joanna C., *Broken Homes.*

Foster, R. G., *Marriage and Family Relationships,* Ch. 16.

Hill, R., and Becker, H., *Marriage and the Family,* Ch. 22.

Meriam, A. S., *The Stepfather in the Family.*

Schmiedeler, Edgar, *An Introductory Study of the Family,* Ch. 13.

U. S. Department of Labor, Children's Bureau, *Services for Unmarried Mothers and their Children.*

Waller, Willard, *The Family,* Ch. 19.

Articles

Baber, R. E., "A Study of 325 Mixed Marriages," *American Sociological Review,* Vol. 2, pp. 705–716.

Eliot, T. D., "The Broken Family," *Annals of the American Academy of Political and Social Science,* Vol. 160, pp. 184–190.

Eliot, T. D., "Of the Shadow of Death," *Annals of the American Academy of Political and Social Science,* Vol. 229, pp. 87–99.

Eliot, T. D., "War Bereavements and their Recovery," *Marriage and Family Living,* Vol. 8, pp. 1–5 and 8.

Locke, Harry J., "Mobility and Family Disorganization," *American Sociological Review,* Vol. 5, pp. 489–494.

Montague, M. F. A., "Some Factors in Family Cohesion," *Psychiatry,* Vol. 7, pp. 349–352.

Weeks, H. Ashley, "Male and Female Broken Home Rates by Types of Delinquency," *American Sociological Review,* Vol. 5, pp. 601–609.

Wires, Emily M., "The Foster Child and Separation," *Mental Hygiene,* Vol. 30, pp. 250–256.

CHAPTER 16

THE INCOMPATIBLE FAMILY

Subjects for Reports

1. Psychoanalytic interpretation of jealousy.
2. Frustration as a source of domestic incompatibility.

3. Cultural differences as a cause of domestic incompatibility.
4. Minor quarreling within the family as a process of adjustment.
5. Delinquency as an expression of emotional tension due to the incompatibility of parents.

REFERENCES

Books

Burgess, E. W., and Locke, H. J., *The Family*, Chs. 11 and 18.

Duvall, Evelyn M., and Hill, Reuben, *When You Get Married*, Ch. 10.

Flügel, J. C., *The Psychoanalytic Study of the Family*, Ch. 3.

Groves, E. R., and Brooks, L. M., *Readings in the Family*, Ch. 16.

Hill, R., and Becker, H., *Marriage and the Family*, Ch. 16.

Mowrer, E. R., *Family Disorganization*, Part 3.

Mowrer, H. R., *Personality Adjustment and Domestic Discord*, Parts 2 and 3.

Articles

Chassell, Joseph, "Family Constellation in the Etiology of Essential Alcoholism," *Psychiatry*, Vol. 1, pp. 473–503.

Ciocco, Antonio, "Disruptive and Cohesive Factors in the Marital Group," *Human Biology*, Vol. 10, pp. 556–574.

Davis, Kingsley, "Jealousy and Sexual Property," *Social Forces*, Vol. 14, pp. 395–425.

Davis, Kingsley, "The Sociology of Parent-Youth Conflict," *American Sociological Review*, Vol. 5, pp. 523–535.

Frazier, E. Franklin, "Certain Aspects of Conflict in the Negro Family," *Social Forces*, Vol. 10, pp. 76–84.

Groves, E. R., "The Psychic Side of Marital Maladjustment," *Social Forces*, Vol. 16, pp. 396–400.

Krueger, E. T., "A Study of Marriage Incompatibility," *Family*, Vol. 9, pp. 53–60.

Levy, David M., "Hostility Patterns," *American Journal of Orthopsychiatry*, Vol. 13, pp. 441–461.

Mowrer, Harriet R., "Clinical Treatment of Marital Conflicts," *American Sociological Review*, Vol. 2, pp. 771–778.

Mowrer, Harriet R., "Personality Disorganization and Domestic Discord," *Social Forces*, Vol. 10, pp. 388–394.

Pratt, George K., "Some Psychiatric Views on Maladjustments in Marriage," *Social Forces*, Vol. 9, pp. 554–559.

Pressey, L. C., "Some Serious Family Maladjustments among College Students," *Social Forces*, Vol. 10, pp. 236–242.

Pritchett, H. L., "The Adjustment of College Students' Family Problems," *Social Forces,* Vol. 10, pp. 84–89.

Punko, H. H., "What do Families Quarrel About?" *School and Society,* Vol. 58, pp. 507–511.

Rienemann, J. O., "Extra-Marital Relations with Fellow Employees in War Industry as a Factor in Disruption of Family Life," *American Sociological Review,* Vol. 10, pp. 399–404.

Stanford, W. R., "Medical Aspects of Marital Incompatibility," *Social Forces,* Vol. 16, pp. 400–406.

CHAPTER 17

DIVORCE AND DESERTION

Subjects for Reports

1. The law regarding divorce in the state of the student reporting.
2. The value and hazards of alimony.
3. The status of migratory divorces.
4. Divorce trends in the United States.
5. Review of Waller's *The Old Love and the New.*

References

Books

Baber, R. E., *Marriage and the Family,* Chs. 14 and 15.

Bowman, H. A., *Marriage for Moderns,* Ch. 16.

Cavan, R. S., *The Family,* Ch. 9.

Clarke, H. I., *Social Legislation,* Ch. 6.

Drummond, Isabel, *Getting a Divorce.*

Duvall, Evelyn M., and Hill, Reuben, *When You Get Married,* Ch. 13.

Elmer, M. C., *The Sociology of the Family,* Ch. 10.

Folsom, J. K., *The Family and Democratic Society,* Ch. 15.

Groves, E. R., *Conserving Marriage and the Family.*

Groves, E. R., *Marriage,* Ch. 28.

Hill, R., and Becker, H., *Marriage and the Family,* Ch. 23.

Lichtenberger, J. P., *Divorce.*

Marshall, Leon, and May, Geoffrey, *The Divorce Court, Maryland.*

Marshall, Leon, and May, Geoffrey, *The Divorce Court, Ohio.*

Vernier, C. G., *American Family Laws,* Vol. 2.

Waller, Willard, *The Old Love and the New,* Chs. 20 and 21.

Weiss, Edward, and English, O. S., *Psychosomatic Medicine,* pp. 605–609.

Articles

Bradway, John S., "Family Dissolution—Limits of the Present Litigious Method," *Iowa Law Review,* Vol. 2, pp. 256–271.

Brearley, H. C., "A Note upon Migratory Divorce of South Carolinians," *Law and Contemporary Problems,* Vol. 2, pp. 329–334.

Cavers, David F., "Migratory Divorce," *Social Forces,* Vol. 16, pp. 96–107.

Daggett, H. S., "Division of Property Upon Dissolution of Marriage," *Law and Contemporary Problems,* Vol. 6, pp. 225–235.

Desvernine, Eugene, "Grounds for the Modification of Alimony Awards," *Law and Contemporary Problems,* Vol. 6, pp. 236–249.

Groves, E. R., "Migratory Divorces," *Law and Contemporary Problems,* Vol. 2, pp. 293–301.

Hart, Hornell, and Bowne, Henrietta, "Divorce, Depression and War," *Social Forces,* Vol. 22, pp. 191–194.

Ingram, F. W., and Ballard, G. A., "The Business of Migratory Divorces in Nevada," *Law and Contemporary Problems,* Vol. 2, pp. 302–309.

Kelso, R. W., "The Changing Social Setting of Alimony Law," *Law and Contemporary Problems,* Vol. 6, pp. 186–196.

Lemkin, Raphael, "Orphans of Living Parents: A Comparative Legal and Sociological View," *Law and Contemporary Problems,* Vol. 10, pp. 834–854.

Lichtenberger, J. P., "Divorce Legislation," *Annals of the American Academy of Political and Social Science,* Vol. 160, pp. 116–123.

Monahan, Thomas P., "The Changing Probability of Divorce," *American Sociological Review,* Vol. 5, pp. 536–545.

Mowrer, Ernest, "Divorce and Readjustment," *Annals of the American Academy of Political and Social Science,* Vol. 160, pp. 191–196.

Neuver, Robert, "Modern Divorce Law—The Compromise Solution," *Iowa Law Review,* Vol. 28, pp. 272–285.

Peele, Catherine Groves, "Social and Psychological Effects of the Availability and the Granting of Alimony on the Spouses," *Law and Contemporary Problems,* Vol. 6, pp. 283–292.

Plant, James S., "The Psychiatrist Views Children of Divorced Parents," *Law and Contemporary Problems,* Vol. 10, pp. 807–818.

Pound, Roscoe, "Foreword to Symposium in Law of Divorce," *Iowa Law Review,* Vol. 28, pp. 179–189.

Sayre, Paul, "Recognition by Other States of Decrees for Judicial Separation and Decrees for Alimony," *Iowa Law Review*, Vol. 28, pp. 321–340.

CHAPTER 18

THE FAMILY ITSELF A PROBLEM

SUBJECTS FOR REPORTS

The theories of reform of the family of:
1. Edward Carpenter
2. V. F. Calverton
3. Ellen Key
4. Edgar Schmiedeler
5. Sidney E. Goldstein
6. Anna Garlin Spencer

REFERENCES

Books

Baber, R. E., *Marriage and the Family,* Ch. 17.

Briffault, R., *Sin and Sex,* Chs. 14 and 15.

Calverton, V. F., *The Bankruptcy of Marriage,* Ch. 4.

Carpenter, Edward, *Love's Coming of Age,* pp. 91–111.

Dell, F., *Love in the Machine Age,* Ch. 7.

Ellis, Havelock, *My Life.*

Ellis, Mrs. Havelock, *James Hinton.*

Goldstein, Sidney E., *The Meaning of Marriage and the Foundations of the Family.*

Groves, E. R., *The Drifting Home,* Ch. 7.

Groves, E. R., *The Family and Its Social Functions,* Ch. 20.

Groves, E. R., *The Marriage Crisis,* Ch. 9.

Key, E., *Love and Marriage,* Ch. 9.

Reed, R., *The Modern Family,* Ch. 11.

Russell, B., *Marriage and Morals.*

Russell, Dora, *The Right to Be Happy.*

Schmalhausen, S. D., and Calverton, V. F., *Woman's Coming of Age,* pp. 260–297.

Schmiedeler, Edgar, *An Introductory Study of the Family,* Ch. 11.

Spencer, Anna Garlin, *The Family and its Members.*

Symposium: Keyserling, H., and others, *The Book of Marriage,* pp. 406–421.

Wieman, Regina W., *The Modern Family and the Church,* Ch. 1.

Wollstonecraft, Mary, *A Vindication of the Rights of Women.*

Articles

Allport, F. H., "Must We Scrap the Family?" *Harper's Magazine,* Vol. 962, pp. 185–194.

Anonymous, "The Single Woman," *Social Forces,* Vol. 9, pp. 91–93.

Ellwood, C. A., "The Family Situation in the United States," *The South Atlantic Quarterly* (October, 1931), pp. 357–365.

Hansheer, Herman, and Moseley, J. O., "A Study of the Unmarried," *Social Forces,* Vol. 10, pp. 394–404.

Taft, J., "The Home Has Lost Its Halo," *Survey Graphic,* Vol. 12, No. 3, pp. 286–287.

Todd, A. J., "The Future of the Family," *Religious Education,* Vol. 24, pp. 480–482.

CHAPTER 19

THE LEGAL APPROACH

SUBJECTS FOR REPORTS

1. Promise to marry and the breach thereof.
2. Community property.
3. The Family Court.
4. History, organization and function of the Juvenile Court.
5. Rights and duties of parents.
6. Common law marriage.
   With suggestions in each report for needed legal changes.

REFERENCES

Books

Baber, R. E., *Marriage and the Family,* Ch. 5.

Breckinridge, S. P., *Marriage and the Civic Rights of Women.*

Clarke, H. I., *Social Legislation*, Part 1.

Daggett, H. S., *Legal Essays on Family Law*.

Elmer, M. C., *The Sociology of the Family*, Ch. 6.

Folsom, J. K., *The Family and Democratic Society*, pp. 466–473.

Goldstein, J. J., *The Family in Court*.

Groves, E. R., *The American Woman*, Ch. 12.

Groves, E. R., *Marriage*, Ch. 10.

Groves, E. R., and Groves, Catherine, *Dynamic Mental Hygiene*, Ch. 9.

Knox, S. T., *The Family and the Law*.

Madden, J. W., and Compton, W. R., *Cases and Materials on Domestic Relations*.

Madden, J. W., *Persons and Domestic Relations*.

May, Geoffrey, *Marriage Laws and Decisions in the United States*.

Meriam, A. S., *The Stepfather in the Family*.

Richmond, Mary E., and Hall, F. S., *Marriage and the State*.

Schmiedeler, Edgar, *An Introductory Study of the Family*, Ch. 16.

Smith, C. E., *Papal Enforcement of Some Medieval Marriage Laws*.

Sowers, Ray, and Mullen, John (eds.), *Understanding Marriage and the Family*, Ch. 3.

Vernier, C. G., *American Family Laws*, Vols. 1 and 3, and 1938 Supplement.

Articles

Bradway, John S., "Needed Legislation for the Family," *Marriage and Family Living*, Vol. 6, pp. 32 and 37.

Daggett, H. S., "The Civil-Law Concept of the Wife's Portion in the Family," *Oregon Law Review*, Vol. 15, pp. 291–305.

Daggett, H. S., "The Oklahoma Community Property Act: A Comparative Study," *Louisiana Law Review*, Vol. 2, pp. 575–596.

Hall, Fred S., "Marriage and the Law," *Annals of the American Academy of Political and Social Science*, Vol. 160, pp. 110–115.

May, Geoffrey, and Bliven, Robert, "Legislation Trends in Family Law," *American Sociological Review*, Vol. 2, pp. 696–704.

Rheinstein, Max, "The Family, the Law, and the State," *Living*, Vol. 2, p. 20.

Sayre, Paul, "Property Rights of Husband and Wife," *Marriage and Family Living*, Vol. 6, pp. 17–20.

Zwally, Margaret, and Mahoney, John F., "Requirements of Premarital Legislation," *Public Health Service*, Bulletin No. 98, U. S. Government Printing Office.

CHAPTER 20

THE BIOLOGICAL APPROACH

SUBJECTS FOR REPORTS

1. Life and work of Sir Francis Galton.
2. The contribution of Leonard Darwin.
3. The Human Betterment Foundation.
4. The operation for the sterilization of the male and female.
5. Eugenic sterilization in California.
6. The laws regarding sterilization in the state of the student reporting.
7. Causes of non-hereditary feeble mindedness.

REFERENCES

Books

Burlingame, *Heredity and Social Problems,* Ch. 18.

Child, C. M., *Physiological Foundations of Behavior,* Chs. 16 and 17.

Corner, G. W., *Ourselves Unborn.*

Davenport, C. B., and Others, *Medical Genetics and Eugenics.*

Elmer, M. C., *The Sociology of the Family,* Ch. 8.

Goodsell, Willystine, *Problems of the Family,* Ch. 15.

Groves, E. R., *Marriage,* Ch. 8.

Groves, E. R., *Preparation for Marriage,* Ch. 2.

Groves, E. R., and Groves, Catherine, *Dynamic Mental Hygiene,* Ch. 2.

Hill, R., and Becker, H. (eds.), *Marriage and the Family,* Ch. 11.

Holmes, S. J., *Human Genetics and Its Social Import.*

Hunt, J. McV. (ed.), *Personality and the Behavior Disorders,* Vol. 1, Chs. 16 and 17.

Jennings, H. S., *The Biological Basis of Human Nature,* Chs. 11 and 15.

Laughlin, H. H., *Eugenical Sterilization: 1926.* American Eugenics Society.

Myerson, Abraham, and Others, *Eugenical Sterilization.*

Nimkoff, M. F., *The Family,* Ch. 7.

Osborn, Frederick, *Preface to Eugenics.*

Perkins, H. F., and Others, *A Decade of Progress in Eugenics.*

Popenoe, Paul, and Johnson, R. H., *Applied Eugenics.*

Scheinfeld, Amram, *You and Heredity.*

Sheldon, W. H., Stevens, S. S., and Tucker, W. B., *The Varieties of Human Physique,* Ch. 7.

Snyder, L. H., *Medical Genetics.*

Sowers, Ray, and Mullen, John (eds.), *Understanding Marriage and the Family,* Ch. 12.

Stockard, C. R., *The Physical Basis of Personality,* Ch. 15.

Symposium: *A Decade of Progress in Eugenics. Third International Congress of Eugenics.*

Yahraes, Herbert, *Epilepsy—The Ghost is Out of the Closet,* Public Affairs Pamphlet No. 98.

Articles

Hartman, C. G., "Biological Basis of the Family," *Marriage and Family Living,* Vol. 2, No. 1, pp. 21–23.

Lennox, W. G., "Marriage and Children for Epileptics," *Eugenical News,* Vol. 10, pp. 107–111.

Liberson, W. T., and Seguin, C. A., "Brain Waves and Heredity in Mental Diseases," *Psychosomatic Medicine,* Vol. 7, pp. 35–38.

MacArthur, Kenneth, "Eugenics and the Church," *Eugenical News,* Vol. 30, pp. 1–4.

Montagu, M. F. A., "Man's Biological Outlook," *Psychiatry,* Vol. 6, pp. 359–360.

Penrose, L. S., "Inheritance of Mental Defect," *Scientific Monthly,* Vol. 52, pp. 359–364.

Popenoe, Paul, "Divorce and Remarriage from the Eugenic Point of View," *Social Forces,* Vol. 12, pp. 48–50.

Rosenhaupt, Heinrich, "The Male Birth Surplus," *Scientific Monthly,* Vol. 48, pp. 163–169.

Snyder, L. H., "The Study of Human Heredity," *Scientific Monthly,* Vol. 51, pp. 536–541.

Strandskov, H. H., "The Rh Blood Factor," *Scientific Monthly,* Vol. 60, pp. 451–454.

Stone, Charles S., "Huntingon's Chorea: A Sociological and Genealogical Study of a New Family," *Mental Hygiene,* Vol. 15, pp. 350–363.

Whelpton, P. K., and Kiser, Clyde, "Social and Psychological Factors Affecting Fertility," *Milbank Quarterly,* Vol. 24, pp. 49–93.

CHAPTER 21

THE MEDICAL APPROACH

SUBJECTS FOR REPORTS

1. The meaning of psychosomatic medicine.
2. The medical examination as a preparation for marriage.
3. Medical insurance.
4. Progress in maternal health.
5. The public-health program and family welfare.

REFERENCES

Books

Benedek, Therese, and Rubenstein, B. B., *The Sexual Cycle in Women.*

Binger, C. A. L., and Others, *Personality in Arterial Hypertension,* Ch. 6.

Chadwick, Mary, *The Psychological Effects of Menstruation.*

Corner, G. W., *The Hormones in Human Reproduction.*

Cowdry, E. V., and Others, *Problems of Aging.*

Davis, Maxine, *Woman's Medical Problems.*

Deutsch, Helene, *Motherhood,* Vol. 2, Chs. 5–8.

Duffus, R. L., and Holt, L. Emmett, Jr., *L. Emmett Holt.*

Elliott, G. L., *Women After Forty.*

Elmer, M. C., *The Sociology of the Family,* Ch. 22.

Finney, R. P., *The Story of Motherhood.*

Foster, R. G., *Marriage and Family Relationships,* Ch. 9.

Gossett, W. B., *What the Public Should Know About Childbirth.*

Groves, E. R., *Marriage,* Ch. 23.

Groves, E. R., *Preparation for Marriage,* Chs. 4 and 5.

Groves, E. R., and Groves, Catherine, *Dynamic Mental Hygiene,* Ch. 3.

Hamblen, E. C., *Endocrine Gynecology.*

Hamblen, E. C., *Endocrinology of Woman,* Part 2.

Hartman, C. G., *Time of Ovulation in Women.*

Hoskins, R. G., *Endocrinology.*

Hotchkiss, R. S., *Fertility in Men.*

Hühner, Max, *Sexual Disorders.*

Kaplan, C. J. (ed.), *Mental Disorders in Later Life,* Ch. 4.

Lane-Roberts, Cedric, and Others, *Sterility and Impaired Fertility.*

Lawton, George (ed.), *New Goals for Old Age.*

Mazer, C., and Israel, S. L., *Diagnosis and Treatment of Menstrual Disorders and Sterility.*

Meaker, S. R., *Human Sterility.*

Novak, Emil, *The Woman Asks the Doctor.*

Parran, Thomas, *Shadow on the Land.*

Richardson, H. B., *Patients Have Families.*

Rosenau, M. J., *Preventive Medicine and Hygiene.*

Siegler, S. L., *Fertility in Women.*

Sowers, Ray, and Mullen, John (eds.), *Understanding Marriage and the Family,* Chs. 10 and 11.

Taylor, H. C., *The Abortion Problem.*

White House Conference on Child Health and Protection, *Fetal, Newborn and Maternal Morbidity and Mortality.*

Weiss, Edward, and English, O. S., *Psychosomatic Medicine,* pp. 616–620.

Articles

Cornell, W. A., "Care of the Aged—A Family Problem," *Social Forces,* Vol. 18, pp. 403–405.

Ingraham, J. N. R., "Health Problems of the Adolescent Period," *Annals of the American Academy of Political and Social Science,* Vol. 236, pp. 117–127.

Lawton, George, "Happiness in Old Age," *Mental Hygiene,* Vol. 27, pp. 231–237.

Lawton, George, "Mental Hygiene at Senescence," *Mental Hygiene,* Vol. 23, pp. 257–267.

Lawton, George (chairman), "Psychological Problems of Later Maturity," *American Journal of Orthopsychiatry,* Vol. 14, pp. 266–284.

MacNider, William deB., "Adjustability of the Life Process to Injurious Agents," *Scientific Monthly,* Vol. 54, pp. 247–250.

Reeve, G. H., "Psychological Factors in Obesity," *American Journal of Orthopsychiatry,* Vol. 12, pp. 674–678.

Stokes, W. R., "Premarital Medical Service," *Psychiatry,* Vol. 5, pp. 361–369.

Tuohy, E. L., "Nutrition for the Aging," *Journal of Home Economics,* Vol. 37, pp. 260–262.

Wermel, M. T., and Gelbaum, Selma, "Work and Retirement in Old Age," *American Journal of Sociology,* Vol. 51, pp. 16–21.

CHAPTER 22

THE MENTAL HYGIENE APPROACH

SUBJECTS FOR REPORTS

1. The family as the promising institution for the development of a mental hygiene program.
2. The Child Guidance Clinic.
3. The development and the function of the Marriage Counselor.
4. The Marriage Counseling Clinic as a mental hygiene agency.
5. The minister as a marriage counselor.
6. The American Association of Marriage Counselors.
7. The training of the Marriage Counselor.

REFERENCES

Books

Benz, M. G., *Family Counseling Service in a University Community.*

Burkhart, Roy A., *Ministerial Counseling and Planned Parenthood.*

Dicks, R. L., *Pastoral Work and Personal Counseling,* Chs. 11 and 12.

Duvall, Evelyn M., and Hill, Reuben, *When You Get Married,* Appendix B.

Goldstein, Sidney E., *Marriage and Family Counseling.*

Groves, E. R., and Groves, Catherine, *Dynamic Mental Hygiene,* Ch. 1 and Part 2.

Groves, Gladys H., *Marriage and Family Life,* Ch. 18.

Holman, C. T., *Getting Down to Cases,* Ch. 5.

Levy, David M., *Maternal Overprotection,* Chs. 9 and 10.

May, Rollo, *The Art of Counseling,* Chs. 3, 6 and 7.

Mowrer, H. R., *Personality Adjustment and Domestic Discord,* Chs. 1 and 2.

Rogers, C. R., *Counseling and Psychotherapy.*

Sowers, Ray, and Mullen, John (eds.), *Understanding Marriage and the Family,* Ch. 5.

Steiner, L. R., *Where Do People Take Their Troubles?*

Stolz, K. R., *The Church and Psychotherapy,* Ch. 6.

Stolz, K. R., *Pastoral Psychology,* Ch. 14.

Articles

Ackerman, N. W., "Psychotherapy and 'Giving Love,'" *Psychiatry*, Vol. 7, pp. 129–137.

Carden, Marie, "Organization of Family Consultation Centers," *Marriage and Family Living*, Vol. 4, pp. 61–62.

Conn, Jacob H., "The Child Reveals Himself through Play; The Method of the Play Interview," *Mental Hygiene*, Vol. 23, pp. 49–69.

Conn, Jacob H., "The Treatment of Fearful Children," *American Journal of Orthopsychiatry*, Vol. 11, pp. 744–751.

Cuber, J. F., "Functions of the Marriage Counselor," *Marriage and Family Living*, Vol. 7, pp. 3–5.

Dearborn, Lester, "Personal and Marriage Counseling in Boston," *Journal of Home Economics*, Vol. 36, pp. 557–559.

Dickerson, Roy E., "Marital Counseling: An Evaluation," *Journal of Home Economics*, Vol. 36, pp. 560–561.

Dicks, R. L., "Methods for Effective Counseling," *Marriage and Family Living*, Vol. 7, p. 85.

Foster, Robert G., "Servicing the Family through Counselling Agencies," *American Sociological Review*, Vol. 2, pp. 764–770.

Gaylord, Gladys, "Marriage Counseling in War Time," *Annals of the American Academy of Political and Social Science*, Vol. 229, pp. 39–45.

Groves, E. R., "A Decade of Marriage Counseling," *Annals of the American Academy of Political and Social Science*, Vol. 212, pp. 72–80.

Groves, E. R., "Professional Training for Marriage and Family Counseling," *Social Forces*, Vol. 23, pp. 447–451.

Hankins, Dorothy, "Mental Hygiene Problems and the Adolescent Period," *Annals of the American Academy of Political and Social Science*, Vol. 236, pp. 128–135.

Hinckley, R. G., and Fenlason, A. F., "Mental Hygiene Interviewing: A Therapeutic Approach," *American Journal of Orthopsychiatry*, Vol. 12, pp. 309–316.

Hixenbaugh, E. R., "Reconciliation of Marital Maladjustment, An Analysis of 101 Cases," *Social Forces*, Vol. 10, pp. 230–236.

Jacoby, Julia, "The Nursery School as an Experience in Therapy," *American Journal of Orthopsychiatry*, Vol. 13, pp. 162–166.

Marcus, Grace, "The Individual and His Family Relationships," *Mental Hygiene*, Vol. 17, pp. 353–368.

Mudd, E. H., "An Analysis of One Hundred Consecutive Cases in the Marriage Counsel of Philadelphia," *Mental Hygiene*, Vol. 21, pp. 198–217.

Plant, James S., "Present Problems in Marriage Counseling," *Mental Hygiene,* Vol. 23, pp. 353–362.

Szurek, S. A., "Child Therapy Procedures," *Psychiatry,* Vol. 7, pp. 9–14.

Trendley, Mary B., "Mental Illness and Family Routines," *Mental Hygiene,* Vol. 30, pp. 235–249.

Ware, Anna Budd, and Goodwin, M. S., "Family Counseling through Family Case Work," *Marriage and Family Living,* Vol. 3, p. 10.

Wortis, S. Bernard, "Counseling in the Premarital Interview," *Marriage and Family Living,* Vol. 7, p. 86.

White, H. C., "The Role of the Family Agency in Counseling," *Living,* Vol. 2, No. 1, p. 29.

CHAPTER 23

THE HOME ECONOMICS APPROACH

SUBJECTS FOR REPORTS

1. Family allowances.
2. Consumer education.
3. New discoveries in nutrition.
4. Home economics courses for high school boys.
5. Budget making.
6. Progress of the co-operative movement in the United States.
7. Needed changes in house construction.

REFERENCES

Books

Abel, M. H., *Successful Family Life on the Moderate Income.*

Andrews, Benjamin R., *Economics of the Household.*

Angell, R. C., *The Family Encounters the Depression.*

Bigelow, H. F., *Family Finance.*

Cushman, E. M., *Management in Homes.*

Douglas, Paul H., *Wages and the Family.*

Duvall, Evelyn M., and Hill, Reuben, *When You Get Married,* Ch. 11.

Elmer, M. C., *The Sociology of the Family,* Ch. 13.

Folsom, J. K., *The Family and Democratic Society,* Chs. 17 and 18.

Folsom, J. K., *Plan for Marriage*, Ch. 8.

Foster, R. G., *Marriage and Family Relationships*, Chs. 11 and 12.

Groves, E. R., and Groves, Catherine, *Dynamic Mental Hygiene*, Ch. 10.

Groves, Gladys H., *Marriage and Family Life*, Ch. 15.

Hill, R., and Becker, H., *Marriage and the Family*, Ch. 17.

Komarovsky, Mirra, *The Unemployed Man and His Family*.

Kyrk, Hazel, *Economic Problems of the Family*.

Nickell, Paulina, and Dorsey, J. M., *Management in Family Living*.

Nimkoff, M. F., *The Family*, Ch. 8.

Rathbone, E. F., *The Disinherited Family*.

Reid, M. G., *Economics and Household Production*.

Sait, U. B., *New Horizons for the Family*, Chs. 21 and 22.

Selling, L. S., and Ferraro, M. A. S., *The Psychology of Diet and Nutrition*.

Stewart, Jean J., *Foods: Production, Marketing, Consumption*.

Zimmerman, C. C., and Frampton, M. E., *Family and Society*, Chs. 27 and 28.

Articles

Amidon, E. P., "Social Change and the Family from the Point of View of the Home Economist," *Journal of Home Economics*, Vol. 32, pp. 526–533.

Andrews, B. R., "The Household Employee," *Journal of Home Economics*, Vol. 34, pp. 158–160.

Blazier, F. E., "Planning Homemaking Rooms," *Journal of Home Economics*, Vol. 37, pp. 498–502.

Burgess, E. W., and Locke, H. J., "Family Allowances for Children," *Marriage and Family Living*, Vol. 7, p. 12.

Brandon, Vera, and Thompson, Susanne, "Persistent Problems in Family Life at the College Level," *Journal of Home Economics*, Vol. 33, pp. 297–301.

Carlson, A. J., "Food and Fitness," *Scientific Monthly*, Vol. 55, pp. 403–407.

Chaney, M. S., "Food Needs in Growth," *Journal of Home Economics*, Vol. 32, pp. 4–10.

Emery, Andree, "Wanted: A House to Fit the Family," *Journal of Home Economics*, Vol. 34, pp. 501–505.

Gibbs, Elizabeth, "Democratic Living in a College Residence Hall," *Journal of Home Economics*, Vol. 31, pp. 365–368.

Gray, Greta, and Stapler, Ruth, "Housing Needs of Children," *Social Forces*, Vol. 7, pp. 250–252.

Hedrick, Blanche E., "The Role of the Trained Homemaker in a Changing Society," *Journal of Home Economics,* Vol. 32, pp. 590–594.

Jones, Lester, "Undergraduate Views on Minimum Budget for Marriage," *Social Forces,* Vol. 22, pp. 199–203.

Lynd, R. S., "Family Members as Consumers," *Annals of the American Academy of Political and Social Science,* Vol. 160, pp. 86–93.

Morgan, Agnes F., "Vitamins and Senescence," *Scientific Monthly,* Vol. 52, pp. 416–421.

Ogburn, W. F., "Economic Basis of Family Life," *Living,* Vol. 2, pp. 24–28.

Reed, Ellery F., "Cost of Living Compared with Family Income in Seven Cities," *American Sociological Review,* Vol. 11, pp. 192–197.

Riemer, Svend, "Maladjustment to the Family Home," *American Sociological Review,* Vol. 10, pp. 642–647.

Spicer, Mildred, "Homemaking Departments Geared to Family Living," *Journal of Home Economics,* Vol. 34, pp. 227–230.

Sweeny, Mary, "Changing Food Habits," *Journal of Home Economics,* Vol. 34, pp. 457–462.

Van Horn, "Forty Years of Consumer Education," *Journal of Home Economics,* Vol. 33, pp. 377–386.

Watson, A. E., "The Reorganization of Household Work," *Annals of the American Academy of Political and Social Science,* Vol. 160, pp. 165–177.

Watson, Maxine, "Problems of Low Income Homemakers," *Journal of Home Economics,* Vol. 35, pp. 560–562.

White, T. E., and Banks, E. L., "Adventures in Housing," *Journal of Home Economics,* Vol. 37, pp. 72–73.

Wilmot, J. S., and Mallory, Bernice, "Economic and Social Problems in Homemaking," *Journal of Home Economics,* Vol. 32, pp. 607–609.

CHAPTER 24

THE EDUCATIONAL APPROACH

SUBJECTS FOR REPORTS

1. An outline of instruction for marriage.
2. Family education in high schools and in the grades.

3. The development of the nursery school as a means of education for parenthood.
4. The training of the college teacher of marriage.
5. The practice house as a training center for family living.
6. Child study in the adult education program.

References

Books

Elmer, M. C., *The Sociology of the Family*, Chs. 23 and 26.

Groves, E. R., *The Family and Its Social Functions*, Ch. 10.

Sait, U. B., *New Horizons for the Family*, Chs. 7, 8, and 9.

Schmiedeler, Edgar, *The Sacred Bond*, Ch. 20.

Sladen, F. J. (ed.), *Psychiatry and the War*, pp. 163–183.

Sowers, Ray, and Mullen, John (eds.), *Understanding Marriage and the Family*, Chs. 7, 8, and 9.

Articles

Abrams, R. H., "The Contribution of Sociology to a Course in Marriage and the Family," *Living*, Vol. 2, No. 3, pp. 82–84.

Andrews, B. R., "Workshop Methods in Family Life Education," *Journal of Home Economics*, Vol. 36, pp. 269–270.

Barach, Meyer, "The Problem of Teaching a Course in the Family," *Social Forces*, Vol. 20, pp. 87–88.

Blau, Abram, and Veo, Louise, "Mental Hygiene in a Special Public School for Maladjusted Children," *American Journal of Orthopsychiatry*, Vol. 11, pp. 691–701.

Bowman, Henry, "The Marriage Course at Stephens College," *Marriage and Family Living*, Vol. 3, pp. 8–9.

Bowman, Henry, "Marriage Education in a Junior College," *Marriage and Family Living*, Vol. 8, pp. 36–37.

Bridgman, Ralph P., "Guidance for Marriage and Family Life," *Annals of the American Academy of Political and Social Science*, Vol. 160, pp. 144–164.

Burgess, J. Stewart, "The College and Preparation for Marriage and Family Relationships," *Living*, Vol. 1, pp. 39–42.

Cooper, R. M., and Others, "Teaching College Marriage Courses: A Symposium," *Marriage and Family Living*, Vol. 8, pp. 32–42.

Denune, P. P., "Education for Marriage at Ohio State University," *Marriage and Family Living*, Vol. 7, pp. 6–8.

Eckert, R. G., "Highlights of a Marriage Course," *Marriage and Family Living*, Vol. 8, pp. 37–40.

Emery, E. Van Norman, "A Biological Perspective for Education during Periods of Social Change," *Mental Hygiene,* Vol. 22, pp. 177–192.

Firth, Maude M., "Teaching Family Relationships to Mixed Classes," *Journal of Home Economics,* Vol. 29, pp. 151–153.

Foster, Robert G., "Family Life Education in a Democratic Society," *Social Forces,* Vol. 17, pp. 396–405.

Frank, Lawrence K., "Eugenics and Education," *Mental Hygiene,* Vol. 22, pp. 72–78.

Gesell, Arnold, "The Kindergarten as a Mental-Hygiene Agency," *Mental Hygiene,* Vol. 10, pp. 27–37.

Groves, E. R. (chairman), "Education for Marriage and the Family," *Living,* Vol. 2, pp. 46–48.

Groves, E. R., "Parent Education," *Annals of the American Academy of Political and Social Science,* Vol. 160, pp. 216–222.

Groves, E. R., "Professional Training for Family Life Education," *Marriage and Family Living,* Vol. 8, pp. 25–26.

Groves, E. R., "Professional Training for Marriage and Family Counseling," *Social Forces,* Vol. 23, pp. 447–451.

Groves, E. R., "Teaching Marriage at the University of North Carolina," *Social Forces,* Vol. 16, pp. 87–96.

Johnson, Adelaide, and Others, "School Phobia," *American Journal of Orthopsychiatry,* Vol. 11, pp. 702–711.

Landis, P. H., "Courses in Marriage and the Family by Sociologists and Home Economists," *Social Forces,* Vol. 24, pp. 336–339.

Landis, P. H., and Day, K. H., "Education as a Factor in Mate Selection," *American Sociological Review,* Vol. 10, pp. 558–563.

Liss, Edward, "The Psychiatrist in School," *Mental Hygiene,* Vol. 20, pp. 37–40.

Lynd, H. M., "Parent Education and the Colleges," *Annals of the American Academy of Political and Social Science,* Vol. 160, pp. 197–204.

Macleod, Annie L., "Home Economics: A Liberal Education," *Journal of Home Economics,* Vol. 37, pp. 547–550.

McGinnis, Esther, "The College Girl Goes to Nursery School," *Journal of Home Economics,* Vol. 34, pp. 506–507.

Miller, Ellen, "Elementary Education for Family Living," *Journal of Home Economics,* Vol. 33, pp. 237–240.

Peller, Lili E., "Significant Symptoms in the Behavior of Young Children," *Mental Hygiene,* Vol. 30, pp. 285–295.

Peretz, Josephine, "A High School for Homemaking," *Journal of Home Economics,* Vol. 33, pp. 646–651.

Popenoe, Paul, "Trends in Teaching Family Relations," *Marriage and Family Living,* Vol. 8, pp. 35–36.

Risedorph, Allan E., and Risedorph, Jeanne R., "Education for Marriage and the Family as a Means of Strengthening National Security in the Community," *Marriage and Family Living,* Vol. 4, pp. 56–58.

Rockwood, L. D., "Courses in Marriage and Family Relations," *Marriage and Family Living,* Vol. 8, pp. 40–41.

Ruben, Margarete, "A Contribution to the Education of a Parent," *The Psychoanalytic Study of the Child,* pp. 247–262.

Rustad, R. M., and Reubin, P. B., "Child Study in High School," *Journal of Home Economics,* Vol. 37, pp. 321–323.

Schweinitz, Karl de, "The Dangers and Advantages of Sex Instruction for Children," *Mental Hygiene,* Vol. 15, pp. 561–569.

Wilkening, H. E., "The Purdue University Marriage Course," *Marriage and Family Living,* Vol. 7, pp. 25–27.

CHAPTER 25

THE SUCCESSFUL FAMILY

SUBJECTS FOR REPORTS

1. The qualities of a successful family.
2. Predicting success and failure in marriage.
3. The Catholic philosophy of marriage.
4. The Jewish philosophy of marriage.
5. The Protestant philosophy of marriage.
6. Review of Binkley and Binkley's *What is Right with Marriage.*
7. Review of Swedenborg's *Marital Love.*
8. The program for a successful marriage of the students reporting.

REFERENCES

Books

Baber, R. E., *Marriage and the Family,* Ch. 18.
Duvall, Evelyn M., and Hill, Reuben, *When You Marry,* Ch. 14.
Folsom, J. K., *Plan for Marriage,* Ch. 12.
Goodsell, Willystine, *Problems of the Family,* Ch. 20.
Groves, E. R., *The Family and Its Social Functions,* Ch. 21.
Groves, E. R., and Brooks, L. M., *Readings in the Family,* Ch. 25.
Groves, Gladys H., *Marriage and Family Life,* Ch. 20.

Hill, R., and Becker, H., *Marriage and the Family*, Ch. 14.

Lindquist, Ruth, *The Family in the Present Social Order*, Chs. 4 and 9.

Parsons, E. C., *The Family*, Ch. 15.

Sait, U. B., *New Horizons for the Family*, Ch. 25.

Sowers, Ray, and Mullen, John (eds.), *Understanding Marriage and the Family*, Chs. 4 and 6.

Swedenborg, Emanuel, *Marital Love*.

Articles

Bernard, Jessie, "Distribution of Success in Marriage," *American Journal of Sociology*, Vol. 39, pp. 194–203.

Ferguson, Leonard, "Correlates of Marital Happiness," *Journal of Psychology*, Vol. 6, pp. 285–294.

Mayo, Elton, "Should Marriage be Monotonous?" *Harper's Magazine*, Vol. 151, pp. 420–427.

Overstreet, H. A., "Training for Successful Marriage," *Journal of Social Hygiene*, Vol. 16, pp. 134–139.

Popenoe, Paul, and Wicks, Donna, "Marital Happiness in Two Generations," *Mental Hygiene*, Vol. 21, pp. 218–223.

Richardson, Anna E., "The Art of Family Life," *Journal of Social Hygiene*, Vol. 14, pp. 81–90.

Toops, Laura C., "The Measurement of Success in Marriage and Parenthood," *Teachers College Record*, Vol. 30, pp. 579–588.

Woodhouse, C. G., "A Study of 250 Successful Families," *Social Forces*, Vol. 8, pp. 511–532.

Appendix C

TO THE INSTRUCTOR

This book attempts to keep to its proper province as an introductory text to the American family for the college student. It is not a source book of encyclopedic detail but assumes that the instructor is familiar with and will help his students to become familiar with the quantities of specific, detailed studies of marriage and family experience that are now available. The volume also is not a drill book, but instead it aims to guide the student in building background. Because of this it has seemed best not to include topics for discussion, in the belief that if the class is not too large discussion will come spontaneously, thereby being closer to the interests of the students than can ever come from a formal manual. In very large classes it is difficult to get more than a minimum of free discussion. Then the instructor must rely largely upon personal conferences for the opportunity of giving the students answers to the questions which trouble them.

In class discussions it is important for the student to realize and to keep in mind the difference between assertions of personal opinion and those based upon some degree of factual knowledge. The expression of the first should not be discouraged because it leads to statements of individual prejudices and preferences and thus forces an awareness of the differences that exist when thoughtful people discuss marriage and the family. These expressions of personal judgments are themselves facts. Their origin, however, may be individual experience or group suggestion rather than objective information.

Effort has been made to prevent the student's thinking of the family as something static. Even the most reliable and statistically based findings should be recognized by the student as a portrayal of an existing situation similar to the camera's picture which records in an instant an ever changing scene. Family life is living experience and it is unfortunate whenever a student gets any idea of finality with reference to any phase of domestic life as he becomes convinced of the value of some specific study to which his attention has been attracted.

Subjects for report have been suggested. They are purposely wide in meaning and are offered as a means of reinforcing the text. They can easily be limited by the instructor when he wishes a more specific detailed interpretation of the subject to be reported. They invite the student to explore for himself along lines of importance in understanding the American family. They are likely to be most profitable when they are self-chosen by the individual student rather than given as an assignment. He may understand that this reporting is part of the work he has to do, but if he feels that he selects the topic himself and presents his own interests the work is more likely to be profitable.

If there is opportunity, the worth of these reports is enhanced by having them given to the class. This permits the student to gain the educational value of the work. The instructor needs to impress upon the student that the purpose of the report is not merely the gathering of information but that there is also a problem of delivery. Too seldom during his college career is a student impressed with the significance of his assignments as a means of increasing his ability to do things. It can be assumed that every student later in life will be called upon at times to deliver information to other people. Students, as a rule, do not find the reports of their colleagues very interesting. Their reaction is usually natural because the reports are in fact not interesting. The person reporting is too likely to be satisfied merely with the gathering of information and preparing it for the assignment without much thought of how to present it to the class. It is of distinct value to him to seek to make it interesting by considering how to write or speak it before the class. It will help to remind him that he should make his material as dramatic and concrete as possible. The report must not be overloaded with detail. He should keep to the point and his material should seem not only convincing but practical as well. Many reports are made dull because they are too long. If the student has his time limited and if emphasis is made upon his talking to the students rather than to the instructor, the appeal of the report is generally increased. Friendly criticism publicly, for the benefit of the class, or privately, with constant attention on the problem of delivery, will greatly help the student to think of reports not as tasks but as opportunities to be appreciated since they give training which will prove useful in later life. References are included to help the student get started in preparing these reports.

The authors have kept in mind in the writing of this part of the book, as in the main text, that it is their business to help the student realize his goal, not to know about family life but to know family life, and that in order to accomplish this he must draw not only from the information that has been gathered by specialists but also from his own observations and personal experience as he has contacts with other families as well as his own. Thus he gains the insight and information which make his study of the family worth while.

Appendix D

BIBLIOGRAPHIES

Many of the college texts in the field of marriage and the family have excellent bibliographies. In addition, the following will prove useful to the student.

Briffault, R., *The Mothers,* Vol. 3, pp. 523–719. (Bibliography on Primitive Family.)

Calhoun, A. W., *Social History of the American Family,* Vol. 3, pp. 333–358. (Bibliography on History of Family.)

Jacobs, A. C., and Angell, R. C., *A Research in Family Law,* Vol. 2, Part 5. (Select Bibliography on Family Law.)

Robertson, A. I., *Guide to Literature of Home and Family Life.*

Thurston, F. M., *A Bibliography on Family Relationships.*

Groves, E. R., and Groves, Catherine, *Dynamic Mental Hygiene,* has a quantity of reference material concerning family experience.

Groves, E. R., is the author of annotated *Bibliographies 1–4,* published by *Social Forces* in 1940, 1942, 1943, and 1946 and reprinted by the Institute for Research in the Social Sciences, Chapel Hill, N. C.

Pearl, Raymond, *Natural History of Population,* has a large bibliography concerning the arrested family and fertility.

Scheinfeld, Amram, *You and Heredity,* contains a small but valuable bibliography on the problems of heredity as they concern the family.

Unwin, J. D., *Sex and Culture,* has a carefully selected bibliography relating to the primitive family.

INDEX